HIV, AIDS and Childbearing

HIV, AIDS and Childbearing

Public Policy, Private Lives

Edited by

RUTH R. FADEN
Johns Hopkins University

NANCY E. KASS
Johns Hopkins University

New York   Oxford
Oxford University Press
1996

Oxford University Press

Oxford New York
Athens Auckland Bangkok Bombay
Calcutta Cape Town Dar es Salaam Delhi
Florence Hong Kong Istanbul Karachi
Kuala Lumpur Madras Madrid Melbourne
Mexico City Nairobi Paris Singapore
Taipei Tokyo Toronto

and associated companies in
Berlin Ibadan

Copyright © 1996 by Oxford University Press, Inc.

Published by Oxford University Press, Inc.,
198 Madison Avenue, New York, New York 10016

Oxford is a registered trademark of Oxford University Press

All rights reserved. No part of this publication may be reproduced,
stored in a retrieval system, or transmitted, in any form or by any means,
electronic, mechanical, photocopying, recording, or otherwise,
without the prior permission of Oxford University Press.

Library of Congress Cataloging-in-Publication Data
HIV, AIDS and childbearing : public policy, private lives / edited by
Ruth R. Faden, Nancy E. Kass.
p. cm. Includes index.
ISBN 0-19-509958-3
1. AIDS (Disease) in pregnancy.
2. AIDS (Disease) in infants.
3. HIV-positive women—Legal status, laws, etc.
4. Human reproduction—Law and legislation.
I. Faden, Ruth R. II. Kass, Nancy E.
RG580.A44H57 1996
618.3—dc20   95-50070

9 8 7 6 5 4 3 2 1

Printed in the United States of America
on acid-free paper

For the women,
For their children,
For our children

PREFACE

Whether, with whom, and when to have children are among the most precious of private decisions in a person's life. Increasingly, however, the interests of others in the outcomes of these decisions are raising difficult questions about the proper role of government and health-care professionals in influencing reproductive choice. Nowhere is this tension more keenly felt than in the context of HIV infection and AIDS since about one-quarter of all children born to HIV-infected women contract the infection, if there is no intervention, and virtually all children who are not infected are orphaned at some point during childhood. This book addresses head-on the complex ethical, legal, social, medical, and public health issues raised by childbearing in the context of HIV infection. Written by a group of leading scholars in these fields, it analyzes both alternative policy options for the public and private sectors of health care and alternative clinical and counseling options for those who provide that care.

A unique feature of this volume is that it blends normative and legal reflections about reproductive choice and public policy with original empirical research. To enrich the analysis presented, over 150 HIV-infected women and 50 of their health-care providers have been interviewed. The results of these interviews, which provide needed insight into the values and life circumstances of the people directly engaged in confronting and influencing reproductive choices, are reported in this volume. Moreover, the recommendations defended herein are grounded in the lived experiences of these respondents.

Although the book focuses on HIV and AIDS in its analysis of public responses to reproductive choice, it is not only about the AIDS epidemic. In some respects, it sets the stage for the next generation of debate about interference with reproductive choice. For example, the discussion of how health professionals should approach questions of reproductive choice is carried to a new level by challenging as the appropriate model for professional behavior what has often been referred to as non-directive counseling. Similarly, the book includes analyses of the moral right to have children, the nature of social influence, and the role of cultural and personal values in evaluating the ethics of reproductive behavior, all of which have implications not only for AIDS but also for debates about reproductive choice and public and private conduct in such varied contexts as genetic disease, substance use, adolescence, persons receiving welfare benefits, and homosexuality.

Background

Women are becoming infected with HIV at an alarming rate. Nearly 10% of all cases of AIDS reported to the Centers for Disease Control (CDC) since the onset of the epidemic have been among women. In the last year, the percentage of AIDS cases among women has climbed to 18%, and there is every expectation that the proportion of women among all persons with AIDS will continue to rise. Virtually all HIV-infected women are of childbearing age. The increase in cases of children diagnosed with AIDS parallels this rise in the infection rate among women. Currently, vertical transmission from mother to fetus or newborn accounts for almost all new cases of AIDS in children under 13 years of age. It is estimated that, absent medical intervention, about 25% of infants born to HIV-infected women contract the infection. Research suggests that by administering antiretroviral therapy to pregnant women and newborns the rate of transmission can be reduced to less than 10%. Despite advances in the medical management of HIV, very few HIV-infected women are likely to live long enough to raise their children to maturity. Thus, although most children born to HIV-infected women escape the infection, almost all of them are orphaned by their biological mothers sometime during childhood. Moreover, because HIV-infected women often became infected from their male sexual partners, many of their children are orphaned by their biological fathers as well.

These "facts" have led many commentators and health-care professionals to question the appropriateness of childbearing by women who are infected. Any attempt to influence childbearing raises profound moral, legal, and policy issues, however. Reproductive choice is among the most elemental and most cherished components of our rights to autonomy and privacy. Any interference with reproductive choice, even directive counseling, requires justification. When only a small segment of society is singled out for such interference, the potential for moral wrong is great. In the context of HIV disease, the target group is disproportionately poor women of color; issues of sexism, racism, and even genocide must be squarely addressed.

A grant from the Health Resources Services Administration (HRSA) has made possible an unusual process for creating this edited volume of original contributions. A working group[1] of 18 colleagues from the disciplines of obstetrics/gynecology, pediatrics, medicine, public health, ethics, and law held ten meetings over a period of 2 years. We discussed and debated policy and clinical options related to childbearing and HIV disease. In addition, we met in smaller interdisciplinary groups to critique one another's chapter drafts.

The grant also supported the conduct of interviews with 159 HIV-infected women and 51 health-care providers from Baltimore, Miami, Los Angeles, and New York. Through these audiotaped, qualitative interviews, we learned these women's stories. We asked them when they learned they were HIV-infected, what childbearing means to them generally, whether being HIV-infected affected those feelings, whether **they** think HIV-infected women should have children, what health-care providers have said to them concerning reproductive issues, and what health-care providers ought to say. We asked health-care providers what they say to women concerning reproduction, how they think women ought to be counseled, and what their perceptions are of what is occurring elsewhere in the field, as well as what their own opinions and values are concerning HIV-infected women having children. As might be anticipated, rich experiences and anecdotes were reported, which had a profound effect on our thinking.

Our recommendations for public policy and clinical practice derive from the arguments and analyses presented in the chapters as well as the interviews with women and providers. Drafts of these recommendations were presented for review and critique at two public conferences, one invitational conference and two academic colloquia. Our final position is put forward in Chapter 17.

Two problems are raised by writing a book focused on women, HIV, and reproduction. One is the impression that the only issues about women and HIV worthy of public policy consideration concern reproduction. The other is the impression that reproduction is only a women's issue and that public policies need not concern, or be directed toward, men. Both of these impressions are false. Attention to women in the HIV/AIDS epidemic began largely in response to the recognition that HIV could be transmitted from pregnant women to their babies. As we have argued elsewhere,[2] important interests of women suffered as a consequence. Female manifestations of HIV infection were not identified, little was known about how women responded to anti-HIV agents, barrier methods of prevention that women could control were not developed, and innumerable diagnoses of HIV in women were missed. At the same time, although vertical transmission became the focus of considerable attention, little notice was taken of the fact that most HIV-infected women became infected from HIV-infected men. The "problem" of vertical transmission is as much a consequence of the behavior of men as of women. We focused on women and reproduction in this volume because of our concerns about the targeting of women for interventions and policies specifically related to reproduction and vertical transmission, not because we believe that reproduction is the only area related to women and HIV where attention ought to be focused.

This volume is divided into four sections. Section 1 covers the medical and public health issues related to HIV and childbearing. In Chapter 1, Alfred Saah describes the epidemiology of HIV infection in women and how the changes in the CDC surveillance definition of AIDS have affected projections of numbers of cases among women and children. In Chapter 2, Lois Eldred and Richard Chaisson relate the clinical course of HIV among women. Included in this chapter are the major manifestations of HIV in women and the impact of therapies on the natural history of HIV in women. Chapter 3 addresses gynecological and obstetrical issues for HIV-infected women. In this chapter, Jean Anderson reviews vertical transmission and the effect of HIV on pregnant women, as well as the gynecological manifestations of HIV infection. Chapters 4 and 5 focus on the children of HIV-infected women. In Chapter 4, Nancy Hutton discusses the natural history of HIV infection in children as well as the medical management of the HIV-infected child. In Chapter 5, Lawrence Wissow, Nancy Hutton, and Deven C. McGraw address the psychosocial implications of being the child of an HIV-infected mother, for both children who are themselves infected and children who are uninfected. The chapter confronts the impact of grief, orphaning, and stigmatization on the well-being of children. In Chapter 6, Liza Solomon and Sylvia Cohn examine access to medical care for women who are infected with HIV, including the special problems generated by having a socially stigmatizing condition. Concluding this section is Chapter 7, authored by Mary E. McCaul, Marsha Lillie-Blanton, and Dace S. Svikis. In this chapter, the complex interaction of drug use and HIV infection for women is explored.

Section 2 focuses on the legal issues surrounding HIV and childbearing. In Chapter 8, Taunya Lovell Banks focuses on constitutional and statutory challenges to state intervention in reproductive choice. In Chapter 9, Karen Rothenberg examines the potential for provider and maternal tort liability within the context of reproductive decision-making and HIV-infected women. In Chapter 10, Katherine Acuff reviews state interventions that have been used to control and monitor the behaviors of pregnant or postpartum drug users, with particular focus on the implications of these interventions on HIV-infected women.

Section 3 examines ethical and social issues. In Chapter 11, M. Gregg Bloche challenges the conventional understanding of social influence in the clinical context, with implications for the normative evaluation of reproductive counseling of HIV-infected women. Chapter 12, authored by Madison Powers, analyzes the status and justification of moral rights to have children. In Chapter 13, Patricia A. King considers, first, the special issues surrounding reproductive choice when the woman is an adolescent, and, second, the further implications when the adolescent woman is HIV-infected. In Chapter 14, Anita Allen examines the moral claim that HIV-infected women ought to avoid reproduction in light of competing multicultural and universalist understandings of moral judgment. Her analysis is grounded in the interviews with HIV-infected women.

Section 4 provides in greater detail our findings from the interviews. In Chapter 15, we report what health-care providers told us about how they actually counsel HIV-infected women and what their own beliefs are concerning HIV infection and childbearing. In Chapter 16, we relay in the women's words whether they intend to have children, the importance they place on motherhood, and what they have experienced and expect from health-care providers.

The final chapter of the book is authored by all of the members of the Working Group. In this chapter we put forward a policy proposal for whether and how others should attempt to influence, counsel, or otherwise interfere with the reproductive choices of HIV infected women based on the analyses, arguments, and findings presented in the earlier chapters.

Baltimore　　　　　　　　　　　　　　　　　　　　　　　　　　　　R.R.F.
February 1995　　　　　　　　　　　　　　　　　　　　　　　　　　N.E.K.

Notes

1. Members of the Working Group: Ruth R. Faden, Nancy E. Kass, Katherine L. Acuff, Anita Allen, Jean Anderson, Taunya Lovell Banks, M. Gregg Bloche, Richard Chaisson, Sylvia Cohn, Nancy Hutton, Patricia A. King, Marsha Lillie-Blanton, Mary E. McCaul, Madison Powers, Karen H. Rothenberg, Alfred Saah, Liza Solomon, and Lawrence Wissow.
2. R. Faden, N. Kass, and D. McGraw, "Women as Vessels and Vectors: Lessons from the HIV Epidemic," in *Feminism and Bioethics: Beyond Reproduction,* ed. Susan Wolf (New York: Oxford University Press, 1996, in press).

ACKNOWLEDGMENTS

This volume would not have been possible without support from the Health Resources Services Administration (HRSA). A grant from HRSA, entitled "Societal Responses to the Reproductive Choices of HIV-Infected Women," allowed us to convene the Working Group and interview HIV-infected women and their health-care providers. We are particularly indebted to Irene Forsman, our project officer, for her support of, and enthusiasm for, this project.

The position defended in Chapter 17 benefitted considerably from constructive and critical comments received in response to presentations of earlier versions of the chapter. We are indebted to colleagues at the Kennedy Institute of Ethics, Georgetown University, and the Center for AIDS Research, Johns Hopkins University, as well as to individuals who attended sessions of the American Public Health Association meetings in which our work was discussed.

We also wish to acknowledge the many people who helped us identify appropriate clinics and other settings in which to conduct our interviews. These interviews would not have been possible without the cooperation of administrators and other personnel, who permitted and facilitated our work on the days of the interviews. Sylvia Cohn, Monica Schoch-Spana, and Carol Slocum were outstanding interviewers; because of their sensitivity and good judgment, the empirical part of this project was a success. Linda Fogarty also contributed significantly to the success of the empirical part of our project through her careful management, analysis, and understanding of both the quantitative and qualitative data. In her work, Ms. Fogarty was assisted by Nahla Abdel-Tawab, Agatha Eke, Juanita Gupton, Karen McDonnell, and Bahar Moussavian, whose contributions we also acknowledge here.

We were fortunate in having the able assistance of Nancy Gregory in editing this volume. She was the force that kept the book moving at crucial times in its production. We also had editorial assistance from Meghan Dunleavy, Ruta Virkutis, and Kathleen Lester to whom we also give our thanks.

This project would not have been possible without the able assistance of our office staff. From start to finish, Gwendolyn Thomas and Adria Carey-Oduniyi helped in innumerable and often unseen ways.

Our greatest thanks go to the women and health-care providers who opened their lives to us. They entrusted us with the responsibility to share their stories. We hope we have been true to them.

CONTENTS

Contributors xvii

PART I MEDICAL AND PUBLIC HEALTH ISSUES

1. **The Epidemiology of HIV and AIDS in Women** 3
   ALFRED SAAH

2. **The Clinical Course of HIV Infection in Women** 15
   LOIS ELDRED AND RICHARD CHAISSON

3. **Gynecological and Obstetrical Issues for HIV-Infected Women** 31
   JEAN ANDERSON

4. **Health Prospects for Children Born to HIV-Infected Women** 63
   NANCY HUTTON

5. **Psychosocial Issues for Children Born to HIV-Infected Mothers** 78
   LAWRENCE WISSOW, NANCY HUTTON, AND DEVEN C. MCGRAW

6. **Access to, and Utilization of, Health Services for HIV-Infected Women** 96
   LIZA SOLOMON AND SYLVIA COHN

7. **Drug Use, HIV Status, and Reproduction** 110
   MARY E. MCCAUL, MARSHA LILLIE-BLANTON, AND DACE S. SVIKIS

PART II LEGAL ISSUES

8. **Legal Challenges: State Intervention, Reproduction, and HIV-Infected Women** 143
   TAUNYA LOVELL BANKS

9. Reproductive Choice and Reality: An Assessment of Tort Liability for Health-Care Providers and Women With HIV/AIDS 178
   KAREN H. ROTHENBERG

10. Perinatal Drug Use: State Interventions and the Implications for HIV-Infected Women 214
    KATHERINE ACUFF

PART III ETHICAL AND SOCIAL ISSUES

11. Clinical Counseling and the Problem of Autonomy-Negating Influence 257
    M. GREGG BLOCHE

12. The Moral Right to Have Children 320
    MADISON POWERS

13. Reproductive Choices of Adolescent Females with HIV/AIDS 345
    PATRICIA A. KING

14. Moral Multiculturalism, Childbearing, and AIDS 367
    ANITA ALLEN

PART IV VOICES FROM THE COMMUNITY

15. Practices and Opinions of Health-Care Providers Serving HIV-Infected Women 411
    NANCY KASS AND RUTH FADEN

16. In Women's Words: The Values and Lived Experiences of HIV-Infected Women 426
    NANCY KASS AND RUTH FADEN

PART V CONCLUSION

17. HIV Infection and Childbearing: A Proposal for Public Policy and Clinical Practice 447
    RUTH R. FADEN, NANCY E. KASS, KATHERINE L. ACUFF, ANITA ALLEN, JEAN ANDERSON, TAUNYA LOVELL BANKS, M. GREGG BLOCHE, RICHARD CHAISSON, SYLVIA COHN, NANCY HUTTON, PATRICIA A. KING, MARSHA LILLIE-BLANTON, MARY E. MCCAUL, MADISON POWERS, KAREN H. ROTHENBERG, ALFRED SAAH, LIZA SOLOMON, AND LAWRENCE WISSOW

Index 463

CONTRIBUTORS

Katherine L. Acuff, J.D., M.P.H.
Program in Law, Ethics and Health
The Johns Hopkins University School of Hygiene and Public Health
Baltimore, Maryland

Anita Allen, J.D., Ph.D.
Professor
Georgetown University Law Center
Washington, D.C.

Jean Anderson, M.D.
Associate Professor, Department of Obstetrics and Gynecology
The Johns Hopkins University School of Medicine
Baltimore, Maryland

Taunya Lovell Banks, J.D.
Jacob A. France Professor
University of Maryland School of Law
Baltimore, Maryland

M. Gregg Bloche, M.D., J.D.
Professor
Georgetown University Law Center
Washington, D.C.

Richard Chaisson, M.D.
Associate Professor of Medicine, Epidemiology and International Health
The Johns Hopkins University School of Medicine
Baltimore, Maryland

Sylvia Cohn, M.P.H., M.Sc.
Department of Epidemiology
The Johns Hopkins University School of Hygiene and Public Health
Baltimore, Maryland

Lois Eldred, M.P.H.
AIDS Service
The Johns Hopkins University School of Medicine
Baltimore, Maryland

Ruth Faden, Ph.D., M.P.H.
Philip Franklin Wagley Professor of Biomedical Ethics
Director, The Bioethics Institute
The Johns Hopkins University
Baltimore, Maryland

Senior Research Scholar
Kennedy Institute of Ethics
Georgetown University
Washington, D.C.

Nancy Hutton, M.D.
Director, Pediatric HIV/AIDS Program
Johns Hopkins Children's Center
The Johns Hopkins University School of Medicine
Baltimore, Maryland

Nancy Kass, Sc.D.
Assistant Professor
Program in Law, Ethics, and Health
The Johns Hopkins University School of Hygiene and Public Health
Baltimore, Maryland

Patricia A. King, J.D.
Professor
Georgetown University Law Center
Washington, D.C.

Marsha Lillie-Blanton, Dr.P.H.
Assistant Professor
Department of Health Policy and Management
The Johns Hopkins University School of Hygiene and Public Health
Baltimore, Maryland

CONTRIBUTORS

Mary E. McCaul, Ph.D.
Associate Professor
Director, Johns Hopkins Hospital Comprehensive Women's Center
Department of Psychiatry and Behavioral Sciences
The Johns Hopkins University School of Medicine
Baltimore, Maryland

Deven C. McGraw, J.D., M.P.H.
Georgetown University Law Center
Washington, D.C.
The Johns Hopkins University School of Hygiene and Public Health
Baltimore, MD

Madison Powers, J.D., D.Phil.
Associate Professor, Department of Philosophy
Senior Research Scholar, Kennedy Institute of Ethics
Georgetown University
Washington, D.C.

Karen H. Rothenberg, J.D., M.P.A.
Marjorie Cook Professor and Director,
Law and Health Care Program
University of Maryland School of Law
Baltimore, Maryland

Alfred Saah, M.D., M.P.H.
Associate Professor
Epidemiology and Infectious Disease Program
The Johns Hopkins University School of Hygiene and Public Health
Baltimore, Maryland

Liza Solomon, M.H.S, Dr.P.H.*
Director, AIDS Administration
Maryland Department of Health and Mental Hygiene
Baltimore, Maryland

Dace S. Svikis, Ph.D.
Assistant Professor
Department of Psychiatry and Behavioral Sciences
The Johns Hopkins University School of Medicine
Baltimore, Maryland

*Formerly with The Johns Hopkins School of Hygiene and Public Health

Lawrence Wissow, M.D., M.P.H.
Associate Professor, Pediatrics
The Johns Hopkins University School of Medicine
Baltimore, Maryland

I
MEDICAL AND PUBLIC HEALTH ISSUES

1

The Epidemiology of HIV and AIDS in Women

ALFRED SAAH

> I would certainly like to see more research, more clinical research, more statistics on it because obviously I want to know what's going on. I think there are probably women out there and will be in the future to justify research . . .
>
> *woman from New York*

Reported Cases of AIDS

AIDS was first recognized in gay/bisexual men in 1981 and was described in a woman in the United States that same year.[1] In 1983, a report described the first 43 women with AIDS: 30% apparently became infected through heterosexual intercourse, while injection drug use was responsible for the other 70% of cases.[2] Injection drug use has remained a major cause of HIV infection and AIDS in women in the United States, both by needle-sharing and through sexual transmission to non-drug-using female partners of drug using men. As HIV infection has become more prevalent, women are accounting for an ever-increasing proportion of reported AIDS cases in the United States. Women made up 7% of reported AIDS cases by 1986, 10% during 1988, and 18% during the period July 1993–June 1994.[3]

After five years of the epidemic, heterosexual transmission (for both men and women) made up 1% of the 16,227 reported cases in adults, injection drug use 17%, and male homosexual transmission 73%. Pediatric cases of AIDS, important epidemiologically because they often reflect unrecognized HIV infection in women, added another 231 to the total. Ten years of the epidemic produced 202,921 total cases of AIDS, but the proportions of the various subpopulations changed dramatically. For cases reported in 1990 and 1991,[4] gay men comprised 63% and 59% of the 42,564 and 44,823 total annual cases, respectively; injection drug use accounted for 24% and 25%, respectively. Women accounted for 10,618 (12%) cases of AIDS during these 2 years combined, with slightly less than half directly due to injection drug use and fully a third due to heterosexual transmission.

During the last year for which data are available (July 1993–June 1994),[5] the trend continued: 14,309 women with AIDS were reported nationwide. Of these

3

cases 38% were due to heterosexual contact, injection drug use accounted for 43%, and another 16% were in the category "risk-not-identified," which means that these cases remain under investigation. The heterosexual contact category can only increase because some of the risk-not-identified group eventually will be classified as heterosexual contact.

After 10 years of the HIV and AIDS epidemics, the racial distribution also has changed dramatically. During the first half of the AIDS epidemic, reported cases overwhelmingly were Caucasian. As HIV spread by use of contaminated needles, the demographic picture of AIDS in the United States changed to encompass more minority persons. By 1991, 46% of all men with AIDS and 75% of all women with AIDS were African-American or Hispanic,[6] despite the fact that these two groups comprise only 21% of the U.S. population. AIDS clearly has become a disease of poor, mostly urban minorities in the United States, but the epidemic is not confined to large urban centers.

Reports of HIV infection among migrant farm workers in the southeastern United States provide a glimpse of a new epidemic of AIDS yet to come. A report from Florida[7] showed that, of 310 migrant farm workers (80% male in this sample) who participated in screening for HIV infection, syphilis, and tuberculosis (TB), 5% (=15) were HIV-positive and 8% (=26) had reactive tests for syphilis. Those born in the United States were more likely than those who were foreign-born to have positive HIV tests and reactive syphilis tests (11% vs. 3%). Positive tests for TB were similar among those born in the United States and those foreign-born. Overall, 44% (=118 of 267) had tests indicating infection with TB. HIV seropositivity was associated with having more than two sex partners during the previous 6 months, a prior history of syphilis, and, among men, having ever paid for sex. Injection drug use and male-to-male sexual intercourse were reported rarely, regardless of HIV infection. None of those who were HIV-positive reported injection drug use, one male reported male-to-male sexual behavior, and one female reported bisexual behavior. Almost half had never used a condom. These rates of HIV infection were higher than similar populations in the South. Three and one-half percent of farm workers tested in Belle Glade, Florida (an agricultural community) and 2.6% of those tested in North Carolina were HIV-positive. In all of these populations, the risk factor for HIV infection was heterosexual intercourse.

Ellerbrock and colleagues[8] report a descriptive analysis comparing women with AIDS to heterosexual men with AIDS during the years 1981 through 1990. At the time of diagnosis of AIDS, the median age for women was 34 and for men 36 years. More women were in their twenties than men (27% vs. 16%), indicating that many were infected with HIV as adolescents. Geographically, ten areas accounted for 72% of reported AIDS cases in women: Puerto Rico, New York, New Jersey, Connecticut, Maryland, Delaware, Rhode Island, Massachusetts,

Georgia, and the District of Columbia, with the overwhelming majority (73%) of female cases found in large urban centers at the time of diagnosis. The geographic distribution of AIDS in heterosexual men is very similar to that of women. Survival rates were examined in this study for women and men who were diagnosed with AIDS as of December 31, 1989. Median survival after diagnosis of AIDS was 9.8 months for women and 9.3 months for heterosexual men, not a significant difference. The 3-year survival rate after AIDS diagnosis was 20% for women and 19% for heterosexual men, also not significant. These data do not provide information on the duration of asymptomatic HIV infection in either women or heterosexual men, so the natural history of HIV infection (i.e., its duration prior to symptomatic disease) cannot be inferred.

Analysis of AIDS cases indicates a far greater problem than may be evident from such surveillance data because AIDS (clinically manifest immune deficiency disease) results from HIV infection that has been present for some years. In other words, AIDS surveillance data reflect HIV transmission that occurred 5–8 years prior to the reporting of the clinical case of AIDS. Seroprevalence studies, however, measure the presence of antibodies to HIV and, thus, are a more accurate reflection of who is currently infected, providing data with which to plan for the expected cases of AIDS.

New Definition of AIDS

During the most recent revision of the surveillance definition for AIDS in the United States,[9] there was much controversy regarding whether clinical conditions should continue to be included in the definition. An effort was made by some to change the definition of AIDS from a clinical one to a strict laboratory one (i.e., number of CD4 cells below 200). The difficulty with a strict laboratory definition was that many forms of serious HIV-related diseases, especially gynecological conditions, occur above 200 CD4 cells and would, therefore, not be considered AIDS-related or AIDS-defining conditions, limiting access to medical care. Moreover, as many as 25%–30% of individuals whose CD4 cells fall below 200 are completely asymptomatic for 1–2 years thereafter, thus making the diagnosis of AIDS (traditionally meaning clinically significant disease) irrelevant to the delivery of preventive or therapeutic clinical care. The argument for an exclusively laboratory definition did not succeed, however, and the changes in the latest revision resulted in the inclusion of specific conditions that now define AIDS and AIDS-related conditions in women. There is yet another advantage of the newly adopted surveillance definition: previous versions were simply classification systems of disease as opposed to staging systems of progressive HIV infection. While the two systems may sound similar, there are significant differences between them. In an HIV staging system, disorders affecting women may

TABLE 1.1. 1993 Revised Classification System of Three Clinical Categories for HIV Infection and Expanded AIDS Surveillance Case Definition for Adolescents and Adults

CD4 T-Cell Categories	(A) Asymptomatic, Acute (Primary) HIV or PGL[a]	(B) Symptomatic, not (A) or (C) Conditions	(C) AIDS-Indicator Conditions
(1) ≥500[b]	A1	B1	C1
(2) 200–499	A2	B2	C2
(3) <200	A3	B3	C3

Centers for Disease Control, "1993 Revised Classification System for HIV Infection," *Morbidity and Mortality Weekly Report* 41 (No. RR—17; 1992:1–19.
[a] Persistent generalized lymphadenopathy.
[b] Cells × 10^6 per liter.

now be studied in a systematic fashion, and results may be validly compared and/or grouped across different populations of women; such capability will permit data on the course of HIV infection and disease in women to be much more rapidly collected and put to clinical use.

The new surveillance definition for AIDS in the United States has produced great leeway for clinicians in the diagnosis of AIDS. Table 1.1 depicts the combined staging and classification system for the new surveillance definition.

Everyone in column C and everyone in row 3 is now classified as meeting the surveillance definition for AIDS. The clinical categories are for adolescents or adults with documented HIV infection. Category A includes asymptomatic HIV infection, persistent generalized lymphadenopathy, or acute (primary) HIV infection with accompanying illness or history of acute HIV infection. Category B conditions are those attributable to HIV infection, those that indicate a defect in cell-mediated immunity, or those that require management that is complicated by HIV infection. Such conditions include (conditions specific to women are in italics) bacillary angiomatosis; oropharyngeal candidiasis (thrush); *vulvovaginal candidiasis that is persistent, frequent, or poorly responsive to therapy; moderate or severe cervical dysplasia or carcinoma in situ*; constitutional symptoms, such as fever (38.5° C) or diarrhea lasting longer than 1 month; oral hairy leukoplakia; herpes zoster involving at least two distinct episodes or more than one dermatome; idiopathic thrombocytopenic purpura, listeriosis, *pelvic inflammatory disease (PID)*; and peripheral neuropathy. These categories are hierarchical in one direction so that someone who is treated successfully for a category B condition and becomes asymptomatic remains in category B. Category C conditions are those that have previously defined clinical AIDS, with the addition of pulmonary TB, recurrent pneumonia, and *invasive cervical carcinoma*, now AIDS-defining conditions. The laboratory definition of AIDS also applies, but it is not the sole criterion by which AIDS is defined. Clinicians thus have much more flexibility in diagnosing AIDS based on gynecological conditions.

Mortality Due to AIDS

AIDS is rapidly becoming a major killer of young women in the United States.[10] Figures 1.1 and 1.2 report the death rates, by cause, for all women and men (for comparison) aged 25–44 years in the United States from 1982 to 1992. It can be seen that death due to AIDS in women aged 25–44 years soon will overtake heart disease and become the second leading cause of death in women in the United States within 5–7 years. Death in this age group is particularly devastating to society because of the loss of productive years of life and the impact of these deaths on families, workplaces, and children who are orphaned.

In addition to demonstrating the increasing importance of HIV/AIDS as a cause of death in women between the ages of 25 and 44 years, Table 1.2 provides data on the total number of deaths in women and the proportion of deaths that are due to HIV/AIDS in women by year. Note that the difference in total deaths from 1987 is almost exactly the number of deaths due to AIDS for that particular year. The implication is that HIV/AIDS is producing excess mortality—i.e., AIDS is killing women who otherwise would not have died of other causes.

FIGURE 1.1. Death rates[a] from leading causes of death among men aged 25–44 years, by year—United States, 1982–1992[b]

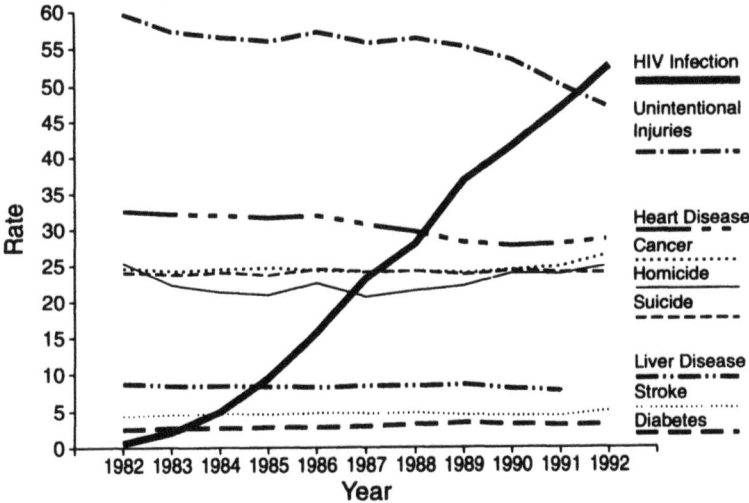

[a]Per 100,000 population.
[b]National vital statistics based on underlying cause of death, using final date for 1982–1991 and provisional data for 1992. Data for liver disease in 1992 are unavailable.

FIGURE 1.2. Death rates[a] from leading causes of death among women aged 25–44 years, by year—United States, 1982–1992[b]

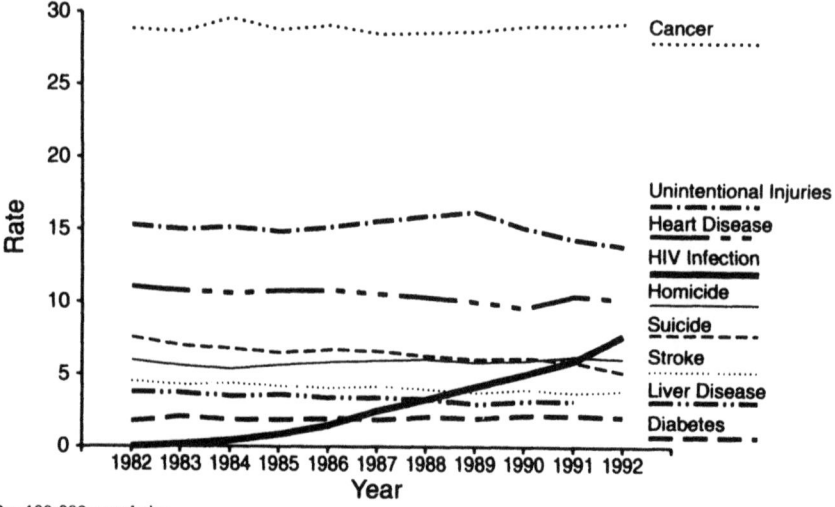

[a] Per 100,000 population.
[b] National vital statistics based on underlying cause of death, using final date for 1982–1991 and provisional data for 1992. Data for liver disease in 1992 are unavailable.

The data are even more informative when mortality is stratified by race and ethnicity. HIV/AIDS mortality is heavily concentrated in minority women. While HIV/AIDS ranked fourth as the cause of death in all women in 1992, it was second among African-American women (data not shown). For Hispanic women, AIDS accounted for 11% of deaths in 1990 and 12.4% in 1991; mortal-

TABLE 1.2. Percentage of Deaths Caused by HIV/AIDS, Rank of HIV/AIDS Among All Causes of Death, and Death Rate of HIV/AIDS for U.S. Women Aged 25–44 Years[a]

Year	Total Deaths	HIV/AIDS Deaths	Percent	Rank	Death Rate
1987	40,082	953	2.4	8	2.5
1988	41,172	1,285	3.1	8	3.3
1989	41,961	1,676	4.0	6	4.2
1990	42,134	2,031	4.8	6	5.0
1991	42,960	2,670	6.2	5	6.4
1992[b]	43,610	3,200	7.3	4	7.8

Centers for Disease Control (CDC), "1993 Revised Classification System for HIV Infection," *Morbidity and Mortality Weekly Report* 41 (No. RR—17; 1992:1–19; CDC, "Update: Mortality Attributable to HIV Infections/AIDS Among Persons Aged 25–44—United States, 1990 and 1991," *Morbidity and Mortality Weekly Report* 42 (1993): 481–486; CDC, "Update: Mortality Attributable to HIV Infection/AIDS Among Persons Aged 25–44—United States, 1991 and 1992," *Morbidity and Mortality Weekly Report* 42 (1993): 869–872.
[a] Death rates are calculated per 100,000.
[b] Provisional data

TABLE 1.3. Percentage of Deaths Caused by HIV/AIDS, Rank of HIV/AIDS Among All Causes of Death, and Death Rate of HIV/AIDS for U.S. Women Aged 25–44 Years by Race and Ethnicity During 1990[a]

Race/Ethnicity	Total Deaths	HIV/AIDS Deaths	Percent	Rank	Death Rate
Non-Hispanic					
White	25,354	434	1.7	9	1.5
Black	10,584	1,160	11.0	3	24.4
Hispanic					
Puerto Rican	644	192	29.8	1	—
Cuban	106	10	9.4	5	—
Mexican	1,287	31	2.4	8	—
Other	366	21	5.7	4	—
Unspecified	459	58	12.6	3	—
Total Hispanic	2,862	312	10.9	3	8.8

Centers for Disease Control, "1993 Revised Classification System for HIV Infection," *Morbidity and Mortality Weekly Report* 41 (No. RR—17; 1992: 1–19.
[a]Death rates are calculated per 100,000.

ity among Hispanic women varied greatly by national origin. AIDS was the leading cause of death among women of Puerto Rican origin, accounting for approximately 30% of all deaths during 1990. Table 1.3 shows racial and ethnic categories of women who died of AIDS in the United States in 1990 (the latest year when complete data are available). Note that while the percentage of deaths due to HIV/AIDS among African-American women (11.0%) is very similar to that of Hispanic women (10.9%), the death rate is threefold higher among African-American women than among Hispanic women (24.4% vs. 8.8%). This probably reflects the "maturity" of the epidemic in the respective populations.

HIV Seroprevalence

United States

Various serosurveys in the United States have demonstrated that HIV has achieved high levels of infection in women, particularly in coastal cities. Initial studies relied upon the anonymous testing of the blood of newborns to obtain an estimate of seroprevalence in pregnant women since HIV seroreactivity in newborns reflects maternal infection with HIV. In a 1989 national survey of more than 1.6 million anonymously tested newborns, Wasser and colleagues[11] found regional and urban/nonurban differences in HIV seroprevalence. Urban areas in the Northeast and South had much higher prevalences of HIV seroreactivity than urban areas in the West and Midwest. Urban areas of New York State had the highest estimated rate (8.4 per 1,000) of HIV-infected women, followed by urban areas in Florida, New Jersey, California, and Maryland. In nonurban health districts, seroprevalence rates were high in New York (1.3 per 1,000), South Carolina (1.3 per 1,000), Florida (2.0 per 1,000), and Georgia and Delaware (1.2 per 1,000). Race had the strongest association with seropositivity. African-American childbearing women were 12 times more likely to be infected than white women in the Northeast and seven times more likely in the South. While the highest concentration of HIV infection in childbearing women occurs in urban areas on the East Coast, this study also showed that HIV infection in nonurban areas, especially in the South, is widespread.

Hoff and associates[12] reported a study in which newborns were tested in Massachusetts for evidence of serological HIV reactivity. These specimens were collected routinely for testing by public health officials for evidence of metabolic disorders in newborns. Testing was of specimens collected largely during 1987. Rates of seropositivity were highest in inner-city hospitals (8.0 per 1,000), lower in mixed urban and suburban hospitals (2.5 per 1,000), and lowest in suburban and rural hospitals (0.9 per 1,000). These rates were higher than those found in the Department of Defense's screening of recruits: during a comparable period, seroprevalence was found to be 1 per 1,000 in female recruits.[13]

Novick and colleagues[14] tested blood specimens from virtually all newborns in the state of New York for 12 months during 1987 and 1988. HIV seroprevalence was found to be 0.13% for white, 1.82% for African-American, and 1.31% for Hispanic mothers. (Note that these prevalence rates are per 100 and that the rates in Massachusetts are per 1,000.) Of 1,186 births to HIV-infected mothers, 54% occurred among African-American women and 30% among Hispanic women.

In a national serosurvey, Gwinn and colleagues[15] reported the results of a population-based sample of pregnant women who delivered during 1988 and 1989. The states with the highest rates of seroprevalence were New York, New Jersey, and Florida. Overall, HIV infection was more prevalent among women residing in metropolitan counties than in other areas. Broken down by ethnicity, seroprevalence rates in African-American women were generally five to 15 times higher than in white women in the same states. Hispanic women had rates between those of African-American and white women in several states, including New York. High prevalence areas, such as the states noted above, generally had overall HIV seroprevalence rates above 4.5 per 1,000. The District of Columbia had a rate of 5.5 per 1,000.

St. Louis and colleagues[16] conducted a national survey by studying admissions to selected hospitals during 1988 and 1989. Seroprevalence for HIV among women who were admitted for non-AIDS-related conditions ranged from 0% to 7.8% in women 25–44 years old. The highest rates of seroprevalence were found in women aged 25–34 years; this age group is also the one with the highest frequency of AIDS in women. (Age at diagnosis of HIV infection was adjusted downward by 3 years from age at diagnosis of AIDS to partially account for the incubation period from infection to onset of symptoms.) Seroprevalence was lowest in the western and midwestern United States, intermediate in the South, and highest in the Northeast. Rates of infection were found to be high in communities in which there were high rates of injection drug use; these communities also were comprised largely of African-American and Hispanic persons. Data from the Department of Defense[17] showed rates of seropositivity in those being recruited for military service to be highest in the nation in the northeastern United States and within and around Washington D.C. From 1985 through 1989, 358,584 civilian women applying for military service were tested for HIV seroreactivity: 225 (0.06%) were seropositive. Seroprevalence was 0.02% for whites, 0.15% for African-Americans, and 0.08% for Hispanics. A quarter of the seropositive applicants were from New York.

International

The epidemic of HIV and AIDS in countries outside of North America and Europe has been and remains largely a heterosexual one. Illnesses characteristic of severe immune deficiency were being recognized in central Africa and Haiti at the same time that they were first being observed in the United States. By January 1992, there were an estimated cumulative worldwide total of 11.8 million adults and 1.1 million children with HIV infection, a number that is expected to increase threefold by the end of the century. It is estimated that 40% (4.7 million) of HIV-infected adults are women and that most reside in Africa. The cumulative proportion of HIV infection, attributable to heterosexual contact, for both men and women is 71% worldwide.[18]

Prevalence of infection in African populations ranges from less than 1% in many rural areas[19] to higher than 30% in certain cities.[20] Recent evidence indicates that infection is spreading rapidly outside of the cities because of the level of commercial interaction and exchange among the many regions on the continent.[21] Genital ulcer disease has been shown to be a significant risk factor for HIV infection. Sexually transmitted infections, such as chancroid, syphilis, and herpes simplex, promote transmission of HIV by disruption of normal skin and mucosal barriers.[22] Other sexually transmitted diseases, such as gonorrhea and chlamydia, also have been shown to be associated with HIV infection in certain studies.

The highest frequency of HIV infection is found among central African women between the ages of 15 and 29 years.[23] In a large commercial area in Malawi, in central Africa, incidence of HIV infection was estimated to be 10% annually during the late 1980s.[24] During 1984–1985, seroprevalence in women presenting for prenatal care was approximately 2%; this rose to more than 28% in the same population by the end of 1992. AIDS is currently the leading cause of death in young adults in Abidjian, Ivory Coast,[25] and is probably the leading cause of death among young adults in many parts of Africa.

Conclusion

Of the estimated 11.8 million adults infected with HIV worldwide in early 1992, 4.7 million (40%) were women. Unfortunately, an effective vaccine against HIV is years away. While efforts at improving the social empowerment of women throughout the world continue, and while we struggle to understand the determinants of sexual behavior to effect a lasting change in this difficult area, we should move quickly toward identifying an effective method of protection that women themselves can use. The female condom, one such method under study, is meeting with mixed reviews at the time of this writing. A safe and effective vaginally applied microbicide would be extremely valuable in preventing HIV infection, as well as other sexually transmitted diseases. Funding agencies are encouraging research in this area, which seems technologically quite feasible.

There are a number of studies that address the natural history of HIV infection in women in the United States and that seek to understand which factors affect HIV transmission and clinical disease, particularly in women. In addition to heterosexual transmission, significant numbers of women are becoming infected through injection drug use. Efforts must be made to alter illicit drug behavior through treatment and by changing the socially bankrupt conditions in which women, or their male partners, seek drugs in the first place. A short-term plan must be devised and implemented to prevent some sexually mediated and drug use–mediated infections and to treat those who are infected already. Such activities, however, should not come at the expense of very serious long-term planning to prevent conditions that result in HIV infection in women.

Notes

1. Centers for Disease Control, "Follow-up on Kaposi's Sarcoma and Pneumocystis Pneumonia," *Morbidity and Mortality Weekly Report* 30 (1981): 409–410.
2. Centers for Disease Control, "Immunodeficiency Among Female Sexual Partners of Males with Acquired Immune Deficiency Syndrome (AIDS)—New York," *Morbidity and Mortality Weekly Report* 31 (1983): 697–698.
3. Centers for Disease Control, "Update: Acquired Immunodeficiency Syndrome—United States," *Morbidity and Mortality Weekly Report* 35 (1986): 757–766; Centers for Disease Control, *HIV/AIDS Surveillance Report*, January (Atlanta, GA: CDC, 1990): 1–22; Centers for Disease Control, *HIV/AIDS Surveillance Report*, 6 (Atlanta, GA: CDC, 1994): 1–23.
4. Centers for Disease Control, *HIV/AIDS Surveillance Report*, January (Atlanta, GA: CDC, 1993): 1–23.
5. Centers for Disease Control, *HIV/AIDS Surveillance Report*, 6 (Atlanta, GA: CDC, 1994): 10.
6. Centers for Disease Control, *HIV/AIDS Surveillance Report*, January (Atlanta, GA: CDC, 1993): 1–23.
7. Centers for Disease Control, "HIV Infection, Syphilis, and Tuberculosis Screening

Among Migrant Farm Workers—Florida, 1992," *Morbidity and Mortality Weekly Report* 41 (1992): 723–725.
8. T. V. Ellerbrock, T. J. Bush, M. E. Chamberland, and M. J. Oxtoby, "Epidemiology of Women with AIDS in the United States, a Comparison with Heterosexual Men with AIDS, 1981 through 1990," *Journal of the American Medical Association* 265 (1991): 2971–2975.
9. Centers for Disease Control, "1993 Revised Classification System for HIV Infection and Expanded Surveillance Case Definition for AIDS Among Adolescents and Adults," *Morbidity and Mortality Weekly Report* 41 (No. RR—17; 1992): 1–19.
10. Centers for Disease Control, "Update: Mortality Attributable to HIV Infection/AIDS Among Persons Aged 25–44—United States, 1990 and 1991," *Morbidity and Mortality Weekly Report* 42 (1993): 481–486; Centers for Disease Control, "Update: Mortality Attributable to HIV Infection Among Persons Aged 25–44 years—United States, 1991 and 1992," *Morbidity and Mortality Weekly Report* 42 (1993): 869–872.
11. S. C. Wasser, M. Gwinn, and P. Fleming, "Urban–nonurban Distribution of HIV Infection in Childbearing Women in the United States," *Journal of Acquired Immune Deficiency Syndromes* 6 (1993): 1035–1042.
12. R. Hoff, V. P. Berardi, B. J. Weiblen, L. Mahoney-Trout, M. L. Mitchell, and G. F. Grady, "Seroprevalence of Human Immunodeficiency Virus Among Childbearing Women," *New England Journal of Medicine* 318 (1988): 525–530.
13. D. S. Burke, J. F. Brundage, J. R. Herbold, et al., "Human Immunodeficiency Virus Infections Among Civilian Applicants for United States Military Service—October 1985 to March 1986," *New England Journal of Medicine* 317 (1987): 131–136.
14. L. F. Novick, D. Berns, R. Stricof, R. Stevens, K. Pass, and J. Wethers, "HIV Seroprevalence in Newborns in New York State," *Journal of the American Medical Association* 261 (1989): 1745–1750.
15. M. Gwinn, M. Pappaioanou, J. R. George, et al., "Prevalence of HIV Infection in Childbearing Women in the United States," *Journal of the American Medical Association* 265 (1991): 1704–1708.
16. M. E. St. Louis, K. J. Rauch, L. R. Petersen, et al., "Seroprevalence Rates of Human Immunodeficiency Virus Infection at Sentinel Hospitals in the United States," *New England Journal of Medicine* 323 (1990): 213–218.
17. D. S. Burke, J. F. Brundage, J. R. Herbold, et al., "Human Immunodeficiency Virus Infections Among Civilian Applicants," (1987): 131–136.
18. J. M. Mann, D.J.M. Tarantola, and T. W. Netter, "The HIV Pandemic: Status and Trends," in *AIDS in the World*, eds. J. M. Mann, D.J.M. Tarantola, and T. W. Netter (Cambridge, MA: Harvard University Press, 1992): 11–109.
19. N. Nzilambi, K. M. DeCock, D. N. Forthal, et al., "The Prevalence of Infection with HIV over a 10-Year Period in Rural Zaire," *New England Journal of Medicine* 318 (1988): 276–279.
20. S. Allen, C. Lindan, A. Serufilira, et al., "HIV Infection in Urban Rwanda: Demographic and Behavioral Correlates in a Representative Sample of Childbearing Women," *Journal of the American Medical Association* 266 (1991): 1657–1663.
21. Mann et al., "The HIV Pandemic," pp. 40–47.
22. J. N. Simonsen, D. W. Cameron, M. N. Gakinya, et al., "HIV Among Men with Sexually Transmitted Diseases," *New England Journal of Medicine* 319 (1988): 274–278.

23. P. G. Miotti, G. Dallabetta, E. Ndovi, G. Liomba, A. J. Saah, and J. Chiphangwi, "HIV-1 and Pregnant Women: Associated Factors, Prevalence, Estimate of Incidence and Role in Fetal Wastage in Central Africa," *Journal of Acquired Immune Deficiency Syndromes* 4 (1990): 733–736.
24. Ibid.
25. K. M. De Cock, B. Barrere, L. Diaby, et al., "AIDS—The Leading Cause of Adult Death in the West African City of Abidjan, Ivory Coast," *Science* 249 (1990): 793–796.

2
The Clinical Course of HIV Infection in Women

LOIS ELDRED AND RICHARD CHAISSON

> It has been great but now it's getting bad. I feel weak, tired, very exhausted. From all that time, it was great, a normal life, but now it's really affecting me. The more years it takes, it seems like it's getting to me more. It's very hard.
>
> *woman from Los Angeles*

Women account for a growing proportion of HIV infection in the United States as injection drug use and heterosexual contact become the predominant modes of HIV transmission. In seroprevalence studies of inner-city populations, the female-to-male ratio of HIV seropositivity approaches 1:1.[1] In 1991, 74% of reported AIDS cases in women were among African-American and Hispanic women.[2] AIDS is the fourth leading cause of death among women of childbearing age nationally[3] and the leading cause of death among women of childbearing age in several urban areas.[4]

Recognition of early manifestations of HIV disease in women is essential for the initiation of antiretroviral and chemoprophylactic therapy since the effectiveness and tolerance of many therapeutic regimens diminishes with advanced HIV disease.[5] Until recently, however, manifestations of HIV that may be unique to, or more prevalent in, women have not been studied. The primary focus of research in HIV-infected women has been vertical transmission, examining rates of transmission of HIV from mother to child during pregnancy.[6] Frequently, HIV infection in women is identified through routine prenatal screening in areas of high HIV infection, where a majority of women are unaware of exposure to HIV.[7] Despite the high prevalence of gynecological manifestations in women, HIV infection often remains undiagnosed until advanced immunodeficiency is present since clinicians may not suspect HIV when women present with gynecological complications.

Few studies have compared gender-specific differences in terms of progression of infection, clinical manifestations, therapeutic interventions, or survival. Early studies suggested that HIV-infected women have a poorer prognosis than men; however, recent studies have found no gender-specific survival difference in women who have equal access to health-care services.[8] While the social, economic, and political circumstances of women with HIV infection may differ from those of men, the biological consequences of HIV are, for the most part, similar.[9]

Progression of Disease

HIV infection leads to an inevitable decline in cellular immune response. Manifestations of HIV disease are directly related to the degree of cellular immunodeficiency, which is determined primarily by the CD4 cell count. While useful in the clinical setting, large inter- and intralaboratory fluctuations limit the value of the CD4 cell count in detecting true changes in cellular immune function.[10] Other markers of immune activation are predictive of disease progression but are applied primarily in a research setting. More sensitive markers of immunodeficiency and HIV activity are under investigation.[11]

Gender differences in expression of immunological markers of HIV disease progression have not been studied. However, sex steroid receptors are found on the CD8 lymphocyte,[12] and alterations in exogenous estrogens have affected the threshold for opportunistic infections in mice.[13] The effects of pregnancy, oral contraception, and estrogen use on immune function are unlikely to be clinically significant in healthy women; the effect of gender-specific hormonal interactions on immunoregulatory mechanisms in HIV-infected women is unknown.

The average CD4 cell count in healthy, nonimmunosuppressed individuals is approximately $1,000/mm^3$.[14] HIV-infected persons lose an average of $200-300/mm^3$ CD4 cells in the first year after infection, followed by an average decline of $50-80/mm^3$ in each subsequent year. By the tenth year after infection, most individuals have a CD4 count less than $200/mm^3$,[15] the range where opportunistic conditions develop. The probability of developing an AIDS-defining condition within 18 months in untreated HIV-infected adults is given in Table 2.1.

Many factors influence progression of HIV disease: virulence of HIV strain, inoculum size or route of infection, health and nutritional status of the infected person, age, concomitant infections, and use of antiretroviral and chemoprophylactic agents.[16] All studies have shown an increasing risk of developing AIDS with time; indeed, time remains the most significant prognostic indicator of HIV-associated mortality. Estimates from cohorts of gay men indicate that the median time from acquisition of HIV infection to development of AIDS is 11 years,[17] though some persons have progressed to serious HIV-related disease within 2 years of acquisition of HIV, while others have remained asymptomatic longer than 14 years.[18]

The natural histories of HIV infection in homosexual men, injection drug users (IDUs), and transfusion recipients has been studied.[19] Prospective studies of the natural history of HIV infection in women in the United States first recruited subjects in 1993; any differences in progression to AIDS and survival among men and women will take several years to determine. The population-based

TABLE 2.1. Probability of Developing an AIDS-Defining Condition within 18 Months for Untreated HIV-Infected Adults[a]

CD4 Cell Count	18-Month Probability of AIDS
100/mm^3	60%
200/mm^3	30%
300/mm^3	15%
400/mm^3	8%
500/mm^3	3%

D. S. Stein, J. A. Korvick, and S. H. Vermund, "CD4+ Lymphocyte Cell Enumeration for Prediction of Clinical Course of Human Immunodeficiency Virus Disease: A Review," *Journal of Infectious Diseases* 165 (1992): 352–363.
[a]Refers to AIDS as defined by 1987–1992 case definition criteria [*Morbidity and Mortality Weekly Report* 36 (1987): 35].

natural history of progression to AIDS in adults in the absence of intervening antiretroviral and prophylactic therapy is given in Table 2.2.

Studies of gender differences in the progression of HIV disease in the United States are limited by small numbers or brief periods of evaluation. Studies from populations in developing countries are not comparable to the United States in baseline health status, concomitant infections, and access to medical care. An incident cohort study in Italy evaluated 854 HIV-infected patients, followed for up to 9 years after seroconversion, and found no gender differences in disease progression.[20] Gender differences in HIV disease among 2,606 men and 252 women with 24 months of follow-up were analyzed by Creagh and associates in Atlanta.[21] No differences were detected in the development of specific opportunistic infections when stratified by CD4 count, but women with a baseline CD4 count < 100 had significantly more rapid disease progression and shorter survival than men (25 months vs. 29 months). Although patients were not stratified by use of antiretroviral therapy, all patients were receiving medical care. This finding has not been validated by other studies.

A retrospective review of patients followed in an inner-city hospital-based clinic in New York found no differences in patterns of opportunistic infection, survival, or disease progression between men and women.[22] In another study, primarily of non-Hispanic white women with equal access to medical care across socioeconomic groups, no gender differences in disease progression were found.[23] Chaisson and colleagues measured progression of HIV infection and survival in an urban cohort of 1372 HIV seropositive patients. Thirty percent of the patients were women. The median follow-up was 1.6 years, with 2170 person-years of observation. There were no gender-specific differences in the disease progression or survival.[24]

TABLE 2.2. Natural History of HIV Infection[a]

Time from Transmission (Average)	Observation[b]	CD4 Cell Count
0	Viral transmission	Normal: 1,000 ± 500/cu mm
2–4 weeks	Self-limited infectious mononucleosis-like illness with fever, adenopathy, splenomegaly, morbilliform rash, leukopenia with atypical lymphocytes; may present with aseptic meningitis	Transient decrease
6–12 weeks	Serconversion (rarely requires ≥ 3 months for seroconversion)	Normal
0–8 years	Asymptomatic HIV infection ± PGL, ± recurrent vaginal candidiasis	Gradual reduction, with average decrease of 50–80 cu mm/year
4–8 years	ARC or early symptomatic HIV infection; thrush, oral hairy leukoplakia, ITP, constitutional symptoms (fever, weight loss, fatigue), bacterial infections, pelvic inflammatory disease, genital ulcerative disease, progressive cervical dysplasia	50–300/cu mm
6–10 years	AIDS[c]; most common late complications are AIDS-defining opportunistic infections. AIDS-defining diagnosiss: *P. carinii, Candida esophagitis*, wasting syndrome, Kaposi's sarcoma, HIV-associated dementia, disseminated *M. avium*, lymphoma, cryptococcal meningitis, invasive cervical carcinoma	<200/cu mm (mean count is 50–100/cu mm)
8–12 months	Deaths after AIDS-defining diagnosis[c]	<50/cu mm

Revised from John G. Bartlett, "Recommendations for the Medical Care of Persons with HIV Infection, 1992–1993," *Critical Care America* (Johns Hopkins Medical Institutions, 1992).

[a] Natural history indicates course of HIV infection in absence of antiretroviral treatment.

[b] ARC, AIDS-related complex; ITP, immune thrombocytopenia; PGL, peripheral generalized lymphadenopathy.

[c] The AIDS-defining diagnoses utilize the CDC criteria of 1987–1992 [*Morbidity and Mortality Weekly Report* 36 (1987): 35].

Survival after a diagnosis of AIDS depends on the initial AIDS-defining illness, CD4 count, age, and use of antiretroviral and chemoprophylactic agents.[25] Early studies in the pretherapeutic era in New York City showed that women, African-Americans, and IDUs had poorer survival rates than men, whites, and homosexuals.[26] These differences have been explained largely by differences in socioeconomic status; delay in detecting HIV infection in women, African-Americans, and IDUs; and inequities in access to care. The occurrence of Kaposi's sarcoma almost exclusively in homosexual men further creates a lead-time bias which confounds survival comparisons in men and women, as Kaposi's sarcoma occurs earlier in the course of HIV infection than other opportunistic conditions and is associated with longer survival.[27]

Moore and colleagues[28] examined differences in the natural history of AIDS in Maryland residents diagnosed after the licensing of zidovudine (also known as azidothymidine or AZT), the first available antiretroviral medication for HIV infection. Gender and ethnic differences were evaluated using AZT as a marker of access to medical services. While 49% of the total cohort received AZT, only 33% of the women received therapy as compared to 53% of the men. In addition, non-Hispanic whites were significantly more likely than minorities to receive AZT (63% vs. 43%). Median survival in persons receiving AZT was 770 days compared to 190 days in persons not receiving AZT. Gender and race differences were accounted for by differential use of AZT.

A prospective study of survival after a diagnosis of AIDS analyzed all reported AIDS patients in San Francisco between July 1981 and December 1990 and followed them prospectively through May 1991.[29] Despite significantly improved survival rates in recent years for both men and women, women still experienced significantly shorter survival than men. However, when stratified by use of antiretroviral therapy, gender-based survival differences disappeared. Easterbrook and associates[30] studied a large heterogeneous group of patients with advanced HIV disease, all of whom received AZT; although women accounted for only 5% of study subjects, no gender differences in survival were observed.

Clinical Course of HIV Disease

The clinical manifestations of HIV disease are highly variable. Two to 4 weeks after infection, 53%–93% of patients experience symptomatic primary HIV infection, variably characterized by fever, muscle aches, malaise, rash, swollen lymph glands, and headache.[31] Gender differences in the experience of symptomatic primary HIV infection are not known. In a study by Carpenter and colleagues,[32] only eight of 117 women identified symptomatic primary HIV infection; however, women were interviewed about seroconversion symptoms retrospectively, so poor recall could greatly underestimate this phenomenon.

HIV seroconversion generally occurs 2–12 weeks after exposure and is followed by a relatively asymptomatic phase of HIV disease, usually lasting for several years. Patients may develop peripheral generalized lymphadenopathy, but most are asymptomatic and often unaware of their infection. The most frequent initial manifestation of HIV in women is recurrent vaginal candidiasis (yeast infections), which may develop in women who otherwise are asymptomatic and have a normal CD4 cell count.[33] Gynecological disease is extremely common in HIV-infected women, yet HIV infection is likely to go undetected at early stages unless the patient or her clinician have a high index of suspicion.

As HIV-induced immunosuppression progresses, nonspecific symptoms develop. The most reliable clinical predictors of HIV disease progression in studies of homosexual men are thrush, persistent fever, unexplained diarrhea, and involuntary weight loss.[34] These constitutional symptoms do not differ significantly from those experienced by women. Late complications of HIV disease typically manifest when the CD4 count drops to below 200/mm³.[35] At this advanced stage of immunodeficiency, patients become susceptible to opportunistic infections and malignancies, wasting syndrome, HIV dementia, and recurrent PID. Despite the profound degree of immunosuppression (i.e., having an extremely low CD4 count), some HIV-infected patients remain asymptomatic for months to years (see Table 2.1).

Early in the AIDS epidemic, the CDC developed a clinical definition of AIDS to include opportunistic conditions indicative of profound cellular immunodeficiency.[36] In 1987, the CDC revised the case definition to include HIV wasting syndrome, HIV dementia, disseminated TB, and other opportunistic conditions.[37] As the scope of AIDS-indicator conditions broadened, more AIDS cases among women were reported.[38] In 1993, the CDC AIDS case definition was expanded again in an effort to be more inclusive of IDUs, women, and populations that may have been underrepresented in the previous definitions.[39] The 1993 definition includes the 1987 AIDS-indicator conditions, a CD4 cell count $< 200/mm^3$, or one of the following indicator conditions: pulmonary TB, recurrent bacterial pneumonia within a period of 12 months, or invasive cervical carcinoma.

In a study conducted at the Johns Hopkins Hospital HIV Clinic, the 1993 revision of the AIDS case definition doubled the number of prevalent AIDS cases, with significant increases in the proportion of women and IDUs.[40] Patients meeting only the 1993 case definition were less immunocompromised and more likely to be asymptomatic than patients with opportunistic diseases meeting the 1987 case definition. Not surprisingly, median survival rates were significantly longer for patients meeting the 1993 definition exclusively. Although 126 new AIDS cases were identified in the Johns Hopkins study using the 1993 case definition, only nine of them met the definition by indicator criteria alone (three had pulmonary TB, six had recurrent pneumonia, and none had invasive cervical carcinoma); the rest were included because the CD4 count fell below 200.

The 1993 CDC AIDS definition resulted in an additional 48,915 cases of AIDS reported nationally through September, 1993.[41] The majority of this increase (44,176 cases) was due to the reporting of severe HIV-related immunosuppression (CD4 < 200); invasive cervical carcinoma accounted for 123 AIDS cases. Reported cases of invasive cervical carcinoma among HIV-infected women are likely to increase due to expanded awareness and gynecological screening of HIV-infected women and a rapid rise in the incidence of cervical dysplasia, the precursor to invasive cervical carcinoma. As the life expectancy of persons with AIDS increases due to improved prophylaxis and treatment of AIDS-related conditions, invasive cervical carcinoma and other malignancies will increase.

Gynecological disease in HIV-infected women is extremely common (see Chapter 3). In one study, 34% of women attending an inner-city HIV clinic presented with gynecological disease.[42] Genital ulcerative disease may be more severe, persistent, and atypical in HIV-infected women and may recur more frequently as immunodeficiency progresses.[43] Human papillomavirus (HPV) is prevalent in HIV-infected women; consequently, cervical dysplasia that is severe, extensive, and multifocal has been associated with immunosuppression in HIV-infected women.[44] Similarly, invasive cervical carcinoma in HIV-infected women appears to be associated with a more advanced stage of the disease, poor response to therapy, and cancer recurrence.[45] HIV seroprevalence in women with PID ranges from 6.7% to 46%.[46] PID may be more severe and recurrent in HIV-infected women and more likely to require surgical intervention.[47]

Nongynecological Manifestations of HIV in Women

The majority of AIDS cases reported to the CDC are among men; by June of 1994, women accounted for 13% of cumulative reported AIDS cases.[48] Gender differences in CDC-defined AIDS are most pronounced in persons with Kaposi's sarcoma, an HIV-related malignancy seen primarily in homosexual men. Kaposi's sarcoma is a rare complication of HIV disease in women[49] and is decreasing in all risk groups. Among HIV-infected women with Kaposi's sarcoma there is a 4:1 predominance in sexual partners of bisexual men, evidence that a sexually transmitted agent is responsible.[50] The difference in incidence of Kaposi's sarcoma among risk groups confounds comparisons of gender-related opportunistic conditions. Stratification of opportunistic conditions by mode of transmission and gender (e.g., comparing male drug users to female drug users) can elucidate potential biological differences between men and women.

Fleming and colleagues[51] analyzed gender differences in AIDS cases reported to the CDC from January 1988 to June 1991. *Pneumocystis carinii* pneumonia (PCP) was the most common AIDS-defining illness, regardless of race, ethnicity, gender, or mode of HIV transmission, accounting for over 50% of reported AIDS cases in men and women. *Candida* esophagitis accounted for 19.6% of AIDS-defining diseases in women, compared with 14.6% in heterosexual men and 12.3% in homosexual men. Wasting syndrome accounted for 18.9% of AIDS-defining conditions in women, 19.0% in heterosexual men, and 16.1% in homosexual/bisexual men. In a multivariate analysis of IDUs, three opportunistic infections (herpes simplex virus [HSV], *Candida* esophagitis, and cytomegalovirus [CMV] disease) were reported significantly more frequently among women than men.

In a study of 200 HIV-infected Rhode Island women, opportunistic infections occurred at the same rate as for men, with comparable levels of profound immunodeficiency[52] but with some variation in manifestations of immunosuppressive conditions.[53] When compared with national data, this cohort was disproportionately white IDUs and had more uniform access to medical care across socioeconomic strata. *Candida* esophagitis was the most frequent AIDS-defining illness (34%), followed by PCP (20%), and chronic mucocutaneous HSV infections (18%). Other HIV-related diseases accounted for 27% of AIDS-defining illnesses, with no individual syndrome accounting for more than 4.5% of the total. The relatively low incidence of PCP is at least partly related to the use of prophylaxis against PCP in this cohort, though previous reports of AIDS in Rhode Island also revealed a low incidence of this opportunistic infection.

Bacterial infections frequently complicate HIV disease. Uninfected IDUs have a higher prevalence of bacterial infections caused by nonhygienic injection practices, smoking, and poorer socioeconomic status than do persons who do not inject drugs.[54] Among HIV-infected drug users, the incidence and manifestations of bacterial infection is compounded by progressive immunodeficiency. While endocarditis, cellulitis, osteomyelitis, and bacteremia are well-documented infections of drug users directly related to injection, HIV infection increases drug users' susceptibility to bacterial sinusitis, pneumonia, and other common bacterial infections.

Increased incidence and severity of bacterial infections among HIV-infected women are reported by several authors.[55] In the study by Carpenter and colleagues,[56] bacterial pneumonia was the third most common clinical manifestation on presentation. In a New York City study of 2,983 outpatients, women were significantly more likely than men to experience bacterial pneumonia and endocarditis.[57] However, women in this study largely were IDUs (49%) or sexual partners of IDUs (26%), so the incidence of bacterial infections could be confounded by drug use and socioeconomic status. In a retrospective review of clinical manifestations of HIV infection in women in Louisiana, bacterial infections were implicated in at least 11% of deaths.[58] Bacterial pneumonia and septicemia accounted for 14% and 10% of HIV-related deaths, respectively, in a review of death certificate data among women of childbearing age.[59]

Antiretroviral Therapy

The first antiretroviral agent, AZT, became available in the United States in 1986. AZT has been shown to increase time to first AIDS-defining illness, improve survival, and decrease opportunistic infections.[60] Large clinical trials evaluating the effectiveness of AZT were conducted by the AIDS Clinical Trials

Group with men and women, and a recent analysis of two studies (ACTG 016 and 019) revealed no gender-specific difference in benefit from AZT.[61] Subsequently, three other nucleoside analogues, didianosine, zalcitabine and stavudine, were approved for use in patients who are either intolerant to AZT or demonstrate clinical or immunological deterioration as evidenced by new opportunistic conditions or a decline in CD4 count while taking AZT. The efficacy of these agents is similar to AZT but toxicities differ. Didanosine and zalcitabine may cause rash, peripheral neuropathy, diarrhea, and pancreatitis; stavudine may cause peripheral neuropathy and pancreatitis. These conditions are not associated with gender-specific biological differences. Recently recognized resistance to AZT, developing as early as 16 weeks after initiation of therapy, have led to a range of clinical practices, including use of combination antiretroviral therapy and alternating therapeutic regimens.

Efficacy of antiretroviral treatment and tolerance of therapy is related to disease status at initiation of therapy. AZT is approved by the Food and Drug Administration (FDA) for HIV-infected patients with a CD4 cell count less than $500/mm^3$; however, its use in asymptomatic patients with CD4 cell counts between $200-500/mm^3$ is controversial. The 1993 National Institute of Allergy and Infectious Diseases (NIAID) State of the Art Conference on Antiretroviral Therapy for HIV Infection concluded that AZT shall be considered optional for this group.[62] In patients with CD4 cell counts $<200/mm^3$, AZT is recommended regardless of symptoms. When initiated in late-stage disease (CD4 cell count $< 50/mm^3$), AZT has been shown to prolong life, but resistance and dose-limiting toxicity are more common.[63] There are no differences in dosage recommendations of antiretroviral therapy between women and men, though lower mean hemoglobin in women potentially could affect therapeutic regimens of AZT commonly associated with anemia. Genital tract tumors in female mice and rats have been associated with AZT.[64] No similar association has been seen in women, though studies are early and it is possible that a relationship could be revealed at a later time.

Prophylaxis of Opportunistic Infections

Major advances have occurred in the prevention of opportunistic infections in HIV-infected patients. Indications for prophylaxis vary according to CD4 cell count and likelihood of acquisition of infections. The use of trimethoprim-sulfa and other agents to prevent PCP has significantly decreased morbidity and mortality related to the disease.[65] The use of trimethoprim-sulfa as first-line preventive therapy for PCP in patients with CD4 cell counts $<200/mm^3$ has the added advantage of effectiveness in preventing *Toxoplasma gondii*, as well as HIV-related bacterial infections.[66] Rifabutin has recently been approved for prevention of disseminated *Mycobacterium avium* complex infection in patients with

CD4 cell counts <100/mm^3.[67] Secondary prophylaxis to prevent recurrence of opportunistic infection is recommended for cryptococcal meningitis, *Candida* esophagitis, recurrent HSV infection, and recurrent salmonella bacteremia.[68] There are no gender-specific recommendations for use of prophylactic agents as the occurrence of opportunistic infection is similar in men and women. The use of prophylactic agents for recurrent vaginal candidiasis is dependent on severity of symptoms and frequency of recurrence. TB chemoprophylaxis is recommended for HIV-infected patients with reactive skin tests (PPD) or significant exposure to TB.[69] The CDC recommends consideration of TB chemoprophylaxis for HIV-infected anergic patients from high-prevalence groups, including IDUs. These recommendations are not gender-specific.

Potential Pharmacokinetic Differences

The exclusion of women from clinical trials has limited the knowledge of pharmacokinetics (i.e., how drugs are metabolized) in women. Women may require different doses of drugs from men to maximize effectiveness and minimize intolerance. In 1990, only 6.7% of the ACTG participants were women, at a time when 9.8% of the AIDS diagnoses were among women.[70] Most clinical trials of antiretroviral HIV agents in the United States are actively recruiting women, but male participants still predominate due to the larger number of HIV-infected men and differential access to, and knowledge of, clinical trials. Therefore, knowledge of how drugs for HIV are metabolized among women remains limited.

Access to Care

Nonbiological factors greatly affect the medical care of HIV-infected women. Clinicians have a low index of suspicion of HIV disease in women in developed countries due to the prior predominance of HIV infection in men. Underutilization of available health services by women is exacerbated by generally inadequate nonpregnancy-related health services for poor inner-city women. HIV-infected drug-using women often have competing demands of addiction, family, and poverty overshadowing their ability to obtain medical care (see Chapter 6).

Women are the fastest growing group of HIV-infected persons in the United States. While there are differences in disease manifestations between HIV-infected women and men, particularly the gynecological manifestations, there is little difference in progression of disease, response to therapy, or survival among persons with access to medical care. The development of health services, clinical trials, and family support for HIV-infected women will improve medical outcomes for this underserved population. Further recognition of HIV manifestations in women will allow earlier treatment of both HIV disease and the consequences of immunodeficiency.

Notes

1. Centers for Disease Control, "Trends in Human Immunodeficiency Virus Infection Among Civilian Applicants for Military Service—United States, October 1985–March 1988," *Morbidity and Mortality Weekly Report* 37 (1988): 677–699; S. P. Donegan, K. C. Edelkin, and D. E. Craven, "HIV Seroprevalence Rate at Boston City Hospital," *New England Journal of Medicine* 319 (1988): 653–654; J. Horton, L. Alexander, and J. Brundage, "HIV Prevalence Among Military Women: An Examination of Military Applicant, Active Duty and Reserve Testing Data" (abstract M.A.P.2) p. 78, *5th International Conference on AIDS* (Montreal, Canada, June 1989); D. S. Burke, J. F. Brundage, M. Goldenbaum, et al., "Human Immunodeficiency Virus Infection in Teenagers: Seroprevalence Among Applicants for U.S. Military Service," *Journal of the American Medical Association* 263 (1990): 2074–2077; M. E. St. Louis, K. J. Rauch, L. R. Peterson, et al., "Seroprevalence Rates of Human Immunodeficiency Virus Infection at Sentinel Hospitals in the United States," *New England Journal of Medicine* 323 (1990): 213–218.
2. Centers for Disease Control, "Surveillance for AIDS and HIV Infection Among Black and Hispanic Children and Women of Childbearing Age, 1981–1989," *Morbidity and Mortality Weekly Report* 39, (1990): 23–30.
3. Centers for Disease Control, "Update: Mortality Attributable to HIV Infection Among Persons Aged 25–44 Years—United States, 1991 and 1992," *Morbidity and Mortality Weekly Report* 42 (1993): 481–486.
4. Centers for Disease Control, "HIV Prevalence Estimated and AIDS Case Projections for the United States: Report Based on a Workshop," *Morbidity and Mortality Weekly Report* 39 (1990): 1–31.
5. D. D. Richman, J. M. Grimes, and S. W. Lagakos, "Effect of Stage of Disease and Drug Dose on Susceptibilities of Isolates of Human Immunodeficiency Virus," *Journal of Acquired Immune Deficiency Syndromes* 3 (1990): 743–746; F. M. Gordin, G. L. Simon, C. D. Wofsy, et al., "Adverse Reactions to Trimethoprim-Sulfamethoxazole in Patients with Acquired Immunodeficiency Syndrome," *Annals of Internal Medicine* 100 (1984): 495–499.
6. C. A. Hankin and M. A. Handley, "HIV Disease and AIDS in Women: Current Knowledge and a Research Agenda," *Journal of Acquired Immune Deficiency Syndromes* 5 (1992): 957–971.
7. M. D. Barbacci, G. A. Dallabetta, J. T. Repke, et al., "Human Immunodeficiency Virus Infection in Women Attending an Inner-City Prenatal Clinic: Ineffectiveness of Targeted Screening," *Sexually Transmitted Diseases* 17 (1990): 122–126.
8. R. C. Horsburgh, R. Hanson, S. A. Fann, et al., "Predictors of Survival in HIV Infection Including CD4 Cell Counts, AIDS-Defining Conditions and Therapy but no Sex, Age, Race or Risk Activity" (Abstract MC3175), *7th International Conference on AIDS* (Florence, Italy, 1991); G. F. Lemp, A. N. Hirozawa, J. B. Cohen, et al., "Survival for Women and Men with AIDS," *Journal of Infectious Disease* 166 (1992): 74–79; T. V. Ellerbrock, T. J. Bush, M. E. Chamerland, et al., "Epidemiology of Women with AIDS in the U.S. 1981 through 1990," *Journal of the American Medical Association* 265 (1991): 2971–2975.
9. R. P. Brettle and C.L.S. Leen, "The Natural History of HIV and AIDS in Women," *AIDS* 5 (1991): 1283–1292.
10. J. L. Malone, T. E. Simms, G. C. Gray, et al., "Sources of Variability in Repeated T-Helper Lymphocyte Counts from Immunodeficiency Virus Type 1-Infected Pa-

tient: Total Lymphocyte Count Fluctuations and Diurnal Cycle are Important," *Journal of Acquired Immune Deficiency Syndromes* 3 (1990): 144–151.
11. M. S. Saag, "AIDS Testing: Now and in the Future," in *Medical Management of AIDS*, eds. M. D. Sande and P. A. Volberding (Philadelphia: W. B. Saunders, 1992): p. 33.
12. J.H.M. Cohen, L. Daniel, G. Cordier, et al., "Sex Steroid Receptors in Peripheral T Cells," *Journal of Immunology* 131 (1981): 2767–2771.
13. C. Grossman, "Possible Underlying Mechanisms of Sexual Dimorphism in the Immune Response, Fact and Hypotheses," *Journal of Steroid Biochemistry* 34 (1987): 241–251.
14. D. S. Stein, J. A. Korvick, and S. H. Vermund, "CD4+ Lymphocyte Cell Enumeration for Prediction of Clinical Course of Human Immunodeficiency Virus Disease: A Review," *Journal of Infectious Diseases* 165 (1992): 352–363.
15. R. B. Nieman, J. Fleming, and R. J. Coker, "The Effect of Cigarette Smoking on the Development of AIDS in HIV-1 Seropositive Individuals," *AIDS* 7 (1993): 705–710.
16. D. C. DesJarlais, S. R. Friedman, M. Marmor et al., "Development of AIDS, HIV Seroconversion, and Potential Cofactors for T4 Cell Loss in a Cohort of Intravenous Drug Users," *AIDS* 1 (1987): 105–111; R. D. Semba, N. M. Graham, W. T. Caiaffa, et al., "Increased Mortality Associated with Vitamin A Deficiency Virus Type 1 Infection," *Archives of Internal Medicine* 153 (1993): 2149–2154; R. B. Nieman, J. Fleming, and R. J. Coker, "The Effect of Cigarette Smoking on the Development of AIDS in HIV-1 Seropositive Individuals," *AIDS* 7 (1993): 705–710; J. A. Levy, "Human Immunodeficiency Viruses and the Pathogenesis of AIDS," *Journal of the American Medical Association* 261 (1989): 2997; R. A. Kaslow, J. P. Phair, and H. B. Friedman, "Infection with the Human Immunodeficiency Virus: Clinical Manifestations and their Relationship to Immune Deficiency—A Report from the Multicenter AIDS Cohort Study," *Annals of Internal Medicine* 107 (1987): 474–480; W. W. Darrow, D. F. Echenberg, H. W. Jaffe, et al., "Risk Factors for Human Immunodeficiency Virus (HIV) Infections in Homosexual Men," *American Journal of Public Health* 77 (1987): 479–483; R. D. Moore, T. Creagh-Kirk, S. C. Keruly, et al., "Long-Term Safety and Efficacy of In-Patients with Advanced Human Immunodeficiency Virus Disease," *Archives of Internal Medicine* 151 (1991): 981–986; M. A. Fischl, D. D. Richman, M. H. Grieco, et al., "The Efficacy of Azidothymidine (AZT) in the Treatment of Patients with AIDS and AIDS-Related Complex," *New England Journal of Medicine* 317 (1987): 185–191.
17. G. W. Rutherford, A. R. Lifson, N. A. Hessol, et al., "Course of HIV-1 Infection in a Cohort of Homosexual Men and Bisexual Men: An 11 Year Follow-Up Study," *British Medical Journal* 301 (1990): 1183–1188.
18. A. M. Hardy, "Characterization of Long-Term Survivors of Acquired Immunodeficiency Syndrome" (The Long-Term Survivor Collaborative Study Group), *Journal of Acquired Immune Deficiency Syndromes* 4 (1991): 386–391.
19. B. F. Polk, R. Fox, R. Brookmeyer, et al., "Predictors of the Acquired Immunodeficiency Syndrome Developing in a Cohort of Seropositive Homosexual Men," *New England Journal of Medicine* 316 (1987): 61–66; A. R. Lifson, G. W. Rutherford, H. W. Jaffe, "The Natural History of Human Immunodeficiency Virus Infection," *Journal of Infectious Diseases* 158 (1988): 1360–1367; G. Rezza, A. Lazzarin, G. Angarano, et al., "The Natural History of HIV Infection in Intravenous

Drug Users: Risk of Disease Progression in a Cohort of Seroconverters," *AIDS* 3 (1989): 87–90; J. W. Ward, T. J. Bush, H. A. Perkins, et al., "The Natural History of Transfusion-Associated Infection with Human Immunodeficiency Virus: Factors Influencing the Rate of Progression to Disease," *New England Journal of Medicine* 321 (1989): 947–957.

20. A. C. Lepri, P. Pezzotti, M. Dorrucci, A. N. Phillips and G. Rezza, "HIV Disease Progression in 854 Women and Men infected through injecting drug use and heterosexual sex and followed for up to nine years from seroconversion. Italian Seroconversion Study," *BMJ* 309 (1994): 1537–1542.
21. T. Creagh, M. Thompson, and A. Morris, "Gender Differences in the Spectrum of HIV Disease" (Abstract MoC0032), *8th International Conference on AIDS* (Amsterdam, The Netherlands, 1992): M010.
22. S. Szabo, L. H. Miller, H. S. Sacks, et al., "Gender Differences in the Natural History of HIV Infection" (Abstract MoC0030), *8th International Conference on AIDS* (Amsterdam, The Netherlands, 1992): M010.
23. C. C. Carpenter, K. H. Mayer, M. D. Stein, et al., "Human Immunodeficiency Virus Infection in North American Women: Experience with 200 Cases and a Review of the Literature," *Medicine* 70 (1991): 307–324.
24 R. E. Chiasson, J. C. Keruly, and R. D. Moore, "Race, Sex, Drug Use and Progression of HIV Disease," *New England Journal of Medicine* (in press).
25. R. A. Kaslow, J. P. Phai, H. B. Friedman, "Infection with the Human Immunodeficiency Virus: Clinical Manifestations and Their Relationship to Immune Deficiency—A Report from the Multicenter AIDS Cohort Study," *Annals of Internal Medicine* 107 (1987): 474–480; M. R. Moore, J. Hidalgo, B. Sugland, et al., "Zidovudine and the Natural History of the Acquired Immunodeficiency Syndrome," *New England Journal of Medicine* 324 (1991): 1412–1416.
26. New York City Department of Health, *AIDS Surveillance Update* (New York: NYC/DOH 1–8, March 1989); G. Rothenberg, M. Woelfel, R. Stoneburner, et al., "Survival with the Acquired Immunodeficiency Syndrome," *New England Journal of Medicine* 317 (1987): 1297–1302.
27. L. P. Jacobson, A. Munoz, R. Fox, et al., "Incidence of Kaposi's Sarcoma in a Cohort of Homosexual Men Infected with Human Immunodeficiency Virus Type 1," *Journal of Acquired Immune Deficiency Syndromes* 3 (1990): 534–531; A. R. Lifson, W. W. Darrow, N. A. Hessol, et al., "Kaposi's Sarcoma in a Cohort of Homosexual and Bisexual Men," *American Journal of Epidemiology* 131 (1990): 221–231.
28. M. R. Moore, J. Hidalgo, B. Sugland, et al., "Zidovudine and the Natural History of the Acquired Immunodeficiency Syndrome," *New England Journal of Medicine* 324 (1991): 1412–1416.
29. G. F. Lemp, A. N. Hirozawa, J. B. Cohen, et al., "Survival for Women and Men with AIDS," *Journal of Infectious Diseases* 166 (1992): 74–79.
30. P. J. Easterbrook, J. C. Keruly, T. Creagh-Kirk, et al., "Racial and Ethnic Differences in Outcome in Treated Patients with Advanced HIV Disease," *Journal of the American Medical Association* 266 (1991): 2713–2718.
31. R. Fox, L. J. Eldred, E. J. Fuchs, et al., "Clinical Manifestations of Acute Infection with Human Immunodeficiency Virus in a Cohort of Gay Men," *AIDS* 1 (1987): 35–38; B. Tindall, S. Barker, B. Donovan, et al., "Characteristics of the Acute Clinical Illness Associated with Human Immunodeficiency Virus Infection," *Archives of Internal Medicine* 148 (1988): 945–949; C. Pederson, B. O. Lindhardt,

B. L. Jensen, et al., "Clinical Course of Primary HIV Infection: Consequences for Subsequent Course of Infection," *British Medical Journal* 299 (1989): 154–157.
32. C. C. Carpenter, K. H. Mayer, M. D. Stein, et al., "Human Immunodeficiency Virus Infection in North American Women: Experience with 200 Cases and a Review of the Literature," *Medicine* 70 (1991): 307–324.
33. W. Imam, C. J. Carpenter, K. Mayer, et al., "Hierarchical Pattern of Mucosal Candida Infections in HIV Seropositive Women," *American Journal of Medicine* (1990): 142–146.
34. R. A. Kaslow, J. P. Phair, and H. B. Friedman, "Infection with the Human Immunodeficiency Virus: Clinical Manifestations and their Relationship to Immune Deficiency—A Report from the Multicenter AIDS Cohort Study," *Annals of Internal Medicine* 107 (1987): 474–480; A. R. Lifson, G. W. Rutherford, and H. W. Jaffe, "The Natural History of Human Immunodeficiency Virus Infection," *Journal of Infectious Diseases* 158 (1988): 1360–1367; R. Melbye, R. Biggar, P. Ebbesen, et al., "Long-Term Seropositivity for Human T-Lymphotrophic Virus Type II in Homosexual Men without the Acquired Immunodeficiency Syndrome: Development of Immunologic and Clinical Abnormalities," *Annals of Internal Medicine* 104 (1986): 496–500; J. Phair, A. Munoz, R. Detels, et al., "The Risk of Pneumocystis Carinii Pneumonia Among Men Infected with Human Immunodeficiency Virus Type 1," *New England Journal of Medicine* 322 (1990): 161–165.
35. A. R. Lifson, G. W. Rutherford, and H. W. Jaffe, "The Natural History of Human Immunodeficiency Virus Infection," *Journal of Infectious Diseases* 158 (1988): 1360–1367; A. R. Moss, P. Bacchetti, D. Osmond, et al., "Seropositivity for HIV and the Development of AIDS or ARC: Three Year Follow-Up of the San Francisco General Hospital Cohort," *British Medical Journal* 296 (1988): 745–750.
36. Centers for Disease Control, "Update on Acquired Immunodeficiency Syndrome (AIDS)—United States," *Morbidity and Mortality Weekly Report* 31 (1982): 353–361.
37. Centers for Disease Control, "Revision of the CDC Surveillance Case Definition for Acquired Immunodeficiency Syndrome," *Morbidity and Mortality Weekly Report* 36 (1987): 3S–14S.
38. R. M. Selik, H. W. Buehler, J. M. Karon, et al., "Impact of the 1987 Revision of the Case Definition of Acquired Immune Deficiency Syndrome in the United States," *Journal of Acquired Immune Deficiency Syndromes* 3 (1990): 73–82.
39. Centers for Disease Control, "1993 Revised Classification System for HIV Infection and Expanded Surveillance Case Definition for AIDS Among Adolescents and Adults," *Morbidity and Mortality Weekly Report* 41 (1992): 1–19.
40. R. E Chaisson, D. L. Stanton, J. E. Gallant, et al., "Impact of the 1993 Revision of the AIDS Case Definition on the Prevalence of AIDS in a Clinical Setting," *AIDS* 7 (1993): 857–862.
41. Centers for Disease Control, *HIV/AIDS Surveillance Report* 5 (Atlanta, GA: CDC, 1993): 13.
42. J. R. Anderson, J. Horn, R. King, et al., "A Descriptive Analysis of Patients Attending the Women's HIV Clinic at the Johns Hopkins Hospital" (abstract Th.D.P.10), *5th International Conference on AIDS* (Montreal, Canada, June 4–9, 1989): 760.
43. J. A. Maier, A. Bergman, and M. G. Ross, "Acquired Immunodeficiency Syndrome Manifested by Chronic Primary Genital Herpes," *American Journal of Obstetrics and Gynecology* 155 (1986): 756–758.
44. M. A. Byrne, D. Taylor-Robinson, P. E. Muday, et al., "The Common Occurrence

of Human Papilloma-Virus Infection and Intraepithelial Neoplasia in Women Infected by HIV," *AIDS* 3 (1989): 379–382; M. J. Henry, M. W. Stanley, S. Cruikshank, et al., "Association of Human Immunodeficiency Virus-Induced Immunosuppression with Human Papilloma-Virus Infection and Cervical Intraepithelial Neoplasia," *American Journal of Obstetrics and Gynecology* 160 (1989): 352–353; B. Spurrett, D. S. Jones, G. Steward, "Cervical Dysplasia and HIV Infection" (letter), *Lancet* (1988): 237–238.

45. M. Maiman, N. Tarricone, J. Vieira, et al., "Colposcopic Evaluation of Human Immunodeficiency Virus Seropositive Women," *American Journal of Obstetrics and Gynecology* 78 (1991): 84–88.

46. S. Safrin, B. J. Dattel, L. Hauer, et al., "Seroprevalence and Epidemiologic Correlates of Human Immunodeficiency Virus Infection in Women with Acute Pelvic Inflammatory Disease," *American Journal of Obstetrics and Gynecology* 75 (1990): 666–670; R. S. Sperling, F. Friedman, Jr., M. Brodman, et al., "Seroprevalence of Human Immunodeficiency Virus in Women Admitted to the Hospital with Pelvic Inflammatory Disease," *Journal of Reproductive Medicine* 36 (1991): 122–124; B. Hoegsberg, O. Abulafia, A. Sedlis, et al., "Sexually Transmitted Diseases and Human Immunodeficiency Virus Infection among Women with Pelvic Inflammatory Disease," *American Journal of Obstetrics and Gynecology* 163 (1990): 1135–1139.

47. V. Beral, T. A. Peterman, R. L. Berkelman, and H. W. Jaffe, "Kaposi's Sarcoma Among Persons with AIDS: A Sexually Transmitted Infection?" *Lancet* 335 (1990): 123–128.

48. Centers for Disease Control, *HIV/AIDS Surveillance Report*, 6 (Atlanta, GA: CDC, 1994): 5, 10.

49. Beral, et al., "Kaposi's Sarcoma." 123–128.

50. T. A. Peterman, H. W. Jaffe, and V. Beral, "Epidemiologic Clues to the Etiology of Kaposi's Sarcoma," *AIDS* 7 (1993): 605–611.

51. P. L. Fleming, C. A. Ciesieki, R. H. Byers, et al., "Gender Differences in AIDS-Indicative Diagnosis Conference on AIDS," *Journal of Infectious Diseases* 168 (1993): 61–67.

52. Grossman, "Possible Underlying Mechanisms." 241–251.

53. Carpenter et al., "Human Immunodeficiency Virus Infection in North American Women." 307–324.

54. P. A. Selwyn, P. Alcabes, D. Hartel, et al., "Clinical Manifestations and Predictors of Disease Progression in Drug Users with Human Immunodeficiency Virus Infection," *New England Journal of Medicine* 327 (1992): 1697–1703.

55. R. A. Clark, W. Brandon, J. Dumestre, et al., "Clinical Manifestations of Infection with Human Immunodeficiency Virus in Women in Louisiana," *Clinical Infectious Diseases* 17 (1993): 165–172; Carpenter et al., "Human Immunodeficiency Virus Infection in North American Women" 307–324; A. Greenberg, P. Thomas, S. Landesman, and D. Mildvan, "The Spectrum of HIV-1 Related Disease Among Outpatients in New York City," *AIDS* 6 (1992): 849–859.

56. Carpenter et al., "Human Immunodeficiency Virus Infection in North American Women," 307–324.

57. S. Y. Chu, J. W. Buehler, and R. L. Berkelman, "Impact of the Human Immunodeficiency Virus Epidemic on Mortality in Women of Reproductive Age, United States," *Journal of the American Medical Association* 264 (1990): 225–229.

58. Greenberg et al., "The Spectrum of HIV-1 Related Disease," 849–859.

59. Chu et al., "Impact of the Human Immunodeficiency Virus," 225–229.

60. T. Creagh-Kirk, P. Doi, E. Andrew, et al., "Survival Experience Among Patients with AIDS Receiving Zidovudine: Follow-up of Patients in a Compassionate Plea Program," *Journal of the American Medical Association* 260 (1988): 3009–3015; M. A. Fischl, D. D. Richman, N. Hansen, et al., "The Safety and Efficacy of AZT in the Treatment of Subjects with Mildly Symptomatic Human Immunodeficiency Virus Type 1 (HIV) Infection: A Double-Blind, Placebo-Controlled Trial," *Annals of Internal Medicine* 112 (1990): 727–737; Moore et al., "Zidovudine and the Natural History." 1412–1416.
61. Easterbrook et al., "Racial and Ethnic Differences" 2713–2718; S. Lagakos, M. A. Fischl, D. S. Stein, et al., "Effects of Therapy in Minority and Other Subpopulations with Early HIV Infection," *Journal of the American Medical Association* 266 (1991): 2709–2712; M. A. Fischl, D. D. Richman, M. H. Grieco, et al., "The Efficacy of Azidothymidine (AZT) in the Treatment of Patients with AIDS and AIDS-Related Complex: A Double-Blind, Placebo-Controlled Trial," *New England Journal of Medicine* 317 (1987): 185–191.
62. M. A. Sande, C. C. Carpenter, C. G. Cobbs, et al., "Antiretroviral Therapy for Adult HIV-Infected Patients: Recommendations from a State-of-the-Art Conference," *Journal of the American Medical Association* 270 (1993): 2583.
63. G. X. McLeod and S. M. Hammer, "Five Years Later," *Annals of Internal Medicine* 117 (1987): 487–501.
64. Burroughs-Wellcome, *Physician Desk Reference* (Medical Economics Company, Montuale, New Jersey, 1994).
65. S. M. McAvinue, J. E. Gallant, D. L. Stanton, et al., "The Effect of Prophylaxis on Outcome of *Pneumocystis carinii* Pneumonia (PCP)" (Abstract PuB 7350), *8th International Conference on AIDS* (Amsterdam, The Netherlands, 1992); 107. W. D. Hardy, J. Feinberg, D. M. Finkelstein, et al., "A Controlled Trial of Trimethoprim-Sulfamethoxazole or Aerosolized Pentamidine for Secondary Prophylaxis of *Pneumocystis carinii* Pneumonia in Patients with the Acquired Immunodeficiency Syndrome, AIDS Clinical Trials Group Protocol 021," *New England Journal of Medicine* 327 (1992): 1842–8; M.M.E. Schneider, A.I.M. Hoepelman, J.K.M.E. Schattenkerk, et al., "A Controlled Trial of Aerosolized Pentamidine or Trimethoprim-Sulfamethoxazole as Primary Prophylaxis Against *Pneumocystis carinii* Pneumonia in Patients with Human Immunodeficiency Virus Infection," *New England Journal of Medicine* 327 (1992): 1836–1841.
66. J. E. Gallant, R. D. Moore, R. E. Chaisson, "Prophylaxis of Opportunistic Infections in HIV-Infected Patients," *Annals of Internal Medicine* 120 (1994): 932–944.
67. H. Masur, D. Cohn, M. Cynamon, et al., "Recommendations on Prophylaxis and Therapy for Disseminated *Mycobacterial Avium* Complex for Adults and Adolescents Infected with Human Immunodeficiency Virus," *New England Journal of Medicine*, 329 (1993): 898–904.
68. J. E. Gallant, R. D. Moore, and R. E. Chaisson, "Prophylaxis of Opportunistic Infections in HIV-Infected Patients,": 932–944.
69. Centers for Disease Control, "Purified Protein Derivative (PPD)—Tuberculin Anergy and HIV Infection: Guidelines for Anergy Testing and Management of Anergic Persons at Risk for Tuberculosis," *Morbidity and Mortality Weekly Report* 40 (Atlanta, GA: CDC, 1991): 27–33.
70. D. Cotton, J. Feinberg, D. Finkelstein, AIDS Clinical Trials Group, Statistical Data Analysis Center, "Participation of Women in a Multicenter HIV Clinical Trials Program in the United States" (Abstract Tu.D.114), *7th International Conference on AIDS* (Florence, Italy, 1991): 87.

3

Gynecological and Obstetrical Issues for HIV-Infected Women

JEAN ANDERSON

> I want to know what are the statistics, what are the chances that my child is going to be HIV-positive and what can I do to increase the chances of a negative baby. And it is frustrating that there aren't that many answers.
>
> *woman from New York*

Women now account for over 50,000 cases of AIDS diagnosed in the United States, representing 13% of total cumulative AIDS cases among adolescents and adults in this country.[1] Furthermore, AIDS is now the fourth leading cause of death for U.S. women between the ages of 25 and 44 years and is the number one cause of death in certain regions of the country.[2] Nevertheless, these statistics, as sobering as they are, both misrepresent and underestimate the reality of HIV disease today. The World Health Organization (WHO) estimates that some 16 million people are infected with HIV worldwide and that 7–8 million of these are women of childbearing age.[3]

Despite evidence that the face of HIV is increasingly female, the importance of gender-specific issues and gynecological manifestations of HIV has been underrecognized and poorly studied. Fortunately, this has begun to change, and these are now major targeted areas for research nationally and internationally.

This chapter reviews our current understanding of the interaction between HIV infection and both gynecological and obstetrical health, as well as the range of psychosocial issues that cannot be ignored when caring for an HIV-infected woman.

Sexual Activity, Contraception, and the Prevention of Infection

Most HIV-infected women, like men, continue to be sexually active after learning of their infection. Not only is sex an expression of love and a source of pleasure, for women at highest risk for HIV infection it may also represent tangible evidence of support and the absence of emotional isolation, a means for establishing proprietary rights in a relationship, or a source of economic support. Furthermore, because of the long latency period from initial infection to development of AIDS, most HIV-infected women, the majority of whom are under the age of 40 years, remain asymptomatic for many years and for much of this time may not know they are infected. One of the major determinants of declining sexual activity may be progressive immunological decline, as measured by lowering CD4 counts and the development of symptoms.

Education and counseling for HIV-infected individuals has centered around safer sexual practices in an effort to prevent transmission to others. For the HIV-infected woman, an associated but separate agenda is the prevention of unintended pregnancy. It is estimated that greater than 50% of pregnancies in the United States each year are unplanned.[4] A recent study investigating HIV risk reduction practices in an inner-city obstetrical clinic population with a high prevalence of HIV found that 72% of pregnancies were unintended.[5] Unintended pregnancy is a particular risk in the setting of substance abuse, domestic violence, psychiatric illness, mental retardation, adolescence, and dementia. These situations also describe women at high risk for HIV.

It is important to distinguish the issues and counseling concepts relevant to the prevention of pregnancy from those related to the prevention of infection. Contraceptive methods available to the HIV-infected or at-risk woman need to be considered in terms of several factors: effectiveness, potential for serious complications and contraindications, side effects, convenience and cost, noncontraceptive benefits, potential role in HIV transmission or progression, and general acceptability to the woman.

The most reliable forms of contraception are permanent sterilization with tubal interruption or, if there is a single long-term male partner, vasectomy. Tubal ligation has no long-term effects on sexual or menstrual function and no known direct role in transmission or progression of HIV. However, there is evidence that sterilized women are less likely to use condoms after tubal ligation, as compared to nonsterilized women, even when significant sexual risk factors remain.[6] As for other women, for the HIV-infected woman, the permanence of this procedure may be either an advantage or disadvantage, depending on the personal context.

Norplant is a progestin-only implant, consisting of matchstick-sized capsules typically inserted under the skin of the upper arm. It was approved by the FDA in 1990 and has a first-year failure rate of 0.04 pregnancies per 100 users, making it the most effective reversible form of contraception available.[7] It is effective for 5 years and also requires no ongoing action on the part of the woman. A major advantage is its total and immediate reversibility upon removal, making it a significantly more acceptable method than sterilization to women unwilling to forego the possibility of future childbearing. Its potential role in HIV transmission has not been studied, but there are theoretical concerns that the menstrual cycle changes, including irregular bleeding, experienced by over half of Norplant users in the first year, might contribute to an increased risk of transmission. This method has been touted as ideal for many HIV-infected women because of its reversibility, which would be particularly relevant should a vaccine protecting against perinatal transmission become available or should the woman decide she wanted to become pregnant. It is also particularly useful for women with generally disorganized lives, including those with active substance abuse problems, who may be unable to use effectively methods that are user-dependent. Nevertheless, careful counseling is important, and concerns have been raised about the potential for abuse or coercion.

In 1992, the FDA approved the long-acting injectable contraceptive depot medroxyprogesterone acetate (DMPA, also known as depo provera). DMPA has been used by over 30 million women worldwide and has been approved for use in over 90 countries.[8] It generally is given by intramuscular injection every 3 months. Irregular bleeding and spotting are common during the first few months of DMPA use, but there is a 50% incidence of amenorrhea (i.e., not having menstrual periods) after 1 year of use. The amenorrhea is not harmful and may have the advantage of decreasing the frequency of anemia.[9] Its benefits are similar to those of Norplant, including long action, reversibility, freedom from estrogen-related side effects, and lack of interference with intercourse. The primary advantage is its high effectiveness (failure rate 0.3%) without requiring ongoing user action. However, it is dependent on the woman returning to the health-care setting every 3 months to receive her injection.

Oral contraceptives (OCs) are the most commonly used form of contraception in the United States today and have a failure rate of up to 7.3% in the first 12 months of use.[10] Although a woman using this method must remember to take a pill each day, correct and consistent use ("use effectiveness") is increased by its coital independence. Absolute contraindications include thromboembolic disease, coronary artery or cerebrovascular disease, history of breast cancer, and liver disease or history of liver tumor, but major complications are rare. Important noncontraceptive benefits of OCs have been recognized, including decreased incidence of benign breast disease, endometrial and ovarian cancer, salpingitis, and decreased blood loss and anemia. Minor side effects, including nausea, breakthrough bleeding or missed menses, headaches, and mood changes, can occur and may result in user discontinuation. Furthermore, certain other medications may interact with OCs, resulting in possible altered efficacy for either or both.

OCs have been implicated as an independent risk factor for HIV infection in only one study of 123 uninfected Nairobi prostitutes followed for up to 30 months. Increased risk persisted when controlled for condom use, number of sexual partners, and history of sexually transmitted diseases (STDs).[11] However, other investigators have shown no association between OC use and HIV infection in case-control studies involving heterosexual couples in Central Africa and a cross-sectional study of 640 U.S. prostitutes.[12] More recently, a cross-sectional study of 368 Italian women, who were steady partners of HIV-infected men, found OC use to be negatively associated with transmission of HIV infection (odds ratio 0.5, 95% confidence interval 0.3–1.0).[13] Although the issue of the relationship between OC use and HIV transmission has yet to be resolved definitively, OCs appear to be safe for infected women and women at risk, provided condoms are used consistently as well.

The intrauterine device (IUD), although highly effective, reversible, and independent of user-compliance issues, probably is not a good choice for contraception for the HIV-infected or at-risk woman. It is associated with an increased risk of PID, particularly in women likely to be exposed to other STDs, and generally results in heavier and more painful menses. It also has been associated with an increased risk of HIV infection.[14]

Spermicides containing nonoxynol-9 provide a chemical barrier which offers protection against both pregnancy and certain STDs. Although theoretical effectiveness for pregnancy prevention is approximately 97%, a recent analysis of data from the 1988 National Survey of Family Growth found a 30% failure rate in the first 12 months of use.[15] Traditionally, spermicides have been used in combination with other barrier methods of contraception, which increases their effectiveness. Safe and easy to use, a major drawback is that optimal effectiveness requires consistent use with each act of intercourse.

Under laboratory conditions, spermicides containing nonoxynol-9 have been shown to inactivate both free and cell-based HIV.[16] Furthermore, in experiments simulating intercourse, HIV in a cylinder was inactivated when condoms containing nonoxynol-9 lubricant were ruptured.[17] Preliminary data from a study in Cameroon examining the effect of spermicide and condom use on the rate of HIV infection among 273 women at high risk for HIV infection show that consistent spermicide users had a 70–80% reduction in rate of HIV infection.[18] However, preliminary reports from two other ongoing studies of HIV infection in discordant couples in Rwanda[19] and Zambia[20] have failed to demonstrate a protective effect of spermicides. This issue is complicated by growing concerns about safety. Reports of local irritation and genital ulceration, particularly with use of large and/or frequent doses of spermicide, raise concerns that the potential protective effects of spermicides may be outweighed by increased susceptibility to HIV with damage and/or disruption to the genital epithelium.[21] There is currently no information that this problem applies to women using nonoxynol-9 infrequently, though what frequency of use confers increased risk is unknown and likely relates to several additional variables, such as concomitant infections, dose, use of physical barriers, and individual susceptibility.

Physical barrier methods of contraception include the spermicide-impregnated sponge, cervical cap, diaphragm, and male and female condoms, with typical user failure rates of 16%–22% in the first year of use.[22] Inconsistent use probably accounts for the majority of failures since the theoretical effectiveness of these methods is greater than 90%.[23] Current evidence suggests that, for user-dependent methods of birth control, younger women who are unmarried, poor, and from minority racial and ethnic groups are more likely to experience contraceptive failure.[24] These same variables demographically describe women who are at higher risk for HIV infection.

Barrier methods offer significant protection against STDs. In fact, women using the contraceptive sponge or diaphragm (presumably with spermicide)—both female-dependent methods—have experienced greater protection against gonorrhea (GC), chlamydia, and trichomonas than those depending only on male condoms.[25] However, a recent prospective randomized trial of the sponge and a placebo glycerine vaginal suppository in 116 uninfected Kenyan prostitutes found that nonoxynol-9 sponge use was associated with an increased frequency of genital ulcers and vulvitis. There was no evidence that sponge use was effective in reducing the risk of HIV transmission among these highly exposed women.[26]

The new polyurethane vaginal pouch, or female condom, offers an alternative to the male condom and is the first product to receive expedited review by the Obstetrics and Gynecology Devices Panel of the FDA because of its potential role in preventing the spread of HIV and other STDs. Made in one size, prelubricated with silicone, and twice as thick as the latex rubber used in condoms, laboratory tests suggest that viral permeability is less than that of latex.[27] Preliminary data suggest that its contraceptive efficacy is comparable to other barrier methods.[28] However, cost (approximately three times the cost of male condoms) and issues of acceptability to both men and women may limit its effectiveness.

Only male condoms have been intensively studied in terms of protective effect for HIV transmission or acquisition. Over ten cross-sectional and cohort studies in heterosexual populations show significant reductions in HIV infection with use of latex condoms.[29] Both inconsistent and incorrect use are responsible for condom failure in prevention of infection, as well as pregnancy. Average condom breakage rates range from 0%–13%.[30] Although breakage may be related to manufacturing defects, most likely it is secondary to incorrect storage or use. Storage in hot and humid conditions causes a steady deterioration in condom strength. The most common practices related to condom breakage are incorrect methods of putting on condoms, use of oil-based lubricants, reuse of condoms, and prolonged duration or intensity of coitus. Anal intercourse, practiced at least sporadically by over 15% of sexually active U.S. female college students,[31] has also been shown to result in high levels of breakage.[32] Natural skin condoms, as opposed to latex, do not offer an adequate barrier to HIV.

The use of condoms has been associated with a number of factors: (1) belief in their effectiveness in preventing HIV transmission; (2) low perceived costs (e.g., embarrassment, reduced pleasure); (3) perception of personal susceptibility to HIV; (4) cultural peer norms; and (5) good sexual communication skills.[33] Association of sex with drug or alcohol use, imbalances of power in male–female relationships, and socioeconomic and cultural influences promoting pregnancy have been associated with reduced likelihood of condom use.[34] Less frequent use of condoms has been demonstrated among individuals at high risk for STDs, including persons with multiple sexual partners and those with previous history of STDs.[35] These findings have significant implications for health education and design of intervention programs in populations most at risk for HIV.

Most adults in the United States still do not see themselves as being at risk for HIV. The 1990 National Health Interview Survey found that approximately 72% and 20% of adults surveyed felt that there was no chance or a low chance, respectively, of personally becoming HIV-infected.[36] Furthermore, only 28% of African-American and non-Hispanic white adults rated condoms as "very effective" in preventing sexual transmission of HIV, whereas 44% of African-Americans and 54% of whites believed condoms were "somewhat effective." These beliefs are directly related to educational level and inversely proportional to age. African-American women were substantially less likely than African-American men to rate condoms as "very effective" in preventing transmission of HIV.[37]

STDs are transmitted more easily from man to woman than from woman to man, and one recent study suggested that women are up to 17 times more likely to be infected with HIV by male partners than men are by female partners.[38] Factors, in addition to nonuse of condoms, which may increase the risk for heterosexual transmission of HIV to women include number of contacts with an infected partner, later stage infection in the partner, anal intercourse, bleeding during intercourse, and the presence of ulcerative and nonulcerative genital tract infections.[39]

However, there is a pressing need for development of more effective and acceptable woman-controlled methods for HIV and STD prevention. Anecdotal reports of physical and verbal abuse in response to women's request that their partners use condoms highlight the problem. Cultural norms for sexual behavior may stigmatize women for taking an active role in promoting HIV-preventive practices with their partners. For the woman who is HIV-infected, it is not unusual to find uninfected partners still refusing to use condoms consistently, thereby placing themselves at risk for infection and women at risk for other STDs.

Health-care providers should place a high priority on educating all individuals about the risks associated with sexual activity, and each individual should have access to the knowledge and practical resources needed to prevent unintended pregnancy and infection with sexually transmissible organisms, including HIV. Inevitably, this will involve efforts to empower women and encourage responsibility in sexual matters on the part of both women and men. Abstinence is an appropriate alternative to discuss, as is noncoital sexual expression, but these messages must be tempered with reality and understanding and provision of the full spectrum of options for protection.

For the HIV-infected woman, a full range of sexual expression may be supported in a context of mutual knowledge, consent, and disclosure. It is important to make a distinction between prevention of pregnancy and prevention of infection. The most effective forms of contraception do not offer protection against the transmission or acquisition of HIV or most other STDs. The use of condoms for HIV prevention is also more demanding than their use for contraception: if condoms are to protect against HIV transmission, they must be used with every act of intercourse, during menses, during pregnancy, and in the presence of infertility or after sterilization.

Gynecological Problems

Both infectious and noninfectious gynecological problems are prevalent in HIV-infected women.

In a 1989 retrospective review of 168 women attending an inner-city HIV clinic, 34% had an active gynecological problem at their first visit.[40] These included disorders, such as STDs, with behavioral and epidemiological links to HIV infection, as well as those manifestations directly related to the evolving immunosuppression associated with HIV. Gynecological pathology without an apparent link to HIV infection also was identified. It becomes clear that HIV-infected women often will be identified first in reproductive-health settings.

STDs are a major cause of morbidity among women and achieve their peak incidence and prevalence in the reproductive years, which are also the years with the highest prevalence of HIV infection. Each year, 2.5 million U.S. women acquire chlamydia infections and a half-million are diagnosed with GC.[41] One million women are treated for upper genital tract infection or PID.[42] Worldwide, it is estimated that 15–20 million women are chronically infected with HPV and genital HSV, and one quarter of a million women newly acquire these infections annually.[43] Given our current understanding of the high prevalence of asymptomatic HPV and HSV infections, these numbers may be significant underestimates.[44] HIV also is an STD; because women with one STD are concomitantly at higher risk for others, many HIV-infected women can be expected to have, or develop, other STDs. In the Baltimore City Health Department STD clinics, the prevalence of STDs was compared between 183 HIV-infected and 238 uninfected women. At their initial clinic visit, HIV-infected women had more syphilis (14.8% vs. 5.0%), more GC (19.7% vs. 13%), more trichomonas (27.9% vs. 15.5%), and more PID (7.7% vs. 5.9%) than uninfected controls.[45] Nevertheless, the exact relationship between various STDs and HIV remains unclear. Data come primarily from studies of male heterosexual or homosexual populations in

Western Europe and the United States and female prostitutes in Africa; their applicability to U.S. women is uncertain.

Review of the best designed studies of STDs and HIV acquisition/transmission suggests that both ulcerative and nonulcerative STDs increase the risk of HIV approximately three- to five-fold.[46] The possible role of STDs in HIV progression has not been examined in women. Most attention has been focused on the effect of HIV on the incidence, clinical manifestations, natural history, diagnosis, and response to treatment of various STDs. Methodological weaknesses abound in the available literature: The failure to consider confounding factors such as sexual behavior, drug use, coinfection with other STDs, and health-care utilization; the overabundance of anecdotal reports and case series; and the frequent lack of an uninfected control group. Nevertheless, the implications are clear:

> If coinfection with HIV prolongs or augments the infectiousness of individuals with STDs and if the same STDs facilitate transmission of HIV, these infections may greatly amplify one another. This epidemiological synergy may underpin the explosive growth of the HIV pandemic in some populations.[47]

Incidence rates for primary and secondary syphilis among women have recently climbed dramatically, and the rate of congenital syphilis increased from 4.3 to 174.7 cases per 100,000 live births between 1983 and 1990.[48] This acceleration has been linked geographically and epidemiologically to the use of illegal drugs, especially crack cocaine, and mirrors HIV infection rates among injection drug-using inner-city populations. Atypical clinical presentations, accelerated progression to tertiary disease, an increase in false-positive and false-negative serological tests, and failure of standard therapy all have been reported, bringing into question the validity of standard diagnostic, treatment, and follow-up modalities for syphilis in the presence of HIV disease.[49] Because of the strong epidemiological association, the CDC recommends that any patient diagnosed with syphilis be counseled about HIV and offered screening and that HIV-infected individuals should be tested for syphilis.[50] Neurosyphilis should be considered in the differential diagnosis of neurological disease in HIV-infected persons.

Information on the effect of HIV infection on other genital ulcerative diseases, such as genital herpes and chancroid, suggests that herpetic outbreaks may be more severe, atypical, or persistent and may recur more frequently as HIV-related immunosuppression progresses.[51] There are no data on the accuracy of HSV detection by culture, but HSV strains resistant to standard treatment with acyclovir have been reported.[52] Chancroid, usually considered a minor STD found mostly in tropical and subtropical climates, is increasing in incidence in the United States. Atypical presentation and increased incidence of treatment failures as compared to uninfected controls have been reported in HIV-infected patients.[53] There is little information on the effect of HIV on trichomonas, GC, and chlamydial infections; but nothing suggests an alteration in the clinical presentation, diagnosis, or response to treatment.

However, in a cross-sectional survey of 1,033 women attending an inner-city gynecological emergency department and undergoing HIV antibody testing, Lindsay and colleagues[54] found that HIV-infected women were more likely to have clinical symptoms consistent with PID than uninfected women (18% vs. 3%, P < .01). Women admitted to the hospital with a clinical diagnosis of PID also appear to have an increased likelihood of being HIV-infected, with the prevalence of HIV infection ranging from 6.7% to 16.7% in published studies.[55] HIV-infected women with PID are more likely to have multiple admissions[56] and lower white blood cell counts on admission,[57] as compared to uninfected patients. Furthermore, Korn et al.,[58] in a retrospective review of 131 women hospitalized with PID in San Francisco, found that HIV-infected women were more likely to require surgical intervention than uninfected women. Health-care providers should have a high index of suspicion for pelvic infection in the presence of lower abdominal and pelvic pain in the HIV-infected woman.

The majority of studies of gender-specific disorders in HIV-infected women have focused on HPV and preinvasive cervical cancer (i.e., cervical dysplasia or cervical intraepithelial neoplasia [CIN]). Most show an increased prevalence of HPV (especially with progressive immunosuppression) utilizing DNA hybridization techniques or polymerase chain reaction (PCR) for diagnosis.[59] Since HPV is considered a cofactor in carcinogenesis of the lower genital tract, and given its association with both sexual transmission and immune compromise, it is not surprising that abnormal Pap smears appear to be significantly more common among populations of HIV-infected women, as compared to uninfected women.[60] The reported frequency of abnormal Pap smears in HIV-infected women ranges from 18% to 50%.[61] Furthermore, the frequency and severity of cervical dysplasia diagnosed by both Pap smear and biopsy appear to increase with declining immune status.[62] Maiman and colleagues[63] have demonstrated that CIN appears to be not only more severe in HIV-infected women but also more extensive and multifocal, often involving the vagina, vulva, and perianal regions, as well as the cervix. Although Maiman has raised concerns that cervical cytology may be less accurate as a screening tool in HIV-infected women and has suggested consideration of periodic colposcopic examination as a standard,[64] Korn et al.[65] and Adachi et al.[66] have found no difference in sensitivity of Pap smear in HIV-infected women compared to uninfected controls. Nevertheless, periodic or baseline colposcopy—particularly if easily available—deserves consideration in this population because of the higher prevalence of dysplasia with resultant lower negative predictive values for Pap smear; the general life-style disorganization, which is common and may interfere with medical care compliance; and the opportunity colposcopy offers to detect occult vaginal, vulvar, and perianal lesions, which are commonly found but are less well detected by Pap smear. Williams and associates[67] have reported that anal HPV infection and dysplasia are at least as common as cervical infection and disease among HIV-infected women. Abercrombie et al.[68] reported vulvar intraepithelial neoplasia (VIN) in 14 of 58 (24%) HIV-infected women as compared to 1 of 85 (.01%) HIV-uninfected women. Standard treatment of CIN in HIV-infected women has been associated with increased rates of recurrence, and recurrences appear to be related to the degree of immune compromise in this population.[69]

Will these findings be reflected in more rapid progression to invasive malignancy and a new epidemic of cervical cancer, the most common genital tract malignancy in women throughout much of the world? Will this be an evolving problem as development of newer antiviral, prophylactic, and other therapies allow more prolonged survival for women with HIV infection? The answers to these questions are unclear. In the only published series to date, Maiman and coworkers[70] examined 37 women with invasive cervical cancer under the age of 50 years. Among the seven women (19%) who were HIV-infected, there was a higher stage of disease and a poorer response to standard therapy. Median time to recurrence was 1 month in HIV-infected women and 9 months in uninfected women. Median time to death was 10 months in HIV-infected women and 23 months in uninfected women. In January 1993, invasive cervical cancer became the first gender-specific AIDS indicator condition.[71]

Current recommendations from the Agency for Health Care Policy and Research (AHCPR)[72] call for a Pap smear to be performed as part of the initial evaluation in all women with HIV infection and to be repeated twice in the first year and annually thereafter. Pap smears should be performed every 6 months when there is evidence of a history of HPV infection, previous abnormal Pap, or symptomatic HIV infection. Colposcopy should be utilized to evaluate even minor degrees of abnormality noted with cervical cytology.

Vaginal candidiasis as a marker for immunosuppression in HIV-infected women was first reported in 1987 when seven of 28 HIV-infected women at Walter Reed Hospital presented with chronic recurrent vaginal yeast infections as their only symptom of immune dysfunction.[73] Subsequently, investigators at Brown University confirmed these findings and demonstrated a hierarchical relationship between CD4 count and the different types of mucosal candidiasis, with vaginal candidiasis appearing earliest, followed by oral and then esophageal candidiasis with more severe CD4 depletion.[74] Carpenter and colleagues,[75] in a further examination of the same cohort of women, reported that recurrent vaginal candidiasis was the first sign of immunosuppression in 43 of 113 (38%) women and was the most frequently occurring opportunistic infection over the 4-year follow-up, (89 of 200, 44.5%).

Menstrual disturbances have been noted by many HIV-infected women. In a study by the WHO, amenorrhea was noted by 26% of HIV-infected women in

Uganda, with a positive predictive value of 89% as a symptom indicative of HIV infection.[76] A recent cross-sectional controlled study by Shah and associates,[77] however, found no clinically significant effect on menstruation associated with HIV or related immunosuppression. Ellerbrock and colleagues[78] also reported no significant differences in several menstrual parameters, including dysmenorrhea, amenorrhea, intermenstrual- or postcoital- bleeding, between a cohort of HIV-infected and -uninfected women. Nevertheless, because of frequently coexistent substance abuse and/or weight loss associated with chronic illness, menstrual disorders may be commonly seen. Furthermore, genital tract infections (e.g., cervicitis, endometritis) or progestins used for contraception (e.g., Norplant, DMPA) or appetite stimulation (e.g., Megace) frequently cause unpredictable vaginal bleeding. Finally, a missed menses in a sexually active woman of reproductive age who is not using a reliable method of contraception consistently should always prompt consideration of pregnancy.

CMV cervicitis and endometritis have been described in HIV-infected women,[79] and other opportunistic infections also may affect the reproductive tract in women. There is some evidence that genital ulcers may be caused by HIV infection itself, in the absence of other pathogens.[80] Recently at Johns Hopkins Hospital, we have seen several instances of deep genital ulceration and even rectovaginal fistula formation in women with late-stage HIV infection (i.e., CD4 cell counts (50/mm^3). Culture, histology, and serology have generally failed to reveal an etiology for these ulcers; and empiric therapy, including antibiotics, antivirals, and systemic steroids, has had little effect.

It is important for all health-care providers to develop a heightened awareness of HIV-related gynecological disorders and for providers of reproductive health care to women to be aware of these issues. HIV must be considered in the context of other STDs, abnormal Pap smears, and recurrent or chronic vaginal yeast infections; and HIV screening should be offered, along with appropriate counseling. When a genital tract problem is discovered in a woman known to be HIV-infected, careful attention to diagnosis, treatment, and follow-up is crucial since natural history, diagnostic standards, and response to treatment may be affected by the presence of HIV.

Pregnancy and HIV Infection

AIDS during pregnancy was first described in 1983.[81] Six years later, an estimated 1.5 per 1,000 women giving birth in the United States were infected with HIV.[82] As with general prevalence of HIV infection, rates of infection among pregnant women vary widely with geographic location and the specific population of women studied. The highest prevalence rates were observed in New York (5.8 per 1,000), the District of Columbia (5.5 per 1,000), New Jersey (4.9 per 1,000), and Florida (4.5 per 1,000). In general, prevalence of HIV infection in

African-American pregnant women was 5–15 times higher than in white pregnant women in the same states.[83]

Using newborn blood as an indication of maternal infection status with 276,609 specimens in 1987–1988, Novick and colleagues[84] found a prevalence rate of 1.25% in New York City and 2.2% in zip code areas having high rates of drug use. In a prenatal population in Atlanta undergoing routine voluntary HIV screening from 1987 to 1990, approximately 95% of all registrants agreed to testing, and prevalence increased from 3.5 per 1,000 to 5.3 per 1,000. Of significance, 70% of HIV-infected women denied traditional risk factors, though a history of crack cocaine use was significantly associated with infection.[85] Inner-city parturients who did not register for prenatal care but delivered at the same hospital were approximately three times more likely to be HIV-infected.[86] This study and others document the inadequacy of targeted screening[87] and the acceptability of routine voluntary screening[88] and underscore the need to provide all pregnant women with information about HIV infection and to offer screening on a voluntary basis with appropriate counseling.[89]

Once an HIV-infected woman becomes pregnant, termination of pregnancy may be a legal option, depending on gestational age and regulations in her jurisdiction. However, studies—most focusing on injection drug users (IDUs) or sexual partners of IDUs—generally have not shown a significant difference in decisions regarding pregnancy continuation between HIV-infected and uninfected women.[90] An exception was a recent study of 108 uninfected women and 98 HIV-infected women followed for an average of 1.5 years after an index pregnancy. In this cohort, HIV-positivity did correlate with a decision to terminate pregnancies but did not correlate with subsequent fertility.[91] Nevertheless, the majority of HIV-infected women who become pregnant, whether knowing of their infected status before pregnancy or first learning of it during pregnancy, choose to continue the pregnancy. While knowledge of HIV status does influence such decisions, it frequently is overshadowed by other factors. Desire for a child, religious beliefs, and family or partner pressures play a significant role in decision-making.

Denial, depression, anger, and drug use may act singly or in combination to immobilize the HIV-infected woman and prevent her from making a decision or following through on that decision. Drug-using women may see pregnancy as a positive step, enabling them to abstain from drug use and seek treatment for their addiction. A substantial minority in the African-American community view both HIV disease and abortion as genocidal, raising particular concerns for some women who are both HIV-infected and pregnant.[92] Finally, accessibility, availability, and affordability of services in general, and for low-income women in particular, may have a significant impact on pregnancy decisions. A recent random survey of 30 abortion clinics in New York City found that 20 refused services to a woman identifying herself as HIV-infected, despite the fact that discrimination against HIV-infected individuals is illegal in New York State.[93]

Effect of pregnancy on HIV infection

Observations of an alteration in immune function during pregnancy and increased morbidity and mortality from a variety of viral illnesses in pregnant women have led to concerns about an adverse effect of pregnancy on HIV progression. Seeming to confirm these concerns were early reports of a high incidence of progression to clinical illness in short-term follow-up of asymptomatic HIV-infected women who were identified because of delivery of a child who developed AIDS.[94] However, most subsequent studies comparing HIV-infected pregnant and nonpregnant women fail to demonstrate a significant influence of pregnancy (in the absence of HIV-associated symptoms or injection drug use) on the rate of clinical or immunological decline.[95] Nevertheless, definitive conclusions about a lack of correlation between pregnancy and HIV progression await well-designed studies with sufficient length of follow-up that control for clinical and immunological stage of disease, as well as potential cofactors, such as drug use, associated with morbidity in women.[96]

A recent study by Miotti and associates[97] of HIV-infected and uninfected pregnant women in Malawi reported an increase in the absolute number of CD4 and CD8 lymphocytes between late pregnancy and early postpartum, while percentages of CD4 and CD8 cells remained virtually unchanged. They suggested that percentage, rather than absolute number, should be used when monitoring immune function in HIV-infected pregnant women to avoid the effect of the higher volume of distribution during pregnancy on absolute number of CD4 cells.

Perinatal transmission

Prospective studies from the United States and Europe through 1991 place the overall rate of perinatal transmission between 13% and 40%, averaging approximately 29% in the United States.[98] Perinatal transmission derived from published studies of African populations approximates 41%, possibly reflecting various cofactors, such as a larger proportion of mothers in a more advanced disease stage; the effect of malaria or other parasites, poor nutrition, or a potential bias in follow-up, selecting for poor health in the mothers or sicker babies, both likely to retain a higher proportion of infected infants.[99]

Perinatal transmission may occur before, during, or after birth via breastfeeding. HIV-DNA has been identified in fetal tissue as early as 8–9 weeks or early in the second trimester of pregnancy.[100] Furthermore, the presence of p24 antigen or a positive HIV culture in approximately 50% of newborns to HIV-infected mothers[101] and the existence of a bimodal clinical pattern of perinatal disease, with approximately one-quarter of HIV-infected infants demonstrating early onset and rapidly progressive HIV infection,[102] suggests that transmission may occur prior to delivery.

However, a synthesis of available data suggests that HIV transmission most commonly occurs around the time of birth, analogous to the vertical transmission of hepatitis B. The inability of available laboratory methods to reliably detect HIV infection directly or indirectly prior to 3–6 months of age[103] and the disproportionately higher risk for first-born twins with more extensive exposure to maternal blood and genital tract secretions,[104] as compared to second twins, support the notion that transmission commonly occurs close to, or at, delivery.

Mother–infant transmission via breast-feeding is possible but has been thought to be rare. However, a recent meta-analysis of published prospective studies estimates that the additional risk of transmission secondary to breastfeeding when the mother was infected prenatally is 14% (95% confidence interval 7–22%) and 29% (95% confidence interval 16–42%) if the mother develops her primary infection in the postpartum period.[105] General recommendations in the United States are to avoid breast-feeding when the mother is HIV-infected. The benefits of breast-feeding in terms of neonatal health are significant, however, and this recommendation is less applicable in the developing world (and perhaps in parts of the United States as well), where there are no safe alternatives to breast-feeding.

Precise mechanisms for transmission of HIV between mother and fetus are unknown. HIV antigens have been localized in placental tissue,[106] and the transplacental passage of virus may occur under certain conditions where there is disruption of the placental barrier (e.g., chorioamnionitis, abruption). HIV has been isolated from amniotic fluid,[107] and contact with maternal blood and secretions at delivery is unavoidable.

Factors modulating the risk or rate of HIV transmission from mother to child are not well defined, and there is inconsistent transmission from a single infected mother with different pregnancies. The weight of available evidence indicates an increased risk of transmission with advanced clinical disease, high viral load (i.e., high titers of HIV virus or p24 antigenemia), and depressed maternal CD4 lymphocyte count.[108]

ACTG study 076, sponsored by the NIAID, was a Phase III, randomized, double-blind, and placebo-controlled clinical trial designed to evaluate the safety and efficacy of zidovudine (also known as AZT) administered to HIV-infected pregnant women and their infants in reducing the rate of transmission from mother to infant. HIV-infected pregnant women with CD4 lymphocyte counts greater than 200 cells/mm^3 who were not receiving AZT as part of their medical care were eligible for participation and received daily AZT or placebo initiated between the 14th and 34th weeks of pregnancy and continued through the remainder of the pregnancy and the intrapartum period. Infants born to women in the study received the same medication as their mothers, beginning 8–12 hours after birth and continuing for 6 weeks.

Enrollment into this study was stopped in February 1994 after interim analysis of 364 infants demonstrated a significant reduction in HIV infection in the group receiving AZT as compared to placebo (8.3% vs. 25.5%, P = 0.00006). Reported maternal and infant side effects were balanced between the groups receiving AZT and placebo, with the exception of mild (and reversible) anemia in infants receiving AZT. No congenital anomalies were believed to be related to AZT.[109] A subsequent report by the CDC, summarizing data from the Antiretroviral Pregnancy Registry for the period January 1989 through December 1993, described neither a higher incidence nor a consistent pattern of structural birth defects in babies born to mothers who received AZT during pregnancy.[110] Boyer and colleagues[111] have recently presented data suggesting that the beneficial effects of AZT therapy given during pregnancy and/or labor and delivery in reducing maternal–fetal transmission may extend to women with lower CD4 cell counts and that prolonged treatment of infants may not be necessary.

The level and type of maternal immune response to HIV may play a role in transmission as well. Several studies have focused on antibodies to certain epitopes of the gp120 envelope protein, the V3 region, suggesting that high titers may be protective against vertical transmission.[112] However, other investigators have been unable to replicate these findings.[113] A recent study reported that antibody to gp41, another envelope protein, was lower in women who transmitted HIV to their infants, as compared to non-transmitting mothers.[114] Other potential (but unproven) variables related to perinatal transmission may include: (1) genotype of mother or infant (genes potentially influencing susceptibility to infection or transmission include the human leukocyte antigen (HLA) complex, T-cell receptors, immunoglobulins, and interferons);[115] (2) prematurity;[116] (3) intrapartum events, such as mode of delivery, duration of labor, status of membranes, chorioamnionitis or other maternal genital tract infections, placental abruption, or invasive procedures (e.g., fetal scalp monitoring, episiotomy);[117] (4) maternal drug use or smoking; (5) maternal malnutrition;[118] and 5) genetic variants or quasispecies of HIV, which may vary in biological activity, tropism, or virulence. These variants may be able to escape maternal immune surveillance or may actually be enhanced by maternal antibody with possible promotion of transmission.[119] These variants have been postulated to be involved in the progression of HIV infection through development of resistance to antiretroviral therapy. Recent work by Wolinsky and associates[120] suggesting selective transmission of HIV-1 variants from mother to infant, if substantiated, could have a major impact on the design of prevention strategies.

Based on our current understanding, maternal-fetal HIV transmission may be reduced by: prevention or treatment of cofactors; reducing viral load; restricting viral replication; blocking viral entry; and/or stimulating the immune response. The success of future interventions will depend upon gaining a better understanding of the mechanisms and timing of transmission, as well as the costs, availability, safety, and feasibility or ease of use of these therapies.

Strategies currently under investigation or under consideration for study include: (1) vaginal lavage with a virucidal agent during the intrapartum period; (2) treatment with other antiretroviral medications; (3) administration of a CD4 analogue for competitive inhibition of HIV binding; (4) passive immunization with HIV immune globulin (currently in clinical trials) or with monoclonal antibodies or multivalent preparations; and (5) active immunization with an HIV vaccine, which could potentially stimulate both humoral and cell-mediated immune responses, and may provide clinical benefit to the mother as well.

Effect of HIV infection and drug use on pregnancy

There is conflicting evidence concerning whether HIV infection adversely affects the course of pregnancy and pregnancy outcome. Significant increases in low birth weight, premature delivery, and chorioamnionitis were found in a study from Zaire using uninfected controls.[121] Furthermore, these complications were more common among women with AIDS than among those with asymptomatic HIV infection. In an age- and parity-matched cohort of HIV-infected and uninfected pregnant women in Kenya, HIV infection was significantly associated with low birth weight, prematurity, and postpartum endometritis, with a trend toward a higher stillbirth rate in HIV-infected mothers.[122] Similarly, Halsey and colleagues[123] reported a greater proportion of low birth weight and preterm infants born to HIV-infected women in Haiti, as compared to uninfected controls. However, studies in the United States, when controlling for drug use, have not shown a significant increase in obstetrical/perinatal complications,[124] possibly because the overwhelming majority of HIV-infected women delivering in the United States to date have been relatively early in the course of the disease. Nevertheless, a 1989 report summarizing 26 identified pregnancy-associated deaths due to AIDS in the United States noted that each pregnancy had an obstetrical complication, including 15 preterm deliveries and four with stillbirths or fetal deaths.[125]

Of much more significance is the role that drug use plays in adverse pregnancy outcome. It has been estimated that between 554,400 and 739,200 infants are exposed in utero each year to one or more illicit drugs, with additional annual costs of neonatal care ranging from $385 million to $3 billion.[126] Fetal anomalies, low birth weight, premature delivery, intrauterine growth retardation, placental abruption, intracranial hemorrhage, small head circumference, and neurobehavioral deficits have been associated with use of illicit drugs. In a report describing obstetrical and perinatal outcomes in 81 HIV-infected women, injection drug use (practiced by 48% of subjects) was associated with preterm delivery in 36% of cases (vs. 15% in non-IDUs) and a 500 g decrease in mean birth weight. Unintended pregnancy was common in both groups of women but occurred in 93% of IDUs vs. 65% of non-IDUs.[127]

The use of cheap, smokable crack cocaine has risen to epidemic proportions, and national estimates of fetal cocaine exposure range upward of 240,000.[128] Cocaine use in particular is closely linked both to acquisition of HIV infection and inadequate prenatal care,[129] which is a major factor in the occurrence of obstetrical and perinatal complications and neonatal costs. It has been shown that provision of prenatal care and helping cocaine or alcohol using women to abstain during pregnancy significantly reduce the incidence of prematurity, low birth weight, and other perinatal complications.[130]

Clinical course and management of HIV infection in pregnancy

Antepartum

Clinical care of the HIV-infected pregnant woman should be individualized and based on the clinical and immunological stage of HIV disease, as well as other medical, psychosocial, and/or obstetrical risk factors or conditions. An HIV-infected woman early in the course of her infection and in the absence of other non-HIV risk factors should not be considered high risk and need not be referred to a tertiary care setting. Consistency of care is important and has been associated with increased compliance during both the antenatal and postpartum periods.[131]

Counseling about HIV-related issues in pregnancy is a particularly critical component of the health-care system. Many women are learning that they have a chronic, life-threatening, and probably fatal disease at a time which is traditionally an occasion of joy and celebration. In such a time of crisis, information often is assimilated slowly, and both patience and repetition are required. Confidentiality must be held as a basic tenet of HIV care, and the patient must be assured of this. Decisions about continuation of pregnancy should be approached gently but directly, with counseling that is factual, supportive, and noncoercive.

At the initial prenatal visit and throughout the pregnancy, education about pregnancy, HIV, and other issues relevant to each individual woman is essential to support the partnership between patient and provider that is the goal of optimal health care. Communication between provider and patient always should be clear, sensitive, culturally appropriate, and in language adjusted to the woman's level of understanding. All HIV-infected pregnant women should be informed about the results of ACTG-076, and the provider should place this in the context of the individual clinical circumstances of the woman in helping her make a decision about AZT use during pregnancy. It is important to emphasize that no current therapy reliably eliminates the risk of HIV transmission and that there is no technology available to diagnose HIV infection in a fetus prior to birth. Furthermore, the potential for long-term toxicity with AZT cannot be excluded.

In addition to the standard history and physical examination obtained at each routine obstetrical visit, special emphasis should be placed on review of systems and examination targeted to HIV-related signs and symptoms. Attention must be given to the myriad psychosocial issues consuming the lives of many HIV-infected women, such as homelessness, drug use, domestic violence, and mental illness. Drug treatment programs and other supportive services and assistance should be made available.

Pap smears and screening for STDs, including hepatitis, should be a routine part of prenatal care for HIV-infected women. With the emergence of multiple drug-resistant strains of mycobacterium TB, screening for TB in HIV-infected individuals and others at increased risk has taken on added importance. Safer sexual practices, including condom use, should be emphasized throughout pregnancy, as well as education about available methods of postpartum contraception. Procedures which potentially may increase the risk of perinatal transmission, such as chorionic villus sampling (CVS) and amniocentesis, should be avoided if possible. Antepartum biophysical fetal heart rate testing should be considered in HIV-infected women who are significantly immunosuppressed or who have risk factors for fetal compromise, such as active drug use. Certain immunizations, such as influenza, hepatitis B, and pneumococcal vaccines, may be given during pregnancy[132] and may be indicated for certain HIV-infected women.

Other obstetrical and medical management should be based on the immunological stage of disease. Baseline CD4 cell counts (or percentages) should be performed at entry into prenatal care and repeated at intervals during the pregnancy. If the initial cell count is greater than 600/mm^3, Sperling and colleagues[133] recommend repeat testing in 6 months and at 3-month intervals with lower cell counts. However, given the often extreme variability of CD4 cell count results and our still imperfect state of knowledge regarding the nature of pregnancy and HIV progression, many obstetrical experts currently recommend repeat testing each trimester. Furthermore, very low counts (i.e., CD4 less than 200/mm^3) should be confirmed in 1 week.

Given the significant risk for opportunistic infections, there is consensus that pregnant women with CD4 counts below 200/mm^3 should be given AZT with delay, if possible, past the first trimester.[134] Other currently approved antiretroviral regimens in the United States include didanosine (ddI), dideoxycytidine (ddC), and stavudine (D4T); however, there are no data at this time on their use during pregnancy. Given the results of ACTG-076, AZT should be offered to all pregnant women, with appropriate consent.

CD4 cell count results should guide the need for prophylactic medical treatment of HIV infection during pregnancy, as they would for the nonpregnant individual. Furthermore, the standards for treatment should be identical unless there are documented and significant maternal or fetal risks that would justify modification of recommendations during pregnancy. In all circumstances, full discussion with the HIV-infected individual should assist in guiding treatment decisions.

CD4 cell counts below 200/mm^3 have been associated with development of PCP in approximately 10% of nonpregnant HIV-infected individuals within 10 months,[135] and PCP also has been associated with low CD4 counts during pregnancy.[136] Therefore, HIV-infected pregnant women with a history of PCP or with CD4 counts less than 200/mm^3 should receive prophylactic treatment. Low-dose intermittent therapy with trimethoprim-sulfamethizole currently is the first-line regimen for both primary and secondary PCP prophylaxis and can be used safely during pregnancy. Many obstetricians have chosen to substitute aerosolized pentamidine during the first trimester and at term because of theoretical concerns about teratogenicity or newborn kernicterus (jaundice) with trimethoprim-sulfamethizole. Aerosolized pentamidine has limited systemic absorption and may have the benefit of increasing compliance with once-a-month dosing; however, it is costly and has been associated with local treatment failure and systemic pneumocystis.[137] There also are concerns about environmental contamination and a lack of information on alveolar distribution during pregnancy. Dapsone is a third drug used for PCP prophylaxis in nonpregnant adults, but there is minimal experience with its use in pregnancy at this time. Depending on CD4 level and/or other individual variables, prophylaxis for opportunistic infections other than PCP (e.g. toxoplasmosis, mycobacterium avium, mycobacterium tuberculosis) should be considered.

Appropriate therapy for opportunistic infections to prevent mortality or significant morbidity should not be withheld because of pregnancy. However, if more than one treatment is available and effective, pregnancy should be an important factor in therapeutic decision-making.

Intrapartum

Obstetrical management during the intrapartum period is altered little for the HIV-infected individual. Universal precautions should be employed for all patients within health-care settings and must include adequate eye protection during delivery. Mode of delivery should be determined based on standard obstetrical indications. However, procedures which theoretically may increase the risk of perinatal transmission, such as placement of fetal scalp electrodes or fetal scalp sampling, should be avoided if possible. Consistent with ACTG 076 findings, AZT should be considered for intravenous administration during the intrapartum period. The need and/or efficacy of routine intrapartum antibiotic prophylaxis in reducing peripartum infections is unclear.

Postpartum

Postpartum care is focused on: (1) assessment of healing after delivery and appropriate resolution of other obstetrical complications; (2) postpartum medical needs, including appropriate immunizations; (3) follow-up of contraceptive plans; (4) reinforcement of safer sexual practices and other health maintenance issues; (5) assessment of current psychosocial or social service needs; and (6) plans for further HIV-related medical care.

Pregnancy-related care may be the point of identification of HIV infection in many women and should be the gateway to subsequent appropriate medical care. Studies suggesting shortened survival for women with HIV, as compared to HIV-infected men, may partially reflect inadequate utilization of health-care services by women. Moore and colleagues[138] found in a recent study in Maryland that 2-year survival after a diagnosis of AIDS was greater among men than women and that this disparity was most strongly associated with AZT therapy, which was received by 53% of men but only 33% of women (see Chapter 6).

The birth of a new baby, who also may be ill, dramatically increases the complexity of appropriate medical care for the mother, resulting in competing needs and responsibilities. After institution of a project providing care to HIV-infected pregnant women utilizing a midwifery model, DeFerrari and colleagues[139] showed significantly improved compliance with HIV follow-up within 3 months postpartum, as compared to women followed previously in the general obstetrical clinic. This model emphasized continuity and consistency of care throughout pregnancy, delivery, and the postpartum period. Care was provided by a nurse-midwife (CNM) in collaboration with an obstetrician. CNMs have a recognized record of providing safe, effective, and satisfying care to women living in high-risk social situations, including those that involve alcohol and drug abuse.[140] In addition, liaison during prenatal care with future pediatric and adult medical providers and the provision of supportive services were characteristics of this model, which promoted maternal access to, and utilization of, care.

Psychosocial Issues

There can be no meaningful discussion of the gender-specific medical issues faced by HIV-infected women without recognition of the social context of their lives. Because of poverty, frequent minority status, and, ultimately, gender, many women with HIV infection come from a milieu of social and economic disenfranchisement. This further is complicated in many situations by drug use and domestic violence. It is the women most unempowered who are at greatest risk for becoming HIV-infected. "Like every other epidemic, AIDS develops in the cracks and crevices of society's inequalities."[141]

Disenfranchisement further engenders isolation, and HIV-infected women often struggle virtually alone with the knowledge of their illness, lacking a support structure that promises acceptance and assistance. Fear of abandonment, physical violence, or withdrawal of economic support is a potent force that may keep the HIV-infected woman "in the closet." This has been potentiated by the lack of acknowledgment of HIV as a disease affecting women.

Utilization of health care commonly is sporadic and crisis-oriented (see Chapter 6). It may be unavailable because of lack of insurance or access to drug treatment programs; inaccessible because of child-care responsibilities, limited hours, or lack of transportation; and, finally, a low priority because of overriding concerns about food, shelter, drugs, or health care for family members. Women infected with HIV, like most women in our culture, usually are caretakers. Both her sexual partner and children also may be infected, and the woman must balance her health-care needs with theirs. In a study of health-care utilization by 90 HIV-infected women and their infants, Butz and associates[142] found that, although there was 73% adherence with infant immunization schedules by 9 months, only 41 (45.6%) of the mothers ever had sought health care at a specialized HIV clinic during pregnancy or in the first 12 months postpartum.

The issues surrounding fertility, contraception, and childbearing are uniquely female. For the woman with HIV, having a child may represent a responsibility to God and family, a way to achieve personal immortality, a means to ensure survival of her community or culture, a symbol of status or security, tangible evidence of having been loved or touched by another, something that gives meaning to her life, or simply something of her own to love and be loved by.[143] The approximately one in four chance that she will bear an infected child often seems like better odds than others with which she lives on a daily basis.

When women have been considered separately as a population affected by HIV, the implied or stated emphasis of epidemiological, treatment, and prevention studies too often has been only on their relationships to men or children. Yet, as Kathryn Carovano[144] eloquently has argued, HIV-infected women are "more than mothers and whores," more than reservoirs of infection or vehicles of transmission. HIV-infected women have their own health needs, which must be given attention.

We return over and over again to the intersection of the medical problems of HIV infection in women and the social context of their lives. Societal responses and solutions are necessary, but individuals can make a difference as well. Acknowledgment of these issues and their power in women's lives is the first step; learning of their relevance in the life of the individual comes next. Utilizing available resources or developing new ones to address problems such as drug addiction, domestic violence, homelessness, and discrimination ultimately empowers all of us, but in particular the women battling these demons. This is of critical importance in the face of HIV. As long as women can say "HIV is not my worst problem," our efforts toward prevention and treatment likely will fail.

Notes

1. Centers for Disease Control, *HIV/AIDS Surveillance Report,* 6 (Atlanta, GA: CDC, 1994): 5–10.

2. Centers for Disease Control, "Mortality Attributable to HIV Infection/AIDS—United States, 1981–1990," *Morbidity and Mortality Weekly Report* 42 (1993): 869–872.
3. United Press International, "HIV Infection Trend Moving Toward Women" (February 8, 1995).
4. F. Stewart, F. Guest, G. Stewart, and R. Hatcher, *Understanding Your Body* (New York: Bantam Books, 1987).
5. A. C. Gielen, R. R. Faden, P. O'Campo, N. Kass, and J. Anderson, "Women's Protective Sexual Behaviors: A Test of the Health Belief Model," *AIDS Education and Prevention* 6 (1994): 1–11.
6. J. S. Santelli, L. G. Burwell, C. Rozsenich, et al., "Surgical Sterilization Among Women and Use of Condoms—Baltimore, 1989–1990," *Morbidity and Mortality Weekly Report* 41 (1992): 568–575.
7. "Implants, Injections, and Other Progestin-Only Contraceptives," in *Contraceptive Technology 1990–1992*, 15th ed., eds. R. A. Hatcher, F. Stewart, J. Trussell, D. Kowal, F. Guest, G. K. Stewart, and W. Cates (New York: Irvington, 1992): 301–334.
8. A. M. Kaunitz, "Injectable Contraception," *Clinical Obstetrics and Gynecology* 32 (1989): 356–367; *FDC Reports* 54 (1992): 3–4.
9. Food and Drug Administration Drugs Advisory Committee, "Fertility and Maternal Health" (transcript) (Washington, DC: U.S. Department of Health and Human Services, 1992).
10. E. F. Jones and J. D. Forrest, "Contraceptive Failure Rates Based on the 1988 NSFG," *Family Planning Perspectives* 24 (1992): 12–19.
11. F. A. Plummer, N. J. Simonsen, D. W. Cameron, et al., "Cofactors in Male–Female Transmission of Human Immunodeficiency Virus Type 1," *Journal of Infectious Diseases* 163 (1991): 233–239.
12. M. Carael, P. Van dePierre, P. LePage, et al., "Human Immunodeficiency Virus Transmission Among Heterosexual Couples in Central Africa," *AIDS* 2 (1988): 201–205; W. W. Darrow, W. Bigler, D. Deppe, et al., "HIV Antibody in 640 U.S. Prostitutes with No Evidence of Intravenous (IV) Drug Abuse" (Abstract 4054), *4th International Conference on AIDS*, 1 (Stockholm, Sweden, June 12–16, 1988): 273.
13. A. Lazzarin, A. Saracco, M. Musicco, and A. Nicolosi, "Man-to-Woman Sexual Transmission of the Human Immunodeficiency Virus," *Archives of Internal Medicine* 151 (1991): 2411–2416.
14. A. Lazzarin, A. Saracco, M. Musicco, A. Nicolosi, G. Angarano, et al., "Man-to-Woman Sexual Transmission of HIV: Longitudinal Study of 343 Steady Partners of Infected Men," *Journal of Acquired Immune Deficiency Syndromes* 6 (1993): 497–502.
15. Jones and Forrest, "Contraceptive Failure Rates," 12.
16. R. P. Eglin, "*In Vitro* HIV Anti-Viral Studies with Nonoxynol-9 and Nonoxynol-11 Spermicidal Preparations," *British Journal of Sexual Medicine* 16 (1989): 112–114.
17. F. N. Judson, J. M. Ehret, G. F. Bodin, M. J. Levin, and C. A. Reitmeijer, "*In Vitro* Evaluations of Condoms With and Without Nonoxynol-9 as Physical and Chemical Barriers Against *Chlamydia trachomatis*, Herpes Simplex Virus Type 2, and Human Immunodeficiency Virus," *Sexually Transmitted Diseases* 16 (1989): 51–56.
18. L. Zekeng, P. J. Feldblum, R. M. Oliver, and L. Kaptue, "Barrier Contraceptive

Use and HIV Infection Among High-Risk Women in Cameroon" *AIDS* 7 (1993): 725–731.
19. S. Allen, A. Serufilira, J. Bogaerts, et al., "Confidential HIV Testing and Condom Promotion in Africa. Impact on HIV and Gonorrhea Rates," *JAMA* 268 (1992): 3338–3343.
20. P. J. Feldblum, J. Kamanga, G. K. Mukelabai, et al., "Anti-HIV Efficacy of Barrier Contraceptives Among Discordant Couples," (Abstract A112) in *7th Regional Conference of African Union Against Venereal Diseases and Treponemaoses* (Lusaka, Zambia March 17–20, 1991): 33.
21. S. Niruthisard, R. E. Roddy, and S. Chutivongse, "The Effects of Frequent Nonoxynol-9 Use on the Vaginal and Cervical Mucosa," *Sexually Transmitted Diseases* 18 (1991): 176–179.
22. Jones and Forrest, "Contraceptive Failure Rates," 12.
23. "Choosing a Contraceptive: Effectiveness, Safety, and Noncontraceptive Benefits," in *Contraceptive Technology 1990–1992*, 15th ed., eds. R. A. Hatcher, F. Stewart, J. Trussell, D. Kowal, F. Guest, G. K. Stewart, and W. Cates (New York: Irvington, 1992): 131–154.
24. Jones and Forrest, "Contraceptive Failure Rates," 12.
25. M. J. Rosenberg, A. J. Davidson, J.-H. Chen, F. N. Judson, and J. M. Douglas, "Barrier Contraceptives and Sexually Transmitted Diseases in Women: A Comparison of Female-Dependent Methods and Condoms," *American Journal of Public Health* 82 (1992): 669–674.
26. J. Kreiss, E. Ngugi, K. Holmes, et al., "Efficacy of Nonoxynol-9 Contraceptive Sponge Use in Preventing Heterosexual Acquisition of HIV in Nairobi Prostitutes," *Journal of the American Medical Association* 268 (1992): 477–482.
27. B. Voeller, S. L. Coulter, and K. G. Mayhan, "Gas, Dye, and Viral Transport Through Polyurethane Condoms" (letter), *Journal of the American Medical Association* 266 (1991): 2986–2987.
28. Food and Drug Administration Obstetrics and Gynecology Devices Panel, "Forty-Eighth Meeting" (transcript), (Washington, DC: U.S. Department of Health and Human Services, 1992).
29. W. Cates and K. M. Stone, "Family Planning, Sexually Transmitted Diseases and Contraceptive Choice: A Literature Update—Part I," *Family Planning Perspectives* 24 (1992): 75–84.
30. L. Liskin, C. Wharton, and R. Blackburn, "Condoms—Now More Than Ever," *Population Reports*, Series H, 8 (1990).
31. N. E. MacDonald, G. A. Wells, W. A. Fisher, et al., "High-Risk STD/HIV Behavior Among College Students," *Journal of the American Medical Association* 263 (1990): 3155–3159.
32. S. Golombok, J. Sketchley, and J. Rust, "Condom Failure Among Homosexual Men," *Journal of Acquired Immune Deficiency Syndromes* 2 (1989): 404–409.
33. R. DiClemente, "Predictors of HIV-Preventive Sexual Behavior in a High-Risk Adolescent Population: The Influence of Perceived Peer Norms and Sexual Communication on Incarcerated Adolescent's Consistent Use of Condoms," *Journal of Adolescent Health* 12 (1991): 385–390; R. DiClemente, M. Durbin, D. Siegel, F. Krasnovsky, N. Lazarus, and T. Comacho, "Determinants of Condom Use Among Junior High School Students in a Minority, Inner-City School District," *Pediatrics* 89 (1992): 197–202.
34. D. Worth, "Sexual Decision-Making and AIDS: Why Condom Promotion Among

Vulnerable Women is Likely to Fail," *Studies in Family Planning* 20 (1989): 297–307; H. S. Weinstock, C. Lindan, G. Bolan, S. M. Kegeles, and N. Hearst, "Factors Associated with Condom Use in a High-Risk Heterosexual Population," *Sexually Transmitted Diseases* 20 (1993): 14–20.
35. DiClemente et al., "Determinants of Condom Use," 197.
36. A. M. Hardy and A. E. Biddlecom, "AIDS Knowledge and Attitudes of Black Americans: United States, 1990—Provisional Data from the National Health Interview Survey" (Advance Data No. 206), (Washington, D.C.: National Center for Health Statistics, U.S. Department of Health and Human Services, October 1991).
37. Ibid.
38. N. S. Padian, S. C. Shiboski, and N. P. Jewell, "Female-to-Male Transmission of Human Immunodeficiency Virus," *Journal of the American Medical Association* 266 (1991): 1664–1667.
39. K. K. Holmes and J. Kreiss, "Heterosexual Transmission of Human Immunodeficiency Virus: Overview of a Neglected Aspect of the AIDS Epidemic," *Journal of Acquired Immune Deficiency Syndromes* 1 (1988): 602–610; N. S. Padian, S. C. Shiboski, and N. P. Jewell, "The Effect of Number of Exposures on the Risk of Heterosexual HIV Transmission," *Journal of Infectious Diseases* 161 (1990): 883–887.
40. J. R. Anderson, J. Horn, R. King, J. Keller, B. Herbert, M. Barbacci, et al., "Selected Gynecologic Issues in Women with HIV Infection" (abstract), *5th International Conference on AIDS*, (Montreal, Canada, June 1989), 760.
41. Division of Sexually Transmitted Disease/HIV Prevention, Center for Prevention Services, *Annual Report—1990* (Atlanta, GA: Centers for Disease Control, 1990).
42. Centers for Disease Control, "Pelvic Inflammatory Disease: Guidelines for Prevention and Management," *Morbidity and Mortality Weekly Report* 40 (suppl. RR-5) (1991): 1–23.
43. A. Meheus, Director of the Sexually Transmitted Disease Division of the World Health Organization, personal communication.
44. L. A. Koutsky, C. E. Stevens, K. K. Holmes, R. L. Ashley, N. B. Kiviat, C. W. Critchlow, and L. Corey, "Underdiagnosis of Genital Herpes by Current Clinical and Viral-Isolation Procedures," *New England Journal of Medicine* 326 (1992): 1533–1539; J. Paavonen, "Pathophysiologic Aspects of Human Papillomavirus Infection," *Current Opinion in Infectious Diseases* 6 (1993): 21–26.
45. J. M. Zenilman, B. Erickson, R. Fox, C. A. Reichart, and E. W. Hook, "Effect of Posttest Counseling on STD Incidence," *Journal of the American Medical Association* 267 (1992): 843–845.
46. J. N. Wasserheit, "Epidemiological Synergy: Inter-Relationships Between HIV Infection and Other STDs," *Sexually Transmitted Diseases* 19 (1992): 61–77.
47. Ibid.
48. R. A. Dunn and R. T. Rolfs, "The Resurgence of Syphilis in the United States," *Current Opinion in Infectious Diseases* 4 (1991): 3–11.
49. Wasserheit, "Epidemiological Synergy," 61; C. M. Hutchinson and E. W. Hook, III, "Syphilis in Adults," *Medical Clinics of North America* 74 (1990): 1389–1416; P.D.R. Johnson, S. R. Graves, L. Stewart, R. Warren, B. Dwyer, and C. R. Lucas, "Specific Syphilis Serological Tests May Become Negative in HIV Infection," *AIDS* 5 (1991): 419–423.
50. Centers for Disease Control, "Syphilis," *Morbidity and Mortality Weekly Report* 38 (suppl. 8, 1989): 5–13.
51. F. P. Siegal, C. Lopez, G. S. Hammer, et al., "Severe Acquired Immunodeficiency

in Male Homosexuals, Manifested by Chronic Perianal Ulcerative Herpes Simplex Lesions," *New England Journal of Medicine* 305 (1981): 1439–1444; J. A. Maier, A. Bergman, and M. G. Ross, "Acquired Immunodeficiency Syndrome Manifested by Chronic Primary Genital Herpes," *American Journal of Obstetrics and Gynecology* 155 (1986): 756–758; M. A. Conant, "Prophylactic and Suppressive Treatment with Acyclovir and the Management of Herpes in Patients with Acquired Immunodeficiency Syndrome," *Journal of the American Academy of Dermatology* 18 (1988): 186–188.

52. K. Erlich, J. Mills, P. Chatis, et al., "Acyclovir-Resistant Herpes Simplex Virus Infections in Patients with the Acquired Immunodeficiency Syndrome," *New England Journal of Medicine* 320 (1989): 293–296.

53. D. W. Cameron, F. A. Plummer, L. J. D'Costa, et al., "Prediction of HIV Infection by Treatment Failure for Chancroid, a Genital Ulcer Disease" (Abstract 7637), *4th International Conference on AIDS*, 2 (Stockholm, Sweden 1988) 334; J. Quale, E. Teplitz, and M. Augenbraun, "Atypical Presentation of Chancroid in a Patient Infected with the Human Immunodeficiency Virus," *American Journal of Medicine* 88 (1990): 5–44N.

54. M. K. Lindsay, J. Grant, H. B. Peterson, J. Risby, H. Williams, L. Klein, "Human Immunodeficiency Virus Infection Among Patients in a Gynecology Emergency Department," *Obstetrics and Gynecology* 81 (1993): 1012–1015.

55. S. Safrin, B. J. Dattel, L. Hauer, and R. L. Sweet, "Seroprevalence and Epidemiologic Correlates of Human Immunodeficiency Virus Infection in Women with Acute Pelvic Inflammatory Disease," *Obstetrics and Gynecology* 75 (1990): 666–670; R. S. Sperling, F. Friedman, M. Joyner, M. Brodman, and P. Dottino, "Seroprevalence of Human Immunodeficiency Virus in Women Admitted to the Hospital with Pelvic Inflammatory Disease," *Journal of Reproductive Medicine* 36 (1991): 122–124; B. Hoegsberg, O. Abulafia, A. Sedlis, J. Feldman, D. DesJarlais, S. Landesman, and H. Minkoff, "Sexually Transmitted Diseases and Human Immunodeficiency Virus Infection Among Women with Pelvic Inflammatory Disease," *American Journal of Obstetrics and Gynecology* 163 (1990): 1135–1139.

56. J. Anderson, D. Howard, J. Abrams, and J. Keller, "HIV Infection in Pelvic Inflammatory Disease" (abstract), *4th Annual B. Frank Polk Symposium* (Baltimore, Maryland April 1993): 41–42.

57. Hoegsberg et al., "Sexually Transmitted Diseases," 1135; A. P. Korn, D. V. Landers, J. R. Green, and R. L. Sweet, "Pelvic Inflammatory Disease in Human Immunodeficiency Virus-Infected Women," *Obstetrics and Gynecology* 82 (1993): 765–768.

58. Korn et al., "Pelvic Inflammatory Disease," 765.

59. S. H. Vermund, K. F. Kelley, R. S. Klein, A. R. Feingold, K. Schreiber, G. Munk, and R. D. Burk, "High Risk of Human Papillomavirus Infection and Cervical Squamous Intraepithelial Lesions Among Women with Symptomatic Human Immunodeficiency Virus Infection," *American Journal of Obstetrics and Gynecology* 165 (1991): 392–400; M. Laga, J. P. Icenogle, R. Marsella, A. T. Manoka, N. Nzila, R. W. Ryder, S. H. Vermund, W. L. Heyward, A. Nelson, and W. C. Reeves, "Genital Papillomavirus Infection and Cervical Dysplasia—Opportunistic Complications of HIV Infection," *International Journal of Cancer* 50 (1992): 45–48; A. B. Williams, T. M. Darragh, K. Vranizan, C. Ochia, A. R. Moss, and J. M. Palefsky, "Anal and Cervical Human Papilloma Virus Infection and Risk of Anal

and Cervical Epithelial Abnormalities in Human Immunodeficiency Virus-Infected Women," *Obstetrics and Gynecology* 83 (1994): 205–211.
60. Laga et al., "Genital Papillomavirus Infection," 45; J. S. Mandelblatt, M. Fahs, K. Garibaldi, R. T. Senie, and H. B. Peterson, "Association Between HIV Infection and Cervical Neoplasia: Implications for Clinical Care of Women at Risk for Both Conditions," *AIDS* 6 (1992): 173–178.
61. A. Schafer, W. Friedmann, M. Mielke, B. Schwartlander, and M. A. Koch, "The Increased Frequency of Cervical Dysplasia–Neoplasia in Women Infected with the Human Immunodeficiency Virus is Related to the Degree of Immunosuppression," *American Journal of Obstetrics and Gynecology* 164 (1991): 593–599; A. P. Korn, M. Autrey, P. A. DeRemer, and W. Tan, "Sensitivity of the Papanicolaou Smear in Human Immunodeficiency Virus-Infected Women," *Obstetrics and Gynecology* 83 (1994): 401–404; M. Conti, A. Agarossi, F. Parazzini, M. L. Muggiasca, A. Boschini, E. Negri, and E. Casolati, "HPV, HIV Infection, and Risk of Cervical Intraepithelial Neoplasia in Former Intravenous Drug Abusers," *Gynecologic Oncology* 49 (1993): 344–348.
62. Schafer et al., "The Increased Frequency of Cervical Dysplasia–Neoplasia," 593; A. Spinillo, P. Tenti, R. Zappatore, G. Barbarini, A. Maccabruni, L. Carratta, and S. Guaschino, "Prevalence, Diagnosis and Treatment of Lower Genital Neoplasia in Women with Human Immunodeficiency Virus Infection," *European Journal of Obstetrics, Gynecology and Reproductive Biology* 43 (1992): 235–241.
63. M. Maiman, R. G. Fruchter, E. Serur, J. C. Remy, G. Feuer, and J. Boyce, "Human Immunodeficiency Virus Infection and Cervical Neoplasia," *Gynecologic Oncology* 38 (1990): 377–382.
64. M. Maiman, N. Tarricone, J. Vieira, J. Suarez, E. Serur, and J. G. Boyce, "Colposcopic Evaluation of Human Immunodeficiency Virus Seropositive Women," *Obstetrics and Gynecology* 78 (1991): 84–88.
65. Korn et al., "Sensitivity of the Papanicolaou Smear," 401.
66. A. Adachi, I. Fleming, R. D. Burk, G. Y. Ho, and R. S. Klein, "Women with Human Immunodeficiency Virus Infection and Abnormal Papanicolaou Smears: A Prospective Study of Colposcopy and Clinical Outcome," *Obstetrics and Gynecology* 3 (1993): 372–377.
67. Williams et al., "Anal and Cervical Human Papilloma Virus Infection," 205.
68. P. D. Abercrombie and A. P. Korn, "Vulvar Intraepithelial Neoplasia (VIN) in HIV-Infected Women" (Abstract FC2-209), *HIV Infection in Women: Setting a New Agenda*, (Washington, D.C., February 22–24, 1995): S59.
69. M. Maiman, R. G. Fruchter, E. Serur, P. A. Levine, C. D. Arrastia, and A. Sedlis, "Recurrent Cervical Intraepithelial Neoplasia in Human Immunodeficiency Virus-Seropositive Women," *Obstetrics and Gynecology* 82 (1993): 170–174.
70. Maiman et al., "Human Immunodeficiency Virus Infection and Cervical Neoplasia," 84.
71. Centers for Disease Control, "1993 Revised Classification System for HIV Infection and Expanded Surveillance Case Definition for AIDS Among Adolescents and Adults," *Morbidity and Mortality Weekly Report* 41 (1992): 1–19.
72. Agency for Health Care Policy and Research, *Clinical Practice Guidelines No. 7: Evaluation and Management of Early HIV Infection* (AHCPR No. 94–0572) (Washington D.C.: U.S. Department of Health and Human Services, January 1994).
73. J. L. Rhoads, C. Wright, R. R. Redfield, and D. S. Burke, "Chronic Vaginal

Candidiasis in Women with Human Immunodeficiency Virus Infection," *Journal of the American Medical Association* 257 (1987): 3105–3107.
74. N. Imam, C.C.J. Carpenter, K. H. Mayer, A. Fisher, M. Stein, and S. B. Danforth, "Hierarchical Pattern of Mucosal Candida Infections in HIV-Seropositive Women," *American Journal of Medicine* 89 (1990): 142–146.
75. C.C.J. Carpenter, K. H. Mayer, M. D. Stein, B. D. Leibman, A. Fisher, and T. C. Fiore, "Human Immunodeficiency Virus Infection in North American Women: Experience with 200 Cases and a Review of the Literature," *Medicine* 70 (1991): 307–325.
76. R. Widy-Wirski, S. Berkley, R. Downing, S. Okware, U. Recine, R. Mugerwa, A. Lwegaba, and S. Sempala, "Evaluation of the WHO Clinical Case Definition for AIDS in Uganda," *Journal of the American Medical Association* 260 (1988): 3286–3289.
77. P. N. Shah, J. R. Smith, C. Wells, S. E. Barton, V. S. Kitchen, and P. J. Steer, "Menstrual Symptoms in Women Infected by the Human Immunodeficiency Virus," *Obstetrics and Gynecology* 83 (1994): 397–400.
78. T. Ellerbrock, T. Wright, M. A. Chiasson, T. J. Bush, "Characteristics of Menstruation in HIV-Infected (HIV+) Women" (Abstract TP-449), *HIV Infection in Women: Setting a New Agenda,* (Washington, DC, February 22–24, 1995): P104.
79. S. Brown, E. K. Senekjian, and A. G. Montag, "Cytomegalovirus Infection of the Uterine Cervix in a Patient with Acquired Immunodeficiency Syndrome," *Obstetrics and Gynecology* 71 (1988): 489–491; M. Brodman and L. Deligdisch, "Cytomegalovirus Endometritis in a Patient with AIDS," *Mount Sinai Journal of Medicine* 53 (1986): 673–675.
80. J. P. Covino and W. McCormick, "Vulvar Ulcer of Unknown Etiology in Human Immunodeficiency Virus Infected Women: Response to Treatment with Zidovudine," *American Journal of Obstetrics and Gynecology* 163 (1990): 116–118; J. K. Kreiss, R. Coombs, F. Plummer, K. K. Holmes, B. Nikora, W. Cameron, E. Ngugi, J.O.N. Achola, and L. Corey, "Isolation of Human Immunodeficiency Virus from Genital Ulcers in Nairobi Prostitutes," *Journal of Infectious Diseases* 160 (1989): 380–384.
81. C. V. Wetli, E. O. Roldan, and R. M. Fojaco, "Listeriosis as a Cause of Maternal Death: An Obstetric Complication of the Acquired Immunodeficiency Syndrome (AIDS)," *American Journal of Obstetrics and Gynecology* 147 (1983): 7–9.
82. M. Gwinn, M. Pappaioanou, J. R. George, W. H. Hannon, S. C. Wasser, M. A. Redus, R. Hoff, G. F. Grady, A. Willoughby, A. C. Novello, L. R. Petersen, T. J. Dondero, and J. W. Curran, "Prevalence of HIV Infection in Childbearing Women in the United States," *Journal of the American Medical Association* 265 (1991): 1704–1708.
83. Ibid., 1704.
84. L. F. Novick, D. Berns, R. Stricof, R. Stevens, K. Pass, and J. Wethers, "HIV Seroprevalence in Newborns in New York State," *Journal of the American Medical Association* 261 (1989): 1745–1750.
85. M. K. Lindsay, H. B. Peterson, S. Willis, B. A. Slade, J. Gramling, H. Williams, and L. Klein, "Incidence and Prevalence of Human Immunodeficiency Virus Infection in a Prenatal Population Undergoing Routine Voluntary Human Immunodeficiency Virus Screening, July 1987 to June 1990," *American Journal of Obstetrics and Gynecology* 165 (1991): 961–964.
86. M. K. Lindsay, T. I. Feng, H. B. Peterson, B. A. Slade, S. Willis, and L. Klein,

"Routine Human Immunodeficiency Virus Infection Screening in Unregistered and Registered Inner-City Parturients," *Obstetrics and Gynecology* 77 (1991): 599–603.
87. M. D. Barbacci, G. A. Dallabetta, J. T. Repke, et al., "Human Immunodeficiency Virus Infection in Women Attending an Inner-City Prenatal Clinic: Ineffectiveness of Targeted Screening," *Sexually Transmitted Diseases* 17 (1990): 122–126.
88. N. E. Kass, R. R. Faden, P. O'Campo, and A. C. Gielen, "Policy Options for Prenatal Screening Programs for HIV: The Preferences of Inner-City Pregnant Women," *AIDS and Public Policy Journal* 7 (1992): 225–233.
89. Working Group on HIV Testing of Pregnant Women and Newborns, "HIV Infection, Pregnant Women, and Newborns: A Policy Proposal for Information and Testing," *Journal of the American Medical Association* 264 (1990): 2416–2420.
90. P. A. Selwyn, R. J. Carter, E. E. Schoenbaum, V. J. Robertson, R. S. Klein, and M. F. Rogers, "Knowledge of HIV Antibody Status and Decisions to Continue or Terminate Pregnancy Among Intravenous Drug Users," *Journal of the American Medical Association* 261 (1989): 3567–3571; F. D. Johnstone, R. P. Brettle, L. R. MacCallum, J. Mok, J. F. Peutherer, and S. Burns, "Women's Knowledge of Their HIV Antibody State: Its Effect on Their Decision Whether to Continue the Pregnancy," *British Medical Journal* 300 (1990): 23–24.
91. A. Sunderland, H. L. Minkoff, J. Handte, G. Moroso, and S. Landesman, "The Impact of Human Immunodeficiency Virus Serostatus on Reproductive Decisions of Women," *Obstetrics and Gynecology* 79 (1992): 1027–1031.
92. A. Sunderland, "Influence of Human Immunodeficiency Virus Infection on Reproductive Decisions," *Obstetrics and Gynecology Clinics of North America* 17 (1990): 585–590.
93. K. M. Franke, "Discrimination Against HIV Positive Women by Abortion Clinics in New York City" (Abstract TEP52), *5th International Conference on AIDS*, (Montreal, Canada, June 1989). 855.
94. G. B. Scott, M. A. Fischl, N. Klimas, M. A. Fletcher, G. M. Dickinson, R. S. Levine, and W. P. Parks, "Mothers of Infants with the Acquired Immunodeficiency Syndrome: Evidence for Both Symptomatic and Asymptomatic Carriers," *Journal of the American Medical Association* 253 (1985): 363–366.
95. F. D. Johnstone, L. MacCallum, R. Brettle, J. M. Inglis, and J. F. Peutherer, "Does Infection with HIV Affect the Outcome of Pregnancy?" *British Medical Journal* 296 (1988): 467; A. Berrebi, J. Chraibi, W. E. Kobuch, J. Puel, H. Grandjean, and A. Fournie, "Influence of Pregnancy on HIV Disease" (Abstract WB2046), *7th International Conference on AIDS*, (Florence, Italy, 1991: 193; G. Mazzarello, A. Canessa, F. Melica, G. Carrega, and A. Terragna, "Influence of Pregnancy on HIV Disease Progression" (Abstract WC3235), *7th International Conference on AIDS*, (Florence, Italy, 1991): 354; M. M. Deschamps, J. W. Pape, M. Desvarieux, P. Williams-Russo, S. Madhavan, J. L. Ho, and W. D. Johnson, "A Prospective Study of HIV-Seropositive Asymptomatic Women of Childbearing Age in a Developing Country," *Journal of Acquired Immune Deficiency Syndromes* 6 (1993): 446–451.
96. C. A. Hankins and M. A. Handley, "HIV Disease and AIDS in Women: Current Knowledge and a Research Agenda," *Journal of Acquired Immune Deficiency Syndromes* 5 (1992): 957–971.
97. P. G. Miotti, G. Liomba, G. A. Dallabetta, D. R. Hoover, J. D. Chiphangwi, and

A. J. Saah, "T Lymphocyte Subsets During and After Pregnancy: Analysis in Human Immunodeficiency Virus Type-1-Infected and Uninfected Malawian Mothers," *Journal of Infectious Diseases* 165 (1992): 1116–1119.
98. L. Boylan and Z. Stein, "The Epidemiology of HIV Infection in Children and Their Mothers—Vertical Transmission," *Epidemiologic Reviews* 13 (1991): 143–177.
99. Ibid., 143.
100. S. H. Lewis, C. Reynolds-Kohler, H. E. Fox, and J. A. Nelson, "HIV-1 in Trophoblastic and Villous Hofbauer Cells, and Haematological Precursors in Eight-Week Fetuses," *Lancet* 335 (1990): 565–568; V. Courgnaud, F. Laure, A. Brossard, C. Bignozzi, A. Goudeau, F. Barin, and C. Brechot, "Frequent and Early *In Utero* HIV-1 Infection," *AIDS Research and Human Retroviruses* 7 (1991): 337–341; H. Mano and J.-C. Cherman, "Fetal Human Immunodeficiency Virus Type 1 Infection of Different Organs in the Second Trimester," *AIDS Research and Human Retroviruses* 7 (1991): 83–88.
101. "Early Diagnosis of HIV Infection in Infants: Report of a Consensus Workshop," *Journal of Acquired Immune Deficiency Syndromes* 5 (1992): 1169–1178.
102. S. Blanche, M. Tardieu, A.-M. Duliege, C. Rouzioux, F. LeDeist, K. Fukunaga, M. Caniglia, C. Jacomet, A. Messiah, and C. Griscelli, "Longitudinal Study of 94 Symptomatic Infants with Perinatally Acquired Human Immunodeficiency Virus Infection," *American Journal of Diseases of Children* 144 (1990): 1210–1215.
103. "Early Diagnosis of HIV Infection in Infants." 1169.
104. J. J. Goedert, A.-M. Duliege, C. I. Amos, S. Felton, and R. J. Biggar, "International Registry of HIV-Exposed Twins," *Lancet* 338 (1991): 1471–1475.
105. D. T. Dunn, M. L. Newell, A. E. Ades, C. S. Peckham, "Risk of Human Immunodeficiency Virus Type 1 Transmission Through Breastfeeding" *Lancet* 340 (1992): 585.
106. Lewis et al., "HIV-1 in Trophoblastic and Villous Hofbauer Cells," 565.
107. D. C. Mundy, R. F. Schinazi, A. R. Gerber, A. J. Nahmias, and H. W. Randall, "Human Immunodeficiency Virus Isolated from Amniotic Fluid," *Lancet* 2 (1987): 459–460.
108. "Maternal Factors Involved in Mother-to-Child Transmission of HIV-1: Report of a Consensus Workshop," *Journal of Acquired Immune Deficiency Syndromes* 5 (1992): 1019–1029; B. Weiser, S. Nachman, P. Tropper, K. H. Visces, R. Grimson, G. Baxter, G. Fang, C. Reyelt, N. Hutcheon, H. Burger, "Quantitation of Human Immunodeficiency Virus Type 1 During Pregnancy: Relationship of Viral Titer to Mother-to-Child Transmission and Stability of Viral Load," *Proceedings of the National Academy of Sciences of the United States of America* 91 (1994): 8037–8041.
109. Centers for Disease Control, "Zidovudine for the Prevention of HIV Transmission from Mother to Infant," *Morbidity and Mortality Weekly Report* 43 (1994): 285–287.
110. Centers for Disease Control, "Birth Outcomes Following Zidovudine Therapy in Pregnant Women," *Morbidity and Mortality Weekly Report* 43 (1994): 409–416.
111. P. J. Boyer, M. Dillon, M. Navaie, A. Deveikis, M. Keller, S. O'Rourke, and Y. Bryson, "Factors Predictive of Maternal-Fetal Transmission of HIV-1: Preliminary Analysis of Zidovudine Given During Pregnancy and/or Delivery," *Journal of the American Medical Association* 271 (1994): 1925–1930.
112. P. Rossi, V. Moschese, P. A. Broliden, C. Fundaro, I. Quinti, A. Plebani,

C. Giaquinto, P. A. Tovo, K. L. Junggren, J. Rosen, H. Wigzell, M. Jondal, and B. Wahren, "Presence of Maternal Antibodies to Human Immunodeficiency Virus 1 Envelope Glycoprotein gp120 Epitopes Correlates with the Uninfected Status of Children Born to Seropositive Mothers," *Proceedings of the National Academy of Sciences of the United States of America* 86 (1989): 8055–8058; Y. Devash, T. A. Calvelli, D. G. Wood, K. J. Reagan, and A. Rubinstein, "Vertical Transmission of Human Immunodeficiency Virus is Correlated with the Absence of High-Affinity/Avidity Maternal Antibodies to the gp120 Principal Neutralizing Domain," *Proceedings of the National Academy of Sciences of the United States of America* 87 (1990): 3445–3449.

113. B. S. Parekh, N. Shaffer, C.-P. Pau, et al., "Lack of Correlation Between Maternal Antibodies to V3 Loop Peptides of gp120 and Perinatal Transmission," *AIDS* 5 (1991): 1179–1184; N. A. Halsey, R. Markham, B. Wahren, et al., "Lack of Association Between Maternal Antibodies to V3 Loop Peptides and Maternal-Infant HIV-1 Transmission," *Journal of Acquired Immune Deficiency Syndromes* 5 (1992): 153–157.

114. K. E. Ugen, J. J. Goeder, J. Boyer, Y. Refaeli, J. Frank, W. V. Williams, A. Willoughby, S. Landesman, H. Mendez, A. Rubenstein, "Vertical transmission of human immunodeficiency virus infection: reactivity of maternal sera with glycoprotein 120 and 41 peptides from HIV type 1," *J. Clin. Invest* 89 (1992): 1923–1930.

115. L. Louie, B. Nauman, and M.-C. King, "Genetic Susceptibility to Progression to AIDS Following HIV-1 Infection: The San Francisco Men's Health Study" (Abstract THC-676), *6th International Conference on AIDS* (San Francisco, California, June 1990): 294.

116. J. J. Goedert, H. Mendez, J. E. Drummond, et al., "Mother-to-Infant Transmission of Human Immunodeficiency Virus Type 1: Association with Prematurity or Low Anti-gp 120," *Lancet* 2 (1989): 1351–1354; European Collaborative Study, "Risk Factors for Mother-to-Child Transmission of HIV-1," *Lancet* 339 (1992): 1007–1012.

117. Boyer et al., "Factors Predictive of Maternal–Fetal Transmission," 1925; European Collaborative Study, "Risk Factors for Mother-to-Child Transmission," 1007; M. E. St. Louis, M. Kamenga, C. Brown, et al., "Risk for Perinatal HIV-1 Transmission According to Maternal Immunologic, Virologic, and Placental Factors," *Journal of the American Medical Association* 269 (1993): 2853–2859; D. N. Burns, S. Landesman, L. R. Muenz, R. P. Nugent, J. J. Goedert, H. Minkoff, J. H. Walsh, H. Mendez, A. Rubinstein, A. Willoughby, "Cigarette Smoking, Premature Rupture of Membranes, and Vertical Transmission of HIV-1 among Women with Low CD4+ Levels," *J Acquir Immun Defic Syndr* 7 (1994): 718–726; The European Collaborative Study," Caesarean Section and Risk of Vertical Transmission of HIV-1 Infection," *Lancet* 343 (1994): 1464.

118. R. D. Semba, P. G. Miotti, J. D. Chiphangwi, A. J. Saah, J. K. Canner, G. A. Dallabetta, and D. R. Hoover, "Maternal Vitamin A Deficiency and Mother-to-Child Transmission of HIV-1," *Lancet* 343 (1994): 1593–1597.

119. G. Scarlatti, J. Albert, P. Rossi, V. Hodara, P. Biragli, L. Muggiascq, E. M. Fenyo, "Mother-to-Child Transmission of Human Immunodeficiency Virus type 1: Correlation with Neutralizing Antibodies against Primary Isolate," *J. Infect Dis* 168 (1993): 207–210; S. C. Kliks, D. W. Wara, D. V. Landers, J. A. Levy, "Features of

HIV-1 that Could Influence Maternal-Child Transmission," *JAMA* 272 (1994): 467-674.
120. S. M. Wolinsky, C. M. Wike, B.T.M. Korber, C. Hutto, W. Parks, L. L. Rosenblum, K. J. Kunstman, M. R. Furtado, and J. L. Munoz, "Selective Transmission of Human Immunodeficiency Virus Type-1 Variants from Mothers to Infants," *Science* 255 (1992): 1134-1137.
121. R. W. Ryder, W. Nsa, S. E. Hassig, et al., "Perinatal Transmission of the Human Immunodeficiency Virus Type 1 to Infants of Seropositive Women in Zaire," *New England Journal of Medicine* 320 (1989): 1637-1642.
122. M. Temmerman, F. A. Plummer, N. B. Mirza, J. O. Ndinya-Achola, I. A. Wamola, N. Nagelkerke, R. C. Brunham, and P. Piot, "Infection with HIV as a Risk Factor for Adverse Obstetrical Outcome," *AIDS* 4 (1990): 1087-1093.
123. N. A. Halsey, R. Boulos, E. Holt, A. Ruff, J.-R. Brutus, P. Kissinger, T. C. Quinn, J. S. Coberly, M. Adrien, and C. Boulos, "Transmission of HIV-1 Infections from Mothers to Infants in Haiti: Impact on Childhood Mortality and Malnutrition," *Journal of the American Medical Association* 264 (1990): 2088-2092.
124. P. A. Selwyn, E. E. Schoenbaum, K. Davenny, V. J. Robertson, A. R. Feingold, J. F. Shulman, M. M. Mayers, R. S. Klein, G. H. Friedland, and M. F. Rogers, "Prospective Study of Human Immunodeficiency Virus Infection and Pregnancy Outcomes in Intravenous Drug Users," *Journal of the American Medical Association* 261 (1989): 1289-1294; H. L. Minkoff, C. Henderson, H. Mendez, M. H. Gail, S. Holman, A. Willoughby, J. J. Goedett, A. Rubinstein, P. Stratton, J. H. Walsh, and S. H. Landesman, "Pregnancy Outcomes Among Mothers Infected with Human Immunodeficiency Virus and Uninfected Control Subjects," *American Journal of Obstetrics and Gynecology* 163 (1990): 1598-1604.
125. L. M. Koonin, T. V. Ellerbrock, H. K. Atrash, M. F. Rogers, J. C. Smith, C.J.R. Hogue, M. A. Harris, W. Chavkin, A. L. Parker, and G. J. Halpin, "Pregnancy-Associated Deaths Due to AIDS in the United States," *Journal of the American Medical Association* 261 (1989): 1306-1309.
126. I. J. Chasnoff, "Drugs, Alcohol, Pregnancy, and the Neonate: Pay Now or Pay Later," *Journal of the American Medical Association* 266 (1991): 1567-1568.
127. T. Feng, J. Anderson, L. Ofstead, E. DeFerrari, L. Rocco, and N. Hutton, "Obstetric and Perinatal Outcomes in HIV-Infected Pregnant Women" (abstract), *8th International Conference on AIDS* (Amsterdam, The Netherlands, July 1992): B205.
128. C. S. Phibbs, D. A. Bateman, and R. M. Schwartz, "The Neonatal Costs of Maternal Cocaine Use," *Journal of the American Medical Association* 266 (1991): 1521-1526.
129. H. L. Minkoff, S. McCalla, I. Delke, R. Stevens, M. Salwen, and J. Feldman, "The Relationship of Cocaine Use to Syphilis and Human Immunodeficiency Virus Infections Among Inner City Parturient Women," *American Journal of Obstetrics and Gynecology* 163 (1990): 521-526.
130. I. J. Chasnoff, D. R. Griffith, S. MacGregor, K. Dirkes, and K. A. Burna, "Temporal Patterns of Cocaine Use in Pregnancy," *Journal of the American Medical Association* 261 (1989): 1741-1744; R. E. Little, A. Young, A. O. Streissguth, and C. N. Ukl, *Preventing Fetal Alcohol Effects: Effectiveness of a Demonstration Project* (Marshfield, MA: Pitman Publishers, 1984).
131. E. DeFerrari, J. Anderson, J. White-Hamilton, R. Frazier, J. Keller, and L. Ofstead, "A Midwifery Model of Care for HIV-Infected Pregnant Women" (abstract),

8th International Conference on AIDS (Amsterdam, The Netherlands, July 1992): 155.
132. American College of Obstetricians and Gynecologists, *Immunization During Pregnancy, ACOG Technical Bulletin, No. 160* (Washington, D.C.: American College of Obstetricians and Gynecologists, 1991).
133. R. S. Sperling, P. Stratton, and the Obstetric–Gynecologic Working Group of the AIDS Clinical Trials Group of the National Institute of Allergy and Infectious Diseases, "Treatment Options for Human Immunodeficiency Virus-Infected Pregnant Women," *Obstetrics and Gynecology* 79 (1992): 443–448.
134. Ibid., 443.
135. J. Phair, A. Munoz, R. Deteis, et al., "The Risk of *Pneumocystis carinii* Pneumonia Among Men Infected with Human Immunodeficiency Virus Type 1," *New England Journal of Medicine* 322 (1990): 161–165.
136. H.L. Minkoff, A. Willoughby, H. Mendez, G. Moroso, S. Holman, J. J. Goedert, and S. H. Landesman, "Serious Infections During Pregnancy Among Women with Advanced Human Immunodeficiency Virus Infection," *American Journal of Obstetrics and Gynecology* 162 (1990): 30–34.
137. E. E. Telzak, R. J. Cote, J.W.M. Gold, S. W. Campbell, and D. Armstrong, "Extrapulmonary *Pneumocystis carinii* Infections," *Journal of Infectious Diseases* 12 (1990): 380–386.
138. R. D. Moore, J. Hidalgo, B. W. Sugland, and R. E. Chaisson, "Zidovudine and the Natural History of the Acquired Immunodeficiency Syndrome," *New England Journal of Medicine* 324 (1991): 1412–1416.
139. DeFerrari et al., "A Midwifery Model of Care," 155.
140. C. Cavero, J. Fullerton, and J. Bartlome, "Assessment of the Process and Outcomes of the First 1000 Births of a Nurse-Midwifery Service," *Journal of Nurse-Midwifery* 36 (1991): 104–110; H. C. Heins, Jr., N. W. Nancy, B. J. McCarthy, and C. M. Efird, "A Randomized Trial of Nurse-Midwifery Prenatal Care to Reduce Low Birth Weight," *Obstetrics and Gynecology* 75 (1990): 341–345; S. L. Piechnik and M. A. Corbett, "Reducing Low Birth Weight Among Socioeconomically High-Risk Pregnancies: Successful Intervention with Certified Nurse-Midwife-Managed Care and a Multidisciplinary Team," *Journal of Nurse-Midwifery* 30 (1985): 88–98.
141. D. H. Vida, *Antes da Morte/Life Before Death* (Rio de Janiero, Brazil: Escritorio e Tipografia Jaboti Ltda, 1989): 37.
142. A. M. Butz, N. Hutton, M. Joyner, J. Vogelhut, D. Greenberg-Friedman, D. Schreibeis, and J. Anderson, "HIV-Infected Women and Infants: Social and Health Factors Impeding Utilization of Health Care," *Journal of Nurse-Midwifery* 38 (1993): 103–109.
143. C. Levine and N. Dubler, "Uncertain Risks and Bitter Realities: The Reproductive Choices of HIV-Infected Women," *The Milbank Quarterly* 68 (1990): 321–351.
144. K. Carovano, "More than Mothers and Whores: Redefining the AIDS Prevention Needs of Women," *International Journal of Health Services* 21 (1991): 121–142.

4

Health Prospects for Children Born to HIV-Infected Women

NANCY HUTTON

> I mean I look at my son all the time and it just kills me that he might not grow up to have a future. You know. I mean up to this point, he's here now, but there's times when you know, and I mean it's—I don't mean to sound like I don't want children, but there's time[s] when I think, you know "God I wish I didn't have him yet," you know, that I could have—would have—known and I would have saved him all this pain. Cause I got to see him get his blood drawn all the time and giving him medicine every day. I mean it's not easy.
> *woman from Los Angeles*

> [My daughter] weighs 21 pounds. She's eleven months old. She looks like a normal baby, like a healthy baby. And no one can believe me, but she is HIV-positive.
> *woman from Los Angeles*

In making reproductive decisions, women may consider a number of different issues affecting many domains of their lives. A particularly poignant one for women with HIV infection is the potential for their children also to be HIV-infected and what that might mean for their children's well-being. This discussion reviews what is currently known about the risks of mother-to-child transmission of HIV, the natural history of HIV disease in children, and the health interventions available to children infected with HIV.

Epidemiology of HIV in Children

As of June 1994, the CDC reports 5,734 cases of AIDS in children under the age of 13 years. Of the cases reported, 19% are white, 56% African-American, 24% Hispanic, and fewer than 1% were Asian/Pacific Islander or Native American. Eighty-nine percent of children with AIDS were born to women with, or at risk of, HIV infection, though almost all new cases of HIV infection in children are the result of mother-to-child transmission given that transfusion-associated transmission virtually has been eliminated.[1] HIV infection is currently the seventh leading cause of death for children aged 1–4 years.[2]

Mother-to-Child Transmission of HIV

From the early days of the AIDS epidemic, it was clear that HIV could cause congenital infection. There have been numerous reports from different parts of the globe about the rate of transmission, ranging from 12% to 50%.[3] In the United States, the rate of transmission ranges from 25% to 30%.[4] All infants are born with their mothers' antibodies, passed to them through the placenta. Therefore, all infants born to women with HIV infection are HIV antibody–seropositive at birth. The 70% of the infants who are not truly infected usually lose their maternal antibody by 15–18 months of age, after which time they test negative for the HIV antibody.[5] It is estimated that 6,000 HIV-infected women gave birth in the United States in 1990; therefore, as many as 30% of those infants (1,800) will be truly HIV-infected and eventually die from AIDS.[6]

It appears that HIV can be transmitted from mother to baby at any time during the pregnancy, at the time of birth, or after birth via breast-feeding. There is evidence from studies of aborted fetuses that HIV can be transmitted across the placenta as early as 15 weeks of gestation.[7] It is presumed that HIV also is transmitted at the time of birth because the newborn is exposed to maternal blood and secretions.[8] There also is evidence that transmission can occur when mothers breast-feed their infants after birth.[9] Although evidence suggests that the majority of infants are infected in utero or at the time of delivery, the frequency or proportion of transmission which occurs at these different points has not been determined.[10] There is currently no conclusive answer to these questions. Investigators have, therefore, studied newborn blood specimens, looking for evidence of HIV infection, using a variety of techniques.

CDC criteria for diagnosing children with HIV infection are presented in Table 4.1.

Viral detection tests, such as HIV culture, PCR, and p24 antigen, demonstrate that more than half of all infected newborns show no evidence of HIV infection at the time of birth but develop it quickly thereafter.[11] These data have been interpreted in different ways. Some investigators believe that this viral evidence indicates that those newborns with HIV detected within hours to days after birth were infected during the pregnancy whereas those whose initial virus tests were negative but became positive during the first weeks of life were exposed to HIV at the time of birth.[12] Other investigators believe that this same viral evidence supports the hypothesis that most of the HIV infection takes place during the pregnancy and that the birth process activates virus growth so that it becomes detectable several weeks after birth.[13] It seems clear that infection can occur during both pregnancy and the birth process. Moreover, postnatal transmission during breast-feeding[14] may account for some of the differences in transmission rates seen worldwide.

Many attempts have been made to identify predictors of transmission. None has been found conclusively. Women who already have transmitted HIV to one child may go on to have several uninfected children. Women who have had uninfected children may transmit infection to a later child. Some women transmit HIV to all of their children, some to none. How a woman acquired her own HIV infection does not predict her risk of transmitting. Whether her partner has HIV

TABLE 4.1. Diagnosis of HIV Infection in Children

Child < 18 months of age

Requires diagnosis of AIDS based on the 1987 case definition or a positive test result on blood samples drawn at two different time points using one or any combination of the following tests:
1. HIV culture
2. HIV PCR[a]
3. HIV p24 antigen test

Child > 18 months of age

Repeatedly reactive ELISA with confirmation by Western blot or immunofluorescence test

Centers for Disease Control, "1994 Revised Classification System for Human Immunodeficiency Virus Infection in Children Less that 13 Years of Age," *Morbidity and Mortality Weekly Report*, 43 (1994): 1–10.

[a]PCR, polymerase chain reaction.

does not predict transmission. Her own health status may influence the risk that she can transmit. Some studies indicate that women with more advanced HIV disease and/or lower CD4 counts are more likely to transmit HIV infection to their children.[15] However, there are anecdotes of women dying of PCP within days of giving birth to an uninfected infant.

Work is ongoing in the areas of whether specific strains of virus are more transmissible[16] or whether specific maternal immune factors are more or less protective.[17] Mode of delivery may have an impact on the likelihood of transmission. Several studies have observed that cesarean delivery appears to have a protective effect.[18] In one study of twins, the firstborn twin was more likely to be infected with HIV than the second, particularly if the birth was vaginal.[19] Fetal scalp monitoring does not appear to affect transmission.

Interventions are being developed and tested to block the transmission of HIV from mother to infant. A large randomized, placebo-controlled trial of AZT given to mothers during pregnancy and childbirth and to newborns for the first 6 weeks of life was conducted within the ACTG. Enrollment in this study, known as ACTG 076, was stopped earlier than planned because the mothers and infants who were treated with AZT were substantially less likely to exhibit mother-to-infant transmission than those treated with placebo. Forty of 184 newborns in the placebo-treated group developed HIV infection, a transmission rate of 25.5%, which is well within the range of previously reported transmission rates. However, in the group in which mothers received AZT during their pregnancies and labors and the newborns received AZT until 6 weeks of age, only 13 of 180 newborns (8.3%) developed HIV infection, a two-thirds reduction. In August of 1994, the U.S. Public Health Service outlined the following principles regarding the use of AZT to reduce perinatal transmission:

1. HIV-infected women should be informed of the substantial benefit and short-term safety of AZT administered during pregnancy and the neonatal period observed in ACTG Protocol 076.

2. However, they must also must be informed that the long-term risks of AZT therapy to themselves and their children are unknown. A woman's decision to reduce the risk for HIV transmission to her infant should be based on a balance of the benefits and potential risks of the regimen to herself and to her child.
3. Discussion of treatment options should be noncoercive, and the final decision to accept or reject AZT treatment recommended for herself and her child is the right and responsibility of the woman. A decision not to accept treatment should not result in punitive action or denial of care, nor should AZT be denied to a woman who decides to receive the regimen.[20]

Other strategies to prevent or mediate perinatal transmission, including antibody preparations and vaccines, are currently under investigation. To prevent postnatal transmission, it is recommended that women avoid breast-feeding when a safe, alternative infant formula is available (for additional details, see Chapter 3).

It must be remembered, however, that even the 70%–90% of infants who are not HIV-infected are not "unaffected." All of them have HIV-infected mothers who likely will die from AIDS, and many others may have fathers or other family members also infected with the virus. Although only a minority of children born to HIV-infected women will themselves be infected, all children are subject to the difficulties of losing their mothers, and perhaps other family members, to the disease (see Chapter 5).

Natural History of HIV Infection in Young Children

Much of the early descriptive work on the clinical expression of HIV in children was limited to children with severe and fatal disease. This left the impression that most children with congenital HIV infection are seriously ill during infancy and can expect to survive only a few years at best. We now know that, as with adults, the incubation period between infection with HIV and onset of clinical signs and symptoms varies among children, as does the time from onset of signs and symptoms to death. Especially with the advent of early intervention (e.g., PCP prophylaxis), the time from infection to diagnosis with AIDS has been substantially lengthened.

In general, children with congenital HIV infection fall into two categories: those who develop AIDS during their first 2 years of life and those who do not and survive into older childhood or early adolescence.[21] While it remains true that the age at diagnosis of AIDS is correlated with child survival and that infants diagnosed with AIDS before age 1 year have the worst prognosis and shortest expected survival time, more recent prospective studies of infants born to HIV-infected women and our own clinical experience reveal that the majority of children do not develop serious illness early in life.[22] Even prior to the availability of antiretroviral therapy, such as AZT, many children were asymptomatic well into their elementary school years.[23] With continued improvements in early recognition of HIV infection, its related complications, and more effective prophylactic regimens, mean survival times are likely to improve.[24]

The median age of onset of symptoms for children with perinatally acquired HIV infection is 5–10 months.[25] The median age of diagnosis with AIDS is more difficult to define because many HIV-infected children have not yet been diagnosed; the average age of onset and median survival time are available only from children who already have been identified. Existing figures for median age at diagnosis and survival time, therefore, undoubtedly are biased to be lower than the actual numbers since children who have not yet been diagnosed—but may be older than children who have been diagnosed—cannot be included in the averages. This should be understood in examining the research in this area. One study reports that median age of diagnosis with AIDS for children is 1 year and that median survival from time of diagnosis is 14.3 months.[26] In another study, which included 209 surviving HIV-infected children, 50% were 4–7 years old and 13% were 8–13 years old.[27] In addition, three large cohort studies report mean survival times of 67, 77, and 96 months.[28] In one of these studies, 32% of 94 infected infants followed, developed progressive disease before 2 years of age and the remaining 68% of infants had a 97% survival rate at age 3 years.[29] Of 600 infected infants being studied in Italy, 80% are alive, 60% are over 6 years, the cumulative proportion surviving at age 9 years is 49.5%, and median survival is 96.2 months.[30] Of 190 children in another study, 93 are above 6 and 50 are above 9 years.[31]

The clinical manifestations of HIV infection in children depend on which body systems are affected, at what age, and to what degree of severity. The primary target of the HIV virus is the CD4, or T-helper, cell. CD4 cells are an important component of the immune system, which helps the body fight infection. There are multiple complex mechanisms by which HIV depletes the body's CD4 cells.[32] One direct way that HIV destroys CD4 cells is through its ability to attach to them. The structure of the CD4 receptor on the surface of the cells matches the structure of the projections from the surface envelope of the HIV virus. The virus attaches to the CD4 receptor site, enters the cell, its genetic material is integrated into the genetic material of the host CD4 cell, and it remains there quietly for varying lengths of time. When prompted to manufacture new viruses, the cell is damaged or destroyed in the process of releasing these new viruses into the body. Once free, these new viruses find and infect new cells. Over time, a person infected with HIV gradually loses most of his or her CD4 cells.

The loss of CD4 cells is a potent method for HIV to cause the disorganization and deficient functioning of the body's immune system. The CD4 cell's role is as a "helper"; it orchestrates the immune response. CD4 cells circulate through the body in search of foreign particles. Once they identify a foreign body they exert their protective effects by mobilizing other cells involved in the immune response. When the number of CD4 cells is depleted to the point where they cannot function adequately, the immune system cannot orchestrate an effective immune response, causing greater susceptibility to infections, more difficulty controlling or clearing infections, and greater susceptibility to becoming clinically ill from pathogens that do not ordinarily cause disease. This immune deficiency state is the hallmark of HIV disease.

Clinical signs of HIV infection in the newborn may be hard to identify. Specifically, investigators have found no significant clinical differences between infants born to HIV-infected women compared to infants born to uninfected women.[33] However, infected infants, compared to uninfected controls and infants who have seroreverted (lost their mothers' antibodies for HIV), are more likely to manifest signs of infection, such as a slowing of growth patterns and some motor and cognitive developmental delays, during infancy.[34]

Once the state of immune deficiency begins to affect the HIV-infected infant's ability to mount a proper immune response, HIV disease manifests itself in a variety of ways, including chronic infections, diseases of vital organ systems, and, in rare cases, malignancies. The most frequently reported indicator conditions among pediatric AIDS cases are a definitive diagnosis of PCP (22%), multiple or recurrent bacterial infections (17%), HIV encephalopathy (15%), and HIV wasting syndrome (15%). The AIDS case definition for infants and children is similar to the definition for adults but includes a number of diseases specific to this age group.[35]

HIV-infected infants and children may experience repeated or chronic infections, such as ear infections, urinary tract infections, diaper rashes, diarrhea, pneumonias, blood infections, and thrush.[36] Generally, these opportunistic infections occur in only a small proportion of HIV-infected children (approximately 10%) until the end of life, at which time almost all HIV-infected children become quite immunocompromised and are susceptible to multiple infections. The approximately 10% of children who develop serious and repeated infections during the first year of life often have numerous other health problems and experience repeated bouts of illness, with a deteriorating course. These children have a life expectancy of only a few years. Immunodeficiency also may cause common childhood diseases, such as chicken pox, to be more serious and in rare cases even to progress to life-threatening infection.

HIV may damage vital body organs. The lungs are susceptible to repeated bouts of pneumonia in some children with HIV. Usually, pneumonia can be treated successfully if it is detected and treated promptly. Some types of pneumonia are more devastating, such as PCP, and can result in permanent lung damage or even death. Given the morbidity and mortality caused by PCP, preventive therapy is essential. In our clinical experience, approximately one in six

HIV-infected children develops a progressive infiltrative process called lymphoid interstitial pneumonitis (LIP).[37] Although initially clinically silent, after several years it may interfere with the lungs' ability to oxygenate the blood, which may cause exercise intolerance and a need to be on oxygen for the rest of the child's life.

The heart is another vital organ that can be damaged by HIV. The heart muscle may become thickened or flabby and less efficient in its ability to pump blood. The heart's electrical system may be damaged, causing arrhythmia. Although not painful, all of these may interfere with a child's energy and ability to keep up with other children in physical activities due to shortness of breath. Children may require special tests and medicines. Although 62%–93% of HIV-infected children have abnormal electrocardiograms, it is rare for children to have enough heart disease to have the symptoms mentioned above.[38] When it does occur, it is usually in older children and can be managed with medications. Sometimes it occurs as part of a complex of serious problems in the terminal phase of AIDS.

The gastrointestinal (GI) tract is responsible for digesting and absorbing nutrients and acting as a barrier to infection. The GI tract may be damaged in HIV infection directly by HIV or by other infections. It can malfunction if the neurological controls malfunction. These problems can cause malabsorption of food, diarrhea, and weight loss or failure to thrive. A child may develop anorexia or loss of appetite. The malnutrition that may result from these complications also may play a role in the progression of HIV disease.[39] Children may require special diets; nutritional supplements; special methods of feeding, such as feeding tubes or central lines; and alternatives to oral therapy, such as AZT, used to treat HIV infection.[40] Most children, however, eat normal diets and grow well for many years. A few infants, usually the same small group that has multiple problems early in life, develop severe nutritional and growth problems. Some older children exhibit a plateau in their growth, not associated with visible illness. They should be provided with nutritional supplementation.

Approximately 3%–4% of HIV-infected children develop significant kidney disease.[41] Unusual but more frequent is the appearance of protein in the urine, indicating a malfunction in the kidneys' filtration function. This is painless and, unless quite severe, will remain unnoticed unless the urine is tested for the presence of protein. Another malfunction sometimes detected when blood tests are done is the kidneys' loss of bicarbonate in the urine, causing a metabolic acidosis in the blood. This can be replaced with oral medications.

The manufacture and survival of the blood components may be affected, causing anemia (low red blood cells), leukopenia (low white blood cells), or thrombocytopenia (low platelets). Mild anemia is a relatively common finding in the general population. It is also relatively common in children with HIV. It may be caused by HIV, by the medicines used to treat it, or by other causes of childhood anemia, such as iron deficiency. In unusual circumstances, generally in the context of complex and severe illness, the anemia may be severe, requiring blood transfusions, or a very low platelet count may occur. This is potentially life-threatening if not detected and managed effectively. When thrombocytopenia appears as an early sign of HIV, the child otherwise may be well. In this setting, standard supportive treatment is effective initially, and specific anti-HIV therapy, such as AZT, is effective in the long-term.

Skin disorders are common in HIV-infected children. The skin is an important barrier to infection. It is also a sensory organ. Significantly, it is the part of the body that is visible to others. The skin of HIV-infected children may become more dry or more sensitive to chemicals or allergens. Hair may thin or fall out. Rashes and infections may be recurrent or difficult to treat. In our population of HIV-infected children at Johns Hopkins, seborrheic dermatitis and eczema are particularly common and can be managed successfully.

The brain can be damaged directly by the HIV virus, causing changes in its control of muscle tone, strength, and coordination. In our experience, fewer than 10% of HIV-infected infants and children will experience a clinically significant level of neurological dysfunction. This can limit or cause deterioration in a child's ability to sit, crawl, walk, run, feed him or herself, build with toys, or write his or her name. Cognitive abilities can also be damaged, causing learning disability, memory loss, and cognitive delay or deterioration. This may limit a child's ability to carry on a conversation, understand instructions, or express frustrations. A steady decline in language, motor, and adaptive skills may be indicative of a progressive HIV-related brain disease. Severe neurological disease is rare; milder symptoms are moderately common.

Compared to adults with HIV disease, malignancies are fairly uncommon in children. For a summary of the indicators of vital organ dysfunction in infants and children with AIDS, see Table 4.2.

Although HIV may affect any body system, it rarely affects all systems simultaneously unless children are terminally ill. Most children with HIV infection have abnormalities that are detected on blood tests, physical exams, or chest x-rays but are not "felt" by the child. They do not cause pain or disability. The child more likely notes that he or she needs blood tests when others do not or that he or she takes medicines when others do not or that he or she must stay in the hospital sometimes when others do not. However, this is true of many children with a variety of chronic conditions, such as diabetes, asthma, sickle cell disease, and cystic fibrosis. Children with HIV infection are similar to other children in more respects than they are different.

Ultimately, HIV disease progresses and causes death. Whether death occurs during the first months of life or waits until the teen years cannot be predicted before or during pregnancy. Although death early in infancy may occur after an abrupt, unexpected, severe illness, the more typical scenario involves years of recurrent and progressively more complex health problems, finally ending with

TABLE 4.2. Indicators of Vital Organ Dysfunction in Infants and Children with AIDS

Organ	Symptoms
Lung	Acute or gradual onset of rapid breathing, shortness of breath, or cough associated with lack of oxygen in the blood
Heart	Weakening of heart muscle, arrhythmia, low energy
Gut	Malabsorption of food, diarrhea, weight loss, failure to thrive
Blood	Anemia, low white blood cell count, low platelets
Kidney	Protein in urine, acidosis in blood
Skin	Rashes, seborrheic dermatitis, eczema, hair loss
Brain	Progressive deterioration of motor, adaptive, and language skills

death. Children require more frequent visits to the doctor, more medications, more medical tests, and more hospital admissions. They become tired and unable or unwilling to eat normally. They often develop breathing problems. Many will have pain of some kind, often due to an infection or to sensory nerve damage. These problems can be managed with compassionate skill to promote comfort even when curing the problem is not possible.

Health Care for HIV Infected Children

Children best maintain their health and thereby their functioning and quality of life when problems are anticipated, identified early, and managed aggressively. Medical check-ups are recommended every 1–3 months for the first 2 years of life for children known or suspected to be HIV-infected. Evaluation and management of fever, for instance, permits the prompt identification of serious, but treatable, bacterial infections. The child feels better faster, recovers without sequelae, and can be treated in the least restrictive setting. This management is best provided by pediatric health-care providers in primary-care settings who have experience caring for children with HIV infection and who have access to specialty consultation when needed. Therefore, knowing which infants and children have HIV is crucial to implement this "proactive" approach.

Specific Anti-HIV Treatment

Drugs which work by interfering with HIV's ability to infect new cells or make new copies of itself slow the progression of disease. AZT was the first drug of this kind licensed for use in the treatment of HIV disease. It was approved for use in children in 1990. It is now the standard of care for children with symptomatic HIV disease or evidence of significant immune deficiency in the absence of symptoms.[42] Most children tolerate AZT well, with minimal toxicity. The ACTG 128 protocol seeks to determine whether a lower dose of AZT is equally efficacious and less toxic than the currently approved dosage. Data have been collected for over 4 years and currently are being analyzed. Another trial, ACTG 152, is testing whether initiating treatment with ddI or with a combination of AZT and ddI is more efficacious than treatment with AZT alone. ddI recently has been approved for use in children who cannot tolerate AZT or who have disease progression despite treatment with AZT. Trials that will refine the dosage recommendations for children continue. There has been much discussion recently about the overall effectiveness of nucleoside antiretroviral agents. HIV can develop resistance to individual drugs, permitting progression of disease. In adults, it appears that changing drugs, alternating drugs, or combining drugs helps to control the disease more effectively. Questions remain about the best time to initiate this treatment. The standard of recommending early treatment has been challenged. Our clinical experience has been that children improve or remain stable for years on AZT, with little or no side effects if treatment is started early in the course of disease. Children who are severely ill before receiving antiretroviral treatment have much more difficulty tolerating the treatment. Generally, a smaller range of antiretrovirals is available and prescribed for HIV-infected children than for adults.

Preventing Infections

Several strategies are used to prevent infections in children with HIV. Routine childhood immunizations should be given on the same schedule recommended for other children. Polio vaccine should be administered in the killed virus, injectable form rather than the live, attenuated virus, oral form. In addition, children with HIV should receive pneumococcal and influenza vaccines.[43]

Children at risk for PCP should receive prophylaxis against this infection. Children who already have had PCP always should receive medication to prevent a recurrence (secondary prevention). Children with low CD4 cell counts for their age also are potentially at risk and, therefore, should receive medication to prevent a first episode (primary prevention). Currently, the medication of choice is trimethoprim-sulfamethoxazole; alternative regimens using dapsone or pentamidine also are available.

Some children are particularly prone to recurrent, serious bacterial infections. The most common are blood infections caused by *Streptococcus pneumoniae* (pneumococcus). Sometimes infections are caused by more unusual bacteria. Sometimes they cause soft tissue infection, such as pneumonia or preseptal cellulitis. Recurrent pneumococcal bacteremia can be prevented by daily use of oral penicillin. More complex or resistant patterns of infection require monthly administration of intravenous immunoglobulin (IVIG) to boost the child's antibody levels to fight infections.

Early Identification and Treatment of Problems

Monitoring physical growth and nutritional status permits early identification of problems with appetite, intolerance, and malabsorption. Interventions can be made before serious malnutrition or wasting occurs. High-calorie nutritional supplements can be offered to children whose appetites do not meet their bodies' energy needs. Special formulas are available for those intolerant to certain components of a regular diet. Feedings through either a nasogastric tube or a gastrostomy tube can bypass a child's lack of appetite.

Neurodevelopmental monitoring can detect delays or deterioration which necessitate alteration in anti-HIV treatment and special services, such as physical therapy or special education.

Summary

There is a great deal of available information concerning the health status of children for HIV-infected women considering childbearing. It falls into a few key areas:

1. How likely is it that my baby actually will get HIV infection?
2. If my baby gets HIV, how soon will he or she get sick, how sick will he or she be, and how long will he or she survive?
3. How will I plan for the care of my child if I should become ill or die?

At this time we know that only a minority of children born to HIV-infected women actually get HIV infection themselves. Of this small group, a much smaller subset will become seriously ill during infancy and survive only a few years at best. The majority of HIV-infected children will live well into their school and even teen years with minimal disease. However, it is expected that ultimately all HIV-infected children will succumb to complications of their HIV infection, while the remaining large group of children who escaped HIV infection will have to deal with the grief of losing their mothers to HIV.

Notes

1. Centers for Disease Control, *HIV/AIDS Surveillance Report*, 6 (Atlanta, GA: CDC, 1994): 11.
2. Centers for Disease Control, "Annual Summary of Births, Marriages, Divorces, and Deaths: United States 1992," *Monthly Vital Statistics Report* 42 (suppl. 1993): n2.
3. Italian Multicenter Study, "Epidemiology, Clinical Features, and Prognostic Factors of Paediatric HIV Infection," *Lancet* 2 (1988): 1043–1045; European Collaborative Study, "Children Born to Women with HIV-1 Infection: Natural History and Risk of

Transmission," *Lancet* 337 (1991): 253–260; S. Blanche, C. Rouzioux, M. G. Moscato, et al., "A Prospective Study of Infants Born to Women Seropositive for Human Immunodeficiency Virus Type 1," *New England Journal of Medicine*, 320 (1989): 1643–1648; S. K. Hira, J. Kamanga, G. J. Bhat, et al., "Perinatal Transmission of HIV-1 in Zambia," *British Medical Journal*, 299 (1989): 1250–1252; N. A. Halsey, R. Boulos, E. Holt, et al., "Transmission of HIV-1 Infections from Mothers to Infants in Haiti: Impact on Childhood Mortality and Malnutrition," *Journal of the American Medical Association*, 254 (1990): 2088–2092.

4. L. D. Frenkel and S. Gaur, "Perinatal HIV Infection and AIDS," *Clinics in Perinatology*, 21:1 (1994): 95–107; S. Grubman and J. Oleske, "The Maturation of an Epidemic: Update on Pediatric HIV Infection," *AIDS*, 7 (suppl. 1, 1993): S225–235; Centers for Disease Control, "Recommendations for the Use of Zidovudine to Reduce Perinatal Transmission of Human Immunodeficiency Virus," *Morbidity and Mortality Weekly Report* 43 (1994): 1–20.

5. G. B. Scott, C. Hutto, R. W. Makuch, et al., "Survival in Children with Perinatally Acquired Human Immunodeficiency Virus Type 1 Infection," *New England Journal of Medicine*, 321 (1989): 1791–1796; G. L. Trowbridge, G. S. Marshall, J. B. Fahner, S. D. Barbour, "HIV: Recognizing and Managing the Infant at Risk," *Contemporary Pediatrics* (October 1991): 118–134.

6. Scott et al., "Survival in Children," 1791; Grubman and Oleske, "The Maturation of an Epidemic," S225.

7. S. Sprecher, G. Soumenkoff, F. Puissant, et al., "Vertical Transmission of HIV in a 15-Week Fetus," *Lancet* 2 (1986): 228; E. Jovaisas, M. A. Koch, A. Schafer, et al., "LAV/HTLVIII in 20-Week Fetus," *Lancet* 2 (1985): 1129; W. D. Lyman, Y. Kress, K. Kure, W. K. Rashbaum, A. Rubinstein, and R. Soeiro, "Detection of HIV in Fetal Central Nervous System Tissue," *AIDS* 4 (1990): 917–920; V. Corgnaud, F. Laure, A. Broussard, et al., "Frequent and Early In Utero HIV-1 Infection," *AIDS Research*, 7 (1991): 337–341; A. Ehrnst, S. Lindgren, M. Dictor, et al., "HIV in Pregnant Women and Their Offspring: Evidence for Late Transmission," *Lancet* 338 (1991): 203–207.

8. J. J. Goedert, A. M. Duliege, C. I. Amos, S. Felton, and R. J. Biggar, "International Registry of HIV-Exposed Twins," *Lancet* 338 (1991): 1471–1475; G. B. Scott, "Special Considerations in Children," in S. Broder, T. Merigan, and D. Bolognesi, *Textbook of AIDS Medicine* (Baltimore: Williams & Wilkins, 1994): 169–181; Grubman and Oleske, "The Maturation of an Epidemic", S225.

9. J. B. Zeigler, D. A. Cooper, R. O. Johnson, and J. Gold, "Postnatal Transmission of AIDS-Associated Retrovirus from Mother to Infant," *Lancet* 2 (1985): 896–898; S. K. Hira, U. G. Mangrola, C. Mwale, et al., "Apparent Vertical Transmission of Human Immunodeficiency Virus Type 1 by Breast-Feeding in Zambia," *Journal of Paediatrics*, 117 (1990): 421–424; E. R. Stiehm and P. Vink, "Transmission of Human Immunodeficiency Virus by Breast-Feeding," *Journal of Paediatrics*, 118 (1991): 410–412.

10. E. Connor and G. McSherry, "Treatment of HIV Infection in Infancy," *Clinics in Perinatology*, 21:1 (1994): 163–177; L. G. Hoyt and J. M. Oleske, "The Clinical Spectrum of HIV Infection in Infants and Children: An Overview," in *Management of HIV Infection in Infants and Children*, eds. R. Yogev and E. Connor, (St. Louis, MO: Mosby Year Book, 1992): 227–245; Grubman and Oleske, "The Maturation of an Epidemic," S225.

11. Ehrnst et al., "HIV in Pregnant Women," 203; A. Krivine, G. Firtion, L. Cao, C.

Francoual, R. Henrion, and P. Lebon, "HIV Replication During the First Weeks of Life," *Lancet* 339 (1992): 1187–1189; Y. Bryson, I. Chen, S. Miles, et al., "A Prospective Evaluation of HIV Co-Culture for Early Diagnosis of Perinatal HIV Infection" (abstract book 2, WB2014), in *VII International Conference on AIDS* (Florence, Italy, 1991): 185.

12. Connor and McSherry, "Treatment of HIV," 163; Grubman and Oleske, "The Maturation of an Epidemic," S225.

13. Consensus Workshop Report from Italy, "Maternal Factors Involved in Mother-to-Child Transmission of HIV-1," *Journal of Acquired Immune Deficiency Syndromes* 5 (1992): 1019–1029.

14. P. Van de Perre, A. Siminon, D. G. Hitimana, et al., "Mother to Child Transmission of HIV: First Immunologic and Serologic Features from an Ongoing Cohort Study in Kigali, Rwanda" (Abstract ThC43), in *VI International Conference on AIDS* (San Francisco, 1990), 144; Blanche et al., "A Prospective Study of Infants," 1643, R. W. Ryder, T. Manzila, E. Baende, et al., "Evidence from Zaire that Breast-Feeding by HIV-1 Seropositive Mothers is Not a Major Route for Perinatal HIV-1 Transmission but Does Decrease Morbidity," *AIDS* 5 (1991): 709–714.

15. Blanche et al., "A Prospective Study of Infants," 1643; R. W. Ryder, W. Nsa, S. E. Hassig, et al., "Perinatal Transmission of the Human Immunodeficiency Virus Type 1 to Infants of Seropositive Women in Zaire," *New England Journal of Medicine*, 320 (1988): 1637–1642; J. C. Melchor, C. Gutierrez, R. Larrieta, J. M. Ariceta, and B. Corcostegui, "Vertical Transmission of HIV," *Journal of Acquired Immune Deficiency Syndrome* 5 (1992): 529–530; J. J. Goedert, H. Mendez, J. E. Drummond, et al., "Mother-to-Infant Transmission of Human Immunodeficiency Virus Type 1: Association with Prematurity or Low Anti-gp120," *Lancet* 2 (1989): 1351–1354; European Collaborative Study, "Risk Factors for Mother-to-Child Transmission of HIV-1," *Lancet* 339 (1992): 1007–1012; M. A. d'Arminio, M. Ravizza, M. L. Muggiasca, et al., "HIV Infected Pregnant Women: Possible Predictors of Vertical Transmission" (abstract book 2, WC49), in *VII International Conference on AIDS* (Florence, 1991):35; R. A. Hague, J.Y.Q. Mok, L. MacCallum, S. Burns, P. L. Yap, "Do Maternal Factors Influence the Risk of Vertical Transmission of HIV?" (abstract book 2, WC3237), in *VII International Conference on AIDS* (Florence, 1991):355; C. Tibaldi, E. Palomba, N. Ziarati, M. Sciandra, C. Gabiano, and A. Sinicco, "Maternal Factors Influencing Vertical HIV Transmission" (abstract book 2, WC3277), in *VII International Conference on AIDS* (Florence, 1991):365; P. Datta, J. Embree, J. O. Ndinya-Achola, J. Kreiss, and F. A. Plummer, "Perinatal Transmission in Nairobi, Kenya: 5 Year Follow-Up" (abstract book 1, MC3), in *VII International Conference on AIDS* (Florence, 1991):20; M. E. St. Louis, M. Kamenga, C. Brown, et al., "Risk for Perinatal HIV-1 Transmission According to Maternal Immunologic, Virologic, and Placental Factors," *Journal of the American Medical Association*, 269 (1993): 2853–2859.

16. P. M. Fontelos, M. J. Mellado, J. Villota, et al., "Evolution of a Series of Pediatric AIDS Related to Different Strains of HIV" (abstract book 2, WB2030), in *VII International Conference on AIDS* (Florence, 1991):189; S. M. Wolinsky, C. M. Wike, B.T.M. Korber, et al., "Selective Transmission of Human Immunodeficiency Virus Type-1 Variants from Mothers to Infants," *Science* 255 (1992): 1134–1137.

17. Goedert et al., "International Registry," 1471; P. Van de Perre, P. Lapage, A. Simonon, et al., "Biological Markers Associated with Prolonged Survival in

African Children Maternally Infected by the Human Immunodeficiency Virus Type 1," *AIDS Research*, 8 (1992): 435–441; P. Rossi, V. Moschese, P. A. Broliden, et al., "Presence of Maternal Antibodies to Human Immunodeficiency Virus Type 1 Envelope Glycoprotein gp120 Epitopes Correlates with the Uninfected Status of Children Born to Seropositive Mothers," *Proceedings of the National Academy of Sciences* 86 (1989): 8055–8058; P. Rossi, V. Moschese, H. Wigzell, et al., "Mother-to-Infant Transmission of HIV," *Lancet* 335 (1990): 359–360; B. S. Parekh, N. Shaffer, C. P. Pau, et al., "Lack of Correlation Between Maternal Antibodies to V3 Loop Peptides of gp120 and Perinatal HIV-1 Transmission," *AIDS* 5 (1991): 1179–1184; N. A. Halsey, R. Markham, B. Wahren, et al., "Lack of Association Between Maternal Antibodies to V3 Loop Peptides and Maternal–Infant HIV-1 Transmission," *Journal of Acquired Immune Deficiency Syndromes* 5 (1992): 153–157; J. P. Allain, T. Matthews, R. Coombs, et al., "Antibody to V3 Loop Does Not Predict Vertical Transmission of HIV" (abstract book 2, WC2263), in *VII International Conference on AIDS* (Florence, 1991); N. Malanda, M. St. Louis, J. R. George, et al., "Low Prevalence in HIV-Infected Zairian Mothers of Antibodies Against gp120 Neutralizing Epitopes of the MN HIV-1 Isolate and Lack of Association with Perinatal HIV Transmission" (abstract book 1, MC3065), in *VII International Conference on AIDS* (Florence, 1991):314.

18. Italian Multicenter Study, "Epidemiology, Clinical Features," 1043; European Collaborative Study, "Risk Factors for Mother-to-Child Transmission of HIV-1," *Lancet* 339 (1992): 1007–1012; C. Hutto, W. P. Parks, S. Lai, et al., "A Hospital-Based Prospective Study of Perinatal Infection with Human Immunodeficiency Virus Type 1," *Journal of Pediatrics* 118 (1991): 347–353; Goedert et al., "International Registry," 1471; F. Chiodo, E. Ricci, P. Costigliola, L. Michelacci, L. Bovicelli, and P. Dallascasa, "Vertical Transmission of HTLV-III," *Lancet* 1 (1986): 739; J. Q. Mok, C. Gianquinto, A. DeRossi, I. Grosch-Worner, A. E. Ades, C. S. Peckham, "Infants Born from Mothers Seropositive for Human Immunodeficiency Virus: Preliminary Findings from a Multicentre European Study," *Lancet* 1 (1987): 1164–1168; S. Lindgren, B. Anzen, A. B. Bohlin, K. Lindman, "HIV and Child-Bearing: Clinical Outcome and Aspects of Mother-to-Infant Transmission," *AIDS* 5 (1991): 1111–1116; C. Gabiano, P. A. Tovo, M. deMartino, L. Galli, "Italian Multicenter Study: HIV-1 Transmission Rate in First Born Children to Seropositive Mothers and Interfering Factors" (abstract book 2, WC3241), in *VII International Conference on AIDS* (Florence, 1991):356.
19. Goedert et al., "International Registry," 1471.
20. *Morbidity and Mortality Weekly Report*, "Recommendations for the Use of Zidovudine to Reduce Perinatal Transmission of Human Immunodeficiency Virus," 1994b.
21. Scott et al., "Survival in Children," 1791; Hoyt and Oleske, "The Clinical Spectrum," 227.
22. S. Blanche, M. Tardieu, A. M. Duliege, et al., "Longitudinal Study of 94 Symptomatic Infants with Perinatally Acquired Human Immunodeficiency Virus Infection," *American Journal of Diseases of Childhood*, 144 (1990): 1210–1215; N. Hutton, unpublished data; H. Mendez, "Natural History and Prognostic Factors," in *Management of HIV Infection in Infants and Children*, eds. Yogev, Ram, Connor, and Edward, (St. Louis: Mosby Year Book, 1992), 89–105; Connor and McSherry, "Treatment of HIV," 163.
23. D. Persaud, S. Chandwani, M. Rigaud, et al., "Delayed Recognition of Human

Immunodeficiency Virus Infection in Preadolescent Children," *Pediatrics* 90 (1992): 688–691.
24. Scott et al., "Survival in Children," 1791.
25. Ibid, 1791.
26. Hoyt and Oleske, "The Clinical Spectrum," 227.
27. Scott et al., "Survival in Children," 1791.
28. Scott et al., "Survival in Children," 1791; Blanche et al., "Longitudinal Study of 94 Symptomatic Infants with Perinatally Acquired Human Immunodeficiency Virus Infection," 1210; K. Kraskinski, W. Borkowsky, R. S. Holzman, "Prognosis of Human Immunodeficiency Virus Infection in Children and Adolescents" *Pediatric Infectious Disease Journal* 8 (1989): 216–220.
29. Blanche et al., "Longitudinal Study of 94 Symptomatic Infants with Perinatally Acquired Human Immunodeficiency Virus Infection," 1210.
30. Italian Multicenter Study, "Epidemiology, Clinical Features," 1043.
31. Grubman and Oleske, "The Maturation of an Epidemic," S225.
32. Z. F. Rosenberg and A. S. Fauci, "Immunopathogenesis," in *Textbook of AIDS Medicine* eds. S. Broder, T. Merigan, and D. Bolognesi (Baltimore: Williams & Wilkins, 1994), 55–68.
33. A. Butz, N. Hutton, and E. Larson, "Immunoglobulins and Growth Parameters at Birth of Infants Born to HIV Seropositive and Seronegative Women," *America Journal of Public Health*, 81 (1991): 1323–1326.
34. E. Aylward, A. Butz, N. Hutton, M. Joyner, and J. Vogelhut, "Cognitive and Motor Development in HIV-Risk Infants," *American Journal of Diseases of Childhood*, 115 (1991): 347–349.
35. Scott et al., "Survival in Children," 1791; *Morbidity and Mortality Weekly Report*, "Recommendations for the Use of Zidovudine to Reduce Perinatal Transmission of Human Immunodeficiency Virus," 1994b.
36. Hoyt and Oleske, "The Clinical Spectrum," 227.
37. Trowbridge et al., "HIV: Recognizing and Managing," 118; Scott et al., "Survival in Children," 1791.
38. Scott et al., "Survival in Children," 1791.
39. Hoyt and Oleske, "The Clinical Spectrum," 227.
40. Ibid, 227.
41. Frenkel and Gaur, "Perinatal HIV Infection," 95.
42. W. El-Sadr, J. M. Oleske, B. D. Agins, et al., "Evaluation and Management of Early HIV Infection," in *Agency for Health Care Policy and Research Publication No. 94–0572* (Rockville, MD: Public Health Service, January 1994): 88–90.
43. American Academy of Pediatrics, "HIV Infection and AIDS," in *1994 Red Book: Report of the Committee on Infectious Diseases*, 23rd ed., ed. G. Peter (Elk Grove Village, IL: American Academy of Pediatrics, 1994): 254–270.

5
Psychosocial Issues for Children Born to HIV-Infected Mothers

LAWRENCE WISSOW, NANCY HUTTON,
AND DEVEN C. MCGRAW

> I would hope that they would have a program set up for children of deceased parents that can encourage the children to go on and . . . to become, how to enter into the world, you know, when they get older. I don't, you know, feel they shouldn't leave the children alone, just to be raised by grandparents or foster parents or whatever . . . they should have some kind of social program that steer[s] the children, not towards bureaucracy but actually stay[s] with them and encourage[s] them and motivate[s] them to go on 'cuz they really need that, they need that extra push because now they['ve] lost.
>
> *woman from New York*

> Like my daughter, she is seven. And she can do things for herself. I have been teaching her like, you know, teaching her how to wash the dishes, and she cleans up her room or whatever. Sometimes I lay there and think about when is the time I can't do it and I be having her in the house. And I be working the poor child to death. Get up, get me some water, and do this. And I will say mommy don't feel good. Can you get this and can you get that, you know.
>
> *woman from New York*

This is one of two chapters describing children born to HIV-infected mothers. Chapter 4 described the diagnostic and treatment process from a medical perspective. This chapter focuses on psychological well-being and care, including issues of stigma, parental loss, living with chronic illness, and the need for services. The information in this chapter comes from a variety of sources. While some of it comes from investigations of HIV-infected children themselves, much is extrapolated from studies of childhood illness and development in general. Much of the chapter derives from experience caring for children and parents at one particular medical institution. We believe that this experience is representative of what happens at other institutions but recognize the need for more systematic investigations.

The Population

The term "born to HIV-infected mothers" describes children with a wide range of potential medical and social problems. Children born before their mothers became infected or who escape infection despite being born to HIV-infected mothers have no greater risk of medical problems than any other children. Current estimates are that as many as 75% of children born to HIV-infected women who did not receive zidovudine (also known as AZT) during pregnancy will escape infection. At the other end of the spectrum, of the 20–25% born infected, about 25% will have severe disease in infancy. The remaining 75% of those born infected will have a variable course, with some surviving only into their preschool years but others living well into the second decade of life. Taken as a whole, this is a group of children who, in the large majority, are physically healthy or who have a chronic but relatively stable illness that allows them to function in the community and in school. Some of these children will have delays in both their physical and cognitive development, but the exact proportion and the extent of the disability is not known.[1] In some studies, as many as 90% of infected children appear to have some impairment at any one time, but these figures are likely to fall as greater numbers of asymptomatic but infected children come to clinical attention. A finite minority, however, will have serious illness striking either during infancy or the preschool years. At the present time, no method exists to identify at birth which course an exposed child will take.

Three Vignettes*

An infant with AIDS

B. T., now 9 months old, was first referred to the pediatric HIV clinic at age 4 months for evaluation of his poor growth and lagging development. He weighed little more than he had at birth, his muscles were floppy, and he frequently choked as he tried to nurse. His first visit to the clinic led directly to a 3-month stay in the hospital, part of it in the intensive care unit. He recovered from an episode of PCP and was diagnosed as having an HIV infection of the brain, which left him mentally retarded and unable to coordinate swallowing or sucking. Ultimately, he had a feeding tube placed in his stomach to enable him to eat safely.

B. T.'s mother, Ms. R., had learned of her HIV-infected status during her prenatal care. She is 19 years old and single, though she now lives with B. T., his father, Mr. T., and Mr. T.'s parents. B. T.'s long hospitalization was particularly difficult for Ms. R. Mr. T. could visit only infrequently because of the long distance from their rural home. Their aging car frequently broke down, and the hospital had only limited space for two parents to remain overnight with a child.

Throughout her pregnancy and until B. T.'s hospitalization, Ms. R. had worked in a grocery store, deriving much pride from her job and enjoying the

---

*Initials and circumstances have been altered to protect the confidentiality of the families described in these case histories.

support of her friends. She resigned herself to caring for B. T. on a full-time basis. She has a distant relationship with her own family, stemming from her mother's alcoholism and physical abuse at the hands of her father. She feels well-cared for by Mr. T.'s family, though there is tension in the relationship because Mr. T. declines to be tested for HIV. Ms. R. has no known risk factors for HIV exposure; she had one brief sexual relationship prior to meeting Mr. T.

Ms. R. describes B. T. as "my whole reason for living." She became very depressed as his hospitalization lengthened and the degree of his impairment became apparent. During the hospitalization she accepted her first consultation for her own infection. She has not returned for care for herself since then, however, feeling that the bulk of her energies should go into caring for her son.

An uninfected preschool child whose mother has end-stage HIV illness

J. A. is a 4 year old boy whose mother, Ms. B., has end-stage AIDS. In the past few months she has spent more time in the hospital than out. While she is hospitalized, J. A. is cared for by one of his aunts, but at other times J. A. and his mother live together.

Ms. B. frequently is confused and irritable, conditions probably caused by central nervous system (CNS) infection, malnutrition, and possible depression. One aspect of her irritability is an unwillingness to discuss any future arrangements for J. A.'s care or to acknowledge the difficulty she has feeding and supervising him during the time they are together.

J. A. has been followed in the pediatric HIV clinic since birth. He has been HIV-negative since age 15 months and is thought to be uninfected. His growth and development are normal. He has been in a Head Start program since age 2 and appears ready to start kindergarten, though the Head Start teachers feel he may be hyperactive. They note that his attendance and dress are erratic during the periods he spends with his mother. At one point, they called child protective services after J. A. answered a telephone call to Ms. B.'s apartment, saying that his mother was sick and unable to come to the phone. A visit to the apartment found it to be disorderly but safe and adequately stocked with food.

An 11-year-old girl with probably perinatally acquired HIV infection

P. K. is a normally developed fifth-grader from a middle-class family. Her perinatal and childhood health history reveal no apparent risk factors for HIV infection. For several years, however, she has had chronic sinus and ear infections along with several episodes of pneumonia. Ultimately, an HIV test was performed and she was found to be infected.

It is now 1 year since the test was obtained, but P. K.'s parents insist that she not be told the results. Mr. and Ms. K. initially refused any HIV-specific treatment but then agreed when P. K.'s CD4 lymphocyte count became dangerously low. They continued to insist, however, that neither the patient nor other family members be told the nature of her illness or the name of the medication she was receiving. They declined supportive counseling offered to help them respond to their daughter's illness and to the likelihood that one or both of them also were infected.

P. K.'s parents cited several reasons for not wanting to tell her about her HIV infection, including fear that she would be upset, lose hope, or be unwilling to continue treatment. They also feared that she might inadvertently disclose the diagnosis, causing them to have problems in their neighborhood or at work.

P. K. herself seemed aware that she was not to ask questions about her illness or the nature of the clinic she was visiting. To the clinic staff she appeared a quiet, well-behaved child who spoke appropriately with other patients and her younger brother, who had been tested and was uninfected. Her parents reported that she did moderately well in school and had several neighborhood friends. She looked forward to her twelfth birthday and was planning a party, to which she would invite several of her classmates.

The Unique Nature of HIV Infection

It is tempting to look to other chronic childhood illnesses for a framework within which to assess the impact of being born into an HIV-infected family. Tay-Sachs disease and other inborn errors of metabolism cause fatal illness in infancy; cystic fibrosis and sickle cell disease produce illness with a spectrum of severity ranging from serious disability to near-normal functioning. Children also are born to mothers with other serious and even terminal illnesses, including cancer, multiple sclerosis, and lupus erythematosus. In all of these cases, families wrestle with the odds that a child will be affected or that a parent will not survive to see his or her child grow to maturity. In all of these illnesses, families have, to some extent, faced difficulties securing adequate medical care, equal educational opportunities, and support for the burdens of living with chronic illness. HIV-related illness, however, presents families with a constellation of challenges not found previously in any single condition.

Stigma

Perhaps most importantly, HIV infection has been more highly stigmatized than nearly any other illness. Other illnesses have been equally feared[2] and caused those afflicted to be shunned, but none has so strongly been associated in the public mind with socially unacceptable etiologies, such as homosexuality or substance abuse. This stigma was responsible for an early lack of attention to AIDS as a disease worthy of response;[3] it persists as a barrier to educating the public on the mechanisms by which the transmission of HIV infection can be prevented. Stigma, and its resulting need for secrecy, remain among the primary concerns of families with HIV-infected children, often surpassing concerns about obtaining health care and isolating them from supportive services and even other family members.[4]

An illness of families

HIV infection also differs from other serious diseases of childhood in the extent to which other family members are affected. Parents bearing a child affected by sickle cell disease or cystic fibrosis may be carriers of the illness and may even have borne other affected children, but they are unlikely to be affected themselves. The vast majority of HIV-infected children acquire the infection during gestation or at the time of birth;[5] by definition, their mothers, and in many cases their fathers, also are infected. Children who are infected and ill probably will be cared for by parents who themselves are ill and becoming progressively weaker. One estimate placed at 60% the proportion of children with AIDS who were being cared for by extended families or foster parents.[6] Surviving children of HIV-infected women are almost certain to be orphaned sometime during childhood; the median age at death of women with AIDS is 33 years.[7] The CDC estimates that from 93,000 to 112,000 uninfected children will be born to HIV-infected women in the decade 1992–2002.[8] The task of caring for surviving children may be shifted to relatives, older children, or the foster care system.

A disease concentrated among the disadvantaged

Finally, HIV infection in children differs from most other serious illnesses of childhood in its overwhelming concentration among persons of minority status and low income. Over three-quarters of children with AIDS are of African-American or Hispanic background.[9] Minority children historically have been medically underserved in the United States;[10] in addition, their families are more likely to be fragmented and struggling with difficulties that may take priority even over caring for a sick child, such as finding adequate housing, food, and employment. Disadvantaged families also have more trouble accessing and utilizing complex health services. Relatively minor obstacles, such as transportation, child care during visits, and maintaining communication via telephone or mail, frequently become significant barriers to effective use of services.[11]

Comorbidity among HIV-infected children

Because of the ways in which HIV infection is transmitted, many affected children have other obstacles that put them at further risk for problems with psychosocial development. Figures from one pediatric HIV clinic in New York City are illustrative, though they are not representative of children from affected families. (Hospital clinics are more likely to care for children from low income multiproblem families, while affected children from middle-class settings are more likely to receive care from community physicians.) Of 126 children cared for in the clinic, 60% had been exposed to drugs in utero, 50% were considered to be neglected, and 20% were alleged to have been sexually abused.[12]

Issues in the Care of Families with HIV Infection

The following describes issues that frequently arise during the care of HIV-affected families with young children. We cannot speak to relative frequency of these issues, though we know that many, if not most, families function fairly well. Similarly, we suspect that, in the majority of cases, children are highly cherished within HIV-affected families and serve as important sources of emotional support for infected adults.[13] Nonetheless, serious problems that present a risk to child welfare do arise in an important minority of families.

Situations in which a parent is unable or unwilling to seek medical care or special services for an infected or at-risk child

Children are largely dependent on their parents for access to medical care and for ongoing care at home. Extended family members and organized medical or social services can offer support, but ill parents must first acknowledge the need and then allow for a sharing of responsibilities and even for a sharing of decision-making.

Parents may decline help for a variety of reasons. Well-meaning helpers may usurp the parents' role, in effect setting up a competition for "best parent" to the child. Acknowledging the need for help may make the parent vulnerable to old but unresolved conflicts with other family members. It may be difficult, for example, for a mother to accept help from her mother, when the two have frequently quarreled in the past about childrearing issues. Accepting help also may be a symbolic marker of infirmity for the HIV-infected parent. The point at which she no longer can care fully for her children marks both an advancing stage of a mother's illness and the loss of her status as a caregiver and, thus, as a "useful" person. It foreshadows the day when she will die and the care of her children will be completely out of her hands. Potential helpers must be aware of these dynamics and address them directly as part of the package of aid to a family.

Undiagnosed or untreated mental health problems—both those that are previously existing and those that arise as a result of HIV infection—also may lie behind the refusal of parents to seek care for themselves or their children. The onset of these conditions may be subtle and the symptoms missed or misinterpreted in superficial medical interactions. Some evidence suggests that certain psychiatric illnesses, including depression, anxiety disorders, and impulsive or dependent personality traits, are more prevalent among persons currently at risk for HIV infection than in the general population.[14] Possible explanations for this increased prevalence include the higher rates of depression among the poor[15] or the extent to which mental illness or certain personality traits are risk factors for the acquisition of HIV infection through their impact on behavior, judgment, or susceptibility to substance abuse. All of these conditions may be exacerbated at the time HIV infection is diagnosed and subsequently at significant events in the course of treatment. Both depressed and overly anxious parents may deny the need to seek care for themselves or their children. Even moderately impaired parents may find it difficult to provide their children with emotional support on a day-to-day basis. Impulsive traits may also reappear in previously well-compensated parents, leading to seemingly irrational treatment decisions or a relapse of substance abuse.

At the point at which HIV infection becomes clinically apparent, parents may become demented, delirious, manic, or depressed, even when they had not been so before. The dementia found among HIV-infected persons typically involves loss of memory, decreased attention, apathy, and global difficulty with reasoning. The first signs of dementia may be subtle and attributed to anxiety, lack of sleep, or the "understandable" stress of illness. Later, changes in personality and understanding can become more obvious, especially to other family members or to clinicians who have known the parent over an extended period of time. Demented parents may develop delusional beliefs about providers, medications, or their child's state of health. Paranoid feelings are especially common and result in seemingly irrational mistrust of attempts to offer services or treatment. At the same time, paranoid feelings may be fueled by true discriminatory practices and hostile attitudes experienced in the community.

Dementia and even severe depression raise questions about the cognitive competency of parents to consent to medical care on behalf of their children. Care of HIV-infected children involves decisions about research protocols, use of toxic medications, and the provision or withdrawal of treatment at critical points in the child's illness. Depressed parents also may be less attentive to their children or become more punitive in their childrearing if they perceive children as more irritating or more of a burden.

Situations in which the birth of an HIV-infected child provokes a crisis and dissolution of the family

Mothers often first learn of their own HIV-infected status during prenatal care or at the time of childbirth. Repercussions within the family vary, depending on the state of relationships prior to the pregnancy. In some cases, the family is drawn closer together to support those affected, but among other families, the diagnosis comes as a sign of betrayal. Of 72 HiV-infected mothers interviewed in a pediatric AIDS clinic, only 53% said they had the support of a partner, and only 65% had the support of parents.[16]

The group of newly diagnosed women is comprised of many individuals who did not feel that they were at risk of HIV infection, only to discover that a present or past sexual partner had been infected. To the extent that these partners are still present as sources of support, their help may be lost as the women experience feelings of anger and betrayal. In a minority of cases, the mother also may choose to reject her newborn baby as well as the infected father.

Custody and decision-making issues

As their own illness progresses, HIV-infected parents must make arrangements for ongoing care of their children. While the process of choosing caretakers and drawing up custody documents is a vivid reminder of their own impending death, many parents report feeling comforted with the knowledge that their children will be well cared for and that they will have a role, albeit by proxy, in determining how their children will be raised. HIV-infected parents report concern over the fate of their children as one of their main sources of anxiety as they face death.

Even before the onset of the epidemic, extended family members constituted the first potential source of caretakers in many poor and minority communities, in which HIV infection currently is most prevalent. Extended family may not be available for several reasons, however, including HIV-related illness or interpersonal conflict. Rates of single parenthood are also high in these communities, in many cases further reducing the pool of available family members. In addition, child custody laws may not correspond to the family's vision of how its members are related. In many African-American families, for example, children routinely are raised by relatives other than their parents.[17] Courts, however, may interpret the law as giving noncustodial parents a stronger claim to a child than a grandmother who already has had a role as primary caretaker.

The child welfare system, as it is presently constituted, has been overwhelmed by the volume and complexity of issues surrounding HIV infection.[18] In Newark, New Jersey, upward of 50% of children treated for HIV infection become involved with child welfare agencies at some point.[19] While parents are still living but in failing health, agencies may become involved because of concerns about child neglect. Although designed to offer help to children in need and their families, child protection agencies frequently are seen as punitive and their involvement in a family as stigmatizing. Child welfare laws draw only a hazy boundary between criminal neglect of children and the difficulties in caregiving encountered as parents reach the limits of their capabilities. Unfortunately, medical and other social agencies generally are unable to provide the full range of services needed for the care of chronically ill children, such as day care, respite care, in-home medical support, and transportation assistance. In many areas, only child protection agencies have priority access to these resources but with a degree of intrusiveness that families may not be willing to accept.

Another failing of the child welfare system is the impossibility for parents to make legally binding choices about guardianship for their children. Laws passed recently in Maryland, New York, and Illinois have codified the concept of standby guardianship, allowing parents to make placement decisions and even to initiate a shift in custody prior to death. In most states, however, orphans' courts or the equivalent automatically intervene after the parent's death to reassign guardianship, following either state custody law or the results of a hearing in which contending parties are represented. Courts have been ill-equipped to handle the complexity of family issues in these cases and often lack resources to assure that children and surviving family members have adequate legal representation.

Some children ultimately must be placed in foster homes, but intensive support still may be necessary. Foster families need special training to raise children who may be developmentally disabled or have special medical needs, and foster care systems must develop new ways to assure permanency of placement for children who have no family of origin to which they can return.

Parenthood and Parenting by HIV-Infected Women

Studies of parents of children with chronic illness find that some experience periods of severe anxiety, depression, guilt, and grief about the fate of their children.[20] Parents may blame themselves for a child's illness, worry about the child's fate, or experience a roller-coaster of emotions as the child's condition improves and then worsens. Clinicians treating HIV-infected children also worry that sometimes parents will refuse care for themselves in an attempt to deny their child's illness and suffer more to the extent that their child's illness prefigures their own fate.[21] The burdens of caring for a child clearly add to the physical demands on the parent. Parents of all infants suffer loss of sleep and disruption of normal routines until the child develops more mature eating and sleeping cycles. Ill children may develop irregular patterns of eating and sleeping or require medical care during the night as well as during the day. Having a child greatly increases transportation problems for low-income families who depend on buses or walking. Frequently, a parent's activity is limited because no one is available to care for the child while the parent goes shopping or for his or her own medical care. Financial burdens also increase; while in some cases having children may qualify a family for housing or other benefits to which it otherwise would not be entitled, overall costs increase, and housing and food can be more difficult to obtain.

Despite this long list of difficulties, clinicians also comment on the very positive effects children have on many HIV-infected women.[22] Mothers comment that caring for children gives them a reason for living and helps them maintain hope for the future and for themselves. By continuing to care for their children, they maintain a sense of usefulness and position in society that they otherwise might lack. If transportation barriers can be broken, children can help to overcome the isolation and denial experienced by many HIV-infected women.

Mothers can be drawn into activities and support networks at the source of their child's medical care. They have the opportunity to meet other HIV-infected women in a sheltered, nonstigmatizing setting, and the opportunity exists to share advice and even material resources. Contacts at the child's clinic also help encourage the mother to seek care for herself or notice early signs of illness that can be treated more effectively.

Children also may help a mother overcome barriers within her own family. The need to unite to care for surviving children or to help the mother as her own condition declines draws in relatives and friends who otherwise might have remained aloof. It also may be easier for an ill mother to seek help for her children than for herself.

The Outlook for Children Born to HIV-Affected Families

The most difficult task in assessing the social impact of being born into an HIV-affected family is separating issues related specifically to HIV from those related to poverty, substance abuse, discrimination, and other problems faced by many in the groups at highest risk of infection. For example, children whose parents are substance abusers or who have been incarcerated have higher rates of delinquency and aggression,[23] and children of depressed parents are themselves at greater risk of depression.[24] Furthermore, although HIV infection is one reason why children increasingly are growing up in the custody of relatives or in foster care, many other causes also contribute, including interpersonal violence and substance abuse. Estimates by the Annie E. Casey Foundation place at nearly 10% the proportion of American children living in a household headed by someone other than a parent, compared to about 6.7% in 1970.[25] Many of these children have serious problems with social adjustment and school performance.

Children with other chronic illnesses also have well-documented vulnerabilities for psychosocial development, as will be outlined below. On the one hand, there are reasons to believe that the burdens of HIV infection, especially stigma and secrecy, may be worse than for other illnesses. On the other hand, HIV infection, in some communities, entitles those affected to enhanced access to medical and social services that are sorely needed but generally unavailable to many poor adults and children.[26] Detailed, population-based research will be necessary to determine whether HIV infection per se contributes additional burdens to disadvantaged children. The following outlines specific issues likely to influence the lives of children living in HIV-affected families.

Children and death

Children born into HIV-infected families face a greater than average risk that they will experience the death of a parent or sibling. While death is a universal and inescapable experience, it is one from which children usually are shielded.

Despite parental efforts, however, even toddlers are aware that life has an end, and children have some understanding of the finality of death by age 3 or 4 years. Awareness of death as an inevitable part of life appears to be nearly universal among children by age 6–7 years.

At least in times of peace and relative prosperity, children are buffered from death by two main factors: the faith that their parents always will be there to rescue them and the belief that only old people die. Both of these defenses are likely to be threatened in an HIV-infected family.

The loss of a parent or sibling is a major influence on a child's development and can be catastrophic. In addition to becoming fearful of their own death, children may feel guilty for having magically caused the death by wishing it in the heat of Oedipal fantasies or sibling conflicts. Other reactions include anger for having been deserted and feelings of helplessness or vulnerability that may lead to depression or shame.

The effects of early losses, especially of a parent, appear to be long-lasting. Early parental or sibling loss is overrepresented among schizophrenic, depressed, and suicidal adults compared to the general population, suggesting that early, severe trauma may be one factor leading to the development of mental illness.[27] Even children who appear to be functioning normally may remain distressed for extended periods of time, up to several years. The dead parent frequently is idealized, with the child's anger and hostility being projected onto surviving adults.

Many children, however, adapt and go on to develop apparently normal lives. The ability to cope probably depends on several factors, including the child's age at the time of the loss, the quality of the child's remaining support network, the way in which the death is handled, and the level of stress or impairment in the family prior to the death. The highest-risk age groups for children appear to be about 3–4 years old and early adolescence.[28] Insecurity, chaos, or a marked change in environment after the parent's death also are associated with greater difficulties. The types of reassurance that often best help children—that they will continue to live, that they will not die in the same way, that they do not have the same problem—may not be possible for an HIV-infected child whose parent dies of AIDS. Children who lose a parent to AIDS are likely to face multiple factors that predict a poor adjustment to the loss: an unstable support network, an already chaotic family, and, for about a quarter of them, a shared fate.

Psychosocial adjustment of children with chronic illness
Children with a chronic illness, such as cystic fibrosis, sickle cell disease, or any other condition that requires constant medical care and frequent hospitalizations, develop emotional and behavioral problems at a rate 1.5–3 times greater than healthy children.[29] Behavioral problems surrounding issues of anxiety, dependency, and separation are common among infants and toddlers, while older

children may manifest a decreased sense of social competence and have difficulty adjusting to normal home and school life. Chronically ill children may become depressed at any age. The symptoms may be masked, however, against the background of social and physiological disturbances caused by the illness. Listlessness or increased aggressive activity, either of which can be signs of depression in children, may be attributed to pain, malnutrition, or disruption in family routines imposed by medical care. Changes in sleep and appetite may be difficult to assess against a background of round-the-clock care or treatment with medications that induce nausea or abdominal pain.

Many factors probably cause behavioral problems in chronically ill children. Importantly, there does not appear to be a close, one-to-one correlation with the severity of a child's illness.[30] There is even the suggestion that children with less severe problems may have more difficulties perhaps because they are sufficiently ill to require some modification of their routines or expectations but not ill enough to receive the intensive support accorded children with more life-threatening problems. Uncertainty about the future also may play a role in producing distress among children with milder chronic illness. Their current good level of functioning may give them the outward appearance of a normal life and social expectancy, while at the same time they live constantly under the threat that complications of their illness could shorten, or seriously disrupt, their lives.

Children with cancer, a condition potentially analogous to HIV infection in its emotional impact and need for chronic medical care, frequently experience emotional difficulties.[31] Weakness, fatigue, and vulnerability to infection often serve as pretexts for limiting social interactions, but the limitation also may be caused by fear of rejection or ridicule. Changes in appearance caused by medication or surgery make the child stand out and invite questions from, or different treatment by, peers and adults. For many reasons, children with chronic illnesses frequently do not grow normally. Their small stature and reduced muscle mass also serves to set them apart from peers and may limit participation in age-appropriate activities.

Children with cancer can require hospitalizations frequently and without warning; this is also true among HIV-infected children. Some children and families view the hospital as a safe haven. At the hospital, they are relieved of the fear that a sudden medical catastrophe will arise before help can be obtained. The hospital provides some respite to the parents, who otherwise may be unable to find baby-sitters or day-care providers willing to care for an ill child. For low-income patients, the hospital may offer comforts, food, shelter, and companionship that they find difficult to obtain at home. Most of the time, however, these positive aspects of hospitalization are outweighed by the fear of worsening disease. Each hospitalization risks being a rehearsal for the child's death and may disrupt whatever fragile emotional equilibrium the family has been able to establish. It is common for children to regress behaviorally during a hospitalization and, after discharge, only slowly return to their prior level of functioning.

Perhaps the greatest impact on the emotional development of children with chronic illness comes from alterations in their ability to develop independence and a sense of competency. Ill children learn to live with a variety of restrictions and potentially with a much higher level of parental vigilance. Toddlers may be deprived of opportunities to separate, socialize, and explore, while older children may rebel against restrictive medical routines that they clearly perceive as different from the experiences of their peers. Chronically ill children also frequently have to make confusing choices among an enlarged set of parental figures and caretakers. Their identification with a powerful and protective parent may be disrupted by the presence of an authoritative medical provider, who is also nurturing and who, from time to time, usurps the parents' role. The result of these confusions may be a child who is reluctant to function outside of the family or the medical setting.

It may not be fair, however, to make comparisons between chronically ill and well children. Some of the coping mechanisms observed among chronically ill children, including pseudomaturity, seeming lack of stranger anxiety, or an ability to adapt quickly to, and enjoy, "unnatural" surroundings such as a hospital ward, may represent appropriate adaptations to a life-style that is markedly different from that of other children. Debate continues over just how "normally" children with chronic illnesses should be treated. As with all children, they need a combination of nurturing and limit-setting if they are to gain independence and self-discipline; whether they need the same combination as normal children is not clear.

Several types of intervention can help children in their adjustment to chronic illness. Medical services can be made more child-friendly by providing toys, appropriate-sized furniture, and staff capable of accommodating a child's pace and activity level. Physicians can be attentive to issues of pain and fear and respond with appropriate medications or a limit on the number of invasive procedures. Child life-workers can help teach children about their illness and its treatment, providing rehearsals with dolls and other props. This sort of teaching has been shown to hasten children's postoperative recovery and to decrease length of stay in the hospital.[32] Early in the course of the child's illness, social workers, psychologists, or psychiatrists can assess the family, outlining ways in which strengths can be exploited and vulnerabilities addressed before they lead to crisis. Last, but far from least, medical workers can maintain close contacts with schools and other community agencies to assure that appropriate accommodation, where needed, is made for the child's disabilities. Regular school attendance, in particular, appears to be very important to the long-term adjustment of children with chronic illness.[33] Schools have heretofore presented HIV-infected children with one of their most difficult social challenges. Many school systems are ill equipped to aid children with any form of chronic illness. Budget cutbacks have limited the availability of school nurses to dispense medicines or to assess minor problems that otherwise would result in a child being sent home. Home or hospital teaching services frequently cannot adequately assure that children will be able to stay abreast of their classes during episodes of illness. Although many professional groups, including the CDC, the American Academy of Pediatrics, and the National Education Association, have issued guidelines stressing the unrestricted schooling of HIV-infected children, several highly publicized cases have, over the years, demonstrated the fear communities can feel in relation to such children and the publicity and ostracism that can result.[34] Schools are slowly coming into compliance with public health regulations requiring the use of universal blood and body fluid precautions and evolving policies about responsible disclosure of pertinent student medical information.

Impact on Uninfected Siblings and Children

HIV-infected children frequently have uninfected siblings. Brothers and sisters may have been born before their mother became infected or they may be among those who escape perinatal transmission. Siblings of chronically ill children frequently develop behavioral and emotional problems related to the family's adjustment to illness; often their emotional adjustment is worse than that of the child who is ill.[35] Children may feel resentful of attention given to their ill brother or sister, only to later feel guilty about the feelings or about their inability to help.[36] Unaffected children frequently feel anxious about their own health. HIV infection raises specific fears about acquiring the infection through household contact. Although this possibility is considered remote, at least one case has been reported of transmission from a hemophiliac child to his brother.[37] Siblings of HIV-infected children also may feel uncertain about whom they can trust to share concerns.[38] Along with other family members, they learn that they must be circumspect in their disclosures to friends or schoolmates.

Siblings of children with chronic disease frequently are required to take on additional responsibilities within the family.[39] This may take place to a greater extent among HIV-affected families than among those with other chronic illnesses, either because the parents are ill themselves or because of the high prevalence of single parents.[40] Unaffected siblings of chronically ill children are likely to receive the least emotional support.[41] They may fare well if they are resilient children who enjoy feeling needed; being involved in family and illness-related chores may get them attention and support they otherwise would miss. One factor that seems to promote poor adjustment is parental withholding of information about the sick sibling's condition. Again, this problem may be more common among HIV-affected families as parents struggle with the decision to disclose their HIV-infected status to their children and others.[42]

The vulnerable child

The "vulnerable child" syndrome has long been used to describe the manner in which parents treat a child who at one point was seriously ill but now is, in reality, healthy.[43] A child also may become "vulnerable" after the death or illness of a sibling, another significant person in the parent's life, or life-threatening illness in the parent.

Even though healthy, the vulnerable child may be brought frequently for medical care, be overly supervised and protected around the home, and receive little discipline. The parent may have a great deal of difficulty separating from the child, resulting in decreased school attendance or problems with bedtime routines. No studies as yet have looked for the incidence of special treatment among siblings of HIV-infected children, nor at how the vulnerable child syndrome is transformed when the primary caretaker is not the child's parent.

Recommended Interventions

While there is no doubt that HIV infection can devastate families and change the lives of affected and healthy members alike, a variety of services and interventions have the potential to ease problems and promote optimal adaptation.

A most important task is to break barriers of isolation and shame. Clinicians generally suggest that the diagnosis of HIV infection not be kept a secret within the family, even from young children. It may be reasonable for parents to be circumspect outside the home, but professionals must be careful to assure that their interactions with the family create an atmosphere in which the diagnosis can be discussed freely. Eventually, parents and children can be helped to gain the confidence required when inevitable unwanted disclosures take place.

Both parents and children benefit when parents are given a participatory role in the child's medical care. Parents gain needed self-esteem, while children gain the comfort of having their parents closely involved. Adherence to treatment is also likely to be enhanced if parents feel their concerns are understood and respected. No two families respond to HIV infection in precisely the same way, and, therefore, even the most innovative care programs risk failing if they cannot adapt to individual needs.

Medical services can take a central role in the lives of HIV-affected families, obliging medical providers to organize care in the most accessible way possible. This generally requires that services be well coordinated, even spanning adult and child services in the same setting. Attention must be given to transportation, child care, and cost issues. Perhaps most importantly, the medical-care site must be a welcoming environment that caters to the family's need for comfort and belonging as well as its physical health needs. Available services must include both home and hospice care.

Those helping HIV-affected families must be sensitive to cultural and individual differences among families. Mental health services, in particular, may have to be provided in ways that the family is willing to accept. Long-term relationships between patients and providers are essential to create the proper match between needs and services.

Finally, community agencies, including schools and social services, need to develop flexible approaches to meet the needs of HIV-affected families. Assessments often must be made more quickly than usual for families with seriously ill parents or children. Regulations regarding guardianship and consent for medical procedures may have to be loosened or modified to reflect the role of the extended family in caring for surviving children or adults. Schools must create an atmosphere of respect and tolerance that welcomes families with special needs, and programs that assist adults and children with bereavement need to be more widely available.[44]

Conclusion

The majority of children born to HIV-infected mothers will not be infected. Of those who are, some will die in their early years, but the majority will live well into childhood, though with a fairly high rate of medical and psychological morbidity. The majority who will not develop medical illness will face an unusually turbulent childhood marked by the near certain loss of parents, siblings, and possibly other relatives. Studies of families and of child resiliency support the notion, however, that these adversities are not insurmountable if survivors can be adequately supported and if those who are ill can be helped to live meaningfully for as long as possible and to die with dignity. Medical and social service knowledge exists to provide this type of support.

Notes

1. L. Spiegel and A. Mayers, "Psychosocial Aspects of AIDS in Children and Adolescents," *Pediatric Clinics of North America* 38 (1991): 153–167.
2. New York State Association for Retarded Children, Inc. v. Hugh L. Carey; Thomas A. Coughlin III v. Board of Education of the City of New York; Christine West v. Board of Education of the City of New York, 612 F.2d 644 (1979) (case involving children with hepatitis and right to attend school); A. H. Malcolm, "Experts Try to Allay Fears on Herpes," *New York Times*, Jan. 12, 1985, p. 6.
3. R. Shilts, *And the Band Played On: Politics, People, and the AIDS Epidemic* (New York: St. Martin's Press, 1987).
4. L. S. Baker, "The Perspective of Families," in *Children and Aids*, ed. M. L. Stuber (Washington DC: The American Psychiatric Press, 1992): 147–161.
5. Centers for Disease Control, "Acquired Immunodeficiency Syndrome—United States, 1992," *Morbidity and Mortality Weekly Report* 42 (1993): 547–551.
6. A. Septimus, "Psychosocial Aspects of Caring for Families of Infants Infected with Human Immunodeficiency Virus," *Seminars in Perinatology* 13 (1989): 49–54; C. Levine, "AIDS and Changing Concepts of Family," *The Milbank Quarterly* 68 (suppl. 1, 1990): 33–58.
7. M. B. Caldwell, P. L. Fleming, and M. J. Oxtoby, "Estimated Number of AIDS Orphans in the United States" (letter), *Pediatrics* 90 (1992): 482.
8. Ibid.

9. M. B. Caldwell, L. Mascola, W. Smith, et al., "Biologic, Foster, and Adoptive Parents: Care Givers of Children Exposed Perinatally to Human Immunodeficiency Virus in the United States," *Pediatrics* 90 (1992): 603–607.
10. P. H. Wise and A. Meyers, "Poverty and Child Health," *Pediatric Clinics of North America* 35 (1988): 1169–1186.
11. L. J. Cornelius, "Access to Medical Care for Black Americans with an Episode of Illness," *Journal of the National Medical Association* 83 (1991): 617–626; V. C. McLoyd, "The Impact of Economic Hardship on Black Families and Children: Psychological Distress, Parenting, and Socioemotional Development," *Child Development* 61 (1990): 311–346.
12. S. M. McAuliffe, "HIV-Infected Children, Adolescents: Role of the Child Psychiatrist Expands," *Psychiatric Times* (February, 1994): 12–13.
13. S. Andrews, A. B. Williams, and K. Neil, "The Mother–Child Relationship in the HIV-1 Positive Family," *IMAGE: Journal of Nursing Scholarship* 25 (1993): 193–198.
14. G. J. Treisman, C. G. Lyketsos, and M. Fishman, et al., "Psychiatric Care for Patients with HIV Infection," *Psychosomatics* 34 (1993): 432–439.
15. R. F. Mollica, "Mood Disorders: Epidemiology," in *Comprehensive Textbook of Psychiatry* 5th ed., eds. H. I. Kaplan and B. J. Saddock (Baltimore: Williams & Wilkens, 1989): 859–867.
16. Andrews et al., "The Mother–Child Relationship," 193.
17. J. L. Pearson, A. G. Hinter, M. E. Ensminger, and S. G. Kellam, "Black Grandmothers in Multigenerational Households: Diversity in Family Structure and Parenting Development in the Woodlawn Community," *Child Development* 61 (1990): 434–442; L. Richardson, "Adoptions That Lack Papers, Not Purpose," *New York Times*, Nov. 25, 1993, p. C1; J. Gross, "Collapse of Inner-City Families Creates America's New Orphans," *New York Times*, March 29, 1992, p. 1.
18. Levine, "AIDS and Changing Concepts," 33.
19. S. Taylor-Brown, "The Impact of AIDS on Foster Care: A Family Centered Approach to Services in the United States," *Child Welfare* 70 (1991): 193–209.
20. A. Strauss, *Chronic Illness and the Quality of Life* (St. Louis: Mosby, 1984).
21. M. G. Boland, L. Czarniecki, and H. J. Haiken, "Coordinated Care for Children with HIV Infection," in *Children and AIDS*, ed. M. L. Stuber (Washington, DC: The American Psychiatric Press, 1992): 165–181.
22. Andrews et al., "The Mother–Child Relationship," 193; Boland et al., "Coordinated Care for Children," 165.
23. S. Gabel and R. Shindledecker, "Characteristics of Children whose Parents Have Been Incarcerated," *Hospital and Community Psychiatry* 44 (1993): 656–660.
24. G. Downey and J. C. Coyne, "Children of Depressed Parents: An Integrative Review," *Psychology Bulletin* 108 (1990): 50–76.
25. Gross, "Collapse of Inner-City Families," 1.
26. M. Navarro, "AIDS Plan for Poor Seen as a Model for Other Ills," *New York Times*, Feb. 22, 1994, p. 1.
27. M. Osterweis, F. Solomon, and M. Green, *Bereavement: Reactions, Consequences, and Care* (Washington, D.C.: National Academy Press, 1984): 115; I. D. Yalom, *Existential Psychotherapy*, (New York: Basic Books, 1980): 104.
28. Osterweis et al., *Bereavement: Reactions, Consequences, and Care* 115.
29. J. M. Perrin and W. E. MacLean, Jr., "Children with Chronic Illness," *Pediatric Clinics of North America* 35 (1988): 1329.

30. D. J. Jessop and R.E.K. Stein, "The Psychological and Social Correlates of Chronic Illness in Children," *Social Science and Medicine* 10 (1985): 993–999.
31. J.E.W.M. Van Dongen-Melman and J.A.R. Sanders-Woudstra, "Psychosocial Aspects of Childhood Cancer: A Review of the Literature," *Journal of Child Psychology* 27 (1986): 150–155.
32. R. P. Pinto and J. G. Hollandsworth, Jr., "Using Videotape Modeling to Prepare Children Psychologically for Surgery: Influence of Parents and Costs Versus Benefits of Providing Preparation Services," *Health Psychology* 8 (1989): 79–95; J. Wolfer, L. Gaynard, J. Goldberger, et al., "An Experimental Evaluation of a Model Child Life Program," *Children's Health Care* 16 (1988): 244–254.
33. Perrin and MacLean, "Children with Chronic Illness," 1329; J. J. Spinetta P. Deasy-Spinetta, and S. Brandt, *Living with Childhood Cancer* (St. Louis, MO: Mosby, 1981).
34. A. Rubenstein, "Schooling for Children with Acquired Immunodeficiency Syndrome," *Journal of Pediatrics* 109 (1986): 242–244.
35. Perrin and MacLean, "Children with Chronic Illness," 1329.
36. Ibid.
37. Centers for Disease Control, "HIV Transmission between Two Adolescent Brothers with Hemophilia," *Morbidity and Mortality Weekly Report* 42 (1993): 948–951.
38. W. Nehring, K. Malm, and D. Harris, "Family and Living Issues for HIV-Infected Children," in *Women, Children, and HIV/AIDS*, eds. F. L. Cohen and J. D. Durham (New York: Springer, 1993): 211–227.
39. Perrin and MacLean, "Children with Chronic Illness," 1329.
40. Septimus, "Psychosocial Aspects of Caring for Families," 49.
41. Van Dongen-Melman and Sanders-Woudstra, "Psychosocial Aspects of Childhood Cancer," 150.
42. Septimus, "Psychosocial Aspects of Caring for Families," 49.
43. M. G. Green and A. J. Solnit, "Reactions to the Threatened Loss of a Child: A Vulnerable Child Syndrome," *Pediatrics* 34 (1964): 58–66.
44. T. Keyser, "Lessons of Grief," *Baltimore Sun*, Oct. 31, 1993, p. B1.

6

Access to, and Utilization of, Health Services for HIV-Infected Women

LIZA SOLOMON AND SYLVIA COHN

> Well I have a very good doctor, but I haven't been a good patient because I don't have any transportation to get . . . I live on one side of the world and the doctor's office is way on the other side. And I just don't have a way to get there. So I don't follow up. I haven't been taking my AZT or any medications because I have no way of getting here.
>
> *woman from Baltimore*

> So, I had —all the blood work was done. I had gotten a phone call at home saying, "We can no longer care for you. Do not return to our clinic. We cannot give you any type of medical attention. You are HIV-positive."
>
> *woman from Miami*

Access to health-care services and patient participation in ongoing care are important elements in reducing HIV-related morbidity and mortality. In addition, attempts to engage women in discussions concerning the health consequences of their reproductive decisions are predicated on the existence of a relationship between a woman and a health-care provider. In the absence of contact between women and the health-care system, women will make decisions concerning their health care, as well as decisions concerning childbearing, without the benefit of consultation with medical experts. This chapter explores factors which affect the availability and quality of health-care services for HIV-infected women, as well as barriers to service use. An appreciation of these factors is necessary to understand the obstacles which must be overcome before the specific goal of counseling a woman regarding pregnancy can be contemplated. This chapter stresses access to health services for HIV-infected women; as we discuss the use of health services, however, we must be mindful that barriers to care, which function generally to keep women outside the health-care system, will contribute to our inability to communicate with them regarding reproductive decision-making.

Problems of health-care availability to disadvantaged groups have existed independent of the HIV epidemic. Recent reports have noted the disparity between whites and minorities in the use of health services for many diseases, including glaucoma, hypertension, and heart disease.[1] Given the history of inadequate use of health services by minority individuals, it is not surprising to find this pattern repeated in response to HIV disease. What is of particular concern, however, is that the individuals most affected in the second wave of the HIV epidemic are, by virtue of their ethnic and sociodemographic characteristics, even more poorly equipped to cope with the myriad problems associated with this disease. Thus, HIV disease has added an additional burden to individuals who are already coping with poverty, poor health, and, frequently, substance abuse. This chapter first reviews data on the use of HIV-related services and medications and then discusses factors affecting the use of health services by HIV-infected women. Some of the factors addressed in this chapter are specific to HIV disease, while others are not. Each of these factors, however, may influence the ultimate utilization of health-care services by HIV-infected women.

HIV Disease and Treatment

Since the first cases of AIDS were identified in 1981, advances in the treatment of HIV infection have resulted in effective strategies to reduce morbidity and to extend lives.[2] HIV and AIDS-related treatment strategies have focused on improvements in antiretroviral and antibacterial therapies in addition to efforts to postpone or prevent initial opportunistic infections.

In 1987, the CDC issued recommendations for the use of zidovudine (AZT) for HIV-infected individuals with CD4 cell counts below 200 cells/μl.[3] In January 1990, this recommendation was expanded to include the use of AZT by individuals with CD4 cell counts between 200 cells/μl and 500 cells/μl. These recommendations and the growing body of literature which has established the benefits of AZT in increasing AIDS-free time and survival[4] have been reconsidered in light of the conflicting results of the recent Concorde trial[5] and the European–Australian study.[6] Although new recommendations for early use of antiretroviral medications are likely to be forthcoming, early studies have demonstrated that women are receiving AZT significantly less often than men[7] and, as compared to men, have a shorter survival period after an AIDS diagnosis.[8]

Although treatment studies have continued to show a shorter survival period for women with AIDS, more recent studies have suggested that this shortened survival may be due to lack of HIV treatment as opposed to gender-related differences in HIV mortality. In a study of Maryland Medicaid recipients by Moore and colleagues,[9] women with AIDS had a median survival of 290 days compared to 490 days for men; however, only 33% of women received AZT compared to 53% of men. Lagakos and associates[10] reported a median survival of 11.1 months for women with AIDS compared to 14.6 months for men. In this study, women were less likely than men to receive antiretroviral therapy. In a more recent study of 880 symptomatic HIV-infected individuals receiving care in public hospitals and community-based organizations in nine cities, Stein and colleagues[11] found that, after adjusting for disease severity, injection drug use, insurance status, and race, men were three times more likely to have been offered AZT than women.

Although new recommendations for early use of antiretroviral medications will continue to evolve, the importance of PCP prophylaxis, use of antiretroviral therapy in later stages of HIV disease, and ongoing monitoring of immune parameters remains uncontested. The challenge of understanding factors affecting use of health services remains of critical importance because, unless women are participating in the health-care system, they will not receive care as clinical recommendations change. In the following section we analyze factors that may explain why women with HIV disease are not participating in the health-care system.

Framework for Evaluating Health-Service Utilization

Utilization of HIV-related health services by women can be seen as an interplay of the desire, or "need," for services, as well as the availability and accessibility of services. The need for health services may be determined by the individual herself or by some external assessment of need. For example, need simply may be a personal assessment by a woman that she is not feeling well and will benefit from health-care services. However, even when a woman believes she needs a service she may not believe that she can obtain it. A personal assessment of need, therefore, may not necessarily translate into a request for services if the woman does not believe the service is beneficial or obtainable. Need also may result from a practitioner identifying a condition and conveying the sense of need to the patient. This is often the case when considering preventive treatment, such as vaccines or early interventions for HIV, since patients may not yet feel ill and may not identify the need for any medical intervention.

Availability and accessibility of health-care services refer more to institutional factors, such as whether specific services exist within the community and how the organization of these services affects an individual's ability to use them. Availability of services often applies to whether the appropriate service exists, while accessibility pertains to characteristics of the service which may influence utilization. Particularly important aspects of accessibility include when services are available, distance to the service facility, convenience of transportation, hours of services, and cost.

Perceived need for services, availability, and accessibility clearly affect, and may limit, an HIV-infected woman's options in making treatment choices, potentially resulting in her not obtaining treatment. Any barrier, or perceived barrier, to access tends to shift the balance toward not obtaining treatment. We discuss each of these factors and its influence on utilization of services by HIV-infected women. Although recommendations for HIV treatment are evolving, it is our assumption that women must be integrated into the health-care system in order to participate in advances in HIV clinical care as they become available.

Need for Services

With advances in medical care for HIV, the treatment of this infection has taken on many of the characteristics of a chronic disease, including the necessity of prolonged medical management occurring months or even years prior to the development of symptoms. Treatment for any chronic illness may pose problems for patients. Medication regimens can be burdensome, and drugs may have distressing or dangerous side effects. For asymptomatic patients, postponing or discontinuing treatment until symptoms appear may seem intuitively correct. Preventive medicine always has struggled to convince patients that, even in the absence of symptoms, some diseases—such as hypertension, diabetes, and glaucoma—require continuous, even lifelong, treatment. For many women, the ordinary concerns and reluctance which may be associated with the decision to initiate medical treatment are compounded by issues particular to AIDS.

Knowledge

Many women are unaware of their HIV status either because of the unrecognized risk practices of their partners, through their own avoidance of testing due to fear of a positive result,[12] or the failure of health-care professionals to offer testing. In a study of patients seeking treatment at an emergency room in New York, HIV disease was recognized three times more often among men than women.[13] Although awareness of the importance of HIV infection in women is increasing, many women with HIV disease remain unrecognized for years due to unappreciated exposure risks.

Even after women are informed of their HIV-infected status, a decision to begin treatment presupposes knowledge of available treatment possibilities. Although there are scant data specifically addressing women's knowledge of recommended HIV care, studies have suggested that minority populations, in general, have limited knowledge of recommended HIV therapeutics. For example, in an investigation of injection drug users (IDUs) in Baltimore, all of whom were aware of their HIV status and had been given extensive education about HIV, only 56% knew of the existence of antiretroviral medications.[14] Although many IDUs rely on mass communication (e.g., radio and television) to inform them of HIV-related matters,[15] educational messages broadcast through public service announcements focus on the importance of prevention of HIV transmission and describe dire consequences of acquiring the infection. The emphasis on transmission and the relative scarcity of messages concerning the importance of treatment may reinforce the impression that there is little that can be done after HIV infection occurs. Studies involving women have suggested that they have a greater awareness of how HIV is transmitted than they do of whether and what treatments exist.[16]

Stigma

HIV disease carries enormous social stigma, which inhibits care-seeking behavior. Many infected persons, or those suspected of being infected, have experienced harassment, family and social rejection, threat to employment, and loss of insurance.[17] Participating in medical care may make concealment of HIV infection difficult. There are practical limits to the protection of confidentiality and privacy, even with the best efforts of health-care providers. Being seen at an HIV specialty clinic or having medications used for treating HIV disease may put a woman at real or perceived risk of discrimination. Although men with HIV disease also have experienced such discrimination, women with HIV disease may be dependent on family members or partners for financial support or have child-care responsibilities that make them particularly vulnerable to potential rejection.

HIV infection is associated with high-risk and socially disfavored behaviors such as injection drug use. As a result, women may wish to conceal their HIV infection from family members and others for fear of indirectly revealing their drug use or the drug use of sexual partners. Likewise, women who use drugs may fear that entering the health-care system will make them vulnerable to identification by child-protective services and pose a possible threat to child custody (see Chapter 10). Several well-publicized cases in which pregnant drug users have been arrested for child abuse may contribute to a woman's reluctance to be identified as HIV-infected and, hence, a drug user.

Although there is little empirical evidence documenting adverse consequences accompanying disclosure of a woman's HIV infection, health-care workers have reported episodes of physical abuse when sexual partners become aware of a woman's HIV infection.[18] These factors, whether representing actual or feared consequences, may inhibit a woman's willingness to be identified as being HIV-infected.

Hopelessness and competing needs

The difficulty of making HIV-infected women aware of the value of early treatment must be seen within the context of the life conditions of the affected communities. The majority of women currently diagnosed with AIDS are racial and ethnic minorities of lower socioeconomic status. Thus, the burdens of HIV disease fall disproportionately upon women who are struggling with long-standing poverty, poor health status, and the accompanying hopelessness that these situations often engender. Studies have demonstrated that African-Americans and Hispanic-Americans receive significantly fewer preventive and curative services than other Americans.[19] Thus, the failure to use outpatient HIV-related health services is similar to health-care utilization patterns seen in response to other illnesses in these populations.

Tragically, HIV disease frequently involves multiple members of the same family. This presents additional obstacles to a woman trying to obtain care. The need to tend to sick partners and/or children who are themselves HIV-infected may compete with and overwhelm a woman's ability to care for herself.

Suspicion

Some poor, minority women are hesitant to obtain care for HIV disease due to suspicion of the health-care system. Articles in African-American newspapers have articulated the suspicion that HIV is part of a genocidal plot perpetuated on minority people. The reasons for this distrust are complex but are due in part to the historical experience of minorities in the health-care system, an experience which has frequently been characterized by discrimination, hostility, and injustice. The residue of decades of inadequate services and experiences, such as the Tuskegee experiments,[20] have contributed to a profound suspicion and avoidance of the health-care system by many minority individuals.[21]

Availability of Services

Lack of participation in clinical trials

Participation in clinical trials has become, for many individuals, an essential vehicle for obtaining medical care. In addition, participation in these trials is important since recommendations for standards of care evolve from them. The absence of women from clinical trials has meant that recommendations for care have been made without the opportunity to fully examine the effect of these clinical modalities on women.

Possibly more than with any other illness, treatment of HIV has evolved rapidly with the dissemination of experimental treatments into mainstream clinical care. Experimental protocols quickly have become integrated into large clinical trials through either the ACTG, community-based trials or buyers' clubs (informal organizations which import and distribute experimental or unlicensed therapies to individuals). For many individuals, participation in clinical trials has become the mechanism for early access to experimental drugs at no cost. In addition, clinical trials can make HIV treatment accessible to undocumented immigrants, the uninsured, those whose insurance does not cover medications, and those who fear loss of insurance coverage if their HIV infection is revealed.

In addition to the important role of giving HIV-infected individuals access to experimental drugs, clinical trials provide data which form the basis for general recommendations for standards of care. To date, the inclusion and participation of women in HIV-related clinical trials has lagged in relation to the proportion of

HIV-infected women generally. By the end of 1990, only 6.7% (cumulative) of ACTG participants were women, while 9.8% of cumulative AIDS cases in the United States had occurred in women. In 1991, only 8.3% of women enrolled in trials through the ACTG were not pregnant.[22] By 1994, the cumulative total of female participants in ACTG trials had increased to 17% due to enrollment in perinatal transmission studies, studies for treatment of cervical dysplasia and *candida vaginitis*, and special efforts to include women in protocols examining the effect of drug combination therapy.[23] Although this increase is evidence of expanded efforts on the part of the ACTG to include women, the number of women involved still lags far behind the number of those eligible.

Even among the women participating in clinical trials, the racial and ethnic composition is not reflective of the population of HIV-infected women. Nonwhite women accounted for 52% of study enrollees in 1986–1990 compared to 74% of the female national AIDS cases.[24]

Women with substance abuse problems also have remained under-represented in clinical trials. The proportion of women in ACTG trials with a history of drug use was 22% in 1986–1990, compared to 51% of women reported with AIDS.[25] In addition, most ACTG trials have excluded enrollment of active drug users. As of July 1994, of a total of 33,400 ACTG participants, only 256 were active IDUs.[26] Thus, there has been no opportunity to obtain information regarding the interaction of HIV therapeutics and illicit drugs or drugs used in addiction treatment, despite the fact that these therapies, once licensed, will be used widely in HIV-infected female IDUs.

Accessibility of Services

Organization of health-care services

The majority of HIV-related services have been provided in specialty HIV clinics in urban teaching hospitals. Although these clinics provide sophisticated medical services, the rotation of medical residents into outpatient clinics results in the lack of a primary health-care provider who knows about the medical history of the patient, as well as details concerning her family. This discontinuity of care can contribute to a sense of being misunderstood or anonymous and undermines the patient's desire to return for care.

Additional barriers are created by long waiting times for HIV treatment in these large urban clinics. Appointments for HIV services are frequently scheduled weeks and even months in advance. In addition, on the day of the appointment there often are long waits for care at the clinic. These long waiting periods are particularly problematic for women with young children, who either must try to supervise them for hours or obtain child-care at home. Few facilities have designated areas for children and fewer still offer child-care services. The needs of women with HIV to obtain care for their children, many of whom may also be

HIV-infected, have not yet been incorporated into services for women in most facilities.

HIV clinics are still more geared to homosexual and drug-using men than women. This unfamiliar atmosphere may seem threatening to women accustomed to female-dominated clinics, such as gynecological/obstetrical clinics and pediatric clinics. The perception that these clinics may be inhospitable, or at least unfamiliar, may discourage women from obtaining service.

Integrated services for women and children

Although frequently both women and their children have HIV disease, it is still the exceptional clinical service that integrates pediatric and adult HIV care into one visit. Most clinical services are organized by specialty clinics, which can result in multiple separate visits for adult HIV care, pediatric services, and gynecological care. Infectious disease clinics may not provide necessary gynecological services due in part to the specialty orientation of physician training, which has left nongynecologists with little instruction in providing services to women. Infectious disease clinics are also frequently poorly equipped for gynecological examinations. Although new programs to incorporate HIV and pediatric care are evolving, significant problems in integrating these services remain.

Financial barriers

It is estimated that the yearly cost of treating a person with asymptomatic HIV infection ranges from $3,384 to $10,880; this increases to a yearly cost of $33,000 for a person with AIDS and a lifetime cost of $119,000.[27] As HIV disease has increasingly shifted from populations of gay men to women and IDUs, the costs of treating HIV disease and AIDS have shifted from private insurance to Medicaid or to individuals without health insurance. In a study of insurance coverage among Philadelphia residents diagnosed with AIDS, the proportion of patients with private medical insurance decreased from 51.9% in July–December 1988 to 28.6% in July–December 1991. This coincides with the increasing proportion of AIDS cases among women, minorities, and IDUs.[28] In addition, several studies of insurance coverage among HIV-infected individuals have noted that the proportion of individuals without any health insurance is approximately 30%.[29] For many people, the lack of any type of health insurance has resulted in reduced access to health-care services and decreased use of preventive and early intervention health services. In a study of insurance status among people living with AIDS, those without insurance were admitted as inpatients less often than those with private insurance and had shorter lengths of stay once admitted.[30]

As greater numbers of HIV-infected people have needed to depend on publicly funded programs to obtain health care, the increasing volume of patients has been accompanied by a decrease in the number of private physicians accepting

Medicaid and increased reliance on publicly funded health-care institutions.[31] The "Medicaidization" of AIDS[32] has also resulted in a demand for services that often outstrips supply. The frequently inadequate reimbursement structure for Medicaid services has contributed to the reluctance of private physicians to treat patients and has put considerable stress on small community-based organizations which serve large numbers of Medicaid recipients with AIDS.

Inadequate services and facilities in urban areas

Racial and ethnic minorities and poor people receive their health care disproportionately from public clinics or emergency rooms.[33] In addition to the health-care services traditionally provided in these facilities, urban public health clinics have had the responsibility of providing HIV-related medical services to a greater extent than other facilities. As the number of poor HIV-infected persons has risen, the increasing demand for services has overwhelmed these clinics. Hospitals serving large numbers of HIV-infected patients have reported waiting times for appointments that average from 1 to 6 months.[34] Inadequate or overburdened public health facilities often are the only option for women trying to obtain health-care services.

Furthermore, few private physicians are available or willing to treat HIV-infected persons.[35] In one study of physician attitudes, 23% of physicians reported that, if given a choice, they would not take care of patients with AIDS.[36] This may be due to a perception by physicians that people with HIV are undesirable patients because of their status as drug users, minorities, or homosexuals. The low level of reimbursement for public financing of care for indigent people with HIV disease offers an additional disincentive for physicians to provide care.

Rural health-care services

Health-care services for people with HIV are even more limited in rural areas.[37] First, public hospitals or clinics with the expertise to treat HIV disease are rare.[38] The problems associated with traveling to a city for health-care services, including transportation expenses and lack of child care, constrain a woman's opportunity to obtain services. Second, individuals in rural areas may have difficulty finding practitioners with expertise in HIV or the willingness to provide care, despite attempts to educate primary-care practitioners in HIV-related clinical care. Health-care providers have resisted treating HIV-infected patients due to concerns about their expertise in managing this complex disease and about possibly unfavorable reactions from other patients.

Conclusion

Women with AIDS comprise the fastest growing segment of the HIV-infected population, yet there is considerable evidence that women are not receiving necessary HIV-related medical services. Circumstances that involve the choices and perceptions of individual women and the patterns and organization of institutions combine to hinder women from obtaining appropriate care.

Women often remain outside the health-care system for months and even years after HIV infection occurs because the women themselves and society in general fail to recognize their infection. Women may fail to seek testing due to a lack of appreciation of their risk, while medical practitioners contribute to a pervasive myopia concerning women and HIV disease. Even after diagnosis, many women face significant barriers to obtaining care. For many women, HIV disease becomes yet another entry in a long list of problems that must be dealt with, a list that often incudes poverty, substance abuse, and family members afflicted by HIV disease.

HIV disease among women disproportionately affects poor women of color. Thus, a disease which requires intensive medical surveillance and treatment is superimposed upon long-standing inadequacies in society's ability to provide health care for this population. The dismantling of the public health service, the erosion of efforts to bring health care into impoverished communities, and the long-standing suspicion of the health-care structure by people of color all have contributed to a system in which minorities are least likely of any of our citizens to receive health-care services.

The effect of women's hesitancy to obtain health-care services has been exacerbated by the inadequate response of the health-care system. The apparatus of the HIV research community has been slow to recognize the need to include women in all drug trials. Although significant progress has been made in redesigning clinical trials to include women, ongoing efforts will be necessary to ensure that women, representing all exposure categories and racial and ethnic backgrounds, are involved in substantial numbers in all clinical trials.

Fundamental changes in the organization of health services will be necessary if we are to successfully care for women and other vulnerable populations. Increased utilization of primary-care practitioners and coordination of services for women and children will reduce some obstacles to care. Other approaches which must be explored include integrated services for substance abuse, case management, and primary care. Innovative strategies designed to increase women's participation in health-care services, including on-site child care, support groups, "buddy systems," vouchers for transportation, meal coupons, and monetary subsidies, should be investigated.

Finally, any discussion of the problems associated with access to health-care services must confront the fact that, at the present time in the United States, health care remains a luxury that many cannot afford. Although AIDS is not responsible for the shortcomings of our health-care system, the inadequacies that have emerged within the context of the HIV epidemic may be prescient. AIDS has brought the shortcomings of the American health-care system into high relief. Health-care reform offers the hope of an approach to medical care that would have as a primary goal guaranteed access to health services. Access to health-care institutions alone will not solve the problems of women with HIV disease, but without it there can be no hope of progress.

Notes

1. J. M. Tielsch, A. Sommer, J. Katz, R. M. Royall, et al., "Racial Variations in the Prevalence of Primary Open-Angle Glaucoma," *Journal of the American Medical Association* 266 (1991): 369–174; K. C. Goldberg, A. J. Hartz, S. J. Jacabsen, H. Krakauer, and A. A. Rimm, "Racial and Community Factors Influencing Coronary Artery Bypass Graft Surgery Rates for all 1986 Medicare Patients," *Journal of the American Medical Association* 267 (1992): 1473–1477; E. L. Hannan, H. J. Kilburn, J. F. O'Donnell, G. Lukacik, and E. P. Shield, "Interracial Access to Selected Cardiac Procedures for Patients Hospitalized with Coronary Artery Disease in New York State," *Medical Care* 29 (1991): 430–441; J. Z. Ayanian, B. A. Kohler, T. Abe, and A. M. Epstein, "The Relation Between Health Insurance Coverage and Clinical Outcomes Among Women with Breast Cancer," *New England Journal of Medicine* 329 (1993): 326–331; J. Whittle, J. Conigliaro, C. B. Good, and R. P. Lofgren, "Racial Differences in the Use of Invasive Cardiovascular Procedures in the Department of Veterans Affairs Medical System," *New England Journal of Medicine* 329 (1993): 621–627; M. B. Wenneker and A. M. Epstein, "Racial Inequalities in the Use of Procedures for Patients with Ischemic Heart Disease in Massachusetts," *Journal of the American Medical Association* 261 (1989): 253–257.
2. M. A. Fischl, D. D. Richman, M. H. Grieco, M. S. Gottlieb, P. A. Volberding, O. L. Laskin, J. M. Leedom, J. E. Groopman, D. Mildvan, R. T. Schooley, et al., "The Efficacy of Azidothymidine (AZT) in the Treatment of Patients with AIDS and AIDS-Related Complex: A Double-Blind, Placebo-Controlled Trial," *New England Journal of Medicine* 317 (1987): 185–191; M. A. Fischl, D. D. Richman, D. M. Causey, M. H. Grieco, Y. Bryson, D. Mildvan, O. L. Laskin, J. E. Groopman, P. A. Volberding, R. T. Schooley, et al., "Prolonged Zidovudine Therapy in Patients with AIDS and Advanced AIDS-Related Complex: AZT Collaborative Working Group," *Journal of the American Medical Association* 262 (1989): 2405–2410; P. A. Volberding, S. W. Lagakos, M. A. Koch, C. Pettinelli, M. W. Myers, D. K. Booth, H. H. Balfour, Jr., R. C. Reichman, J. A. Bartlett, M. S. Hirsch, et al., "Zidovudine in Asymptomatic Human Immunodeficiency Virus Infection: A Controlled Trial in Persons with Fewer than 500 CD4-Positive Cells per Cubic Millimeter," *New England Journal of Medicine* 322 (1990): 941–949; J. E. Harris, "Improved Short-Term Survival of AIDS Patients Initially Diagnosed with *Pneumocystis carinii* Pneumonia, 1984 through 1987," *Journal of the American Medical Association* 263 (1990): 397–401; N.M.H. Graham, S. L. Zeger, L. P. Park, J. P. Phair, R. Detels, S. Vermund, M. Ho, A. J. Saah, and the Multicenter AIDS Cohort Study, "Effect of Zidovudine and *Pneumocystis carinii* Pneumonia Prophylaxis on Progression of HIV-1 Infection to AIDS," *Lancet* 338 (1991): 265–270.
3. Centers for Disease Control, "Guidelines for Prophylaxis Against *Pneumocystis carinii* Pneumonia for Persons Infected with Human Immunodeficiency Virus," *Morbidity and Mortality Weekly Report* 38 (1989): 1–9.

4. Fischl et al., "The Efficacy of Azidothymidine," 185; Volberding et al., "Zidovudine in Asymptomatic Human Immunodeficiency Virus Infection" 941; Graham et al., "Effect of Zidovudine," 265; N.M.H. Graham, S. L. Zeger, L. P. Park, S. H. Vermund, R. Detels, C. R. Rinaldo, and J. P. Phair, "The Effects on Survival of Early Treatment of Human Immunodeficiency Virus Infection," *New England Journal of Medicine* 326 (1992): 1037–1042; G. F. Lemp, S. F. Payne, D. Neal, T. Temelso, and G. W. Rutherford, "Survival Trends for Patients with AIDS," *Journal of the American Medical Association* 263 (1990): 402–406; S. Vella, M. Giuliano, P. Pezzotti, M. G. Agresti, C. Tomino, M. Floridia, D. Greco, M. Moroni, G. Visco, F. Milazzo, F. Giannelli, G. Angarano, L. Ortona, C. Zanussi, and Italian Evaluation Group, "Survival of Zidovudine-Treated Patients with AIDS Compared with that of Contemporary Untreated Patients," *Journal of the American Medical Association* 267 (1992): 1232–1236; P. A. Selwyn, P. Alcabes, D. Hartel, D. Buono, E. E. Schoenbaum, R. S. Klein, K. Davenny, and G. H. Friedland, "Clinical Manifestations and Predictors of Disease Progression in Drug Users with Human Immunodeficiency Virus Infection," *New England Journal of Medicine* 327 (1992): 1697–1703; M. A. Fischl, D. D. Richman, N. Hansen, A. C. Collier, J. T. Carey, M. F. Para, W. D. Hardy, R. Dolin, W. G. Powderly, J. D. Allan, B. Wong, T. C. Merigan, V. J. McAuliffe, N. E. Hyslop, F. S. Rhame, H. H. Balfour, S. A. Spector, P. Volberding, C. Pettinelli, J. Anderson, and AIDS Clinical Trials Group, "The Safety and Efficacy of Zidovudine (AZT) in the Treatment of Subjects with Mildly Symptomatic Human Immunodeficiency Virus Type 1 (HIV) Infection," *Annals of Internal Medicine* 112 (1990): 727–737.
5. J. P. Aboulker, A. M. Swart, and the Concorde Coordinating Committee, "Preliminary Analysis of the Concorde Trial," *Lancet* 341 (1993): 889–890.
6. D. A. Cooper, J. M. Gatell, S. Kroon, N. Clumeck, J. Millard, F. Goebel, J. N. Bruun, G. Stingl, R. L. Melville, J. Gonzalez-Lahoz, J. W. Stevens, A. P. Fiddian, and The European–Australian Collaborative Group, "Zidovudine in Persons with Asymptomatic HIV Infection and CD4+ Cell Counts Greater than 400 per Cubic Millimeter," *New England Journal of Medicine* 329 (1993): 297–303.
7. M. D. Stein, J. Piette, V. Mor, T. J. Wachtel, J. Fleishman, K. H. Mayer, and C.C.J. Carpenter, "Differences in Access to Zidovudine (AZT) Among Symptomatic HIV-Infected Persons," *Journal of General Internal Medicine* 6 (1991): 35–40; R. D. Moore, J. Hidalgo, S. W. Sugland, and R. E. Chaisson, "Zidovudine and the Natural History of the Acquired Immunodeficiency Syndrome," *New England Journal of Medicine* 324 (1991): 1412–1416.
8. Vella et al., "Survival of Zidovudine-Treated Patients," 1232; Moore et al., "Zidovudine and the Natural History," 1412; V. Mor, J. A. Fleishman, M. Dresser, and J. Piette, "Variation in Health Service Use Among HIV-Infected Patients," *Medical Care* 30 (1992): 17–29; G. F. Lemp, A. M. Hirozawa, J. B. Cohen, P. A. Derish, K. C. McKinney, and S. R. Hernandez, "Survival for Women and Men with AIDS," *Journal of Infectious Diseases* 166 (1992): 74–79; L. Bastian, C. L. Bennett, J. Adams, H. Waskin, G. Divine, and B. R. Edlin, "Differences Between Men and Women with HIV-Related *Pneumoncystis carinii* Pneumonia: Experience from 3,070 Cases in New York City in 1987," *Journal of Acquired Immune Deficiency Syndromes* 6 (1993): 617–623.
9. Moore et al., "Zidovudine and the Natural History," 1412.
10. S. Lagakos, M. A. Fischl, D. S. Stein, L. Lim, and P. A. Volberding, "Effects of

Zidovudine Therapy in Minority and Other Subpopulations with Early HIV Infection," *Journal of the American Medical Association* 266 (1991): 2709–2712.
11. Stein et al., "Differences in Access to Zidovudine," 35.
12. R. Eversley, "Lack of Knowledge and Fear of Seropositivity Keeps Minority Women from Getting HIV Tested" (Abstract PO DO3-3495), in *9th International Conference on AIDS*, (Berlin, Germany, June 1993): 800.
13. E. E. Schoenbaum and M. P. Webber, "The Underrecognition of HIV Infection in Women in an Inner-City Emergency Room," *American Journal of Public Health* 83 (1993): 363–368.
14. M. D. Smith, D. D. Celentano, L. Solomon, J. Astemborski, and D. Vlahov, "Knowledge of HIV Therapeutics Among IVDUs," *Journal of Infectious Diseases* 166 (1992): 685–686.
15. L. Solomon, D. Vlahov, and D. D. Celentano, "Infection Prevention Message for Injecting Drug Users: Sources of Information and Use of Mass Media—Baltimore, 1989," *Morbidity and Mortality Weekly Report* 40 (1991): 465–469; J. Jason, L. Solomon, and D. Vlahov, "Potential Media Channels for Intravenous Drug Users AIDS Prevention Messages," *International Journal of Addictions* 28 (1993): 837–851.
16. N. Kass, R. Faden, A. Gielen, and P. O'Campo, "Pregnant Women's Knowledge of HIV: Implications for Education and Counseling," *Women's Health Issues* 2 (1992): 17–25.
17. L. O. Gostin, "The AIDS Litigation Project: A National Review of Court and Human Rights Commission Decisions, Part II: Discrimination," *Journal of the American Medical Association* 263 (1990): 2086–2093.
18. R. North and K. Rothenberg, "Partner Notification and the Threat of Domestic Violence Against Women with HIV Infection," *New England Journal of Medicine* 329 (1993): 1194–1196.
19. Tielsch et al., "Racial Variations in the Prevalence," 369; Goldberg et al., "Racial and Community Factors," 1473; R. Andersen, M. Chen, L. Aday, and L. Cornelius, "Health Status and Medical Care Utilization," *Health Affairs* (Spring 1987): 136–153; C. Muller, "Review of Twenty Years of Research on Medical Care Utilization," *Health Services Research* 21 (1986): 129–144.
20. J. H. Jones, *Bad Blood the Tuskegee Syphilis Experiment: A Tragedy of Race and Medicine* (New York: The Free Press, 1981).
21. S. B. Thomas and S. C. Quinn, "The Tuskegee Syphilis Study, 1932 to 1972: Implications for HIV Education and AIDS Risk Education Programs in the Black Community," *American Journal of Public Health* 81 (1991): 1498–1504.
22. D. J. Cotton, D. M. Finkelstein, W. He, J. Feinberg, and The AIDS Clinical Trials Group, "Determinants of Accrual of Women to a Large Multicenter Clinical Trials Program of Human Immunodeficiency Virus Infection," *Journal of Acquired Immune Deficiency Syndromes* 6 (1993): 1322–1328.
23. Sharon March, AIDS Clinical Trials Information Service, Centers for Disease Control and Prevention Clearinghouse on AIDS, personal communication.
24. Cotton et al., "Determinants of Accrual of Women," 1322.
25. Ibid.
26. Sharon March, AIDS Clinical Trials Information Service, Centers for Disease Control and Prevention Clearinghouse on AIDS, personal communication.
27. F. J. Hellinger, "The Lifetime Cost of Treating a Person with HIV," *Journal of the American Medical Association* 270 (1993): 474–478.

28. D. Fife and J. McAnaney, "Private Medical Insurance Among Philadelphia Residents Diagnosed with AIDS," *Journal of Acquired Immune Deficiency Syndromes* 6 (1993): 512–517.
29. J. A. Fleishman and V. Mor, "Insurance Status Among People with AIDS: Relationships with Sociodemographic Characteristics and Service Use," *Inquiry* 30 (1993): 180–188; L. Solomon, R. Frank, D. Vlahov, and J. Astemborski, "Utilization of Health Services in a Cohort of Intravenous Drug Users with Known HIV-1 Serostatus," *American Journal of Public Health* 81 (1991): 1285–1290.
30. Solomon et al., "Utilization of Health Services," 1285.
31. D. P. Andrulis, V. S. Beers, J. D. Bentley, and L. S. Gage, "The Provision and Financing of Medical Care for AIDS Patients in U.S. Public and Private Teaching Hospitals," *Journal of the American Medical Association* 258 (1987): 1343–1346.
32. J. Green and P. S. Arno, "The 'Medicaidization' of AIDS," *Journal of the American Medical Association* 264 (1990): 1261–1266.
33. N. Lewin-Epstein, "Determinants of Regular Source of Health Care in Black, Mexican, Puerto Rican, and Non-Hispanic White Populations," *Medical Care* 29 (1991): 543–557.
34. United States Conference of Mayors, *The Impact of AIDS Upon America's Cities: A 26 city report for USCM Task force on AIDS* (Washington, DC: United States Conference of Mayors, June, 1991).
35. B. Gerbert, B. T. Maguire, T. Bleecker, T. J. Coates, and S. J. McPhee, "Primary Care Physicians and AIDS: Attitudinal and Structural Barriers to Care," *Journal of the American Medical Association* 266 (1991): 2837–2842; P. M. Arnow, L. A. Pottenger, C. B. Stocking, M. Siegler, and H. W. DeLeeuw, "Orthopedic Surgeons' Attitudes and Practices Concerning Treatment of Patients with HIV Infection," *Public Health Reports* 104 (1989): 121–129; M. F. Shapiro, R. A. Hayward, D. Guillemot, and D. Jayle, "Residents' Experiences in, and Attitudes Toward, the Care of Persons with AIDS in Canada, France, and the United States," *Journal of the American Medical Association* 268 (1992): 510–515.
36. R. A. Hayward and M. F. Shapiro, "A National Study of AIDS and Residency Training: Experiences, Concerns, and Consequences," *Annals of Internal Medicine*, 114 (1991): 23–32.
37. J. E. Smith, J. Landau, and G. R. Bahr, "AIDS in Rural and Small Town America," *AIDS Patient Care* (June 1990): 18–21; K. A. Rounds, "AIDS in Rural Areas: Challenges to Providing Care," *Social Work* (May–June 1988): 257–261.
38. Office of Rural Health Policy, *HIV Infection in Rural Areas: Issues in Prevention and Services, Report of an Invitational Workshop July 16–17, 1990,* (Washington DC, April 1991).

7

Drug Use, HIV Status, and Reproduction

MARY E. MCCAUL, MARSHA LILLIE-BLANTON, AND DACE S. SVIKIS

> I've did it thirteen times one day. And you know why I didn't do it fourteen, because I didn't have nowhere else to shoot. Thirteen times in one day with a human thing in my stomach. Now if that's not insanity. . . . It's like poking a baby thirteen times.
>
> *woman from Los Angeles*

> After I had him, I got high three more days. Then I tried to get clean. I stayed clean for six months, then I relapsed, then I did it again. I'm trying. I believe I would have still been on drugs, still getting high, until I came here a couple weeks and found out he was positive and that was like . . . you know. I just felt like I had to not only live for myself but also live to take care of my son.
>
> *woman from New York*

Whereas approximately 35% of all reported AIDS cases in the United States are related directly or indirectly to injection drug use,[1] for women, these rates are even higher, with approximately 48% of cases resulting from injection drug use by the woman herself and an additional 19% from injection drug use by her sexual partner(s).[2]

A drug-using woman often experiences a variety of problems associated with her drug use, particularly if she is addicted. On a personal level, she is at elevated risk to develop medical complications from her drug use and to suffer from anxiety, depression, or lowered self-esteem.[3] At an interpersonal level, she is likely to have a drug user as her sexual partner or spouse[4] and to experience abuse or abandonment by that partner.[5] At a societal level, she is often stigmatized and potentially threatened with prosecution because of the effects of her disorder on her family and on society.

A woman's drug use also can affect her child through a variety of mechanisms: prenatally as a result of in utero drug exposure, postnatally as a result of impaired caregiving attributable to the mother's potential deterioration associated with drug use, and indirectly via the disorganized, chaotic environment in which the child may be raised.[6] At present, a history of maternal drug use is the leading risk factor for HIV infection in newborns in the United States.[7]

This chapter explores some of the ways that drug use affects reproductive health, behaviors, and choices. First, we review the prevalence of drug use and associated problems among women and examine drug-related risk factors for HIV infection. Second, we discuss the effects of drug use on sexual activity, contraceptive practices, termination of pregnancy, and childbirth. Third, we review the effects of drug use on women's help-seeking behaviors and the availability and effectiveness of drug treatment services for women. Finally, we identify some of the ethical and policy issues that must be considered in the ongoing debate of the reproductive rights of drug-using women, irrespective of their HIV status.

Prevalence of Drug Use, Abuse, and Dependence in Women

The 1991 National Institute on Drug Abuse (NIDA) Household Survey estimated that, during the preceding year, 15% of men and 11% of women over 12 years of age had used an illicit drug.[8] These rates are especially high for 18–25 year olds, with 31% of men and 27% of women in this age range reporting illicit drug use during the preceding year. Alcohol use is even more widespread. In the U.S. population over 12 years of age, 73% of men and 64% of women reported alcohol use in the last year; of these, 29% of men and 14% of women reported drinking alcohol once a week or more.

These high rates of drug and alcohol use lead to elevated rates of drug- and alcohol-related problems. It is estimated that over a lifetime, 14% of the U.S. population will experience symptoms of alcoholism and 6% will experience symptoms of drug abuse or dependence.[9] While lifetime prevalence of alcohol abuse[10] is known to be significantly higher in males than females, gender differences in drug abuse are not as striking, with approximately 7% of males and 5% of females experiencing the disorder during their lifetimes. Among those reporting drug abuse, rates of alcoholism are strikingly high; for example, 84% of those reporting cocaine abuse also meet criteria for alcohol abuse at some time in their lives.[11] At present, multiple drug abuse (including alcohol) is the most common presenting complaint reported by persons entering substance abuse treatment.[12] Injection drug use represents the most extreme method of drug self-administration, with less than 1% of the general population reporting use of this method.[13] Men are roughly three times more likely to report injection drug use than women;[14] further, women are less likely to report needle-sharing in high-risk situations like shooting galleries as compared to men.[15]

Among pregnant women drug abuse also is a significant problem. It has been estimated that 11%–20% of pregnant women in the United States have a problematic pattern of illicit drug use.[16] Cocaine abuse has been found to account for up to half of these cases, with the prevalence of cocaine abuse running between 3% and 17%.[17] These figures most likely represent a gross underestimate of the problem due to social and psychological pressures to deny substance use during pregnancy and the illicit nature of much of this drug use.[18] Other drugs often detected in pregnant women include alcohol and marijuana.[19] It is important to point out that, as in the larger population of drug abusers, polydrug abuse seems to be the rule rather than the exception among pregnant women who use drugs.[20]

In early reports, drug abuse estimates in publicly funded, inner-city obstetrical populations were reported to be higher than in general obstetrical populations.[21] However, a recent study by Chasnoff and colleagues[22] has demonstrated that women in both public and private obstetrical clinic settings need to be considered at risk for drug abuse and screened appropriately. Specifically, urine toxicology screens were obtained on all women enrolled in prenatal care at five county health clinics and 12 private obstetrical practices in Florida during the first 6 months of 1989. Pregnant women seen at public clinics and those examined in private practices tested positive for alcohol and/or illicit drugs at approximately the same rate: 16.3% positive in public clinics and 13.1% in private clinics. Similarly, African-American and white pregnant women tested positive at comparable rates, with approximately 15% of both groups testing positive for alcohol or any illicit drug.[23]

In Florida, Minnesota, and Illinois, it is legally required that women known to have used alcohol or illicit drugs during pregnancy be reported to health authorities.[24] Such policies will likely have consequences for the reporting of drug use by race and ethnicity. For example, Chasnoff[25] and colleagues found that, despite comparability in the prevalence of drug use among white and African-American obstetrical patients, physicians reported drug use among African-American women at approximately ten times the rate of white women. Overall, these findings suggest that drug use is common in pregnant women regardless of race and socioeconomic status; however, there may be differences in detection and reporting as a function of the sociodemographic characteristics of the obstetrical patient.

Drug-Related Risk Factors for HIV Infection in Women

Injection drug use by women

Personal injection drug use has been the identified risk factor for approximately half of female AIDS cases in the United States.[26] To date, rates of infection have been higher for African-American and Hispanic than for white female drug users.[27] For both male and female IDUs, current research suggests that the primary sources of risk are related to drug injection itself, including needle-sharing, use of shooting galleries, and failing to effectively clean the syringe between injections.[28] There is some suggestive evidence that cocaine use may be associated with increased risk of HIV infection as well.[29]

The relationship between ongoing drug use and disease progression remains unclear. In one study, a survival analysis of a large cohort of AIDS patients in San Francisco failed to demonstrate a poorer prognosis for ongoing IDUs.[30] In contrast, another study reported a positive relationship between frequency of injection drug use and loss of CD4 lymphocytes;[31] however, these findings have not been supported in more recent research.[32] There also is some evidence of more rapid progression from HIV infection to AIDS in persistent drug users as compared to methadone-treated or former users.[33] Possible explanations for the reported positive relationship between ongoing substance use and disease progression include infection with different strains of HIV as a result of ongoing high-risk behavior, immune compromise by injection drug use itself, and high rates of cigarette smoking by IDUs since there is some evidence that smoking accelerates disease progression.[34]

It has been suggested that risk of HIV exposure by IDUs may be best understood in the overall context of risk-taking and management by this group. In a street ethnography study of IDUs, Connors[35] found that drug users typically demonstrated an adequate knowledge about HIV transmission but often reported great difficulty in converting this knowledge into practice. There were two predominant explanations for this difficulty: HIV-risk behaviors were often based in interpersonal relationships and thus required changing not only the individual's behavior but also the behavior of drug-using and sexual partners and HIV-risk behaviors ranked fairly low in the risk hierarchy to which active IDUs generally were exposed. For example, stealing to obtain money, dealing drugs, carrying a needle, and obtaining drugs were all considered more risky than needle-sharing. Thus, reducing HIV risk by reducing needle-sharing was perceived to directly increase the greater risk of carrying a needle and risking arrest. The perceived conflict between reducing HIV risk and increasing risk in other drug-related areas was particularly pronounced for women. For example, women generally reported avoiding such high-risk crimes as armed robbery and larceny and instead often prostituted to obtain drugs, thus further increasing their exposure to HIV. Indeed, for women, needle-sharing was perceived as a networking strategy to increase access to low- or no-cost drugs.

Despite these challenges, recent research has suggested that IDUs are reducing drug-related HIV-risk behaviors in response to targeted interventions. Across a number of studies, over half of interviewed drug users reported reductions in such risk behaviors as injecting drugs, needle-sharing, or not effectively cleaning the syringe between uses.[36] Reductions in high-risk needle-use behaviors appear to be greatest among patients enrolled in drug-treatment services.[37]

Increased risk of sexual transmission among injection drug-using women

In addition to risk behaviors directly related to drug injection, the HIV status of sexual partners is another significant risk factor for injection drug-using women. Female IDUs are more likely than male IDUs to have a sexual partner who is also an IDU.[38] Indeed, a third to half of substance-abusing women enrolled in treatment reported living with a substance-abusing male.[39] An even larger proportion of injection drug-using women report sexual activity with injection drug-using men. For example, 83% of female methadone patients in one clinic reported having had sex with an active IDU.[40] As a result, there has been concern that sexual transmission represents another significant source of HIV risk for drug-abusing women, particularly in light of findings that sexual transmission is far more efficient man to woman than woman to man.[41] In a recent study of gender-specific risk factors for HIV-1 infection among IDUs, a history of three or more sexual partners was positively related to infection only for female participants.[42] However, conflicting findings have suggested that in active male and female IDUs, transmission via needle-sharing is so predominant that the HIV status of sexual partners contributes little additional risk.[43] As risky drug-injection behaviors are decreased, it might be expected that the choice of sexual partners will be an increasingly important factor in the HIV status of injection drug-abusing women.

Injection drug use by male sexual partners

Even women who do not inject drugs themselves are at significant risk for HIV infection as a result of injection drug use by their male sexual partners. Approximately one-third of female AIDS cases have become infected through heterosexual contact with infected men, and approximately two-thirds of those men were IDUs.[44] Such risk is particularly great for African-American and Hispanic women.[45]

An ethnographic study of steady female sexual partners of male IDUs, who themselves did not inject drugs, revealed a number of behaviors that may increase risk for HIV exposure.[46] More than 75% of the female partners used street drugs, with the majority reporting intranasal use; thus, many of them were caught up in the need for a regular drug supply. Only 9% of the women reported consistent use of condoms with their partners, despite widespread knowledge (89% of sample) that condom use could protect them from HIV exposure. As with the IDUs themselves, the daily struggles associated with poverty, under- or unemployment, and drug use interfered with a focus on avoiding the more long-term risks associated with HIV. Finally, many couples established "house rules" which prohibited injection drug use in the home and, thereby, distanced the female partner from the ongoing drug use; indeed, many couples lived quite independently and came together primarily for companionship and sex. These relationship styles generally suppressed discussion of household problems and disagreements, making negotiations about condom use quite difficult.

Influence of Drug Use on Reproductive Behaviors and Choices

Sexual activity among drug-abusing women

The clear majority of male and female drug abusers are sexually active. In a recent treatment-based study, 18% of patients reported not having a sexual partner during the last year, whereas 47% reported one sexual partner and 34% reported two or more partners on average.[47] In a large survey of IDUs not in treatment, almost half of male and female participants reported having two or more partners in the 6 months prior to the interview.[48] Further, female drug abusers have been found to report a greater number of partners as compared to male drug abusers. In a drug-treatment program survey, 18% of interviewed women, but no men, reported more than ten partners during the previous 12 months.[49] Finally, in a sample of single women with unplanned pregnancies drawn from an urban hospital-based obstetrical clinic without regard to their drug use, women with two or more partners (26%) were twice as likely to report drug use during sex than were women with only one partner (13%).[50]

One contributing factor to the greater number of sexual partners among injection drug-abusing women is their elevated rate of prostitution, often directly related to the acquisition of drugs. In one study, approximately 25% of women attending a drug-treatment program reported having sexual intercourse for money in the previous 12 months.[51] Drug abusers also have reported a direct exchange of sexual intercourse for drugs, particularly crack cocaine.[52] Indeed, use of crack cocaine has been implicated in increased HIV risk in several ways: higher-risk sexual practices, including unprotected oral, vaginal, and anal intercourse; increased number of sexual partners; increased likelihood of exchanging sex for money or drugs; and higher rates of sexually transmitted diseases (STDs).[53]

In line with the elevated rates of prostitution reported among female IDUs, high rates of injection drug use and HIV infection also have been reported in samples of women engaged in prostitution, though this varies widely as a function of geographic region. For example, 82% of sex workers who participated in a study in Amsterdam, reported injection drug use, and 30% were HIV-infected, all but one of whom were IDUs.[54] At present, injection drug use appears to be the predominant risk factor for HIV infection in female sex workers.[55] In a study of female prostitutes in the United States, a variety of factors related to drug use were found to correlate with HIV infection: a history of injection drug use, the presence of needle marks, use of shooting galleries, needle-sharing, and duration and frequency of drug use.[56] In a small-scale ethnographic study of female prostitutes in California,[57] the women were found to be almost exclusively IDUs. Both male clients and female sex workers indicated that condom use was infrequent due to potential incrimination resulting from possession of large numbers of condoms should a woman be stopped by the police and fear that if the client were asked to use a condom, he would assume that the sex worker was HIV-infected and refuse the service. Also, there is some evidence that women may receive higher pay for sex without condoms.[58]

The impact of targeted interventions on the high-risk sexual behaviors of drug abusers generally has been slower and less successful than the effects seen on drug-related risk behaviors.[59] For example, Hart and colleagues[60] found that 62% of drug-treatment patients reported changes in drug-use behaviors to reduce HIV risk, whereas only 31% reported any change in sexual behaviors. Nonetheless, in a recent study,[61] 61% of drug-using participants reported engaging in some form of sexual risk reduction, including condom use (44%), reduction in the number of partners (18%), or reduction in the number of injection drug-using partners (2%). For women, there were three predictors for the successful implementation of a sexual risk-reduction strategy: having implemented a drug risk-reduction strategy, having a friend or acquaintance who practices sexual risk reduction, and wanting to have a(nother) child. Thus, reproductive intention appears to be a motivational factor in women's decisions to practice sexual risk-reduction behaviors.

Not surprisingly, drug-treatment personnel focus intervention primarily on high-risk drug-use behaviors rather than sexual risk behaviors, which are not as high a priority for intervention. Further, most staff members have not received special training on sexual risk-reduction counseling and, as a result, may be reluctant to discuss these issues in treatment, thus contributing to the slow progress in modification of sexual risk behaviors among drug abusers.[62] There is evidence, however, that targeted skills-building programs introduced in the drug-treatment setting by specially trained staff may decrease risky sexual behaviors. Specifically, in one study, sexual risk behaviors were compared for drug-abusing women assigned to a single session AIDS information group routinely provided by the clinic vs. a five session skills-building program that identified high-risk sexual behaviors and rehearsed communication skills to promote partner condom use.[63] At posttest, women in the skills-building group were more likely to report increased initiation of safe sex discussions with partners, routinely carrying condoms, and use of condoms during intercourse. Further, participants in the skills-building group reported an increased sense of control over HIV exposure and generally high satisfaction with the group content. Two important conclusions can be drawn from this study: first, detailed and frank discussions of sexual risk behaviors and opportunities to practice risk-related communication skills can significantly increase risk-reduction practices by drug-abusing women and, second, such groups can receive excellent acceptance and attendance in the drug-treatment setting.

Contraceptive practices of drug-using women

Female drug abusers experience more general medical problems than male drug abusers. Common complaints include infections, anemia, STDs (particularly gonorrhea, trichomonas, and chlamydia), hepatitis, urinary tract infections, and gynecological problems.[64] Further, substance-abusing women are at increased risk for a variety of reproductive dysfunctions as compared with other women. Some of the major disorders include amenorrhea, anovulation, luteal phase dysfunction, ovarian atrophy, spontaneous abortion, and early menopause.[65] These general medical and reproductive disorders have an impact on contraceptive behavior in several ways: reducing the perceived need for birth control; increasing the irregularity of the menstrual cycle, making it more difficult to predict periods of fertility; and reducing the ability to conceive.

Generally, research has suggested that female IDUs are less consistent in contraception use compared to non-drug-using women of similar socioeconomic status.[66] For example, Ralph and Spigner[67] reported that approximately 25% of female patients enrolled in a California methadone maintenance clinic used any type of contraceptive method compared to almost 50% in a national sample matched for age, income level, ethnic group, and marital status. Interestingly, drug-abusing women who were never married had rates comparable to the national sample, whereas rates among married and formerly married drug-abusing women were less than half those of women in the national survey. Failure to use contraception often was related to amenorrhea as women reported the belief that the absence of menses indicated infertility.

Although condoms offer the dual benefits of contraception and HIV risk reduction, a minority of drug abusers report use of this risk-reduction strategy, and, in one study, fewer drug abusers reported consistent condom use than non-drug-users.[68] Interestingly, condom use is more likely in sexual activity with casual partners than with monogamous partners,[69] even when steady partners are known to be HIV-infected.[70]

Not surprisingly, partner willingness and support has been found to be a significant predictor of condom use, particularly for African-American and Hispanic women.[71] The perceived need to accommodate the sexual preferences of male partners may be increased for female drug abusers by several factors. First, drug-abusing women have elevated rates of anxiety and depressive disorders;[72] in turn, such disorders often are associated with passive and nonassertive communication patterns, making negotiations about condom use extremely stressful and often unsuccessful.[73] Second, drug-abusing women often obtain their drug supplies from their boyfriends and conjugal partners;[74] thus, a disagreement can mean not only loss of social support but also immediate termination of the drug supply. Third, a third to half of substance-abusing women live with a substance-abusing man[75] and are at increased risk of violence from these partners.[76] Finally, substance use by the women themselves increases their risk to become victims of violence; women are at elevated risk for assault when they and/or their sexual partners are intoxicated, typically using alcohol.[77] Such risk appears to be particularly increased during pregnancy.[78] Thus, there are multiple and serious intra- and interpersonal issues which make effective contraceptive use, particularly condom use, difficult for drug-abusing women.

Decisions to terminate pregnancy

In a study of women enrolled in New York City methadone clinics, 96% reported having been pregnant at least once and 56% reported having had at least one abortion.[79] Thus, the decision to continue or terminate pregnancy is faced by many drug-abusing women. This decision is made particularly complex for this population by the potential for fetal drug exposure and the elevated risk of HIV infection.

A recent descriptive study explored reproductive beliefs and behaviors of women at risk for HIV infection either through their own injection drug use or the injection drug use of their sexual partners.[80] The majority of women believed that all children born to HIV-infected women would be infected with the virus in utero. This assumption was based on their beliefs about fetal drug exposure since both HIV infection and drug exposure were known to involve blood exchange. Based on this belief of universal transmission, all but one of the women interviewed for the study strongly believed that abortion was the most caring, compassionate decision that an HIV-infected pregnant woman could make to avoid suffering by the child. In spite of these stated beliefs, of the four women in the study who recently had been or currently were pregnant, none terminated the pregnancy through abortion. Continuing the pregnancy appeared to be related to a number of factors, including an extreme fear of learning their HIV status, fear of the abortion procedure, and the belief that the pregnancy could be their last. For almost all participants, their maternal role was pivotal to their self-image and their children represented their most important emotional attachment. Indeed, several women indicated that they were able to reduce or discontinue drug use only during pregnancy or as a result of having children.

Other, larger-scale studies have reported similar findings. For example, a study of female IDUs in a New York City methadone treatment program reported no difference in the rates of elective abortion between HIV-infected and uninfected participants.[81] In contrast, Pivnick and colleagues[82] reported that approximately twice as many HIV-infected as uninfected women in drug treatment terminated pregnancy by elective abortion; however, this difference did not reach statistical significance possibly due to the small number of pregnancies observed in the sample. Interestingly, among HIV-infected drug-abusing women, three factors were significantly associated with the decision to terminate pregnancy. First, all of the HIV-infected women who chose to terminate had lived with one previous child, or more, for the child's entire life; in contrast, all of the HIV-infected women who had been separated from their earlier children elected to continue their pregnancies. Second, women who terminated their pregnancies had known of their HIV-infected status for a significantly longer period than women who elected to continue their pregnancies; this difference may reflect higher rates of HIV-related illness and associated disabilities in women electing abortion. Finally, women who elected to terminate their pregnancies had a higher abortion rate for earlier pregnancies than women who continued their current pregnancies. In other studies of the impact of knowledge of HIV status on decisions to continue pregnancy, women have reported a number of additional explanations for continuing pregnancy, including current good health, religious or moral opposition to abortion, personal knowledge of other infected women whose children were well and apparently not infected, and a decision to turn events over to fate.[83]

Childbirth and neonatal outcomes among drug-using women

It is well documented across a variety of drug classes that drug-using women experience a clinically significant increase in obstetrical complications as compared to non-drug-using women. For example, complications specifically associated with cocaine use include lower maternal weight gain, precipitous delivery, placental abruption (usually occurring shortly after drug use), preterm labor and delivery, and spontaneous abortion.[84] It has also been reliably observed that drug-using women generally receive fewer prenatal services than non-drug-using women, thus compromising the delivery of adequate prenatal care for these more complicated pregnancies.[85] In one study,[86] pregnant cocaine-abusing women averaged 6.5 prenatal visits as compared to 9.2 visits in non-drug-using patients.

Maternal drug use negatively affects not only the mother's health but also the health of her newborn. The most obvious neonatal complication associated with maternal drug dependence is drug withdrawal, including tremors, irritability, high-pitched and excessive crying, vigorous sucking, and hyperactivity.[87] It is estimated that 68%–94% of newborns exposed to narcotic drugs (e.g., heroin, methadone) experience some form of neonatal abstinence syndrome.[88] Common withdrawal symptoms in opiate-exposed neonates include CNS hyperirritability, loose stools and other GI dysfunctions, nasal stuffiness, yawning, sneezing, increased lacrimation, and fever.[89] In addition to the direct risks of neonatal drug withdrawal, there is a high frequency of other fetal/neonatal complications associated with maternal drug use. Overall morbidity incidence for drug-exposed neonates is reported to be over twice that of neonates not exposed to drugs, with the overall mortality rate being two to three times higher in drug-exposed infants.[90] This increased morbidity has been associated in some reports with a higher percentage of drug-exposed neonates achieving suboptimal APGAR scores as a reflection of lower responsivity and poorer appearance immediately after birth.[91] Intrauterine growth retardation also has been reported in the fetuses of almost 50% of pregnant cocaine addicts,[92] with associated reductions in weight, length, and head circumference at birth.[93] In general, the percentage of low birthweight infants is three to six times higher in drug-exposed compared to control neonates.[94]

Finally, there have been reports of an increased incidence of malformations, particularly genitourinary, cardiac, and CNS malformations, in infants delivered to cocaine-using mothers.[95] However, in one large-scale study, the relationship between cocaine use and malformations was not significant when other confounding variables were controlled.[96] Across studies, risk of congenital anomalies was elevated 1.9 to 5.3 times that of the general population rate (2.7% of newborns). Combined use of alcohol and illicit drugs further complicates obstetrical outcomes as a result of the well-established teratological effects of heavy alcohol consumption, which have been described in fetal alcohol syndrome.[97]

This variety of complications associated with fetal drug exposure is reflected in an almost fourfold increase in days hospitalized for drug-exposed neonates.[98]

In addition to the direct, toxic effects of drug exposure on mother and child, substance abuse is associated with increased risk for a variety of other problems, many of which have the potential to adversely affect pregnancy and postdelivery outcomes. For example, parenting skills have been reported to be impaired among women who are actively abusing drugs. Chasnoff cites one study that found that a disproportionate number of child abuse cases were among substance-abusing parents.[99] As discussed earlier, the economic burden of supporting illicit drug use often leads to other illegal activities, including prostitution, which decrease the likelihood of the drug-abusing woman seeking health care of any kind, while making her more susceptible to problems such as STDs.[100] For IDUs, use of unsterile or contaminated needles leads to such medical problems as cellulitis, hepatitis,[101] endocarditis,[102] and, most recently, HIV. Such infections in the mother can result in intrauterine or perinatal infections in the fetus. Evidence of the interaction of HIV infection and drug use during pregnancy is mixed. Selwyn and colleagues[103] found few differences in antenatal, intrapartum, or neonatal complications between HIV-infected and uninfected injection drug-abusing women enrolled in methadone maintenance treatment.

Finally, HIV-infected drug-abusing pregnant women have been reported to have higher levels of psychopathology than HIV-infected women with no history of drug abuse. In a study by James and associates,[104] substance-abusing HIV-infected women experienced a greater frequency of severe depression and higher rates of personality disorders, with the onset of these disorders generally appearing before the diagnosis of HIV. Thus, clearly, childbirth and childrearing are made more complex and challenging by the mother's drug abuse and associated problems. These obstetrical and postpartum complications have the potential to impact women's decisions to become pregnant and to continue pregnancy and, over the long-term, to affect childrearing practices and parent–child relationships.

Help-Seeking by, and Drug Treatment Services for, Women

Help-seeking behaviors of drug-abusing women

Although recent efforts to increase the number of women in drug-treatment have had modest success, women are still underrepresented in traditional drug-treatment programs.[105] Indeed, it is estimated that women enrolled in treatment represent only about 30% of the 1.5 million women estimated to have a clear or probable need for treatment.[106] This underrepresentation may be even more severe for minority women in need of substance-abuse services. For example, in a survey of drug-abusing women recruited from methadone detoxification programs and from street settings in low-income neighborhoods, African-American women were significantly less likely either to be currently enrolled in treatment or to have been in treatment during the previous 5 years as compared to white women.[107] In this study, only approximately one-third of the African-American respondents had made contact with a treatment agency during the 5 years preceding the interview. Given that drug treatment is known to reduce HIV risk behaviors related to needle use, nonenrollment in treatment clearly increases risk of HIV infection in this population.

At present, there is a significant overall shortage of drug-treatment slots in our country, and, as a consequence, many substance abusers are not able to enter treatment promptly when the decision to seek help has been made. Women suffer from not only this general lack of resources but also a variety of unique gender-specific barriers believed to decrease their ability to receive treatment. Such barriers include lack of outreach targeted at women who are not highly motivated to enter treatment, exclusion of pregnant women from treatment programs, gender and cultural insensitivity in program content, threat of legal sanction such as loss of custody of children, lack of child care, lack of transportation, ineligibility of women for treatment medications if pregnant or not using a reliable form of birth control, lack of heath insurance coverage, the caretaker role that women generally assume within the family such that no one else is available to care for dependent family members, and the societal intolerance and stigmatization of female drug abusers.[108]

A recent survey of the principal investigators of the 1989 NIDA research demonstration projects for pregnant and postpartum women was conducted to further clarify perceived barriers to help-seeking behavior by drug-abusing women.[109] Traditional male referral networks (i.e., employers, criminal justice system) failed to account for the majority of treatment referrals for women served by these projects; instead, medical providers and child-protective services represented the primary referral agencies for these female drug abusers. The most frequently cited positive influence on help-seeking for female patients was the encouragement of family members other than the partner or spouse (e.g., children, parents, siblings). The most frequently cited factor perceived as discouraging help-seeking was concern about children, including both child-custody issues and availability of child-care services. Program characteristics, including geographic location and gender-sensitive programming, also were reported as influencing women's access to care.[110] Providers reported incorporating such services as on-site obstetrical and psychiatric care, child care, and transportation to better meet women's specific treatment needs. While these findings are limited by the small number of projects sampled and the potentially unique resources available to these federally funded programs, they are important in suggesting both perceived barriers and potential solutions to enhancing enrollment of women in drug-treatment services.

Barriers to care are further complicated for pregnant or HIV-infected drug-abusing women. Although improved in recent years, many drug-treatment programs prohibit access by pregnant drug abusers due to perceived liability risks associated with their care (see Chapter 9). For many drug-abusing women, the medical needs associated with pregnancy or HIV are seen as less urgent than the day-to-day survival needs associated with poverty and drug use.[111] Indeed, there is already some suggestion that the poorer outcomes reported for drug-abusing women with HIV/AIDS may be associated with lack of access to medical care rather than gender- or drug-related differences in disease progression.[112] Clearly, we must develop strategies for enhancing access to, and effectiveness of, drug treatment and medical services if we are to impact the complex personal and interpersonal needs of HIV-infected drug-abusing women.

The need for specialized treatment services for women

Historically, men have represented approximately 75%–80% of substance-abuse treatment program patients; not surprisingly, most treatment programs have been male-oriented in content.[113] Yet, the biopsychosocial differences between male and female substance abusers suggest the need for development of women's treatment programs to address the unique and gender-specific needs of female drug abusers. At present, there exists little information on the relative effectiveness of traditional vs. specialized treatment services for women.[114] For years, however, anecdotal evidence has suggested that women fare more poorly in mixed-gender settings where they are a clear minority of program patients. Recent treatment outcome findings from a large, publicly funded, mixed-gender outpatient substance-abuse program indicate that gender is an important predictor of treatment program retention.[115] Specifically, female patients were found to remain in mixed-gender treatment for a significantly shorter period of time and to participate in significantly fewer treatment sessions than male patients. These decreased levels of attendance were particularly striking for African-American female patients. Several factors may contribute to these poorer retention rates for women: the imbalance of male and female patients in the program; the perceived irrelevance of much of the traditional, male-oriented program content; and the lack of opportunity to address relationship issues, including frequent histories of physical and sexual abuse.

Rather than asking simply if women fare better or worse than men in traditional drug-treatment settings, the more critical question is: Can we improve treatment enrollment, retention, and outcome for women by providing programs or services that more specifically address women's needs (i.e., family therapy, child care, health care)? To date, only one published clinical trial has explicitly compared specialized women's treatment vs. traditional mixed-gender treatment.[116] In this study, patients were women in the early phases of alcohol dependence with no prior treatment history and no evidence of psychotic symptoms or narcotic drug use. Services were relatively comparable across the two treatment sites and included individual and group counseling, occupational therapy, and medical care; however, one treatment site was exclusively for female patients and the other served both male and female patients. Women in specialized services remained in treatment longer and had higher rates of program completion than women in the mixed-gender setting. Also, at 2-year, posttreatment follow-up, women's program patients reported improved outcomes on a variety of alcohol use, psychosocial, and morbidity measures as compared to mixed-gender program patients. Of particular interest, the children of women in specialized treatment were five times less likely to be placed in foster care during the follow-up period than were the children of women treated in the mixed-gender program. Clearly, further research is needed to replicate and extend these findings and to identify those aspects of specialized care that may have contributed to the superior outcomes.

Comprehensive models for women's drug-treatment services have been proposed.[117] Program components include medical services for women and their children, substance-abuse education, relapse prevention therapy, psychiatric assessment, social and life management skills development, and early child development and parenting skills courses. Additionally, outreach mechanisms, including indigenous workers, liaison with community-based organizations, and transportation, are needed to enhance women's access to care.

Integration of substance abuse and health-care services

One increasingly popular strategy for both improved outreach and service delivery for drug-abusing women is the integration of substance abuse–treatment services into health-care and social service delivery sites; this strategy may offer particular promise for identifying and serving HIV-infected drug abusers. Substance-abusing women experience a wide range of service needs for themselves and their children. This introduces a dilemma for health services delivery systems not only in assuring the availability of the basic programs to meet these needs but also in maximizing the coordination of these myriad services. For example, substance-abusing women are often in need of drug treatment, health care, social services, and family support services. Similarly, their children may need specialized educational and developmental interventions in addition to standard health-care services and nutritional support.

To begin to better address these needs, a "one-stop shopping" model for health-care delivery has been recommended.[118] Under this model, the variety of services needed by women and their children would be housed under one roof, creating an opportunity for coordination and continuity of care that often is not currently available. A single appointment would gain access to all needed services, and a single staff member, functioning as case manager, would promote compliance with the delivery system demands. Certainly, pregnant and nonpregnant, HIV-infected and uninfected drug-abusing women would benefit from access to these coordinated services. To date, the majority of such model one-stop programs have focused on pregnant drug abusers. Examples of such models include the integration of drug-treatment services into obstetrical clinics and, conversely, the integration of obstetrical services into drug-treatment settings. It is expected that by combining services the number of women who receive needed services can be maximized and that maternal and infant outcomes can be improved.

Recent efforts to integrate drug-intervention services into the prenatal care clinic of a large, inner-city hospital[119] may serve as an example. Using the traditional hospital consultation model for substance-abuse intervention,[120] fewer than 5% of substance-abusing pregnant patients kept their initial intake appointments at the substance abuse–treatment program to which they were referred. In response to this poor outcome, a number of changes were introduced to improve the integration of drug-treatment services into the obstetrical clinic: first, weekly substance abuse–support groups were introduced on-site in the clinic; second, substance-abusing women were assigned to a special high-risk clinic session, which was coordinated with the support group meeting; and third, lunch was provided for support group attenders to ease the burden of the additional time spent in the clinic. The support group was led by a trained substance-abuse therapist but functioned primarily under a peer-support model in which the women shared their experiences, concerns, and successful strategies for reducing drug use during pregnancy. Over a 2-year period, approximately 40% of referrals attended two or more support group sessions, a striking increase over the 5% of women who accepted formal treatment referral using the traditional consultation model. When pregnancy outcomes were compared for women who had and had not attended the group, attenders[121] were found to have significantly higher mean maternal weight gain and their infants to have significantly higher mean birthweight (including a reduced incidence of low birthweight) and higher mean 1-minute APGAR scores. These improved clinical outcomes for group attenders were paralleled by a significant reduction in short-term health-care costs for both mother and infant. While these findings are suggestive, as results are limited by patient self-selection of support group attendance, a prospective, randomized clinical trial is currently under way to further clarify the utility of substance-abuse support groups in the obstetrical clinic setting. If preliminary findings are confirmed, this would highlight the positive impact of integrating drug treatment with other health-care services and the potentially robust impact of minimal interventions that are cost-effective and easily implemented.[122]

An alternative to providing substance-abuse services in the obstetrical clinic setting is providing obstetrical services in a substance abuse–treatment program. One such program has provided on-site obstetrical services in the context of an outpatient methadone maintenance program, which includes individual and group counseling and random urinalysis for illicit drug use.[123] Pregnant women in this program receive an enriched schedule of obstetrical services, including an initial evaluation, biweekly visits until the middle of the third trimester, and then weekly visits until delivery by the clinic obstetrician. In addition, program counselors, nurses, and the obstetrician meet weekly to discuss treatment issues for all pregnant women enrolled in the program. Preliminary data[124] based on 91 opioid-dependent women receiving integrated services indicate excellent compliance with prenatal care; specifically, participants kept 96% of scheduled prenatal care appointments. Further, there have been few intrapartum or antepartum complications; for example, outcomes include 14% cesarean deliveries, 15% meconium staining, and good APGAR scores (i.e., 8–9) for all infants. The most prevalent antepartum complication has been intrauterine growth retardation, with a mean birthweight of 2,690 g. These initial findings support the notion that the provision of obstetrical services on-site at a drug-treatment program can improve treatment participation and retention in both drug treatment and prenatal care for pregnant opiate-dependent women and can improve birth outcomes for mothers and neonates.

The final step in the integration of care is the development of specialized, comprehensive, interdisciplinary programs established explicitly for the care of pregnant drug-abusing women and their children. One such model program integrates substance abuse, obstetrical, pediatric, and psychiatric care at a single service delivery site.[125] Additional resources include a developmental play program, created so that children under age 5 years can accompany their mothers, and van transportation to and from the site. While such programs may initially appear costly to establish and maintain, the improved maternal and infant outcomes associated with such enriched drug-treatment resources should result in long-term savings in health-care and social service costs for the mothers and their children.

Policy and Ethical Issues Concerning the Reproductive Choices of Drug-Abusing Women

Present policy and practice

The reproductive choices of drug-using women have been shaped by many distinct and yet interrelated forces, including legal and social issues, the responses of the health-care system, and the personal circumstances of the women themselves. In the absence of explicit public policies, these forces have converged to constrain the reproductive choices of drug-using women. Most of the messages have been directed toward pregnant and postpartum women, leaving their male partners out of the equation entirely. The implicit, if not explicit, messages have been to discourage childbearing; yet paradoxically, these messages may result in more, not fewer, infants who have been exposed in utero to drugs and are at increased risk for HIV infection.

Legal and social issues

Societal admonitions, to some extent, reflect societal attitudes about drug use. However, it is the legal status of the abused drug that largely has guided the advice given to drug-using women. A number of state and local governments, fueled by aggressive federal law-enforcement practices established in the mid-1980s, proposed or initiated punitive practices in the management of pregnant drug-involved women, particularly those using crack cocaine. In contrast, punitive measures rarely are proposed in the management of pregnant women using alcohol and tobacco, despite considerable evidence of their harmful effects to newborn infants. For example, alcohol abuse during pregnancy can result in fetal alcohol syndrome, the leading known preventable cause of mental retardation in the United States. Government, in these cases, has instead adopted health education approaches for informing women of the risks of alcohol and tobacco use during pregnancy.

Drug toxicology screens, used for diagnostic purposes, have been the most commonly used basis for government to intervene in the management of drug-using women. When a drug test is positive for an illegal drug, child abuse and neglect laws or other relevant statutes (e.g., possession of a controlled substance) have been used as the basis for government to intervene in the management of the mother and/or child. Legal sanctions range from civil actions (e.g., compelling women to enter treatment, removing a child from the mother's custody, civil commitment) to criminal sanctions (e.g., criminal prosecution or the threat of prosecution if treatment is not obtained; see Chapter 10). However, drug-screening programs and the adverse legal consequences of a positive drug test disproportionately impact low-income and minority women in part because the most frequently used screening criteria (e.g., no or late prenatal care) are more prevalent in these populations and drug-screening programs are more common in public, as opposed to private, settings.

The number of states involving the legal system in the management of perinatal drug use appears to have peaked during the early 1990s; however, the consequences of law-enforcement strategies are not well known. There is concern, fueled by many anecdotal reports,[126] that involvement of the legal system, paradoxically, deters help-seeking among drug-involved women, thereby decreasing their prospects of obtaining medical care and entering drug treatment. Furthermore, if the consequence of legal involvement has been to increase barriers to care, then the opportunity for women to participate in informed reproductive decision-making is reduced by the use of such strategies.

Social role expectations also influence women's reproductive choices. Since women continue to be primarily responsible for the health and well-being of children, they are more likely than men to have their competence as a parent appraised when identified by a service provider as a drug user. When male drug users are arrested or are in treatment, issues regarding family planning rarely are discussed and efforts to restrict the reproductive choices of men are almost unthinkable. Also, because for women a key time of contact with health-care providers is labor and delivery, their role as a parent is the primary frame of reference. Thus, women more than men interact with service providers who discourage childbearing and place the burden of reproductive decision-making solely on women.

The societal costs of caring for infants and young children of drug-using women is often the justification for the different approaches used in the management of drug-using men vs. women or for users of legal vs. illegal drugs. It cannot be assumed, however, that the medical and social costs of drug-exposed children are solely or primarily a consequence of drug use by women. There is growing evidence that the adverse consequences of male drug use include sperm damage, which in turn has consequences in fetal growth and development. In addition, many drug-using female parents who rely on public services were in relationships with drug-using male partners, who by their failure to financially support their children contribute to the social costs of drug-exposed children. Moreover, while the use of crack cocaine generally is considered to be related to infants abandoned in hospitals and to the increase in reported cases of child abuse and neglect, there is little evidence attributing these problems primarily to the use of illegal as opposed to legal drugs. Polydrug use is so prevalent that distinguishing the effects of specific drugs is difficult. Thus, not only should public health policies reflect the medical and social contributions of drug use by men to the problems of drug-exposed newborns, but genuine ethical issues of fairness are raised by the varying management approaches.

Health-care delivery system
Societal attitudes influence public policy as well as the behaviors of service delivery providers. Several states, with federal and private sector funding, have developed innovative systems of care for pregnant drug-using women.[127] However, the nation's drug-treatment capacity for women remains sorely inadequate, and the limited supply of treatment services available to women contributes to the lack of demand for services. Although only a small share of drug-using women enter drug treatment, most women report using general health services within a year, clearly representing a missed opportunity for identification and referral.[128] Inadequate training of health-care providers in identifying problem substance users presents a key barrier in the referral process. Furthermore, because health-care providers are the initial link among a drug-involved woman, a drug-treatment program, and a government authority, their role as caregivers,

coupled with enforcers of legal sanctions, creates additional barriers to a drug-involved woman in need of treatment.

For women who successfully enter drug treatment, efforts to provide advice regarding reproductive decisions are further complicated by the organization of health services in specialty areas. Drug-treatment programs with a predominantly male client mix seldom address adequately the psychosocial problems of women or directly provide female-specific medical services (e.g., obstetrical-gynecological services). Furthermore, because drug-treatment services are generally organizationally separate from primary-care providers, coordination with general medical services is complicated. For drug-involved pregnant women, this lack of coordination of care undermines any effort to provide the support needed for successful drug treatment or informed decision-making about reproduction. With service needs cutting across so many disciplinary areas, the lack of strong organizational linkages delays, if not blocks, the use of appropriate services. Thus, both the lack and the inadequacy of services compromises the reproductive choices of drug-using women.

Personal issues

Complicated and unfulfilled daily lives, combined with psychoactive drug use, can influence judgment about reproductive choices. For example, the lack of stable housing and/or employment can result in a preoccupation with the daily necessities of life to the exclusion of conscious decision-making about sexual activity. Many drug-using women report experiencing isolation; abuse; illness; and grief for loss of health, sexuality, and childbearing potential.[129] Thus, some drug-using women's emotional state of well-being may compromise decision-making and life-style choices. Although these problems also occur among women who are not drug users, health-care providers and the state intervene less frequently in reproductive choices when illegal drug use is not present.

Interpersonal relationships, particularly with sexual partners and in social networks, also influence decision-making, although the direction of the influence depends on the nature of the relationship. A relationship may kindle a desire to have children or hamper use of contraceptive methods. A relationship may also discourage reproductive intentions if it reinforces society's perception of the woman as an unfit parent. Gender inequalities in relationships also influence the reproductive choices of female drug users. For example, condom use, important in the prevention of disease and pregnancy, must be negotiated in relationships where there often is inequality in decision-making. When a male partner is also a woman's drug supplier, circumstances are further complicated by the dynamics of a customer-supplier relationship, as well as a social relationship. In such cases, women must be doubly skilled in their ability to negotiate the interpersonal contexts in which reproductive decisions are made.

Does the HIV status of drug-using women raise new policy issues?

As previously discussed, a woman's drug use has been implicated as the most likely risk factor for infection for nearly half of HIV-infected women. This subset of dually affected women (i.e., drug users who are also HIV-infected) are subjected to the societal stigmas associated with both illegal drug use and HIV infection. Additionally, drug use and HIV infection are subject to very different public policy frameworks, generating confusion for providers and women. While drug use is perceived and managed primarily as a personal/legal problem, HIV infection is managed largely as a medical/public health problem. This leads to the perverse public health context in which HIV-infected drug-using women may have greater access to the medical-care system than women who are drug users but uninfected. However, the potential disincentive for seeking health care associated with the involvement of the legal system in the management of drug-using women could compromise access to quality medical services.

A dually affected woman's continued involvement in drug-seeking and drug-taking behaviors has potential implications for reproductive decision-making. Drug use can impair judgment, affecting use of contraceptives, participation in other high-risk behaviors, as well as compliance with a treatment regimen for HIV infection. A drug-involved woman's HIV-infected status may also result in increased emotional distress, further compromising her judgment. Nonetheless, society generally does not assess whether a parent is emotionally or physically capable of childbearing. Legal precedent has been set for persons who are mentally incompetent, but even those standards are changing.

Women dually affected face uncertainties about their physical health not necessarily experienced by uninfected drug users. If an uninfected woman succeeds in controlling her drug use, the long-term prognosis is a healthier physical future. While controlling drug use will improve the quality of life of an HIV-infected drug-involved woman, it will not appreciably change her long-term prognosis. Drug use, however, may adversely influence the progression of HIV disease by impairing the immune system and increasing exposure to many infectious agents. Given the stage and progression of the disease, dually-affected women may be less capable of caring for a child physically than uninfected drug-involved women. Effective treatment for HIV infection would alter this medical prognosis; however, as new treatments for HIV disease become available, knowledge about the interaction of these treatments with the abused drug would be needed. Women and their health-care providers should enter into informed conversations based on the individual's life circumstances, not societal stereotypes.

Finally, the costs borne by society in caring for children who may be dually affected is an issue for consideration. The stigma of infants being substance-exposed and/or HIV-infected has been, until recently, as damaging as that of adults. Some of the social costs attributed to drug use by women are related to fears about HIV infection. For example, the increase in abandoned infants who are medically ready for hospital discharge is related to many factors, including difficulties in securing placements for infants exposed to HIV. Thus, the social costs of drug-exposed and/or HIV-exposed infants are intertwined. Ironically, dually exposed infants, given the risk of developing AIDS, ultimately may have lower direct service costs than, for example, children with fetal alcohol syndrome because of their shorter life expectancy. Also, the service costs may be similar because of the aggressive use of life-sustaining technology. Identifying the specific and overlapping dimensions of the costs is necessary to clarify whether there are unique social costs to be considered for dually affected children.

Dually affected women are at great risk of having their reproductive rights compromised because of negative social stereotypes of drug users. Although there are some unique issues that affect women who both are HIV-infected and use drugs, the impact of these factors will vary for the particular individual. Thus, the differences would not serve as the basis for sound public policy that differentiates HIV-infected women based on their drug-using status. This nation's history of abuses in the area of reproductive rights (e.g., coerced sterilizations) has occurred largely in socially or economically disadvantaged populations. This pattern suggests the need for safeguards to assure that a dually affected woman's right to informed reproductive decision-making is not compromised.

Conclusion

Concern about the epidemics of drug use and HIV infection has prompted considerable debate about the role and responsibility of the service delivery systems that intervene to assist women, children, and families in crisis. Direct and indirect communication by service providers has discouraged childbearing among drug-using and HIV-infected women. Societal disapproval of births to drug-using women has been conveyed with equal, if not greater, force as the messages from service providers. For dually affected women to have genuine choices and to make informed reproductive decisions, it is necessary to substantially reduce barriers to drug treatment. Managing drug abuse as a public health/medical problem rather than a legal/personal problem is one of the first steps toward assuring that a woman's right to make choices about her life is not compromised.

Public policy regarding the reproductive choices of drug-using and/or HIV-infected women has focused almost exclusively on influencing their personal behavior. Neglected in the policy debate has been the behavior of men and society's responsibility to women and children, regardless of their status as drug-involved or HIV-infected. The challenge is to develop public policy that balances society's obligation to protect those compromised in their ability to care for themselves with people's rights to make choices about their own lives.

Notes

1. Centers for Disease Control, *HIV/AIDS Surveillance Report* 6 (Atlanta, GA: CDC, 1994): 8.
2. Ibid., 8–10.
3. J. E. Helzer and T. R. Pryzbeck, "The Co-Occurrence of Alcoholism with Other Psychiatric Disorders in the General Population and Its Impact on Treatment," *Journal of Studies on Alcohol* 49 (1988): 219–224; E. Oppenheimer, "Alcohol and Drug Misuse Among Women: An Overview," *British Journal of Psychiatry* 158 (1991): 36–44.
4. J. C. Marsh and N. A. Miller, "Female Clients in Substance Abuse Treatment," *International Journal of the Addictions* 20 (1985): 995–1019; M. Rosenbaum, "When Drugs Come in the Picture, Love Flies Out the Window: Women Addicts' Love Relationships," *International Journal of the Addictions* 16 (1981): 1197–1206.
5. H. Amaro, L. E. Fried, H. Cabral, and B. Zuckerman, "Violence During Pregnancy and Substance Use," *American Journal of Public Health* 80 (1990): 575–579.
6. E. Vanderveen, "Public Health Policy: Maternal Substance Use and Child Health," *Annals of the New York Academy of Sciences* (1992): 255–-259.
7. Centers for Disease Control, "AIDS in Women—United States," *Morbidity and Mortality Weekly Report*, 39 (1990): 845–846.
8. In the National Institute of Drug Abuse (NIDA) Household Survey, illicit drugs include marijuana, inhalants, cocaine, hallucinogens, heroin, or nonmedical use of psychotherapeutics.
9. Helzer and Pryzbeck, "The Co-Occurrence of Alcoholism," 220. Research by Helzer and Pryzbeck used the definitions of psychoactive substance abuse and dependence as published in the American Psychiatric Association's *Diagnostic and Statistical Manual of Mental Disorders* (DSM-IIIR), 3rd ed. (Washington, DC: American Psychiatric Association, 1987): 165–185. *Dependence* is defined as a cluster of cognitive, behavioral, and physiological symptoms that indicate impaired control of psychoactive substance use and continued use of the substance despite adverse consequences. *Abuse* is a residual category for noting maladaptive patterns of psychoactive substance use that have never met the criteria for dependence for that particular class of substance.
10. Throughout this chapter, the diagnostic term "abuse" will be used inclusively to refer to both abuse and dependence.
11. Helzer and Pryzbeck, "The Co-Occurrence of Alcoholism," 222.
12. R. H. Price, A. C. Burke, T. A. D'Aunno, D. M. Klingel, W. C. McCaughrin, J. A. Rafferty, and T. E. Vaughn, "Outpatient Drug Abuse Treatment Services, 1988: Results of a National Survey," in *Improving Drug Abuse Treatment* (National Institute on Drug Abuse Research Monograph 106, DHHS #[ADM], 91–1754), eds. R. W. Pickens, C. G. Leukfeld, and C. R. Schusters (Washington, D.C.: U.S. Government Printing Office, 1991): 63–92; K. M. Carroll, B. J. Rounsaville, and K. J. Bryant, "Alcoholism in Treatment-Seeking Cocaine Abusers: Clinical and Prognostic Significance," *Journal of Studies on Alcohol*, 54 (1993): 199–208.
13. L. P. Finnegan, K. Davenny, and D. Hartel, "Drug Use in HIV-Infected Women,"

in *HIV Infection in Women*, eds. F. D. Johnstone and M. Johnson (Edinburgh: Churchill Livingstone, 1993): 133–155.
14. E. Drucker, "AIDS and Addiction in New York City," *American Journal of Drug and Alcohol Abuse* 12 (1986): 165–181.
15. Finnegan et al., "Drug Use in HIV-Infected Women," 135.
16. E. L. Abel and R. J. Sokol, "Incidence of Fetal Alcohol Syndrome and Economic Impact of FAS-Related Anomalies," *Drug and Alcohol Dependence* 19 (1987): 51–70; I. J. Chasnoff, W. J. Burns, S. H. Schnoll, and K. A. Burns, "Cocaine Use in Pregnancy," *New England Journal of Medicine* 313 (1985): 666–669; K. C. Edelin, L. Gurganious, K. Golar, D. Oellerich, K. Kyei-Aboagye, and M. A. Hamid, "Methadone Maintenance in Pregnancy: Consequences to Care and Outcome," *Obstetrics and Gynecology* 71 (1988): 399–404; B. B. Little, L. M. Snell, M. K. Palmore, and L. C. Gilstrap, "Cocaine Use in Pregnant Women in a Large Public Hospital," *American Journal of Perinatology* 5 (1988): 206–207; R. J. Sokol, S. I. Miller, S. Debanne, N. Golden, G. Collins, J. Kaplan, and S. Martier, "The Cleveland NIAAA Prospective Alcohol-in-Pregnancy Study: The First Year," *Neurobehavioral Toxicology and Teratology* 3 (1981): 203–209.
17. Chasnoff et al., "Cocaine Use in Pregnancy," 668; J. R. Janke, "Prenatal Cocaine Use: Effects on Perinatal Outcome," *Journal of Nurse Midwifery* 35 (1990): 74–77; Little et al., "Cocaine Use in Pregnant Women," 206.
18. C. B. Ernhart, M. Morrow-Tlucak, R. J. Sokol, and S. Martier, "Underreporting of Alcohol Use in Pregnancy," *Alcoholism: Clinical and Experimental Research* 12 (1988): 506–511.
19. I. J. Chasnoff, H. J. Landress, and M. E. Barrett, "The Prevalence of Illicit Drug or Alcohol Use During Pregnancy and Discrepancies in Mandatory Reporting in Pinellas County, Florida," *New England Journal of Medicine* 322 (1990): 1202–1206; I. E. Smith, J. S. Lancaster, S. Moss-Wells, C. D. Coles, and A. Falek, "Identifying High-Risk Pregnant Drinkers: Biological and Behavioral Correlates of Continuous Heavy Drinking During Pregnancy," *Journal of Studies on Alcohol* 48 (1987): 304–309; B. Zuckerman, D. A. Frank, R. Hingson, et al., "Effects of Maternal Marijuana and Cocaine Use on Fetal Growth," *New England Journal of Medicine* 320 (1989): 762–768.
20. Edelin et al., "Methadone Maintenance in Pregnancy," 401; B. B. Little, L. M. Snell, V. R. Klein, and L. C. Gilstrap, "Cocaine Abuse During Pregnancy: Maternal and Fetal Implications," *Obstetrics and Gynecology* 73 (1989): 157–160; Little et al., "Cocaine Use in Pregnant Women," 206; T. S. Rosen and H. L. Johnson, "Drug-Addicted Mothers, Their Infants and SIDS," *Annals of the New York Academy of Science* 533 (1988): 89–95.
21. I. J. Chasnoff, "Drug Use and Women: Establishing a Standard of Care," Annals of the New York Academy of Science 562 (1989): 208–210.
22. Chasnoff et al., "The Prevalence of Illicit Drug or Alcohol Use," 1202–1206.
23. There was an interesting difference in the type of drug most commonly used by black vs. white pregnant women: cocaine use was evident in 7.5% of black patients and 1.8% of white patients, whereas marijuana use was evident in 14.4% of white patients and 6% of black patients.
24. See Chapter 10 of this volume for a discussion of legal sanctions for drug use during pregnancy.
25. Chasnoff et al., "The Prevalence of Illicit Drug or Alcohol Use," 1204.
26. Centers for Disease Control, "AIDS in Women," 845; M. E. Guinan and A. Hardy,

"Epidemiology of AIDS in Women in the United States," *Journal of the American Medical Association* 257 (1987): 2039–2042; R. P. Brettle and C. Leen, "The Natural History of HIV and AIDS in Women," *AIDS* 5 (1991): 1283–1292.

27. T. V. Ellerbock, T. J. Bush, M. E. Chamberland, M. J. Oxtoby, "Epidemiology of women with AIDS in the United States, 1981 through 1990," *Journal of the American Medical Association* 265 (1991): 2971–2975; D. K. Lewis and J. K. Watters, "Human Immunodeficiency Virus Seroprevalence in Female Intravenous Drug Users: The Puzzle of Black Women's Risk," *Social Science and Medicine* 29 (1989): 1071–1076; M. Marmor, K. Krasinski, M. Sanchez, H. Cohen, N. Dubin, L. Weiss, A. Manning, D. Bebenroth, N. Saphier, C. Harrison, and D. J. Ribble, "Sex, Drugs, and HIV Infection in a New York City Hospital Outpatient Population," *Journal of Acquired Immune Deficiency Syndromes* 3 (1990): 307–318.

28. D. C. Des Jarlais and S. R. Friedman, "HIV Infection Among Intravenous Drug Users: Epidemiology and Risk Reduction," *AIDS* 1 (1987): 67–76.

29. J. C. Anthony, D. Vlahov, K. E. Nelson, S. Cohn, J. Astemborski, and L. Solomon, "New Evidence on Intravenous Cocaine Use and the Risk of Infection with Human Immunodeficiency Virus Type 1," *American Journal of Epidemiology* 134 (1991): 1175–1189; R. E. Chaisson, P. Bacchetti, D. Osmond, et al., "Cocaine Use and HIV Infection in Intravenous Drug Users in San Francisco," *Journal of the American Medical Association* 261 (1989): 561–565.

30. G. F. Lemp, S. F. Payne, D. Neal, T. Temelso, and G. W. Rutherford, "Survival Trends for Patients with AIDS," *Journal of the American Medical Association* 263 (1990): 402–406.

31. Des Jarlais and Friedman, "HIV Infection Among Intravenous Drug Users," 74.

32. J. B. Margolick, A. Munoz, D. Vlahav, et al., "Changes in T-Lymphocyte Subsets in Intravenous Drug Users with HIV-1 Infection," *Journal of the American Medical Association* 267 (1992): 1631–1636.

33. R. Weber, B. Ledergerber, M. Opravil, W. Siegenthaler, and R. Luthy, "Progression of HIV Infection in Misusers of Injected Drugs Who Stop Injecting or Follow a Programme of Maintenance Treatment With Methadone," *British Medical Journal* 301 (1990): 1362–1365.

34. Brettle and Leen, "The Natural History," 1284.

35. M. M. Connors, "Risk Perception, Risk Taking and Risk Management Among Intravenous Drug Users: Implications for AIDS Prevention," *Social Science and Medicine* 34 (1992): 591–601.

36. S. R. Friedman, D. C. Des Jarlais, J. L. Sotheran, et al., "AIDS and Self-Organization Among Intravenous Drug Users," *International Journal of Addictions* 22 (1987): 201–219; P. H. Kleinman, D. S. Goldsmith, S. R. Friedman, et al., "Knowledge About and Behaviors Affecting the Spread of AIDS: A Street Survey of Intravenous Drug Users and Their Associates in New York City," *International Journal of Addictions* 25 (1990): 345–361; P. A. Selwyn, C. Feiner, C. P. Cox, C. Lipshutz, and R. L. Cohen, "Knowledge About AIDS and High-Risk Behavior Among Intravenous Drug Users in New York City," *AIDS* 1 (1987): 247–254.

37. Selwyn et al., "Knowledge About AIDS," 250.

38. R. J. Battjes, R. W. Pickens, Z. Amsel, and L. S. Brown, "Heterosexual Transmission of Human Immunodeficiency Virus Among Intravenous Drug Users," *Journal of Infectious Diseases* 162 (1990): 1007–1011; D. C. Des Jarlais, M. E. Chamberland, S. R. Yacovitz, P. Weinberg, and S. R. Friedman, "Heterosexual Partners: A Large Risk Group for AIDS" (letter), *Lancet* (1984): 1346–1347.

39. M. L. Griffin, R. D. Weiss, S. M. Mirin, and U. Lange, "A Comparison of Male and Female Cocaine Abusers," *Archives of General Psychiatry* 46 (1989): 122–126; M. N. Hesselbrock, R. E. Meyer, and J. J. Keener, "Psychopathology in Hospitalized Alcoholics," *Archives of General Psychiatry* 42 (1985): 1050–1055; T. R. Kosten, B. J. Rounsaville and H. D. Kleber, "Ethnic and Gender Differences Among Opiate Addicts," *International Journal of the Addictions* 20 (1985): 1143–1162.
40. R. F. Schilling, N. El-Bassel, S. P. Schinke, K. Gordon, and S. Nichols, "Building Skills of Recovering Women Drug Users to Reduce Heterosexual AIDS Transmission," *Public Health Reports* 106 (1991): 297–303.
41. H. W. Haverkos and R. Edelman, "The Epidemiology of Acquired Immune Deficiency Syndrome Among Heterosexuals," *Journal of the American Medical Association* 260 (1988): 1922–1929; H. Handsfield, "Heterosexual Transmission of Human Immunodeficiency Virus," *Journal of the American Medical Association* 260 (1988): 1943–1944.
42. L. Solomon, J. Artemborski, D. Warren, A. Munoz, S. Cohn, D. Vlahov, and K. E. Nelson, "Differences in Risk Factors for Human Immunodeficiency Virus Type 1 Seroconversion Among Male and Female Intravenous Drug Users," *American Journal of Epidemiology* 137 (1993): 892–898.
43. Battjes et al., "Heterosexual Transmission," 1009.
44. Centers for Disease Control, "AIDS in Women," 845; Guinan and Hardy, "Epidemiology of AIDS," 2040.
45. Centers for Disease Control, "AIDS in Women," 845.
46. S. Kane, "HIV, Heroin and Heterosexual Relations," *Social Science Medicine* 32 (1991): 1037–1050.
47. A. S. Abdul-Quader, S. Tross, S. R. Friedman, A. C. Kouzi, and D. C. Des Jarlais, "Street-Recruited Intravenous Drug Users and Sexual Risk Reduction in New York City," *AIDS* 4 (1990): 1075–1079.
48. W. W. Weddington, R. Nemeth-Coslett, M. Anderson, et al., "Risk Behaviors for HIV Transmission Among Intravenous Drug Users Not in Drug Treatment—United States," *Morbidity and Mortality Weekly Report* 39 (1990): 273–276.
49. G. J. Hart, C. Sonnex, A. Petherick, A. M. Johnson, C. Feinmann, and M. W. Adler, "Risk Behaviors for HIV Infection Among Injecting Drug Users Attending a Drug Dependency Clinic," *British Medical Journal* 298 (1989): 1081–1083.
50. P. O'Campo, R. R. Faden, A. C. Gielen, N. Kass, and J. Anderson, "Contraceptive and Sexual Practices Among Single Women with Unplanned Pregnancies: Partner Influences," *Family Planning Perspectives* 25 (September 1, 1993): 215–219.
51. Hart et al., "Risk Behaviors for HIV Infection," 1082.
52. B. P. Bowser, "Crack and AIDS: An Ethnographic Impression," *Journal of the National Medical Association* 81 (1989): 538–540.
53. R. E. Fullilove, M. T. Fullilove, B. P. Bowser, and S. A. Gross, "Risk of Sexually Transmitted Disease Among Black Adolescent Crack Users in Oakland and San Francisco, California," *Journal of the American Medical Association* 263 (1990): 851–855.
54. J.A.R. Van Den Hoek, H.J.A. Van Haastrecht, B. Scheeringa-Troost, J. Goudsmit, and R. A. Coutinho, "HIV Infection and STD in Drug Addicted Prostitutes in Amsterdam: Potential for Heterosexual HIV Transmission," *Genitourinary Medicine* 65 (1989): 146–150.

55. J. B. Cohen, C. Wofsy, P. Gill, et al., "Antibody to Human Immunodeficiency Virus in Female Prostitutes," *Morbidity and Mortality Weekly Report* 36 (1987): 157–161.
56. R. F. Khabbaz, W. W. Darrow, T. M. Hartley, J. Witte, J. B. Cohen, et al., "Seroprevalence and Risk Factors for HTLV-I/II Infection Among Female Prostitutes in the United States," *Journal of the American Medical Association* 263 (1990): 60–64.
57. J. R. Magana, "Sex, Drugs and HIV: An Ethnographic Approach," *Social Science and Medicine* 33 (1991): 5–9.
58. N. P. McKeganey, M. Barnard, and H. Watson, "HIV-Related Risk Behavior Among Injecting Drug Users," *British Journal of Addiction* 84 (1990): 1481–1490.
59. M. C. Donoghoe, "Sex, HIV and the Injecting Drug User," *British Journal of Addiction* 87 (1992): 405–416; Schilling et al., "Building Skills of Recovering Women," 298.
60. Hart et al., "Risk Behaviors for HIV Infection," 1082.
61. Abdul-Quader et al., "Street-Recruited Intravenous Drug Users," 1077.
62. A. J. France, C. A. Skidmore, J. R. Robertson, R. P. Brettle, J.J.K. Roberts, S. M. Burns, C. A. Foster, et al., "Heterosexual Spread of Human Immunodeficiency Virus in Edinburgh," *British Medical Journal* 296 (1988): 526–529.
63. Schilling et al., "Building Skills of Recovering Women," 300–301.
64. J. Mondanaro, "Community-Based AIDS Prevention Interventions: Special Issues of Women Intravenous Drug Users," in *AIDS and Intravenous Drug Use: Future Directions for Community-Based Prevention Research* (NIDA Research Monograph Series # 93), eds. C. G. Leukefeld, R. J. Battjes, and Z. Amsel (Rockville, MD: National Institute on Drug Abuse, 1990): 68–82.
65. B. Lex, "Some Gender Differences in Alcohol and Polysubstance Users," *Health Psychology* 10 (1991): 121–132.
66. L. S. Brown, J. L. Mitchell, S. L. DeVore, and B. J. Primm, "Female Intravenous Drug Users and Perinatal HIV Transmission" (letter), *New England Journal of Medicine* 320 (1989): 1493–1494.
67. N. Ralph and C. Spigner, "Contraceptive Practices Among Female Heroin Addicts," *American Journal of Public Health* 76 (1986): 1016–1017.
68. V. L. King, R. K. Brooner, G. E. Bigelow, C. W. Schmidt, L. J. Felch, and P. M. Gazaway, "Condom Use Rates for Specific Sexual Behaviors Among Opiate Abusers Entering Treatment," *Drug and Alcohol Dependence* 35 (1994): 231–238.
69. J. Catania, J. Coates, R. Stall, et al., "Prevalence of AIDS-Related Risk Factors and Condom Use in the United States," *Science* 258 (1992): 1101–1106; Hart et al., "Risk Behaviors for HIV Infection," 1082.
70. G. Mulleady, D. White, K. Philips, and C. Cupitt, "Reducing Sexual Transmission of HIV for Injecting Drug Users: The Challenge for Counseling," *Counseling Psychology Quarterly* 3 (1990): 325–341.
71. Lewis and Watters, "Human Immunodeficiency Virus," 1074–1075; Ralph and Spigner, "Contraceptive Practices," 1016; Schilling et al., "Building Skills of Recovering Women," 297.
72. B. G. Reed, "Intervention Strategies for Drug Dependent Women: An Introduction," in *Treatment Services for Drug Dependent Women*, eds. G. M. Beschner, B. G. Reed, and J. Mondanaro (Rockville, MD: National Institute on Drug Abuse, 1981): 1–24.
73. Mondanaro, "Community-Based AIDS Prevention Interventions," 76.

74. R. G. Ferrence and P. C. Whitehead, "Sex Differences in Psychoactive Drug Use: Recent Epidemiology," in *Research Advances and Drug Problems, Volume 5: Alcohol and Drug Problems in Women*, ed. O. J. Kalant (New York: Plenum, 1980): 125–201.
75. Griffin et al., "A Comparison of Male and Female Cocaine Abusers," 123; Kosten et al., "Ethnic and Gender Differences," 1147.
76. H. Amaro, L. E. Fried, H. Cabral, and B. Zuckerman, "Violence During Pregnancy and Substance Use," *American Journal of Public Health* 80 (1990): 575–579.
77. G. K. Kantor and M. A. Straus, "Substance Abuse as a Precipitant of Wife Abuse Victimizations," *American Journal of Drug and Alcohol Abuse* 15 (1989): 173–189.
78. Amaro et al., "Violence During Pregnancy," 576.
79. D. C. Ajuluchukwu, L. S. Brown, J. Mitchel, R. Thompson, and A. M. Harris, "HIV Infection in Female Intravenous Drug Abusers (IVDAs) of Childbearing Age in New York City Drug Clinics and Their Demographic Profile" (abstract), in *Problems of Drug Dependence, 1990* (National Institute on Drug Research Monograph 105, DHHS#[ADM], 91–1753), ed. L. Harris (Washington, DC: U.S. Government Printing Office, 1991): 346–347.
80. A. B. Williams, "Reproductive Concerns of Women at Risk for HIV Infection," *Journal of Nurse Midwifery* 35 (1990): 292–298.
81. P. A. Selwyn, E. E. Schoenbaum, K. Davenny, V. J. Robertson, A. R. Feingold, et al., "Prospective Study of Human Immunodeficiency Virus Infection in Pregnancy Outcomes in Intravenous Drug Users," *Journal of the American Medical Association* 261 (1989): 1289–1294.
82. A. Pivnick, A. Jacobson, K. Eric, M. Mulvihill, M. A. Hsu, and E. Drucker, "Reproductive Decisions Among HIV-Infected, Drug-Using Women: The Importance of Mother–Child Coresidence," *Medical Anthropology Quarterly* 5 (1991): 153–169.
83. M. E. James, C. P. Rubin, and S. E. Willis, "Drug Abuse and Psychiatric Findings in HIV-Seropositive Pregnant Patients," *General Hospital Psychiatry* 13 (1991): 4–8; F. D. Johnstone, R. P. Brettle, L. R. MacCallum, J. Mok, J. F. Peutherer, and S. Burns, "Women's Knowledge of Their HIV Antibody State: Its Effect on their Decision Whether to Continue the Pregnancy," *British Medical Journal* 300 (1990): 23–24.
84. I. J. Chasnoff, K. A. Burns, and W. J. Burns, "Cocaine Use in Pregnancy: Perinatal Morbidity and Mortality," *Neurotoxicology and Teratology* 9 (1987): 291–293; R. Cherukuri, H. Minkoff, J. Feldman, et al., "A Cohort Study of Alkaloidal Cocaine ('Crack') in Pregnancy," *Obstetrics and Gynecology* 72 (1988): 147–151; L. P. Finnegan, "Management of Maternal and Neonatal Substance Abuse Problems," in *Problems of Drug Dependence NIDA Research Monograph #90*, ed. L. Harris (Washington, D.C.: U.S. Government Printing Office, 1988): 177–182; Janke, "Prenatal Cocaine Use," 75–76; Little et al., "Cocaine Use in Pregnant Women," 207; Zuckerman et al., "Effects of Maternal Marijuana and Cocaine Use," 764–765.
85. Zuckerman et al., "Effects of Maternal Marijuana and Cocaine Use," 766; Finnegan, "Management of Maternal and Neonatal Substance Abuse," 178; A. W. Funkhouser, A. M. Butz, T. I. Feng, M. E. McCaul, and B. J. Rosenstein, "Prenatal Care and Drug Use in Pregnant Women," *Drug and Alcohol Dependence* 33 (1993): 1–9; Edelin et al., "Methadone Maintenance," 401.

86. Zuckerman et al., "Effects of Maternal Marijuana and Cocaine Use," 766.
87. N. Bingol, M. Fuchs, V. Diaz, R. K. Stone, and D. S. Gromisch, "Teratogenicity of Cocaine in Humans," *Journal of Pediatrics* 110 (1987): 93–96; Cherukuri et al., "A Cohort Study," 150; Janke, "Prenatal Cocaine Use," 75–76; A. Oro and S. Dixon, "Perinatal Cocaine and Methamphetamine Exposure: Maternal and Neonatal Correlates," *Journal of Pediatrics* 111 (1987): 577–578.
88. I. J. Chasnoff, "Drug Use in Pregnancy: Parameters of Risk," *Pediatric Clinics of North America* 35 (1988): 1403–1412.
89. M. C. O'Connor, "Drugs of Abuse in Pregnancy: An Overview," *Medical Journal of Australia* 147 (1987): 180–183; B. D. Rodgers and R. V. Lee, "Drug Abuse," in *Medical Complications During Pregnancy*, eds. G. N. Burrow and T. F. Ferris (Philadelphia: W. B. Saunders, 1988): 570–579; Finnegan, "Management of Maternal and Neonatal Substance Abuse," 178.
90. Finnegan, "Management of Maternal and Neonatal Substance Abuse," 178; J. F. Connaughton, D. Reeser, J. Schut, and L. P. Finnegan, "Perinatal Addiction: Outcome and Management," *American Journal of Obstetrics and Gynecology* 129 (1977): 679–686.
91. Edelin et al., "Methadone Maintenance," 403; M. Russel and J. B. Skinner, "Early Measures of Maternal Alcohol Misuse as Predictors of Adverse Pregnancy Outcomes," *Alcoholism: Clinical and Experimental Research* 12 (1988): 824–830; L. Ryan, S. Ehrlich, and L. Finnegan, "Cocaine Abuse in Pregnancy: Effects on the Fetus and Newborn," *Neurotoxicology and Teratology* 9 (1987): 295–299.
92. M. Mitchell, R. E. Sabbagha, L. Keith, S. MacGregor, J. M. Mota, and J. Minoque, "Ultrasonic Growth Parameters in Fetuses of Mothers with Primary Addiction to Cocaine," *American Journal of Obstetrics and Gynecology* 159 (1988): 1104–1109.
93. I. J. Chasnoff, D. R. Griffith, C. Freir and J. Murray, "Cocaine/Polydrug Use in Pregnancy: Two-Year Follow-up," Pediatrics 89 (1992): 284–289; Zuckerman et al., "Effects of Maternal Marijuana and Cocaine Use," 765; L. Slutsker, "Risks Associated with Cocaine Use During Pregnancy," *Obstetrics and Gynecology* 79 (1992): 778–789.
94. Slutsker, "Risks Associated with Cocaine Use," 783; Edelin et al., "Methadone Maintenance," 403; S. MacGregor, L. Keith, J. Bachicha, and I. Chasnoff, "Cocaine Abuse During Pregnancy: Correlation Between Prenatal Care and Perinatal Outcome," *Obstetrics and Gynecology* 74 (1989): 882–885.
95. Chasnoff et al., "Cocaine Use in Pregnancy," 667; MacGregor et al., "Cocaine Abuse During Pregnancy," 883. N. Bingol, M. Fuchs, V. Diaz, et al., "Teratogenicity of Cocaine in Human," *Journal of Pediatrics* 110 (1987): 93–96.
96. Zuckerman et al., "Effects of Maternal Marijuana and Cocaine Use," 765.
97. H. L. Rosett, L. Weiner, A. Lee, B. Zuckerman, E. Dooling, and E. Openheimer, "Patterns of Alcohol Consumption and Fetal Development," *Obstetrics and Gynecology* 61 (1983): 539–546.
98. Connaughton et al., "Perinatal Addiction," 681–682.
99. Chasnoff, "Drug Use in Pregnancy, Parameters of Risk," 1404.
100. Chaisson et al., "Cocaine Use and HIV Infection," 565; Zuckerman et al., "Effects of Maternal Marijuana and Cocaine Use," 766.
101. Connaughton et al., "Perinatal Addiction," 681–682.
102. Chaisson et al., "Cocaine Use and HIV Infection," 562.
103. Selwyn et al., "Prospective Study," 1290–1292.

104. James et al., "Drug Abuse and Psychiatric Findings," 5.
105. Finnegan et al., "Drug Use in HIV-Infected Women," 147–148; Mondanaro, "Community-Based AIDS Prevention," 69.
106. Institute of Medicine, *Prevention and Treatment of Alcohol Problems: Research Opportunities* (Washington, D.C.: National Academy Press, 1989); National Council on Alcoholism (NCA), *A Federal Response to a Hidden Epidemic: Alcohol and Other Drug Problems Among Women* (New York: National Council on Alcoholism, 1987).
107. Lewis and Watters, "Human Immunodeficiency Virus," 1072.
108. I. J. Chasnoff, "Drugs, Alcohol, Pregnancy and the Neonate: Pay Now or Pay Later," *Journal of the American Medical Association* 266 (1991): 1567–1568; National Institute on Drug Abuse, "Pregnant Drug Abusers Face Obstacles to Receiving Treatment," *NIDA Notes* (Fall 1990): 11–12.
109. M. Lillie-Blanton and M. Hall, "Women and Drug Treatment: Providers Offer Perceptions About Help-seeking," (unpublished manuscript).
110. Ibid.
111. C. B. Wofsy, "Human Immunodeficiency Virus Infection in Women," *Journal of the American Medical Association* 257 (1987): 2074–2076.
112. Brettle and Leen, "The Natural History," 1288.
113. M. Vannicelli, "Treatment Outcome of Alcoholic Women: The State of the Art in Relation to Sex Bias and Expectancy Effects," in *Alcohol Problems in Women: Antecedents, Consequences, and Intervention*, eds. S. C. Wilsnack and L. J. Beckman (New York: Guilford, 1984): 369–412.
114. Institute of Medicine, *Broadening the Base of Treatment for Alcohol Problems*, (Washington, DC: National Academy Press, 1990).
115. M. E. McCaul, D. S. Svikis, R. D. Moore, A. Gupman, and R. Gopalan, "Does Drug Use Predict Poor Treatment Retention?" *Alcoholism: Clinical and Experimental Research* 18 (1994): 494.
116. L. Dahlgren and A. Willander, "Are Special Treatment Facilities for Female Alcoholics Needed? A Controlled 2-Year Follow-Up Study from a Specialized Female Unit (EWA) Versus a Mixed Male/Female Treatment Facility," *Alcoholism: Clinical and Experimental Research* 13 (1989): 499–504.
117. Finnegan, "Management of Maternal and Neonatal Substance Abuse," 180; Finnegan et al., "Drug Use in HIV-Infected Women," 147–148.
118. L. C. Mayes, R. H. Granger, M. H. Bornstein, and B. Zuckerman, "The Problem of Prenatal Cocaine Exposure," *Journal of the American Medical Association* 267 (1992): 406–408.
119. M. E. McCaul, D. S. Svikis, and T. Feng, "Pregnancy and Addiction: Outcomes and Interventions," *Maryland Medical Journal* 40 (1991): 995–1001; D. S. Svikis, M. E. McCaul, T. Feng, T.B.R. Johnson, and E. J. Stokes, "Can a Weekly Support Group for Pregnant Addicts Improve Maternal and Fetal Outcome?"(abstract) in *Problems of Drug Dependence 1991* (National Institute on Drug Abuse Research Monograph 119, DHHS#[ADM], 92–1888), ed. L. Harris (Washington, DC: U.S. Government Printing Office, 1992): 271.
120. Patients were seen by a trained substance abuse counselor who conducted a comprehensive psychosocial evaluation of the patient and, when appropriate, made a referral for formal substance abuse treatment.
121. Attenders were defined as women who had participated in a minimum of two groups; nonattenders were women who had participated in one or fewer groups.

122. G. A. Elvy, J. E. Wells, and K. A. Baird, "Attempted Referral as Intervention for Problem Drinking in the General Hospital," *British Journal of Addictions* 83 (1988): 83–89.
123. B. A. Shipley, P. M. Gazaway, R. K. Brooner, and L. J. Felch, "Prenatal Care Delivered in a Drug Abuse Setting: Birth Outcome Compared to ACOG Standards," in *Problems of Drug Dependence 1990: Proceedings of the 54th Annual Meeting of the College on Problems of Drug Dependence* (National Institute on Drug Abuse Research Monograph #132), ed. L. S. Harris (Washington, DC: U.S. Government Printing Office, 1993): 301.
124. Shipley et al., "Prenatal Care Delivered in a Drug Abuse Setting," 301.
125. L. Jansson, D. Svikis, J. Lee, P. Paluzzi, P. Rutigliano, F. Hackerman, "Pregnancy and Addiction: A Comprehensive Care Model," (submitted manuscript).
126. General Accounting Office (GAO), *Drug-Exposed Infants: A Generation at Risk*, Report to the Chairman, Committee on Finance, United States Senate (GAO/HRD-90-138, (Washington DC: U.S. Government Printing Office, 1990).
127. J. Breyel and I. Hill, *Creating Systems of Care for Substance-Using Pregnant Women and Their Children* (Washington, D.C.: Health Policy Studies Center for Policy Research, National Governor's Association, 1993).
128. Women's Research and Education Institute, *Women's Health Insurance Costs and Expenditures* (Washington, DC: Kaiser Family Foundation, 1994).
129. Amaro et al., "Violence During Pregnancy," 577; James et al., "Drug Abuse and Psychiatric Findings," 5–6; Reed, "Intervention Strategies," 3–4.

II
LEGAL ISSUES

8

Legal Challenges: State Intervention, Reproduction, and HIV-Infected Women

TAUNYA LOVELL BANKS

> We have the same rights as other people have. You know, let us have our babies, whether they're sick or not.
>
> *woman from Miami*

Although women account for only 13% of all reported AIDS cases in the United States,[1] AIDS is now the fourth leading cause of death among all women between the ages of 25 and 44 years—the childbearing years.[2] As of June 1994, the CDC reported 5,734 cases of AIDS in children under the age of 13 years.[3] In the vast majority of pediatric AIDS cases, the virus was acquired perinatally.[4] Experts expect the number of pediatric AIDS cases to continue to increase over the next few years. As a result, much attention has been focused on minimizing the risk of maternal–fetal transmission of the virus because most infected women are of reproductive age.[5]

Because of the substantial social and medical resources required to care for children infected with HIV, public health policies are being developed to minimize the risk of perinatal transmission of the virus. For example, in 1985 the increased incidence of perinatally transmitted HIV/AIDS cases caused the CDC to recommend that women infected with HIV delay or forego childbearing, a recommendation seconded in 1987 by the American College of Obstetrics and Gynecology (ACOG).[6] Many health-care providers have adopted these recommendations and are counseling HIV-infected women not to have children.[7] The primary justification for directing the reproductive choices of HIV-infected women is the need to minimize maternal–fetal transmission of HIV.

The demographics of HIV/AIDS among women in the United States is such that there is not much public sympathy for these women.[8] The vast majority of women currently infected with HIV come from poor urban communities of color.[9] More specifically, 70% of women with AIDS in the United States are African-American or Hispanic.[10] Approximately one-half of these women have histories of injection drug use and another quarter were infected as a result of heterosexual contact with HIV-infected drug users.[11] This association with a drug-using culture, coupled with the historical antagonism toward childbearing

143

by poor women of color and women with disabilities, only reinforces public sentiment that favors limiting the reproductive freedom of these women. Women with HIV/AIDS are seen as irresponsible people, whose voluntary conduct is responsible for their condition and who are inappropriate parents because of their drug use or association with drug users. Therefore, there is less societal resistance to government-initiated policies aimed at discouraging these women from bearing children.

While the focus of the CDC's concern is on minimizing the birth of children infected with HIV, little attention has been paid to the legal ramifications of public health policies that direct women's reproductive decisions. Both the CDC recommendations about delaying or foregoing pregnancy and the trend toward directing HIV-infected women not to have children raise certain legal issues when the government is involved in counseling these women on reproductive matters. The extent to which the federal, state, or local government legally can interfere with the reproductive decisions of women is unclear.

In the context of HIV, legal issues about reproduction are most likely to arise in two settings. In the first, a woman of childbearing age infected with HIV is faced with deciding whether or not to become pregnant. In the second, a woman infected with HIV already is pregnant and must decide whether to continue or terminate her pregnancy. Both decisions are difficult when a woman has no life-threatening illness, but a woman infected with HIV does have a decreased life expectancy and may not live to parent her child throughout childhood. In addition, the fact that HIV may be transmitted from mother to child perinatally presents special problems for HIV-infected women.

History of Discrimination

Low-income women and women of color

With the introduction in the late 1960s of the birth control pill and the legalization in 1973 of abortion,[12] women in this country started having greater control over childbearing. However, certain groups of women have less control over reproductive decision-making than others. For example, federal and state governments were active participants in a well-documented history of sterilization abuse directed against women of color in the United States.[13] The last widely reported case of government-supported involuntary sterilization occurred in the early 1970s and involved two black sisters, Minnie Lee and Mary Alice Relf, 14 and 12 years old, who were sterilized using federal funds designed to help eliminate poverty.[14] Much has been written about the Relf sisters and the federal regulations promulgated after their involuntary sterilizations were exposed.[15] It would be a mistake, however, to conclude that these regulations effectively ended such abuse. Evidence exists that countless other women of color continue to be sterilized involuntarily with the support of government funds.[16]

"Classism and racism lead physicians and other health care providers to urge sterilization on patients they believe incapable of using other methods (of birth control) effectively."[17] The emphasis seems to be on methods that provide permanent or long-term contraception. For example, government-financed sterilization is readily available, while abortion is not.[18] Almost every state provides Medicaid funds for voluntary surgical implants of Norplant, a temporary, long-term form of sterilization.[19]

In addition, there is a trend among medical authorities to seek court-ordered obstetrical intervention to force women, most of whom are low-income women of color, to have cesarean sections and intrauterine transfusions.[20] In one study, all of these women were patients in public hospitals.[21] There also are a sprinkling of cases in which pregnant women who abuse illicit drugs or alcohol or who are charged with child abuse or neglect have been ordered by state courts to use contraceptives.[22] The states are divided over the constitutionality of such measures.

Women with disabilities

In the United States, women of reproductive age who have a disability "encounter substantial legal, medical, and familial resistance to their choice of motherhood."[23] While some disabilities compromise the biological capacity to reproduce, and a few disabilities are made worse by pregnancy, the choices of most women with disabilities are restricted for nonmedical reasons. They simply are not expected to become mothers.[24] For example, despite the absence of scientific evidence on the effect of pregnancy on the progression of multiple sclerosis, many physicians counsel women with this condition not to have children.[25]

Public sentiment against reproduction in the context of disability extends to disability in the offspring as well as the mother. Recently, Bree Walker Lampley, a television anchor in Kansas City, received much criticism when she decided to become pregnant a second time after giving birth to one child who had a rare genetic anomaly, ectrodactyly, in which a person's hands and toes are partially fused and appear to be webbed, a condition she also has.[26] The public reaction to Bree Walker Lampley's decision is not surprising. Recent studies suggest that more than three-quarters of all Americans view a woman's physical disability as an acceptable reason for her to have an abortion.[27] Implicit in many reproductive technologies, and explicit in others, is the goal of preventing future disability.[28] Many Americans believe that a pregnant woman should abort a fetus that will be born with a disability and that women with disabilities are inappropriate mothers.[29] Disability in either mother or potential offspring is seen as a negative.

Women infected with HIV have a disabling condition; but unlike many women with disabilities, some HIV-infected women also transmit the virus to their children.[30] Many people in this country believe that no woman infected with HIV should bear children[31] due, no doubt, to the risk of perinatal transmission of the virus coupled with the attitudes of both the general public and the medical community about controlling the reproductive choices of low-income women, women of color, and women with disabilities. This strong public sentiment against childbearing by HIV-infected women has resulted in calls for government policies that compel these women to forego childbearing. The issue is the extent to which either the United States Constitution or federal laws preclude government from substantially interfering with the reproductive choices of women, especially women infected with HIV.

Constitutional Right to Procreate

The United States Supreme Court directly addressed the right to procreate in only two cases, *Buck* v. *Bell*[32] and *Skinner* v. *Oklahoma*.[33] In *Buck* v. *Bell*, the Court upheld the constitutionality of a Virginia sterilization statute designed to prevent reproduction by institutionalized "mentally defective people," ruling that the state statute did not violate the substantive due process requirements of the Fourteenth Amendment. In other words, the state can involuntarily sterilize institutionalized individuals with mental impairments without violating the constitutional rights of those individuals.

The Supreme Court in *Skinner,* another sterilization case, relied on an equal protection analysis and distinguished, rather than overruled, *Buck.*[34] The *Skinner* Court struck down an Oklahoma statute which authorized sterilization of habitual criminals, characterizing the right to procreate as basic and finding no basis to exempt so-called white collar offenses.[35] The Court indicated that procreational decision-making is "fundamental" and state-initiated compulsory sterilization classifications should be strictly scrutinized.[36] The Court did hold that the right to procreate is not absolute,[37] but it did not elaborate on this point. The Court's decision in *Skinner* also can be read to suggest that the state can authorize involuntary sterilization of habitual criminals, provided it does not unfairly discriminate between classes of criminals.

The most recent discussions by the Supreme Court concerning the right to control procreation occur in the abortion cases, starting with *Roe* v. *Wade*[38] and ending with *Planned Parenthood of Southern Pennsylvania* v. *Casey.*[39] In *Roe* the Court held that the state's interest in protecting maternal health cannot prohibit a woman's access to abortion during the first trimester of pregnancy.[40] Once the fetus becomes viable, however, the state may prohibit abortion unless it is necessary to protect the life of the mother. In *Casey* a plurality of the Court reaffirmed the essential holding of *Roe:* that a woman has a right to have an abortion before viability without "undue interference from the State."[41]

The *Casey* Court reexamined the source of this right to an abortion, characterizing it as rooted in the Fourteenth Amendment's due process clause guarantee of liberty and acknowledging that this liberty guarantee encompasses areas of personal liberty, including decisions relating to procreation.[42] In this area, the state's right to interfere is limited and can be justified only where there is an "important and legitimate interest in protecting the potentiality of human life."[43] However, the plurality in *Casey* also suggests that the right to procreate carries with it an obligation to be responsible in making procreational decisions, and it is this aspect of the right which the Court attempts to protect in *Roe*.[44]

At the same time, the plurality in *Casey* reaffirms the state's interest in protecting the life of the unborn child, saying that, at a later point in the fetus's development, this governmental interest justifies placing restrictions on the liberty interests of a pregnant woman.[45] The plurality in *Casey* held that state-imposed restrictions on abortion are permissible, as long as they do not unduly burden a woman's access to abortion.[46] The state cannot totally bar a woman from obtaining an abortion, though states lawfully may refuse to finance or permit state agencies to perform abortions, authorize parental notification or consent requirements for minors, and impose waiting periods or other restrictions on access to abortion.

In accordance with these decisions, a pregnant HIV-infected woman seeking an abortion will be treated like any other pregnant woman seeking an abortion: a state cannot prohibit her from obtaining an abortion during the first trimester of her pregnancy. However, a state will not be required to finance an abortion for a woman who lacks the necessary financial resources. If the pregnant HIV-infected woman is a minor, some states require parental consent or notice unless the minor woman obtains consent from a court.

While the *Casey* decision may have clarified certain issues surrounding the extent to which government may restrict women's access to abortion, it does not squarely address whether government may coerce HIV-infected women to have an abortion or not become pregnant. However, there is dicta in *Casey* where the plurality justifies retaining the *Roe* rationale as necessary to protect both a woman's right to abortion and her right to decide "whether to bear and beget a child."[47] They cite two lower court cases where governmental agencies tried to prohibit minor women from bearing children. In *Arnold v. Board of Education of Escambia County, Alabama* a federal appellate court used the *Roe* rationale to conclude that the state government violated the Constitution by coercing a minor woman to have an abortion.[48] In *Avery v. County of Burke* another federal appellate court also relied on *Roe* in holding that the county agency unconstitutionally induced a minor woman to undergo an unwanted sterilization by misrepresenting that she had the trait for sickle cell anemia.[49] The dicta in *Casey* suggests that some members of the current United States Supreme Court would closely scrutinize government efforts aimed at influencing women to obtain unwanted abortions or sterilizations, at least where minor women are involved.

There are other Supreme Court decisions that focus on regulation of contraceptives designed to prevent pregnancy rather than terminate it, but most of these cases are linked to other so-called fundamental rights, such as the right to marry[50] or parent children.[51] Even in *Skinner*, the compelled sterilization case, the Court characterized the right to procreate as an important component of the marital relationship.[52] As a result, the parameters of any constitutional right to procreate are not entirely clear.

There are, however, cases where the Court stresses that freedom to rear children is an important private interest with which the state should not interfere "absent powerful and countervailing interests."[53] State policies which embody unsupported generalizations about one's ability to parent are suspect. Thus, in *Stanley v. Illinois* the Court struck down, as violative of the due process clause of the Fourteenth Amendment, a state law denying custody to an unwed father based on the presumption that all unwed fathers are unfit parents.[54] Therefore, it seems fairly well established that a state cannot summarily conclude that certain women are presumptively unfit to parent. However, these cases involve children already born and take into account the mutual interests of parent and child in companionship and familial relationship. They do not define more clearly the parameters of the constitutional right to procreate.

The most recent decisions involving regulation of pregnancy termination suggest that procreational decision-making is considered simply a liberty interest under the due process clause of the Fourteenth Amendment, rather than a separate fundamental right. This distinction is significant since, with liberty interest claims, the Court applies a less demanding standard of review to the challenged government action than with rights classified as fundamental. This means that the interest of the government in implementing the policy needs only to be important and legitimate, as opposed to compelling. However, since there is no direct opinion on this issue and only dicta from various decisions, it is not entirely clear what standard of review the Court will actual apply where government is trying to restrict women from bearing children. As mentioned previously, the rationale used to recognize a woman's right to an abortion also recognizes that states may balance that right against the state's interest in the fetus, at least after viability.[55] However, the state's interest in the fetus under the abortion cases is to protect, not prevent, potential life.

The Court's somewhat superficial analysis of the right to control procreation probably reflects its reluctance to elaborate on the nature and scope of this right since any detailed analysis is likely to generate controversy. For example, legal commentators generally presuppose that there are some limits on the right to procreate, even under a compelling interest standard of review, but few are willing to decide which women should not be allowed to do so.[56] However, there is nothing in the abortion cases to suggest that a state is prohibited from supporting a woman's decision to terminate her pregnancy by either subsidizing or providing free abortions, provided there is no force or coercion. What is not clear is whether or under what circumstances the state can counsel, compel, or coerce a woman to terminate a pregnancy. The reason proffered for any such policy may be important in determining its constitutionality. Thus, it is important to look at instances where government attempts to prevent or constrain procreation by women.

Examples of Governmental Intervention in Reproductive Decision-Making

Involuntary sterilization cases

It is conceivable that, in some circumstances, government can legally compel HIV-infected women to not bear children. There are cases in which government has legally compelled a woman to be sterilized because of a disabling condition which either interferes with her ability to parent or may be passed on to any children she bears, the latter being an often unwarranted fear. The most well-known cases involve the involuntary sterilization of developmentally disabled women. The women whose involuntary sterilization was upheld by the United States Supreme Court in *Buck* were characterized as mentally deficient, and the Court's decision was influenced by the belief that this condition could be passed on to their children.[57] Because this belief is now suspect, there is some question whether *Buck* would be decided the same way were it presented today. Nevertheless, many state courts currently permit the involuntary sterilization of mentally deficient individuals.

Some state statutes authorize the involuntary sterilization of mentally impaired individuals, a policy that has a disproportionate impact on women.[58] Most state courts will deny petitions for involuntary sterilization of mentally disabled individuals in the absence of specific statutory authorization;[59] however, some courts permit court-authorized sterilization in the absence of such a mandate.[60] The Supreme Court has not directly ruled on these cases and the lower courts are divided over the validity of these laws. However, these modern involuntary sterilization cases involve women who lack the legal capacity to consent to sterilization.[61] In these cases, the judgment of someone else is substituted for that of the incapacitated woman and is allowed to control the decision. Arguably, these cases are distinguishable from most cases involving women infected with HIV. There may be a few HIV-infected women who suffer some preexisting disability affecting their legal capacity or who, as a result of HIV, are so neurologically impaired as to lack legal capacity. Those cases would be most analogous to the current involuntary sterilization cases. Since most women infected with HIV are legally competent, the question is whether there are other reasons why government could legitimately intervene in their reproductive decisions. Once more, the rationale in the involuntary sterilization cases is instructive.

Currently, some people defend the involuntary sterilization of the developmentally disabled by arguing that mentally impaired people are incapable of adequate parenting and that, therefore, their offspring will become a financial burden on the state. This financial burden argument has been advanced in several cases.[62] A number of courts reject financial burden as a justification for authorizing involuntary sterilization, reasoning that the issue in each case is the best interest of the woman, not the welfare of society.[63] Nevertheless, a few courts accept this rationale,[64] and two states, by statute, expressly authorize involuntary sterilization solely on the ground of benefit to society.[65]

Courts that accept the financial burden rationale often rely on Justice Holmes's language in *Buck* v. *Bell*—that society benefits from sterilizing those who "sap the strength of the State"[66]—to justify overriding the procreational rights of the women who are involuntarily sterilized. This conflict—between the procreational rights of women with disabilities and the financial costs to society—is reflected in some of the arguments asserted today to justify discouraging HIV-infected women from bearing children.[67] Existing case law on both the federal and state levels does not clearly support either position.

A second argument asserted to justify the involuntary sterilization of mentally impaired individuals is preventing the birth of children with physical or mental disabilities. Some proponents of this rationale argue that the burden of living with a disability is too great to impose on a person.[68] This conclusion denigrates the personal worth of people with disabilities and certainly is one that many in the disability community, as well as the community at large, would dispute.[69] A quality-of-life argument in support of discouraging the birth of infants with disabilities may also mask a variant of the financial burden rationale: the presumption is made that the care of children with disabilities will be shared in whole or in part by the taxpayers, rather than the biological or adoptive parents. Unfortunately, that outcome currently is a real possibility for many children whose mothers are infected with HIV.

Taking this argument a step further, some philosophers and lawyers argue that there is a moral limit on the exercise of reproductive freedom when others may be injured.[70] They advance this "harm principle" to justify government intervention in the reproductive decisions of women infected with HIV.[71] These arguments, focusing either on concern for the child or on financial cost to society, are being used as a basis for restricting the ability of an HIV-infected woman to procreate.

Unfortunately, case law in this area is unclear. Most courts have never squarely addressed these questions, and the Supreme Court has not directly ruled on the appropriateness of these rationales for government-imposed restrictions on childbearing. It can be argued that these rationales are inconsistent with the spirit of the Americans With Disabilities Act (ADA) of 1990, a federal antidiscrimination provision designed to protect persons with disabilities (a point that will be addressed later in this chapter), but even the ADA provides no clear answer.

Court-ordered contraception and medical intervention cases

The law presumes that the biological parents of a child, especially the child's mother, will care for the emotional, physical, and financial needs of the child. There are some HIV-infected women who are ready and able to take care of a child. However, the lives of other HIV-infected women are so disorganized due to illness, drug use, and financial and family problems that they have little interest or ability to care for a child; but even assuming that parenting ability is not a problem, as the preceding discussion indicates, there may be another reason asserted to justify compelling pregnant women infected with HIV to abort: concern about the health of the potential offspring. There are a few cases in which pregnant women who used illicit drugs were charged with child abuse or neglect under the theory that their conduct while pregnant was harmful to their fetuses. State-initiated attempts to prosecute these women, when contested, have been unsuccessful (see Chapter 10).[72]

Medical intervention cases suggest that there is a growing conflict within both law and medicine over maternal–fetal rights. Many in the legal and medical profession see a pregnant woman as two patients, not one: the pregnant woman and her fetus.[73] This perspective is adopted by courts, which reason that court-ordered medical inventions for the sake of the fetus are permissible, even over the objection of the woman, because a pregnant woman who does not place the health of her fetus above her own is a bad mother.[74] Unfortunately, this conflict has not been clearly resolved by most state courts or the United States Supreme Court.[75] Concern about the health of the potential fetus, specifically concern about maternal–fetal transmission of the virus resulting in the birth of an HIV-infected child, may not always be a sufficient basis on which to justify even mildly intrusive government policies designed to discourage procreation. However, in light of the current demographics of HIV/AIDS in women and the history of court-ordered fetal interventions, it is foreseeable that HIV-infected women who become pregnant will be likely targets for forced medical interventions on behalf of the fetus.

Special problems posed by minor women

Currently, approximately 1% of women with AIDS are between the ages of 13 and 19 years.[76] The number of teenagers who are infected with the virus but asymptomatic is unknown. However, the rate of HIV infection among teenagers, especially females, is expected to increase significantly by the year 2000. Some authorities predict that, increasingly, women with HIV will be younger and more sexually active.[77] Teenagers often are more sexually active and less likely to take precautions to prevent pregnancy and transmission of HIV than adults. Therefore, it is not surprising that the rate of unintended pregnancies among adolescent females is increasing.[78]

When women infected with HIV are minors (under 18 years old), there are additional legal problems. The state is deemed to have a stronger interest in regulating the behavior of minors; however, the case law is somewhat contradictory. For example, some state policies that discourage sexual activity by adolescent women have been upheld. In 1981, the Supreme Court ruled that the state's interest in preventing illegitimate pregnancy gives it the authority to criminalize consensual sexual intercourse with underage women.[79] Several years earlier, however, the Court struck down a state statute that prohibited the distribution of contraceptives to minors.[80]

Today, every state allows adolescents to be treated for STDs without parental consent or notice,[81] many states allow adolescents to receive counseling about contraceptives without parental consent or notice,[82] and some states also allow adolescent women to receive prenatal treatment without parental consent or notice.[83] Thus, both courts and legislative bodies recognize that minor women have a right to personal autonomy in reproductive matters that often outweighs parental or state interests. In addition, the *Arnold* and *Avery* cases, discussed earlier, suggest that coercive or fraudulent methods aimed at limiting childbearing by minor women may violate the Constitution. At the very least, government-initiated policies with this aim will be closely scrutinized by the courts.

Infected teenage women who are not pregnant undoubtedly will be encouraged to use some permanent or long-term contraceptive. Some health-care providers are justifiably reluctant to recommend permanent sterilization of minor women, especially those who have no children, since minors may not fully appreciate the consequences of sterilization and may later regret this action. Permanent sterilization also is not likely if the teenager is unable to pay for the procedure. Federal regulations prohibit the use of federal Medicaid funds to subsidize the cost of sterilizing minors.[84] Any attempt to obtain a waiver of this regulation would be met with opposition within those communities of color with histories of sterilization abuse, the same communities that are disproportionately impacted by HIV.

To date, much of the AIDS education directed at sexually active teenagers has focused on condom use, among the least effective contraceptive devices in practice because the method relies heavily on someone other than the woman for its proper use. Because condoms often are ineffective in preventing pregnancy, it is more likely that, in the future, infected teens will be strongly urged to use Norplant, a surgically implanted contraceptive that is effective for up to 5 years. Almost all state Medicaid programs will cover the cost of implanting the contraceptive. While Norplant, by precluding pregnancy, may prevent perinatal transmission of HIV, it does not prevent transmission from one sexual partner to another. In light of *Avery* and *Arnold,* it seems unlikely that government can compel a teenager to use Norplant when both the female and her parents object; but it is less clear whether government can compel use of Norplant when the health-care provider and the parents favor use of the contraceptive, given the often contradictory treatment of minor women in regard to sexuality.

There are other problems when an HIV-infected minor woman is pregnant. Following *Roe* v. *Wade*,[85] the Supreme Court recognized that minor women, like adult women, have a right to an abortion that neither parents nor the state can veto.[86] In a series of cases, however, the Court conditioned this right, with limited exceptions, on obtaining parental consent or parental notification.[87] Today, some states do not allow teenagers to obtain abortions without parental consent or notice. Since this policy has the approval of the United States Supreme Court and is unlikely to change in the near future, it is unlikely that HIV-infected adolescent women could lawfully be coerced into aborting without a parent's knowledge in states that require parental notification. However, adolescents in states without such restrictions may be prime candidates for coercive counseling to abort since teenagers generally are considered less prepared to parent than adult women. Federal antidiscrimination laws aimed at protecting the rights of persons with disabilities, however, may place more clear restrictions on government interventions in reproductive decision-making by women infected with HIV.

Federal Statutory Protections

The Rehabilitation Act of 1977

Even if the Constitution is construed to permit implementation of government policies that compel or coerce HIV-infected women not to bear children, some of these policies may violate federal statutes enacted to protect individuals with certain disabilities. For example, the Rehabilitation Act of 1977 prohibits discrimination against individuals with disabilities by federal entities and recipients of federal funds.[88] The Supreme Court, in *School Board of Nassau County* v. *Arline*, ruled that individuals with infectious or contagious diseases may be considered disabled under the statute.[89] Although not specifically mentioned in the original act or the *Arline* decision, it now is well established that persons infected with HIV may be considered disabled under the statute.[90]

The focus of the Rehabilitation Act is limited to programs and activities conducted by the federal executive or federal contractors or other recipients of federal funds.[91] Thus, state and local programs and activities that do not receive federal monies are not covered. Absent a state antidiscrimination law designed to protect individuals with disabilities, state and local governments could discriminate on the basis of disability, provided they could articulate some legitimate governmental interest.[92] There are other deficiencies in the statutory protection provided individuals with disabilities under the Rehabilitation Act: in addition to the problems with its limited scope, problems abound with its wording, interpretation, and enforcement.[93] However, with the passage of the more comprehensive ADA in 1990,[94] the Rehabilitation Act has become a secondary source of protection against unlawful discrimination against persons with disabilities.

The ADA of 1990
General

Title II of the ADA prohibits discrimination by a public entity against a "qualified individual with a disability" if the discrimination is "by reason of such disability."[95] The language in title II tracks the language in section 504 of the Rehabilitation Act, but the ADA extends coverage to all programs, services, and activities of state and local governments, not just those programs that receive federal funds. The statutory definition of the term "public entity" also is very broad and would include health departments and "other structures or means by which a state or local government takes action or involves itself in activities or programs."[96]

Title III of the act covers public accommodations and provides that "[n]o individual shall be discriminated against on the basis of disability."[97] Public accommodations are privately operated facilities that are used by the general public. Under the act, public accommodations include hospitals and professional offices of health-care providers.[98] This title also prohibits a public accommodation from providing different or separate benefits to individuals with disabilities, unless a separate benefit is necessary to ensure access or service that is as effective as those granted to individuals without a disability.[99]

One goal of the ADA was the elimination of discrimination in access to health care.[100] However, Congress did not intend to require health-care providers to render treatment outside the providers' areas of specialty.[101] Thus, the ADA does not prevent a health-care provider from referring a patient with a disability to another health-care provider, as long as it is on the same basis the provider would refer other patients with the same condition. The act also does not require that a health-care provider render treatment in a situation in which the disability creates specialized complications for the patient's health which the provider lacks either the knowledge or experience to address.[102]

To some extent, the ADA modifies the common law. According to common law, health-care providers were under no legal obligation to treat any patient in need. Even where the required care fell within the health-care providers' competence, physicians could base their decision not to treat upon cost (refusing poor patients), prejudice (on the basis of race or use of illicit drugs), liability concerns,[103] or subtle judgments about which patients deserve scarce health-care resources.[104] Without question, the ADA prohibits physician decisions not to treat that are based solely on prejudice stemming from a person's disability. Nevertheless, most commentators agree that the ADA does not guarantee access to health care but simply prohibits denial of equal access based on a person's disability. However, private provider decisions based on liability concerns or subtle judgments about patient access to scarce health-care resources are less clear. Further, a private health-care provider still may lawfully refuse to treat based on a patient's inability to pay.

There is some question about whether a public, as opposed to a private, health-care provider can refuse to treat a person with a protected disability based on cost. In August 1992, the Bush administration refused to give Oregon an exception under the federal Medicaid program so that the state could institute an experimental health-care rationing program designed to significantly increase access to care for people in that state. The administration reasoned that by restricting certain highly expensive categories from Medicaid coverage, the Oregon plan would violate the ADA because it would have a disproportionate impact on people with disabilities.[105] Undoubtedly, some of these issues will arise in the context of treating HIV-infected women of childbearing age.[106]

Under title III, the ADA's guarantee of access to public accommodations is qualified. The act does not require a public accommodation to permit an individual with a disability to participate in, or benefit from, its services when the individual poses a direct threat to the health or safety of others.[107] The ADA defines "direct threat" as "a significant risk to health or safety of others that cannot be eliminated" by modifying policies, practices, or procedures or by providing auxiliary aids or services.[108] The act sets forth the test to be used to determine whether an individual poses a direct threat to the health or safety of others. It requires a three-pronged individualized assessment based on reasonable judgment that relies on (1) current medical evidence, or the best available objective evidence, to determine the nature, duration, and severity of the risk; (2) the probability that the potential injury will actually occur; and (3) whether reasonable modifications of policies, practices, or procedures will mitigate the risk.[109] This is essentially the same approach adopted under the Rehabilitation Act[110] and is thus applicable to title II of the ADA. Under the ADA, no covered health-care provider can refuse to provide a patient with a disability all the services and benefits provided other patients unless it can be shown either that the treatment required is outside the provider's area of specialty or that the person poses a direct threat to the health or safety of others, including the health-care provider.

In theory, at least, it is unlikely that a health-care provider lawfully could refuse to treat a person infected with HIV under the direct threat exception. While it is possible that HIV can be transmitted from patient to provider, there are few reported cases of such transmission.[111] It also is true that infection with HIV is considered a fatal condition. However, the risk of infection in a health-care setting varies significantly according to the type of medical procedure being performed. Where the procedure is noninvasive, the risk of transmission of the virus is extremely low, if not nonexistent. When invasive procedures are warranted and the health-care provider is likely to be exposed to blood and other bodily fluid, the risk of transmission of HIV is greater. Nevertheless, according to the CDC, this risk of transmission may be significantly reduced by adopting the recommended universal safety precautions.[112] In light of the foregoing, a strong argument can be made that HIV infection alone, more likely than not, is an insufficient basis for denying medical treatment to an otherwise qualified patient.[113]

Nevertheless, the test set out in the ADA may not help courts clearly distinguish a lawful refusal to treat based on genuine clinical judgment from an unlawful refusal based on an individual's disability. Distinguishing sound medical judgment from personal prejudice will be crucial in assessing whether a physician's refusal to provide reproductive medical treatment or services is lawful under the ADA.

> While the Act certainly prohibits a refusal to treat based upon prejudice or irrational fear, some medical practices are far more subtle. Practitioners are defending their decisions to not treat or to refer patients with communicable conditions by arguing that this is an exercise of clinical judgment and does not constitute discrimination, and that to restrict the physician's right to decide whom to treat or when to refer is to dictate the practice of medicine.[114]

Unfortunately, the ADA provides no real guidance on the extent to which courts will review medical decisions involving patients with disabilities.[115]

Application to HIV-infected women

GENERAL ACCESS TO MEDICAL SERVICES. There is little relevant case law on determining when a decision not to provide medical services is based on legitimate clinical judgment and when the decision constitutes unlawful discrimination. In the one analogous Rehabilitation Act case, *Doe v. Jamaica Hospital,* the state court never reached these substantive issues because it ruled that, since the physician/hospital employee did not directly receive any federal funds, he was not personally liable under the statute.[116] Nevertheless, the plaintiff's allegation illustrates the problems inherent when courts are inclined, often out of necessity, to rely on medical judgment that may be biased or unscientific.

In this case, the plaintiff, Carol Doe, learned that she was pregnant in 1988. Because she was 38 years old, weighed over 300 pounds, and had previously given birth to a child born with spina bifida, she chose to attend a high-risk prenatal clinic at Jamaica Hospital. When her HIV test proved positive, she alleged that both the social worker and a prenatal clinic specialist informed her that her chances of having a baby infected with HIV were great and that she should have an abortion. Then Carol Doe was referred to the Chief of Obstetrics and Gynecology, who referred her to another hospital which, the physician claimed, was better qualified to treat a pregnant woman infected with HIV. Ultimately, she had the abortion performed at the second hospital.

In a subsequent civil action, Carol Doe complained that she had been denied treatment at Jamaica Hospital because of her HIV-infected status and had received separate, different, unequal, and ineffective counseling upon which to make her reproductive choice based on that status. She also sued the hospital that performed the abortion, arguing that it had failed to counsel her about the reproductive choices available to her based on her HIV-infected status.[117] This seems like an easy case under the ADA, which speaks directly to Jamaica Hospital's refusal to care for Carol Doe. Unless the health-care provider could establish that the patient's HIV-infected status created specialized complications for her health for which the provider lacked either the knowledge or experience to address or that it caused some direct threat to others, there appears to be a violation of the ADA. It would seem that the health-care provider has a difficult burden to meet in this case.

In 1990, the New York City Commission on Human Rights conducted an investigation of 50 health centers that offered abortions, including both freestanding clinics and abortion clinics in hospitals.[118] Twenty of these clinics refused to provide medical services once they were told that the patient seeking an abortion was infected with HIV.[119] Most often, these clinics cited "medical" factors, like the lack of appropriate sterilization equipment and inexperience in treating HIV-infected patients, to justify their refusal to perform the abortions.[120] The commission learned from medical experts that the abortion procedure for women infected with HIV is no different from the procedure used for uninfected women and that sterilization of equipment used on women infected with HIV is no different from standard sterilization procedures. Further, the risk of transmission of the virus from patient to provider is "very small, but finite" if providers follow universal blood precaution procedures.[121]

However, if the provider claimed that a patient was referred to another facility because of some other risk factor, like drug use, and the provider could prove that drug-using pregnant women always were referred to other facilities, the action might not violate federal antidiscrimination law; but there might be a situation in which a blanket policy to exclude drug-using pregnant women from certain medical services is merely a cover to avoid treating women infected with HIV, a disproportionate number of whom are identified as having drug histories.[122] It would be difficult under the ADA to separate a lawful denial of services because of current drug use from an intent to discriminate against a protected disabled group, some of whom also are drug users.

The ADA makes a distinction between use of an illegal substance and the status of being addicted. Addiction is considered a disability, but in most instances, the ADA excludes current illegal drug users from coverage.[123] The law provides a limited exception for health services or services provided in connection with drug rehabilitation if the individual otherwise is entitled to such services.[124] Under the regulations promulgated to implement the act, a health-care provider or other public accommodation may exclude an individual whose current illegal use of drugs poses a direct threat to the health or safety of others.[125] A public accommodation also may impose or apply eligibility criteria for the provision of services and legitimate safety requirements.[126]

Under the ADA, Carol Doe's claim that she received "separate, different, unequal, and ineffective counseling" would require more analysis. According to her complaint, Carol Doe was "directed" to abort by the social worker and the prenatal clinic specialist at Jamaica Hospital. In other words, she alleged that hospital personnel, because she was infected with HIV, did not give her an unbiased assessment of her medical condition, and thus she was denied the opportunity to make an informed personal decision about continuing her pregnancy. To prevail under the ADA, Carol Doe would have to demonstrate that the actions of the hospital personnel were based on facts applicable to her particular medical condition and not on presumptions as to what women infected with HIV, as a class, can or cannot do. The ADA is intended to prohibit exclusion or segregation of individuals with disabilities based on, among other things, presumptions, patronizing attitudes, fears, and stereotypes. This issue is discussed in more detail later in this chapter.

ACCESS TO FERTILITY SERVICES. In light of CDC recommendations that a woman infected with HIV delay or forego pregnancy, it is foreseeable that health-care providers will advise a woman with infertility problems, who wants to become pregnant even after learning of her HIV-infected status, against seeking fertility services. It also is likely that in vitro clinics will elect not to provide services to this woman. However, it is unclear whether a health-care provider can refuse to assist an HIV-infected woman who has fertility problems and wants to bear a child.[127] Most in vitro clinics are highly selective and often use factors like health, marital, and socioeconomic status to screen potential patients.[128]

While it may not violate the federal Constitution's protection of the right to bear children, denying fertility services may violate the ADA unless the health-care provider can affirmatively demonstrate that the HIV-infected woman does not meet legitimate eligibility criteria or that she poses a direct threat to the health or safety of others. This may not be an easy determination; however, a blanket policy against providing infertility services to HIV-infected women would be suspect since, under the ADA, individual assessment is required in each case. To support any blanket exclusion, the provider of infertility services would have to affirmatively demonstrate that there are accepted scientific reasons why financially able women with HIV did not meet eligibility requirements.

COUNSELING AGAINST PREGNANCY. Whether or not a woman should become pregnant or continue her pregnancy once she discovers she is infected with HIV is a value-ladened decision. This is a situation ripe for potential abuse of power by the health-care provider. For example, patients may be led into accepting treatments or undergoing procedures which strip them of their bodily autonomy.[129] Health-care providers may innocently or negligently misrepresent the rate of vertical transmission of HIV. Providers may not clearly distinguish between advice related to childbearing that is based on current medical information and advice that represents the provider's personal opinion about what is best for the patient's, or potential child's, well-being. When the provider is a government employee, these actions have constitutional dimensions because they undercut a woman's interests in procreation and personal autonomy. In addition, coercive policies that favor sterilization or abortion may impermissibly interfere with the religious liberty of some patients. Even when the provider is not a government employee, these actions may constitute questionable practices under existing federal law governing discrimination against people with disabilities.

There even may be an appearance of coercion when there is no conscious attempt to coerce. The likelihood of this impression is great since the women at highest risk of becoming infected with HIV today are also the women who historically have been most subject to sterilization abuse, forced contraception, and court-ordered medical interventions during pregnancy.[130] Many women, irrespective of race, income, or education, do not question advice given by health-care providers. This is particularly true of low-income women.[131] Therefore, so-called medically based advice can have a powerful, and perhaps coercive, effect on some women's reproductive decision-making.

COUNSELING WOMEN WHO ARE NOT PREGNANT. Currently, the CDC recommends that all fertile women be routinely tested for the virus.[132] Given the sharp increase in HIV infection among women and the risk of perinatal transmission, it seems likely that future recommendations will continue to advise testing women of childbearing age to prevent perinatal transmission of HIV. Any HIV testing of fertile women designed to minimize the risk of vertical transmission raises the issue of what information should be provided to fertile HIV-infected women.

Counseling is an essential component of any HIV testing program. When counseling on reproductive matters, an approach which fully respects and facilitates patient autonomy in the decision-making process is most appropriate. Currently, HIV counseling is not regulated, and many health-care professionals are quietly advocating directive counseling for HIV-infected fertile women.[133] Directive counseling occurs when the patient or client is denied the opportunity to receive an unbiased assessment of her medical situation and to make an informed personal decision free of coercive, or even persuasive, influences.

Assuming a government entity's directive counseling not to bear children is constitutional, this practice may violate the ADA. A counselor may have to justify why directive counseling is appropriate for HIV counseling but not appropriate for genetic counseling or for women who are not infected with HIV but who are otherwise considered "high-risk" because of a health concern. HIV counseling designed to minimize vertical transmission of the virus is analogous in many ways to reproductive counseling for genetic diseases. HIV infection is similar to a genetic disorder which can be transmitted vertically from mother to child. Following this line of reasoning, HIV reproductive counseling is much like many types of genetic reproductive counseling in that currently there is no medical cure for the infection and the fetus cannot be treated prior to birth.[134] Therefore, it can be argued that HIV reproductive counseling should be treated the same way as reproductive counseling for genetic diseases which are not treatable prior to birth.[135] Since directive genetic counseling is considered inappropriate,[136] it should be similarly considered for reproductive HIV counseling.

However, proponents of directive counseling argue that HIV infection is different from genetic disorders not only because there is the chance of vertical transmission but also because the mother will have a decreased life expectancy. Therefore, it is argued that the mother's decreased life expectancy makes the two situations sufficiently disanalogous to support or justify different counseling procedures. In practice, however, decreased life expectancy of the mother generally is not seen as a reason to direct, as opposed to advise, women not to become pregnant. There are numerous instances where childbearing by women with terminal or life-threatening illnesses was considered by many to be noble and self-sacrificing.[137] Concern about decreased life expectancy of HIV-infected mothers may have more to do with societal concerns that, because of their socioeconomic and marital status, their offspring will become burdens on the community. These are thorny issues that courts have yet to address, and the ADA also is silent on these issues. Any court faced with these problems probably will engage in some balancing of the competing interests, and the outcome may vary from jurisdiction to jurisdiction.

COUNSELING PREGNANT WOMEN. There are calls for routine HIV testing of pregnant women.[138] Prenatal HIV testing is proposed as a means of allowing health-care providers to counsel HIV-infected women about the impact of the virus on pregnancy and the effect of pregnancy on progression of the disease, the risk of transmission of HIV to the fetus, the risk of transmission to sexual partners, and the possibility of infection in older children.[139] If, however, the primary reason for prenatal HIV testing is to identify infected pregnant women and counsel them to abort, then the health-care provider arguably is interfering with the reproductive choices of women with a protected disability, in violation of federal and some state law.[140]

What is not completely clear is whether directing a woman not to become pregnant, or to abort if she becomes pregnant, because of the risk of maternal–fetal transmission of HIV is a violation of either the Rehabilitation Act or the ADA because it discriminates against potential children who are perceived as disabled. As used in the Rehabilitation Act, "handicapped individual" includes infants born with congenital defects. Thus, protected seriously ill newborns who are "otherwise qualified" cannot be discriminated against in the provision of health care solely due to their disability.[141] The Supreme Court recognizes that in these situations the decision whether or not to treat ultimately rests with the parents, not government.[142] Since the ADA closely tracks the Rehabilitation Act, it is certain that newborns infected with HIV would be protected from discrimination based on their disability.

What complicates the analysis here is that there are government policies, like public funding of amniocentesis, which encourage the elimination of newborns with disabilities.[143] In fact, public funds for an abortion can be obtained in some states by labeling the abortion a medical necessity because the "fetus is physically deformed, mentally deficient, or afflicted with a congenital illness."[144] As applied to women with HIV, this means that a health-care provider, by labeling these abortions as "therapeutic" (i.e., pregnancy poses a risk of a child with HIV), could make it easier for infected women to obtain abortions using public funds. At least one commentator contends that government policy which makes it easier to obtain publicly funded abortion for disability, as opposed to elective abortion, violates both the equal protection clause of the Fourteenth Amendment and the ADA because it constitutes a "killing" of disabled "children." This commentator acknowledges, however, that this government conduct is widely practiced and seldom challenged.[145]

A second, but concededly weaker, argument against directive counseling is that where government is the health-care provider, directive counseling to abort also may violate a woman's right to privacy.[146] Since this constitutionally protected right applies only to the government or its agents, this argument would not address directive counseling by private health-care providers; but if government urges or counsels a pregnant woman to abort, then it could be argued that government is not encouraging potential life but is trying to prevent life through coerced or forced abortions. Even in *Roe* v. *Wade*, the Court recognized that at some point government has an interest in protecting the fetus and that this interest justifies restricting the liberty interests of a pregnant woman.[147] This interest in protecting potential life, and thus a fetus, conflicts with the financial arguments advanced for discouraging HIV-infected women from bearing children, such as the need to limit the cost to society of caring for seriously ill newborns and orphans. However, as mentioned earlier, this conflict seems to go unchallenged in the courts.

Neonatal Testing—Implications for the Mother

HIV neonatal testing may be important to the newborn because early detection of potential HIV exposure will determine what treatment regimes are needed. However, mandatory or routine unconsented HIV neonatal testing poses some problems. Arguments for unconsented testing presuppose that the care of newborns who test positive will be vastly improved if their HIV status is known. While some medical studies suggest this may be true,[148] unconsented neonatal testing poses real risks for HIV-infected mothers.[149] Specifically, the newborn's test result also indicates the mother's HIV status, and this information will go on her medical records, becoming available to many health and social service staff members. Inappropriate disclosure of this information by any of these individuals may subject the mother to unlawful discrimination.

It is unlikely that an infected woman whose HIV status is disclosed via neonatal testing will be prosecuted criminally if she knew she was HIV-infected prior to becoming pregnant. No such prosecutions have been brought to date. However, there have been attempts to prosecute pregnant drug users for "knowingly" transmitting drugs to their children perinatally.[150] In addition, a woman who decides to become pregnant after learning of her HIV status may be characterized as a neglectful or abusive parent because she gives birth to a child who may be HIV-infected.[151] Such a determination could result in loss of custody by the mother. While it is unlikely that such actions would be successful, the possibility that they might be initiated against an HIV-infected woman should not be discounted. More importantly, some people believe that women infected with HIV may avoid health care because they fear that disclosure of their infected status will cause them to lose their children or suffer discrimination.[152] Thus, informed consent to neonatal testing also serves an educational purpose that may counter a woman's fears about HIV testing. Since HIV neonatal testing threatens the mother's right to confidentiality, it should be performed only without her informed consent in cases where knowledge of the newborn's status will prevent significant morbidity or mortality. The current question is whether the risks to the mother of unconsented testing outweigh the extent to which testing prevents morbidity. This too is an issue not squarely addressed by the courts. In applying a balancing test, however, at least some courts may strike the balance in favor of the child since early diagnosis may prolong the child's life and there are legal remedies, although woefully inadequate, for the mother should the information regarding her infected status be misused. However, there is continuing medical controversy about how much early identification actually means for the infected newborn. Thus, other courts may strike the balance in favor of the mother. The resolution of this issue may well depend on future medical developments in this area.

Conclusion

The language in some Supreme Court cases involving abortion suggests that government-sponsored directive counseling to abort or forego childbearing raises serious constitutional issues. Directive counseling to abort or forego childbearing also may violate the Rehabilitation Act, if done by a federal entity or recipient of federal funds, or the ADA, if done by state or local government or a covered place of public accommodation. Unfortunately, both the case and statutory law in this area are not entirely clear. However, it does seem clear that under the Rehabilitation Act or the ADA, any blanket policy which discourages women infected with HIV from bearing children or directs them to abort because of their disability is suspect.

Policies developed to address the issue of reproductive choices of HIV-infected women should encourage independent, informed decision-making by each woman and should be based on current medical knowledge. In addition, policy-makers should be sensitive to the special nonmedical needs of the many HIV-infected women. Since women infected with HIV are considered "disabled" under two federal laws designed to discourage discrimination against, and increase independence for, persons with disabilities, reproductive decision-making policies which tend to exclude, segregate, or treat HIV-infected women different from uninfected women need to be closely scrutinized. Blanket policies, based on a woman's disability, that discourage reproduction may be unlawful. Counseling and treatment policies should be flexible and encourage individual assessment of each woman's circumstances.

Notes

1. D. Michaels, "Estimates of the Number of Motherless Youth Orphaned by AIDS in the United States," *Journal of the American Medical Association*, 268 (1992): 3456–3461; Centers For Disease Control, *HIV/AIDS Surveillance Report*, 6 (Atlanta, GA: CDC, 1994): 1–24. Between 1981 and March, 1992 women accounted for 10% of the 218,301 cases of AIDS reported to the CDC; when these figures are examined more closely, women comprised 9% of the first 100,000 reported AIDS cases but 12% of the second 100,000 cases.
2. Centers for Disease Control, "Update: Mortality Attributable to HIV Infection Among Persons Aged 25–44 Years—United States, 1991 and 1992," *Morbidity and Mortality Weekly Report* 42 (1993): 481–486.
3. Centers for Disease Control, *HIV/AIDS Surveillance Report*, 5 (Atlanta, GA: CDC, 1993): 10.
4. Ibid., 11. 5,095 cases of pediatric AIDS (89%) involved children of mothers with/at risk for HIV infection.
5. There have been systematic efforts to discourage pregnancy in HIV-infected women by state health departments and professional medical associations. R. Bayer, "AIDS and the Future of Reproductive Freedom," *The Milbank Quarterly*, 68 (suppl. 2, 1990): 191–193. A survey of two pediatric residency programs in New York indicated that residents were substantially more likely to agree that women infected with HIV should not have babies than women at risk for Tay-Sachs disease and cystic fibrosis, both painful and life-shortening illnesses. Ibid., 193.
6. Centers for Disease Control, "Recommendations for Assisting in the Prevention of Perinatal Transmission of HTLV-III/LAV and Acquired Immunodeficiency Syn-

drome," *Morbidity and Mortality Weekly Report* 34 (1985): 721–731; American College of Obstetrics and Gynecology, *Prevention of Human Immune Deficiency Virus Infection and Acquired Immune Deficiency Syndrome*, ACOG Committee Statement no. 53 (Washington, DC: American College of Obstetrics and Gynecologists, 1987): 1–4. This statement was withdrawn in December 1988, but the most recent ACOG statement does not address counseling HIV-infected women who are not pregnant about future pregnancies. "Human Immunodeficiency Virus Infections," in *ACOG Technical Bulletin* (Washington, DC: American College of Obstetricians and Gynecologists, 1992): 4. A joint statement of the American Academy of Pediatrics and ACOG contains the following statement on HIV infections: "The identification of an HIV-infected pregnant woman early in pregnancy is important to ensure appropriate counseling and medical care, including pregnancy termination if this is her choice; to plan medical care for the infant; and to provide counseling about family planning, future pregnancies, and the risk of sexual transmission of HIV to others."

American Academy of Pediatrics and American College of Obstetricians and Gynecologists, *Guidelines for Perinatal Care*, eds. R. Freeman and R. Poland (Washington, DC: American Academy of Pediatrics and American College of Obstetricians and Gynecologists, 1992): 126. This book also does not address the issue of HIV-infected women seeking counseling about future pregnancies.

7. Bayer, "AIDS and the Future," 191–193.
8. For example, Ronald Bayer, in discussing the trend by physicians to direct women infected with HIV not to become pregnant, admits that the class and racial/ethnic background of the women currently infected may also influence physician's attitudes, as well as drug use by many of these women. Bayer, "AIDS and the Future," 194.
9. Michaels, "Estimates of the Number of Motherless Youth," 3459. For example, "[t]he 1988 death rate for HIV/AIDS in black women 15 to 44 years of age was nine times the rate for white women the same age." HIV/AIDS-related causes is the leading cause of death among African-American women between the ages of 25 and 44 years in the states of New York and New Jersey. S. Y. Chu, J. W. Buehler, and R. L. Berkelman, "Impact of the Human Immunodeficiency Virus Epidemic on Mortality in Women of Reproductive Age," *Journal of the American Medical Association* 264 (1990): 225–227. Thus, it is not surprising that the number of children whose mothers have died from AIDS are concentrated in cities like New York, Newark, Miami, San Juan, Puerto Rico, Los Angeles, and the District of Columbia. Michaels, "Estimates of the Number of Motherless Youth," 3459.
10. Working Group on HIV Testing of Pregnant Women and Newborns, "HIV Infection, Pregnant Women, and Newborns: A Policy Proposal for Information and Testing," *Journal of the American Medical Association* 264 (1990): 2416–2420 (citing Centers for Disease Control, *HIV/AIDS Surveillance Report* [August, 1990]: 1–18).
11. Michaels, "Estimates of the Number of Motherless Youth," 3456.
12. *Roe v. Wade*, 410 U.S. 113 (1972).
13. See, generally, B. Hartmann, *Reproductive Rights and Wrongs* (New York: Harper & Row, 1987): 240. She notes that poor women and women of color often are given unnecessary hysterectomies rather than the less dangerous form of sterilization, tubal ligation.
14. See, for example, L. Nsiah-Jefferson, "Reproductive Laws, Women of Color, and

Low-Income Women," *Women's Rights Law Report* 11 (1989): 15–38; D. Kelves, *In the Name of Eugenics: Genetics and the Uses of Human Heredity* (New York: Knopf, 1985): 275–276; A. Asaro, "The Judicial Portrayal of the Physician in Abortion and Sterilization Decisions: The Use and Abuse of Medical Discretion," *Harvard Women's Law Journal* 6 (1983): 93–101; D. Grosboll, "Sterilization Abuse: Current State of the Law and Remedies for Abuse," *Golden Gate Law Review* 10 (1980): 1147–1156.

15. Federal regulations require that a woman give written informed consent before sterilization. These regulations also mandate a waiting period of 30–180 days before the sterilization is performed. 42 C.F.R. Sections 441.250–441.259 (1992); 42 C.F.R. Sections 50.201–50.210 (1992). Unfortunately, these provisions are not very effective at deterring sterilization abuse since there are no criminal or civil sanctions imposed when they are violated. The only consequence is loss of government-financed reimbursement. 42 C.F.R. Section 441.256(a)(1992); 42 C.F.R. Section 50.209 (1992).

16. For a more complete discussion of this point, see A. Clarke, "Subtle Forms of Sterilization Abuse: A Reproductive Rights Analysis," in *Test-Tube Women: What Future for Motherhood*, eds. R. Arditti, R. Klein, and S. Minden (Boston: Pandora Press, 1984): 188–212.

17. L. Nsiah-Jefferson, "Reproductive Laws, Women of Color, and Low-Income Women," in *Reproductive Laws for the 1990s*, eds. S. Cohen and N. Taub (Clifton, NJ: Humana Press, 1989): 23–67.

18. B. Brotman, "Mixed Emotions, Jumbled Laws in Wake of Webster, States to Vary More on Abortion Statutes," *Chicago Tribune*, Jan. 14, 1990, p. 1 (noting that 37 states have passed laws forbidding the use of Medicaid funds for abortion in almost all circumstances since 1977). The unavailability of less costly and more temporary means of contraception may explain why African-American women currently have a higher abortion rate than white women. G. Kolata, "Abortion Rate is Found to be Staying Constant," *New York Times*, Oct. 6, 1988, p. Y13 (young, poor, black, unmarried women are most likely to have an abortion). Abortion may be seen by some women as a better alternative to permanent sterilization because access to abortion as a means of contraception does not permanently foreclose a woman's ability to choose to become pregnant, whereas sterilization does. Thus, the choice of abortion over government-financed sterilization suggests that many African-American women are not ready to permanently forego their procreational choice. Some view the willingness of states to allow Medicaid funds to be used to provide Norplant, a long-lasting contraceptive, to poor women as yet another instance where government policy restricts, rather than expands, the reproductive choices of some women. A disproportionate number of these poor women who are being encouraged to use Norplant are women of color.

19. M. Rees, "Shot in the Arm: The Use and Abuse of Norplant," *The New Republic*, Dec. 9, 1991, p. 16.

20. V.E.B. Kolder, J. Gallagher, and M. T. Parsons, "Court-Ordered Obstetrical Interventions," *New England Journal of Medicine* 316 (1987): 1192–1196. The Massachusetts study found that 81% of the women subjected to court-ordered obstetrical interventions were women of color, 44% were unmarried, and none were private patients. Ibid., 1195. A Baltimore study made a similar finding, as did a 1972 National Natality survey. Nsiah-Jefferson, "Reproductive Laws," 63 n80 (citing L. K. Gibbons, "Analysis of the Risk of C-Section in Baltimore," Doctoral diss.,

School of Hygiene and Public Health, The Johns Hopkins University, Baltimore, 1976); P. J. Black, "Type of Delivery Associated with Social and Demographic Maternal Health, Infant Health, and Health Insurance Factors: Findings from the 1972 U.S. National Natality Survey." Paper presented at the American Statistical Association Meeting, Chicago, August 1977.
21. Kolder, "Court-Ordered Obstetrical Interventions," 1195.
22. For example, Darlene Johnson, a 27-year-old pregnant African-American woman, was convicted of child abuse (beating two of her four children with an electric cord) after she found them engaging in potentially harmful activities. The state judge gave her the option of spending 1 year in prison and 3 years on probation or 4 months in prison and 3 years on probation if she agreed to use the contraceptive Norplant for 3 years. *Johnson v. California*, No. 29390 (Cal. App. Dep't Super. Ct. plea entered Dec. 3, 1990). In 1991 the state of Kansas introduced legislation that would require use of Norplant for fertile women convicted of felony possession and distribution of certain illegal drugs. Rees, "Shot in the Arm," 16. See, generally, D. E. Roberts, "Punishing Drug Addicts Who Have Babies: Women of Color, Equality, and the Right of Privacy," *Harvard Law Review* 104 (1991): 1419–1482 (discussing this point in relation to drug-using women).
23. A. Asch, "Reproductive Technology and Disability," in *Reproductive Laws for the 1990s*, eds. S. Cohen and N. Taub (Clifton, NJ: Humana Press, 1989): 69–124.
24. Asch, "Reproductive Technology," 79 (citing D. Hyler, "To Choose a Child," in *With the Power of Each Breath*, eds. S. E. Browne, D. Connors, and N. Stern, [Pittsburgh: Cleis Press, 1985]): 280–283; J. Le Maistre, "Parenting," in *With the Power of Each Breath*, eds. S. E. Browne, D. Connors, and N. Stern (Pittsburgh: Cleis Press, 1985): 285–291; S. Shaul, P. Dowling, and B. I. Laden, "Like Other Women: Perspectives of Mothers with Physical Disabilities," in *Women and Disability: The Double Handicap*, eds. M. J. Deegan and N. A. Brooks (New Brunswick, NJ: Transaction Publishers, 1985): 133–142; S. K. Thurman, *Children of Handicapped Parents* (San Diego, CA: Academic Press, 1985).
25. D. Kaplan, "Disability Rights Perspectives On Reproductive Technologies and Public Policy," in *Reproductive Laws for the 1990s*, eds. S. Cohen and N. Taub (Clifton, NJ: Humana Press, 1989): 242.
26. J. Matthews, "The Debate over Her Baby: Bree Walker Lampley has a Deformity. Some People Think She Shouldn't Have Kids," *Washington Post*, Oct. 20, 1991, p. F1. It should be noted that there is a 50–50 chance that this condition will be inherited.
27. Asch, "Reproductive Technology," 80 (citing M. A. Lamanna, "Social Science and Ethical Issues: The Policy Implications of Poll Data on Abortion," in *Abortion: Understanding Differences*, eds. S. Callahan and D. Callahan (New York: Plenum Press, 1984): 1–24.)
28. There is subtle and even overt pressure for users of prenatal diagnosis to abort after detection of a disability. Asch, "Reproductive Technology," 83. For some, this is the goal of prenatal diagnosis in the first place.
29. Lamanna, "Social Science and Ethical Issues," 1–5.
30. For a discussion of transmission rates see Chapter 3 in this volume.
31. For a discussion of this point see Bayer, "AIDS and the Future."
32. *Buck v. Bell*, 274 U.S. 200 (1927).
33. *Skinner v. Oklahoma*, 316 U.S. 535 (1942).
34. Ibid., 540–541.

35. In *Buck* the Virginia law treated all institutionalized "mentally defective people" the same way, whereas in *Skinner* the Oklahoma law treated differently persons who had committed essentially the same crime and thus had impermissibly discriminated "as if it had selected a particular race or nationality for oppressive treatment." Ibid., 540–541.
36. Ibid., 541.
37. Ibid. Ultimately, the fundamental rights analysis used by the Court in *Skinner* was abandoned in a string of contraceptive cases involving state intrusions on procreative choices. In *Griswold* v. *Connecticut* the Court struck down a state law criminalizing contraceptive use and counseling, relying on a "zone of privacy" which encompasses the marital relationship. *Griswold* v. *Connecticut*, 381 U.S. 479, 484–485 (1965). In *Eisenstadt* v. *Baird* the Court extended this protection to single persons, striking down a statute criminalizing the distribution of contraceptives to single people while allowing distribution to married persons. *Eisenstadt* v. *Baird*, 405 U.S. 438 (1972). However, in *Eisenstadt* the Court clearly refused to base its holding on a fundamental rights theory, relying instead on the even more ambiguously based privacy guarantee. 405 U.S. at 453.
38. *Roe* v. *Wade*, 410 U.S. 113 (1973). In *Roe* v. *Wade* the Court, while extending the right to privacy to encompasses a woman's decision to terminate a pregnancy, cited *Buck* in support of its claim that a woman does not have an unlimited right to control her body. Nevertheless, the Court indicated that state regulations limiting this right to bodily autonomy must be compelling and, while compelling, must nonetheless be narrowly drawn. Ibid., 164.
39. *Planned Parenthood of Southern Pennsylvania* v. *Casey*, 112 S. Ct. 2791 (1992).
40. It should be noted that the majority in *Roe* v. *Wade* cite *Buck* v. *Bell* in support of the claim that the right of privacy does not give a woman "an unlimited right to do with (her) body as (she) pleases." *Roe* v. *Wade*, 154.
41. *Planned Parenthood* v. *Casey*, 2804.
42. Ibid., 2804–2807 (citing *Carey* v. *Population Services International*, 431 U.S. at 685; *Eisenstadt* v. *Baird*, 405 U.S. at 453).
43. Ibid., 2817 (citing *Roe* v. *Wade*, 410 U.S. 113, 162 [1973]).
44. See, for example, the following language from *Casey*: "[These Supreme Court decisions] support the reasoning in *Roe* relating to the woman's liberty because they involve personal decisions concerning not only the meaning of procreation but also *human responsibility and respect for it*." Ibid., 2807. While some people believe that each pregnancy is so wonderful that it should be continued without regard to any difficulties posed in caring for a child, the Court notes that "the inability to provide for the nurture and care of the infant is a cruelty to the child and an anguish to the parent." Ibid., 2808.
45. Ibid., 2816–2817.
46. Ibid. So at least in the context of abortion, the most recent Supreme Court decisions suggest that almost nothing short of an absolute prohibition on first trimester abortion will be considered unduly burdensome.
47. Ibid., 2811. The plurality also suggests that even if *Roe* is overruled, the cases relying on *Roe* that involve government restrictions on the right to bear children would still be sound because *Roe*'s scope is confined by the facts of that case. In other words, *Roe* deals with "post conception potential life," whereas forced abortion or sterilization cases involve situations where government is sanctioning the destruction of potential life. Ibid. Even some of the dissenting justices in *Casey*

seem to agree with this distinction. For example, Chief Justice Rehnquist notes that the court's decision in *Harris v. McRae*, 448 U.S. 297, 325 (1980) distinguishes marriage, procreation, and contraception from abortion because the latter "involves the purposeful termination of potential life." Ibid., 2859. Justice Scalia, in a footnote to his separate dissenting opinion, says that there is a liberty interest in childbirth protected by the Constitution. Ibid., 2874.

48. *Arnold v. Board of Education of Escambia County, Alabama*, 880 F.2d 305, 311 (CA11 1989).
49. *Avery v. County of Burke*, 660 F.2d 111, 115 (CA 4 1981).
50. See *Griswold v. Connecticut*, 381 U.S. at 485 (striking down a state law banning the use of contraceptives because it has "maximum destructive impact" on the marital relationship).
51. See *Carey v. Population Services Int'l.*, 431 U.S. at 708 (Justice Powell concurring agreeing with the majority that a New York state law prohibiting the sale of contraceptives to minors unjustifiably interferes with the interests of parents in rearing their children).
52. *Skinner v. Oklahoma*, 541: "We are dealing here with legislation which involves one of the basic civil rights of men. Marriage and procreation are fundamental to the very existence and survival of the race."
53. *Stanley v. Illinois*, 405 U.S. 645, 651 (1972). See also, *Meyer v. Nebraska*, 262 U.S. 390, 399 (1923) (the right to conceive and raise one's children is "essential"); *Kovacs v. Cooper*, 336 U.S. 77, 95 (1949) (Justice Frankfurter concurring); *May v. Anderson*, 345 U.S. 528, 533 (1953) ("rights more precious . . . than property rights").
54. *Stanley v. Illinois*, 405 U.S. 645 (1972).
55. *Planned Parenthood v. Casey*, 2817.
56. See, generally, J. A. Robertson, "Procreative Liberty and the Control of Conception, Pregnancy and Childbirth," *Virginia Law Review* 69 (1983): 405–420; E. S. Scott, "Sterilization of Mentally Retarded Persons: Reproductive Rights and Family Practice," *Duke Law Journal* (1986): 806–840.
57. For a complete discussion of this point see P. A. Lombardo, "Three Generations, No Imbeciles: New Light on *Buck v. Bell*," *New York University Law Review* 60 (1985): 30.
58. Approximately 14 states have statutes authorizing involuntary sterilization of persons with mental impairments who are deemed incapable of consent. G. P. Smith, "Limitations on Reproductive Autonomy for the Mentally Handicapped," *Journal of Contemporary Health Law & Policy* 4 (1988): 71–77.
59. Most of these cases were decided before the United States Supreme Court's holding in *Stump v. Sparkman*, 435 U.S. 349 (1978), where a judge who authorized the sterilization of a "somewhat retarded" minor in a state without an enabling statute was found to be immune from suit. Although the Supreme Court never addressed the specific issue of whether a judge could legally authorize involuntary sterilization in the absence of any state law, post-*Stump* decisions often cite the case for that principle. See, for example, *C.D.M.*, 627 P.2d 607, 611 (Alaska, 1981); *In re Terwilliger*, 450 A.2d 1376, 1379–80 (Pa, 1982).
60. See, for example, *In re P.S.*, 452 N.E.2d 969, 976 (Ind., 1983) (rejecting the idea that the courts cannot decide to involuntarily sterilize incompetent individuals without express legislative authority); *In re Matejski*, 419 N.W.2d 576, 578–80 (Iowa,

1988); *In re Moe*, 432 N.E.2d 712, 718–719 (Mass., 1982); *In re Hayes*, 608 P. 2d 635, 638 (Wash., 1980).
61. See, for example, *Guardianship of Kemp*, 118 Cal. Rptr. 64, 65 (Ct. App. 1974); *Wentzel v. Montgomery General Hospital Inc.*, 447 A.2d 1244, 1247–1248, 1254 (Md, 1982); *In re Simpson*, 180 N.E.2d 206, 208 (Ohio P. Ct., 1962); *Frazier v. Levi*, 440 S.W.2d 393, 394–95 (Tex. Civ. App., 1969).
62. See, for example, *In re Simpson*, 180 N.E.2d 207, 208 (Ohio Prob. Ct., 1962) (suit by the mother of 18-year-old "physically attractive" developmentally disabled woman who has one child and had applied for welfare); *Frazier v. Levi*, 440 S.W.2d 393, 394 (Ct. of Civ. App. Tx., 1969) (suit by a mother who was supporting the two children of her developmentally disabled daughter); *Holmes v. Powers*, 439 S.W.2d 579, 580 (Ky., 1969) (county officials sought involuntary sterilization of single developmentally disabled mother of two "illegitimate" children); *In re Kemp*, 43 Cal. App.3d 758, 760 (1974) (parents of an adult developmentally disabled daughter claimed financial burden to both them and the general public); *Wentzel v. Montgomery General Hospital, Inc.*, 447 A.2d 1244, 1247–48 (Md, 1982) (suit by the grandmother of a physically and mentally impaired 13-year-old girl, claiming she, the grandmother, would be unable to support any offspring).
63. *Wentzel v. Montgomery General Hospital, Inc.*, 1254; *In re Grady*, 426 A.2d 467, 481n.8 (N.J., 1981).
64. See, for example, *North Carolina Association for Retarded Children v. North Carolina*, 420 F. Suppl. 451, 457–8 (M.D.N.C., 1976); *In re Simpson*, 206, 208.
65. Mississippi Code Annotated 41–45–1–45–11 (1972 and Suppl. 1990); North Carolina General Statutes Annotated 35–36–50 (1990).
66. *Buck v. Bell*, 207.
67. See, for example, *Doe v. Jamaica Hospital*, Kings County, Supreme Court, *New York Law Journal* (May 6, 1991): 27 (involving an HIV-infected woman who was told by a health-care provider that abortion was the best alternative because a baby infected with HIV "would suffer and become a burden on society").
68. See the discussion of the Bree Walker Lampley case in Matthews, "The Debate over Her Baby," F1.
69. See, for example, Asch, "Reproductive Technology."
70. Bayer, "AIDS and the Future," 194 (citing other authorities), but compare C. Levine and N. Neveloff Dubler, "Uncertain Risks and Bitter Realities: The Reproductive Choices of HIV-Infected Women," *The Milbank Quarterly* 68 (1990): 321–351. Levine and Dubler "do not agree that there is an absolute standard by which the birth of an HIV-infected baby is morally unacceptable. There is no intent to create harm. . . . There is no certainty that harm will in fact be done." Ibid., 346. They urge a multipoint approach: (1) meaningful sex education beginning in elementary school, (2) access to medical services for all poor people, (3) increased access to prenatal care to reduce poor pregnancy outcomes, (4) timely access to abortion for HIV-infected women who desire it, and (5) improved housing and support services that will allow mothers to maintain relationships with their children and reduce incidences of separation and loss of custody. Ibid., 346–347.
71. Bayer, "AIDS and the Future," 194 (philosophers like John Arras and some lawyers assert moral principles like the "harm principle," which they argue should be counterbalanced against concepts of autonomy).
72. See T. Lewin, "Drug Verdict Over Infants Is Voided," *New York Times*, July 24,

1992, p. B6. Of the 160 women who have been arrested in 24 states for drug use during pregnancy, none of those who contested were convicted, but most of the women pled guilty; *Johnson* v. *State*, 578 So.2d 419 (Fla. Dist. Ct. App., 1991) is an interesting variation. Jennifer Johnson, a user of cocaine, was charged with delivering a controlled substance to a minor after suffering a crack overdose while pregnant and using rock cocaine while in labor. She was prosecuted and convicted on a theory that she delivered cocaine to her child between the time the child emerged from the birth canal and the moment the doctor cut the umbilical cord. Ibid., 421–422 (Sharp, J., dissenting). Her conviction was overturned by the Supreme Court of Florida. *Johnson* v. *State*, 602 So.2d 1288 (Fla., 1992).

73. A. R. Fleischman, "The Fetus Is a Patient," in *Reproductive Laws for the 1990s*, eds. S. Cohen and N. Taub (Clifton, NJ: Humana Press, 1989): 249; D. Johnson, "The Creation of Fetal Rights: Conflicts with Women's Constitutional Rights to Liberty, Privacy, and Equal Protection," *Yale Law Journal* 95 (1986): 599.

74. Kolder, "Court-Ordered Obstetrical Interventions," 1194 and accompanying text; L. C. Ikemoto, "The Code of Perfect Pregnancy: At the Intersection of the Ideology of Motherhood, the Practice of Defaulting to Science, and the Interventionist Mindset of Law," *Ohio State Law Journal* 53 (1992): 1236–1240.

75. Just recently the United States Supreme Court refused, without explanation, to hear an emergency petition by the public guardian for the fetus of a pregnant woman who refused, for religious reasons, to undergo a cesarean operation or to accept attempts to induce labor in order to improve the fetus's chances of being born alive. A state trial court and two state appellate courts had refused to order the procedures. R. Brownstein and T. Shryer, "Refusal to Undergo Cesarean Supported," *Los Angeles Times*, Dec. 19, 1993, p. 24A. There are few state cases that directly address this issue. In 1981 a Georgia court addressed the issue of whether and when a court should order a cesarean section in a case involving a woman in her 39th week who refused the procedure for religious reasons. In that case, the state court also ordered the cesarean, reasoning that the fetus was capable of living outside its mother. *Jefferson* v. *Griffin Spalding County Hospital Authority*, 247 Ga. 86 (1981). Several years later, a three judge motions division of the District of Columbia appellate court upheld a trial court-ordered cesarean of a woman dying of cancer who was in her 26th week of pregnancy. *In re A.C.*, 533 A.2d 611 (Ct. App. D.C.1988). The judges reasoned that the procedure would not have significantly affected the mother's health or shortened her life, so there was no infringement upon the mother's right to bodily integrity, and there was a significant chance that the fetus would be born alive. Ibid., 617. The fetus did not survive and the mother died 2 days after the cesarean procedure. Subsequently, the appellate court sitting en banc vacated and remanded the case. *In re A.C.*, 573 A.2d 1235 (Ct. App. D.C., 1990). The full appellate court acknowledged that a pregnant woman had a right to bodily integrity and that government can lawfully override a pregnant woman's objection to medical intervention only when there is a compelling state interest. Ibid., 1247. The court ruled that the question of medical treatment in this case was a matter to be decided by the patient on behalf of herself and the fetus. Ibid., 1237.

76. Centers for Disease Control, *HIV/AIDS Surveillance Report*, 6 (Atlanta, GA: CDC 1994) 16. Less than 1% of males in the same age group are reported as having AIDS. M. F. Goldsmith, "'Invisible' Epidemic Now Becoming Visible as HIV/AIDS Pandemic Reaches Adolescents," *Journal of the American Medical Association* 270 (1993): 16. "Heterosexual transmission accounted for a greater

proportion of AIDS cases among women aged 20–29 years than women aged >30 years.... The increase in cases among women aged 20–29 years primarily reflects persons who were infected as adolescents." Centers for Disease Control and Preventions, "Update: Acquired Immunodeficiency Syndrome—United States, 1992," *Journal of the American Medical Association* 270 (1993): 930–933.

77. Goldsmith, "'Invisible' Epidemic," 16 (reporting that the number of 13–21 year olds in the United States infected with HIV rose 77% in the past 2 years and that half of the transmissions occurred through heterosexual intercourse). During the 1980s there was an increase in the number of women aged 10–19 years who reported having premarital sexual intercourse. During this period there also was an increased incidence of gonorrhea, which some authorities believe puts this group of individuals at increased risk of HIV infection. L. A. Webster, S. M. Berman, and J. R. Greenspan, "Surveillance for Gonorrhea and Primary and Secondary Syphilis Among Adolescents, United States—1981–1991," *Morbidity and Mortality Weekly Report* 42 (1993): 1–11.

78. J. Moore, J. Campana, M. Lam et al., "Selected Behaviors That Increase Risk for HIV Infection, Other Sexually Transmitted Diseases, and Unintended Pregnancy Among High School Students—United States," *Journal of the American Medical Association* 269 (1993): 329–330 (finding "that a substantial proportion of students throughout the United States engage in behaviors that simultaneously place them at risk for HIV infection, other STDs, and unintended pregnancy"). "[T]he teenagers and young women who are particularly at risk for HIV infection do not have access to economic or educational institutions that reward postponed childbearing." Levine and Dubler, "Uncertain Risks," 330. "The role of sex in these children's lives is neither an erotic expression nor a response to romantic love, but rather a happening—a part of the 'warm body syndrome' or the search for comfort. For many urban poor there is neither privacy nor time for loving sexual encounters." Ibid. "As a result of these conditions, the rate of unintended pregnancy is considerably higher among poor teens of all races than among the teenage population as a whole. There is a low level of knowledge about and use of contraceptives." Ibid. (citing V. M. Mays and S. D. Cochran, "Issues in the Perception of AIDS Risk and Risk Reduction Activities by Black and Hispanic/Latina Women," *American Psychologists* 43 [1988]): 949–957. Attempts to educate young women about the possible negative effects of teenage pregnancy have been largely unsuccessful. The only exceptions have been programs that provide consistent, well-supported services and messages throughout the community. Ibid. (citing J. W. Stout and F. P. Rivara, "Schools and Sex Education: Does It Work?" *Pediatrics* 83 [1989]: 375–379). Of teenage mothers, 80% did not consciously want to get pregnant but did so anyway because of a lack of knowledge about contraception or a desire to be liked by a particular boy. When they do get pregnant, poor teenagers are less likely to get an abortion (citing National Research Council, Panel on Adolescent Pregnancy and Childbearing, *Risking the Future* [Washington, D.C.: National Academy Press, 1987]). "They do not abort because having a baby carries the possibility of love and purpose." Ibid., 330–331.

79. *Michael M. v. Superior Court*, 450 U.S. 464 (1981). Justice Rehnquist, writing for the plurality, concluded that a California statutory rape law, making it illegal to have sexual intercourse with a woman under the age of 18, did not violate the equal protection clause of the Fourteenth Amendment by making men alone criminally liable for the act of sexual intercourse. Ibid., 473. He concluded that because the

harmful consequence of teenage sexual intercourse (pregnancy) disproportionately impacts women, the state could lawfully punish young men because they suffer fewer consequences of their act. Ibid., 471–473.
80. *Carey v. Population Services International*, 678 (the statute banned distribution of contraceptives to minors under 16 years of age).
81. Goldsmith, "'Invisible' Epidemic," 16.
82. A. English, "Adolescent Health Care—Barriers to Access: Consent, Confidentiality, and Payment," *Clearinghouse Review* 20 (1986): 484.
83. Ibid.
84. 42 C.R.F. section 441.253 (1992) (requiring that all mentally competent individuals must be at least 21 years old when they consent to be sterilized).
85. Ibid. In *Roe* the Court held that the right of privacy contained in the due process clause of the Fourteenth Amendment encompassed a woman's right to choose to terminate her pregnancy.
86. *Planned Parenthood of Central Missouri v. Danforth*, 428 U.S. 52 (1976) (striking down a Missouri abortion law requiring parental consent unless a physician certified that the abortion was needed to save the minor woman's life). The United States Supreme Court recognizes that minors, like adults, have constitutional rights. *In re Gault*, 387 U.S. 1 (1967) (holding that the due process guarantee applies to juveniles as well as adults). However, their rights are not always equal to adult rights, and this is especially true in reproductive matters.
87. See, for example, *Bellotti v. Baird*, 428 U.S. 132 (1976) (upholding a Massachusetts parental consent law that allowed minors to go to court to override a denial of consent and waived the consent requirement when parents were unavailable). *H.L. v. Matheson*, 450 U.S. 398 (1981) (upholding a parental notification statute as not violative of a minor woman's right of privacy). *Hodgson v. Minnesota*, 110 S.Ct. 2926 (1990) (upholding a Minnesota law that required notification of both parents unless the minor obtains a judicial bypass). *Ohio v. Akron Center for Reproductive Health*, 110 S. Ct. 2972 (1990) (upholding an Ohio parental notification requirement that also had a judicial bypass provision). Currently, 12 states have parental notification laws and 24 have parental consent statutes. However, few of these laws are operational. J. S. Ehrlich and J. A. Sabino, "A Minor's Right to Abortion—The Unconstitutionality of Parental Participation in Bypass Hearings," *New England Law Review* 25 (1991): 1194 n.30.
88. 29 U.S.C. Sections 701–761 (1988 and Suppl. III 1991). Section 504 applies to recipients of federal funds and covers all health-care providers who accept Medicare and Medicaid patients (codified as amended at 29 U.S.C. Section 794 [1988 and Suppl. III 1991]); 45 C.R.F. § 84.3 app. A at 376 (1992).
89. *School Board of Nassau County v. Arline*, 480 U.S. 273 (1987) (school teacher with TB).
90. See, for example, *Doe v. Centinela Hospital*, No. CV 87–2514, 1988 U.S. Dist. LEXIS 8401, at 32 (C.D. Cal. July 7, 1988).
91. 29 U.S.C. Section 794.
92. *City of Cleburne v. Cleburne Living Center*, 473 U.S. 432 (1985) (holding that individuals with disabilities are not a suspect group entitled to higher standard of scrutiny under the equal protection clause).
93. For a more complete discussion of this point, see National Council on the Handicapped, *Toward Independence* A-6-A-30 (Washington, D.C.: National Council on the Handicapped, 1986) (appendix describes these deficiencies).

94. Public Law 101–336, 104 Stat. 327 (codified at 42 U.S.C. Sections 12101–12213 [1992]).
95. 42 U.S.C. Section 12132 (1992).
96. R. L. Burgdorf, Jr., "The Americans with Disabilities Act: Analysis and Implications of a Second-Generation Civil Rights Statute," *Harvard Civil Rights–Civil Law Review* 26 (1991): 465. Burgdorf suggests that judicial and legislative activities also may be subject to the nondiscrimination requirements of the ADA. Ibid., 465 n. 266.
97. 42 U.S.C. Section 12182 (1992).
98. 42 U.S.C. Section 12181(7)(F) (1992).
99. 42 U.S.C. Section 12182(a)(1)(A)(iii) (1992).
100. The House Committee on Education and Labor's report on the ADA explicitly mentioned that individuals with disabilities continue to experience discrimination in medical treatment. H.R. Rep. No. 487 (or 485), 101st Cong., 2d Sess. pt. 2 at 31 (1989). The report quotes from the United States Commission on Civil Rights' earlier report, U.S. Commission on Civil Rights, *Accommodating the Spectrum of Individual Abilities* (Clearinghouse Publication 81 Sept. 1983): 17–45.
101. H.R. Rep. No. 485 (II), 101st Cong., 2d Sess. at 388–389, reprinted in 1990 U.S.C.C.A.N. 482.
102. H.R. Rep. No. 485 (II), 101st Cong., 2d Sess. at 389, reprinted in 1990 U.S.C.C.A.N. 482.
103. For example, today some physicians refuse to deliver babies, fearing medical malpractice suits for children born with certain disabilities. See Chapter 9 of this volume.
104. L. O. Gostin, "The Americans with Disabilities Act and the U.S. Health System," *Public Affairs* 11 (1992): 250.
105. S. Rich, "Oregon Medicaid Rationing Program Rejected as Biased Against Disabled," *Washington Post*, Aug. 4, 1992, p. A2.
106. For example, some physicians might be concerned about their legal liability for counseling an HIV-infected woman to become pregnant because they fear a child born with HIV might file a civil action for wrongful life. However, as a general rule, most courts have refused to entertain these suits because they require courts to find that living with an impairment is worse than ever having been born. W. Page Keeton, D. B. Dobbs, R. E. Keeton, et al., *Prosser and Keeton on Torts*, 5th ed. (St. Paul, MN: West Publishing Company, 1988): 370–373. Physicians also fear that parents will bring a wrongful birth action to recover for injuries the parents incurred from the birth of an unwanted and impaired child. Generally, wrongful birth suits have been brought where there was a genetically transmissible disorder and the physician failed to recognize the risk, failed to test for the disorder, or failed to inform the parents of the risk of transmission. For a more complete discussion of the question of health-care provider tort liability and women with HIV, see Chapter 9 of this volume. An example of a situation where a health-care provider might claim limited resources as a basis for refusing to treat a woman infected with HIV is a request for infertility services, an issue discussed in more depth later in this chapter.
107. 42 U.S.C. Section 12182(b)(3) (West, 1992); 28 C.R.F. Section 36.208(a) (citing to *School Board of Nassau County v. Arline*, 480 U.S. 273 [1987]).
108. 42 U.S.C. Section 12182(b)(3) (West, 1992); see 28 C.F.R. Sections 36.208, 36.302, 36.303 (1992).

109. 42 U.S.C. Section 12182(c) (West, 1992).
110. See, for example, *Doe* v. *Centinela Hospital*, 1988 U.S. Dist. LEXIS 8401 (D. 1988) (HIV-infected man excluded from residential drug-treatment program because of his infection).
111. Centers for Disease Control, "Surveillance of Occupationally Acquired HIV Infection—United States, 1981–1992," *Journal of the American Medical Association* 268 (1992): 3294 (reporting that, as of September 1992, there were 32 documented and 69 possible occupationally acquired cases of HIV infection).
112. Centers for Disease Control, "Recommendations for Preventing Transmission of Human Immunodeficiency Virus and Hepatitis B Virus to Patients During Exposure-Prone Invasive Procedures," *Morbidity and Mortality Weekly Report, Recommendations and Reports* 40 (1991): 5–6.
113. Lawrence Gostin, Executive Director of the American Society of Law and Medicine, agrees with this conclusion: "Courts . . . are unlikely to accept occupational risk as a justification for discrimination: the risk is exceedingly low and can be kept low through the 'reasonable accommodation' of strict adherence to infection control procedures. Health care professionals will probably be expected to accept some level of risk in carrying out their jobs in the same way that fire fighters or police officers cannot excuse themselves from particularly dangerous assignments." Gostin, "The Americans With Disabilities Act," 251.
114. Ibid., 251.
115. However, the United States Supreme Court in *School Board of Nassau County* v. *Arline*, a Rehabilitation Act case, said that "courts should normally defer to the reasonable medical judgments of public health officials." 103 S. Ct.1123, 1131 (1987). However, Lawrence Gostin claims that "increasingly courts are looking beyond the mantle of clinical judgment and are examining patterns of behavior that may be masking prejudice." Gostin, "The Americans With Disabilities Act," 251.
116. *Doe* v. *Jamaica Hospital*, *New York Law Journal* (May 6, 1991): 27.
117. Ibid. In 1989 Carole Doe filed a civil action against both hospitals and the physician, alleging arbitrary discrimination on the basis of a physical disability, HIV, in violation of section 504 of the Rehabilitation Act of 1973 and state human and civil rights laws.
118. E. Rosenthal, "Abortion Clinics Often Reject Patients with the AIDS Virus," *New York Times*, Oct. 23, 1990, p. A1.
119. Ibid.
120. Ibid.
121. Ibid. Note that these problems continue today for HIV-infected women seeking abortions.
122. Michaels, "Estimates of the Number of Motherless Youth," 3456.
123. 42 U.S.C. Section 12210 (1992). Current illegal use of drugs is defined in 28 C.F.R. Section 36.104 (1992) to mean use that occurred recently enough to justify a reasonable belief that a person's drug use is current or that continuing use is a real and ongoing problem.
124. 42 U.S.C. Section 12210; see 28 C.F.R. Section 36.209(b) (1992).
125. 128 C.F.R. Section 36.208 (1992).
126. 28 C.F. R. Section 36.301 (1992).
127. See, for example, J. R. Smith et al., "Infertility Management in HIV Positive Couples: A Dilemma," *British Medical Journal* 302 (1991): 1447–1450 (describing

a case study of an HIV-infected couple, who, after learning of their infected status and receiving pregnancy counseling, opted to continue with infertility management).

128. G. Corea, *The Mother Machine: Reproductive Technologies from Artificial Insemination to Artificial Wombs* (New York: Harper Collins, 1985): 145.

129. For example, the health-care provider is concerned about both the pregnant woman and her potential child. The provider may believe that there are some treatments or medical procedures designed to benefit the potential child which the pregnant woman resists. As a result, the woman may be coerced or ordered to undergo the treatment or medical procedure and be labeled a bad or uncaring mother for resisting medical advice. The increased incidence of court-ordered medical interventions involving pregnant women suggests that some courts consider these women to be obligated to do all that is necessary, short of giving up their lives, to enhance the health and survival of their potential children. See Nsiah-Jefferson, "Reproductive Laws"; Kelves, *In the Name of Eugenics*, 275–276; Asaro, "The Judicial Portrayal," 93–101; Grosboll, "Sterilization Abuse," 1153–1156; Clarke, "Subtle Forms of Sterilization Abuse," 188–212.

130. See Hartmann, *Reproductive Rights and Wrongs*, 240; Nsiah-Jefferson, "Reproductive Laws," 17; Kelves, *In the Name of Eugenics*, 275–276; Asaro, "The Judicial Portrayal," 93–101; Grosboll, "Sterilization Abuse," 1153–1156; Clarke, "Subtle Forms of Sterilization Abuse," 188–212; Brotman, "Mixed Emotions," 1; Kolata, "Abortion Rate," 13; Rees, "Shot in the Arm," 16; Kolder, "Court-Ordered Obstetrical Interventions," 1192–1195.

131. Nsiah-Jefferson, "Reproductive Laws," 39.

132. Originally CDC recommended that only fertile women "at risk" for HIV infection be routinely tested. H. L. Minkoff, "Care of Pregnant Women Infected with Human Immunodeficiency Virus," *Journal of the American Medical Association* 258 (1987): 2714–2717. However, draft recommendations currently being circulated recommend HIV counseling and testing for all pregnant women. Centers for Disease Control, "Draft U.S. Public Health Service Recommendations for HIV Counseling and Testing for Pregnant Women," *Federal Register* 60 (1995): 10086–10087.

133. See Bayer, "AIDS and the Future."

134. A child born with HIV antibodies may not be infected with HIV, and it may take up to 16 months before an accurate diagnosis can be made. C. Levine and R. Bayer, "The Ethics of Screening for Early Intervention in HIV Disease," *American Journal of Public Health* 79 (1989): 1661–1662 The level of test accuracy for infants varies quite a bit since infants born to infected mothers may test positive for up to 15 or 16 months following birth but not be infected.

135. Ibid., 1664–1665. Traditionally, routine prenatal genetic testing has not been performed for medical conditions which cannot be treated prior to delivery and can be avoided only by not becoming pregnant or by abortion. (In the context of HIV, however, if evidence increases that medical intervention during pregnancy can affect pregnancy outcomes, HIV counseling would be less analogous to genetic counseling.)

136. Ibid., 1666.

137. See, for example, the diabetic daughter in the movie *Steel Magnolias*, who, against the advice of both her physician and her mother, elects to become pregnant and subsequently dies while her child is still a baby. The daughter's death is portrayed as

a sad but noble sacrifice to ensure that the bloodlines of both her husband and herself continue. Traditionally, childbearing is viewed as a way to ensure one's immortality, a concern that may be even more pressing for someone who knows that her life expectancy is shortened. This point also is made by Levine and Dubler, "Uncertain Risks," 323.

138. M. Angell, "A Dual Approach To The AIDS Epidemic," *New England Journal of Medicine* 324 (1991): 1498–1500. Centers for Disease Control, "Draft U.S. Public Health Service Recommendations for HIV Counseling and Testing for Pregnant Women," *Federal Register* 60 (1995): 10086–10087.

139. H. L. Minkoff, "Care of Pregnant Women Infected With Human Immunodeficiency Virus," *Journal of the American Medical Association* 258 (1987): 2714–2717. S. Grubman, J. M. Oleske, R. J. Simonds, et al., "1995 Revised Guidelines for Prophylaxis Against Pneumocycstis Carinii Pneumonia for Children Infected with or Perinatally Exposed to Human Immunodeficiency Virus," *Morbidity and Mortality Weekly Report* 44 (1995): 1–11.

140. See, for example, the Rehabilitation Act of 1973, 29 U.S.C. 794 (1982 and Suppl. V 1987). The Civil Rights Restoration Act of 1987 amended Sections 503 and 504 of the Rehabilitation Act to include persons with contagious diseases and infections. Pub. L. No. 100–259, 102 Stat. 31 (current version at 29 U.S.C. Section 706 [Suppl. 1989]; recipients of federal funds); the Americans With Disabilities Act of 1990, Pub. L. 101–336, 104 Stat. 327 (1990). While this act greatly increases protection against discrimination based on HIV, it does not apply to any public accommodations until January 1992. Pub. L. 101–336 Section 310, 104 Stat. 365.

141. *Bowen v. American Hospital Association*, 476 U.S. 614, 624 (1986).

142. Ibid., 631–633. The issue in this case was whether under the Rehabilitation Act covered providers had a duty to provide nourishment and treatment for a seriously ill newborns. The United States Supreme Court said that there was no duty in the absence of parental consent.

143. For example, one study found that all of the states pay for amniocentesis through their Medicaid programs. "Study Tracks Payments for Abortions," *Mod. Healthcare* 20 (June 4, 1990): 12–14.

144. 1991 Iowa Legis. Serv. 270 Section 103 (West); Va. Code Ann. Section 32.1–92.2 (Michie 1982) ("the fetus will be born with a gross and totally incapacitating physical deformity").

145. M. Field, "Pregnancy and AIDS," *Maryland Law Review* 52 (1993): 420–421, 421 n.74; but compare C. S. Rush, "Note, Genetic Screening, Eugenic Abortion, and Roe v. Wade: How Viable is Roe's Viability Standard," *Brookings Law Review* 50 (1983): 142, where the author argues that states that ban postviability abortions must make exceptions for pregnant women who learn that their fetuses will have serious disabilities because there is a constitutional right to abort and choose not to have a child who would have a disabling condition.

146. The Supreme Court's decision in *Casey* raises questions about the exact standard to be applied in these cases. However, *Casey* and *Roe v. Wade* involve individual choice about not bearing a child postconception, whereas *Skinner*, *Griswold*, and *Baird* involve individual preconception choice. Arguably, once a woman has exercised her right to procreate, any governmental action which interferes with procreation is more personal and invasive.

147. *Roe v. Wade*, 150 (prenatal life).

148. See, for example, M. Gwinn, M. Pappaioanou, J. R. George, et al., "Prevalence of

HIV Infection in Childbearing Women in the United States: Surveillance Using Newborn Blood Samples," *Journal of the American Medical Association* 265 (1991): 1704–1708 (suggesting that recent progress in early diagnostic testing, clinical trials under way in children, and FDA approval of AZT for pediatric use are reasons why early diagnosis in newborns may be desirable but recommending against unconsented testing); E. M. Connor, R. S. Sperling, R. Gelber, et al., "Reduction of Maternal-Infant Transmission of Human Immunodeficiency Virus Type 1 With Zidovudine Treatment," *New England Journal of Medicine* 331 (1994): 1173–1181.

149. For a general discussion of this issue, see Working Group on HIV Testing of Pregnant Women and Newborns, "HIV Infection, Pregnant Women, and Newborns," 2416 (rejecting unconsented testing of newborns because "[a]t present, the expected benefits to newborns from HIV testing do not clearly outweigh these risks (discrimination, possible abandonment) or the privacy and autonomy interests of their mothers"). Ibid., 2418.

150. In *State v. Johnson*, No. 89–890-CFA (Fla. Cir. Ct., 1989) a woman was criminally prosecuted for delivering drugs to her newborn through the umbilical cord moments after birth.

151. *In re Baby X*, 97 Misc. App. 111, 293 N.W.2d 736 (1980) a state court allowed evidence of a mother's drug use during pregnancy to be used as proof of neglect or abuse in a state-initiated proceeding to deprive the woman of her newborn child.

152. M. Navarro, "Testing Newborns for AIDS Virus Raises Issue of Mothers' Privacy," *New York Times*, Aug. 8, 1993, p. A1.

9

Reproductive Choice and Reality: an Assessment of Tort Liability for Health-Care Providers and Women with HIV/AIDS

KAREN H. ROTHENBERG

> I found out when I got pregnant with the baby in '91. And I was told—the routine was to take an AIDS test. I took it not knowing. They told me it came out positive, I just took it because they said take it. . . . I thought I was dying, you know, dead tomorrow. I didn't understand what HIV was. . . . I had to find out what that mean[t] on my own, . . . (and) they didn't refer me to anybody.
>
> *woman from New York*

When HIV began infecting women[1] of childbearing age in increasing numbers,[2] it prompted public scrutiny of the reproductive choices of HIV-infected women.[3] This public scrutiny remains largely focused on limiting childbearing among HIV-infected women as a means of reducing the incidence of pediatric AIDS, rather than on the impact of HIV/AIDS on the health and well-being of infected women.[4] The public debate seeks to establish whether, and to what extent, an HIV-infected woman has a moral or legal duty to make socially "responsible" reproductive choices,[5] a focus which concentrates on women as "*posing* a risk rather than being at risk,"[6] reduces women to vectors of transmission, and suggests that HIV-infected women may have a responsibility to not bear children.

Since the epidemic currently affects poor African-American and Hispanic women disproportionately,[7] the debate regarding responsible reproductive choices for HIV-infected women is, ironically, focused on a group of women already beset by a well-documented lack of access to health care[8]—particularly for reproductive health services[9]—and whose reproductive choices are already correspondingly circumscribed.[10]

While this situation is indicative of the deficiencies in the American health-care delivery system as a whole,[11] it also is related, at least in part, to an unwillingness by physicians to treat these women.[12] The reluctance of physicians to treat poor and minority women is often attributed to three factors—rate of reimbursement, health status of the patient, and perception of increased malpractice liability[13]—that intertwine in a vicious cycle, contributing to the exclusion of low-income and minority women from health care.

Both the prospect and the reality of insufficient or nonexistent reimbursement for provider services produce an unwillingness to accept poor and poorly insured patients. This reluctance is reinforced by rising medical malpractice premiums, particularly for obstetrician/gynecologists (OB/GYNs),[14] and the perception that the reduced rate of reimbursement for low-income patients does not justify the increased risk of malpractice liability.[15] Low-income patients are viewed as "more litigious"[16] than middle-class or wealthy patients, despite mounting evidence to the contrary. Indeed, because they are disenfranchised from the health and justice systems, minorities and the poor may be less inclined to assert claims for wrongful injury.[17] At the same time, they may be more likely to suffer adverse outcomes.[18] Although the relationship between minority status and adverse outcomes has not been adequately investigated,[19] statistically higher adverse outcomes for the poor may be attributable to lack of access to the system, especially for primary and prenatal care, or discriminatory and inadequate care once in the system.[20]

The predicament of pregnant women who use illegal drugs is a case in point. Currently, many HIV-infected women are IDUs or the partners of IDUs.[21] Viewed as noncompliant[22] and obstetrically risky patients,[23] low-income, drug-addicted women have little chance of enlisting professional help to get clean during their pregnancy. The overwhelming majority of drug-treatment programs refuse to accept pregnant women in part because they fear "pregnancy-related legal liability."[24] This almost blanket exclusion from drug-treatment programs continues despite new studies which indicate that intensive prenatal care for pregnant drug addicts results in substantially improved obstetrical outcomes.[25] Thus, misfounded perceptions of potential liability contribute to the exclusion of drug-addicted women from treatment and to the disproportionate detriment of poor and minority women and the children they bear.

HIV/AIDS is becoming increasingly prevalent among women, especially poor and minority women. The impact of excluding poor and minority women from health care is even greater when these women have a serious medical condition. Moreover, provider fear of contracting HIV produces a reluctance to treat HIV-infected patients and can lead to refusals to treat or abandonment of HIV-infected patients. Since providers, in effect, are the gatekeepers to health care, provider response to HIV/AIDS will determine in large part the level of access poor and minority women have to care and any resulting liability. Within the context of HIV infection, race, class, and gender-based differences[26] among providers and patients are thought to lead to notably different risk calculations and decisions about whether to bear a child when HIV-infected.[27] When a female patient's decision-making processes and ultimate decisions are markedly different from those of the treating physician's,[28] the specter of "directive" medical practice, which may lead to unwanted procedures and potential liability, is raised.

In any case, to prevent HIV from further eroding access to health care and limiting the reproductive choices of these women, the myths surrounding reproductive liability must be separated from reality. Fear of tort liability in this context is far out of proportion to the liability risk and is one factor which may erode access to both primary and reproductive health care for poor and minority women.[29]

The subset of American jurisprudence which is concerned with defining those junctures in social interactions when one individual owes another individual a legal duty of care is known as tort law.[30] The legal duty of care which the law of torts defines is the duty to avoid intentionally or negligently[31] harming another, through either acts or omissions that are unreasonably risky. Tort law "is the mechanism this society uses to discourage individuals from subjecting others to unreasonable risks, and to compensate those individuals who have been injured by unreasonably risky behavior."[32] It is concerned with a broad array of intentionally or negligently inflicted injuries, including physical and emotional harm to the person (e.g., battery and the intentional infliction of emotion distress), harm to personal interests (e.g., invasion of privacy), and harm to economic interests (e.g., interference with contractual relations). While tort principles and the goals of tort law—deterrence, compensation, and justice—are universal in theory, in practice, tort law varies widely from state to state.

This chapter examines the potential for provider and maternal tort liability within the context of reproductive decision-making and HIV-infected women. It traces provider liability issues and current legal standards at various points along the woman's decision-making continuum, beginning at the point where the woman is informed she is HIV-infected and branching off to follow her reproductive options. It then provides a general and realistic assessment of provider liability, as well as an analysis of potential maternal liability. Since case law addressing issues of reproduction in the context of HIV is virtually nonexistent, analogy is made to other similar areas, such as liability associated with reproductive decision-making and genetically transmitted diseases, where legal precedent is better established.

Liability Issues for Health-Care Providers

Health-care providers[33] may be held liable for a wide range of torts[34] and may be sued for more than one tort arising from the same set of facts.[35] Medical malpractice, the most commonly occurring tort in the health-care setting, provides a good illustration of the application of basic tort principles to the complexities of medical practice and the patient–provider relationship. To sustain a medical malpractice action, an injured party must establish by a preponderance of the evidence[36] the existence of each of the four legal elements of negligence: "[1] a duty, recognized by law to conform to a certain standard of conduct; [2] failure on the defendant's part to conform to that standard of care (i.e., a breach of that duty); [3] a reasonably close causal connection between the conduct and the injury (proximate cause and cause in fact); and [4] an injury denoted by the actual loss or damage to the victim."[37]

In the context of patient–provider relationships, a legally recognized duty of care attaches when a patient–provider relationship is established and continues until the relationship is terminated properly under the law.[38] Under certain circumstances, the duty of care continues even after the relationship is properly terminated (e.g., the duty of confidentiality).

The scope of the duty of care is defined by the "standard of care," which is a standard of conduct. Each provider is required to act with that level of skill and learning which is possessed by members in good standing of the provider's particular health-care profession.[39] Because reproductive services to HIV-infected women are rendered by a variety of health-care providers, it is important to note several things about provider liability. First, in actuality, the standard of conduct or care is profession-specific: it is directly related to the level of expertise, or "skill and learning," of the particular profession. Generally, a social worker would be held to a different standard of care from a general practitioner, while an OB/GYN would be held to a higher standard than a general practitioner for obstetrical and gynecological services. Second, because of the technical nature of medicine and the inability of judges and juries to adequately substitute their judgment for that of medical professionals, the standard of care is customarily defined by the particular profession.

To establish the second element of negligence, the provider's breach of the duty of care, the plaintiff must prove that the provider departed from the applicable standard of care by some act or failure to act. As described above, except in the most obvious negligence cases in which common knowledge would dictate that negligence could be found, plaintiffs rely on expert testimony to establish a provider's breach of duty of care.

The third legal element of negligence requires that the provider's breach of duty, the act or failure to act, be the factual and legal cause of the plaintiff's injury.[40] Establishing proximate cause is an inherently arduous task due to the difficulties associated with establishing the fact that the harm resulted from the breach.

Fourth, for a court to provide a remedy for the harm imposed, the harm—whether a detriment, loss, or injury—must be measurable in terms of damages. In tort suits, nominal, compensatory, or punitive damages may be awarded. Nominal or token damages may be awarded when an injury is insignificant or the amount of actual damages is incalculable. Compensatory damages shift the cost of the injury back to the party which caused the injury, or in some instances to the party best able to bear the cost of the injury, by compensating the injured party for damages measured in terms of the nature and amount of actual harm suffered (e.g., medical expenses, lost wages). A court may award punitive or exemplary damages to further tort law's public policy goals of punishment and deterrence if the defendant's conduct was intentional or sufficiently outrageous to warrant punishment or if the awarding of such damages serves as an example to deter other potential defendants.

In summary then, liability may arise when a legally owed duty of care is breached and the breach proximately causes actual, legally measurable harm. A provider's failure to diagnose, failure to inform a patient of the diagnosis, or misdiagnosis of a patient's HIV status exposes the provider to liability for the harm caused by the provider's breach of the standard of conduct.[41] For the purposes of this chapter, it is assumed that the diagnosis of HIV infection is correctly made and properly communicated to the woman. In the context of reproductive decision-making for HIV-infected women, provider liability may arise at a few points along the continuum: reproductive counseling, the decision not to conceive, and the pregnancy.

Reproductive counseling
The scope of the duty to provide reproductive counseling

Many women learn they are HIV-infected only after their newborns become ill or when the women experience symptoms of AIDS.[42] The diagnosis of HIV infection[43] may be communicated to the infected woman from a wide range of providers and in circumstances totally unrelated to reproduction. What level of reproductive counseling should accompany any diagnosis of HIV infection in a female patient of childbearing age?[44]

It is widely recognized that the highly communicable and lethal nature of the virus, coupled with the social stigma and devastating emotional impact which often accompanies a diagnosis of HIV infection, requires providers who communicate the initial diagnosis to discuss more than mere test results.[45] When test results are conveyed, the session must include both an educational and an informational component, as well as posttest counseling.

The educational component must contain at least minimal levels of information on risk factors and modes of transmission, including sexual and perinatal transmission. The accuracy and adequacy of the information provided are important in preventing harm and in assessing liability for a failure to counsel or negligent counseling. For example, any provider who informs a woman she is HIV-infected but fails to inform, or fails to accurately inform, of the risk of perinatal transmission may be found tortiously liable for the birth of a child the woman would not have conceived had she known of the risk of perinatal transmission. A provider has the duty to keep as current with the professional literature as required to act with that level of skill and learning which is possessed by members in good standing of the provider's particular healthcare profession. The standard of care for the accuracy and adequacy of the content of the information provided can never be greater than the existing level of scientific knowledge at the time: a health-care provider cannot be held responsible for information which is currently unknown or unknowable; but as medical knowledge increases, a provider may, in some instances, have a duty to supplement communications with patients and former patients.

When HIV-infected women seek to make informed reproductive decisions regarding whether to conceive, terminate a pregnancy, or carry a pregnancy to term and seek reproductive services to implement such decisions, they need more than minimal information on risk and modes of transmission. HIV-infected pregnant women "should be provided accurate, understandable information to enable them to make fully informed choices about their reproductive lives."[46] Information relevant to such reproductive decision-making for HIV-infected pregnant and nonpregnant women may include the following:

1. The impact of contraception, pregnancy, and abortion on the progression of HIV/AIDS.
2. The impact of HIV/AIDS on pregnancy and abortion.
3. The life expectancy and course of disease progression in women and children.
4. The fact that a child of an HIV-infected woman will be born with maternal HIV antibodies but that 70%–80% of the children born to untreated HIV-infected mothers will be HIV antibody-free by 18 months of age.[47]

However, in addition to expanded information requirements, reproductive counseling requires discussion of psychosocial issues:

[W]hat distinguishes counseling from health education is the component of the counseling session that examines psychological issues. If there is a *decision* to be made, such as whether to terminate a pregnancy or whether to take a drug whose risks in pregnancy are unknown, it is crucial to sort out the counselee's values and feelings in regard to the decision. Even when there is *not* a decision to be made, a counseling session includes a psychological component. In the context of HIV testing, this may include determining and facilitating a patient's ability to tap her own support system and typical coping mechanisms.[48]

Similarly, a recent study on reproductive decision-making by HIV-infected women[49] revealed the importance of psychosocial factors such as coping mechanisms (e.g., faith in God or medicine), "systems of thought" (e.g., positive thinking), the "locus of decision making" (e.g., the woman or another), and the value placed on motherhood in decisions regarding whether they chose to carry the pregnancy to term or to terminate it.[50]

The failure to counsel a woman, or negligently conducted counseling that fails to provide accurate and complete information about the impact of HIV on reproductive issues, strips the woman of her opportunity for informed autonomous decision-making and deprives her of counseling which is supportive and enhancing of her decision. As a result, it may lead to an unwanted pregnancy and birth or a coerced abortion, harms which may expose a provider to liability.

Breaches of the duty to provide reproductive counseling
THE FAILURE TO COUNSEL. Wrongful conception or pregnancy, wrongful birth, and wrongful life claims are negligence actions which developed as abortion became legally obtainable and as prenatal diagnostic testing became technologically available.[51] These suits share the common goal of protecting reproductive decision-making—particularly the right not to have children—and seek to hold the provider liable for the birth of an unwanted child. The cornerstone of these suits is that "but for" the provider's negligent act or omission (e.g., failure to inform of perinatal transmission) the unwanted child would never have been born. Although confusion exists as to the proper definitions of the terms "wrongful pregnancy," "birth," and "life," the actions can be differentiated by determining which party, parent or child, brings the suit and whether the child was born healthy or impaired.[52]

Wrongful conception or pregnancy suits are brought by parents for the birth of a healthy but unwanted child. Typically, in a wrongful conception/pregnancy suit, the birth of the child is the injury which results from a negligently performed abortion or sterilization procedure, including vasectomies, or from the erroneous filling of oral-contraceptive prescriptions. Initially, courts refused to award damages in wrongful conception/pregnancy suits based on the premise that the parental benefits derived from the birth of a healthy, albeit unwanted, child far outweighed the burdens associated with the unwanted birth. Now, however, many jurisdictions will permit the recovery of compensatory damages for the costs and pain associated with the pregnancy and childbirth, though damage awards generally have not been expanded to include other expenses incurred by the unwanted birth, such as childrearing and educational costs.

In wrongful birth suits, parents seek to recover for the injuries they incurred resulting from the birth of an unwanted child with disabilities. The parents generally seek to recover compensatory damages for the medical expenses incurred for the pregnancy and delivery, the costs of rearing and educating the child, special medical and educational costs arising from the impairment, and the parents' own pain and suffering.

Wrongful life suits are brought on behalf of the impaired child and often in conjunction with the parents' suits. The child with disabilities does not claim the provider caused the medical problems in not providing counseling or prenatal testing, for example, but rather that the provider's negligence caused the child's life. Life with disability is the harm for which the child seeks a remedy. Wrongful life suits are unlikely to succeed: courts generally deny recovery due to the inability to measure the value of never having been born as compared to a life with impairment.

Typically, wrongful birth suits arise for pre- and postconception injuries.[53] Preconception injuries result from harm to the parents in being denied the decision as to whether to conceive; postconception injuries result from the parents being denied the right to abort.[54] Preconception injuries often involve genetically transmitted disorders,[55] particularly those where a parent or previously born child was afflicted by an inheritable disease, but also include instances of negligence that have an impact on future pregnancies.[56] Postconception injuries include prenatal injuries which result from maternal illness (e.g., exposure to rubella)[57] and failure to provide diagnostic testing for genetically transmitted disorders.

In essence, these suits are based on provider acts or omissions which "prevent parents from getting appropriate counseling and information"[58] needed to make reproductive choices. In such suits brought in the context of genetically transmitted disorders, providers have been sued for negligence in failing to "(1) recognize the parents were at risk for transmitting a genetic disease (e.g., failure to take the appropriate family history); (2) diagnose a genetically transmitted disease in a previous child; (3) diagnose due to negligently performed laboratory testing; and (4) inform the parents of the consequences of an appropriately diagnosed genetic disease."[59]

While no case law exists concerning wrongful pregnancy or birth actions in the context of HIV, it is reasonable to predict that judicial precedents in the area of genetic disease may be extended to HIV if sufficiently analogous. Similarly substandard medical practice in the context of HIV might be implicated for diagnosing- and counseling-related failures to (1) perceive a woman was at risk for HIV infection (e.g., failure to take an adequate history); (2) diagnose HIV/AIDS in previous children; (3) diagnose HIV due to laboratory error; (4) communicate the risk of perinatal transmission, means of reducing the transmission risk, and/or the consequences of HIV transmission to the child.

However, HIV is not (yet) directly analogous to genetic disease. With some diseases, genetic and prenatal diagnostic testing can determine whether a particular fetus is afflicted with a particular disease or disorder. The failure to provide such testing, or the negligent provision of such testing and posttest counseling, denies the parents' right to make an informed reproductive choice about a specific fetus who would be born with disability and is an injury courts are willing to recognize. In contrast, once pregnant, no reliable prenatal diagnostic tools are yet available to diagnose HIV infection in a particular fetus, which destroys the needed causal connection between the specific identification of an impaired fetus and the missed opportunity to have an abortion. This may change when accurate HIV prenatal diagnostic testing becomes available.

Wrongful life suits remain controversial and are unlikely to succeed in most jurisdictions.[60] Generally, courts are philosophically disinclined to hold that life with disability is worse than never having been born and are likewise reluctant to attempt to measure this harm.[61] Under traditional tort theory in an HIV-based wrongful life suit, the issue before the court would be whether an HIV-infected child may claim that never having been born is preferable to life with HIV infection. Since the manifestations of pediatric HIV/AIDS are sufficiently analogous to other pediatric diseases and disorders,[62] HIV-based wrongful life claims are unlikely to succeed as well.

"DIRECTIVE" COUNSELING AND ITS IMPLICATIONS. Posttest (as well as pretest) counseling is closely aligned with public health efforts to curb the spread of HIV. Since public health efforts emphasize prevention of transmission, those aspects of counseling which have been related to reproduction often have been directive in nature: preventing pregnancy or birth prevents perinatal transmission. Not surprisingly, since 1985[63] the CDC has advocated directive counseling, recommending that women "should be advised to consider delaying pregnancy until more is known about the perinatal transmission of the virus."[64] The American College of Obstetrics and Gynecology (ACOG) has also been directive in nature, issuing a statement in 1987 that "[w]omen infected with HIV . . . should be strongly encouraged not to become pregnant. . . . Those who do become pregnant should be counseled again about the risks to themselves and their child and should be informed about the option of pregnancy termination."[65]

Usually the standard of care is determined by the profession, and recommendations of such organizations as the CDC and ACOG could be evidence of the standard. However, in the case of HIV infection and reproductive decision-making, a professionally determined, directive counseling standard creates significant problems.[66] The greatest danger presented by directive counseling may lie in its potential for manipulating or coercing a woman into making an unwanted reproductive decision, a decision which is based on the health-care provider's perceived need to protect future children or society from harms associated with "irresponsible" choices. Such counseling may lead to liability: consider *Doe v. Jamaica Hospital*,[67] a recent New York case.

According to the allegations in the complaint in *Doe*, the plaintiff, an obese, diabetic pregnant woman who had previously given birth to a child with spina bifida, was accepted at Jamaica Hospital's high-risk prenatal care unit.[68] At the time of registration, the plaintiff was offered a "volunteer" HIV test, which she accepted because she had received numerous blood transfusions during past surgeries.[69] Some 2 weeks later, a registered nurse and a social worker communicated the diagnosis of HIV infection to the plaintiff and "counseled" the plaintiff that: "[1] the chance of having a baby with AIDS was very high . . . ; [2] she should have an abortion . . . ; [3] she should go home and immediately write a will for her daughter . . . ; [4] not to tell anyone of the test results except the father."[70] As a result of this counseling the plaintiff believed her death was imminent.[71]

Several days later, when the plaintiff returned for a regular checkup, she was "counseled" by the Chief of Obstetrics and Gynecology and the Chief of Residents, as well as the registered nurse and social worker she met with previously.[72] During that "counseling session," the defendants "told the plaintiff . . . that having a baby with AIDS is worse than having a child with Spinabifida[sic]; that she would be wrong not to give up the baby to abortion; and that she would be adding another burden to society to have this child."[73] Although the plaintiff wished to continue her pregnancy, the defendants apparently refused to continue to treat the plaintiff at the high-risk clinic and referred her to Kings County Hospital for an abortion.[74] Negligent counseling contributed to the injuries the plaintiff then suffered at Kings County Hospital, where she was first treated on an outpatient basis and then admitted for a second trimester abortion.[75] Prior to performing the abortion, the staff at Kings County Hospital failed to provide counseling and secure informed consent for the procedure.[76]

The plaintiff filed a six-count lawsuit against Jamaica Hospital, its Chief of Obstetrics and Gynecology, its Chief of Residents, the registered nurse and social worker, as well as the New York City Health and Hospitals Corporation as manager of Kings County Hospital, the physician at Kings County Hospital to which the plaintiff was referred, and the physician who induced labor.[77]

The first three counts were based on discrimination claims.[78] The fourth count, directed against all defendants, was for the intentional infliction of emotional distress.[79] The fifth count was a negligence claim. The final claim was directed only against the Kings County Hospital defendants and was based on a lack of informed consent and failure to disclose alternative treatments and reasonably foreseeable risks and benefits so that the plaintiff could have fully consented to the abortion procedure. The plaintiff asked for one million dollars in compensatory damages and one-half million dollars in punitive damages.[80]

While ultimately the plaintiff may not prevail on these claims, other tort claims, including abandonment, corporate negligence in failing to develop counseling policies and supervise counseling staff, vicarious liability imputed to the defending hospitals for the negligence of the health-care workers, lack of informed consent for the HIV test, battery (if recognized in the jurisdiction), and the negligent infliction of emotional distress[81] could arise from such a fact pattern.

This case illustrates the important role reproductive counseling plays in preventing injury and subsequent liability. Compare the counseling revealed by these facts[82] to the counseling suggested by some, which contains an educational–informational component plus a psychosocial component, and the recent trend away from directive counseling.[83] The trend toward a nondirective standard encourages the provider/counselor to assist the HIV-infected woman in reaching her own decision by providing information, options, and assistance in adjusting to her reproductive decision.

When was the accurate, current, and understandable information provided which Carole Doe needed to make an informed choice about her pregnancy? When was she provided with accurate information on the impact of pregnancy and abortion on the progression of HIV/AIDS or, conversely, the impact of HIV/AIDS on pregnancy and abortion; the life expectancy and course of disease progression in women and children; and the risk of perinatal transmission? When did any of the health-care providers discuss Carole Doe's values or feelings in regard to a decision to continue or terminate the pregnancy or her ability to cope with her disease?

Note the series of counseling failures which occurred. First, informed consent pretest counseling did not occur and the plaintiff was not informed that HIV infection was a "high-risk" condition the high-risk clinic was not prepared to undertake. Nor was information made available regarding the true rate of perinatal transmission or the progression of HIV infection in women and children. A discussion of relevant medical information not all of which is known—the effect of pregnancy and abortion on HIV and the effect of HIV on pregnancy and abortion—did not occur. Second, the information which was provided during the posttest counseling session was substandard, erroneous, and distorted. Third, the information was inappropriately laced with provider-held value judgments. Fourth, it was rendered in an intimidating manner, not only because she was told what to do but also because she was told in an intimidating fashion by two to four providers, including two high-ranking male providers, what she should do. A significant power imbalance existed in this counseling. As a result of these factors, Carole Doe felt she was left with no choices and no options. While the lines separating influence, manipulation, and coercion may blur depending on the circumstances in any given situation, the providers in this case clearly went beyond being directive by intimidating the patient into making an unwanted reproductive choice.

The duty to maintain confidentiality and the duty to warn

Provider intimidation, which can lead to an unwanted reproductive choice, may also occur when a provider decides to warn a third party of the infected woman's HIV status.[84] In cases in which partners do not know the HIV status of the HIV-infected woman and the woman does not want them to know, a tension arises between a provider's (1) duty of confidentiality owed to the patient, (2) desire to protect third parties from the harm of contracting HIV by disclosing a patient's infected status as a means of warning the third party, and (3) legal obligations to public health initiatives aimed at controlling the spread of the virus. Thus, the interplay between the provider's decision to disclose a woman's HIV status to a partner and a woman's decision whether to conceive may exist in a delicate, yet fluid, balance. Fear of disclosure might prompt an HIV-infected woman not to conceive, and, conversely, a decision not to conceive may sway a provider not to disclose.

Confidentiality is the fiduciary duty a provider owes to a current or former patient to safeguard the patient's confidences, as well as information contained in the patient's medical records, from disclosure to third parties. Breaches of confidentiality—the willful or negligent divulgence of information the provider is professionally obligated to keep secret—can expose providers to tort claims for invasion of privacy,[85] breach of a confidential relationship, or wrongful disclosure, medical malpractice, the intentional infliction of emotional distress, and defamation.[86]

However, the duty of confidentiality is not and never has been absolute. Confidentiality breached for the protection of others, or for the public good, may be sanctioned by the health-care profession and the law. The dilemma for the provider is determining when confidentiality may be breached with impunity to warn a third party.

The legal duty to warn is an exception to the generally recognized tort principle that "a person has no legal obligation to care for or look after the welfare of a stranger, adult or child"[87] and arises only when a "special relationship" is deemed to exist. Whether the relationship between a patient and provider is special enough to give rise to a duty to warn a third party is open to debate, particularly in the context of HIV.[88] An HIV-infected woman's decision to conceive clearly implicates an intention to engage in unprotected sexual intercourse (unless she's considering artificial insemination), which could infect her partner. The knowledge of the patient's intent to potentially transmit HIV to her partner raises a classic confidentiality–duty to warn dilemma in the event that the partner is uninfected and does not already know of her HIV status.

However, the consequences of disclosure for the HIV-infected woman may be more complicated than other dilemmas of this nature if disclosure could expose her to domestic violence, jeopardize custody of her children, endanger her relationship with her partner as well as her children's means of support, and erode her trust and future participation in the health-care system.[89] If it is foreseeable that the patient's partner will harm the patient if her infection status is revealed, the physician "could become legally liable if [the] warning proximately causes injury, even if there is a statute in [the] state which grants immunity from civil suit for breaching confidentiality."[90]

Since the provider should be knowledgeable about the implications of disclosure–nondisclosure, the provider is in a good position to manage the tension between the harm of possible transmission to a noninfected third party if disclosure is not made vs. the harm of violence to the infected woman if disclosure is made. The conflicting tensions may be systematically balanced through the use of risk-benefit analysis. Such an analysis should evaluate five components:

1. Measuring the potential for violent harm to the patient if the provider discloses her status to her sexual and needle-sharing partners.
2. Identifying the third parties at risk.
3. Considering the foreseeability of harm to the identified third parties.
4. Analyzing the connection between the physician's decision to disclose or not disclose and the injury to third parties.
5. Balancing confidentiality principles with public health strategies to increase public awareness and prevent transmission through testing.[91]

In measuring the potential for harm to the patient, the provider should determine the woman's fear of violence and consider the use of drugs and alcohol by the woman and her partner(s). Studies reveal an increased likelihood of violence if the woman uses alcohol and her partner uses drugs.[92] If the woman and her partner have a history of or she fears domestic violence the partner should not be informed unless the woman consents and can somehow be protected.[93]

If in the provider's estimation the woman will not be harmed and she consents to the disclosure, the provider may proceed to identify third parties at risk. Since, in addition, a duty to warn may attach to "foreseeable victims within the zone of danger,"[94] the provider may identify third parties entitled to protection because they fall within the zone of danger. If an HIV-infected woman has had many sexual and needle-sharing partners, the zone of danger potentially becomes unmanageably large and the task of tracking down all those at risk may be too burdensome or futile to pursue. Nevertheless, a provider should attempt to ascertain the following: (1) the identity of the patient's current and former sexual and needle-sharing partners, (2) whether the patient has or intends to disclose her status to those partners, and (3) whether the patient contemplates future pregnancies and by whom. The provider may be required to ask the patient about the sexual and needle-sharing partners of any of these identifiable partners.

When evaluating the foreseeability of harm to third parties, the provider should consider the patient's sexual and needle-sharing practices and whether (1) partners know the woman's HIV status, (2) condoms will be used, (3) cofactors exist which increase the risk of transmission, (4) the partner is already infected, and (5) warning will impact on prevention of transmission.

In analyzing the causal connection between the physician's decision to disclose or not disclose and the potential for injury to third parties, the physician should consider whether the third parties are at risk from other behavior and individuals. If, for example, an identifiable third party engages in multiple high-risk behaviors with multiple partners, then preserving confidentiality may be favored. Finally, the provider must balance this isolated disclosure against the effect that disclosure has on public health initiatives designed to increase public awareness and prevent transmission through testing.

The decision not to conceive

When a woman decides not to conceive[95] and seeks medical advice and assistance in preventing conception, potential tort liability can attach to providers who negligently provide birth control services. HIV has a special impact on the provision of birth control services, as it has on all aspects of reproductive medical care: it raises questions about the continually evolving standard of care developing from sparsely available data. In fact, the harms which result from substandard medical practice and nondisclosure in the area of contraceptive services implicate many of the tort actions already discussed.

When an HIV-infected woman seeks contraception, the type of information that should be disclosed to her includes:

1. The effect of various birth control methods on the progression of HIV and, conversely, the effect of HIV infection on the reliability of various types of birth control.
2. The existence of contraindications for certain forms of birth control, such as IUDs.
3. The potentiality of drug interactions between oral and implanted contraceptives, such as Norplant, and drug therapy for HIV/AIDS.[96]

Additionally, while latex condoms containing spermicide (nonoxynol-9) may be the best way, next to abstinence, to prevent transmission of the virus, alone they may not be the best choice to prevent pregnancy due to their failure rate[97] and the level of partner cooperation required.[98] For many of the women currently affected by HIV, condom use is culturally unacceptable and the suggestion to a male partner that he use condoms may result in domestic violence against, or the abandonment of, the woman.[99] As an alternative, providers do encourage sterilization, though this may also be culturally unacceptable. In fact, many HIV-infected women are from ethnic groups that have been victimized by sterilization abuses (see Chapter 8).

Pregnancy

Once the duty to treat a pregnant HIV-infected woman attaches, the provider is obligated to continue to treat her throughout the course of the pregnancy and labor or, if requested by the woman, to terminate the pregnancy,[100] unless the relationship is properly terminated under the law. The establishment of the patient–provider relationship is based on the existence of an implied or expressed contract. When a patient seeks services from a provider and the provider undertakes to render those services, an implied contract generally is formed and the duty of care attaches. In alternative delivery systems, such as health maintenance organizations (HMOs), the provider expressly contracts with the patient or the patient's employer to provide services under the terms of the contract.

Historically, the provider had the power to accept or reject the patient's offer to purchase provider services. Correspondingly, the provider had no obligation to treat patients the provider had not agreed or undertaken to treat.[101] Recent law suits, such as the *Doe* case, seek to prevent providers from limiting their practices to HIV-negative patients or terminating services to HIV-infected patients once infection is known. These suits, which are based on federal and state antidiscrimination legislation,[102] threaten to alter the traditional contractual basis of the patient–provider relationship: HIV status is not sufficient justification for refusing to treat a patient. The extent to which this will alter or erode the contractual basis of the patient–provider relationship remains to be seen.

As noted above, once a relationship exists, "[t]he obligation of continuing attention can be terminated only by the cessation of the necessity which gave rise to the relationship, or by the discharge of the physician by the patient, or by the withdrawal from the case by the physician after giving the patient reasonable notice so as to enable the patient to secure other medical attention."[103] Notice is adequate if it gives the patient the opportunity to locate another provider who can meet his or her needs. If an HIV-infected person cannot find another provider willing to meet those needs, then termination of the patient–provider relationship may be tortious. However, if the medical needs of an AIDS patient are beyond the treating physician's skill, the treating physician is obligated to refer the patient to a specialist. (The need to observe universal precautions does not justify referral.) In some instances, a provider's duty of care is continuous in nature and may survive the termination of the relationship (e.g., duty to maintain confidentiality continues after the duty to treat ceases).

If the legal requirements for terminating the patient–provider relationship are not met, the provider may be found liable for the tort of abandonment. Damages could include harm suffered as a direct result of the abandonment (e.g., complications or worsening of the condition).

When an HIV-infected woman seeks to obtain medical services and procedures related to pregnancy, the treating physician has the traditional affirmative duties as with other medical conditions to (1) engage in a dialogue which discloses the relevant risks entailed in the procedure[104] and culminates in obtaining informed consent to perform the procedure[105] and (2) perform the procedure nonnegligently. The duty to disclose and the doctrine of informed consent are interrelated: consent cannot be informed unless there has been disclosure.[106]

Termination of the pregnancy

Termination of the pregnancy is one option an HIV-infected woman may choose. Specifically, for the abortion procedure, the provider owes a duty to the woman to disclose information on the nature of the procedure, the risks and benefits associated with the procedure chosen, alternative procedures, and the effect of abortion on HIV progression and the effect of HIV on abortion. Whether the lethal nature of HIV infection creates a special obligation to counsel the woman that this pregnancy may be her last opportunity to bear a child is a provocative question.

The provider is further obligated to be cognizant of, and adhere to, any statutorily imposed requirements on abortion, such as written informed consent requirements. In performing the abortion and during follow-up care, the provider has the duty to provide care and treatment which conforms to the applicable standard of care.

The complaint in *Doe* alleged that the physician did not obtain informed consent prior to inducing labor in the second trimester abortion. The complaint further alleged that the abortion was negligently performed. The allegedly negligent medical care consisted of assigning the plaintiff to a room labeled "isolation," where labor was induced and she was "left unattended for 15 minutes after the fetus was expelled," screaming in pain in a pool of blood with the expelled and developed fetus visible.[107] When the staff returned, the plaintiff was informed that the abortion was incomplete, and "[c]ontrary to sound medical practice, while plaintiff was hemorrhaging, she was made to walk a great distance to the examining room for the next procedure."[108]

As further alleged in *Doe*, abortion should not be used as a way to quickly terminate the patient–provider relationship. Such actions may result in claims of abandonment and discrimination based on HIV status.

Continuation of the pregnancy

The real challenge faced by most HIV-infected women is obtaining access to HIV-related therapies during pregnancy, as well as overcoming barriers to primary and prenatal care due to poverty and minority status, in addition to their HIV status. The CDC estimates that 7,000 HIV-infected women gave birth annually for the years 1989–1992. Yet, "[p]erhaps in an effort to avoid harm to the fetus, Public Health Service guidelines have avoided recommendations for therapies in pregnancy and in fact have specifically recommended deferring prophylaxis against *pneumocystis carinii* pneumonia (PCP) until after pregnancy,"[109] even though PCP can be deadly.[110] It was not until 1995, however, that the CDC recommended PCP prophylaxis to women while they were pregnant.[111] These new CDC guidelines now reflect the practice of many physicians who have suggested that "therapies potentially beneficial to women should not be withheld during pregnancy unless adverse maternal, fetal or neonatal effect is known and outweighs the potential maternal benefits of therapy."[112]

Treatment issues for women who wish to carry their pregnancies to term will reflect the evolving standard of care. While providers have the duty to conform to the standard of care during pregnancy, delivery, and postnatal care as it evolves, since it preliminarily appears that gender-specific manifestations of HIV infection affect the reproductive system, obstetricians and gynecologists should be especially vigilant in staying current with the medical literature for the development of protocols for managing HIV infection. For example, although data are scant, preliminary research indicates that medical management of *candida vaginitis*, HSV types I and II, primary and secondary syphilis, PID,[113] and cervical diseases including human papillomavirus and cervical neoplasia[114] in HIV-infected women demand special attention.[115] Second, medically indicated differences in routine gynecological evaluations (e.g., more frequent Pap smears) and protocols for invasive obstetrical procedures (e.g., avoidance of chorionic villus sampling [CVS] and amniocentesis) have also been implicated and need to be disclosed to the woman. Decisions may include whether vaginal or cesarean section delivery is appropriate as knowledge of the mechanisms of perinatal transmission develops.

These differences, coupled with concerns for fetal safety, are relevant during pregnancy, when decisions must be made regarding prenatal testing and monitoring, treatment and drug therapy, and delivery. Disclosure is important: the woman must be informed of the risks to her and her fetus so that she may come to an informed decision about the management of her HIV infection and her pregnancy. A recent clinical trial has indicated that "administration of zidovudine (ZDV) to HIV infected pregnant women and their newborns reduced the risk for perinatal transmission of HIV by approximately two thirds."[116] These findings have prompted the CDC to issue recommendations for routine HIV counseling, including discussion of the benefits and risks of ZDV to both the pregnant woman and her fetus.[117]

Throughout the continuum of care, some providers experience significant levels of anxiety when treating HIV-infected patients,[118] though the risk of contracting HIV is small. Fear of accidentally contracting HIV through treating HIV-infected patients may be intensified for reproductive services, such as childbirth, due to significant provider involvement with blood and body fluids and potentially explosive splatterings of such fluids during procedures.[119] If provider fear of contracting HIV infection leads to discriminatory treatment, discriminatory refusals to treat, and provider coercion in reproductive decision-making, providers may expose themselves to liability for discriminatory and coercive acts and omissions, as well as tortuous acts and omissions.

Although there are numerous points along the continuum at which provider liability may potentially attach, it is important to place provider liability in its proper perspective. Otherwise, unfounded fear of liability will further reduce access to care.

Assessing the Reality of Provider Tort Liability

Most HIV-infected women are poor minority women, statistically no more likely to sue than other patients, and maybe less likely to recognize an injury or assert their rights. Like HIV infection, medical injury may be just one more problem in a life characterized by unrelenting adversity and social and economic impoverishment.

In general, despite the popular belief that too many malpractice suits are brought, in reality there is little risk of tort liability for negligent medical care and its accompanying injuries in this context. Litigation "only infrequently compensates patients injured by medical negligence and rarely identifies, and holds providers accountable for, substandard care."[120] This is true in part because the structure of the tort system itself effectively minimizes provider liability. When a typical tort suit is dissected into its component parts, the reasons why liability is virtually nonexistent become apparent. The beginnings of any tort suit necessarily lie in the recognition that some injury or harm, which should not have occurred, did occur; but how often can lay people recognize negligence in an area as complex as medicine? The ability to recognize the occurrence of a negligent medical injury may be contingent upon socioeconomic factors, such as educational level and past familiarity with the health-care system, as well as access to further care, which may identify the occurrence of an injury.[121] As studies of actual malpractice claims document, ethnic minorities and the poor are no more likely to sue,[122] and may be statistically less likely to sue,[123] than other socioeconomic groups, though they may experience statistically higher occurrences of adverse events.[124] Minorities and the poor, already disenfranchised from the health and justice systems, also may be disinclined to work within the system to assert claims to address wrongful injuries.[125] Disenfranchisement may also lead to different expectations as to quality of care and redressability of wrongs.

If a negligently induced injury is recognized, legal representation must be obtained in order to sue. Unlike some legal disputes (e.g., small claims), the complexity of most medical negligence cases necessitates legal representation. However, the tort system functions as a barrier, preventing many poor people from obtaining legal counsel for medical malpractice actions.[126] Plaintiffs' attorneys accept tort cases on a contingency basis, with the attorney receiving a percentage of the amount recovered for the client plus the costs of litigating the claim, which may be substantial depending on the complexities of the case. Contingency fees are inherently financially risky: losing the suit means no compensation for the attorney, as well as the client, even though the attorney expended considerable time and money pursuing the claim.[127]

Since recovery in tort is based on compensatory damages, which are measured at least in part by the economic impact of the injury (e.g., lost income and impaired earning ability), undereducated, unskilled, unemployed, and underemployed people will be awarded substantially less in compensatory damages than well-educated, higher earning people for the same injury. Furthermore, in the context of HIV/AIDS, damages are likely to be limited or difficult to quantify.[128]

If legal representation is obtained, the plaintiff must be prepared to wait a substantial period for settlement or litigation as lawsuits can take years to wind through the courts. Many HIV-infected women will be too sick to cope with, or survive, a lengthy lawsuit through its trial and appellate phases. If the woman becomes too ill or dies, will her family continue the suit? Since AIDS is a disease which devastates entire families, often claiming the woman last, no family members may be left living or be in sufficiently good health to carry the suit forward. Also, the family, in its struggle to care for those the woman left behind, such as her children who may also be infected and ill, may not be able to cope with protracted litigation. Even in those relatively few jurisdictions which funnel cases through alternative dispute resolution mechanisms toward a more rapid conclusion, defense counsel can often circumvent final settlement for years.

If the woman and her family are committed to spending years litigating the suit, who will provide financial support during that time? If damages ultimately are recovered, the resultant boost in income may remove the woman and her children from eligibility for governmental benefits, especially health-care benefits.[129] On balance, the loss of governmental assistance may not be worth the cost of settling or winning the suit.[130]

In fact, the HIV/AIDS epidemic may increase uncompensated injury to greater numbers of people. A recent malpractice study[131] conducted in New York State correlated malpractice claims to actual adverse events caused by negligence by matching malpractice claims to inpatient medical records. The study estimated that New York's statewide ratio of actually occurring adverse events caused by negligence to malpractice claims filed was 7.6 to 1.[132] When translated into percentages, this relative frequency means that "the fraction of medical negligence which leads to claims is probably under 2%."[133] If substandard care is a serious and largely unaddressed problem, HIV/AIDS is likely to exacerbate it. If significant levels of uncompensated negligent injuries already occur, and HIV-related medical knowledge evolves more rapidly than with other diseases, the adequacy with which providers meet the challenges posed by the evolving standard of care may influence the amount of injury which results in the future.

Liability Issues for Women

While preventing harm to children and costs to society may be desirable goals, attempts to punish women for bearing children—rather than providing the needed prenatal and drug treatment care to communities already plagued by third-world infant mortality rates and overwhelmed by poverty, drug abuse, and HIV—seem to be counterproductive. Nevertheless, in addition to criminal prosecution, civil remedies for maternally inflicted prenatal injuries are discussed increasingly.[134]

Overview of liability

The decision by HIV-infected women to bear children often is met with condemnation.[135] This condemnation is part of a larger societal frustration with the spread of substance abuse and HIV infection to women of childbearing age and the corresponding detrimental effects maternal substance abuse and HIV have on the children they bear. The notion of utilizing tort law to influence, manipulate, or coerce pregnant women into making "socially responsible" reproductive decisions[136] mirrors recent attempts to use criminal law to deter pregnant substance abusers from bearing children or to punish substance-abusing mothers for prenatally injuring children.[137] These proposals are flip sides of a legal coin which seeks to solve complex social problems through coercive legal action.

Using tort law to deter the birth of HIV-infected children or to fiscally punish HIV-infected mothers who bear children requires establishing the existence of a maternal legal duty owed to the child, which, if breached, results in some form of legally cognizable harm that is measurable in damages. Until relatively recently in our legal history, children could not sustain personal injury actions against their parents or other third parties, such as health-care providers, for injuries inflicted prenatally (i.e., no duty existed).[138]

It was not until the late 1940s and early 1950s that a series of state courts recognized a cause of action:

> If a child after birth has no right of action for prenatal injuries, we have a wrong inflicted for which there is no remedy, for, although the father may be entitled to compensation for the loss he has incurred and the mother for what she has suffered, yet there is a residuum of injury for which compensation cannot be had save at the suit of the child. If a right of action be denied to the child it will be compelled, without any fault on its part, to go through life carrying the seal of another's fault and bearing a very heavy burden of infirmity and inconvenience without any compensation therefore.[139]

The effect of this shift in perception, the recognition of a previously categorically excluded class of injured parties, opened the door to third-party liability for prenatal injuries;[140] but when the door to third-party liability finally opened, it opened wider for providers than for parents:[141] parents continue to have greater protection from tort liability than unrelated third parties due to the doctrine of intrafamily or parental tort immunity.

The doctrine of parental immunity is a defense which bars recovery by children who are tortiously injured by a parent, even though recovery would be permitted if the family relationship did not exist. No longer justified for social policy reasons (e.g., a tort suit would disrupt family harmony by pitting child against parent or could lead to collusion between family members and result in fraudulently based lawsuits), parental immunity has been abrogated in most states.[142]

Many states do retain remnants of parental immunity for noninsured "parental functions" where parental authority and discretion are deemed to exist. Whether reproductive decisions are deemed to be parental functions and whether a standard of care could be established for them ultimately will depend on state law, which is likely to vary from state to state. For example, in *Goller* v. *White*,[143] the Wisconsin Supreme Court adopted Michigan's often cited Plumley Rule, generally abrogating parental immunity but reserving it

> (1) [w]here the alleged negligent act involves an exercise of parental authority over the child; and (2) where the alleged negligent act involves an exercise of ordinary parental discretion with respect to the provision of food, clothing, housing, medical and dental services, and other care.[144]

What constitutes parental authority or discretion remains unclear. Arguably, the decision to bear a child (assuming the pregnancy is not accidental) is the most discretionary of all parental functions and is a necessary precursor to all other parental functions. Yet is it the same kind of discretionary parental function, like providing food, clothing, shelter, and care, for which immunity is granted? Or could the consequence of being HIV-infected, and the potential inability of an HIV-infected parent to provide food, clothing, shelter, and care for the child, place it outside of discretionary parental function?

Another court[145] "reject[ed] the implication of *Goller* that the parent has carte blanche to act negligently toward his child"[146] and adopted a reasonable parent standard:

> Although a parent has the prerogative and the duty to exercise authority over his minor child, this prerogative must be exercised within reasonable limits. The standard to be applied is the traditional one of reasonableness, but viewed in light of the parental role. Thus we think the proper test of a parent's conduct is this: what would an ordinarily reasonable and prudent parent have done in similar circumstances?[147]

Adopting such an objective person standard in the context of HIV raises many questions. What is a reasonable reproductive choice for an asymptomatic HIV-infected woman? What for a symptomatic woman? Considering that HIV currently disproportionately affects poor and minority women, will an objectively reasonable standard accommodate cultural and socioeconomic differences?[148] (See Chapter 14.)

Establishing a maternal duty and standard of care related to the mother's health status would be breaking new ground. Most reported case law on prenatal injury and parental immunity addresses prenatal injuries sustained in automobile or similar accidents or postnatal injuries sustained through negligent parental supervision. No case law on the transmission of HIV infection as a prenatal injury exists, and only one case, *Grodin v. Grodin*,[149] exists for drug-induced prenatal injury. *Grodin* is a Michigan case involving a child who sued his mother for discolored teeth, which resulted from his mother taking tetracycline while pregnant.[150] The court in *Grodin* found that the ingestion of tetracycline during pregnancy was an exercise of parental discretion and remanded it for a determination of whether the decision to continue taking tetracycline while pregnant was "reasonable,"[151] a question of fact to be determined by a jury. Maintaining that "justice requires that a child has a legal right to begin life with a sound mind and body,"[152] this court was willing to entertain holding a mother liable for her conduct during pregnancy to the same degree of liability as a third party.[153]

Other state courts also have been willing to accord children the right to begin life with a sound mind and body. If such a right is deemed to exist, by implication, the mother would have a corresponding legal duty to prenatally foster or ensure the child's sound mind and body. What would such a duty require from the mother? That she take AZT during pregnancy? That the baby not be born? When would any such duty attach? For example, would it attach only if HIV infection had been confirmed medically or when the mother had reason to believe she may have been infected?

Various maternal duties may be imposed along the continuum of an HIV-infected woman's decision-making about reproduction. A nonpregnant HIV-infected woman may be deemed to have a duty not to conceive to prevent the harm of transmission. Currently, to effectuate such a duty, an HIV-infected woman would need to avoid conceiving any children. Why should such a duty exist for HIV infection but not for other diseases? Although some have suggested such a duty in the context of genetically transmitted diseases,[154] parental reproductive decision-making for genetic and other diagnosable prenatal diseases and disorders is typically a matter of private choice, not socially legislated or judicial choice.

When medical technology evolves to a point where medical interventions can prevent perinatal transmission,[155] conception would be legally allowed if the intervention was used; but medical interventions may be contraindicated for some and/or unaffordable for others. Will this provide a defense to liability? Interventions may also be simply unwanted. Will women be liable for not using the interventions when available? Will unwanted procedures be coerced? Coerced interventions run counter to the common law right to refuse treatment and to bodily integrity, as well as judicially and legislatively recognized rights to informed consent.

If pregnant, an HIV-infected woman may be deemed to have a duty to terminate the pregnancy. Some view abortion as a way to rescue impaired fetuses from a burdensome life.[156] However, a social policy that requires abortion of all HIV-infected pregnant women would mean that the approximately 70%–80% of fetuses that (absent intervention) are uninfected would be terminated to prevent perceived harm to the 20%–30% who are born infected. When technology permits accurate prenatal diagnosis of HIV infection, the situation would be more analogous to genetically transmitted diseases, in which, to date, a woman does not have a legal duty to terminate a pregnancy.

Pregnant HIV-infected women may be deemed to have a duty to take medications and undergo invasive procedures (e.g., cesarean sections) to prevent transmission, already a controversial issue in other contexts. In fact, such coercive practices are most likely to be imposed on low-income and minority women when they refuse cesarean sections for religious or cultural reasons.[157]

In any case, the problems with establishing any such legal maternal duty are twofold. First, it has virtually no legal support: there is no well-established fetal right to be born healthy, either constitutionally or under tort law. Second, it extracts a tremendous cost from women. As noted by the Supreme Court of Illinois in *Stallman v. Youngquist*:

> It is clear that the recognition of a legal right to begin life with a sound mind and body on the part of the fetus which is assertable after birth against the mother would have serious ramifications for all women and their families, and for the way in which society views women and women's reproductive abilities. The recognition of such a right by a fetus would necessitate the recognition of a legal duty on the part of the woman who is the mother; a legal duty as opposed to a moral duty, to effectuate the best prenatal environment possible. The recognition of such a legal duty would create a new tort: a cause of action assertable by a fetus, subsequently born alive, against its mother for the unintentional infliction of prenatal injuries.[158]

The imposition of tort liability on HIV-infected women is the equivalent of requiring them to be guarantors of their children's health: "[a] legal right for a fetus to begin life with a sound mind and body assertable against a mother would make a pregnant woman the guarantor of the mind and body of her child at birth. A legal guarantee to the mental and physical health of another has never been recognized in law."[159]

Conclusion

The real dangers presented by the HIV/AIDS epidemic are not increased provider liability but (1) increased uncompensated injury to greater numbers of people and (2) the potential to use the myth of medical malpractice to further erode access to medical care and limit reproductive choices for poor and minority women. Serious questions of public policy and social justice are also raised by an attempt to impose tort liability on HIV-infected women for their reproductive decisions. Imposing maternal liability would have little practical benefit to the HIV-infected child and would further threaten women who have already experienced overwhelming social neglect.

Notes

1. The role that decision-making about reproduction plays in the lives of HIV-positive men and the male sexual partners of HIV-positive women is beyond the scope of this chapter but needs to be explored. See, generally, J. D. Arras, "AIDS and Reproductive Decisions: Having Children in Fear and Trembling," *The Milbank Quarterly* 68 (1990): 353–359.
2. Centers for Disease Control, "AIDS in Women—United States," *Journal of the American Medical Association* 23 (1991): 265 ("Among all cases of AIDS in women, 85% occurred among women of childbearing age [15–44 years]."); Centers for Disease Control, "Update: Acquired Immunodeficiency Syndrome—United States, 1981–1990," *Morbidity and Mortality Weekly Report* 40 (1991): 358; Centers for Disease Control, "The Second 100,000 Cases of Acquired Immunodeficiency Syndrome—United States," *Journal of the American Medical Association* 267 (1992): 788.
3. See, for example, R. Bayer, "AIDS and the Future of Reproductive Freedom," *The Milbank Quarterly* 68 (suppl. 2, 1990): 179; A. Zarembka and K. M. Franke, "Women in the AIDS Epidemic: A Portrait of Unmet Needs," *St. Louis University Public Law Review* 9 (1990): 519–526. ("Societal contempt for HIV positive women who chose to bear children despite their serostatus derives, in part, from an increasingly popular view of women as reproductive vessels. According to this view, once a woman becomes pregnant, her life, lifestyle, and medical options become subject to public scrutiny and control.")
4. C. Levine and N. N. Dubler, "Uncertain Risks and Bitter Realities: The Reproductive Choices of HIV-Infected Women," *The Milbank Quarterly* 68 (1990): 321. ("The spread of disease to women is rarely described as a concern in and of itself; it is typically linked to the possibility of transmission to infants.")
5. The range of questions raised by the debate includes: Do HIV-positive women have a duty not to become pregnant? Do pregnant HIV-positive women have a duty to abort? Can or should HIV-positive women be held liable for perinatally transmitting HIV to their children?
6. N. D. Hunter, "Complications of Gender: Women and HIV Disease," in *AIDS Agenda: Emerging Issues in Civil Rights* vol. 8, eds. N. D. Hunter and W. B. Rubenstein (1992): 5–39.
7. Centers for Disease Control, "AIDS in Women—United States," *Journal of the American Medical Association* 23 (1991): 265. ("Although black and Hispanic women constitute 19% of all U.S. women, they represent 72% of all U.S. women diagnosed with AIDS.")
8. Levine and Dubler, "Uncertain Risks," 339 ("While interference with reproductive choice is a 'fact of life for most poor women and women of color,' paradoxically these women often experience difficulties in obtaining health care, related or not to reproductive services. Access to health care in the inner city varies from limited to nonexistent. There are few developed patterns of integrated health-care use and preventative care. . . . The system is complex and indistinct, and is entered only in emergency or as a last resort."); Centers for Disease Control, *Health: United States, 1990* (Atlanta, GA: CDC, 1991).
9. Ibid.; J. W. Zylke, "Maternal, Child Health Needs Noted by Two Major National Study Groups," *Journal of the American Medical Association* 261 (1989): 1687.
10. Centers for Disease Control, *Health: United States, 1990* 24.

11. U.S. Bi-Partisan Commission on Comprehensive Health Care (The Pepper Commission), *A Call for Action: Final Report* (Washington, D.C.: U.S. Government Printing Office, 1990).
12. J. Perkins and K. Stoll, "Medical Malpractice: A Crisis for Poor Women," *Clearinghouse Review* 20 (1987): 1277.
13. M. G. Mussman, L. Zawistowich, C. S. Weisman, F. E. Malitz, and L. Morlock, "Medical Malpractice Claims Filed by Medicaid and Non-Medicaid Recipients in Maryland," *Journal of the American Medical Association* 265 (1991): 2992.
14. Perkins and Stoll, "Medical Malpractice," 1277.
15. Mussman et al., "Medical Malpractice Claims," 2992. ("The cost of malpractice insurance is thought to deter physicians from participating because Medicaid payment is insufficient to compensate for rising premiums.")
16. Ibid., 2992.
17. D. Hilfiker, "Are Poor Patients More Likely to Sue for Malpractice?" *Journal of the American Medical Association* 262 (1989): 1391–1392; Perkins and Stoll, "Medical Malpractice," 1278.
18. Perkins and Stoll, "Medical Malpractice," 1278. ("Pregnant women on Medicaid or with no insurance are included in most practitioners' definition of 'high risk,' because these women more often receive no prenatal care and exhibit other indications of pregnancy complications such as inadequate diet and high stress.") See also Chapter 6 of this volume.
19. T. Brennan, L. E. Hebert, N. M. Laird, A. Lawthers, K. E. Thorpe, L. L. Leape, A. R. Localio, S. R. Lipsitz, J. P. Newhouse, P. C. Weiler, and H. H. Haitt, "Hospital Characteristics Associated with Adverse Events and Substandard Care," *Journal of the American Medical Association* 265 (1991): 3265.
20. Ibid.
21. Centers for Disease Control, "Update: Acquired Immunodeficiency Syndrome—United States," 358. ("A history of IV-drug abuse was reported by 2,329 [47.6%] women with AIDS. Heterosexual contact with a man infected with HIV or at high risk for HIV infection accounted for 1,657 [33.9%] cases among women; 64.1% of these male sexual partners were IV-drug users.")
22. C. Levine, "Women and HIV/AIDS Research: The Barriers to Equity," *Evaluation Review* 14 (1990): 447.
23. M. McNulty, "Combating Pregnancy Discrimination in Access to Substance Abuse Treatment for Low-Income Women," *Clearinghouse Review* 23 (May, 1989): 21. ("Most drug treatment programs categorically do not admit pregnant addicts, because clinics lack obstetrical expertise, because a pregnant addict is considered 'high-risk' and drains away a disproportionate share of treatment resources, or because they fear obstetrical malpractice suits. Likewise, prenatal care centers often turn away pregnant women who are addicts, because they lack drug treatment capacity, or because they wish to avoid treating high-risk patients.")
24. See, for example, T. Randall, "Intensive Prenatal Care May Deliver Healthy Babies to Pregnant Drug Abusers," *Journal of the American Medical Association* 265 (1991): 2773.
25. Ibid.
26. The poor African-American and Hispanic women currently hardest hit by the epidemic are culturally and socioeconomically unlike the doctors who treat or refuse to treat them. ("Who the doctor is and where he/she has come from in terms of sociodemographic background, cultural and personality variables, as well as

medical training experience has relevance for how patients are treated and the kind of medicine that will be practiced. Some people are more likely to become doctors than others. The sociodemographic profile which has traditionally characterized the medical profession is disproportionately male, white and upper-middle-class.") D. Roter and J. Hall, *Doctors Talking with Patients/Patients Talking with Doctors: Improving Communication in Medical Visits* (Westport, CT: Auburn House, 1992), 117. (An excellent analysis of the influence of gender, class, and race on the medical care process. See, particularly, "The Influence of Patient Characteristics on Communication between the Doctor and the Patient" [Chapter 3] and "The Influence of Physician Background and Characteristics on Communication Between the Doctor and the Patient" [Chapter 4]). The damaging influence of race, class, and gender bias—conscious or unconscious—on access to, and provision of, medical services and medical technology is well documented and pervasive. See, for example, Council on Ethical and Judicial Affairs, American Medical Association, "Black–White Disparities in Health Care," *Journal of the American Medical Association* 263 (1992): 2344. (Discusses the effect of racial and economic disparities on health status and treatment decisions.)
27. See, generally, Levine and Dubler, "Uncertain Risks," 321.
28. American Medical Association Board of Trustees, "Legal Interventions During Pregnancy: Court-Ordered Medical Treatments and Legal Penalties for Potentially Harmful Behavior by Pregnant Women," *Journal of the American Medical Association* 264 (1990): 2663.
29. J. Glasson and D. Orentlicher, "Caring for the Poor and Professional Liability: Is There a Need for Tort Reform?" *Journal of the American Medical Association* 270 (1993): 1740; K. H. Rothenberg, "Myth and Reality: The Threat of Medical Malpractice Claims by Low Income Women," *Law, Medicine and Health Care* 20 (1992): 403.
30. See W. Keeton, D. Dobbs, R. Keeton, D. Owen, et al., *Prosser and Keeton on the Law of Torts*, 5th ed. Section 1, (St. Paul, MN: West Publishing Company, 1984): 5.
31. Ibid. Section 8, 34. The distinction between intentional vs. negligent acts or omissions is important legally and may impact on the measure of damages awarded. Intentional torts require a "state of mind of intent to exist when the act occurs." Intent includes "Not only . . . having in mind a purpose (or desire) to bring about given consequences but also having in mind a belief (or knowledge) that given consequences are substantially certain to result from the act." Battery is one such intentional tort and is defined as "[a] harmful or offensive contact with a person, resulting from an act intended to cause the plaintiff or third person to suffer such a contact, or apprehension that such contact is imminent." Ibid. Sections 9, 39 (referencing *Second Restatement of Torts*, Section 13.) Negligence, however, requires no intent and refers to conduct which falls below the legal standard established to protect others against unreasonable risk of harm.
32. D. H. Hermann, "Torts: Private Lawsuits about AIDS," in *AIDS and the Law: a Guide for the Public*, eds. H. L. Dalton and S. Burris (New Haven, CT: Yale University Press, 1987): 153.
33. The term "health-care provider" includes individual health-care workers and the institutions (e.g., hospital or nursing home) and organizations (e.g., health-maintenance organizations [HMOs], independent practice associations [IPAs], preferred provider organizations [PPOs]) with which they are affiliated. Both an indi-

vidual health-care worker and the institution or organization may be subject to legal liability for negligently inflicting harm. Since one purpose of tort law is to compensate injured parties for legally cognizable harms, the institution or organization may become the more attractive defendant because it has greater resources than its employee. This shifts the cost of the injury to the party most able to bear the cost. Institutions and organizations may be held vicariously liable for the negligent acts of its employees or directly liable under the theory of corporate negligence. Under the doctrine of vicarious liability, a principle of the law of agency, the employer (master) can be held liable for torts committed by the employee (servant) even though the employer was not itself negligent, provided a master–servant relationship can be established. To establish the existence of such a relationship, the plaintiff must satisfy the legal tests, such as the control, inherent function, or ostensible agency or apparent authority tests used in that jurisdiction. Corporate negligence is liability directly imposed on the corporate entity for its negligence in selecting, supervising, or controlling its staff.

34. In the context of reproductive decision-making, health-care providers are most likely to be held liable for torts based on "harm to the person" or "harm to intangible personal interests." Provider liability associated with harm to property (e.g., trespass) and economic interests (e.g., interference with contractual relations) is unlikely to arise within the context of reproductive decision-making. Intentional torts which allege physical or emotional harm to the person include battery, abandonment, and intentional infliction of mental or emotional distress. Negligence-based torts, other than medical malpractice, which allege physical or emotional harm to the person include negligent infliction of mental distress, negligent nondisclosure, wrongful birth, wrongful conception/pregnancy, wrongful life, breach of confidentiality, and lack of informed consent. These torts are defined throughout the text.

35. For example, Kimberly Bergalis, the young Florida woman who contracted HIV from her dentist during an invasive procedure, sued the dentist's estate and the PPO for which he worked. She sued the PPO under the following three theories: (1) vicarious liability because of the high degree of control the PPO exercised over the dentist; (2) corporate negligence, for failure to investigate and monitor the dentist; and (3) negligent misrepresentation, for advertising that the PPO provided high-quality care. D. Eaton, "The Representation of Kimberly Bergalis: The First Confirmed Transmission of AIDS from a Health Care Worker to a Patient," *Courts, Health Science and the Law* 2 (1991): 14. To establish the tort of negligent misrepresentation, the plaintiff must establish that the provider negligently provided erroneous information in the course of doing business and that the plaintiff relied on this information and suffered some injury due to this reliance.

36. A preponderance of the evidence means a "greater weight of the evidence" and is often explained to juries as a tipping of the scales of justice in favor of one of the parties. F. James, Jr., G. C. Hazard, Jr., and J. Leubsdorf, *Civil Procedure*, Section 7.14 4th edition (Boston: Little, Brown, 1992): 339.

37. R. Schoenstein,"Standards of Conduct, Multiple Defendants, and Full Recovery of Damages in Tort Liability for the Transmission of Human Immunodeficiency Virus," *Hofstra Law Review* 18 (1989): 37. ("This Note focuses on the issue of potential negligence suits against defendants who were unaware of their infection at the time they sexually transmitted HIV.")

38. Improper termination of the relationship by the provider may result in liability for abandonment.

39. Keeton et al., *Prosser and Keeton on the Law of Torts*, see, generally, Section 32, 185–193.
40. Ibid., Sections 41–45.
41. Harms associated with failure to diagnose or failure to inform of a diagnosis would be related to the (1) resultant delay in obtaining proper and available treatment, such as shortened survival time or a worsening of the condition; (2) preventable transmission to third parties; and (3) emotional distress associated with delaying treatment or transmitting HIV to a third party. If a provider misdiagnosed HIV infection as some other condition and treated the patient for a disease or condition the patient did not actually have, the provider could be held liable for injuries caused by improper treatment, such as unneeded and harmful drug therapy or surgery, as well as the harms associated with failure to diagnose HIV. If the provider erroneously diagnosed an individual as HIV-infected, the provider could be held liable for a range of adverse effects caused by the erroneous HIV diagnosis, such as (1) economic harm (e.g., the loss of health insurance, employment, and housing), (2) emotional distress, (3) physical harm (e.g., domestic violence, adverse reactions to needless drug therapy), and (4) suicide, as well as for harms associated with the failure to diagnose the actual disease.
42. See, for example, Centers for Disease Control, "AIDS in Women," 23.
43. Even if the HIV test is negative, there is a possibility that the woman is infected but that the virus is in an incubation period. Liability may result from injuries which stem from not informing the woman of this fact.
44. What reproductive counseling should be provided to HIV-infected men, especially in view of the fact that we do not medically understand the father's role in perinatal transmission? The public health admonition to use condoms may reduce the spread of HIV, but it also prevents male reproduction. Should male reproduction be bounded by public health concerns about preventing sexual transmission any more than female reproduction? Do men have a right to conceive or not conceive a child or to conceive a child at risk for HIV?
45. For these same reasons, informed consent and pretest counseling are recommended requisites to HIV testing (see, for example, Centers for Disease Control, "Recommendations for Prevention of HIV Transmission in Health Care Settings," *Morbidity and Mortality Weekly Report* 36 [1987]: 15S) and, in some instances, legally required by state statute (see, for example, *Maryland Health, General Annotated Code* [1991]: S18–336). Nevertheless, hospitals may not be following these recommendations or requirements consistently. "The fact that a large percentage of women (and men) never return for the results of their HIV test suggests that insufficient time is being devoted to counseling at many test sites." (M. H. Allen and C. Marte, "HIV Infection in Women: Presentations and Protocols," *Hospital Practice* 27 3 [1992]: 160.) This recent observation supports an earlier survey of 561 hospitals, which found that: "One or more officials at 40% of the hospitals reported that patients are never or only occasionally counseled before being tested for HIV infection. . . . At about 15% of the hospitals, at least one official reported that informed consent was not obtained before patients were tested for HIV infection." ("Hospital HIV-Testing Programs Not Protecting Patients," *AIDS Alert* 5 [May 1990]: 81.) Furthermore, it is unclear how much reproductive counseling occurs during the informed consent/pretest counseling phase. Although provider exposure to liability is present at the pretest phase, this chapter is concerned only with the posttest phase of the patient–provider relationship.

46. *Doe* v. *Jamaica Hospital* (affidavit of Vicki Alexander, M.D., at 3). Index no. 31248/89, Supreme Court of New York, Kings County, Nov. 6, 1989 (case reported in *New York Law Journal* [May 6, 1991]: 21). Appeal filed to the Appellate Division, 2d Dept. (1991), Docket No. 92–01085.
47. Ibid., 3–4.
48. N. Kass, "Reproductive Decision Making in the Context of HIV: The Case for Nondirective Counseling," in *AIDS, Women and the Next Generation*, eds. R. R. Faden, G. Geller, and M. Powers (New York: Oxford University Press, 1991): 309.
49. M. Huchinson and A. Kurth, "I Need to Know that I Have a Choice . . . : A Study of Women, HIV, and Reproductive Decision-Making," *AIDS Patient Care* 5 (February, 1991): 17.
50. Ibid.
51. J. R. Botkin, "The Legal Concept of Wrongful Life," *Journal of the American Medical Association*, 259 (1988): 1541.
52. Keeton et al., *Prosser and Keeton on the Law of Torts*, see, generally, Section 55 at 370–373 ("a growing number of 'wrongful conception' or 'wrongful pregnancy' cases are being brought against doctors and others for tortiously failing to prevent the birth of *healthy*, but unwanted children.") Also see, J. Feinberg, "Wrongful Conception and the Right Not to Be Harmed," *Harvard Journal of Law and Public Policy* 8 (1985): 65–66. ("Sometimes, of course, an unplanned and unwanted baby, conceived because of negligence of a third party, is also a deformed or impaired baby, and the suit is both for 'wrongful pregnancy' *and* for 'wrongful birth.'")
53. C. Brown, Editorial Note, "Genetic Malpractice: Avoiding Liability," *University of Cincinnati Law Review* 54 (1986): 857.
54. The judicial acceptance of wrongful birth/life actions is widely attributed to implications inherent in *Roe* v. *Wade*: "For the purposes of this discussion there are two important implications of *Roe*: a woman has a constitutionally protected right to make an informed decision as to whether to terminate a pregnancy; and a geneticist or obstetrician who counsels a woman with respect to her pregnancy has a duty to provide her with any and all available information necessary to make that decision. Thus, one then had an 'injury' for the courts to recognize, that is, a 'wrong' to support the 'wrongful birth' claim." L. Fleisher, "Liability for Prenatal Injury," *Hospital Law* 20 (July, 1987): 97.
55. See, for example, *Park* v. *Chessin*, 400 N.Y.S. 2d 204 (Sup. Ct. 1976), *modified*, 440 N.Y.S. 2d 110 (1977), *modified sub nom. Becker* v. *Schwartz*, 413 N.Y.S. 2d 895 (1978). (Based on the defendant doctor's erroneous assurances that polycystic kidney disease would not occur in subsequent pregnancies, a couple, whose first child died from polycystic kidney disease, gave birth to a second child, who died from the inherited disease prior to the third birthday.)
56. See, for example, *Jorgensen* v. *Meade-Johnson Laboratories*, 483 F.2d 347 (10th Cir. 1973). (Upheld a parental cause of action for prenatal injuries—Down's syndrome—caused by chromosomal damage to the ova of the mother from oral contraceptives ingested prior to conception.)
57. See, for example, *Gleitman* v. *Cosgrove*, 227 A.2d 689 (1967). (Physician wrongfully assured pregnant woman that contracting rubella during pregnancy posed no danger to her developing fetus.)
58. E. Wright Clayton, "What the Law Says About Reproductive Genetic Testing and What It Doesn't," in *Women and Prenatal Testing: Facing the Challenges of Genet-*

ic Technology, eds. K. H. Rothenberg and E. J. Thomson (Columbus: Ohio State University Press, 1994): 131–178.
59. Ibid.
60. Keeton et al., *Prosser and Keeton on the Law of Torts* Section 55, 370–373.
61. Ibid.
62. Arras, "AIDS and Reproductive Decisions," 336.
63. The directive counseling standard has been slowly evolving toward a nondirective standard. The CDC is currently reviewing its counseling standard to be more supportive of women's reproductive choices.
64. Centers for Disease Control, "Recommendations for Assisting in the Prevention of Perinatal Transmission of HTLV-III/LAV and Acquired Immunodeficiency Syndrome," *Morbidity and Mortality Weekly Report* 34 (1985): 721–731.
65. American College of Obstetrics and Gynecology, *Prevention of Human Immune Deficiency Virus Infection and Acquired Immune Deficiency Syndrome* (ACOG Committee Statement no. 53) (Washington, D.C.: American College of Obstetricians and Gynecologists, 1987): 1–4. This statement was withdrawn in December, 1988, but the most recent ACOG statement does not address counseling HIV-infected women who are not pregnant about future pregnancies. "Human Immunodeficiency Virus Infections," in *ACOG Technical Bulletin* (Washington, D.C.: American College of Obstetricians and Gynecologists, 1992): 4.
66. A directive standard, based on public health goals, may be too risky if medicine does not yet understand how abortion or pregnancy affects the course of the disease. Does the lethal nature of HIV infection give women a "special claim" to having children and obligate providers to inform the woman that this may be the only or last child she may ever have? See, for example, K. Nolan, "Ethical Issues in Caring for Pregnant Women and Newborns at Risk for Human Immunodeficiency Virus Infection," *Seminars in Perinatology* 13 (February, 1989): 55. Is a directive standard for women with HIV infection discriminatory because it "counsels HIV-positive women who are pregnant in a manner which is separate, different, unequal and less effective than . . . counseling of other pregnant women who make reproductive choices" (*Doe v. Jamaica Hospital* [Complaint]: 5). Is the directive standard discriminatory because HIV-positive women are predominantly African-American and Hispanic, while nondirective counseling is the standard for genetic reproductive counseling, which predominantly affects white middle-class women?
67. *Doe v. Jamaica Hospital* (Complaint).
68. Ibid., 4–5.
69. Ibid.
70. Ibid.
71. Ibid.
72. Ibid., 5–6.
73. Ibid.
74. Ibid., 6.
75. Ibid., 7.
76. Ibid.
77. Ibid., 9–13.
78. Plaintiff sued both hospitals for discrimination in the provision of medical services under the federal Rehabilitation Act of 1973 and New York State's Human Rights Law. The third count was a violation of equal protection based on discrimination on the basis of handicap and was directed against all the defendants. Ibid.

79. To sustain a claim for the intentional infliction of emotional harm, the plaintiff must prove that the provider intentionally or recklessly engaged in outrageous conduct which caused the plaintiff severe emotional distress. The provider could be liable to members of the patient's family who were present at the time the outrageous conduct occurred or to other witnesses if their emotional distress resulted in physical harm.
80. As reported in P. Mangano, L. Bracken, and J. Ritter, Court Decisions, Kings County, the *New York Law Journal*, May 6, 1991, 27 the court granted the defendant's motion for summary judgment on counts one, three, and four, leaving the plaintiff to go forward on counts two and five. The court's granting of the defendant's motion for summary judgment on those counts is in the process of being appealed. Since this case was first filed, one discrimination count against a physician has been dismissed and an appeal requesting dismissal of the negligence claim has been denied. *Doe v. Jamaica Hospital*, 202 A.D.2d 386, 608 N.Y.S.2d 518 (1994).
81. To sustain a claim for the negligent infliction of emotional harm, the plaintiff must prove that the plaintiff was in the zone of possible physical harm created by the negligence of the provider and that the plaintiff feared for his or her safety. Actual physical contact is not required.
82. The complaint alleged that "[h]ospital personnel failed to provide accurate, understandable information to enable plaintiff to make a fully informed choice about her reproductive life." It further alleged that the type of information the providers should have supplied to the plaintiff included "accurate information about the potential for HIV-positivity in the fetus, about the life expectancy of an asymptomatic HIV-positive person, and about the impact of carrying a pregnancy to term on the health."
83. This shift mirrors the historical development of reproductive counseling for genetic diseases. Kass, "Reproductive Decision Making," 312.
84. For a more detailed discussion, see K. Rothenberg and R. North, "The Duty to Warn 'Dilemma' and Women with AIDS: Redefining the 'Foreseeable Victim,'" *Courts, Health Science and the Law* 2 (1991): 90–96. See also R. North and K. Rothenberg, "Partner Notification and the Threat of Domestic Violence Against Women with HIV Infection," *New England Journal of Medicine* 329 (1993): 1194.
85. Keeton et al., *Prosser and Keeton on the Law of Torts* Section 117. (The tort of invasion of privacy may take several forms, including (1) the appropriation of another's name or likeness, (2) the "unreasonable and highly offensive intrusion upon the seclusion of another," (3) the "public disclosure of private facts," and (4) the placing of another in a "false light in the public eye.")
86. Defamation is an "invasion of the interest in reputation and good name" and may be oral (slander) or written (liable). Ibid., Section 111.
87. Rothenberg and North, "The Duty to Warn," 92 (quoting Keeton et al., *Prosser and Keeton on the Law of Torts* Section 56, 375).
88. Ibid., 93.
89. K. H. Rothenberg, S. J. Paskey, M. N. Reuland, et al., "Domestic Violence and Partner Notification: Implications for Treatment and Counseling of Women with HIV," *Journal of the American Medical Women's Association* 50 (1995): 87.
90. Rothenberg and North, "The Duty to Warn," 94.
91. Ibid., 94–96.

92. G. T. Hotaling and D. B. Sugarman, "An Analysis of Risk Markers in Husband to Wife Violence: The Current State of Knowledge," *Violence Victims*, 1 (1986): 101.
93. K. H. Rothenberg and S. J. Paskey, "The Risk of Domestic Violence and Women with HIV Infection: Implications for Partner Notification, Public Policy and the Law," *American Journal of Public Health* 85 (1995): 1569–1576.
94. Rothenberg and North, "The Duty to Warn," 95.
95. In contrast, the flip side of the decision not to conceive is the decision to conceive. What level of reproductive services should be provided to further the woman's desire to bear a child, particularly if the woman is infertile? Does a provider have a duty to inform about or provide extraordinary means, such as in vitro fertilization, to help the woman conceive? Is there a duty to inform the woman of the process of sperm washing to reduce the risk of reinfection or perhaps perinatal transmission? Since the sweep of the pediatric AIDS epidemic will be determined by the reproductive decisions of HIV-positive women, providers may be reluctant to offer them assisted reproductive services. As a practical matter, since HIV currently disproportionately affects poor minority women, such expensive, high-tech services will not be made available to many of these women due to their inability to pay the costs associated with them (also see Chapter 8 of this volume).
96. See H. L. Minkoff and J. A. DeHovitz, "Care of Women Infected with Human Immunodeficiency Virus," *Journal of the American Medical Association* 266 (1991): 2253–2258.
97. Allen and Marte, "HIV Infection in Women," 155–162.
98. Z. A. Stein, "HIV Prevention: The Need for Methods Women Can Use," *American Journal of Public Health* 80 (1990): 460.
99. Levine and Dubler, "Uncertain Risks," 344.
100. Many state legislatures have enacted conscience clauses which permit providers to refuse to perform abortions based on ethical considerations.
101. As an exception to this general rule, hospitals have a common law and statute-based duty to provide emergency medical care to stabilize those who arrive at the emergency room in need of emergency services. See K. H. Rothenberg, "Who Cares?: The Evolution of the Legal Duty to Provide Emergency Care," *Houston Law Review* 26 (1989): 21–76.
102. See Chapter 8 of this volume for a discussion of antidiscrimination legislation.
103. *Ricks v. Budge*, 64 P.2d 208 (1937).
104. Generally speaking, physicians must disclose information about the (1) diagnosis, (2) preferred course of treatment and risks associated with it, (3) medically recognized alternatives to the preferred course of treatment and risks which accompany them, and (4) prognosis with and without treatment. Risks which are within common knowledge or which the physician did not know of and should not have known of need not be disclosed by the provider. Physicians may have a therapeutic privilege to withhold information from a patient if disclosure would seriously impede treatment or cause significant psychological harm to the patient. Physicians need not disclose information if the patient specifically requests not to be told.
105. Under common law and some state statutes, physicians in emergencies may provide treatment without obtaining consent, consent being presumed in these circumstances.
106. Both the duty to disclose and the doctrine of informed consent seek to protect

patient self-determination and autonomous decision-making as well as bodily integrity. Harm to these interests was originally actionable only under the tort of battery: a nonconsensual touching in the form of a medical procedure or treatment. Battery-based informed consent claims have been abrogated in many states and supplanted by negligence-based torts, such as negligent nondisclosure.

107. Nolan, "Ethical Issues," 7–8.
108. Ibid., 8.
109. R. S. Sperling, P. Stratton, and Obstetric-Gynecologic Working Group of the AIDS Clinical Trials Group of the National Institute of Allergy and Infectious Diseases, "Treatment Options for Human Immunodeficiency Virus–Infected Pregnant Women," *Obstetrics and Gynecology* 79 (1992): 443.
110. Ibid.
111. Centers for Disease Control, Public Health Services and Department of Health and Human Services, "USPHS/IDSA Guidelines for Prevention of Opportunistic Infections in Persons with Human Immunodeficiency Virus: A Summary," *Morbidity and Mortality Weekly Report* 44 (1995).
112. Ibid., 444.
113. Stein, "HIV Prevention," 155–162.
114. Allen and Marte, "HIV Infection in Women," 155–162.
115. See Chapter 3 of this volume.
116. Centers for Disease Control, "U.S. Public Health Service Recommendations for Human Immunodeficiency Virus Counseling and Voluntary Testing for Pregnant Women," *Morbidity and Mortality Weekly Report* 44 (1995): 1.
117. Ibid.
118. See, for example, G. A. Shelley and R. Howard, "A National Survey of Surgeons' Attitudes About Patients with Human Immunodeficiency Virus Infections and Acquired Immunodeficiency Syndrome," *Archives of Surgery* 127 (February 1992): 206–212. When queried in a recent survey whether they would perform a needed colon resection for carcinoma on an HIV-infected patient, "[m]ost (73%) answering surgeons indicated they would perform the surgery, but 18% said they would refer the patient to another medical center, while 4% said they would find a reason not to operate and another 4% admitted they would refuse to operate. If the patient was not only infected with HIV but also had AIDS, fewer (66%) of the surgeons claimed they would operate." When asked whether they would perform an elective procedure, an augmentation mammoplasty, "[o]nly 19% of the surgeons said they would operate on a patient infected with HIV . . . and only 12% said they would do so if the patient had AIDS." While only 13% admitted to ever refusing to operate on an HIV-infected patient and 15% admitted to ever refusing to operate on an AIDS patient, 72% of the surgeons surveyed indicated that they never or almost never had operated on HIV-infected or AIDS patients.
119. B. Almond and C. Ulanowsky, "HIV and Pregnancy," *Hastings Center Report* 19 (March–April, 1990): 16–21.
120. A. R. Localio, A. G. Lawthers, T. A. Brennan, N. M. Laird, L. E. Herbert, L. M. Peterson, J. P. Newhouse, P. C. Weiler, and H. H. Haitt, "Relation Between Malpractice Claims and Adverse Events Due to Negligence: Results of the Harvard Medical Practice Study III," *New England Journal of Medicine* 325 (1991): 245–251. This result corroborates earlier studies and reports, such as one study conducted in California, which concluded that "for each medical malpractice claim, 10 injuries were caused by negligent care," and a report which found that "[n]inety

percent of the potentially successful causes of action due to medical negligence never result in lawsuits." Perkins and Stoll, "Medical Malpractice," 1280.
121. Perkins and Stoll, "Medical Malpractice," 1280.
122. Hilfiker, "Are Poor Patients More Likely to Sue," 1391–1392. ("The perception that poor patients sue more for medical malpractice is a damaging myth.")
123. Ibid.
124. Brennan et al., "Hospital Characteristics," 3265.
125. Allen and Marte, "HIV Infection in Women," 155.
126. Ibid.
127. In contrast, medical malpractice defense work is generally conducted on an hourly charge basis, with the attorney recovering fees regardless of the outcome.
128. For example, damages for a 30-year-old woman with symptomatic AIDS and a projected life span of 5 years who suffered a disabling injury from medical negligence would be less than those for a healthy 30-year-old woman with a normal projected life span suffering an identical disabling injury because of the difference in projected life span.
129. Ibid.
130. When HIV begins to affect increasing numbers of white middle-class women, the risk calculus may change. This group of women may be more likely to recognize the occurrence of an injury, better able to afford to sue, and more likely to have family members able to press the suit and will be likely to recover more. Notwithstanding these advantages, any HIV-positive plaintiff has substantial legal hurdles to overcome once at trial. The burden of proof in a tort action is on the plaintiff. The plaintiff must establish each element of the claim by a preponderance of the evidence. Establishing the standard at the time of treatment, as well as the breach of an evolving standard, and defining and quantifying the harm may be extremely difficult with HIV.
131. Localio et al., "Relation Between Malpractice Claims," 245.
132. Ibid.
133. Ibid., 249. In addition to practicing medicine at the standard required by the profession and reducing overall the occurrence of negligence, empirical evidence suggests that providers can reduce actual malpractice claims by improving their communications with patients. A recent study, which surveyed 127 Floridian families who had filed claims for birth-related injuries, examined the reasons why families filed lawsuits. (G. Hickson, E. Wright Clayton, P. Githens, and F. Sloan, "Factors that Prompted Families to File Medical Malpractice Claims Following Perinatal Injuries," *Journal of the American Medical Association* 267 (1992): 1359–1363.) The reasons why the families filed are illuminating: while 24% filed to obtain funds for long-term care, 20% filed when they realized the child had "no future" and 19% wanted to deter future incidents of malpractice or obtain revenge on the physician; 33% filed because someone, often another doctor, advised them to file (or, alternatively, the families had interpreted comments by the subsequent treating physician as recognition of an injury or advice to sue); 24% filed because their physician was not honest about the circumstances of the injury; and 20% filed because it was the only way they could determine what caused the injury. Families believed physicians failed to recognize fetal distress (53% of sample), manage fetal distress appropriately (57%), or perform a cesarean section (33%) or that physicians were unavailable when needed (29%). (Percentages add up to over 100% because respondents might have more than one reason.) "Of all families interviewed 32%

believed that their physicians would not talk or answer questions, 13% that their physicians would not listen, 48% that their physicians had misled them, and 70% that no one involved in providing medical care during the perinatal period ever told them that their infants might have permanent medical problems or die." 1361.
134. Liability issues for men remain unexplored. Questions to be explored include the following: Can the father of a child bring a wrongful birth action for the birth of an HIV-infected child if the health-care provider failed to inform him of the mother's positive status? How do state confidentiality statutes affect the father or the health-care provider? What remedy does a man have if he has a vasectomy in reliance on a health-care provider's erroneous assessment of risk of perinatal transmission?
135. Bayer, "AIDS and the Future," 179.
136. See, for example, D. Koropp Note, "Setting the Standard: A Mother's Duty During the Prenatal Period," *University of Illinois Law Review* 1989 (1989) 493. ("The Note will suggest that, rather than disallow prenatal tort actions completely, courts should adopt a stringent standard for maternal liability that requires gross negligence and precludes liability for failure to submit to medical procedures designed solely to benefit the fetus.")
137. See, for example, M. Oberman, M. Ruhle, P. Logli et al. "Symposium: Substance Use During Pregnancy: Legal and Social Responses," *Hastings Law Journal* 43 (1992) 505–660.
138. While the historical development of third-party liability for prenatally inflicted injuries has been discussed at length elsewhere (see, for example, R. Beal, "'Can I Sue Mommy?': An Analysis of a Woman's Tort Liability for Prenatal Injuries to her Child Born Alive," *San Diego Law Review* 21 (1984): 325), the notion of maternal liability was prophetically raised at the turn of the century. At that time, when state courts still refused to recognize a child's cause of action against any third parties for prenatally inflicted injuries, one court noted that if such actions could be maintained against third parties "it necessarily follows that an infant may maintain a cause of action against its own mother for injuries occasioned by the negligence of the mother while pregnant with it." (*Allaire* v. *St. Luke's Hospital*, 56 N.E. 638 [Ill. 1900]). The exclusion of prenatally injured children from recovery against third parties was attributed to (1) the lack of a duty to the unborn child, due to the perception that at the time of the injury, the mother and child were a single entity, with "any damage to (the fetus) which was not too remote to be recovered for at all was recoverable by the (mother)"; (2) the difficulty in proving causation between the act or omission and the prenatal injury; and (3) lack of precedent (*Bonbrest* v. *Kotz*, 65 F. Supp. 138, 141–142 [D.C. 1946]).
139. *Bonbrest* v. *Kotz*, 141–142.
140. The shift roughly coincided with technological developments, which caused a corresponding shift in medical perception from viewing the fetus and mother as one patient to viewing them as two patients. (See, for example, S. Mattingly, "The Maternal–Fetal Dyad: Exploring the Two-Patient Obstetric Model," *Hastings Center Report* 22 [January–February, 1992]: 13.)
141. Liability was then conceived of more in terms of parental liability rather than maternal liability. While a shift in perception to gender-based reproductive liability is apparent, it is equally apparent that a similar concept of paternal reproductive liability is not developing.
142. Parental immunity is often abrogated in cases where the parent's liability insurance (e.g., automobile insurance) provides compensation for the injury. Since the parent

purchased insurance protection against accidental injuries, compensation received from the insurer is seen as promoting, rather than harming, family harmony, thereby negating the doctrine underlying the rationale. Parental immunity for perinatal transmission of HIV is not likely to be abrogated due to the availability of liability insurance: even if such coverage were available, the women currently hardest hit by the epidemic would not be underwritten or would be underwritten at an affordable cost.

143. *Goller v. White*, 122 N.W.2d 193 (1963).
144. *Gibson v. Gibson*, 479 P.2d 648, at 652 (Cal. 1971) (quoting *Goller v. White*, 122 N.W.2d 193, 198 [1963]).
145. Ibid.
146. Ibid., 652–653.
147. Ibid.
148. Cognizant of such differences, a New York State court (in the context of negligent parental supervision) rejected a reasonable parent standard because "[e]ach child is different, as is each parent . . . [c]onsidering the different economic, educational, cultural, ethnic and religious backgrounds which must prevail, there are so many combinations and permutations of parent–child relationships that may result that the search for a standard would necessarily be in vain—and properly so." *Holodook v. Spencer*, 324 N.E.2d 338, 346 (N.Y. 1974).
149. *Grodin v. Grodin*, 301 N.W.2d 869 (Mich. Ct. App. 1980).
150. The mother's physician had assured her she could not become pregnant and she did not know she was pregnant until her seventh month. Upon learning she was pregnant, she stopped taking the drug.
151. *Grodin v. Grodin*, 869.
152. Ibid., 870.
153. However, in deciding a later case, *Mayberry v. Pryor*, 352 N.W. 2d 322, (Mich. App. Ct. 1984), the Michigan Court of Appeals stated that *Grodin* was "incorrectly decided" based on a misinterpretation of the Plumley Rule (Ibid., 832, 352 N.W. 2d 324). "Proper application of the Plumley exceptions requires a determination, not of the reasonableness of the defendant's conduct but rather of the scope of 'reasonable parental authority' and of 'reasonable parental discretion.'" (Ibid., 833, 352 N.W. 2d 325): Questions regarding the scope of Plumley exceptions are questions of law to be decided by the judge. The Supreme Court of Michigan declined the opportunity to decide the controversy (*Mayberry v. Pryor*, 374 N.W.2d 683, [Sup. Ct. Mich. 1985]).
154. M. Shaw, "Conditional Prospective Rights of the Fetus," *Journal of Legal Medicine* 5 (1984): 63.
155. At the time of this writing, the administration of zidovudine (AZT) to pregnant HIV-infected women has been shown to reduce the rate of perinatal transmission of the virus under certain circumstances in certain women. Centers for Disease Control, "Zidovudine for the Prevention of HIV Transmission from Mother to Infant," *Morbidity and Mortality Weekly Report* 43 (1994): 285–287.
156. Shaw, "Conditional Prospective Rights," 63.
157. V. Kolder, J. Gallagher, and M. Parsons, "Court-Ordered Obstetrical Interventions," *New England Journal of Medicine* 316 (1987): 1192.
158. *Stallman v. Youngquist*, 473 N.E.2d 400, (1st Dist. 1984), *appeal after remand*, 504 N.E.2d 920 (1st Dist. 1987), *reversed*, 531 N.E.2d 355–359 (Ill. 1988).
159. Ibid., 359.

10

Perinatal Drug Use: State Interventions and the Implications for HIV-Infected Women

KATHERINE ACUFF

> I am an addict, and I did use drugs when I was pregnant. And I am very sorry. And I have many regrets. However, it is an addiction, it is a disease. And you don't punish someone for having cancer. You don't punish someone for having MS. . . . You will always have it, but you can arrest it, if you do the things that need to be done. Punishing someone for being sick is ridiculous. It's ludicrous.
>
> *woman from Baltimore*

> Throwing her in jail, it gets worse. She will come out of there worse, you know. Well, give her the help she needs, all the help they could give her. If it comes to a point that after she gets out she don't, don't . . . then take the kids away from her. I mean, because she is getting the help she needs, and she still does not want to help herself? The kids, they don't need to go through that. Take them away from her and maybe like that, maybe she will realize, maybe like that, she will open her eyes, you know, like it happened to me. Not no jail, no, that is worse.
>
> *woman from New York*

The epidemics of HIV and drug use[1] among women of childbearing age have ignited a tinderbox of public sentiment favoring state interventions to monitor or constrain women's behaviors relating to reproduction. As discussed throughout this volume, alarm about vertical transmission of HIV has prompted some to advocate the rejection of the traditional nondirective reproductive counseling paradigm (developed in the context of counseling women about genetic risks) in favor of advising HIV-infected women not to reproduce.[2] Evidence suggests that frankly directive counseling against having children is often the case.[3] The federal government's only official statement on the issue sanctioned this shift in policy. In 1985, the CDC recommended that HIV-infected women "be advised to consider delaying pregnancy until more is known about the perinatal transmission of the virus."[4] Given the paucity of knowledge both about the course of HIV infection in women and the factors affecting perinatal transmission, the implication of the CDC's recommendation is that HIV-infected women should forego childbearing altogether. Many states' health departments have adopted the

CDC's message, developing materials explicitly recommending that HIV-infected women avoid pregnancy.[5]

Governmental interventions affecting pregnant or postpartum drug users have been considerably more forceful than the reproductive advisories issued for HIV-infected women. The leading edge of the federal drug policy in the current drug epidemic was captioned as a "war on drugs"[6] under the Reagan and Bush administrations and was characterized by a strong emphasis on legal interdiction, punishment, and having "zero tolerance" for drug users, all at the expense of preventive and treatment measures.[7] Although the Clinton administration appears to favor shifting federal dollars to prevention and treatment, it is unclear whether the current administration will significantly change federal policy in this regard.

The preference for legal solutions to drug use has been apparent in governmental responses to pregnant and postpartum women who are discovered to be drug users. Since the mid-1980s there has been widespread legislative, administrative, prosecutorial, and judicial activity concerning perinatal drug use. Hundreds of bills have been introduced in state legislatures and dozens have been passed. Although some of the proposed legislation has been crafted to promote treatment options for drug-dependent pregnant women and their children, much has a decidedly more punitive flavor, implicitly framing the issues in terms of fetal protection (against the woman). These measures include mandated reporting of suspected prenatal drug use to state authorities, mandated drug testing of newborns, and modified civil commitment provisions to target pregnant drug users.

The 1990 National Drug Control Strategy contained an appeal for states to modify their child abuse and neglect statutes to strengthen their response to parental drug use and several have done so.[8] State and local child-protective services (CPS) departments have also been active.[9] Even without statutory modifications to incorporate prenatal exposure to drugs as evidence of harm or neglect, state and county CPS departments frequently have acted aggressively to remove drug-exposed newborns.

Coercive state interventions aimed at controlling prenatal drug use fall into three general categories: (1) criminal justice measures, which include actual and threatened criminal prosecutions of pregnant or postpartum women; (2) coerced treatment measures based generally on a mental health model which may, but need not, operate via formal commitment proceedings; and (3) child protection measures which, although usually activated immediately postpartum, have also been cited to justify interventions affecting pregnant women based on fetal protection. The distinctions between these types of intervention, however, are not always, and perhaps not even usually, crisp.

Consider the following fictitious, but not unrealistic, example. An obstetrician tests a pregnant patient for drugs without her consent and reports the positive results to the medical social worker, who reports the positive test to a local prosecutor, who then threatens prosecution on charges of possession of a controlled substance. Charges will not be filed, provided the woman agrees to seek prenatal care and undergo drug treatment. Upon delivery, when her newborn tests positive, the newborn (and perhaps its siblings) are placed into foster care by CPS. Now the woman is charged not only with possession of a controlled substance but also with criminal child neglect and delivery of drugs to a minor. She plea bargains to the lesser charge of possession, is sentenced to 5 years' probation, and is ordered to submit to the implantation of Norplant.[10] In an agreement with CPS, she agrees to "successfully" be treated for her drug addiction to regain custody of her children. There is no assistance from the child protection agency in finding a treatment program for her.

Rather than encouraging addicted women to seek prenatal care and drug treatment, such state responses to prenatal drug use may do just the opposite. A General Accounting Office (GAO) report noted: "Women are reluctant to seek treatment if there is a possibility of punishment. They also fear that if their children are placed in foster care, they will never get the children back."[11] Because all of these interventions depend upon the cooperation of health professionals to report test results to state authorities, drug-dependent women may well view the health system as an adjunct to the legal system. Although theoretically only criminal prosecution is punitive, because of the unavailability and (often) inadequacy of drug treatment, social support, and child care for pregnant women, it is difficult for a woman to view as benign any intervention that results in the placement of her children into foster care until she is successfully treated for drug addiction.[12] Without the realistic chance of obtaining effective woman-centered drug treatment, even women who are motivated by their pregnancies to enter treatment are likely to view contacts with health-care professionals as brushing too close to the law for comfort. Anecdotal reports suggest that this is often the case.[13] A study based on 150 interviews with drug-involved women in New York City indicated that, although women are particularly motivated during pregnancy to seek drug treatment:

> Penalizing approaches that underscore guilt and shame may be counterproductive and deter women from use of such services, as 42% said that guilt and shame over their drug use was their principal reason for avoiding prenatal care.[14]

The constellation of legal responses to perinatal drug use bears on the reproductive decision-making of pregnant HIV-infected women in several ways. Before enumerating them, however, it is useful to divide HIV-infected women into those who are themselves drug users and those who are not. In the United States, HIV infection among women is inextricably linked to injection drug use: 48% of HIV infections among women are attributable to the woman's own drug use and another 19% to sexual contact with injection drug-using partners.[15]

Among the half of HIV-infected women who are, or were, drug users (i.e., dually affected), legal interventions based on drug use during pregnancy have an impact on reproductive decision-making in at least two ways. First, legal interventions introduce dynamics that may result in the delay or avoidance of HIV testing, prenatal care, and drug treatment. This delay increases the risks of adverse medical, obstetrical, and pediatric outcomes[16] in part because many pregnant women will continue drug use and risk behaviors associated with HIV infection throughout their pregnancies.[17] Second, treatment-seeking delays often make moot the argument about directive vs. nondirective prenatal counseling by shifting the woman's contact with health-care providers until very late in the pregnancy, often to labor and delivery.[18]

Setting aside the constitutional and ethical objections to coercive drug treatment for pregnant women (which is, I acknowledge, no small matter),[19] for women who are dually affected there are some potentially beneficial side effects of coercive state interventions for drug use. For example, it may be that mandating the reporting of prenatal drug use to CPS will increase the vigilance of health professionals in assessing perinatal drug use and, consequently, lead to more women being offered HIV counseling and testing and being identified earlier as HIV-infected. Furthermore, the association of HIV with drug use may lead to compelled treatment for HIV piggybacked onto an order for compelled drug treatment and prenatal care. To the degree that early identification and treatment could preserve an HIV-infected woman's health for a longer period, it may open a window for safer pregnancies (although the research is incomplete in this regard), allowing her to care better for her child(ren). In addition, now that a regimen of zidovudine (AZT) taken by certain pregnant women under certain circumstances has been shown to reduce the rate of vertical transmission of HIV, there is a potential benefit to her newborn as well.[20]

State interventions for prenatal drug use may also have an indirect impact on policies concerning HIV-infected women by offering blueprints for punitive fetal protection policies and generating increased acceptability for them. Although some states have developed policies providing therapeutic interventions for drug-using women and their children, others have taken a harsher approach in their efforts to compel women to accept treatment or to modify their behaviors.[21] Such state interventions are not unique to cases of prenatal drug use,[22] but the illegal nature of drug use has given additional justification for those promoting aggressive fetal protection policies.[23] It is possible that similar state interventions could be applied to shape the reproductive decision-making of HIV-infected women as well.

In this chapter, I examine state interventions that have been used to control and monitor the behaviors of pregnant or postpartum drug users, with a particular focus on the impact of these drug-related interventions on the reproductive behaviors of HIV-infected women.[24] Additionally, I evaluate the potential for direct application of some or all of these drug-related interventions in controlling the reproductive behaviors of HIV-infected women who are not drug users. I do so based not only on the available treatments for HIV but also on the likelihood of medical advances allowing for the prevention or cure of perinatally acquired HIV infection.

Scope of the Drug and HIV Epidemics Among Women

Until recently, there were no national data on the prevalence of drug use among pregnant women. Estimates were based on the numbers of newborns testing positive at largely urban public teaching hospitals. The most widely quoted estimates, based on anonymous testing at delivery, suggest that there may have been at the epidemic's peak as many as 375,000 drug-exposed infants born per year, or about 11% of all births in the United States.[25] The results of the first national survey looking at the prevalence of drug use among pregnant women, announced by the National Institute on Drug Abuse (NIDA) in September 1994, provide substantially lower estimates.[26] NIDA's National Pregnancy and Health Survey, conducted between October 1992 and August 1993, provided estimates of 5.5%, or 221,000, of the approximately four million women giving birth during this time used some illicit drug during pregnancy. Many more women of childbearing age, however, are current drug users. The National Household Survey on Drug Abuse for 1991 indicated that 9.5% of women between the ages of 18 and 34 years had used illicit drugs within the prior month, a figure which jumps to 20.1% within the prior year.[27] Approximately 250,000 of these were IDUs.[28] Although the National Pregnancy and Health Survey data suggest a decline in the prevalence of drug use among pregnant women, there is some cause for concern in the recent report that drug use among eighth graders and high school students was sharply up in 1994.[29]

Although most published studies have focused on drug use among women in large urban hospitals, prenatal drug exposures are not limited to urban areas. A recent study comparing drug exposures of infants in four counties in Illinois found a high prevalence of drug use in rural counties.[30] Another study of public health clinics in Alabama found no difference between urban and rural groups for any drug tested.[31]

Prenatal exposure to illicit drugs, while significant, is dwarfed by the numbers of newborns who have been exposed prenatally to alcohol and nicotine. Not only are the numbers of pregnancies affected much higher for alcohol and nicotine than for illicit drugs but the nature of the harm to the fetus is better understood. Prenatal exposure to alcohol is believed to be the single greatest preventable cause of mental retardation.[32] Nevertheless, state interventions in cases of prenatal drug use have been more aggressive and more harsh than for any other prenatal risk factor.[33]

State Interventions and Drug-Involved Pregnant Women

Although drug use during pregnancy has long been recognized as a potential hazard to the continuation of a pregnancy and to the health of the fetus and newborn, state interventions related to drug use during pregnancy did not reach a crescendo until the cocaine epidemic of the 1980s and early 1990s. This section reviews the use of criminal sanctions, the child abuse and neglect machinery, and the variety of avenues for compelled treatment. I acknowledge, but do not here examine, the therapeutic models of intervention that some states have chosen.

Criminal prosecution

The state intervention generating the most controversy is the criminal prosecution of women for having used drugs during their pregnancies.[34] Although most advocacy and professional groups oppose criminal sanctions (see Table 10.1), a recent study of obstetricians, pediatricians, and hospital-based social workers found that 30%–40% either "somewhat agreed" or "strongly agreed" that criminal sanctions were appropriate in cases of prenatal drug use.[35]

Furthermore, criminal prosecution has considerable popular support. In 1989, an *Atlanta Constitution* opinion poll reported that 71% favored criminal sanctions against women who use illegal drugs during pregnancy and give birth to a seriously damaged newborn.[36]

As a percentage of the number of women believed to use illicit drugs during pregnancy, the number of criminal prosecutions is relatively modest. As of mid-1992, there were over 160 reported cases in over 20 states.[37] Criminal prosecutions have been fairly restricted chronologically, as well as regionally. Only two cases were reported prior to 1985, the year usually cited as the beginning of the recent crack cocaine epidemic, and relatively few have been brought since 1991. This slowing of criminal prosecutions is believed to be, in large part, because of a wait-and-see stance of many prosecutors while the Florida Supreme Court considered the criminal conviction of Jennifer Johnson, a case discussed later in this chapter. Disproportionate numbers of the prosecutions come from only two states, Florida and South Carolina, and are concentrated in two counties within these states.[38]

Although many states have introduced legislation that would criminalize prenatal drug use, none of it has been enacted.[39] In fact, in none of the cases where women have been prosecuted for having taken drugs or alcohol during their pregnancies has the prosecution been based on statutes crafted for that purpose. Rather, the prosecutions have been an outcome of excessively broad prosecutorial discretion in stretching existing laws to fit.[40]

Four legal theories have been used to charge women who have used drugs during their pregnancies:

TABLE 10.1. Organizations Opposing Criminal Prosecution of Women for Prenatal Drug Use[a]

American Academy of Pediatrics
American Civil Liberties Union
American College of Nurse Midwives
American College of Obstetricians and Gynecologists
American Medical Association
American Medical Students Association
American Nurses Association
American Public Health Association
American Society of Addiction Medicine
Association of Marriage and Family Therapists
Association of Maternal and Child Health Programs
Association of Maternal and Child Health Therapists
Center for Child Protection and Family Support
Center for Law and Social Policy
Center for Science in the Public Interest
Child Welfare League of America
Children of Alcoholics Association
Coalition on Alcohol and Drug Dependent Women and Their Children
Criminal Justice Policy Association
Legal Action Center
March of Dimes
National Abortion and Reproductive Rights Action League
National Association for Children of Alcoholics
National Association of Alcoholism and Drug Abuse Counselors
National Association of Perinatal Addiction Research and Education
National Association of Public Child Welfare Administrators
National Black Women's Health Project
National Council of Jewish Women
National Council on Alcohol and Drug Dependence
National Family Planning and Reproductive Health Association
National Mental Health Association
National Women's Health Network
National Women's Law Center
NOW Legal Defense and Education Fund
Southern Regional Project on Infant Mortality
Women's Legal Defense Fund

K. L. Moss, letter, American Civil Liberties Union Reproductive Rights Freedom Project, September 23, 1991: J. Dinsmore, *Pregnant Drug Users: The Debate Over Prosecution* (Alexandria, VA: National Center for the Prevention of Child Abuse, American Prosecutors Research Institute, 1992): Appendix A.

[a]This is only a partial list. Many state medical associations have also registered their opposition to criminal prosecution of pregnant drug users.

1. Possession of a controlled substance.
2. The delivery of a controlled substance to a minor via the umbilicus during the few seconds after birth but before the umbilicus is clamped (this is an attempt to avoid the obvious difficulties of having to find the fetus to be a "minor").

3. Criminal child abuse or neglect.

4. Manslaughter (in cases of stillbirth or death during the neonatal period).[41]

Usually, but not always, the "evidence" of the crime consists of a positive drug test of the woman's newborn.

Courts in these cases overwhelmingly have agreed with defense arguments that the statutes relied on by prosecutors were never intended to be applied to prenatal drug use and have dismissed criminal charges based on these theories.[42] In only two cases have women been tried and found guilty, and both of the convictions have been reversed at the appellate level.[43]

The best known criminal prosecution for drug use during pregnancy is the 1989 conviction of Jennifer Johnson, a case remarkable not only for being the first based on the charge of delivery of drugs to a minor[44] but also for the nature of the sentence.[45] The Florida court accepted the prosecutor's argument that the statutorily proscribed "delivery" occurred via the umbilical cord during the 60–90 seconds after birth before the cord was clamped. Ms. Johnson was sentenced to 15 years of probation, which included at least 1 year in a drug-treatment program. Additionally, Ms. Johnson's probation was conditioned on her not using drugs or alcohol (determined by random drug tests), getting a high school equivalency diploma, remaining employed, and performing 200 hours of community service. Moreover, Ms. Johnson was ordered to notify the court and enter a judicially approved prenatal program should she again become pregnant. The Florida Court of Appeals upheld Ms. Johnson's conviction.[46]

In July of 1992, however, the Florida Supreme Court unanimously overturned Ms. Johnson's conviction, stating that "the court declines the state's invitation to walk down a path that the law, public policy, reason and common sense forbid it to tread."[47] Citing numerous amicus briefs, the court concluded that drug-dependent women faced with a threat of criminal prosecution would tend to avoid prenatal and medical care or even resort to abortion. Criticizing the prosecutor's discretion in charging Ms. Johnson, the court noted that:

> [T]he Legislature never intended for the general drug delivery statute to authorize prosecutions of those mothers who take illegal drugs close enough in time to childbirth that a doctor could testify that a tiny amount passed from mother to child in the few seconds before the umbilical cord was cut. Criminal prosecution of mothers like Johnson will undermine Florida's express policy of "keeping families intact" and could destroy the family by incarcerating the child's mother when alternative measures could protect the child and stabilize the family.[48]

Further, the court noted that "prosecuting women for using drugs and 'delivering' them to newborns appears to be the least effective response to this crisis."[49]

The Florida Supreme Court's reversal of the Johnson conviction, coupled with the refusal of most state courts to try criminal cases against women regarding drug use during pregnancy, demonstrate the judicial resolve not to endorse criminalization of prenatal drug use. Whether prosecutors will abandon their efforts, however, is unclear. In May of 1992, prosecutors filed criminal charges of child abuse against a pregnant Nebraska woman for being an alcoholic, expanding the use of the criminal justice system not only to the prenatal period but also to the use of legal substances.[50] Furthermore, simply tallying the numbers of criminal court proceedings gives a significant underestimate of the power of the criminal law in the context of prenatal drug abuse. The most common outcome of the filing of criminal charges is not a trial but rather for women to plead guilty or plea bargain for a lesser charge, circumventing the courts altogether.[51] Most attorneys representing the women charged fail to challenge the validity of charges even though they are based on statutes that were never intended to be applied to prenatal drug use.[52] As a result, "many women in America are serving jail terms or are on probation for non-existent crimes."[53]

Finally, as discussed in the next section, some prosecutors (and others) believe that the threat of criminal prosecution is an essential adjunct to therapeutic approaches to prenatal drug use by giving women an additional incentive to accept recommended treatment.

Coerced treatment

Pregnancy is often a catalyst for women to seek drug treatment.[54] Women who attempt to get treatment for drug dependencies, however, face formidable barriers. The first of these is a chronic shortage of drug-treatment facilities. The National Association of State Alcohol and Drug Abuse Directors estimates that there are at least 280,000 pregnant women in need of drug treatment, only about 11% of whom are in treatment.[55] Treatment for cocaine dependencies, the drug driving the most recent epidemic, is even more limited in part because there is no pharmacological equivalent to methadone for cocaine to reduce the cravings and allow outpatient treatment. Moreover, the problem of access to treatment is even more severe for pregnant women.[56] Treatment facilities cite inadequate links with the medical community to provide prenatal care and concerns about liability as the principal reasons for their reluctance to treat pregnant women.[57]

Notwithstanding the lack of facilities for women who would voluntarily seek drug treatment, some advocate measures to compel pregnant drug users to enter treatment, arguing that compulsory treatment for pregnant drug users is a more enlightened policy choice than criminal prosecution. This, however, is a false choice. In a recent examination of the potential role of civil commitment in dealing with perinatal substance abuse, David Chavkin notes:

> While a civil commitment system is more enlightened than a criminal justice or CPS model, its implementation is at best premature. Unless and until there are an adequate number of appropriate treatment programs for women seeking alcohol or drug dependency treatment on a voluntary basis, there is no justification for diverting the level of

financial resources necessary to implement a civil commitment system or for bumping women seeking voluntary treatment in favor of court-committed women.[58]

Before discussing the several mechanisms used to institute treatment, it should be pointed out what can constitute treatment in this context. Prenatally, the emphasis of interventions is to promote good birth outcomes via prenatal care and drug abstinence for the duration of the pregnancy. Postpartum, however, the interest in ensuring that women continue to get adequate medical care and drug treatment (which must include counseling) often fades. For women who have been fortunate enough to receive drug treatment during their pregnancies, there is often an inadequate period of follow-up after delivery and little social support to ensure successful outcomes. Furthermore, women who retain custody of their newborns face child-care responsibilities that may interfere with their drug treatment. Finally, postpartum women may find themselves in competition with pregnant women for drug-treatment slots. A few states mandate that priority be given to the drug treatment of pregnant women and, in others, concerns for the fetus/newborn may outweigh those for the postpartum woman.[59] Ironically, with chronic shortages in drug-treatment capacity, pregnancy preference statutes could provide an incentive for women to become pregnant to get access to drug treatment.

In this chapter, I take a broad view of what constitutes "coerced" treatment.[60] I include not only those situations in which the state mandates confinement and treatment but also situations where there is no viable choice but to "agree" to treatment. So defined, I have found at least five variations of coerced treatment applicable to pregnant or postpartum drug users: (1) civil commitment, (2) the criminal prosecution vs. treatment "option," (3) treatment as a condition for retaining or regaining custody of children,[61] (4) the de facto detoxification treatment resulting from harsher sentences for pregnant offenders who test positive for drugs, and (5) the compelled use of contraceptives.

It must be emphasized that information about the frequency with which these strategies are employed in cases of perinatal drug use is generally unavailable either by examination of public records or by reference to published studies. Civil commitment, agreements with CPS, and treatment options in the context of the threat of criminal prosecution usually are not published even though the legal system clearly authorizes such actions. Likewise, the coerced use of contraceptives, which has appeared in conditions for probation or child protection agreements, is unlikely to appear in the public record. Moreover, de facto treatment is part of no official record, published or not, and often is discernible only by parties familiar with particular cases. Finally, I know of no studies of the frequency of coerced treatment for perinatal drug use.[62] As a result, conclusions about the relative significance of coerced treatment as an intervention are impossible to make. Nonetheless, some form of coerced treatment is used at least occasionally in these cases and is often cited as a legitimate option for addressing perinatal drug use.

In all cases where treatment is imposed involuntarily, one must consider that, to the degree that some women (including women who are HIV-infected) who are unwilling to seek care are coerced to enter drug treatment, other women who would voluntarily do so could be squeezed out.

Civil commitment

The clearest example of coerced treatment is the involuntary confinement of a person, generally on the grounds that an individual presents a danger to himself or herself or to others. Civil commitment is a creature of statutory law and expresses a mental health model (as opposed to a criminal justice model) for state intervention to compel persons to undergo treatment. It is defined as follows:

> Involuntary civil commitment is the legal process—operating at the confluence of the public safety, justice, and social service systems—whereby an individual found to pose a harm to self or others as a result of a mental or physical impairment or disability is forced to undergo treatment or care."[63]

Because involuntary confinement for treatment represents such "a massive curtailment of liberty," courts have insisted that states ground involuntary civil commitment on either their *parens patriae* power (danger to self) or their police power (danger to others) and adhere to certain safeguards.[64] The core criteria for involuntary civil commitment for mental illness are danger to self or others.[65] In addition, courts have generally required evidence of the lack of less drastic alternatives and of the likelihood that the respondent will benefit from treatment.

Although most states statutorily provide for the involuntary confinement of the mentally ill, there is considerable variability in whether or not state statutes permit the compulsory treatment of drug users. State statutes fall into five categories, shown in Table 10.2.

Twenty-three states and the District of Columbia clearly have the civil commitment machinery in place to involuntary detain at least some drug-dependent (pregnant) women for treatment. Minnesota alone specifies pregnant women as a category of persons subject to civil commitment.[66] The civil commitment statutes of four states are clear in excluding involuntary detention based on drug dependency. For the remaining 22 states, however, their authority to involuntarily detain pregnant drug users is uncertain, either because they have civil commitment statutes which cover mental illness without reference to drug dependency or because they lack a civil commitment statute altogether.

Identifying the states with the authority to involuntarily commit certain persons for treatment is not particularly revealing about how vulnerable pregnant drug users are to being committed. The law specific to drug use is not well

TABLE 10.2. Classification of States' Civil Commitment Statutes According to Their Application to Drug-Dependent Pregnant Women

Statutes targeting drug-dependent women

Minnesota

Statutes authorizing involuntary civil commitment of drug-dependent persons

Arkansas	California
Missouri	Connecticut
New Mexico	District of Columbia
North Carolina	Florida
North Dakota	Oklahoma
Georgia	Rhode Island
Hawaii	Iowa
South Carolina	South Dakota
Kansas	Texas
Louisiana	Washington
Massachusetts	West Virginia
Mississippi	Wisconsin

Statutes relating to civil commitment for mental illness (with no mention of drug use)

Alabama	Nevada
Indiana	Oregon
Kentucky	Tennessee
Maine	Vermont
Michigan	Virginia
Nebraska	

Statutes with no provisions relating to civil commitment

Colorado	New Jersey
Delaware	Ohio
Idaho	Pennsylvania
Illinois	Utah
Maryland	Wyoming
Montana	

Statutes excluding civil commitment for drug dependency

Alaska	New Hampshire
Arizona	New York

S. Anderson Garcia and I. Keilitz, "Involuntary Civil Commitment of Drug-Dependent Persons With Special Reference to Pregnant Women," *Mental and Physical Disabilities Law Reporter* 15 (1991): 418.

developed, but, in general, civil commitment for mental illness has required a showing of actual and imminent danger to self (*parens patriae*) or others (police power). In these cases, the legal trend has been to make these criteria very difficult for a state to meet and, as a consequence, very difficult to involuntarily confine a person.

In cases of drug dependency, however, the danger to self criterion may be substantially easier to meet; often the civil commitment of drug-dependent persons can be accomplished by merely providing evidence of drug dependency and a "need for treatment."[67] Arguably, any drug-dependent pregnant woman not already in drug treatment, and perhaps prenatal care, could satisfy this standard. Although the need for treatment criterion presumably is based on the danger to self posed by continued drug use, it is not difficult to imagine that the focus of treatment could be primarily prenatal care, with detoxification constituting its drug "treatment." The danger here is the development of a fetus/newborn-only focus to "need for treatment." A troubling scenario would be to confine a woman for the duration of her pregnancy, render only prenatal care, and then release her without having provided adequate drug treatment.[68]

Minnesota's 1989 statute significantly erodes the criterion for civil commitment by eliminating the need to show actual drug dependency (as defined in the substance abuse literature and the DSM III). In the case of a pregnant woman, a mere showing of drug use is sufficient.[69]

Minnesota's statute first defines a "chemically dependent person" as any person

> (a) determined to be incapable of self-management or management of personal affairs by reason of the habitual and excessive use of alcohol or drugs; and (b) whose recent conduct as a result of habitual and excessive use of alcohol or drugs poses a substantial likelihood of physical harm to self or others as demonstrated by (i) a recent attempt or threat to physically harm self or others, (ii) evidence of recent serious physical problems, or, (iii) a failure to obtain necessary food, clothing, shelter, or medical care.[70]

Minnesota's statute then singles out pregnant women as special cases of chemically dependent persons, stating that any woman who

> has engaged during pregnancy in habitual or excessive use, for a non-medical purpose, of any of the following controlled substances or their derivatives: cocaine, heroin, phencyclidine, methamphetamine, amphetamine falls within definition of a "chemically dependent person."[71]

Minnesota's statute does not provide a definition for excessive use, but it is clear that many people, including health professionals (who are instrumental in the civil commitment process), believe that any drug use during pregnancy is excessive.

The alternative criterion for civil commitment is a showing of danger to others. To date, no state has explicitly found that fetal drug exposures satisfy the danger to others criterion, although Minnesota's statute, with its relaxed definition of drug dependency for pregnant women, arguably is based on this justification.

There are no reported cases concerning prenatal drug users challenging the additional criteria that a civil commitment be the least drastic alternative or that treatment be effective.

An alternative argument for the involuntary confinement of pregnant women for their prenatal behavior is not through a civil commitment of the woman but rather straightforwardly, filing a petition with the court based on the state's *parens patriae* power "for custody of the fetus, which would necessarily involve confining the woman."[72] Under this proposal, offered by Denise Cahalane, the two standards for court intervention would be based on the viability of the fetus and the nature of the pregnant woman's behavior. Prior to the third trimester, courts could not intervene unless the woman is incompetent. However, Cahalane argues that "under egregious circumstances where the woman is clearly in her third trimester and her viable fetus is in danger, the court should intervene to override her right to liberty and order confinement for the sake of the viable fetus."[73] Cahalane's example of "egregious" behavior is noncompliance in controlling diabetes. There is no doubt under her proposal that drug use also would be classified as sufficient cause to involuntarily confine pregnant women for the sake of their fetuses.

Criminal prosecution and the link to coerced treatment

For many years, treatment in lieu of prosecution or sentencing has been available to courts in dealing with certain types of offenders who also are confirmed drug users.[74] Although not as much in favor during the current war on drugs as it was in the 1970s, the Treatment Alternatives to Street Crime program (only one of a series of incarnations) continues to receive funding through the Criminal Justice Block Grant. Under this program, a criminal offender who also is found to be addicted may be diverted to a drug-treatment facility either before prosecution or instead of being sentenced to a prison term. This program has not raised controversy as applied to pregnant women who have committed crimes. This concept, however, sometimes has been turned on its head in the context of perinatal drug use: instead of offering drug treatment and rehabilitation as an alternative to prosecution or a jail term for crimes committed, the criminal justice system has created a new category of criminal—drug-using women who become pregnant—and then used the threat of criminal prosecution to compel treatment. The failure to agree to treatment or to "successfully" complete treatment drives the criminal prosecution.

Proponents of this use of the criminal justice system argue that women often are unreachable without the threat of criminal prosecution looming in the background and that actual prosecution is used only as a last resort. This was the approach implemented in Charleston County, South Carolina, which continued in spite of several lawsuits until late 1994.

In 1989, personnel from the Obstetrics Clinic of the Medical University of South Carolina (MUSC) approached the Charleston County solicitor with information about cocaine use[75] detected in pregnant and postpartum women at the MUSC-operated County Memorial Hospital, the county's health-care facility for the indigent. The outcome of this encounter was the October 1989 Interagency Policy on Cocaine Abuse During Pregnancy,[76] which specifies the threat of criminal prosecution as an inducement for women to enter prenatal care and drug treatment.[77]

Consent for drug testing was contained, in very small print, in the Consent for Medical Treatment form required as a condition for treatment at the hospital.[78] Drug testing was done on the basis of a clinical protocol requiring drug testing of women showing certain clinical indicators.[79] The intensity of the interventions triggered by a positive drug test depended on whether the positive drug test was obtained prenatally or at labor and delivery.

Under the policy, a woman testing positive for cocaine prenatally was shown a film on the dangers of prenatal cocaine use and asked to sign a Letter Agreement with the County Solicitor, under which she accepted a referral to the Substance Abuse Commission to *successfully* complete the commission's program, maintain "clean" urine screens, and continue prenatal care (emphasis added).[80] In return, the county solicitor deferred criminal prosecution. Failure to sign or comply with the agreement resulted in arrest.

At labor and delivery, a positive drug test triggered a similar set of events but included a referral to the Department of Social Services to determine the newborn's risk in remaining in the mother's custody. Failure to cooperate at this stage resulted in the mother's arrest and the filing of a charge of unlawful neglect of a child.[81] According to the Charleston Police Department's Operational Guidelines the purpose of the policy was as follows:

> Pregnant women abusing illegal drugs is a growing problem that poses potentially fatal consequences for the unborn child. This threat to human life has necessitated police intervention in those instances where pregnant females have rejected opportunities to *voluntarily* obtain assistance in stopping their abuse of dangerous drugs.[82] (emphasis added).

Sensitive to criticisms, researchers at MUSC, together with the local prosecutor,[83] published a preliminary outcomes report which argued that the success of MUSC's "prospective management protocol" was evidenced by a significant decline in the number of cocaine-positive urine drug screens among obstetrical patients.[84]

The researchers either discounted or failed to address alternative explanations clearly endorsing the view that, at least for prenatal drug use, the end justifies the means:

> This policy was not designed as a punitive measure, but it was felt necessary to add some teeth to our counseling (sic) efforts. The threat of exposure and arrest does appear to be a deterrent to cocaine use. Nonetheless, it must be emphasized strongly that the program goal has been fetal protection, not maternal prosecution. . . . This preliminary report is offered to support a combined medical/legal approach to the cocaine problem.[85]

Between August 1989 and September 1994, more than 90 women in Charleston and Greenville, South Carolina, were charged with either criminal neglect of a child or distribution of drugs to a minor and at least 43 others were forced to undergo treatment.[86] In October 1993, the Center for Reproductive Law and Policy filed suit in federal district court on behalf of two women prosecuted under the MUSC program and a class of other similarly situated women on several constitutional grounds. In January 1994, it filed a complaint with the National Institutes of Health Office for Protection from Research Risks as well, arguing that the hospital's effort constitutes research on human subjects in violation of federal law.[87] On September 1, 1994, under the threat of losing $18 million in federal research money, MUSC reached an agreement to stop reporting perinatal drug use to the police.[88]

Although most professional and advocacy groups interested in women's and children's health are opposed to criminal sanctions, the National Center for Prosecution of Child Abuse of The American Prosecutors Research Institute (APRI) has endorsed criminal sanctions as an important policy component in dealing with women who use drugs during their pregnancies. In March of 1992, APRI published a report, *Pregnant Drug Users: The Debate Over Prosecution*, which addressed a variety of arguments opposing criminal sanctions in this context. The APRI Report states:

> These arguments wrongly assume that prosecution automatically equals incarceration. Prosecution can be an avenue to treatment and does not necessarily involve incarceration at all. . . . The criminal justice system is . . . the most powerful tool available to enforce treatment when [treatment] is refused. It also provides for a range of options including probation, diversion, deferred prosecution, or treatment in lieu of incarceration.[89]

Although conceding that criminal prosecutions for prenatal drug use have disproportionately affected poor, minority women, the APRI report not only discounts the adverse consequences of such prosecutions but also makes the claim that the failure to offer the "benefit" of coerced treatment to poor, minority women could actually be viewed as discrimination in not affirmatively protecting the welfare of poor, minority fetuses and children.

> Some prosecutors have been asked whether they could be accused of being racist if they *ignored* the impact of crack cocaine and other illegal drugs on minority births and older siblings. Although middle class mothers may be using drugs at the same rate, wealthier families have more resources to take care of kids, and they tend not to come to the attention of public agencies. *Poor children need advocates looking out for their rights.*[90] (emphasis added)

For APRI, prosecuting pregnant women is a form of advocacy for poor children. APRI completely disregards the impact of prosecution on women.

Treatment as a condition for retaining or regaining custody of children

"Voluntary" treatment agreements entered into in connection with supervision by CPS constitute the third category of coerced treatment. These so-called agreements are often the outcome of reports of positive newborn drug tests to CPS. The agreements sometimes include the removal of newborns (and siblings) and their placement into foster care; the return of the children is then conditioned upon the woman's successful completion of drug treatment. Unfortunately, CPS agreements often are not accompanied by a guaranteed slot in any treatment program (or even a preference), let alone a program that has child care or is otherwise woman-centered. Thus, it is sometimes difficult, if not impossible, for a woman to fulfill her end of the CPS agreement. Moreover, given the chronic, relapsing nature of drug dependency, the appropriate measure of "successful treatment" is vague, leaving complete discretion to child protection workers.

De facto commitment

Sometimes courts have, de facto, compelled the treatment of pregnant women by ordering jail terms for offenses where probation is the usual and customary sentence or by giving longer sentences, sometimes explicitly for the "duration of the pregnancy," to female offenders who test positive for drugs. The Illinois case of LeeAnn Moore is a good illustration. In this case, a judge who had initially released Ms. Moore without bond on a charge of disorderly conduct, subsequently (after her urine test came back positive for cocaine) put her under 24-hour guard in the Al-Care drug-treatment center in Rockford until her delivery, due later in the month.[91] In the order, the judge omitted mention of Moore's pregnancy or the threat of continued drug use on the fetus. The prosecutor, however, confirmed to reporters that those were the reasons his office had sought the court order.[92]

Coerced birth control or abortion

Drug-using women, particularly pregnant and postpartum women, get strong messages not to reproduce (again) from the negative attitudes of health professionals,[93] drug-treatment counselors, and the courts. These messages probably infrequently are coercive in a strict definition of that term, but given the restricted choices of many poor, drug-using women, they can come very close.

Another source of the message not to reproduce originates in the context of drug treatment where strongly directive counseling to undergo sterilization or to "be Norplanted" apparently is an integral part of some programs which target pregnant women. A nurse practitioner discussing an inpatient program for pregnant cocaine users in Baltimore, Maryland, candidly reported that "we won't *let* our postpartum women leave without some form of birth control. Ninety-five percent of our women agree to be sterilized or get Norplant before they leave the program." This seems to be an unusually high rate of compliance and is unlikely to be solely the result of the drug counselors' persuasive powers.[94] No doubt a contributing influence is the fact that women very often are referred to drug-treatment programs by CPS or the courts, which condition child custody or probation on successfully completing drug treatment.[95] Many courts have registered their disapproval of "some" women reproducing; but as long as courts resist criminalizing drug use during pregnancy per se, compelled contraception or sterilization will not be imposed directly on women for their perinatal drug use.

In other types of case, however, the courts have imposed birth control as a condition of probation, particularly when the case involves child abuse. For example, in 1991, a California judge ordered a woman to submit to the implantation of Norplant as a condition of her probation on child abuse charges.[96] In January 1993, a Tennessee couple, convicted of molesting the woman's two children, was given a choice of each serving 10 years in prison or, provided the woman agreed to sterilization, both being put on probation.[97] Given the efforts to shoehorn prenatal drug use into child protection legislation and the obvious distaste of some courts for drug use by women, the potential for courts to compel birth control for drug-using women is palpable. When judges are more likely to charge women who use drugs or to give them harsher than usual sentences, this risk increases. Women who are dually affected by drugs and HIV infection may well be particularly vulnerable to disproportionate sentencing or conditions for probation.

Coerced abortions may not be as likely as coerced birth control, but at least one author, George Schedler, argues that society has a right to force women who persist in drug abuse during pregnancy to undergo abortions:[98]

> My argument in brief is that, first, society has a duty to insure that infants are born free of avoidable defects, and, second, that those defects caused by chemical abuse of the pregnant mother are easily avoided. Third, it follows that society can prevent pregnant addicts from giving birth.[99]

Schedler rejects arguments that providing improved access to drug treatment would have a significant impact on reducing drug use during pregnancy:

> I remain pessimistic about the prospect that the social costs of drug abuse during pregnancy can be alleviated as much by voluntary programs as by a program of mandating abortions. Women are not likely to participate in voluntary treatment programs in large numbers. . . . Although coercing women into having abortions is regrettable, we cannot be sure that noncoercive measures will avoid injuries to children and tremendous costs for society.[100]

Measures to prevent childbearing by drug-using women are rarely direct components of a state's interventions, but a strong message to women not to have children until drug treatment is complete is a key component of many government-funded drug-treatment programs and CPS and some courts have freely woven birth control into their orders. Concern about directive reproductive counseling of HIV-infected women must be assessed in this context.

Interventions by CPS

The most common engagement of the state by health professionals in the context of perinatal drug use is reporting evidence of prenatal drug use (usually positive newborn drug tests) to CPS. Although all states have child abuse and neglect legislation that mandates reporting of suspected abuse or neglect, only a few states specify that the use of illicit drugs during pregnancy is a covered harm triggering the child protection reporting requirement.[101] Nonetheless, CPS offices have taken reports of prenatal drug exposure as evidence of potential risk of harm to newborns—that is, they have assumed the authority to act—and have prevented newborns from going home upon their mothers' hospital discharge, ordered home visits, removed the newborns (as well as older siblings) to foster care, and frequently persuaded courts to support their actions.

It should be noted that CPS has a range of options (and considerable discretion) open to it in responding to reports of perinatal drug use, including both civil and criminal actions. Both charges of criminal child neglect and CPS agreements that include a mandatory treatment component were discussed earlier in this chapter. This section discusses only civil interventions prompted by a report to CPS.

Early in the drug epidemic, CPS offices often automatically removed newborns who tested positive for drugs, or whose mothers tested positive, and placed them into foster care.[102] In New York, such automatic removal policies resulted in massive expansion in the numbers of children in foster care and sharp increases in the numbers of children kept in hospitals after the discharge of their mothers.[103] The results of these routine removals included not only budgetary and staffing problems for CPS but genuine questions about the suitability of foster placements as compared to offering treatment and supportive services to drug-using women. Automatic removal policies, together with the tendency of CPS to intervene disproportionately in poor families of racial and ethnic minorities, have been soundly, and I believe appropriately, criticized as a "reflex reaction of child protective agencies and courts in the absence of sufficient alternatives to guarantee children's safety."[104] As a result, New York City and other jurisdictions have instituted protocols requiring evidence beyond drug test results to support child protection petitions.[105]

Today, in many jurisdictions CPS will not even accept a report for prenatal drug use unless the newborn tests positive (a positive drug test of the mother is insufficient) and there is additional evidence that the newborn is at high risk (e.g., no prenatal care, maternal behavior).[106] Furthermore, gross understaffing of CPS agencies and growing caseloads limit investigation to only the most egregious cases.[107] Fear of being reported to CPS is a strong disincentive for women to seek medical care and, particularly, to self-report drug use. It is unclear whether "news" of the diminished likelihood of CPS to automatically remove one's children is well enough understood on the streets to mitigate this disincentive.

State Interventions and Reproductive Decision-Making of HIV-Infected Women

The purpose of examining the potential for state interventions concerning pregnant women who use drugs is to assess the cloud such interventions may create in the context of reproductive counseling of, or decision-making by, HIV-infected women. For the most part, this array of state interventions would act only indirectly to constrain a woman's willingness to engage the medical system out of fear of punishment or loss of her children. The risk of such interventions for HIV-infected women is a function of several factors:

1. Whether or not they are pregnant.
2. Whether or not they have other children.
3. Whether or not they are also drug users (i.e., dually affected).
4. Whether or not they have committed a crime (other than using drugs while pregnant) or have another cofactor of legal significance (e.g., child neglect).
5. The development of treatments that can prevent or cure vertically transmitted HIV infection.

In all of the drug use scenarios discussed in this chapter, the state interventions have been initiated (or proposed) in the context of women who are pregnant or who have children. Most concern women who are either pregnant or immediately postpartum and have as their underlying rationale either fetal protection or punishment of the woman or both, though "treatment" for women also usually is provided at some level.

Pregnancy has been the stimulus for criminal prosecutions, harsher sentencing, civil commitment, or agreements with CPS. Although nonpregnant women who use drugs or who are HIV-infected or who are dually affected may be subjected to directive counseling against childbearing, the state is unlikely to intervene to prevent pregnancy unless the woman is before a court for disposition in a child abuse or neglect case. In such cases, the court and CPS may decide to impose birth control to prevent subsequent pregnancies as a condition of probation or for regaining custody of children.

Dually affected pregnant women—those who are both drug users and HIV-infected—may find themselves particularly susceptible to state scrutiny by virtue of the illegal nature of drug use. As a result, they may be subject to compelled treatment not only for their drug use and prenatal care but also for their HIV/AIDS. This is particularly true given the results of the AIDS Clinical Trials

Group (ACTG) 076 study, which showed that an AZT regimen given to certain pregnant women reduced by two-thirds the rate of transmitting HIV infection to their newborns.[108] In addition, their status as dually affected pregnant women may well increase the severity of state criminal sanctions or child protection orders.

Criminal prosecutions of HIV-infected women

The most powerful effect of the criminal law on the reproductive decision-making of HIV-infected women is probably indirect: the threat of prosecution of pregnant women for drug use. As previously discussed, this threat not only jeopardizes the health of both the woman and her fetus by delaying drug treatment and increasing the potential for exposure to HIV but also restricts a woman's access to reproductive counseling, thus limiting her reproductive choices.

It is unlikely that the criminal law could be used to directly prosecute a woman for perinatally transmitting HIV to her fetus or newborn. Although cases have been brought for intentionally exposing another to HIV and for even threatening HIV exposure, these cases generally have been unsuccessful. The arguments supporting prosecution for vertical transmission would be even more difficult to support, particularly if the only sure way to completely avoid vertical transmission is not to reproduce. Even in light of the ACTG 076 results, it seems unlikely that a woman could be successfully prosecuted for failing to take AZT during pregnancy.

Coerced treatment

The justification for any coerced medical treatment is that there is some beneficial intervention available. In the context of treating pregnant drug users, there are two components: (1) cessation or reduction of the drug use, which stops or minimizes fetal exposure; and (2) since the woman is already in the provider's office, the provision of prenatal care which, many drug users either avoid or otherwise fail to get. Provision of either prenatal care or drug treatment improves birth outcomes, and, if effective drug treatment is provided, the woman benefits directly as well. As a result, although rarely legally or ethically justified, coerced treatment of a drug-using pregnant woman at least has a medical benefit.

In contrast, the "state of medicine" regarding the treatment of HIV infection among asymptomatic individuals is in disarray, with no clear guidance about whether AZT delays symptoms of AIDS or prolongs life.[109] Patients and physicians must weigh the costs and benefits of AZT therapy in designing individual treatment plans. Therefore, coerced treatment of an asymptomatic HIV-infected woman, whether or not pregnant, does not offer even the pretext of clear benefit for the woman and would not, at this time, be sufficiently persuasive to fuel civil commitments, treatment in lieu of criminal prosecution, or CPS agreements.

What about a rationale of compelling treatment of pregnant women based on benefit to the fetus? Until recently, there was no intervention shown capable of preventing or reducing vertical HIV transmission, but the 1994 findings of the ACTG 076 study—that AZT reduces to approximately 8% the HIV vertical transmission rate in certain pregnant women under certain circumstances— provides the rationale of potential benefit to the fetus. Although the research is insufficient thus far to allow identification of the cases in which AZT is most likely to interrupt transmission and the long-term effects of AZT treatment of pregnant women and their newborns are still under investigation, the evidence of reduced transmission rates may give states a stronger rationale to require both HIV testing and AZT treatment for HIV-infected, drug-dependent women, particularly if there is potential benefit to the woman as well. Even without a maternal benefit, however, if the treatment caused the woman minimal harm (other than being confined or coerced), it might be attempted.[110]

For a woman with AIDS-related opportunistic infections, some treatment may be medically indicated for her and, if pregnant, for the benefit of her pregnancy. Nevertheless, without a legal mechanism such as civil commitment or a colorable legal cofactor (e.g., probation, child custody), it would be difficult, but perhaps not impossible, for a court to intervene. If a woman were gravely ill with AIDS-related infections and late in her pregnancy, a physician might seek a court order to mandate treatment for the duration of the pregnancy, although the physician would be doing so against the recommendations of the American College of Obstetricians and Gynecologists.[111] Furthermore, if a woman with AIDS were so ill that she was unable to care for her children, then CPS could condition continued custody on her seeking treatment, though inability to care for one's children is not "neglect" in the true sense.

Paradoxically, if an HIV-infected pregnant woman is actually committed for drug abuse treatment, her health options potentially could be improved.[112] In addition to drug treatment, perhaps a woman would receive prenatal care, which could include HIV counseling and (the offer of) testing, resulting in earlier detection and more time to consider reproductive options. Treatment could also include therapy for HIV infection or AIDS, perhaps extending the woman's period of relative health. Counseling about reproduction could also take place; whether or not discussion of abortion would be included in this counseling would be a function of the type of facility and the state of pregnancy at which the woman was detained.

Interventions by CPS

Unless an HIV-infected woman were so ill with AIDS that her ability to care for her children was impaired or she was also a drug user, CPS would not have even colorable jurisdiction to remove her children based solely on her HIV-infected status.

TABLE 10.3. Characteristics of Perinatal Drug Exposure and Maternal HIV Infection

	Perinatal Drug Exposure	Maternal HIV Infection
Ability to detect harm prenatally	Self reports of drug use, medical assessment, and drug testing of woman or newborn are the means used. All have limitations, and no prenatal or postnatal assessment is correlated to level of impairment or harm to newborn.	Infection status of pregnant women is easily established by serum antibody testing. Most tests cannot determine infection of the fetus.
Risk of harm to newborn	Impossible to quantify. Depends upon the drug, the frequency and chronicity of use, and the timing and type of gestational exposure (e.g., polydrug, alcohol and tobacco, lack of prenatal care, poor nutrition).	Approximately 25%–30% risk of vertical transmission without AZT. Drug use and its accompanying pregnancy risk are also present in approx. 50% of cases of maternal infection.
Magnitude of harm	Difficult to assess. The most consistent findings are prematurity, low birth maturity, low birth weight, and small head circumference. A small percentage show evidence of neurological impairment at birth, no longer evident by the age of 2 yr and within the normal range of intelligence.	Approx. 50% of children with HIV show symptoms within 6 months and die by age 2 yr. A small percentage are significantly impaired at birth. Others have remained symptom-free for years, though many require extensive medical intervention. Some are in elementary school and show no signs of illness.
Interventions	Both prenatal care and drug treatment improve birth outcomes. Prenatal care, even without drug treatment, improves birth outcomes.	Clinical trials of AZT in certain pregnant women have shown significant reduction in the rate of vertical transmission under certain circumstances.

Conclusion

Drug use opens an avenue for states to intervene forcefully to constrain the behavior of pregnant and postpartum women. Because of the strong association of drug use with HIV infection, these interventions affect the lives and decision-making of HIV-infected women in ways that must be considered when formulating policies concerning reproductive counseling.

One point about pregnancy in cases of either drug use or HIV infection is that the potential for fetal harm is of uncertain magnitude and cannot by itself explain or justify bringing the coercive power of the state into play, particularly when so few resources are available for women to voluntarily seek treatment, counseling, and support. Table 10.3 shows some of what is known about perinatal drug exposure and maternal HIV infection.

Coercive or punitive state interventions employed in the case of drug-using pregnant and parenting women, including the threat of incarceration, compelled treatment, and lost custody of children, provide strong disincentives to voluntary encounters with health-care providers. Insofar as they result in inadequate utilization of medical care, such state interventions have the perverse public health outcomes of increasing obstetrical and medical risks and reducing the opportunity for reproductive counseling. Once identified as drug-dependent, women additionally are faced with strong implicit, as well as explicit, messages about not reproducing, independent of their HIV status.

In most cases, the application of a similar set of state interventions to HIV-infected women who are not also drug users is unlikely to be significant under the current state of medical knowledge about perinatal transmission (even with the recent ACTG 076 results). Should the means to fully prevent or cure vertical transmission of HIV—without onerous side-effects to the woman or her newborn—become available, the likelihood that women could be mandated to accept treatment would increase.

Appendix-Selected Public Policy Statements Concerning Criminal Prosecutions of Women for Prenatal Drug Use

American Academy of Pediatrics

The public must be assured of nonpunitive access to comprehensive health care which will meet the needs of the substance-abusing pregnant woman and her child.

American Medical Association

Criminal sanctions or civil liability for harmful behavior by the pregnant woman toward her fetus are inappropriate. . . . Therefore be it . . . resolved that the AMA opposes legislation which criminalizes maternal drug addiction.[114]

American Nurses Association

ANA opposes any legislation that focuses on the criminal punishment of the mothers of drug-exposed infants. ANA recognizes alcohol and other drug problems as treatable illnesses. The threat of criminal prosecutions is counterproductive in that it prevents many women from seeking prenatal care and treatment for their alcohol and other drug problems.[115]

American Public Health Association

The APHA believes that no punitive action should be taken against pregnant users of illicit drugs when no other illegal acts, including drug-related offenses, have been committed.[116]

American Society of Addiction Medicine, Inc.

The American Society of Addiction Medicine is deeply committed to the prevention of alcohol and other drug-related harm to the health and well-being of children. The most humane and effective way to achieve this is through education, intervention and treatment.[117]

Coalition on Alcohol and Drug Dependent Women and Their Children

The Coalition opposes the criminal prosecution of women solely because they were pregnant when they used alcohol or drugs. The Coalition also opposes the mandatory reporting of women with positive drug toxicologies to government officials. . . . The criminal prosecution of addicted women solely because they are pregnant is both inappropriate and counterproductive. There is no evidence that a policy of criminal prosecution will either prevent prenatal drug exposure or improve children's health. Rather, prosecution of alcoholic and drug dependent women will very likely deter them from seeking both prenatal care and treatment for their addiction, resulting in increased risks to the health and well-being of women and their children. Moreover, the trend to apply punitive measures in a disproportionate manner to low-income women and women of color, raises serious concerns about discrimination. Prosecution is particularly inappropriate given the lack of drug treatment services available to pregnant women and the nature of addiction and the socioeconomic circumstances of many of these women's lives. Experts agree that alcoholic and drug dependent women need comprehensive services which address not only their addiction and any underlying mental health needs, but also their medical and health needs during pregnancy, and housing and child care needs.[118]

March of Dimes

Punitive approaches to drug addiction may be harmful to pregnant women because they interfere with access to appropriate health care. Fear of punishment may cause women most in need of prenatal services to avoid health care professionals. . . . The March of Dimes is opposed to the use of such sanctions as a method of facilitating good pregnancy outcomes and generally considers such approaches to be contrary to the best interests of the mother and child.[119]

National Association of Public Child Welfare Administrators

If a jurisdiction elects to mandate drug testing of pregnant women and newborns such testing must be universal (i.e., testing would be conducted on all pregnant women and newborns at all medical facilities and not targeted at specific populations). Test results should be used only to identify families in need of treatment and make referrals. Positive test results should not be used for punitive action.[120]

National Council on Alcoholism and Drug Dependence

(A) punitive approach is fundamentally unfair to women suffering from addictive diseases and serves to drive them away from seeking both prenatal care and treatment for their alcoholism and other drug addictions. It thus works against the best interests of infants and children. . . . Moreover, there is increasing evidence of disparities regarding the screening and reporting of positive toxicologies of newborns, with women of color, poor women and women receiving care in public hospitals having the greatest likelihood of being subject to drug testing and subsequent reporting to legal authorities.[121]

Notes

1. Two points should be made about the terminology used in this chapter. First, the term "drug use" means the use of illicit drugs, such as heroin, cocaine, and

marijuana, as well as the nonmedical use of licit drugs, such as barbiturates and amphetamines. Alcohol use is not included unless specifically indicated. Second, drug or substance "abuse" and drug "dependence" have specific medical definitions, though the literature is careless in usage. According to the *Diagnostic and Statistical Manual of Mental Disorders* (4th ed.), ed. M. B. First (Washington, DC: American Psychiatric Association, 1994): (DSM-IV), 175–272. these terms have the following meanings:

Abuse: Defined as a maladaptive pattern of substance use with repeated and adverse consequences recurrently over at least a 12-month period in the absence of tolerance and withdrawal.

Dependence: Characterized by "a cluster of cognitive, behavioral, and psychological symptoms indicating" continued substance use despite significant adverse consequences. Dependence usually results in tolerance, i.e., requiring larger doses to get the same effect, or withdrawal symptoms when regular intake is stopped or curtailed.

It is important to note that determinations of neither abuse nor dependence can be made on the basis of a single toxicology test, which is generally the means used to detect drugs in the pregnant woman or her newborn. To make medical diagnoses of abuse or dependence, it is necessary to inquire about adverse social outcomes, tolerance, withdrawal, and, as evidence for "pathological use," a history of excessive use and inability to reduce use. In the context of drug use by pregnant women, the medical sense of the term "abuse" has shifted to a legal (or moral) sense. Although there is little argument that drug use by pregnant women is a social problem, most of the state interventions described in this chapter apparently are based on the belief that any drug use during pregnancy is abusive to the fetus and justifies state action. A recent law review article captures this view in its coinage of the term "gestational substance abuse" to mean the "abuse of alcohol or drugs by a pregnant woman." The author clearly considers any use during pregnancy to constitute abuse. See K. R. Lichtenberg, "Gestational Substance Abuse: A Call for a Thoughtful Legislative Response," *Washington Law Review* 65 (1990): 377–396.

2. J. D. Arras, "AIDS and Reproductive Decisions: Having Children in Fear and Trembling," *The Milbank Quarterly* 68 (1990): 353–382. Arras argues that in the case of HIV-infected women the nondirective counseling model should be abandoned in favor of a model where women are educated about their moral obligations to their fetuses, including tours of the pediatric AIDS unit at the "local hospital to see for themselves what happens to some of the unlucky infants."

3. One of the concerns about endorsing directive counseling is that, given the knowledge advantage and the inherent power differential between physicians and their patients, "directive" counseling will edge very close to "coercive" counseling. This power differential is magnified in cases of HIV infection by gender and race or ethnicity. See, for example, *Doe v. Jamaica Hospital*, Index No. 31248/89 (Supreme Court of New York, Kings County, Nov. 6, 1989) (case reported in *New York Law Journal* 21 [May 6, 1991]; see Chapter 9 of this volume for discussion).

4. Centers for Disease Control, "Recommendations for Assisting in the Prevention of Perinatal Transmission of Human T-Lymphotropic Virus Type III/Lymphadenopathy-Associated Virus and Acquired Immunodeficiency Syndrome," *Morbidity and Mortality Weekly Report* 34 (1985): 721–732.

5. R. Bayer, "AIDS and the Future of Reproductive Freedom," *The Milbank Quarterly* 68 (1990): 179–204. Bayer's data are based on a survey of state health departments. Bayer notes that while most states unequivocally recommend post-

poning or deferring pregnancy, few have adopted the CDC's formulation that this decision be "considered." A Massachusetts State Health Department brochure, *Family Planning Facts About AIDS*, states: "Women with positive test results should not get pregnant until more is known about HIV infection and pregnancy," (cited by R. Bayer, p. 192).

6. Characterization of public policy concerning the problem of drug use as a "war against drugs" has been the norm since first popularized by President Nixon. This concept permeates the language used to talk about the problems of drug use (e.g., combating) and conceptions of drug users, especially pregnant women, as enemies to be reckoned with. Into this battle zone, many of the punitive legal interventions being honed against pregnant addicts have been born. Senate Committee on Finance, U.S. GAO, No. GAO/HRD-90-138, *Report on Drug Exposed Infants: A Generation at Risk* (June 1990).

7. Ibid.

8. See, for example, "Sullivan Calls Drug Abuse by Pregnant Women Child Abuse," *Alcoholism and Drug Abuse Week*, 2 (June 13, 1990): 6. "'Substance abuse by a pregnant woman is tantamount to child abuse, pure and simple,' said Health and Human Services Secretary Louis W. Sullivan, M.D., in a speech at the 'Symposium on Drug Abuse and Birth Defects: Medical, Legal and Political Issues' at Tufts Medical School in 1990."

9. One of the problems in dealing with perinatal substance abuse is the lack of clear jurisdictional authority. Not only is there a split between the criminal justice, medical, and public health communities as to who "owns" the problem, but within each state government there is a splintering of agency authority. In a given state, the following departments have interests in the issue: the department of alcohol, tobacco, and drug control; corrections; child protective services; social services; maternal and child health; and education. Any successful intervention strategy will require the collaboration of multiple state agencies, as well as stronger links to health professionals and the community.

10. In January 1994, an Illinois statute went into effect prohibiting judges from mandating Norplant or any other form of birth control as part of a criminal sentence.

11. In the GAO study by the Senate Committee on Finance, hospital officials claimed that fear of being reported to authorities not only kept women from seeking prenatal care but resulted in more home births. In 1991, after the court dismissed criminal charges against Kimberly Hardy, brought after she candidly admitted to her physician that she was unable to stop using cocaine during her pregnancy, she noted: "If I'd known things would have turned out this way I would have taken the easier, softer way out and not told anybody. What woman wouldn't be afraid to tell her doctor if she had the threat of prosecution hanging over her?" "Woman Cleared After Drug Use in Pregnancy," *New York Times*, April 3, 1991, p. A14.

12. There is no consensus on what the indicators of successful treatment are. Given that drug dependence is characterized as a chronic condition punctuated by at least occasional relapses, success can be monitored by decreases in the number of positive urine drug tests. Other social indicators of success can be keeping appointments for medical care and drug treatment, keeping appointments for visiting (the woman's) children in foster care, completing GED or other training, getting and maintaining a job, securing stable housing, getting out of abusive relationships, and a host of other complicated social achievements that are hard to measure.

13. See, for example, W. Chavkin and D. Paone, *An Evaluative Study of the Efficacy*

and Availability of Treatment Programs for Pregnant Crack-Cocaine Dependent Women (New York: March of Dimes, 1991).

14. W. Chavkin, "Mandatory Treatment for Drug Use During Pregnancy," *Journal of the American Medical Association* 266 (1991): 1559. For example, at Jackson Memorial Hospital in Miami, a public hospital with over 14,000 births annually, 29% of women arrive at labor with no prenatal care. For women testing positive at labor and delivery, this figure jumps to 60%. Although some of this increase can be attributed to disorganized life-styles associated with drug involvement, providers at Jackson Memorial attribute much of it to the avoidance of health providers in the context of Florida's statute mandating the reporting of perinatal drug use. See K. Acuff, A. Wright-Spolarich, and D. Andrulis, *Vulnerable Women, Visionary Programs: Safety Net Programs for Drug-Involved Women and Their Children* (Washington D.C.: National Public Health and Hospital Institute, 1994).

15. Centers for Disease Control, *HIV/AIDS Surveillance Report*, 6 (Atlanta, GA: CDC, 1994): 10 (mode of transmission based on data reported through June 1994).

16. The possibility of legal interventions, of course, is not the only factor associated with inadequate prenatal care among pregnant women who use drugs. There are physiological, social, and economic barriers as well. Because of menstrual irregularities, including amenorrhea, drug-dependent women are often unaware of their pregnancies until relatively late. Also, the strength of the addiction undoubtedly interferes with the desire to seek prenatal care. In addition, there is inadequate prenatal care available, generally, and for drug-dependent women in particular. Citing a 1990 survey by the National Association of State Alcohol and Drug Abuse Directors, the GAO reported only 14% of the estimated 4 million women who use drugs nationwide were in drug treatment. U.S. General Accounting Office, Report to the Chairman, Subcommittee on Health and the Environment, Committee on Energy and Commerce, House of Representatives. *ADMS Block Grant: Women's Set Aside Does Not Assure Drug Treatment for Pregnant Women* (Washington, DC, May 1991). GAO/HRD-91-80: 1 citing National Association of State Alcohol and Drug Abuse Directors, "Survey of State Alcohol and Drug Use of Fiscal Year 1990 Federal and State Funds." Few drug-treatment facilities are equipped or willing to deal with pregnant women, citing lack of a connection to medical and obstetrical services and concerns about liability. In a frequently cited study of 78 drug-treatment programs in New York City, where treatment was sought by women claiming to be pregnant addicts, 54% of the programs refused to treat pregnant women, 67% denied treatment to pregnant women on Medicaid, and 87% denied treatment to pregnant women on Medicaid who were addicted to crack cocaine. W. Chavkin and D. Paone, "Treatment for Crack Using Mothers: A Study and Guidelines for Program Design," in *An Evaluative Study,*, W. Chavkin and D. Paone, 1. Even when drug treatment is ostensibly available, it is often inadequate to meet the specialized needs of pregnant women, including prenatal care and child care. See, for example, J. Mondanaro, *Chemically Dependent Women: Assessment and Treatment* (Lexington, MA: Lexington Books, 1989); L. P. Finnegan, "Treatment Issues for Opiod-Dependent Women During the Perinatal Period," *Journal of Psychogenic Drugs* 23 (1991): 217–224.

17. In February 1994, the National Institute of Allergy and Infectious Diseases (NIAID) abruptly halted clinical trials begun in 1991 to assess the effectiveness of AZT in reducing the vertical transmission of HIV or in modifying its course in pregnant women and their newborns. One study (ACTG-076) had demonstrated a two-thirds reduction

in the transmission rate, from 25% to 8%. Given this, any legal disincentives for drug-using women to encounter health-care professionals may result in a greater HIV vertical transmission rate and are antithetical to good public health policy.

18. Data from Jackson Memorial Hospital in Miami indicate that 60% of women who have positive drug tests at labor and delivery have not had any prenatal care. See Acuff, Wright-Spolarich, and Andrulis, *Vulnerable Women, Visionary Programs*, 9.
19. See Chapter 8 of this volume by Taunya Lovell Banks for a discussion of constitutional issues raised by coercive drug treatment and Chapter 11 by M. Gregg Bloche for a discussion of ethical considerations raised by coercive governmental action.
20. National Institutes of Health Press Release, "AZT Study Raises Public Policy Concerns," February 22, 1994.
21. States have intervened in other types of cases as well, on the rationale of protecting the interests of the fetus or potential newborn. Courts have routinely ordered pregnant women to undergo blood transfusions and have also ordered bed rest, forbearance from sexual relations, and even cesarean sections.
22. See, for example, V. Kolder, J. Gallagher, and M. T. Parsons, "Court Ordered Obstetrical Interventions," *The New England Journal of Medicine* 316 (1987): 1192–1196.
23. Note the variety of recently proposed efforts to "control" the reproduction of women on welfare through such policies as the offering of cash incentives for agreeing to be implanted with Norplant and reductions in the amount of welfare benefits per child after a certain family size.
24. For those HIV-infected women who are also drug users, it may not be possible to discern the underlying rationale for legal interventions. For example, HIV infection may be viewed as an additional risk factor signaling drug use and result in greater reporting to state child protective services.
25. I. J. Chasnoff, "Drug Use and Women: Establishing a Standard of Care," *Prenatal Abuse of Licit and Illicit Drugs, Annals of the New York Academy of Sciences* 562 (1990): 208–210. Chasnoff's study was based on anonymous testing at 40 urban hospitals and so is believed by many to be an overestimate. Douglas Besharov of the American Enterprise Institute estimates that the number of crack-exposed infants is 30,000–50,000 per year. D. Besharov, "The Children of Crack," *Public Welfare* 51 (Fall 1989): 7–11.
26. "NIDA Releases Survey on Women's Drug Use During Pregnancy," *The Alcoholism Report*, 22 (October 1994): 2. Only two states, Rhode Island and South Carolina, have done statewide prevalence studies.
27. NIDA, "National Household Survey on Drug Abuse: Population Estimates 1991, Revised November 20, 1992," DHHS Publication Number (ADM) 92–1887 (1992) (illicit drugs include marijuana, nonmedical use of psychotherapeutics, inhalants, cocaine, hallucinogens, and heroin).
28. G. Hoegerman and S. Schnoll, "Narcotic Use in Pregnancy," *Clinics in Perinatology* 18 (1991): 51–79.
29. A study by Michigan's Institute for Social Research found that marijuana use among eighth graders has more than doubled since 1991, with 13% of all eight graders surveyed reporting marijuana use at least once in the preceding 12 months. Drug use among high schoolers was also up between 25% and 31%. Daily use of marijuana had increased by 50% among high schoolers. The Associated Press, "Study: Child Drug Use Rising," AP Dec. 12, 1994.
30. I. J. Chasnoff, "1991 National Training Forum on Drugs, Alcohol, Pregnancy and

Parenting", Presentation at the National Association of Perinatal Addiction Research and Education (NAPARE), Chicago, Illinois, December 14–17, 1991. The results reported were as follows:

County	N	% Any Illicit Drug
Cook	1,083	8
East St. Louis	48	4
Rockford[a]	650	13
Carbon[a]	147	11

[a]Considered rural by the presenter.

31. S. K. George, J. Price, J. Harth, D. M. Barnette, and P. Preston, "Drug Abuse Screening of Childbearing Age Women in Alabama Public Health Clinics," *American Journal of Obstetrics and Gynecology* 165 (1991): 924–927. The Alabama study found the statewide prevalence of positive screens for any illicit drugs to be 12.9% for women of childbearing age and 11% for those who were pregnant.
32. The worldwide incidence of fetal alcohol syndrome (FAS) is 1.9 per 1,000 live births. FAS-related mental retardation is the leading known cause of mental retardation in the Western world and may account for as much as 11% of the annual cost of all mentally retarded institutionalized residents in the United States. E. Abel and R. J. Sokol, "Incidence of Fetal Alcohol Syndrome and Economic Impact of FAS-Related Anomalies," *Drug and Alcohol Dependence* 19 (1987): 51–70.
33. The rationale for many of the criminal prosecutions is based on the illegality of the drugs in question. At least one criminal child neglect case, however, has been brought for alcohol use during pregnancy: *Nebraska v. Arandus*, No. CR92-050557, May 1, 1992. For an examination of the distinctions between legal and illegal drugs in cases of various fetal protection policies, see B. Steinbock, "The Relevance of Illegality," *Hastings Center Report* (January–February 1992): 19–22. Steinbock notes: "From a medical or moral point of view, it makes no difference whether the potentially harmful substance is legal or illegal. The risks to fetal health from heavy smoking and drinking are probably comparable to the risks from shooting heroin or smoking crack. It seems arbitrary to prosecute women who use illegal drugs when use of legal drugs such as tobacco and alcohol may cause just as much, if not more, harm to the developing fetus. However, from a constitutional perspective, there is an important distinction between legal and illegal substances. Privacy rights can be infringed only when the behavior in question is legal. If a woman has no right to use cocaine, she has no right to use cocaine when pregnant."
34. *U.S. v. Vaughn* Crim. N., F-2172–88B(DC Super. Ct. Aug. 23, 1988). (The judge in this case sentenced Ms. Vaughn to jail for the duration of her pregnancy after she pled guilty to forging checks, reasoning that the sentence would protect her fetus from maternal drug use. Normally such a plea would not have resulted in jail time.)
35. K. L. Acuff, *Prenatal Alcohol and Drug Abuse Policy Study: Hospital Practice and Policy* (unpublished research for a doctoral dissertation for the Department of Health Policy and Management, The Johns Hopkins School of Hygiene and Public Health, 1994). The percentages responding that it is sometimes or always appropriate to seek criminal prosecutions in the case of positive newborn drug tests were: obstetricians, 38.1% (13.6% responded "always"); pediatricians, 36.5% (13.5% responded "always"); social workers, 39.6% (15.2% responded "always").

36. J. O. Hansen, "Southerners Back Penalties for Moms Whose Drug Use Hurts the Unborn," *The Atlanta Constitution*, July 30, 1989, p. A1. Punishment was favored more by women than men (75% vs. 66%) and by younger respondents more than older ones. A majority of women (51% vs. 39% of men) and 53% of blacks supported criminal sanctions for pregnant women who drink alcohol or smoke cigarettes and who give birth to babies with serious medical problems. Eleven percent of respondents favored prosecuting women who eat or exercise improperly during pregnancy. Party affiliation was not a factor: 74% of Republicans and 72% of Democrats favored punitive interventions.
37. L. M. Paltrow and S. Shende, "Memorandum: State by State Case Summary of Criminal Prosecutions Against Pregnant Women and Appendix of Public Health and Public Interest Groups Opposed to These Prosecutions," American Civil Liberties Union Reproductive Rights Freedom Project, October 29, 1992; see also, L. M. Paltrow, *Criminal Prosecutions Against Pregnant Women: National Update and Overview* (New York: American Civil Liberties Union Reproductive Rights Freedom Project, 1992).
38. Paltrow, *Criminal Prosecutions Against Pregnant Women*, i.
39. In 1990, Delaware, Hawaii, Maryland, Michigan, Missouri, Oklahoma, and Rhode Island introduced such legislation. Legislation introduced in 1991 in Ohio would have made the delivery of an infant addicted at birth a felony and provided that sentencing include completion of a drug-treatment program, the implantation of long-acting birth control (e.g., Norplant), and a 5-year court-supervised monitoring of the birth control. Legislation introduced in 1991 in South Carolina proposed the choice of reversible sterilization or the implantation of Norplant. Legislation introduced in 1994 in Indiana would create a felony for any woman who knows or "should reasonably know" that she is pregnant to intentionally ingest marijuana, cocaine, or any other controlled substance. Under the bill, prosecutors are granted the discretion to withhold prosecution if the woman agrees to treatment and other conditions.
40. D. L. Greene, "Abusive Prosecutors: Gender, Race & Class: Discretion and the Prosecution of Drug Addicted Mothers," *Buffalo Law Review* 39 (1991): 737–775. "The problem of babies born to drug-addicted women is not new, yet criminal prosecution of the mothers involved is new and what has changed is not the law but prosecutors' interpretation and enforcement of already extant general statutes." Greene's well-written law review article uses prosecutions of drug-addicted mothers as an example of prosecutorial discretion gone awry. Greene also notes: "The effects of prosecutorial policy choices on minorities, women and children are obfuscated by calling these choices part of a 'war on drugs.' In the frenzy of rousing drug war hyperbole there is great risk of unrealized and unchecked exercises of prosecutorial discretion. Prosecutors reflect the unstated but operative norms in American courtrooms which are predominantly affluent, white, usually male, and often Protestant perspectives. Instead of unbiased law enforcement which respects the autonomy of women, these prosecutions may be based on pluralistic ignorance, discrimination predicated on class, racial, ethnic and cultural group characteristics, and the lack of women's power and reproductive rights."
41. See, for example, *State v. Grubbs*, No. 4FA S89–415 (Ala. Super. Ct., October 2, 1989). Ms. Grubbs was charged with manslaughter for the death of her 2-week-old son when an autopsy stated that the infant died from a heart attack caused by

prenatal cocaine use. Ms. Grubbs pled no contest to the lesser charge of negligent homicide and was sentenced to 6 months in jail and 5 years' probation.
42. Often prosecutors charge women under several theories at once. A common charge is based on a "delivery statute," which prohibits the sale or distribution of a drug to another party. Delivery to a minor is associated with harsher penalties. See, for example, *People* v. *Cox*, No. 90–53454 FH, slip op. (Mich. Cir. Ct., Jackson County, July 9, 1990) (granting motion to dismiss, finding that Michigan's drug delivery statute was not intended to regulate prenatal conduct and prosecution would not be in the best interest of public health, safety, and welfare); *State* v. *Luster*, A92A0233 and *Luster* v. *State*, No. A92A0415, slip op. (Ga. Ct. App., April 23, 1992) (unanimous ruling affirming the trial court's dismissal of drug delivery charges on the grounds that Georgia did not intend its drug delivery statute to apply to the transfer of cocaine from a woman to her fetus); *Commonwealth* v. *Pellegrini*, No. 87970, slip op. (Mass. Sup. Ct., October 15, 1990) (dismissing charges because the right to privacy and principles of statutory construction, due process, and the separation of powers do not permit extension of Massachusetts's drug delivery statute to women who give birth to drug-exposed infants).
43. *Welch* v. *Commonwealth*, No. 90-CA-1189-MR (Ky. Ct. App., February 7, 1992) (court reversed a criminal child abuse conviction of a woman who allegedly used drugs during her pregnancy, holding the statute did not apply to a fetus); *Reyes* v. *Superior Court*, 75 Cal. App. 3rd 214 (1977) (unanimous opinion holding that California's felony child endangerment statute did not apply to an unborn child or include a woman's prenatal conduct); *People* v. *Hardy*, No. 128458 (Mich. Ct. App., April 1, 1991) (unanimous ruling that Michigan did not intend its drug trafficking statute to apply to pregnant drug users), *appeal denied*, No. 91–346 (Mich. Sup. Ct., July 16, 1991).
44. Ms. Johnson was charged under a Florida statute which makes the delivery of drugs to a minor illegal. Fla. Stat. Section 893.13(1)(c)(1989) states in part: "Except as authorized by this chapter, it is unlawful for any person 18 years of age or older to deliver any controlled substance to a person under the age of 18 years as an agent or employee in the sale or delivery of such a substance, or to use such person to assist in avoiding detection or apprehension for a violation of this chapter."

The Florida legislature was one of the first to amend its child protection statute to include evidence of prenatal drug and alcohol exposures to constitute a "harm" to children. It subsequently amended it again to specify that evidence of drug exposures reported under the child protection statute could not be used as the basis for criminal charges. As a result, the prosecutor in the Jennifer Johnson case was forced to utilize very wide discretion in reading the criminal law to bring charges against her.
45. *State of Florida* v. *Johnson*, No. E89–890-CFA (Fla. Cir. Ct. July 13, 1989).
46. *Johnson* v. *State*, 578 So.2d 419 (Fla. Fifth D.C.A., 1991). The conviction was upheld notwithstanding evidence that Ms. Johnson reported her cocaine use to her doctor and paramedics during her pregnancy and attempted to obtain drug treatment.
47. *State* v. *Johnson*, No. 77,831, slip op. at 2 (Fla. Sup. Ct. July 23, 1992).
48. *Johnson* v. *State* at 1294. The appellate court had certified the question of whether Florida's drug trafficking statute applied to the transfer of a cocaine metabolite through the umbilical cord after a baby is born but before the cord is severed.

49. Ibid., 1295.
50. *Nebraska v. Arandus*, No. CR92–050557, May 1, 1992.
51. See, for example, *State v. Hudson*, No. K88–3435-CFA (Fla. Cir. Ct., July 26, 1989). Ms. Hudson was charged with possession, distribution to a minor, and child endangerment when her newborn tested positive for cocaine. She pled guilty to the possession charge, and the distribution and endangerment charges were dropped. Ms. Hudson was sentenced to 150 days in jail, 5 years' probation, and a $225 fine. A condition of her probation is that she obtain prenatal care if she becomes pregnant.
52. Paltrow, *Criminal Prosecutions Against Pregnant Women*, ii.
53. Ibid.
54. Chavkin, "Mandatory Treatment," 1559. Chavkin interviewed 150 drug-using women in New York City. Three-fourths of the women interviewed reported concern for their child as a major motive for initiating treatment.
55. *Survey of State Alcohol and Drug Use of Fiscal Year 1989 Federal and State Funds* (National Association of State Alcohol and Drug Abuse Directors: Washington, D.C.: 1989).
56. Ibid.
57. This author has been unable to locate a single case where a drug-treatment facility was held liable in the treatment of a pregnant drug user. The risk of liability is greatly overstated.
58. D. F. Chavkin, "For Their Own Good: Civil Commitment of Alcohol and Drug-Dependent Pregnant Women," *South Dakota Law Review* 37 (1992): 701.
59. State laws in Florida, Georgia, Illinois, Louisiana, Missouri, and Wisconsin mandate that priority access to drug treatment be given to pregnant women. A. B. Marshall, "1992 Legislative Review," *Perinatal Addiction Research and Education Update* (October 1992) p 5.
60. M. Gregg Bloche presents a detailed discussion of coercive and persuasive acts in Chapter 11 of this volume.
61. Chavkin, "Mandatory Treatment," 1559. This classification is based largely on Chavkin's analysis.
62. There are very few studies about either the magnitude or efficacy of compelled treatment in the entire drug use/abuse literature, and I have found none where the data are reported by gender. See, for example, C. G. Leukefeld and F. M. Tims, eds., *Compulsory Treatment of Drug Abuse: Research and Clinical Practice*, NIDA Research Monograph 86 (Washington, D.C.: National Institute on Drug Abuse, 1988). This monograph reviews the "compelled drug treatment" literature.
63. S. Anderson Garcia and I. Keilitz, "Involuntary Civil Commitment of Drug-Dependent Persons with Special Reference to Pregnant Women," *Mental and Physical Disabilities Law Reporter* 15 (1991): 418. This article is an excellent review of civil commitment as it relates to drug-dependent persons.
64. *Humphrey v. Cady*, 405 U.S. 504, 509 (1972).
65. The legal authority for the state to involuntarily confine persons for treatment lies is its *parens patriae* interest in "providing care to its citizens who are unable to care for themselves" and its police power to protect the community from persons who may be dangerous because of mental illness. See *Addington v. Texas*, 441 U.S. 418, 428 (1979).
66. Minnesota's pregnancy-specific civil commitment statute was enacted along with

the only mandatory prenatal drug testing and reporting legislation in the country. Minn. Stat. ann. S.253B.02 subd, 2 (West 1982, Supp. 1991).
67. See, for example, Conn. Gen. Stat. 19a-370 to 395 (West 1988, Supp. 1990) (requiring drug dependency and need of compulsory medical treatment); Fla. Stat. Ann 397.011–052 (West 1986, Supp. 1990) (requiring habitual drug use, loss of self-control, danger to self or others, or need of treatment and impaired judgment about care).
68. The harm of this omission of the woman from the scope of the intervention is magnified if child custody issues are then conditioned upon her "successful" treatment.
69. Anderson Garcia and Keilitz, "Involuntary Civil Commitment," 419.
70. Minn. Stat. Ann. Section 253B.02. subd, 2 (West 1982, Supp. 1990).
71. Ibid. Absent from Minnesota's statute is civil commitment for marijuana use.
72. D. Kenneally Cahalane, "Court-Ordered Confinement of Pregnant Women," *New England Journal on Criminal and Civil Confinement* 15: 203–223, at 220. Kenneally Cahalane proposes using a trimester approach to determine whether court-ordered confinement of high-risk pregnant women is appropriate. She supports court intervention in the third trimester if the fetus is at risk.
73. Ibid., 223. Kenneally Cahalane's proposal does not address the fact that the fetus is most vulnerable to exposure to drugs and alcohol at the earlier stages of development, when she would limit the ability of the state to intervene.
74. For a detailed history of these treatment options for the criminal justice system see, generally, Leukefeld and Tims, *Compulsory Treatment of Drug Abuse*.
75. The impetus for the MUSC drug-testing policy was the identification of cocaine use during pregnancy. This was the case even though statewide or countrywide prevalence measures were nonexistent when the policy was implemented. Most of the documents and subsequent publications refer solely to cocaine use and cocaine drug testing. In the Operational Guidelines dated October 12, 1989, from Captain R. H. Roberts of the Charleston Police Department, however, the sanctions are said to apply to illegal drugs, which are defined as: "heroin, crack/cocaine, amphetamines, and any other drug illegally ingested by the patient that medical authorities deem a threat to the life and safety of the unborn child." An extensive statewide prevalence study done in 1991 found that cocaine use ranked sixth among the drugs tested among women giving birth in the state and was apparently lower in prevalence in South Carolina than in the country generally. The statewide prevalence based on urine testing was (1) barbiturates (5.3%), (2) marijuana (2.5%), (3) opiates (2.2%), (4) alcohol (1.9%), (5) benzodiazepines (0.81%), (6) cocaine, and (7) propozyphenes (0.19%). State Council on Maternal, Infant and Child Health, Office of the Governor, *1991 South Carolina Prevalence Study of Drug Use Among Women Giving Birth* Columbia, SC: Published by the state of South Carolina (October 23, 1991). The prevalence study did, however, find significantly higher cocaine use (5.7 times higher) among black women than white women, among women whose intended payment source was Medicaid or "other payment source" (17–18 times higher), and among urban women.
76. Five entities were parties to this agreement: the office of the solicitor, The Medical University, the Charleston County Substance Abuse Commission, the Charleston County Department of Social Services, and law enforcement.
77. There was a similar agreement in place in Greenville, South Carolina.

78. The full consent for medical treatment stated:

> I acknowledge that I am suffering from a condition requiring Medical/Hospital care and thereby voluntarily consent to such Medical/Hospital care encompassing diagnostic procedures and medical treatment by my physician, assistants or designees, as may be necessary in his or her judgment. I further consent to the testing for infectious diseases such as, but not limited to, syphilis, hepatitis, and AIDS *and I further consent to the testing of drugs if deemed advisable by my physician.* I am aware that the practice of medicine and surgery is not an exact science and I acknowledge that no guarantees have been made as to the result of treatments or examinations. I have read or have had read to me this consent and I voluntarily certify that I understand and agree to its contents. (emphasis added)

> There is controversy over the requirement of informed consent for drug testing of pregnant women. Some argue that a general consent for medical treatment is sufficient to support a variety of diagnostic testing, including drug testing. An intermediate view would insert drug testing in the general medical consent for treatment form or notify the woman that she will be tested and give her the opportunity to refuse. I believe the issue of consent turns on the uses to which the drug testing information would be put. If the drug test results are used only for purposes of treatment or referral to treatment, it may be appropriate not to obtain explicit consent for the testing. When drug testing is not related to any meaningful treatment or is used to provide evidence of child abuse or criminal activity, women should be fully informed of the purpose of the testing and potential legal and social consequences of drug testing and consent obtained. The MUSC consenting process certainly is suspect in the information given to pregnant women about the ramifications of testing. In addition, because the MUSC-operated county hospital is the only source of indigent and Medicaid-supported obstetrical care within a 50-mile radius, a genuine question is raised concerning the voluntariness of the consent.

79. Indicators include no prenatal care, late prenatal care (i.e., registration after 24 weeks' gestation), incomplete prenatal care (i.e., noncompliance), abrupto placenta, intrauterine fetal death, preterm labor, intrauterine growth retardation, congenital anomalies, and known prior drug or alcohol abuse.
80. It is not clear whether "successful" refers to a successful obstetrical outcome or a drug-treatment outcome. According to Kary Moss of the ACLU Reproductive Freedom Project in New York, "drug treatment" consists of weekly group meetings and films. At the time the program was instituted, there was only one residential drug-treatment program in the entire state (October 3, 1994 Kary Moss, personal communication). Drug-treatment research, as it pertains to women, is sorely lacking in terms of outcome measures. Most of the attempts to evaluate drug treatment have focused on outcome measures relating to men's employment and decreased criminal activity, which may not be applicable to this population. Also, the requirement of "clean urine screens," given the chronic relapsing nature of drug addiction and the lack of drug-treatment facilities for cocaine addiction, raises the question of whether compliance with the agreement is even possible.
81. As stated in the operational guidelines for the Charleston Police Department, dated October 12, 1989, the charges to be filed depend upon the gestational age:

> a. If the pregnancy is 27 weeks or less:
> Possession of _____ S.C.Code 44–53–370
> b. If the pregnancy is 28 weeks or more:

Possession of _____ S.C.Code 44–53–370
AND
Distribution to persons under eighteen S.C. Code 44–53–440.

A memorandum dated October 17, 1989 (the memorandum) and circulated to the Police Department, the solicitor, and personnel at MUSC includes an additional charge of unlawful child neglect in cases where the fetus is more than 28 weeks. The memorandum also provided that women testing positive at labor and delivery also be chargedwith possession and distribution:

c. If the patient delivers while testing positive for illegal drugs and/or her newborn tests positive for drugs:
Unlawful neglect of a child S.C.Code 20–7-50.

82. Operational guidelines dated October 12, 1989 to the central detectives from Captain R. H. Graves of the City of Charleston Police Department.
83. The county prosecutor, in part because of the popularity of his policies in dealing with prenatal drug use, was elected South Carolina's Attorney General in November 1994.
84. This decline was measured by comparing the average number of positive drug tests in the 6 months following the program's implementation (an average of 3.1 positive cocaine urine tests) to those in the 6 months preceding implementation (an average of 15–16 positive cocaine urine tests). The report discounted alternative theories that the reduction in positive drug tests was because women were either not seeking health care at MUSC or resorting to home births by showing that (1) the number of deliveries at MUSC remained steady or increased slightly over those of the previous 2 years and (2) no increase in the number of home births was reported by the state Office of Vital Records and Public Health Statistics.

The researchers did not discuss the facts that urine drug tests detect cocaine use only within 72 hours of the sample and, because women may have avoided drug use prior to scheduled appointments to escape detection, that the overall fetal drug exposure may not have been reduced. E. O. Horger, III, S. B. Brown, and C. M. Condon, "Cocaine in Pregnancy: Confronting the Problem," *The Journal of the South Carolina Medical Association* 86 (1990): 527–531.
85. Ibid., 530–531.
86. Paltrow, *Criminal Prosecutions Against Pregnant Women,* 24.
87. "South Carolina Hospital Subject of Rights Investigation," *Reproductive Freedom News* III (February 11, 1994): 3. "Federal Judge Lifts Gag Order in Suit Against Hospital Arrest Program," *Reproductive Freedom News* III (January 28, 1994): 3. The basis of the lawsuit is the argument that MUSC is conducting human subject research in violation of federal statutes requiring submission of the research protocol to the institutional review board, which evaluates the risk to the subjects. Members of the MUSC staff have published an article on their research in the *Journal of the South Carolina Medical Association*.
88. A September 30, 1994 letter from the National Institutes of Health's Office for Protection from Research Risks (OPRR) to MUSC's president stated that the university's participation in the unsanctioned program raised "serious concerns about the adequacy of MUSC's institutional system of protections for human subjects." OPRR took the unusually strong action of only provisionally continuing the hospital's Multiple Projects Assurance program needed for the continuation of eligibility for federal funding for research involving human subjects. "National Institutes of

Health Finds South Carolina Hospital Engaged in Unauthorized Research on Pregnant Women," The Center for Reproductive Law & Policy, New York. Press Release, October 4, 1994.
89. J. Dinsmore, *Pregnant Drug Users: The Debate Over Prosecution* (Washington, D.C.: National Center for Prosecution of Child Abuse, American Prosecutors Research Institute, March 1992): 6.
90. Ibid., 24.
91. Ms. Moore's release was conditioned on her obtaining drug treatment. The court-ordered confinement was pursued after she failed to appear for treatment.
92. "Illinois Court Orders Pregnant Woman Confined to Drug Treatment Center," *The Washington Post*, April 12, 1991, p. A3. The prosecutor, Paul Logli, achieved recognition 2 years earlier for unsuccessfully prosecuting a woman for manslaughter for allegedly causing her newborn's death by her prenatal use of cocaine.
93. N. Finkelstein, "Treatment Programming for Alcohol and Drug-Dependent Pregnant Women," *The International Journal of the Addictions* 28 (1993): 1275–1309. Finkelstein notes the negative attitudes and anger toward drug-dependent women not only expressed by laymen but by caretakers as well. Finkelstein cites studies demonstrating these negative attitudes even among drug-treatment providers, despite their training in addiction.
94. These remarks were made by a nurse practitioner from the Francis Scott Key Hospital's Cocaine-Addicted Pregnant Women's Program in Baltimore, Maryland, in a talk given to the Coalition on Alcohol and Drug Dependent Women and Their Children in July 1992, in Washington, D.C.
95. This author has found no information about the policies of private drug-treatment facilities concerning birth control or sterilization.
96. "Judge Orders Birth Control Implant in Defendant," *The Washington Post*, Jan. 4, 1991, p. B1.
97. "Sterilization and Unfit Mothers," Editorial, *New York Times*, Feb. 12, 1993, p. A32.
98. G. Schedler, "Does Society Have the Right to Force Pregnant Drug Addicts to Abort Their Fetuses?" *Social Theory and Practice* 17 (1991): 369–384. Schedler grounds his position in a utilitarian argument:

> It should also be born in mind that the abortion experience is relatively brief and painless (at least in the early stages of pregnancy), whereas giving birth usually involves many hours of discomfort and pain. Compared to giving birth, then, undergoing an abortion is not at all difficult. Since undergoing an abortion is not too onerous and in a certain sense is beneficial to the woman, it is reasonable to describe as easily avoidable the infantile defects that would result from the failure of the pregnant addict to seek an abortion.

99. Ibid., 370.
100. Ibid., 382–383.
101. The states that have amended their child abuse and neglect laws to include drug use during pregnancy are Florida, Illinois, Indiana, Minnesota, Nevada, and Oklahoma.
102. See, for example, *Matter of Stefanel Tyesha C.*, N.Y. App. Div., 1st Dept. *New York Law Journal* (May 31, 1990); *In re Troy D.*, 263 Cal. Rptr. 869 (Cal. App., 4th Dist., 1989); *In re Baby X*, 293 N.W.2d 736 (Ct. App., Mich., 1980).

103. See, for example, "Statement of Wendy Chavkin, MD, MPH, Hearing Before the United States House Select Committee on Children, Youth, and Families," 101st Congress, First Session, April 27, 1989. Chavkin noted that during the first wave of the boarder baby crisis in New York City, maternal substance abuse was the primary reason for boarder by status, accounting for 40% of the more than 300 cases. See also, C. Walker, P. Sangrillo, and J. Smith, *Parental Drug Abuse and African American Children in Foster Care* (Washington, D.C.: National Black Child Development Institute, 1991). Walker and colleagues report that in 1990 parental drug use was reported to be the dominant characteristic of child protective service caseloads in 22 states and the District of Columbia. In New York state, family substance abuse was a contributing factor in 52% of foster care placements.
104. J. R. Fink, "Advocacy on Behalf of Drug-Exposed Children: Legal Perspectives," in *Identifying the Needs of Drug-Affected Children: Public Policy Issues*, OSAP Monograph 11, (Rockville, MD: U.S. Department of Health and Human Services, 1992): 145.
105. See, for example, A. English, "Prenatal Drug Exposure: Grounds for Mandatory Child Abuse Reports," *Youth Law News* XI (1990): 3–8.
106. Acuff, *Prenatal Alcohol and Drug Abuse Policy Study*. In most jurisdictions, if CPS accepts a report of suspected child abuse or neglect, it is legally obligated to investigate. As a result, by requiring more evidence than a positive drug test to even accept the report, CPS shifts the burden of collecting requisite evidence for a child protection petition to hospital social workers. However, because the length of stay for vaginal deliveries is only 24–48 hours, the opportunity for collecting such evidence is often too brief. Some hospitals have responded to this by keeping infants "beyond medical need" (with questionable legal authority) to give a public health nurse the time to make a home visit. (Part of this information came from personal communication with Joanne Rule, Director of Social Work, Johns Hopkins Hospital.) Another solution to this evidentiary problem for hospitals is to define risk factors for perinatal drug use in medical terms, such as "no prenatal care." Note that the use of "no prenatal care" as a risk factor can essentially be used as a proxy for poor, minority women, who are disproportionately medically underserved either because of lack of health insurance or structural barriers to care.
107. Acuff, *Prenatal Alcohol and Drug Abuse Policy Study*.
108. National Institutes of Health Press Release, "AZT Study Raises Public Policy Concerns," Feb. 22, 1994. As a result of data showing a reduction from 25% to 8% in the rate of vertical transmission of HIV, NIAID stopped the study and issued a clinic alert to physicians treating HIV-infected women. The press release notes, without elaborating, that "(t)he study highlights crucial issues related to accessing prenatal care and HIV screening for women who are either pregnant or are considering pregnancy." Further, the press release quotes Mary Boland, Director of the National Pediatric HIV Resource Center: "When aware of her HIV status, an infected woman will now be in a position to make informed decisions regarding pregnancy and risks and benefits of drug treatment for herself and her infant."
109. See, for example, W. R. Linderking, R. D. Gelber, D. J. Cotton, et al. for the AIDS Clinical Trials Group, "Evaluation of the Quality of Life Associated with Zidovudine Treatment in Asymptomatic Human Immunodeficiency Virus Infection," *New England Journal of Medicine* 330 (1994): 348–353; J. D. Lundgren, A. N. Phillips, C. Pederson, et al. for the AIDS in Europe Study Group, "Comparison

of Long-Term Prognosis of Patients with AIDS Treated and Not Treated with Zidovudine," *Journal of the American Medical Association* 271 (1994): 1088–1092.

110. Should it become possible to fully prevent or cure vertical transmission of HIV by treating the woman, mandated testing and treatment may well occur, provided the risks (and perhaps inconvenience) to the woman are minimal. Precedence for this is in the case of testing of pregnant women for syphilis, which was statutorily mandated throughout the country in the late 1930s and early 1940s. Although only the testing for syphilis was mandated, treatment was implicit and quickly became part of routine medical practice more than a decade before penicillin was introduced. K. L. Acuff, "A History of Prenatal and Newborn Screening Programs: Lessons for the Future," in *AIDS, Women and the Next Generation*, eds. R. R. Faden, G. Geller, and M. Powers (New York: Oxford University Press, 1991) 51–93. AZT, however, is not risk-free, and many patients have many unpleasant and even dangerous side effects, including liver damage.

111. Obstetricians who seek court orders to compel treatment in such cases are probably acting outside the recommendations of the ACOG. ACOG Committee on Ethics, "Patient Choice: Maternal–Fetal Conflict," ACOG Committee Opinion Number 55 (October 1987). ACOG's opinion advises against the use of judicial authority:

> Obstetricians should refrain from performing procedures that are unwanted by a pregnant woman. The use of judicial authority to implement treatment regimens in order to protect the fetus violates the pregnant woman's autonomy. Furthermore, inappropriate reliance on judicial authority may lead to undesirable social consequences, such as the criminalization of noncompliance with medical recommendations.

The opinion, however, stops short of saying that seeking judicial support is never appropriate, noting that the "vast majority of pregnant women are willing to assume significant risk for the welfare of the fetus" and that "the use of the courts is almost never warranted." Unpublished research by this author suggests that, although the majority of over 150 obstetricians surveyed agreed that legal measures should be used sparingly, 39% agreed that criminal sanctions should be available as an intervention option and 88% agreed that some sort of legal intervention was appropriate in cases where prenatal drug use continues after counseling and referrals.

112. I note only that there is a potential for better health care. It would depend a great deal on where the woman was confined or ordered to get care. A review of the health care provided for women in most jails or prisons, for example, would not hold the promise of better care, but care through a woman-centered, comprehensive drug-treatment program might.

113. American Academy of Pediatrics Committee on Substance Abuse, "Drug Exposed Infants," *Pediatrics* 639 (1990): 639–641.

114. American Medical Association Board of Trustees Report, "Legal Interventions During Pregnancy," *Journal of the American Medical Association* 264 (1990): 2663.

115. American Nurses Association, New Position Statement, *Opposition to Criminal Prosecution of Women for Use of Drugs While Pregnant* (Washington, DC: American Nurses Association, 1991).

116. American Public Health Association, Policy Statement No. 9020, "Illicit Drug Use by Pregnant Women," *American Journal of Public Health* 8 (1990): 240.

117. American Society of Addiction Medicine, "Public Policy Statement on Chemically Dependent Women and Pregnancy," *American Society of Addiction Medicine News* 6 (September/October, 1989): 47–49.
118. Coalition on Alcohol and Drug Dependent Women and Their Children, "Statement Opposing Prosecution" (Washington, DC: December 1990).
119. March of Dimes, *Statement on Maternal Substance Abuse* (Washington, DC: March of Dimes, December 1990).
120. National Association of Public Child Welfare Administrators, *Guiding Principles for Working With Substance-Abusing Families and Drug-Exposed Children: The Child Welfare Response* (Washington, D.C.: National Association of Public Child Welfare Administrators, January 1991).
121. National Council on Alcoholism and Drug Dependence, Policy Statement, *Women, Alcohol, Other Drugs and Pregnancy* (Washington, DC: National Council on Alcoholism and Drug Dependence, April 29, 1990).

III
ETHICAL AND SOCIAL ISSUES

11

Clinical Counseling and the Problem of Autonomy-Negating Influence

M. GREGG BLOCHE*

> "I was being told that, as a woman, how dare I bring a child into the world that was going to be born sick. . . . He wanted to refer me to someone who would perform an abortion. . . . And I became angry. . . . So I figured God put this child in my life at this particular time when before I couldn't get pregnant and I wanted to. So there was a reason. And I said I wanted to have my child.
>
> *woman from Miami*

> The nurse that I was with in family planning . . . she never said no, but she always explained to me the outcome and how long. . . . That's what made me have an abortion too. . . . And I really felt bad and guilty. . . . But this last time I made up my own mind.
>
> *woman from New York*

On November 14, 1988, during her fifth month of pregnancy, 38-year-old Carol Doe was informed by a nurse at New York City's Jamaica Hospital that she had become infected with the virus that causes AIDS.[1] According to Ms. Doe, a patient in the hospital's high-risk prenatal program, she was told that her chances of giving birth to an HIV-infected child were "very high"[2] and that an abortion was desirable.

Three days later, Ms. Doe met with Dr. Maurice Abitol, chief of obstetrics and gynecology at Jamaica Hospital. By Ms. Doe's account, Dr. Abitol advised that failure to obtain an abortion would be wrong and that having an HIV-infected child would impose a burden on society.[3] Moreover, according to Ms. Doe, Dr. Abitol said she could no longer receive prenatal care at Jamaica Hospital's high-risk clinic. She was referred to Kings County Hospital, where 3 weeks later she had an abortion.[4] A year later, Ms. Doe filed suit against Jamaica Hospital, Kings County Hospital, and her individual caretakers at both institutions. She alleged that their conduct constituted unlawful discrimination on the basis of physical handicap and that they had breached their duties to provide appropriate care and to obtain her informed consent.

*I thank Anita Allen, Ruth Faden, Steven Goldberg, Nancy Kass, Michael Seidman, Mark Tushnet, and participants in Georgetown University Law Center's faculty research workshop for their comments and suggestions. I am grateful to William Anderson, Michelle Cameron, and Kimberly Henderson for their research assistance.

257

Through the distorting lens of an inchoate adversary proceeding, the nuances of Ms. Doe's conversations with her clinical caretakers are not easy to discern. In a motion for summary judgment, Dr. Abitol characterized his conversation with Ms. Doe as considerably less directive, though he acknowledged having referred her to Kings County Hospital.[5] Quite possibly, Dr. Abitol dealt carelessly or abusively with Ms. Doe, misleading her about the risk that she could infect her child or castigating her for considering giving birth to a child that might suffer and impose a financial burden on society. Quite possibly, he barred her from receiving further prenatal services at Jamaica Hospital, thereby cutting off her access to high-risk prenatal care. If so, then Dr. Abitol violated his duty of care, as understood within the medical profession and imposed by the courts.[6] But if he or Ms. Doe's other caretakers merely *recommended* that she end her pregnancy after advising her about the risks of childbearing and abortion and listening respectfully to her concerns, then their actions were consistent with widely accepted clinical norms.

During the mid and late 1980s, a series of articles in leading medical journals and pronouncements by public health and professional authorities took the position that HIV-infected women should be counseled not to bear children. These academic commentaries[7] and official pronouncements[8] focused primarily on the reproductive choices of women prior to conception. However, their unmistakable implication for women who learned of their HIV-infected status during pregnancy was that abortion represented the preferred outcome.[9] If Ms. Doe's obstetrical caretakers advised abortion while reassuring her that the decision was hers, then they acted in accordance with an accepted clinical practice.

This accepted practice is consistent with the jurisprudence of informed consent and the conception of autonomy that undergirds it. Informed consent doctrine contemplates that clinicians will make recommendations to their patients in addition to instructing them about the risks and benefits of medical alternatives.[10] The law of informed consent does not require a physician to withhold his or her opinion when advising patients about alternatives.[11] Rather, it is premised on the belief that a clinician can express his or her opinion without compromising the patient's autonomy. Most leading bioethics commentators adhere to this view.[12] In the event that Ms. Doe was accurately informed about the risks of pregnancy and abortion (including the risk of HIV transmission to the fetus[13]), a recommendation that she terminate her pregnancy would not have undermined her autonomy, as conventionally conceived, and thereby vitiated her consent.[14]

As an application of prevailing legal and bioethics thinking about informed consent and autonomous action, this conclusion is unremarkable. Yet were a court to reach such a conclusion in Ms. Doe's case, it would surely become a focus of bitter dispute. In the context of reproductive decision-making by HIV-infected women, the ability of patients to choose autonomously after being advised not to bear children is being disputed by scholars and others who view such advice as inherently coercive. These critics contend that the unequal relationship between HIV-infected women and their clinical counselors renders advice to abort, or to refrain from conceiving, inconsistent with the preservation of reproductive autonomy.[15]

In making this claim, critics of such opinion-giving can draw support from the genetic counseling context. Among genetic counselors, the prevailing standard of care since the early 1970s has included avoidance of opinion-giving with respect to patients' childbearing decisions.[16] Some advocates of this standard contend that promoting reproductive forbearance for the purpose of preventing genetic disease interferes with autonomous reproductive decision-making.[17]

More broadly, understandings of autonomy-negating influence in clinical settings appear to vary according to context. The different norms that prevail with respect to opinion-giving in medical treatment and genetic counseling relationships are just one example. Another example is the seeming disconnection between the widely held view that coercive pressures bar prisoners from consenting freely to participation in medical research[18] and the belief that even desperately ill inmates can consent autonomously to treatment. Nor is the phenomenon of apparent inconsistency between understandings of autonomy-negating influence in different contexts limited to clinical counseling. As Alan Wertheimer has observed, the law draws varying lines between coercive and noncoercive external influence in different doctrinal settings.[19] For example, many influences that suffice to void a contract fall short of what is needed to establish that a criminal confession was involuntary.[20] Underlying such inconsistencies, as Wertheimer notes, is the law's tendency to incorporate myriad context-based moral judgments into its accounts of coercive influence.[21]

To no small extent, the emerging conflict over the desirability of discouraging childbirth by HIV-infected women is being cast as a debate over whether efforts to influence their decisions preserve or undermine autonomous choice. This essay considers the problem of line-drawing between autonomy-preserving and autonomy-negating influences in clinical relationships. My purpose is not to propose particular boundaries, with respect to either reproductive decisions by HIV-infected women or other clinical choices. Rather, I aspire to shed some light on what drives our disputes about whether one or another influence method is compatible with autonomous choice.

I argue that such disagreements reflect underlying conflicts between normative commitments and that resolving these conflicts is essential to the settlement of controversies over whether particular influences unduly interfere with autonomous choice. Alternative understandings of the prerequisites for autonomous choice are informed by differing normative visions. Although the ideal of a unified conception of autonomy has broad appeal, we live in practice with multiple understandings. Typically, this presents few problems; each governs within its own sphere of clinical or other activity. Indeed, it may be that illusory belief in autonomy as a unified concept, analytically separable from competing normative visions, facilitates the tranquil coexistence of contrary ideas about the scope of personal responsibility.[22]

Yet at times, differing understandings of autonomous choice collide. The counseling of HIV-infected women about their reproductive options represents an example. When this happens, underlying normative commitments need to be candidly explored, with an eye toward the clarification of differences and the discovery of possibilities for accommodation. I conclude by briefly considering how such exploration might proceed with respect to clinical counseling and reproductive choices by HIV-infected women. Unless we probe beneath the notion of autonomy to its normative foundations, our arguments about autonomy-negating influence are likely to be bitter and fruitless, especially in such painful contexts as the AIDS epidemic.

Clinical Counseling, Reproductive Choice, and the Bioethics Treatment of Autonomy

Debate over the meaning of reproductive autonomy for HIV-infected women has been inspired by the implementation of some influence strategies and the anxious anticipation of others. At the clinical level, the counseling of reproductive abstinence has been widely recommended[23] and is probably an established practice.[24] For the purposes of the discussion below, such counseling can be put into two categories, which I shall refer to as "advisory" and "directive." By the former, I mean statements that are phrased as suggestions, recommendations, or personal opinions and framed in a manner that acknowledges the counselee's decision-making role. A counselor might say, for example: "Because of the risks we've been discussing, I advise against having a child. It's important for you to understand, though, that the ultimate decision is yours." Or, after reviewing the relevant risk data (and discussing the satisfactions of parenting), a counselor might offer: "The choice is up to you, but, personally, I don't think I'd do it." By a "directive" approach, I refer to counseling that takes an imperative form and fails to acknowledge the patient's or client's role as ultimate decision-maker.[25] Examples include such statements as "you should not become pregnant" or "don't have this child."

My dichotomy between advisory and directive approaches constitutes an oversimplification: one can easily conjure up clinical remarks that straddle the two categories or are advisory or directive to varying degrees. Moreover, tone of voice matters at least as much as choice of words, and the manner in which data about risks are presented can deliver strong advisory and directive messages.

Nevertheless, I believe my categories will prove useful in developing the argument set forth below.

Comments by health professionals to the effect that they will not provide prenatal or other medical care to women who decide to bear children[26] constitute a more aggressive influence strategy.[27] Although nowhere advocated in print, such pressure may be endemic in clinical practice.[28] If a woman has no alternative source of care, such pressure amounts to the conditioning of access to care upon reproductive abstinence. The reproductive forbearance requested might range from a promise not to become pregnant to the use of a particular contraceptive method or even consent to abortion. In addition, some have expressed concern about a more extreme prospect—that providers could condition their services upon consent to sterilization.[29]

Additional influence strategies are possible at the public health level. These range from the public promotion of reproductive abstinence via mass media campaigns[30] to the creation of financial and other material incentives to refrain from childbearing.[31] These strategies lie beyond the scope of this paper, which focuses on autonomy-negating influence in clinical relationships. Nonetheless, the analysis that follows is applicable, with adaptations, to public health interventions.

Conceptual analysis and moral judgment

The notion that clinical efforts to dissuade HIV-infected women from having children are coercive *per se* and therefore objectionable squares poorly with prevailing bioethics theory. To begin with, an influential body of bioethics scholarship aspires to the definition and analysis of coercion as a *concept*, quite apart from the *moral* status of coercion in particular contexts. For commentators who hold that such a definition is possible, the conclusion that an influence method constitutes coercion does not by itself imply that the method is morally wrong. For them, an additional, explicitly moral argument is necessary to support this second conclusion.[32] Conceptual analysis and moral assessment, in other words, are entirely separate philosophical tasks. However, this view holds; the former is a prerequisite for the latter to be fruitful.[33] An implication of this position is that when the word "coercion" is employed to convey a moral judgment, unsupported by a separate moral explanation, it is used untidily, in a manner that avoids the hard work of moral analysis. Those who object to the counseling of reproductive abstinence on the sole ground that such counseling is coercive provide no analytical basis for their moral judgment in this view, unless they explain why coercion in this context is wrong.

Such explanations are difficult to find in writings by those who oppose the counseling of reproductive forbearance. The premise that coercion is a bad thing per se seems deeply embedded in this work. One might simply dismiss this premise as an instance of fuzzy thinking, a failure of rigor by writers with passionate beliefs. Alternatively, however, one might take it more seriously, as a challenge to the notion that conceptual and moral analysis of coercion are separable.[34] Such a challenge draws support from myriad commentators on the concept of coercion, many of whom take the position that it is intrinsically wrongful.[35] From this perspective, the coerciveness of an action creates a presumption against its desirability,[36] albeit a presumption open to rebuttal under sufficiently compelling circumstances.[37]

Underlying the sense that coercion is intrinsically wrongful is the notion that to call something "coercive" is to render a normative judgment. In recent years, a number of academic writers have endorsed variations on this theme, contending that distinctions between coercive and noncoercive influence cannot be explained intelligibly except by reference to normative standards. Adherents to this view debate the appropriate sources of such norms.[38] Some take the utilitarian position that an influence attempt coerces if it leads to socially suboptimal results.[39] Others pursue more particularized moral inquiries, focusing on the propriety of the would-be influence agent's behavior toward his or her target or the justice of the target individual's circumstances.[40]

This challenge to the separateness of coercion as a concept and as a normative judgment is consonant with a central insight of contemporary semiology—that the connotations of a term are essential to its signifying function. The communicative content of a term is, in semiological theory, an integrated function of the term's denotative meaning (loosely equivalent to what philosophers call conceptual analysis) and its evolving connotations.[41] No term can be used in a purely denotative sense; connotative significance is inescapable. Connotative meaning is "general, global, and diffuse"—a "fragment of ideology."[42] However, it is the mechanism by which language accommodates to changes in society and culture. Through connotation, "the environmental world invades the system,"[43] thereby compelling the language to evolve new denotative meanings.[44] Connotation, in short, is the cutting edge of denotation. To insist that terms like "coercion" and "autonomy" be defined as conceptual abstractions, in isolation from their context-linked, normative valences, is to deny much about these words' actual signifying functions. To a diverse range of writers and speakers, including those opposed to encouraging HIV-infected women not to bear children, coercion connotes something inherently negative.

If coercion is an intrinsically moral (and negative) idea, then those who condemn the clinical advocacy of reproductive abstinence as wrong because it is coercive make a defensible normative claim. This claim is open to a form of rebuttal that I will not discuss here: it is possible to argue that an influence strategy judged to be coercive, and therefore prima facie objectionable, should nevertheless be tolerated because it achieves some overriding good.[45] I leave to others the question of whether coercion can ever be justified in the clinical contexts upon which this chapter focuses. I turn instead to the persuasiveness of the prima facie claim itself—i.e., to whether the clinical advocacy of reproductive abstinence can plausibly be called coercive. I consider this question as part of a larger problem—the making of distinctions between autonomy-preserving and autonomy-negating influence in clinical contexts.

Autonomy-negating influence in contemporary bioethics

Bioethics theory, I submit in this section, provides, at most, equivocal support for the proposition that the clinical pursuit of reproductive abstinence is per se coercive or otherwise inconsistent with autonomous reproductive choice. The diversity of views on autonomy-negating influence in the bioethics literature precludes easy generalization. On the other hand, I suggest below, bioethics commentators concerned with enhancing the patient's role in medical treatment decisions have tended toward understandings of autonomous choice (and of coercion) that tolerate advice-giving and disregard pressures arising from adverse life circumstances.

These understandings, I argue, permit the conclusion that conditioning the provision of medical care upon abstinence from childbearing can preclude autonomous reproductive choice. They are also compatible with the belief that directive counseling (in the sense described above[46]) forecloses autonomous choice, though they leave room for the opposite view. They make it more problematic to assert that the avisory counseling I described above interferes with reproductive autonomy, but they leave some space for arguments to this effect.

Conceptions of autonomous choice that permit advice-giving and disregard, as a rule, pressures arising from adverse life circumstances neatly fit the normative aims of commentators concerned principally with empowering patients in medical treatment settings. Given these aims, such conceptions are appealing, even persuasive, but this persuasiveness is contextual. Other normative ends—e.g., the pursuit of change in the chooser's life circumstances or intrapsychic world—may render other visions of autonomous action more persuasive, within different contexts.

Requiring a purposeful autonomy-negating agent: the Faden and Beauchamp model as an example

No single conception of coercion or autonomy-negating external influence dominates the bioethics literature; but the empowerment of patients as choosers has animated bioethics scholarship and activism,[47] inspiring models of autonomous action that preserve the possibility of patient self-determination in the face of medical authority and the pressures of illness and life circumstances. By contrast with scholars who contend that autonomous choices must cohere with a person's deep and enduring values,[48] bioethics commentators have tended toward less stringent criteria for autonomous action. The work of Tom Beauchamp and James Childress is illustrative. In their influential bioethics textbook,[49] Beauchamp and Childress state that choosers who act "intentionally," "with understanding," and "without controlling influences" act autonomously.[50] Beauchamp and Childress add that the last two requirements can be met by the average person without the reflective effort contemplated by philosophers who demand coherence between a person's choices and enduring values:

> To chain adequate decision making by patients to fully or completely autonomous decision making strips the rules of informed consent of any meaningful place in the practical world, where people's actions are rarely, if ever, fully autonomous. A person's appreciation of information and independence from controlling influences in the health-care setting need not exceed a person's information and independence in making a financial investment, hiring a new employee, or attending a particular college. The goal, realistically, is only that such consequential decisions be substantially autonomous.[51]

Although some commentators on clinical ethics have espoused more stringent requirements for adequately autonomous choice,[52] the Beauchamp and Childress position probably represents the prevailing view.[53] Their pragmatic approach to the question of "controlling" external influence allows for patient self-determination without a radical restructuring of doctor–patient relations[54] or background social circumstances. This approach to autonomy-negating external influence is developed in greater depth by Beauchamp and Ruth Faden.[55] I turn now to their work, especially their definition of coercion, because (1) its clarity facilitates close examination and (2) it is representative of the inclination in bioethics commentary toward conceptions of autonomous action that permit both professional opinion-giving and a high degree of circumstantial pressure. My aim is to offer a sense of how bioethics scholars who share this inclination might analyze claims that the aforementioned efforts to influence reproductive decisions preclude autonomous choice.[56] I also highlight the normative commitments that inform this analysis and question their relevance to the drawing of lines between influences that permit and preclude autonomous choice outside the medical sphere.

Faden and Beauchamp set forth an apparently simple, three-part definition of coercion. First, an "agent of influence" (one or more persons) must "intend to influence" another person "by presenting a severe threat." Second, this threat must be "credible." Third, the threat must be "irresistible."[57] A notable thing about this definition is its requirement of a purposeful coercing agent.[58] Faden and Beauchamp hold categorically that influences bearing on a decision do not diminish the autonomy of the chooser, whether by coercing or by otherwise controlling his or her actions, unless such influences are the product of a purposeful agent.[59] Purposeful agency is an element of some classic philosophical models of coercion,[60] but it is notably absent from definitions that focus on the experience of those being influenced. An example of the latter is Harold Lasswell's influential model of coercion, which requires only "a high degree of constraint and/or inducement."[61]

From a medical ethics perspective, the requirement of a purposeful agent serves an essential strategic function. Without this requirement, fears inspired by illness, dependency, or the impersonality of medical routines could constitute coercion in clinical settings, rendering autonomous patient decision-making impossible in many circumstances.[62] An obvious example is a patient with a life-threatening malignancy who has been advised (accurately) by her physician that only a disfiguring operation can improve her prospects for survival. Absent the requirement of a purposeful agent, this situation would appear to constitute coercion. A "high degree of constraint and/or inducement" is clearly present. On its face, this situation meets the other two tests in the Faden and Beauchamp formula: the patient's cancer poses a threat that is surely "credible" and seemingly "irresistible." Patients often confront such circumstances. Absent a purposeful agency requirement, coercion in clinical work would be commonplace[63] and nonautonomous patient decision-making would be "par for the course." Were nonautonomous patient decision-making to be seen as unavoidable, insistence on respect for the autonomy of patients would seem quixotic. The rationale for requiring informed consent—protection for autonomous choice[64]—would then lack its current moral force. If patients are commonly unable to act autonomously, regardless of how their doctors interact with them, then why look to physician–patient conversation to preserve autonomy? Indeed, why bother to involve patients in medical decision-making at all?

The intent requirement urged by Faden and Beauchamp (and others) nicely averts this dilemma. By drawing a line between "credible," "irresistible" threats posed purposefully by human agents and impersonally by circumstances, Faden and Beauchamp preserve the conceptual possibility of autonomous decisions by patients in the most dire medical straits. Even the most desperate medical (or other) circumstances do not "coerce," once this line is drawn, unless a human agent intervenes by purposefully posing a threat. In Faden and Beauchamp's words, "nonintentional, situational factors can neither coerce nor otherwise control actions so as to compromise autonomy, no matter how desperate the person's circumstance."[65] This definitional strategy channels attention to constraints on choice that are imposed willfully by human agents. By making such constraints decisive with respect to an actor's capacity to decide autonomously, Faden and Beauchamp set their sights on the behavior of those who impose them.[66] Given their project—the alteration of physician behavior to preserve the possibilities for patient self-determination that remain after illness and social circumstances are taken as givens—this definitional strategy makes contextual sense.

Applying the model to reproductive choice: childbearing by HIV-infected women

The Faden and Beauchamp model of autonomy-negating influence yields mixed results—and much indeterminacy—when applied to the above-mentioned methods for influencing the reproductive choices of HIV-infected women. The model permits the conclusion that conditioning medical care upon abstinence from childbearing is incompatible with autonomous reproductive choice, but its analytic framework is equally consonant with the opposite view. This framework is also indeterminate with respect to whether the directive and advisory modes of counseling constitute autonomy-negating influence. This indeterminacy is traceable to the model's pervasive, tacit dependence upon external normative reference points as grounds for making the analytic distinctions upon which it overtly relies.

CONDITIONING MEDICAL CARE UPON REPRODUCTIVE ABSTINENCE: THE PROBLEM OF RESISTIBILITY. A clinician who instructs her patient that continued care is contingent upon reproductive abstinence[67] issues a proposal that is clearly "intentional" and presumably "credible." If seen as a threat (as opposed to an offer), this sort of proposal plainly satisfies two of the three elements in the Faden and Beauchamp definition of coercion. Only its "irresistibility" seems open to question. Intuitively, the resistibility of such propositions would seem to depend on such factors as access to other sources of care, the intensity of the patient's wish for a child, and the particular behavior solicited by the counselor—e.g., a general promise not to become pregnant, a commitment to use a particular contraceptive method, or consent to an abortion. A case could be made against the irresistibility of such proposals in any event on the ground that medical care, though desirable, can be foregone without assured calamity; certainly, this prospect does not seem so constraining as that quintessentially coercive proposition, "your money or your life." On the other hand, a strong emphasis on protection for self-determination by women in reproductive matters might incline one toward the view that such proposals are irresistible under most or all circumstances.

The Faden and Beauchamp approach to autonomy-negating external influence is complicated by another, parallel line of inquiry in which resistibility plays a critical role. Some contingent propositions that do not qualify as coercive can nevertheless preclude autonomous choice if they meet a relaxed nonresistibility standard. Autonomous action, within the Faden and Beauchamp framework, is precluded by some forms of "manipulation" as well as by coercion. Faden and Beauchamp define "manipulation" as "any intentional and successful influence of a person by noncoercively altering the actual choices available to the person or by nonpersuasively altering the other's perception of those choices."[68] Successful threats (and offers[69]) that do not constitute coercion thereby qualify as manipulation since they alter the available range of choices. When such propositions cannot be "reasonably easily resisted" (a seemingly less stringent criterion than "irresistibility"), they preclude autonomous decision-making.[70] Thus, in theory, a proposal to render medical care on condition of reproductive abstinence may be resistible (and hence not coercive) but nevertheless inconsistent with autonomous choice.

Faden and Beauchamp offer little guidance as to how resistibility ought to be assessed. They characterize the resistibility of a proposition as something empirically measurable, via an inquiry into the "subjective responses" of those at whom it is targeted,[71] but they say nothing about how these "subjective responses" might be explored.[72] This open-endedness precludes an incontrovertible answer, within the Faden and Beauchamp framework, to the question of whether conditioning medical care upon reproductive abstinence compromises autonomous choice.

A more basic problem underlies this analytic difficulty. The resistibility of a threat (or offer) cannot be judged without reference to a normative standard—a premise about the degree of external or psychological pressure that a person ought to resist under the circumstances at issue. To see why, consider the alternative proposition—that resistibility is a purely empirical matter. Thus conceived, the question of resistibility calls for a *counterfactual* inquiry into whether a person who in fact yielded to pressure might have withstood its influencing effect. However, such an inquiry into the subjunctive is an act of imagination, not real-world observation. As Douglas Hofstadter observes about counterfactual thinking, "it is obvious that anything that didn't happen didn't happen. There aren't degrees of 'didn't-happen-ness.'"[73] At times, we intuit that a counterfactual possibility almost happened, but "the 'almost' lies in the mind, not in the external facts."[74]

Our ability to think subjunctively may be central to our capacity for creativity.[75] Yet our inclination to do so is curiously selective. As Hofstadter notes, "some counterfactuals strike us as 'less counterfactual' than other counterfactuals."[76] Intuitively, often unconsciously, we set limits to the subjunctive slippage we allow between reality and what might have been. These limits derive from our mental representations of the world, not from unprocessed, external reality. These representations incorporate background assumptions about what should and should not be varied in our subjunctive imaginings. Such assumptions frame our counterfactual thinking. Hofstadter offers a trivial but instructive example. A football player catches a third-down pass and turns upfield toward the end zone. Unfortunately for his team, which trails by a touchdown, his momentum carries him out of bounds. Predictably, the team's frustrated fans imagine what might have been had he been able to stay in bounds. We would be surprised, by contrast, were the fans to focus on what might have happened had the ball been round.[77] We would be similarly surprised if the fans turned to dreaming about what might have been had there not been a rule against going out of bounds.

Why do the last two variations strike us as less plausible, or more counterfactual, than the first? Why, in other words, are we less inclined to vary our background assumptions about the shape of the ball and the rule against stepping out of bounds? An answer is that it makes heuristic sense to take the shape of the ball and the rules of the game as givens if our aim is to understand what the team (and its fans) are hoping to accomplish. By contrast, it makes heuristic sense to vary, in the subjunctive, the player's steps along the sidelines since he wants badly to stay in bounds.[78]

Analogously, in considering the situation of a person confronting a threat (or offer), it is heuristically useful to frame the problem by taking some circumstances as givens and allowing others to vary in the subjunctive. Among the circumstances that might be either varied or held constant are the existence and character of the threat and the possible response(s) of the threatened person. By depicting a threat as irresistible, we hold the threatened person's response constant, in the subjunctive. We assume, in other words, that the threatened person must yield. This assumption frames our counterfactual inquiry. It channels our subjunctive speculation toward other circumstances—e.g., the presence (or absence) and the character of the threat itself. From the perspective of the threatened person, varying these circumstances offers the only (counterfactual) way to avoid yielding to the threat, once the impossibility of resistance to the threat (as actually posed) is assumed.

By depicting a class of threats as merely "difficult to resist,"[79] Faden and Beauchamp make a similar framing choice, but they signal that the frame can be more easily adjusted. They represent the threatened person's response as constant, in the subjunctive, but they leave open the possibility of counterfactual variation in this response. Our subjunctive speculation is thereby guided toward other factual circumstances, such as the presence and nature of the threat posed. On the other hand, we are not so "locked in" to the assumption that the threatened person will yield: resistance to the threat remains an available counterfactual alternative.

In contrast, characterization of a threat as "easily resistible" channels subjunctive attention to the possibility of variation in the threatened person's response. It renders variation in the threatening situation into a less interesting possibility—less interesting because it seems less significant from the perspective of a person confronting such a benign threat.

The choice between these different framing possibilities has critical normative consequences for it determines the focus of creative, counterfactual thinking about how a threatening situation might be addressed. Characterization of a threat as easy to resist casts the threatened person as a responsible agent with feasible options. It thereby focuses attention on his or her moral agency, as opposed to the moral role (and feasible alternatives) of the one posing the threat. By contrast, depiction of a threat as irresistible (or difficult to resist) casts the threatening party as the responsible moral agent. This channels attention to what the threatening party might do differently—i.e., how the threat might be transformed or eliminated. The choice between these frames for counterfactual thinking is not a purely empirical question since, as Hofstadter bluntly puts it, "there aren't degrees of 'didn't-happen-ness.'" Because "the 'almost' lies in the mind, not in the external facts," the choice between frames reflects human aims. Ultimately, therefore, the question of resistibility is normative, not factual: it is about whether we should hold an actor responsible for not resisting.[80]

Differing views about the resistibility of an effort to influence an HIV-infected woman's reproductive choices are likely to reflect myriad underlying normative concerns. A thorough analytical treatment of these concerns lies beyond the scope of this paper, but I will point to some, for purposes of illustration. To begin with, the belief that a particular means of influence is difficult or impossible to resist is likely to be tied to convictions about the moral legitimacy of the leverage it employs. Conditioning the provision of medical care upon reproductive abstinence, for example, will be troubling to those who view access to health care as a baseline moral entitlement, especially if other sources of care are not readily available. The use of clinical abandonment as leverage, after a therapeutic relationship has been established, will disturb those who believe that such abandonment constitutes a wrongful breach of patient faith.

Intuitions about the resistibility of an influence method are also likely to be linked to considerations of fairness and justice relating to the behavior that the influence agent wishes to elicit. Attempts to discourage childbearing by HIV-infected women implicate a host of such considerations. Some involve the sense that asking these women to sacrifice the fulfillment that comes with childbearing is unfair because of the injustice of their circumstances. To the extent that HIV transmission is seen as a product of poverty, racial discrimination, or other social ills, a clinical response that asks victims of these wrongs to endure further deprivation seems unfair.[81] This impression of unfairness is magnified by society's failure to offer other possibilities for fulfillment—e.g., educational and career opportunities—to minority women, who are at disproportionate risk for infection.[82] Awareness that many women contract HIV from male sexual partners who decline to use condoms and, in some cases, impose their sexual will aggressively can add to this sense of unfairness. For some, painful memories of past infringements upon reproductive freedom[83] heighten sensitivities to present sources of unfairness.

On the other side of the moral ledger, concerns about burdening society with medical costs and burdening offspring with the tragedy of terminal, wasting illness invite the belief that discouraging childbirth is a legitimate aim. The prospect that many children of infected mothers will become orphans reinforces this view. More darkly, insensitivity toward the aspirations of HIV-infected women or to the deprivations that many have experienced may influence perceptions about reproductive abstinence as a clinical goal.

One might object that these factors (on both sides of the ledger) are relevant to the question of whether autonomy-negating influence should be exerted but unrelated to whether a particular influence is so difficult to resist that it precludes autonomous choice. There is something to this objection: we tend not to view our unanalyzed intuitions about resistibility as by-products of our beliefs about fairness and justice. Yet if, as I have just argued, the concept of resistibility draws its content from implicit normative premises,[84] then ideas about fairness and justice are central to any analysis of resistibility that goes beyond boilerplate. The gap between this deeper analytic necessity and the common impression that resistibility is empirically measurable suggests that subterfuge[85] is involved when moral judgments are avowedly grounded on determinations of resistibility. By obscuring deeper, substantive conflicts, this subterfuge may yield benefits. Judgments based avowedly on determinations of resistibility enable us to make hard moral decisions without openly affronting intensely felt values[86] and embittering their adherents. This mechanism may contribute to mutual respect and social peace.[87] It may also enable us to resolve value conflicts differently within separate spheres of activity without suffering the cost of explicit logical contradiction. However, by obscuring the sacrifice of some values, this subterfuge may make it harder for disregarded persons and groups to assert their concerns.

Another basis for disagreement about the meaning of resistibility merits brief mention. At a higher level of abstraction, proponents of broader and narrower understandings of resistibility may differ over whether human dignity is best served by broad conceptions of personal responsibility or by a preference against viewing victims of unjust circumstances as authors of their own actions. While the former perspective affirms human dignity by preserving the domain of the self in the face of myriad influences,[88] the latter does so by channeling attention to possibilities for averting the degradation of persons by alleviating injustice. Preferences for one or another of these perspectives may affect judgments about the resistibility of an influence method independently of normative considerations related to the particular leverage employed or behavior sought.

THE FADEN AND BEAUCHAMP MODEL AND THE THREAT/OFFER DISTINCTION. The framing of contingent propositions presents further problems for the Faden and Beauchamp model. Faden and Beauchamp adhere to the classic view that threats coerce while offers do not.[89] Offers, they hold, are manipulative, not coercive.[90] On the other hand, they take the position that not all offers permit autonomous choice. Some manipulations (including some offers) preclude autonomous decision-making. In short, threats (if "severe," "credible," and "irresistible"[91]) preclude autonomous action, but offers do not, unless they are "unwelcome" and cannot be "reasonably easily resisted."[92] This formulation makes the characterization of contingent propositions—as threats, "unwelcome" offers, or "welcome" offers—critical to whether they preclude autonomous decision-making. Yet choices between these characterizations, like conclusions about resistibility, rest ultimately on moral judgments about the substance of the propositions at issue. With respect to the threat/offer distinction, this point has been made elsewhere, and I will touch upon it only briefly. I will focus more closely on the difference between welcome and unwelcome offers, to which I turn first because it bears importantly on the role of the threat/offer distinction in the Faden and Beauchamp model.

What Faden and Beauchamp mean by "welcome" is less than clear. An offer is "welcome," they say, if it "is one the person influenced wants to *receive*, but not necessarily to *accept*." Conversely, they hold, an offer is unwelcome if its recipient would prefer not to receive it, whether or not she chooses to accept it. Beyond this, they do not elaborate, averring that "the complex morass of human motivations that would *cause* such welcoming" is outside their scope.[93]

The idea of an unwelcome offer that a person decides to reject is easy to envision[94] but trivial for our present purposes since its resistibility, shown in retrospect by the act of rejection, renders it compatible with autonomous action. Much more important—and much more problematic—is the notion of an unwelcome offer that the recipient accepts. Faden and Beauchamp suggest just one example: an impoverished mother of five children is offered $25 per day to participate in six day-long sessions of medical research involving painful and invasive procedures. Although she finds the prospect "horrifying" and "wishes desperately" that she had not received this offer, she nevertheless accepts it.[95] The "unwelcomeness" of this offer is hardly self-evident since in the end its recipient's fears are overcome by her desire for the $25 per day. Although her acceptance seems motivated by a sense of duty, not joy, it constitutes an expressed *net* preference, a decision to endure pain to raise money for her children. Put in other terms, her acceptance of this grim offer is a Pareto-superior move,[96] from her perspective, given her desperate, preoffer starting point. She may have conflicting thoughts about making this move (including the waxing and waning wish never to have received such an offer), but in the end she opts to do so.

Once she accepts, characterization of the offer as one she would have preferred not to receive questions the validity of her own summation of preferences. By accepting, she announces that her own net calculus of preferences in the end favors the offer. To hold that the offer is nevertheless unwelcome to her accords privileged status to doubts that have lost out in her mind.[97] This privileging is an act of interpretation by outside observers, not an unfiltered observation about the recipient's desires. As such, it is informed by the observers' normative beliefs about the recipient's preferences and about the choice situation. Such beliefs might arise from empathy with the recipient's situation, the belief that her life circumstances are unjust, or the sense that the researchers are unfairly exploiting her vulnerability.[98] Like the question of resistibility, the question of welcomeness cannot be answered without implicit reliance upon notions of fairness and justice.

The following example illustrates this point in the context of reproductive decision-making by HIV-infected women. A 38-year-old woman without health insurance develops a fever, sore throat, and shortness of breath. She is childless but was married 2 months ago (for the first time), and she is looking forward to fulfilling her dream of motherhood within a committed relationship. She initially forgoes medical attention, but her symptoms become worse. After 2 weeks, she sees a doctor at her town's primary care center, the only clinic within a day's drive that provides free care to uninsured patients. After a thorough evaluation, including an HIV test, the doctor tells her that she is HIV-infected and has contracted an opportunistic infection. The doctor further advises her that the clinic will treat her only if she agrees not to become pregnant and consents to Norplant. She agonizes over this decision, telling her husband that she wishes she had not received this offer, but she accepts the clinic's terms.

By agreeing to the doctor's proposal, this patient indicates her net preference for its terms, as compared with the alternative scenario—reproductive freedom without access to treatment for her infections. One can characterize the doctor's offer as "unwelcome" only by privileging the patient's anguish about the childbearing possibilities she will forgo. A range of beliefs about fairness and justice might lead one to do this.[99] Examination of her "complex morass of . . . motivations,"[100] uninformed by any normative vision, cannot.[101]

Since Faden and Beauchamp hold that welcome offers are compatible per se with autonomous decision-making,[102] this choice between characterizations matters greatly within their model.[103] The threat/offer distinction is at least as important to their theory since threats imply coercion,[104] which precludes autonomous action per se. Faden and Beauchamp do not propose an approach to the parsing of threats from offers, but they suggest that such distinctions can be made without reference to "[q]uestions of . . moral justiciability."[105] A considerable body of recent work supports a different view.

To begin with, there is virtual unanimity about the proposition that threats and offers can be parsed only by reference to an extrinsic baseline. Wertheimer puts the point as follows:

> The crux of the distinction between threats and offers is quite simple: A *threatens* B by proposing to make B *worse* off relative to some baseline; A makes an *offer* to B by proposing to make B *better* off relative to some baseline.[106]

Selecting the appropriate baseline is thus central to distinguishing threats from offers. The making of this selection, moreover, is an inescapably moral enterprise. The role of moral judgment in setting baselines has been much discussed by philosophers[107] and legal scholars.[108] Conceptions of fairness and justice, more often tacit than explicit, determine the baselines we employ.[109] The conditioning of medical care upon reproductive abstinence by HIV-infected women is illustrative. The premise that access to medical care is a right[110] (or that provision of care is a social obligation[111]) yields a baseline that includes the availability of health services. Measured by this baseline, the conditioning of care upon abstinence from childbearing plainly constitutes a threat, absent the availability of other sources of care.[112] By contrast, the belief that access to medical care is neither an individual right nor a social obligation, but rather a question of contractual arrangement,[113] implies a baseline that does not incorporate such access. Relative to this baseline, a proposal to render care contingent upon reproductive forbearance represents an offer.

Some commentators take the position that baselines also can be derived from nonmoral sources, including historical experience,[114] empirically grounded predictions,[115] and the subjective expectations of a proposal's recipients.[116] For example, a society's past failure to provide health care as a right establishes a historical baseline that does not include assured access to care. Relative to this standard, the contingent proposals I have been discussing constitute offers.[117] Alternatively, were the conditioning of medical care upon personal behavior a usual practice, one could characterize such proposals as predictable and thereby infer an empirical baseline that renders these propositions as offers.[118] The subjective expectations approach, by contrast, entails an inquiry into each recipient's beliefs about what is morally required. The belief that a health-care provider is entitled to condition her services upon reproductive abstinence yields a baseline to this effect—and the conclusion that such propositions are offers.[119]

These seemingly nonmoral baselines invite the impression that threats and offers can be distinguished without reliance upon normative premises. This impression is illusory for two fundamental reasons. First, normative thinking is intrinsic to the formulation of the inquiries that these putative baselines demand. As has been widely recognized in recent years by philosophers of the natural and social sciences, observation and description are richly infused by normative imagination.[120] The claim that human observers can discern baselines from history, prediction, or accounts of intrapsychic experience without relying upon morally informed premises flies in the face of this realization. Second, the elaboration of multiple baselines—including some expressly moral standards and others derived from history, prediction, or subjective expectations—presents the challenge of selecting between baselines. Such selection is a necessary element in models of the threat/offer distinction that assert the possibility of both moral and nonmoral baselines.[121] That choosing between baselines entails normative judgment is tacitly acknowledged by commentators who propose reliance upon more than one baseline.[122] The relative import of history, prediction, and intrapsychic experience as grounds for distinguishing threats from offers is a moral question: the legitimacy of each rests on premises about the fairness and justice of the social phenomena upon which it purports to defer.[123]

"ADVISORY" AND "DIRECTIVE" COUNSELING. As defined herein,[124] neither advisory nor directive counseling of reproductive abstinence presents the listener with a proposal that changes her set of available choices. Such counseling thus entails neither a threat nor an offer. As such, it cannot coerce, within the Faden and Beauchamp paradigm or others that abide by the rule that only contingent propositions (threats or offers) can coerce. For the subset of such models that draws a simple dichotomy between coerced and autonomous action, this analysis suffices for the conclusion that advisory and directive counseling are compatible per se with autonomous choice.[125] Within the Faden and Beauchamp model, however, further inquiry is necessary, since some influence attempts that do not constitute threats or offers are nonetheless not compatible with autonomous choice. In particular, influence attempts that "nonpersuasively alter" a person's "perception" of her choices[126] preclude autonomous action if they are not "easily resistible."[127] "Persuasion" is compatible per se with autonomous choice, but only "appeals to reason" can persuade.[128] Appeals to noncognitive mental processes—to guilt, vanity, fear, or other emotions[129]—constitute efforts to "nonpersuasively alter" a listener's perceptions.

Faden and Beauchamp group influence attempts that "nonpersuasively" change perception into two classes: (1) "manipulation of information" upon which a person bases a decision and (2) "psychological manipulation" via intentional acts that "caus[e] changes in mental processes other than those involved in understanding"—i.e., noncognitive processes.[130] The former category encompasses a range of deceptive practices[131] that lie outside the scope of this paper.[132] Absent such deception, clinical counseling unaccompanied by offers or threats can interfere with autonomous choice only if it falls within the latter category *and* is not "easily resistible."

Advisory counseling, as defined herein, would appear to constitute persuasion within the Faden and Beauchamp model and thus would seem compatible with autonomous choice. A dispassionate recommendation against childbearing, accompanied by accurate statements about vertical HIV transmission, difficulties likely to confront mother and child, and even social costs, represents an "appeal to reason," as this term is typically understood.[133] Faden and Beauchamp acknowledge that their approach to dispassionately given advice entails a difficulty: imbalances of power in clinical relationships encourage patients to act in a passive, compliant manner.[134] This may diminish their ability to act autonomously, Faden and Beauchamp warn, especially when patients belong to "particularly vulnerable" groups like the poor and the uneducated.[135] Since HIV-infected women are disproportionately impoverished, African-American and Latino, and poorly educated, this concern applies with special force to them.

Having acknowledged this problem, Faden and Beauchamp allow space for the conclusion that autonomous choice can nonetheless be safeguarded during advisory counseling. They posit that imbalances of power, or "role constraints," preclude autonomous choice only when people "do not act as they would *prefer* to act, and *would otherwise* act, were they not under the peculiarly intense and often oppressive pressures and constraints inherent in the dependent role."[136] This approach limits the autonomy-negating impact of such dependency to situations in which constraint is both consciously experienced[137] and sufficient to meet a variant of the nonresistibility test ("intense" and "oppressive" pressure). It thereby permits clinicians to counteract their own aura of authority by communicating clearly that their recommendations are not "orders" and that decisions contrary to professional advice will be treated with deference.[138] Even where such communication fails to eliminate the conscious experience of role-related constraint, Faden and Beauchamp leave room for the conclusion that advisory counseling is compatible with autonomous choice. In such situations, their reliance upon a resistibility test yields answers that rest on normative judgments external to their analytic scheme.[139]

Directive counseling would appear to present more possibilities for "psychological manipulation" via "changes in mental processes other than those involved in understanding." Statements that take an imperative form and fail to acknowledge the patient's role as ultimate decision-maker pose the problem of "role constraints" more acutely than does the advisory counseling of reproductive abstinence. Such statements seem almost designed to take advantage of the listener's sense of powerlessness relative to the speaker. They draw much of their force from the speaker's aura of authority: indeed, declarations like "you should not become pregnant" or "don't have this child" appear to rely on little else.[140] Even if accompanied by dispassionate reason-giving—e.g., remarks about disease transmission risks or social costs—these statements inject a noncognitive element into the listener's decision-making process. As such, they are strong candidates for characterization as "psychological manipulation."[141] Whether such statements, once so characterized, should be deemed not "easily resistible" and thus incompatible with autonomous choice is a more open question. Like the question of resistibility in other contexts, it cannot be answered without reliance upon normative premises external to the Faden and Beauchamp framework.[142]

SUMMING UP: AUTONOMY-NEGATING INFLUENCE AND THE NORMATIVE AIMS OF BIOETHICAL THEORY. It would be wrong to read the work of Faden and Beauchamp as an authoritative statement of the bioethical understanding of coercion and autonomous action. Scholars within the main currents of American bioethics continue to struggle with these concepts, which are central to the field's aspirations for the empowerment of patients. On the other hand, Faden and Beauchamp elaborate rigorously on some intuitions about the nature of autonomy-negating external influence that are widely shared within the bioethics movement and that play strategic roles in the movement's reformist vision. In particular, their model posits several prerequisites for the occurrence of influence incompatible with autonomous choice that are broadly accepted by commentators on bioethics. These include the presence of a human agent of influence, the existence (in this agent's mind) of conscious intent to exert influence, and the existence (in the mind of the chooser) of a conscious sense of constraint resulting from the influence attempt.[143]

Once these prerequisites are met, other questions take on decisive import with respect to the question of autonomy-negating external influence. These include the resistibility of an influence attempt, the threat/offer distinction, the difference between welcome and unwelcome proposals, and the distinction between appeals to reason and passion. The Faden and Beauchamp model's tacit reliance upon external normative reference points for answering these questions enables it to generate variable conclusions about the possibility of autonomous action in any given context, depending on the normative reference points chosen; but the threshold requirements that influence be consciously intended by a human agent and consciously experienced as constraining rule out lines of reasoning that might lead more directly to the conclusion that an influence precludes autonomous choice. Arguments about the constraining effects of social structure and/or unconscious experience are pushed to the margins by these prerequisites, which tacitly take patients' medical, social, and psychological circumstances as givens. This analytic strategy serves the bioethics movement's aim of advancing liberty in clinical settings within the parameters imposed by illness, personal character, and social structure.[144]

Viewed from this vantage point, the prerequisite that autonomy-negating influence must be both consciously intended and consciously experienced seems justified. Yet beyond the setting of sick patients seeking treatment, the case for this prerequisite is not so clear. Reproductive decision-making by HIV-infected women may represent a clinical context within which differing normative aims merit another, perhaps broader, conception of autonomy-precluding influence.

Alternative Accounts of Autonomy-Negating Influence

Outside the bioethics tradition, broader conceptions of autonomy-negating influence abound. The proposition that such influence must be both consciously intended and consciously experienced is open to dispute from diverse perspectives. In this section, I consider some of these challenges and their implications for our thinking about autonomous choice in clinical contexts. Seen from the normative vantage points that inspire these broader conceptions, each, I argue, is as persuasive as the prerequisite that autonomy-negating influence must be consciously intended and experienced.[145] Any preference between this more restrictive position and broader conceptions must arise from some *extrinsic*, contextual perspective. The tight linkage between our opinions about the limits of autonomy-negating influence and our poorly articulated, context-based moral leanings is my focus in the next and final section. There, I argue for the need to dispense with subterfuge and to probe for underlying, often hidden normative commitments when contrary visions of autonomous action collide.

Dispensing with the intent requirement: coercion as conscious experience

Making the deliberate action of a human agent into a prerequisite for the presence of autonomy-negating influence fits poorly with our intuitions about the experience of being coerced. From the perspective of a person being influenced, as Norman Daniels observes, it is the "context of restricted choice" that engenders a sense of "diminished voluntariness."[146] The "blame" we might ascribe to someone "who plays an active role in creating the unfreedom"[147] is another matter. The experience of "diminished voluntariness," or "unfreedom,"[148] in other words, is something apart from the actions, purposeful or otherwise, that bring about this experience.[149]

Intuitively, therefore, we often understand coercion as Lasswell and Kaplan define it,[150] in terms of the intensity of the constraining or inducing influence experienced by a chooser. To capture this intuition without discarding the requirement of a coercive purpose, Daniels constructs a parallel concept, "quasi-coercion," that, he posits, entails "diminished freedom of action of the same sort which is glaring in the central cases of coercion."[151] Restrictions on choice are "quasi-coercive," Daniels says, if they result from "unjust or unfair social practices and institutions."[152] For Daniels, autonomous choice is no more possible in the context of quasi-coercive restrictions than it is in the face of coercion as understood by Faden and Beauchamp or others who hold to the conscious intent requirement.

As Daniels acknowledges, his definition of "quasi-coercion" is question-begging: a theory of justice and/or fairness is needed to classify a restriction as quasi-coercive. However, once joined to such a theory, the concept of quasi-coercion expands the scope of autonomy-negating influence beyond the boundaries imposed by the requirement of a coercive (or manipulative) purpose. All restrictions that are "socially caused"—i.e., brought about by "act[s] or institution[s] of man, not God or nature"—are quasi-coercive if "unjust or unfair."[153] This formulation allows immense flexibility. Not only is it open to many conceptions of justice and fairness; it also tacitly permits diverse approaches to the making of distinctions between restrictions on choice that are "socially caused" and those that are traceable to the doings of "God or nature." The broader our view of society's affirmative duty to alleviate pressure on personal choice, the more inclined we are to see failure to do so as a consequence of "act[s] or institution[s] of man."[154]

Daniels' notion of quasi-coercion preserves the classic Nozickian approach to coercion[155] in name only, while in practice dispensing with the purposeful agent prerequisite. Were he to expressly enlarge the concept of coercion to encompass conditions he labels quasi-coercive, the implications for autonomous choice would be identical.[156] The practical significance of Daniels' de facto enlargement of the concept of coercion is potentially great, as the context of reproductive decision-making by HIV-infected women illustrates. If justice entitles all persons to health care regardless of reproductive behavior or ability to pay, then society's failure to guarantee universal access to care forms a quasi-coercive backdrop for women's acceptance of proposals to provide care contingent upon reproductive abstinence. Assessed against this backdrop, agreement to such a proposal cannot be autonomous, even if a woman who would otherwise go without health care finds it welcome.[157] Alternatively, if access to medical care is justly seen as purely a matter of private contractual arrangement,[158] then such a proposal is not quasi-coercive, absent some other moral precept that renders the recipient's choice situation unjust or unfair.

The implications of quasi-coercion for the directive and advisory counseling of reproductive abstinence depend in a different way on baseline beliefs about justice and fairness. The precept that justice requires universal access to health care does not in itself compel the judgment that such counseling is quasi-coercive. Other moral input is needed to reach this conclusion. One might, for example, contend that the aura of authority around health professionals unjustly constrains women's sense of freedom when they hear clinical advice on reproductive matters.[159] One could also argue that poor people and members of marginalized social groups experience a pervasive and unjust sense of powerlessness in their transactions with participants in the dominant culture.[160] Either of these positions can give rise to the conclusion that directive or even advisory counseling is quasi-coercive because its influence is amplified by unjust feelings of powerlessness.

The concept of quasi-coercion thus opens new analytic pathways toward the characterization of influence attempts as incompatible with autonomous choice. Yet this elastic concept does not fully capture the intuition that Daniels says inspired him to invent it. The conscious experience of the chooser is central to this intuition. From his or her perspective, as Daniels notes, restrictions on choice can diminish voluntariness (as perceived by the chooser) regardless of who, if anyone, might be to blame for imposing them. The notion of quasi-coercion reflects Daniels' intuition that the intent behind such restrictions is peripheral to the chooser's subjective experience of diminished voluntariness, but

Daniels' prerequisites for characterizing restrictions as "quasi-coercive"—his requirements that they be both "socially caused" and "unfair or unjust"—seem no more relevant than intent to the chooser's subjective sense of voluntariness. Restrictions on choice traceable to natural causes—e.g., earthquakes or epidemics—can impinge upon a chooser's experience of voluntariness as much as can poverty or other constraints that are seen as socially mediated.[161] Likewise, constraints on choice can beget a sense of diminished voluntariness whether or not they are "unfair or unjust" as measured by one or another moral theory.[162]

Daniels' account of quasi-coercion is thus incomplete as an expression of the extent to which restrictions on choice can impinge upon a chooser's experience of voluntariness. However, his account has considerable appeal as a pragmatic answer to the question of whether autonomous choice is possible in the circumstances that concern him. Daniels proposes the notion of quasi-coercion to cope with the question of whether laborers offered hazard pay for work that poses technologically reducible risks can autonomously assent. As Daniels notes, traditional bioethics understandings of coercion do not clearly encompass such proposals.[163] Yet the narrower a person's range of employment options, the greater the pressure he or she is likely to feel to accept such a proposal. The concept of quasi-coercion enables such proposals to be dismissed as autonomy-negating when the offeree's range of options seems unduly restricted.

The prerequisite that restrictions be socially-caused to be quasi-coercive reflects, in part, the liberal aspiration to preserve a measure of responsible human agency (and the dignity this carries with it) in the face of unavoidable, natural misfortune. The requirement that socially caused restrictions be "unfair or unjust" pursues a balance between respect for the agency and dignity of the chooser and paternalistic concern for the decency of the chooser's situation, as measured by our ideas about fairness and justice. Daniels' explicit deference to notions of fairness and justice permits boundaries to be drawn between autonomy-negating and autonomy-permitting circumstances on the basis of judgments about the morality of restrictions on choice. Intuitively, such judgments seem external to the chooser's subjective experience of voluntariness. Yet Daniels makes them central to the construction of domains of autonomous choice. In so doing, Daniels does candidly what we more typically do covertly, even unconsciously: he roots his conclusions about autonomy in his other moral beliefs.

To fully incorporate Daniels' intuition about the centrality of a subjective sense of "diminished voluntariness" to the experience of being coerced, one would have to define coercion as Lasswell and Kaplan do, in terms of the "degree of constraint and/or inducement"[164] operating on the chooser. However, this poses an obvious difficulty: the setting of a threshold level of "constraint and/or inducement" beyond which the influences operating on a chooser constitute coercion. Since the experience of constraint and inducement is ubiquitous in our conscious mental lives, the placement of this threshold is central to this account of coercion;[165] yet this placement problem is no less thoroughly moralized than is the analogous question of resistibility, within the Faden and Beauchamp model.[166] Like the assessment of resistibility, the setting of coercion thresholds in particular cases of subjectively experienced constraint or inducement is dependent upon external moral reference points. This approach to coercion thus makes the delineation of autonomy-negating clinical influence[167] into a moral inquiry no less open-ended than that called for by the concept of quasi-coercion. With respect to directive and advisory counseling or the conditioning of medical care on reproductive abstinence, this approach is therefore indeterminate, absent an accompanying vision of justice or fairness.

Unconscious coercion

The accounts of autonomy-negating outside influence that I have considered thus far share the premise that such influence must be consciously experienced by a chooser to be coercive or to otherwise preclude autonomous decision-making. Other accounts of coercion, however, incorporate the notion of unconsciously experienced autonomy-negating outside influence. The most prominent such accounts have been offered by three groups of writers with very different normative aims: liberal philosophers concerned with authenticity, radical social theorists working within the Marxist and critical theory traditions, and psychoanalysts from the drive theory and object relations schools.

These accounts of unconsciously-mediated outside influence need to be distinguished from the notion of unconscious internal influence. The latter is widely recognized in the law and in bioethics commentary as potentially autonomy-negating—but not as coercive—under the rubric of psychological incapacity. Mental illness—e.g., clinical depression accompanied by suicidal thinking—is the prototypical example.[168] Severe mental illness is conventionally seen as incapacitating its victims via an internally generated process, though environmental stimuli are often seen as playing a precipitating role.[169] On the other hand, unconsciously mediated external influence is not generally viewed by bioethics commentators or the law as potentially incompatible with autonomous choice.

Liberal theory and the question of authenticity

In liberal social theory (and in most bioethics commentary), the question of unconscious external influence is typically cast as part of the problem of authenticity. According to some liberal theorists, autonomous decision-making must be the product of an authentic self, free from control by external forces. Strong models of authenticity require that a person's principles and preferences be self-consciously chosen via a thought process free from unexamined influence by others.[170] Within such models, unconscious influences on choice tend to be seen as inconsistent with authenticity and therefore preclusive of autonomous action.[171] This vision of autonomy renders choices about childbearing, health care, and other aspects of daily living nonautonomous unless they arise from thought processes far more introspective than those in which we usually engage. Assessed in this light, the reproductive decisions of HIV-infected women are typically nonautonomous whether or not clinical counselors employ any of the influence methods herein discussed.

This sets a high, arguably unreachable, standard for autonomous action. If unconscious mental processes are a pervasive part of human decision-making yet incompatible with authenticity, then autonomous choice, thus conceptualized, is rare or even mythic.[172] From the perspective of liberal social theory, the ideal of deliberative and dispassionate politics affirmed by this vision of self-determination is powerfully appealing. Yet from the standpoint of the bioethics movement's ability to employ the principle of respect for autonomy pragmatically as a safeguard against medical paternalism, the implication that autonomous action is atypical in daily life is troublesome.

Not surprisingly, then, bioethics commentators tend to eschew strong models of authenticity in favor of weaker models that allow considerable room for unconscious mental activity. Gerald Dworkin's model, for example, permits preferences to develop via such unconscious processes as identification with individuals and socialization into groups, as long as persons reflect on these preferences before avowing them as their own.[173] Unconscious external influence of this sort precludes neither authenticity nor autonomy (or autonomous action), in Dworkin's view. Faden and Beauchamp go even further, suggesting, on frankly result-oriented grounds,[174] that authenticity be discarded as a condition for autonomous action. Their alternative to authenticity, expansion of their proposed "condition of noncontrol" by others to encompass noncontrol by "self-alienating psychiatric disorders,"[175] leaves no room for the notion that unconsciously experienced external influence can undermine autonomous action.[176]

Radical social theory

In sharp contrast, radical scholars within the Marxist and post-Marxist traditions find unconsciously experienced autonomy-negating influences pervasive in daily life. For such theorists, coercion is much more commonly unconscious than overt: it permeates social relations between dominant and subordinated individuals and groups, and it usually goes unrecognized by its victims. Indeed, these theorists hold, the most potent forms of coercion succeed by remaining invisible to subordinated persons. Radical scholars have discerned hidden coercion in a broad range of power relations, including interaction between upper and lower socioeconomic classes,[177] exchange between dominant and oppressed racial and ethnic groups,[178] and relationships between men and women.[179]

A comprehensive review of the mechanisms of influence by which choices are coerced, according to these radical models, lies beyond the reach of this chapter, but the salient features shared by these theories of coercion deserve some attention, even at the risk of oversimplifying a large and heterogeneous body of scholarship. The central tenet in these models of unconscious coercion is that subordinated persons and groups internalize self-oppressing systems of belief. Such systems of belief enable subordinated individuals to tolerate—indeed, to consciously accept—social structures and practices that benefit others at their expense. By so doing, subordinated persons avoid conscious confrontation with the bitter truth that their daily actions support the social arrangements that oppress them. The internalization of self-oppressing beliefs, these models hold, is a largely unconscious process for both the subordinated and the dominant. The potential of the powerful to impose their will on the oppressed by overtly posing a threat looms in the distance, but the psychological processes by which the powerless learn to comply remain invisible on the conscious surface of daily life.

This deeply skeptical portrayal of overtly cooperative relations between persons and groups in society renders autonomy as largely illusory, especially as regards subordinated persons. For the radical scholars who subscribe to this deterministic picture, it is closely linked to one or another of two, sharply different normative visions. The darker of these two visions proceeds from the pervasiveness of determinism to the desirability of overt, state-sponsored compulsion. It holds that genuinely noncoercive social life, uncontrolled by internalized self-oppression and external compulsion, is impossible.[180] As a consequence, those who aspire to transform society on behalf of the oppressed need have little compunction about the use of state force to pursue their objectives.

On the contrary, in this Leninist view, the transformative vanguard of a society ought first to substitute its own dictatorial rule for the covert, internalized coercion embedded in daily life. Eventually, this model claims, the principles of human relations forcibly imposed by the revolutionary vanguard will be internalized by the people as habits of belief and behavior.[181] At this hypothetical late stage in social transformation, these habits will have become sufficiently ingrained to permit state compulsion to "wither away"; but at this triumphant stage, coercion will remain ubiquitous, albeit internalized and therefore unseen.[182] The "liberation" this model pursues is the casting off of social and economic oppression, not the realization of personal autonomy. From this vantage point, the question of whether the methods of clinical influence discussed herein are compatible with autonomous choice is a pointless distraction. The possibility of autonomous therapeutic or reproductive decision-making is illusory; all that matters is whether clinical influence operates as an instrument of class oppression or a tool for resisting it.[183]

Other radical scholars, in contrast, pursue a normative vision defined by the wide gap between the pervasiveness of unconscious coercion and their almost boundless optimism about the human capacity for autonomy. For such scholars, radical politics is a program for the liberation of people from deterministic interpersonal influences. The work of Jurgen Habermas offers perhaps the richest example. Habermas calls for the transformation of interpersonal relations so as to "extirpat[e] those relations of force that are inconspicuously set in the very structures of communication and that prevent conscious settlement of conflicts, and consensual regulation of conflicts, by intrapsychic as well as interpersonal communicative barriers."[184] Although Habermas aspires toward liberation that is largely intrapsychic, his transformative focus is primarily social and political. For Habermas, "relations of force" are embodied in material conditions and social institutions. "Emancipation" from "power constellations" that "constrain" and "distort" communication and understanding requires the reconstruction of social and political life.[185] The critical legal studies movement pursues a parallel transformative agenda, emphasizing the exposure of myriad ways by which reigning legal categories and forms of argument conceal oppression, injustice, and possibilities for freedom.[186]

From the standpoint of this challenge to pervasive "relations of force" in social life, the methods of clinical influence considered here are poor candidates for compatibility with autonomous choice.[187] The conditioning of medical services upon abstinence from childbearing entails the naked use of material power as a substitute for "consensual regulation of conflicts." Moreover, to the extent that this manner of influence draws strength from patients' feelings of dependence upon particular clinicians (and consequent fears of vulnerability and loss), it employs human connectedness as an instrument of force. Directive counseling derives much of its influence from a different sort of "relation of force," the directive speaker's aura of authority. By contrast with the liberal bioethics perspective, which focuses upon the noncognitive qualities of clinical authority as an obstacle to autonomous choice,[188] the radical critique looks to social structures that create perceptions of authority and thereby distort understanding. The daunting implication of this viewpoint is that the coerciveness of directive counseling cannot be altered without fundamental social change. A similar analysis applies to advisory counseling. However hard well-intentioned professionals work to imbue their counselees with a sense of empowerment, oppressive social structures will pervert clinical communication into a medium of force, radical critics could be expected to argue. Thus, the central normative thrust of this critique is away from an isolated focus on clinical relationships and toward an ambitious agenda of social transformation.

Psychoanalytic models
In contrast, psychoanalytic understandings of unconsciously experienced external influence support an intensely personal transformative agenda that takes existing social conditions as givens. Psychoanalytic thinking about uncon-

sciously experienced outside influence begins from a simple and powerful insight: because threats operate by evoking fear of future pain or loss, a threat cannot be effective unless it triggers some mental representation of the possibility of pain or loss.[189] Put more broadly, no threat or offer can work without evoking some perception of danger or opportunity, growing out of the recipient's internal representation of the world.[190] To this basic idea, psychoanalysis adds the postulate that large portions of every person's mental representation of the world are unconscious. This opens the way to the perception of danger and the experience of threat in response to life situations that somehow evoke unconscious representations of the possibility of pain or loss. Indeed, life situations that seem benign to many people may be experienced as extremely threatening by others since people's unconscious internal representations of the world vary greatly. Phobias offer a paradigmatic example: an object that seems harmless to most of us can evoke terror in a few by activating unconscious representations of pain or loss.[191] However, the influence of such representations is hardly limited to cases of clinically significant phobia; it extends to all life experiences that, by activating these representations, inspire fears that affect our choices.

When mobilized by life events, unconscious representations of pain or loss can exert the influencing force of overt, consciously experienced threats to life. Indeed, as Willard Gaylin observes, these representations derive their emotive power from their symbolization of our most primitive fears—abandonment and death. The infant's abject dependence upon its mother for survival, Gaylin argues, causes it to equate abandonment with death. In time, experiences of rejection, isolation, and humiliation come to symbolize abandonment and, therefore, death. These "symbolic equivalents of death,"[192] as Gaylin calls them, exercise extraordinary influence on our actions, often outside of our conscious awareness. If one is inclined toward an understanding of coercion in terms of the intensity of constraint or inducement, then this psychodynamic model of unconsciously mediated external influence invites the recognition of unconscious coercion.

Gaylin's central claim—that experiences of rejection, isolation, and humiliation derive coercive force from their symbolic equivalence to death—is consonant with diverse streams within the psychoanalytic tradition. Freudian theory, which postulates that instinctual drives propel all human action,[193] models the influence of external stimuli as the product of the ego's restraining effects upon the instincts. These restraining effects result from the ego's interpretation of external stimuli in terms of its previous experiences of trauma. Trauma, in the Freudian sense, derives from the frustration of instinctual cravings.[194] Instinctual frustration, in Freudian theory, evokes unconscious fear of annihilation, dating back to the close link between infantile survival and instinctual gratification. Memories of instinctual frustration and fear of annihilation constitute our histories of traumatic experience. Such experience is minimized in the life of the well-adapted person as he or she learns to obtain instinctual gratification in socially accepted ways, yet this ideal is never entirely achieved: we all experience instinctual frustration and consequent trauma during our psychosocial development.

When the ego senses a parallel between present experience and prior trauma, anxiety and a sense of danger ensues.[195] This anxiety and experience of danger may be either conscious or unconscious. Either way, according to Freudian theory, it exerts immense influence on human behavior in favor of actions that defend against the subjective sense of hazard. The range of life circumstances potentially able to evoke anxiety and a sense of danger is as broad as the diversity of traumatic experience, but what these circumstances have in common is the capacity to inspire fear of such things as isolation, humiliation, and abandonment—all symbolic of the possibility of annihilation.

From this psychodynamic perspective, myriad life situations possess the hidden potential to coerce. Moreover, generalization about whether an influence method precludes autonomous action is futile. The presence of unconsciously mediated coercion can be assessed only on an individualized basis, via in-depth exploration of the affective experiences that are evoked by the influence at issue. Thus, the clinical influence strategies considered here cannot be characterized as incompatible with autonomous choice, absent an individualized psychological inquiry. For example, a woman whose parents were unavailable for long periods during her early childhood might experience intense, unconscious fear of abandonment if told by her doctor to abstain from childbearing as a condition of continued care. Even if she had easy, unconditional access to alternative providers, she might feel (unconsciously) driven to accede to this prerequisite to maintain her current doctor–patient relationship. By contrast, a woman who never experienced such a deprivation during early childhood might be less afraid to sacrifice this relationship and thus more inclined to change physicians.[196]

Along similar lines, a woman accustomed in early childhood to the conditioning of affection upon compliance with parental commands might tend to unconsciously experience a doctor's directive or advisory statements as orders to be obeyed. Even self-consciously nondirective remarks by a clinician seeking to remain neutral may be interpreted unconsciously by such a patient as imperatives to be heeded. On the other hand, a woman unburdened by unconscious associations between disobedience and abandonment might experience even directive statements as opinions to be weighed but not necessarily followed.

For the practicing psychoanalyst, deterministic accounts of this sort lend support to the intimate quest for self-determination via exposure of unconscious memories and fears. The normative import of such accounts for nonpsychotherapeutic clinical relationships is less clear. The singularity of each person's unconscious experience augers against efforts to generalize about the possibility of autonomous action in the face of one or another influence. However, as Jay Katz has argued, psychoanalytic accounts of unconsciously mediated influence suggest possibilities for enhancing patient autonomy through more deeply reflective clinical conversation.[197]

Other psychoanalytic models of unconsciously experienced external influence are less heavily freighted by reliance on instinctual drives. Object relations theory emphasizes the central role of early interpersonal relationships in the development of a person's internal representation of the world.[198] According to object relations theory, this internal representation unconsciously structures a person's perceptions and expectations of the external world. The influence others exercise upon a person's choices is largely determined by the analogies the person unconsciously draws between present and prior human interactions. For example, at the risk of oversimplification, a woman whose parents were harsh and punitive might be more prone to experience a counselor's gently delivered advice as intimidating than would a woman raised by giving and tolerant parents. As a consequence, the woman with punitive parents might be more inclined to comply with the counselor's advice out of fear of the imagined consequences of defiance. Her experience of intimidation and expectation of punishment are unconscious, as is her understanding of the counseling relationship in terms shaped by her remembrances of her relations with her parents.

At the conscious level, she may experience her compliance as her own rational decision.[199] Indeed, if asked to explain her choice, she might very well respond with a plausible reason. Yet according to the object relations model, her choice has in fact been determined by the filtration of her conversation with the counselor through her internal, unconscious representation of the world. Like Freudian drive theory, the object relations model postulates that we wish to avoid unconsciously imagined danger situations—situations that portend, in our fantasies, rejection, humiliation, and abandonment—all symbolic of annihilation. Yet in contrast to the Freudian focus on frustration of instinctual drives as the source of unconscious fantasies of danger, object relations theory looks to our earliest interpersonal ties to understand our present perceptions of danger. For non-psychotherapeutic clinicians, this model invites attention to the possibility that even gentle advice can exert strong influence, by evoking unconscious feelings tied to prior relationships, particularly those with early authority figures.[200] The model suggests that such influence can be attenuated, or at least better appreciated by patients, if clinicians explore their counselees' affective reactions to advice with an eye toward discouraging unreflective compliance.

Recently, some psychoanalytic theorists have begun to reconceive unconsciously experienced danger as the product of personal narratives and myths. This emerging model stresses the substance of personal myths as opposed to their origins. These mostly repressed myths, the model holds, structure our perception and interpretation of present circumstances. Interpersonal differences in these narratives lead some of us to perceive great danger in situations that others experience as benign.[201] In the words of Roy Schafer, a leading exponent of narrative theory in psychoanalysis, unconscious perceptions of danger confine people "in bars and chains of their imaginings and behavior."[202] Within this inner world of "unconsciously developed meanings"—of "unrecognized symbols, concertized metaphors, reductive allegories, or repressed storylines of childhood"—reality is "reconstructed or retold as imprisonment."[203] The coercive power of such narratives of imprisonment typically operates beneath the conscious surface of mental life. It is often obscured, according to Schafer, by an illusory sense of autonomy, a "false freedom" that belies the truth of confinement.[204]

This narrative approach to psychological determinism implies enormous possibilities for personal liberation via the illumination of unconscious myth. It casts the psychotherapist as an interpretive guide to the patient's unconscious storylines, but it charges the patient with growing responsibility for her actions as she becomes more conscious of the narratives that once constrained her.[205] She becomes responsible by "coauthoring" (with the therapist) a revised life narrative that self-consciously defines her identity and the possibilities and limitations it implies.[206] In nonpsychotherapeutic clinical work, this model suggests, opportunities for such liberation are much diminished, owing to the absence of a sustained search for unconscious narratives of constraint.

These three psychoanalytic models share a normative vision: each calls for the pursuit of personal insight and fulfillment via arduous therapeutic work.[207] For their adherents, such work holds out the promise of greater autonomy with respect to myriad life choices. However, these models suggest that prospects for achieving autonomous reproductive (or medical) decision-making by proscribing clinical opinion-giving are modest without individualized, psychoanalytically oriented inquiry. Likewise, these paradigms imply that the prohibition of efforts to condition medical care upon reproductive abstinence (or other behaviors) cannot by itself contribute greatly toward the goal of autonomous choice.

Understandably, this pessimistic view of the possibility for autonomous action without case-by-case psychodynamic inquiry makes these models unappealing to bioethics commentators and others concerned principally with empowering medical patients. The reluctance of many people to take on the difficult task of psychodynamic self-scrutiny, not to mention the prohibitive cost of such work, makes the ideal of autonomy to which these models aspire impractical as a prerequisite for patient self-determination. For similar reasons, this ideal is likely to prove unpersuasive as a standard for autonomous reproductive decision-making.[208]

Summing up: paradigms of influence without intent

The diverse models of external influence discussed above share the premise that the intent of an influence agent is immaterial to whether an influence precludes autonomous choice. These models look to the experience of the chooser as the basis for making this determination, but their paradigms for understanding that experience differ greatly. This variation, as noted above, reflects their divergent normative thrusts. Norman Daniels' notion of quasi-coercion candidly opens the question of autonomy-negating outside influence to arguments about the justice and fairness of the chooser's circumstances. Lasswell and Kaplan look to the chooser's conscious experience of constraint or inducement but, in so doing, must rely upon external normative input to identify influences incompatible with autonomous action. Liberal theories of authenticity concern themselves with unconsciously experienced influence as a threat to an ideal of deliberative, reflective public and personal life.

Psychoanalysts and radical social theorists mount a more basic challenge to the belief that our conscious sense of freedom is an apt measure of its actuality. There is an obvious parallel between the "false freedom" that psychoanalysts believe belies unconscious coercion and the "false consciousness" that radical theorists see as obscuring social relations of domination and subordination. Yet the normative aims of these enterprises differ sharply. Psychoanalytic practice pursues private liberation within existing social constraints,[209] while radical critique aspires to liberation via the exposure and rejection of these constraints.[210]

Each of these paradigms is "true" in an important sense: there is conceptual integrity between it and associated aspirations for change in the self or the world. Recognition of these divergent truths, I argue below, is a necessary starting point for conversation about the normative conflicts that underlie differences about the nature of autonomy-negating influence.

Toward a Reinterpretation of Clinical Autonomy

The connotative import of autonomous action

The claim that coercion is a thoroughly moralized concept, critically dependent on outside normative input, is highly counterintuitive.[211] Yet this proposition offers a compelling explanation for the persistence of differing understandings of coercion. More generally, distinct normative perspectives lie behind differing approaches to the question of whether a given influence is compatible with autonomous choice. Beliefs about justice, fairness, and the good life are linked to conceptions of autonomy-negating influence at multiple levels of model design and application.

The interplay between normative inputs at multiple levels is complex. The Faden and Beauchamp paradigm of autonomy-negating influence illustrates this. The prerequisites that influence be consciously intended by a human agent and consciously experienced as constraining marginalize concerns about social justice and focus attention upon prospects for empowering patients in clinical settings, once the influence of social structure and biological misfortune is taken as given.[212] However, the model's reliance upon resistibility tests, the threat/offer distinction, and a dichotomy between welcome and unwelcome offers permits the tacit entry of beliefs about social justice.

The insight that differing normative visions lie behind contrary understandings of coercion has led Alan Wertheimer to conclude that coercion "drop[s] out of the picture"[213] once its moral content has been exposed. Anticipating the charge of reductionism, he observes (relying upon Nozick): "[W]e tend to describe as reductionist only explanations which reduce what is thought to be more valuable (or interesting) to what is thought to be less valuable (or interesting) and do so in a way which is false."[214] Measured by these criteria, he asserts, it is not reductionistic to "disaggregat[e] coercion claims into more specific moral claims" because once this has been done nothing else of interest remains. The same might be said about conceptions of autonomy-negating external influences more generally since their underlying normative content plays a similarly determinative role.

Yet the case can be made that something interesting and valuable persists about the idea of coercion (and autonomy-negating influence more generally) even after all implicit normative propositions are parsed out. This interesting and valuable thing derives from the evocative power of respect for autonomy as an expression of our belief that persons should be treated as ends, worthy of noninstrumental deference and regard. Although this belief is most closely identified with Kant, it has been expressed in varying theoretical terms over time. Religious versions cast persons as specially worthy because of their ties to the divine, while Kantian and other Enlightenment iterations postulate a singular human capacity to reason.[215] Postmodernist writers rest their cases for such special regard on a variety of nonessentialist grounds.[216] However widely these accounts differ, their common implication that personhood merits deference and regard is powerfully symbolized within the liberal tradition by the idea that autonomous choice should be protected, at least to a point, and that coercion is prima facie wrong.

On the other hand, our shared sense that persons are worthy of noninstrumental regard contrasts awkwardly with our inconsistent answers to the question of what is to be regarded. As Wertheimer notes about the law's disposition of coercion claims and as I have observed here about conceptions of autonomy-negating influence in clinical settings, we treat constraints and inducements differently in varying normative contexts. Modes of influence that we tolerate or even encourage within some spheres of activity are thought to be problematic within others. A proposal that constitutes duress for contract law purposes might not invalidate a criminal confession and a medical recommendation deemed by courts and bioethics commentators to be compatible with autonomous patient choice might nonetheless preclude autonomous action in the eyes of a patient's psychotherapist. Even within a given sphere of activity, we often argue over which aspects of personhood merit special deference and regard. Followers of Nozick and Habermas, for example, differ sharply about which personal choices deserve society's deference, though they share the sense that persons should be treated as ends.

Although these incompatibilities are explicable in terms of underlying normative differences, they present a problem for the credibility of our commitment to persons as ends for they remind us of the distasteful truth that this commitment is neither absolute nor invariant—that different degrees of interference with personal choice are prima facie acceptable in different contexts. In so doing, they invite doubts about the seriousness of this commitment.[217] One might argue that such skepticism is a salutary thing—that the ideal of singular regard for individuals and their choices cannot stand up to the reality of mutual dependence and vulnerability, and that our culture ought to acknowledge this. On the other hand, it may be that the myth of singular regard for persons as ends reinforces, in a diffuse, connotative way, our discomfort over interference with individual choice. This could occur even as the limits of our prima facie tolerance for such interference are denotatively defined, via conceptions of autonomy-negating influence, by reference to externally derived norms.

To the extent that the ideal of special regard for persons (and their choices) operates in this connotative, even passionate manner,[218] it may inspire a measure of mutual respect beyond that implied by the moral premises that inform paradigms of autonomy-negating influence. This effect may be especially important when health professionals and patients encounter each other in impersonal, bureaucratic settings. Such settings are poorly suited for the development of empathic connection, making professional respect particularly important as an adjunct to feelings of care.

If the ideal of noninstrumental regard for persons accomplishes this much, then coercion, and autonomy-negating external influence more generally, are important apart from their component moral premises. They matter because this ideal is evocatively symbolized by the notions that autonomous choice should be protected and that coercion is presumptively wrong. Indeed, the symbolic power of these notions may protect the ideal of noninstrumental regard for persons from the corrosive effects of inconsistency in our tolerance for interferences with choice. Put in other terms, the connotative power of autonomous action as an ideal tends to obscure incompatibilities between conceptions of autonomy-negating influence. This helps us to maintain differing normative stances toward external constraints and inducements within separate spheres of life.

When conceptions of autonomy-negating influence collide

As a rule, we get along more than adequately with multiple, parallel conceptions of autonomy-negating external influence, each pertinent to different spheres of action, yet at times these conceptions collide. Then we must choose, or create anew, the conception that will govern. Such collisions occur most typically when we confront novel choice situations that implicate opposing, passionately-felt normative concerns.[219] Current clinical examples include the debates over efforts to encourage use of long-acting contraceptives[220] and to promote reproductive abstinence by HIV-infected women. In the near future, the most prominent medical example may be the question of whether constraints upon patient choice imposed by managed care organizations are compatible with informed consent.

When conceptions of autonomy-negating influence collide, competing claims that fail to address, or even to acknowledge, the underlying normative questions at stake grate against each other without making analytic contact. At best, the makers of such claims sustain each other's disregard for the normative questions that must be settled to resolve the conflict. At worst, this mutual disregard degenerates into anger and bitterness as partisans to the conflict sense, quite accurately, that their cherished concerns (which have gone unexpressed) are being ignored. Thus, the insulating capacity of claims about coercion and autonomy—the very quality that makes it easier for us to adhere to disparate models of coercion (informed by differing answers to normative questions) within separate spheres of life—presents a barrier to the resolution of conflict when disparate models collide.

To break through this barrier, a dialogue that pursues analytic connection is necessary. Such connection can be achieved only through candid talk about the competing normative premises that animate conflict over whether an influence is compatible with autonomous choice. Candor of this sort carries risk: the suppression of visible conflict between intensely felt concerns may play an important role in the maintenance of public civility, but this risk can be reduced through mutual recognition that conceptions of autonomy-negating influence tend to make sense in terms of one or another plausible vision of human ends.[221] There are limits to the mutual recognition we ought to aspire toward: we need not, for example, grant dialogic recognition to ideas about autonomy-negating influence that rest upon the racial preferences of an apartheid theorist or a Nazi.[222] Yet within such limits, we can accomplish much, in civil conversation, by opening ourselves to the plausibility of the competing normative visions at issue.[223]

Mediating conflict between conceptions of autonomy-negating influence: clinical counseling and the reproductive choices of HIV-infected women

How, then, might such a conversation proceed with respect to whether clinical efforts to dissuade HIV-infected women from bearing children are compatible with autonomous reproductive choice? I will not attempt to anticipate the entire course of such an interchange; nor will I advocate some single, preferred outcome. By their nature, such conversations are unpredictable: they take on direction and momentum of their own, animated by a dialogic rationality of mutual discovery that carries participants beyond their initial intentions.[224] I will, however, highlight some of the normative concerns with which participants must engage if they are to achieve analytic connection. Moreover, I will suggest, without rigorously defending, some possibilities for the emergence of an accommodation.

The normative issues at stake

To begin with, any effort to achieve analytic contact must address the social justice concerns that inspire the claim that promotion of reproductive abstinence coerces HIV-infected women. For the most part, these concerns are tied to the fact that women who contract HIV are disproportionately poor and from disadvantaged minority groups. As noted earlier, the belief that these women's life circumstances are unjust lends force to the conclusion that it is unfair to expect them to give up the fulfillment that comes with childbearing.[225] In particular, to the extent that HIV transmission is seen as a product of unjust personal or social circumstances, asking victims of these ills to endure further deprivation for public health purposes can seem wrong. Society's failure to offer educational and career opportunities to these women adds to the perception of unfairness by shutting the door to other possibilities for fulfillment. The key moral intuition here is a sense of inequitable sacrifice. Having been already victimized by a dread disease that strikes disproportionately at the disadvantaged, these women are asked to suffer further, for purported public health ends, while society provides them with little or nothing in return.

Analogous justice-related concerns arise from women's experience of socioeconomic inequality and infringement upon reproductive and sexual choice. To the degree that women are seen as victims of economic and other forms of discrimination, expecting HIV-infected women to sacrifice the joys of childbearing for the good of society may seem morally troubling. Likewise, awareness of past and present constraints upon procreative choice—e.g., restrictive abortion laws and low levels of public funding for family planning and abortion services—can nurture perceptions that the promotion of reproductive abstinence is unfair.

To make full analytic contact, conversation about whether strategies for discouraging reproduction are compatible with autonomous choice must also address concerns about the social costs of childbearing by HIV-infected women. To dismiss such concerns as stalking horses for sexism or racism is to deny the reality of two kinds of trade-offs—those between alternative uses of social resources and those between different experiences of pain and deprivation. Whether the satisfactions of childbearing justify the allocation of limited resources to medical care for HIV-infected children and public assistance for many whose mothers become unable to provide for them is a question that merits discussion.

Likewise, how a woman's sacrifice of reproductive fulfillment compares to a child's experience of terminal, wasting illness or loss of a mother is a subject that ought to be talked about. It may be that some who cite such concerns as reasons for the promotion of reproductive abstinence are swayed by covert racial or gender bias, but this ugly possibility does not diminish the costly and tragic realities that these concerns reflect. Moreover, frank discussion of the weight that these concerns should receive might expose underlying bias and/or embarrass those afflicted by it into retreating from views informed by prejudice.

The above-mentioned normative concerns bear on all of the influence methods discussed herein—advisory counseling, directive counseling, and the conditioning of health care upon reproductive abstinence. An additional question of social justice—whether access to medical care is a universal entitlement—is germane only to the latter. An affirmative answer mandates the conclusion that conditioning care upon reproductive abstinence is wrong when patients lack access to alternative sources of care. This moral baseline, in turn, invites the inference that such a condition precludes autonomous reproductive choice when care is not otherwise available. A negative answer, on the other hand, leaves room for the judgment that such a condition is morally tolerable and thus compatible with autonomous action.

Another set of concerns relates to the Hippocratic ideal of undivided professional loyalty to patients. Proponents of clinical strategies for discouraging reproduction tacitly accept a measure of deviation from this ideal, at least insofar as the case for reproductive abstinence rests on social cost grounds.[226] That this ideal represents an ethical absolute is belied by the pervasiveness of clinical activities that compromise it. Physicians perform myriad clinical tasks in the service of public health, forensic, and other social ends.[227] Far from condemning all such activity as an intolerable breach of Hippocratic fidelity, society expects its health professionals to perform such functions. These expectations exist in enduring conflict with the Hippocratic ideal of loyalty and with medicine's therapeutic and caring purposes. Up to a point, we tolerate this conflict. Yet some uses of medicine for public purposes so undermine the apparent trustworthiness of clinical caretakers that we place them ethically off limits. Such line-drawing, I have argued elsewhere, requires case-by-case inquiry, sensitive to both the requisites of intimate trust and the weight of public necessity.[228] This inquiry bears on the moral assessment of each of the clinical influence strategies considered here.

This list of normative concerns is surely incomplete. Other considerations abound—e.g., the more abstract question of whether human dignity is best served by broader or narrower conceptions of personal responsibility in the face of unjust circumstances.[229] Moreover, the issues I have raised can be framed in other ways; indeed the problem of framing should itself be a subject of discussion. Nonetheless, the concerns I have cited can serve as a starting point for conversation about the normative questions at stake when conflicting claims are made about the possibility of autonomous action.

Toward an accommodation

I will end with some suggestions about the outlines of an accommodation with respect to the autonomy-precluding effect of efforts to discourage childbearing by HIV-infected women. To begin with, the widely shared premise that access to an "adequate" level of health care is a moral entitlement[230] should by itself suffice to support the conclusion that conditioning care upon reproductive abstinence is wrong when other providers are not readily accessible. The Hippocratic ideal of fidelity supports a more general objection to clinicians' use of their services as leverage to discourage childbearing. Whether or not alternative providers are accessible, conditioning one's willingness to treat upon a patient's compliance with public purposes constitutes a dramatic departure from this ideal. As such, it puts patient trust at risk, especially among poor people and members of minority groups already skeptical about the devotion of upper-middle class professionals. The above-noted social justice objections to reproductive abstinence as a public health measure only add to the case against conditioning care upon such abstinence. One need not deny the legitimacy of public health and social cost-avoidance concerns to infer from these moral difficulties that this method of influence is incompatible with autonomous reproductive choice.

The clinical counseling of reproductive abstinence presents a different configuration of normative concerns. The question of moral entitlement to medical care is not germane to the ethics of advisory or directive counseling since neither entails a refusal to provide care in the event of non-compliance. Such counseling, however, breaks with the ideal of undivided loyalty to patients insofar as the direction given is informed by social purposes. Yet especially for counseling that is only advisory, this breach of fidelity seems less troublesome than does the total abandonment portended by a provider's declared unwillingness to serve unless her patients abstain from childbearing.[231]

More problematic, in my view, are the above-cited social justice concerns. The link between social deprivation and HIV infection risk, combined with the shortage of opportunities for poor and minority women to pursue nonprocreative fulfillment, lends an aura of inequity to expectations that infected women forego childbearing for the good of the rest of society. This aura of inequity is heightened by past and present gender discrimination. Absent a serious effort to redress these concerns, the clinical counseling of reproductive abstinence calls upon HIV-infected women to bear a disproportionate burden of sacrifice for the benefit of a society that treats them with disregard.

This failure of reciprocity, I believe, inspires the charge that even advisory counseling of reproductive abstinence coerces. This claim gains moral force from the potential of other strategies to slow the spread of AIDS without imposing a singularly harsh burden upon infected women of childbearing age. Interventions targeted at the social conditions that engender high-risk sex and substance abuse, as well as toward opportunities for discouraging such behaviors once they become established, signal a concern for the lives of infected people that contrasts with the disregard conveyed by emphasis on reproductive abstinence. This disregard lends force to the claim that clinical advice to refrain from childbearing is incompatible with autonomous procreative choice.

Yet if lack of reciprocity inspires the belief that the counseling of reproductive abstinence coerces, efforts to ameliorate social deprivation could weaken the moral basis for this belief. Advice to abstain from childbearing might be less problematic in social justice terms if accompanied by programs to redress the conditions that catalyze HIV transmission and genuine attempts to provide poor and minority women with chances for nonprocreative fulfillment. Such a melding of individual and social responsibility has the potential to transform the struggle against the spread of AIDS from a dividing practice into a community-affirming endeavor. To the extent that this potential is realized, it might become less objectionable to conclude that clinical advice to abstain from childbearing is compatible with autonomous choice.

These suggestions offer a starting point for conversation about how the boundaries of autonomy-precluding clinical influence should be drawn with respect to the reproductive choices of HIV-infected women. The subsequent course of such a conversation can be neither managed nor predicted. Its development is likely to be a recursive function of its participants' evolving perspectives with respect to myriad normative questions. What can be predicted is that after a set of boundaries is agreed upon, the normative judgments that inform them will recede behind the language of autonomy and coercion. In turn, the connotative power of this language will engender respect for these boundaries and discourage persistent, corrosive criticism of their normative content.

Conclusion

I have noted herein that judgments about whether particular influences are compatible with autonomous action rest upon tacit normative premises. Beliefs about justice, fairness, and the good life inform conceptions of autonomy-negating influence and guide their application in clinical and other settings. Within different spheres of activity, I have also noted, we live with contrary understandings of autonomy-negating influence, arising from conflicting normative visions. Usually, such contradictions present no problem. As a rule, the understandings of autonomy-precluding influence to which we adhere in different spheres of life do not abrade against each other. Indeed, the notions of autonomy and coercion may help us to tolerate such conceptual dissonance by concealing the contradictory normative premises that inform these understandings.

However, sometimes conceptions of autonomy-negating influence collide within a single sphere of activity. Typically, such spheres are either newly emerging or rapidly changing. When this happens, we must choose—or construct—a governing conception. Reproductive decision-making by HIV-infected women represents one such instance. In such circumstances, the otherwise appealing, even useful, myth that autonomy and coercion are single, free-standing conceptions stands in the way of a solution. Competing claims about autonomy-negating influence that fail to pierce this myth by attending to underlying normative issues cannot achieve analytic contact. At best, those who make such claims reinforce each other's disregard for the normative questions at the heart of the conflict. At worst, mutual disregard evolves into anger as the conflict's participants sense that their deeply felt concerns are being neglected.

Accordingly, I have urged an approach to conversation about competing understandings of autonomy-negating influence that promises greater analytic engagement, as well as reduced acrimony and bitterness. Recognition that many such understandings are possible and open discussion of the normative issues that undergird our choices between them are central to this approach. When the boundaries between influences that permit and preclude autonomous action are socially contested, a process of this sort has the potential to reach solutions marked by mutual respect, social reciprocity, and a deepened sense of community.

Such solutions, it should be noted, leave us with an enigma. On the one hand, they are informed by normative conclusions about justice, fairness, and conceptions of the good. Yet on the other hand, the judgment that an influence precludes autonomous choice is not entirely equivalent to the conclusion that it is wrongful. At most, the former judgment establishes a default rule of wrongfulness: if an influence is deemed incompatible with autonomous action, then the burden of proof is on anyone who would nonetheless justify it.[232] Thus, in practice we sometimes separate the ultimate issue of wrongfulness from the question of whether an influence precludes autonomous action, though more typically we conflate these matters without evident ill effect. This curious inconsistency calls out for further exploration.

Notes

1. "Triable Issues of Fact Exist in AIDS Discrimination Claim; *Doe* v. *Jamaica Hospital*," *New York Law Journal*, May 6, 1991, p. 21 (unreported opinion by a New York State trial court, ruling on defendant physician's motion for summary judgment in tort action against Jamaica Hospital, the New York City Health and Hospitals Corporation, and the individual physicians and other professionals who cared

for Ms. Doe) [hereinafter *Doe v. Jamaica Hospital*]; M. M. Gundrum and J. P. Gibbs, Verified Complaint for Declaratory and Monetary Relief and Jury Demand in Doe v. Jamaica Hospital, November 1989 (on file with the Center for Constitutional Rights) [hereinafter Complaint in *Doe v. Jamaica Hospital*]. The following account of Ms. Doe's allegations is drawn from these two sources.
2. Complaint in *Doe v. Jamaica Hospital*.
3. Ms. Doe, who had previously borne a child with spina bifida, also alleged that Dr. Abitol said that having an HIV-infected baby would be even worse. Ibid.
4. According to Ms. Doe, who said she wanted to carry her pregnancy to term, she pleaded with Dr. Abitol and others at Jamaica Hospital to permit her to continue prenatal care in the facility's high-risk program, but she was told she could not do so. Ibid.
5. In an affidavit accompanying his motion, Dr. Abitol said that he counseled Ms. Doe about the physical and emotional ramifications of testing positive for HIV and discussed her fears about giving birth to another child with spina bifida. Dr. Abitol averred that he referred Ms. Doe to Kings County Hospital because it was more qualified than Jamaica Hospital to treat HIV-infected pregnant women. *Doe v. Jamaica Hospital*.
6. See *Martinez v. Long Island Jewish Hillside Medical Center*, 512 N.E.2d 538 (N.Y. 1987) (granting a cause of action for emotional harm suffered when a physician's erroneous prediction of a congenital birth defect in utero prompted a woman to consent to an abortion despite her belief that abortion is sinful, absent extraordinary circumstances). See also *Bloskas v. Murray*, 646 P.2d 907 (Colo. 1982) (holding that inaccurate information negligently given to patients by physicians to obtain consent constitutes negligent misrepresentation).
7. See, e.g., D. P. Francis and J. Chin, "The Prevention of Acquired Immunodeficiency Syndrome in the United States: An Objective Strategy for Medicine, Public Health, Business, and the Community," *Journal of the American Medical Association* 257 (1987): 1357 (asserting that women who are HIV-infected should "avoid pregnancy"); H. L. Minkoff and R. H. Schwarz, "AIDS: Time for Obstetricians to Get Involved," *Obstetrics and Gynecology* 68 (1986): 267 (concluding that "pregnancy should be discouraged" when women test positive prior to conception); A. J. Pinching and D. J. Jeffries, "AIDS and HTLV-III/LAV Infection: Consequences for Obstetrics and Perinatal Medicine," *British Journal of Obstetrics and Gynaecology* 92 (1985): 1211, 1216–1217 (asserting that HIV-infected women "should be strongly advised to avoid pregnancy").
8. In 1985, the CDC recommended that HIV-infected women be advised to "postpone" pregnancy. Centers for Disease Control, "Recommendations for Assisting in the Prevention of Perinatal Transmission of Human T-Lymphotropic Virus Type III/Lymphadenopathy-Associated Virus and Acquired Immunodeficiency Syndrome," *Morbidity and Mortality Weekly Report* 34 (1985): 721. This peculiar choice of words, according to CDC observers, reflected the agency's reluctance to baldly state its evident conclusion: that HIV-infected women should forgo pregnancy. State health departments have shown no such reluctance. Ronald Bayer's 1990 survey of state health departments found that all except New Jersey's advised that HIV-infected women be counseled to avoid pregnancy. J. D. Arras, "AIDS and Reproductive Decisions: Having Children in Fear and Trembling," *Milbank Quarterly* 68 (1990): 353, 367.

In 1987, the American College of Obstetricians and Gynecologists (ACOG) took a similar position, recommending that HIV-infected women be "strongly encouraged not to become pregnant." American College of Obstetricians and Gynecologists, *Prevention of Human Immune Deficiency Virus Infection and Acquired Immune Deficiency Syndrome* (1987) (ACOG Committee Statement No. 53).

9. The politics of abortion probably led the CDC to refrain from recommending that infected women who are pregnant be counseled about pregnancy termination. See D. A. Grimes, "The CDC and Abortion in HIV-Positive Women," *Journal of the American Medical Association* 258 (1987): 1176. (A CDC panel convened to develop guidelines for prevention of perinatal HIV transmission advised that the abortion option be presented to pregnant, HIV-infected women, but this recommendation was deleted from the published CDC report.)

   Academic medical commentators addressed pregnancy termination in almost as gingerly a fashion. Minkoff and Schwarz said elliptically that a pregnant, HIV-infected woman "is entitled to exercise the same options as a woman whose fetus is exposed to any other viral pathogen." Minkoff and Schwarz, "AIDS: Time for Obstetricians," 267. Pinching and Jeffries were more direct, concluding that "termination is advisable" for both fetal and maternal reasons and that all pregnant, HIV-positive women "should be considered for and counselled about" abortion. Pinching and Jeffries, "AIDS and HTLV-III/LAV," 1216. The authors of an HIV screening protocol for pregnant women at Boston's Brigham and Women's and Beth Israel hospitals were less revealing but suggestive regarding their preference for pregnancy termination when patients test positive. In an article describing their approach, the protocol's developers reported that women testing positive at less than 23 weeks' gestation were "offered the option" of abortion. B. P. Sachs, R. Tuomala, and F. Frigoletto, "Acquired Immunodeficiency Syndrome: Suggested Protocol for Counseling and Screening in Pregnancy," *Obstetrics and Gynecology* 70 (1987): 408–410. At another point in this article, however, the authors referred in passing to the abortion "option" as "recommended." Ibid., 409.

10. See, e.g., *Cobbs* v. *Grant*, 8 Cal. 3d 229, 502 P.2d 1 (1972); *Canterbury* v. *Spence*, 464 F.2d 772 (D.C. Cir. 1969) (holding that physicians have a duty to disclose material risks associated with recommended therapies). See, generally, M. Maguire Shultz, "From Informed Consent to Patient Choice: A New Protected Interest," *Yale Law Journal* 95 (1985): 219–256.

11. Ibid. However, some argue that professional restraint in this regard would enhance patient autonomy in clinical relationships. Jay Katz contends that protection for "psychological autonomy" should include a professional obligation to "facilitate patients' opportunities for reflection" by engaging them in exploratory conversation. J. Katz, *The Silent World of Doctor and Patient* (New York: Free Press, 1984): 121–128. Katz proposes that when a patient asks her doctor to choose between alternatives, the doctor consider answering along the following lines: "Of course I shall eventually give you my recommendation, but I prefer not to do so yet. . . . I would like to hear first what your preferences are. After all it is *your* body that I intend to treat . . . and you must have some opinions about which consequences would be easier or more difficult for you to tolerate." Ibid., 126.

12. See, e.g., T. L. Beauchamp and J. F. Childress, *Principles of Biomedical Ethics*, 3rd ed. (New York: Oxford University Press, 1989): 76 (informed consent to a recommended intervention occurs when a person "with substantial *understanding* and in substantial *absence of control* by others *intentionally authorizes* a professional to do something"); Maguire Shultz, "From Informed Consent to Patient Choice,"

257–299 (urging greatly expanded legal protection for informed patient choice, while retaining the premise that physicians are "personally and professionally responsible for recommending" decisions); A. R. Jonsen, M. Siegler, and W. Winslade, *Clinical Ethics: A Practical Approach to Ethical Decisions in Clinical Medicine* (New York: Macmillan, 1982): 99 (physicians are ethically obliged to try to persuade patients to comply with beneficial treatment).

13. Whether Ms. Doe was accurately informed about the risk of maternal transmission cannot be discerned from the available information. The public record does not reveal whether she was given a numerical estimate of the probability of transmission. If, as Ms. Doe alleged, she was told only that the risk was "great," then she was arguably given an exaggerated idea of its magnitude; current estimates put the risk in the 25%–35% range—e.g., J. W. Zylke, "Another Consequence of Uncontrolled Spread of HIV Among Adults: Vertical Transmission," *Journal of the American Medical Association* 265 (1991): 1798. However, estimates employed clinically at the time Ms. Doe tested positive put the probability of transmission as high as 65%. See Sachs et al., "Acquired Immunodeficiency Syndrome," 410 (counselors instructed to tell HIV-positive pregnant women that risk of transmission "is unknown, but may be as high as 65%").

    Recent research suggests that HIV-infected patients with different biological markers may have dramatically different risks of in utero transmission. See M. E. St. Louis, M. Kamenga, C. Brown, and A. M. Nelson, "Risk for Prenatal HIV-1 Transmission According to Maternal Immunologic, Virologic, and Placental Factors," *Journal of the American Medical Association* 269 (1993): 2853 (reporting that vertical transmission risks for identified biological subgroups of HIV-infected women varied from 7% to 71%).

14. However, were such a recommendation accompanied by a threat to discontinue treatment, thereby effectively cutting off Ms. Doe's access to prenatal care, her assent could hardly constitute legitimate informed consent.

15. N. Kass, "Reproductive Decision Making in the Context of HIV: The Case for Nondirective Counseling," in *AIDS, Women and the Next Generation*, eds. R. Faden, G. Geller, and M. Powers (New York: Oxford University Press, 1991): 308–327; K. Nolan, "Ethical Issues in Caring for Pregnant Women and Newborns at Risk for Human Immunodeficiency Virus Infection," *Seminars in Perinatology* 13 (1989): 63 ("unwanted advice by a paternalistic counselor" may "violate the ethical principles of autonomy and procreative freedom"); C. Levine and N. N. Dubler, "Uncertain Risks and Bitter Realities: The Reproductive Choices of HIV-Infected Women," *Milbank Quarterly* 68 (1990): 321, 322 (counseling programs aimed at preventing pregnancies or births "will inevitably give way to widespread and systematic coercive measures").

    Some commentators couple this claim to a parallel objection with respect to intervention at the public health level. They maintain that the public promotion of reproductive restraint, by means ranging from advertising campaigns to the use of government benefits or private charity as levers of influence, also endangers the reproductive autonomy of HIV-positive women. Ibid., 322, 345.

16. See, generally, A. Milunsky, "Genetic Counseling: Principles and Practice," in *The Prevention of Genetic Diseases and Mental Retardation*, ed. A. Milunsky (Philadelphia: Saunders, 1975): 64–71.

17. See, e.g., G. Annas, "Problems of Informed Consent and Confidentiality in Genetic Counseling," in *Genetics and the Law*, ed. G. Annas (New York: Plenum Press,

1975): 111. Annas characterizes the clinical advocacy of reproductive abstinence as "propaganda" that aims to "impos[e] the beliefs of the counselor on the patient" in pursuit of ends that "could be viewed by some as racist or even genocidal." Ibid., 113. Other supporters of the nondirective model of genetic counseling do not go so far as to claim that opinion-giving compromises autonomy. Rather, they present the nondirective model as a means for keeping counselors focused on their patients' concerns and as a safeguard against the influence of counselors' moral beliefs about the social consequences of reproductive decisions. See J. R. Sorenson and A. J. Culbert, "Professional Orientations to Contemporary Genetic Counseling," in *Genetic Counseling: Facts, Values and Norms*, eds. A. M. Capron, M. Lapé, R. S. Murray, et.al. (New York: Alan R. Liss, 1979): 85–102.
18. See, e.g., J. Mitford, "Experiments Behind Bars," in *Biomedical Ethics*, eds. T. A. Mappes and J. S. Zembaty (New York: McGraw-Hill, 1981): 172–176; National Commission for the Protection of Human Subjects of Biomedical and Behavioral Research, *Report and Recommendations* (Washington D.C.: Department of Health, Education and Welfare Publication No. [OS] 76–131, 1976): 61–64; *Kaimowitz* v. *Dept. of Mental Health*, 2 Prison L. Rptr. 433 (Cir. Court of Wayne Co., Mich. 1973). For arguments to the effect that such consent can be given autonomously, see National Commission for the Protection of Human Subjects of Biomedical and Behavioral Research, Staff Paper on Prisoners as Research Subjects, reprinted in J. Areen, P. A. King, S. Goldberg, and A. M. Capron, *Law, Science and Medicine* (Mineola, NY: Foundation Press, 1984): 1049, 1051 (citing arguments by Paul Ramsey and Paul Freund); C. Cohen, "Medical Experimentation on Prisoners," in eds. T. A. Mappes and J. S. Zembaty *Biomedical Ethics*, 177–186.
19. A. Wertheimer, *Coercion* (Princeton, NJ: Princeton University Press, 1987): 19–175 (reviewing the differing approaches judges have taken to defining coercion when confronted with allegations of contractual or other duress, assumption of risk, failure to obtain informed consent, undue influence, blackmail, and use of coercion to obtain confessions or plea bargains).
20. Ibid., 118–121.
21. Ibid., 173–174.
22. Put in other terms, the illusion of a unified conception of autonomy may function as a useful "subterfuge" (a tool for obscuring inevitable but distressing contradictions between cherished values). See, generally, G. Calabresi, *Tragic Choices* (New York: Norton, 1978): 195–196 (arguing that society relies upon subterfuges to avert the high moral cost of conflict between its most cherished concerns), and see text accompanying notes 85–87 and 217.
23. See notes 7–9.
24. The frequency of this practice is unknown, since reproduction counseling styles for HIV-infected women have not been systematically surveyed.
25. My use of the word "directive" is thus narrower than that of some advocates of "nondirective" genetic counseling, who employ the term "directive counseling" to characterize all expressions of opinion as to what a counselee should decide.
26. Such warnings might be given either before or after conception. Provision of clinical services could be conditioned on a woman's promise to use contraception or her consent to abortion.
27. Characterization of all such statements as influence attempts is not appropriate. Such statements may at times reflect the hard reality that obstetrical or other services needed by pregnant women are not provided within a particular facility.

Even if one were to object to the priority choices made by such an institution (e.g., to argue that it ought to provide prenatal care instead of open-heart surgery), a further leap is needed to characterize these choices as an attempt by an individual clinician to influence her counselees' reproductive decisions. Such a leap might be plausible—e.g., if the clinician advocated, or acquiesced in, an institutional decision not to offer the services at issue—but since my focus in this paper is on autonomy-negating influence within the counseling relationship, I will not address this possibility here.

Another possible explanation for some such statements should be noted. Quite apart from any intent a counselor might have to influence a counselee's childbearing decision, the counselor might be a conscientious objector with respect to childbirth by HIV-infected women. Whether or not one thinks conscientious objection legitimate in this context, it is conceivable that a would-be conscientious objector could decline to provide prenatal care to HIV-infected women without in any sense intending to influence their reproductive decisions.

28. Dr. Abitol's alleged statement to the pregnant Ms. Doe that she could not continue in Jamaica Hospital's high-risk prenatal care program, see text accompanying notes 2 and 3, may have been an example.
29. Thus far, there have been no published allegations of such conduct by providers who care for HIV-infected women. However, providers have reportedly conditioned their services upon consent to sterilization in other contexts. See, e.g., *Walker v. Pierce*, 560 F.2d 609, 613 (4th Cir. 1977), *cert.* denied, 434 U.S. 1075 (1978) (physician who conditioned obstetrical services to poor women with two or more children upon their submission to postpartum sterilization held not to have "forced" his views upon patients).
30. Some state health departments have already begun such campaigns.
31. Such incentives, still purely hypothetical as a strategy targeted toward HIV-infected women, might include the provision of public subsidies for contraception or the conditioning of government benefits (e.g., health insurance or welfare payments) on reproductive abstinence.
32. Ruth Faden states this position as follows:

> [T]here is (obviously) no moral conclusion necessarily to be drawn about the rightness or wrongness of a public policy from the determination that the policy is an instance of coercion, manipulation, etc. Some coercive policies will be justified (in the light of our commitments, values, etc.) and others will not. (personal communication, June 22, 1992)

> G. Dworkin, *The Theory and Practice of Autonomy* (New York: Cambridge University Press, 1988): 9, 32 (distinguishing between "conceptual" and "normative" analysis of autonomy and asserting that it is an "intellectual error" to "assimilat[e]" such virtues as sympathy, integrity, and concern for human welfare into our understanding of autonomy).

33. See, e.g., F. Oppenheim, "'Constraints on Freedom' as a Descriptive Concept," *Ethics* 95 (1985): 305 (arguing that conceptual analysis of coercion and freedom must be morally neutral if discussion about the morality of coercive measures is to be intelligent and fruitful).
34. A broader possibility—that the analysis of a concept can never be wholly separated from its moral assessment—will not be considered in this paper.

35. See, e.g., D. Zimmerman, "Coercive Wage Offers," *Philosophy and Public Affairs* 10 (1981): 121, 127 (accurate account of coercion must explain its prima facie wrongfulness); M. D. Bayles, "A Concept of Coercion," in *Coercion*, eds. J. R. Pennock and J. W. Chapman (Chicago: Aldine Atherton, 1972): 16, 29 ("[c]oercion is the most morally offensive form of the exercise of power over others"); V. Held, "Coercion and Coercive Offers," in *Coercion*, eds. Pennock and Chapman, 49, 61–62 (asserting "prima facie" obligation to avoid coercion); R. P. Wolff, "Is Coercion 'Ethically Neutral'?", in *Coercion*, eds. Pennock and Chapman, 144–146 (contending that coercion is "intrinsically evil" because it is degrading).
36. Held, "Coercion and Coercive Offers," 62.
37. E. D. Pellegrino, "Autonomy and Coercion in Disease Prevention and Health Promotion," *Theoretical Medicine* 5 (1984): 83, 88–90.
38. See K. M. Sullivan, "Unconstitutional Conditions," *Harvard Law Review* 102 (1989): 1413, 1442–1450 (reviewing efforts by philosophers, legal scholars, and even some judges to derive definitions of coercion from competing conceptions of utility, autonomy, fairness, and just desert).
39. See, e.g., R. A. Epstein, *Bargaining with the State* (Princeton, NJ: Princeton University Press, 1993): 39–49 (arguing that once ex ante entitlements are accepted as legitimate, influence attempts should be deemed coercive if they impose social welfare losses). For Epstein, the welfare loss experienced by the target of an influence attempt bears on the determination of the attempt's coerciveness only because the target's loss is a good proxy for the social loss. Ibid., 43. Epstein's approach to the legitimacy of ex ante entitlements centers on the potential of voluntary exchanges to maximize welfare: he argues (along Coasean lines) that minimization of transaction costs ought to determine the allocation of initial entitlements. Ibid., 32–38.
40. Alan Wertheimer has developed the most comprehensive account of coercion along these lines. He argues that the allegation that A coerced B is best understood as a claim that B should be deemed not responsible for some action and that such claims are best evaluated via the conduct of two explicitly moral inquiries: (1) Did A propose to make B worse off, relative to some moral baseline? (2) Was B morally entitled to succumb to A's influence? Only if both questions are answered in the affirmative, Wertheimer holds, can A be said to have coerced B. Wertheimer, *Coercion*, 179–310. Taking issue with utilitarian theorists, Wertheimer contends that these moral inquiries should exclude "considerations of social utility" and center instead on "considerations of justice and rights." Ibid., 174, 284–286. Beyond this, he says little about the substantive content of these inquiries, explaining that this lies beyond the scope of his project. See also C. Fried, *Contract as Promise: A Theory of Contractual Obligation* (Cambridge, MA: Harvard University Press, 1981): 95–99 (arguing that a proposal coerces if it offers something that its maker has no "right" to offer, as measured by moral criteria "deeper, more general, or at any rate independent" of the moral issue presented by the proposal).

   R. Nozick, "Coercion," in S. Morgenbesser, P. Suppes, and M. White, eds., *Philosophy, Science, and Method* (New York: Saint Martin's Press, 1969): 440 (arguing that a contingent proposition constitutes a threat and is, therefore, coercive when it makes the recipient's situation worse than what would have been expected in the absence of the proposition and asserting that what would have been expected is informed both by moral requirements and empirical probabilities). Where moral requirements and empirical probabilities diverge, Nozick proposes, the recipient's conscious preference, between the ex ante states implied by each, ought to be determinative. S. F. Kreimer, "Allocational Sanctions: The Problem of Negative Rights in a Positive State," *University of Pennsylvania Law Review* 132 (1984): 1293, 1352–1378 (suggesting that coercive and noncoercive propositions be distinguished by comparing them to baseline states derived from historical experience, the ideal of equality, and predictions of what might happen in a proposition's absence). Kreimer argues that reliance upon history and empirically grounded prediction can constrain but not eliminate the normative discretion inherent in the making of distinctions between coercive and noncoercive proposals.

41. See, e.g., R. Barthes, *Elements of Semiology* (New York: Hill and Wang, 1968): 89–94 (a word or other sign signifies one or more meanings on the plane of denotation; in turn, use of a sign to denote a meaning signifies additional, more "general" and "diffuse" content on another plane, that of connotation).

This usage of the term "connotation" is sharply different from that employed by logicians and some analytical philosophers. Connotation in this latter sense is no less specific or focused than denotation: both are logical relations between linguistic expressions and particular things in the world. A word connotes a quality, in this analytical sense, if possession of that quality is the necessary and sufficient condition for the word's application to a person or thing. See W. P. Alston, *Philosophy of Language* (Englewood Cliffs, NJ: Prentice-Hall, 1964): 16–17 (illustrating the point with the word "courageous," which connotes the "disposition to remain steadfast in the face of danger" because "possession of that disposition by someone is the necessary and sufficient condition of the term 'courageous' being correctly applied to that person"). I thank Anita Allen for bringing this usage to my attention. Within this analytic tradition, the dichotomy between "cognitive meaning" and "emotional meaning" (ibid., 47) comes much closer to capturing semiologists' distinction between denotation and connotation. However, the notion of "emotional meaning" does not fully capture the ideological—indeed, moral—import of connotation in the semiologic sense.

42. Barthes, *Elements of Semiology*, 91.
43. Ibid., 92.
44. The word "discrimination" provides an example. Its denotative meaning involves the drawing of distinctions between things, but in the bitter context of American race relations it has developed a powerful and negative connotative meaning (in the semiologic sense). This meaning has so crystallized—i.e., the term "discrimination" has become so closely linked to invidious differentiation based on race or other social groupings—that it is now arguably denotative in character.
45. Held, "Coercion and Coercive Offers," 61–62. To the extent that coercion is seen as an intrinsically normative concept with a negative moral valence, such an argument would seem to be at war with itself. Its virtue, however, lies in its respectful treatment of the values it proposes to sacrifice: characterization of an influence strategy as coercive acknowledges that a moral price would be paid to achieve a preferred end.
46. See text accompanying note 25.
47. D. J. Rothman, *Strangers at the Bedside: A History of How Law and Bioethics Transformed Medical Decision Making* (New York: Basic Books, 1991): 241–246.
48. See, e.g., H. G. Frankfurt, "Freedom of the Will and the Concept of a Person," *Journal of Philosophy* 69 (1971): 5 (arguing that autonomous action must be motivated by "first-order" preferences with which a subject identifies, via enduring

"second-order" desires upon which "first-order" preferences should be acted). For Frankfurt, actions inconsistent with lasting, "second-order" desires cannot be autonomous, indeed cannot be plausibly regarded as a person's own. Ibid., 13.
49. Beauchamp and Childress, *Principles of Biomedical Ethics*.
50. Ibid., 69.
51. Ibid.
52. Jay Katz argues for a conception of "psychological autonomy" that emphasizes the chooser's capacity to reflect in a manner that takes unconscious mental processes and irrational beliefs into account. Katz, *The Silent World*, 105–121. For Katz, psychologically autonomous choice requires the exercise of this capacity to a greater degree than is now common in clinical practice. Katz ties this challenging conception of autonomous action to a call for enriched doctor–patient conversation, aimed at deepening both parties' awareness of their beliefs and biases. Ibid., 121–164.

Along similar lines, Gerald Dworkin describes autonomy as "a second-order capacity of persons to reflect critically upon their first-order preferences, desires, wishes, and so forth and the capacity to accept or attempt to change these in light of higher-order preferences and values." Dworkin, *The Theory and Practice of Autonomy*, 20. However, unlike Katz, Dworkin provides little guidance (in his extensive discussion of the importance of patient autonomy, ibid., 100–120) as to how his demanding conception of autonomy might translate into prerequisites for autonomous patient choice.
53. The Beauchamp and Childress model of four prima facie principles—nonmaleficence, beneficence, autonomy, and justice—has been broadly and enthusiastically embraced by medical ethicists and health professionals. For nearly a generation, it has been widely taught to ethicists and clinicians who consult in health-care settings, teach in medical schools, and direct centers of bioethics. See E. D. Pellegrino, "The Metamorphosis of Medical Ethics; A 30-Year Retrospective," *Journal of the American Medical Association* 269 (1993): 1158.
54. By contrast, Jay Katz's more demanding approach to the prerequisites for autonomous choice leads him to call for far-reaching change in doctor–patient conversation so as to remake clinical decision-making into a much more deeply reflective enterprise for patients and physicians. See note 52.
55. R. R. Faden and T. L. Beauchamp, *A History and Theory of Informed Consent* (New York: Oxford University Press, 1986): 337–381.
56. Working with a single, richly developed conception of autonomy-negating influence facilitates deeper analysis of such claims than would generalization about the many treatments of autonomous action in bioethics that share the above-described pragmatic stance toward "controlling" influence. This strategy cannot yield broadly validated conclusions about how bioethics as a movement treats such claims, but this in-depth approach permits illustration of the tight linkage between bioethical commentators' understandings of autonomy-negating influence and their aspirations for the reform of doctor–patient relations.
57. Faden and Beauchamp, *A History and Theory*, 339.
58. Faden and Beauchamp appear to use the term "intent" narrowly, as synonymous with purpose, but they nowhere foreclose the possibility of a broader reading—e.g., as knowledge with substantial certainty.
59. Within the Faden and Beauchamp framework, autonomous choice can be compro-

60. Nozick's model of coercion is the most influential contemporary example. See Nozick, note 40. See also Bayles, "A Concept of Coercion," 19–20. These models portray coercion as a relationship between victim and purposeful perpetrator. They take background social forces and pressures as givens, beyond the scope of the personal relationship between victim and perpetrator and thus beyond the reach of the concept of coercion.
61. H. D. Laswell and A. Kaplan, *Power and Society: A Framework for Political Inquiry* (New Haven: Yale University Press, 1950): 97.
62. This presumes, of course, that coercion precludes the possibility of autonomous choice. This assumption is consistent with evident scholarly consensus. To my knowledge, no commentator has proposed that choices understood as coerced be simultaneously deemed autonomous.
63. F. J. Ingelfinger, "Informed (But Uneducated) Consent", *New England Journal of Medicine* 287 (1972): 465, 466 (patients' incapacitation, fears for their health, etc. lend "some element of coercion" to all consents given by human subjects in medical research). Like Lasswell's, Ingelfinger's interpretation of the concept of coercion does not require a purposeful coercive agent.
64. See Beauchamp and Childress, *Principles of Biomedical Ethics*, 75 ("primary function of informed consent is protecting and enabling individual autonomous choice"). See, generally, Maguire Schultz, "From Informed Consent to Patient Choice."
65. Faden and Beauchamp, *A History and Theory*, 368. Faden and Beauchamp acknowledge that a person in dire circumstances "can be described as not free" (ibid., 344), but they contend it is "a serious confusion to move from a correct claim about a deprivation or loss of freedom caused by desperate circumstances to a (fallaciously drawn) conclusion that there has been a loss of autonomy because of a coercive situation" (ibid., 345). They do not explain the difference between their conceptions of freedom and autonomy.
66. Ibid., 345 (noting their decision to "restrict the notions of 'control' and 'coercion' to the intentional acts of others for which they are responsible and which they could eliminate").
67. Such a statement might reflect either the provider's personal preference or the policy of an institution that employs her. The discussion above does not distinguish between these two possibilities nor does it explore an individual counselor's options when faced with such an institutional policy.
68. Ibid., 354.
69. Faden and Beauchamp take the position that offers are never coercive and that the distinction between threats and offers is not purely a matter of how choices are framed—i.e., that a "genuine offer" can be distinguished from a "veiled threat." Ibid., 340–341.
70. Ibid., 360.
71. Ibid., 342, 360.
72. Faden and Beauchamp explicitly decline to make "suggestions as to how to measure or test whether a given threat would prove irresistible to any particular individual." Ibid., 342. They propose, however, that "for policy purposes," resistibility be assessed based on "evidence and predictions about how most people would respond" to a proposition. Ibid. They acknowledge that "[p]iling so much on the

notions of 'resistance' and 'resistibility' without a deeper analysis of these terms . . . leaves a certain incompleteness." Ibid., 360–361.

73. D. R. Hofstadter, *Godel, Escher, Bach: An Eternal Golden Braid* (New York: Basic Books, 1979): 641. Hofstadter drives home this point with an anecdote:

> After reading [a whimsical, counterfactual dialogue written by Hofstadter], a friend said to me, "My uncle was almost President of the U.S.!" "Really?" I said. "Sure," he replied, "he was skipper of the PT 108." (John F. Kennedy was skipper of the PT 109.)

74. Ibid.

75. G. Steiner, *After Babel: Aspects of Language and Translation* (New York: Oxford University Press, 1975), cited in Hofstadter, 642–643. Steiner argues:

> It is unlikely that man, as we know him, would have survived without the fictive, counter-factual, anti-determinist means of language, without the semantic capacity, generated and stored in the "superfluous" zones of the cortex, to conceive of, to articulate possibilities beyond the treadmill of organic decay and death.

76. Ibid., 641. Hofstadter illustrates this point as follows:

> Driving down a country road, you run into a swarm of bees. You don't just duly take note of it; the whole situation is immediately placed in perspective by a swarm of "replays" that crowd into your mind. Typically, you think, "Sure am lucky my window wasn't open!"—or worse, the reverse: "Too bad my window wasn't closed!" "Lucky I wasn't on my bike!" "Too bad I didn't come along five seconds earlier." Strange but possible replays: "if that had been a deer, I could have been killed!" "I bet those bees would have rather had a collision with a rosebush."

77. Ibid., 635–637.

78. These framing decisions make heuristic sense from a football fan's perspective since they are the choices the player has implicitly accepted: instead of questioning the shape of the ball or the out-of-bounds rules, he focuses his attention on catching the ball and then staying in bounds.

79. See text accompanying notes 68–70.

80. Wertheimer, *Coercion*, 267–273 (assertion that the recipient of a "coercive proposal" has "no choice" constitutes a claim that she is "entitled to succumb" to the proposal).

81. This intuition roughly tracks the Rawlsian difference principle, which allows inequities only when they benefit society's worst-off. J. Rawls, *A Theory of Justice* (Cambridge, MA: Belknap Press of Harvard University Press).

82. See T. V. Ellerbrock, T. J. Bush, M. E. Chamberland, and M. J. Oxtoby, "Epidemiology of Women with AIDS in the United States, 1981 through 1990; A Comparison with Heterosexual Men with AIDS," *Journal of the American Medical Association* 265 (1991): 2971 (reporting that 72% of AIDS cases in women compiled by the CDC's AIDS surveillance system before 1991 occurred in African-Americans or Latinos). This study's authors concluded that African-American and Latino women had cumulative AIDS incidence rates eight and 13 times, respectively, that for whites.

83. See, generally, T. M. Shapiro, *Population Control Politics: Women, Sterilization, and Reproductive Choice* (Philadelphia: Temple University Press, 1985); S. Law, "Sterilization Comes Easier for the Disadvantaged," *New York University Law*

Bulletin 23 (1977): 15. See also J. Mohr, *Abortion in America: The Origins and Evolution of National Policy* (New York: Oxford University Press, 1978): 147–170 (interpreting advocacy of restrictive abortion laws by late nineteenth-century physicians as part of an effort to promote their professional authority).

84. See text accompanying notes 71–80.
85. In employing the term "subterfuge," I do not mean to issue a categorical moral judgment, though the adverse connotations of this term are plainly suggestive in this regard. Rather, I mean merely to note that the concept of resistibility (and analogous constructs in the literature on autonomy and coercion) tends to obscure underlying normative choices. Such disingenuity, I suggest above, may have its advantages.
86. Calabresi, *Tragic Choices*, 149–150 (discussing appeal of various decision-making procedures, ranging from juries to markets, that submerge the sacrifice of passionately held values).
87. If so, then analyses like the present work could have the ironic and disturbing effect of undermining mutual respect.
88. M. Dan-Cohen, "Responsibility and the Boundaries of the Self," *Harvard Law Review* 105 (1992): 959 (linking alternative conceptions of individual responsibility to variation in the boundaries that we draw between the self and the external world).
89. Faden and Beauchamp, *A History and Theory*, 340. See also Wertheimer, *Coercion*, 202 (characterizing this position as the "dominant philosophical view about coercion").
90. See note 69 and text accompanying notes 68 and 69.
91. See text accompanying note 57. Successful threats that are not "severe" (a standard that relies overtly on normative judgment about the leverage employed) qualify as "manipulation" within the Faden and Beauchamp model and thereby preclude autonomous choice when they cannot be "reasonably easily resisted." See text accompanying notes 68–70.
92. Decisions influenced by "welcome" offers are autonomous per se, Faden and Beauchamp say, without reference to a resistibility standard. See Faden and Beauchamp, *A History and Theory*, 357 (a choice influenced by a "welcome offer" is "entirely autonomous" because "it proceeds from the dictates of [the chooser's] will"). In contrast, decisions influenced by "unwelcome" offers are autonomous only when such offers can be "reasonably easily resisted."
93. Ibid. (emphasis in original).
94. As an example, consider a physician's offer of free medical care to a happily married patient in return for sexual relations. This offer is both patently offensive and virtually certain to be rejected.
95. Ibid., 358–359.
96. A move from the status quo is Pareto-superior if at least one person is better off and no one else is worse off.
97. It is inconceivable (at least to me) that the recipient of an offer could at once favor its terms (in comparison with her alternatives) and find them unwelcome. Once the recipient has chosen the offer over its alternatives, the notion that it is unwelcome can only make sense (at least to me) as an expression of observer discomfort with her decision or with her limited set of options.
98. Faden and Beauchamp appear to reject the notion that such moral judgments inform determinations of "welcomeness." They cast exploitation of vulnerable persons and failure to ameliorate dire financial circumstances as "moral concerns" distinct from

the question of welcomeness and from "problems of autonomy and control" more generally. Ibid., 359.
99. The same moral premises that underlie perceptions that such propositions are difficult to resist (see text accompanying notes 80–88) can be expected to inform their characterization as unwelcome.
100. Faden and Beauchamp, *A History and Theory*, 357.
101. One might reconstruct the idea of an unwelcome offer by imagining a proposition that imposes on its recipient an emotional or moral cost of deciding (or cost involved in merely learning its dire terms) greater than the benefits yielded by accepting it. G. Calabresi, *Ideas, Beliefs, Attitudes and the Law: Private Law Perspective on a Public Law Problem* (Syracuse, NY: Syracuse University Press, 1985): 69–86 (analyzing the problem of determining which kinds of emotional and moral cost should "count" for legal purposes). Costs of deciding are incurred upon receipt of an offer (or upon learning of its terms), whether or not the recipient accepts. Unless these costs are outweighed by the benefits of acceptance, a rational person will regret receiving such an offer, even if, once having received it, he or she chooses to accept it. This reconstruction relocates the task of normative judgment: underlying moral concerns inform the evaluation of both the costs of deciding and the benefits of acceptance.
102. Unwelcome offers, by contrast, must be subjected to a resistibility test to determine their compatibility with autonomous action. See note 92.
103. Because the same moral beliefs underlie both the inclination to view offers to persons in dire straits as unwelcome and the tendency to see such offers as difficult to resist (see note 98), the characterization of offers as unwelcome within the Faden and Beauchamp model is likely to be linked to the determination that they preclude autonomous decision-making.
104. See text accompanying notes 89–92.
105. Faden and Beauchamp, *A History and Theory*, 341. They state that such questions are "separate matters" from the distinction between a "genuine offer" and a "veiled threat."
106. Wertheimer, *Coercion*, 204 (emphasis in original). Faden and Beauchamp do not indicate disagreement with this view.
107. For a comprehensive review of this philosophical literature, see Ibid., 202–221. Robert Nozick is generally credited for the insight that moral premises inform the baselines tacitly employed to distinguish threats from offers. See Nozick, "Coercion," 447 (arguing that baselines incorporate both moral expectations and predictions of future behavior). Other important contributors include M. Gunderson, "Threats and Coercion," *Canadian Journal of Philosophy* 9 (1979): 247 and V. Haksar, "Coercive Proposals," *Political Theory* 4 (1976): 65. Among philosophers writing on bioethics, Norman Daniels is perhaps the leading exponent of the view that choices between baselines are inescapably moralized. See N. Daniels, *Just Health Care* (New York: Cambridge University Press, 1985): 165–171 (criticizing derivation of baselines from the preoffer status quo).
108. The problem of distinguishing threats (or illegitimate propositions) from offers (or legitimate proposals) arises in many legal contexts, including contract law (duress), constitutional law (the doctrine of unconstitutional conditions), corporate law (the coerciveness of tender offers that involve front-end premiums, followed by the use of condemnation authority to buy out nay-sayers at lower prices), and criminal law and procedure (blackmail, the defense of duress, coerced confessions, and plea

bargaining). A diverse range of commentators hold to the position that threats cannot be parsed from offers in any of these contexts except by reliance on moral baselines. See Fried, *Contract as Promise*, 95–99 (distinguishing coercive and noncoercive contract proposals based on whether a proposal's substance is wrongful, as measured by some general moral criteria); A. Kronman, "Contract Law and Distributive Justice," *Yale Law Journal* 89 (1980): 472, 485–491 (defining legitimate advantage-taking as that which improves the long-term prospects of those whom it disadvantages in the short run); Sullivan, "Unconstitutional Conditions," 1447–1450 (arguing that distinctions between coercion and consent must rest on some normative theory); Kreimer, "Allocational Sanctions," 1363–1371 (urging equality as a moral baseline in distinguishing threats from offers); Epstein, *Bargaining with the State*, 39–68 (arguing for setting of baselines on social welfare-maximizing grounds); P. Westen, "'Freedom' and 'Coercion'—Virtue Words and Vice Words," *Duke Law Journal* (1985): 541, 576–577 (reviewing role of moral baselines in identifying coercive proposals). Fried, Kronman, Sullivan, and Epstein hold that the setting of appropriate baselines is exclusively a moral question, while Kreimer and Westen argue for the relevance of both moral and nonmoral criteria.
109. Sullivan, "Unconstitutional Conditions," 1447–1450.
110. See, e.g., President's Commission on the Health Needs of the Nation, *Report to the President: Building America's Health* (1953): 3 (asserting that access to health care "is a basic human right").
111. President's Commission for the Study of Ethical Problems in Medicine and Biomedical and Behavioral Research, *Securing Access to Health Care: A Report on the Ethical Implications of Differences in the Availability of Health Services* (Washington D.C.: U.S. Government Printing Office, 1983): 22–25, 32–33 (concluding that society has an "ethical obligation" to ensure universal access to "adequate care" and distinguishing this position from the assertion of a universal right to health care).
112. If alternative sources of care are available, the threat/offer distinction becomes more complicated, reflecting the need for a more richly developed baseline. Since my purpose is to point out the decisive role of moral baselines rather than to offer a substantive theory of moral obligation in clinical work, I will not pursue the development of such a baseline here.
113. R. M. Sade, "Medical Care as a Right: A Refutation," *New England Journal of Medicine* 285 (1971): 1288.
114. Kreimer, "Allocational Sanctions," 1359–1363.
115. J. Feinberg, *Harm to Self Series: The Moral Units of the Criminal Law* (New York: Oxford University Press, 1986): 219; Westen, "'Freedom' and 'Coercion,'" 581; Kreimer, "Allocational Sanctions," 1371–1374; Nozick, "Coercion," 447.
116. Wertheimer, *Coercion*, 207.
117. Conversely, a history of universal, unconditional access to medical care establishes a baseline that incorporates such access, yielding the conclusion that such proposals constitute threats.
118. Conversely, were the provision of care without such conditions the standard practice, such proposals would represent a downward departure from the empirical baseline. As such, they would constitute threats.
119. Conversely, a recipient's belief that she is entitled to care without this condition yields a subjective baseline that casts such proposals as threats.
120. A vast literature develops this theme. For a comprehensive, largely sympathetic discussion of this work, see R. J. Bernstein, *Beyond Objectivism and Relativism:*

Science, Hermeneutics and Praxis (Philadelphia: University of Pennsylvania Press, 1988): 1–169 (reviewing and synthesizing contributions by Thomas Kuhn, Peter Winch, Paul Feyerabend, Charles Taylor, Clifford Geertz, Richard Rorty, Hans-Georg Gadamer, Jurgen Habermas, and others).

121. Wertheimer, *Coercion*, 212–213; Kreimer, "Allocational Sanctions," 1374–1378; Nozick, "Coercion," 451.

122. Nozick, who contends that we derive baselines from predictions about the future and from moral expectations, suggests that when baselines from these sources differ, we ought to defer to the baseline accepted by the recipient of the proposal at issue. Nozick, "Coercion," 451. This decision rule elevates the ideal of personal freedom (interpreted within the liberal tradition, as deference to the individual's consciously experienced preferences) over competing moral claims—e.g., conceptions of distributive justice or welfare maximization. Wertheimer proposes a candidly result-oriented approach to the problem of baseline selection. Where the baselines yielded by moral reasoning, prediction, and/or subjective expectations diverge, he recommends that selection should depend on the "moral force" behind the claim that a proposal coerces within a particular context. Wertheimer, *Coercion*, 212.

123. See Sullivan, "*Unconstitutional Conditions*," 1450, n. 150 (observing, in the "unconstitutional conditions" context, that looking to history or prediction "assume[s] that reliance on continuation of the status quo or the statistically likely course of government action is justified").

124. See text accompanying notes 23–25.

125. I ignore here the problem of factual misrepresentation, which lies beyond the scope of this paper.

126. Faden and Beauchamp, *A History and Theory*, 354.

127. Ibid., 367.

128. Ibid., 347 (persuasion operates by inducing a person, "through appeals to reason, to freely accept . . . the beliefs, attitudes, values, intentions, or actions advocated by the persuader"). To constitute an appeal to reason, a communication must target "some dominantly cognitive process" in the listener. Ibid., 351. Appeals to "emotions or affect"—to "reactions and motivations such as hate, fear, disgust, or embarrassment"—represent manipulation, not persuasion.

129. Ibid., 351, 366.

130. Ibid., 355.

131. Ibid., 363–365 (discussing lying, selective withholding of important facts, exaggeration, use of placebos, and exploitation of framing effects).

132. My analysis of "advisory" and "directive" statements departs from the assumption that they are not accompanied by factual misrepresentation. Such misrepresentation impinges upon autonomy, according to Faden and Beauchamp (and many other commentators) by interfering with a decision-maker's understanding of her choice situation. Ibid., 362.

133. Faden and Beauchamp incorporate the modernist distinction between reason and passion, privileging the former, in Kantian fashion, as a basis for ascribing autonomy to actions. Shorn of Kantian metaphysics—in particular, Kant's proposition that the free and rational self exists "independent of determination by causes in the sensible world," (I. Kant, *Groundwork of the Metaphysics of Morals*, H. J. Paton, trans. [New York: Barnes and Noble, 1967]: 120)—ascription of autonomy based on this distinction reflects a preference for decision procedures that eschew overt

reliance upon passion. This preference cannot rest on the implausible proposition that reason and passion differ in their dependence on "determination by causes in the sensible world." Rather, it stems from a view of the good life that distrusts the transforming (and potentially destabilizing) power of passion. See R. Unger, *Passion: An Essay on Personality* (New York: Free Press, 1984): 256 (observing that many "social visions" eschew passionate influence out of concern that it could impede achievement of "more perfect forms of human association"). Whether this distrust is justified is a normative question that bioethical commentators have by and large not addressed.

134. Faden and Beauchamp, *A History and Theory*, 368–373.
135. Ibid., 368–371.
136. Ibid., 369 (emphasis in original).
137. The use of the term "prefer" in this context implies that constraint must be consciously experienced. For Faden and Beauchamp, unconscious preferences and experiences of constraint are matters of authenticity and, as such, not germane to the task of identifying influences that preclude autonomous choice. Ibid., at 262–266 (arguing that authenticity is not a necessary condition for autonomous action).
138. Ibid., 372. Faden and Beauchamp suggest additional strategies for dealing with the "role constraints" problem, including the involvement of family members, friends, clergy, and others who play supportive roles in patients' lives.
139. See text accompanying notes 71–88 (reviewing a wide range of normative concerns that inform answers to the question of resistibility).
140. Such statements engender feelings of interpersonal and social duty, linked, perhaps, to irrational, often unconscious fantasies about the dangers of defying authority. See Katz, *The Silent World*, 114–121 (discussing roles of irrational and unconscious mental processes in self-determination).
141. Absent any associated reason-giving, such statements as "you should not become pregnant" or "don't have this child" plainly constitute "psychological manipulation" within the Faden and Beauchamp model. The copresence of such statements with "appeals to reason" may make the question of "psychological manipulation" vs. "persuasion" into a difficult judgment call. Conversely, the copresence of overtly emotional appeals—e.g., condemnations of childbearing by HIV-infected women as self-indulgent or irresponsible—strengthens the case for characterization of such counseling as "psychological manipulation."
142. See text accompanying notes 71–88 and 138.
143. These prerequisites are not universally accepted. Jay Katz's concern about the potential of unconscious mental processes to interfere with "psychological autonomy" *The Silent World*, (Katz, 110–121) represents one prominent, dissenting view from within the mainstream of biomedical ethics. Norman Daniels' caveat about the autonomy-negating potential of unjust social practices in the absence of a deliberate influence attempt by a human agent (see text accompanying notes 145–157) represents another differing perspective.
144. Biomedical ethics scholarship tends to focus its reformist energies on the doctor-patient relationship and to take personal psychology and social structure as givens. A scholarly enterprise that instead emphasized possibilities for psychological or social change might be expected to conceptualize autonomy quite differently. A. L. Allen, "Book Review: African-American Perspectives on Biomedical Ethics," *Ethics* 104 (1994): 404–405; L. Harris, "Autonomy Under Duress," in *African-American Perspectives on Bioethics*, eds. H. E. Flack and E. D. Pelligrino (Wash-

ington DC: Georgetown University Press, 1992): 133–134 (arguing that prevailing conceptions of autonomy and rational choice in American biomedical ethics fail to take account of fundamental distributional inequalities and thereby risk yielding morally perverse results).

145. I do not argue that every conception of autonomy-negating influence is equally persuasive when viewed from the normative vantage point that inspired it. Rather, I hold to the position (for reasons that are beyond the scope of this paper) that persuasive and implausible conceptions can be distinguished, even from the most sympathetic of normative vantage points, based on interpretive ideals of consistency and integrity. Each of the conceptions I discuss herein (including the Faden and Beauchamp framework) is persuasive from some normative vantage point.

146. Daniels, *Just Health Care*, 171; Wertheimer, *Coercion*, 243, 287 (referring to the belief that coercion has to do with the amount of "pressure" on an actor as the "preanalytic sense of coercion").

147. Daniels, *Just Health Care*, 170.

148. Daniels employs the terms "voluntariness," "freedom," and "autonomy" in a more or less synonymous fashion, in contradistinction to scholars who ascribe divergent meanings to these three words.

149. However, the intentionality of influence efforts can affect the subjective experience of persons targeted by such efforts. Awareness that somebody else has deliberately restricted one's choices or otherwise concocted a pressure-filled situation to influence one's behavior can lead one to feel degraded and embittered. Such feelings may enlarge one's sense of "diminished voluntariness" or "unfreedom."

150. See Lasswell and Kaplan, *Power and Society*, 97.

151. Daniels, *Just Health Care*, 171.

152. Ibid., 172.

153. Ibid.

154. The distinction between "socially" and "naturally" caused pressures is thus thoroughly moralized, something that Daniels does not acknowledge in proposing his concept of "quasi-coercion."

155. Daniels professes fealty to the Nozickian requirement (which he refers to as part of all "standard analyses" of coercion) that a human agent act intentionally to alter the chooser's range of options. Ibid., 165.

156. Such an enlargement could be achieved without abandoning the intent requirement entirely. This could be accomplished by interpreting intent less specifically—i.e., as mere knowledge of the consequences at issue. Were knowledge of the restrictions on choice that result from "unjust or unfair social practices and institutions" held to satisfy the intent requirement, then society could be charged with intentionally restricting choice by perpetuating such practices and institutions in the face of knowledge of their restrictive impact. Even if such knowledge is not widespread—e.g., if many Americans are unaware that some HIV-infected women lack access to health care—it might plausibly be imputed to society on the ground that a just society has a duty to identify and redress intrusions on its members' autonomy.

157. Ibid., 172–173 (performing similar analysis for proposals to provide extra "hazard pay" to workers when the risks at issue are technologically reducible). Faden and Beauchamp, it should be noted, could arrive at the same conclusion (tacitly rooted in the moral premise that all people are entitled to medical care regardless of reproductive behavior or ability to pay) by characterizing the proposal as a threat or unwelcome offer that meets their relevant resistibility criteria, but such a descriptive

move would be awkward indeed if the proposal's recipient insisted on characterizing it as welcome.
158. Sade, "Medical Care as a Right," 112.
159. Such an argument might roughly track Faden's and Beauchamp's concerns about "role constraints" in clinical settings. See text accompanying notes 133–138. Alternatively, it could take a radical turn toward the notion that the perceived authority of health professionals is per se oppressive and unjust.
160. C. R. Lawrence III, "The Id, the Ego, and Equal Protection: Reckoning with Unconscious Racism," *Stanford Law Review*, 39 (1987): 317, 326; P. C. Davis, "Law As Microaggression," *Yale Law Journal*, 98 (1989): 1559, 1567–1568, n40.
161. The line between social and natural causes is hardly as clear as Daniels seems to assume. Constraints on choice that result from natural phenomena invariably have a socially mediated component. For example, economic conditions and prior decisions about building safety play critical roles in the harm done (and constraints created) by earthquakes. The ascription of consequences to natural vs. social causes is an inescapably moral question, tied to the problem of delineating duties to prevent harm. See note 153.
162. It is true that the experience of diminished voluntariness is often linked to the intuition that a situation is unfair, but this preanalytical intuition does not always reflect moral judgment. The occurrence of terminal cancer in a teenager, for example, evokes a sense of tragic unfairness in the absence of any conceivable moral agent.
163. Daniels, *Just Health Care*, 170.
164. Lasswell and Kaplan, *Power and Society*, 97.
165. Alternatively, all constraints and inducements could be considered coercive. R. Hale, *Freedom Through Law: Public Control of Private Governing Power* (New York: Columbia University Press, 1952): 294–295 (asserting that every "[e]xaction of a price" in the marketplace "restricts freedom" and thereby coerces because the state limits the ability of "non-owners" to make "unauthorized use" of property). However, this move toward global determinism would beg the question implicit in Daniels' intuition: How are we to identify prima facie morally problematic cases of "diminished voluntariness?"
166. See text accompanying notes 71–88.
167. I here presume an identity between coercion and all autonomy-negating external influence (and thus a simple dichotomy between coerced and autonomous choice). I omit, for simplicity's sake, the possibility of other categories of potentially autonomy-negating influence. I also ignore problems of misinformation (e.g., deception and ignorance), which lie beyond the scope of this paper.
168. See, e.g., D. L. Jackson and S. Youngner, "Patient Autonomy and 'Death with Dignity': Some Clinical Caveats," *New England Journal of Medicine*, 301 (1979): 404 (depression and other psychiatric problems undermine autonomy in intensive care unit patients).
169. To the extent that environmental (external) stimuli play any role, the distinction between internal and external stimuli cannot be pure.
170. S. Benn, "Freedom, Autonomy, and the Concept of a Person," *Proceedings of the Aristotelian Society*, 76 (1976): 109, 123–128. R. Young, "Autonomy and Socialization," *Mind* 89 (1980): 565 (contending that unconscious mental activity undermines autonomy by coercing or manipulating and that socialization thereby impairs autonomy unless it is made conscious); D. T. Meyers, *Self, Society and Personal*

Choice (New York: Columbia University Press, 1989): 187–188 (arguing that some unconscious forces are compatible with autonomy—indeed, are "constitutive of the uniqueness of persons" and protective of their integrity—while others "sabotage the use of autonomy skills to formulate life plans" or "splinter the personality").

171. This portrayal of unconscious mental processes casts them as external to the self and thus as alien influences. Alternatively, unconscious mental life might be characterized as part of the essential self and thus consistent with authenticity. Even models of authenticity that require the self-conscious embrace of principles and preferences leave conceptual room for underlying, unconscious concomitants of conscious choice. However, theorists who equate authenticity with the conscious election of principles and preferences tend to be disinclined to incorporate unconscious mental life into their conceptions of the essential self.

172. Jay Katz, whose approach to autonomy demands a higher degree of reflection than that called for by many bioethics theorists, maneuvers around this problem by postulating that a "functional definition of psychological autonomy" must "take into account that an ideational system can exercise motivational force without being introspectively accessible." Katz, *The Silent World*, 115. Katz thereby allows for the possibility of autonomy in the presence of some unconscious motives, even as he argues that more reflective clinical decision-making, aimed in part at diminishing the influence of unconscious determinants, is needed to adequately respect the right to self-determination.

173. Dworkin, *The Theory and Practice of Autonomy*, 15–20. Dworkin holds that such reflection need not be "a conscious, fully articulated, and explicit process," warning that otherwise "it will appear that it is mainly professors of philosophy who exercise autonomy." Ibid., 17.

174. Faden and Beauchamp explain: "If authenticity were made a necessary condition of autonomous actions, many familiar acts of consenting and refusing would fail to qualify as autonomous, and thus would not qualify for protection from interference by the principle of respect for autonomy." Faden and Beauchamp, *A History and Theory*, 265.

175. Ibid., 268.

176. Faden and Beauchamp do not explicitly rule out the possibility that unconsciously mediated external influence might at times undermine autonomous choice. Rather, they eschew exploration of the problem of unconscious influence on the ground that "what really is or belongs to the self" and "the correct explanations of human behavior in terms of its causes and underlying reasons" are "unknowns." In so doing, however, Faden and Beauchamp reject by default the idea that unconsciously experienced outside influence can preclude autonomous action. The only forms of external influence that Faden and Beauchamp explicitly find capable of negating autonomous choice are "coercion" and "manipulation," which, as they define them, are consciously experienced. Ibid.

177. See, generally, J. Reiman, "Exploitation, Force, and the Moral Assessment of Capitalism: Thoughts on Roemer and Cohen," *Philosophy and Public Affairs*, 16 (1987): 3; G. A. Cohen, "Robert Nozick and Wilt Chamberlain: How Patterns Preserve Liberty," in *Justice and Economic Distribution*, eds. J. Arthur and W. Shaw (Englewood Cliffs, NJ: Prentice-Hall, 1978): 246.

178. K. Williams Crenshaw, "Race, Reform, and Retrenchment: Transformation and Legitimation in Antidiscrimination Law," *Harvard Law Review* 101 (1988): 1331, 1357 n98; see also Lawrence, "The Id, the Ego, and Equal Protection, 326.

179. C. MacKinnon, "Feminism, Marxism, Method, and the State: Toward Feminist Jurisprudence," *Signs: Journal of Women in Culture and Society* 8 (1983): 635.
180. W. L. McBride, "Noncoercive Society: Some Doubts, Leninist and Contemporary," in *Coercion*, eds. J. R. Pennock and J. W. Chapman (Chicago: Aldine Atherton, 1972): 178, 185 (critique of Leninist analysis of coercion).
181. V. I. Lenin, *The State and Revolution*, 2nd ed., R. Service trans. (London: Penguin Books, 1992).
182. McBride, "Noncoercive Society," 183. This deterministic vision was reflected in the Pavlovian model of human behavior adhered to by academic psychologists in the Soviet Union during Stalin's rule. The Pavlovian paradigm represented all human actions as the products of complex networks of environmentally conditioned reflexes. In theory, this paradigm predicted, these networks of conditioned reflexes could be engineered (by tight controls on environmental experience) to generate behavior consistent with Leninist political ideals. M. G. Bloche, "Law, Theory, and Politics: The Dilemma of Soviet Psychiatry," *Yale Journal of International Law* 11 (1986): 297, 308–311.
183. A committed Leninist would almost certainly view the influence strategies discussed here as falling into the former category under capitalist conditions. It seems equally likely that a Leninist would view these strategies as legitimate tools of class struggle if administered by the revolutionary vanguard. The treatment of women's reproductive freedom by the government of the Peoples Republic of China is, at the least, suggestive in this regard.
184. J. Habermas, *Communication and the Evolution of Society*, T. McCarthy, trans. (Boston: Beacon Press, 1979).
185. See, generally, ibid.
186. See, generally, M. Kelman, *A Guide to Critical Legal Studies* (Cambridge, MA: Harvard University Press, 1987): 242–268.
187. The elaboration of a theory of autonomous clinical choice, from this radical perspective, is a project far beyond the scope of this paper. My comments in this paragraph are meant only to be suggestive of how scholars from this perspective might approach the question of autonomy-negating clinical influence.
188. See text accompanying notes 137–140.
189. W. Gaylin, "On the Borders of Persuasion: A Psychoanalytic Look at Coercion," *Psychiatry* 37 (1974): 1–3.
190. Willard Gaylin offers a telling example: were one to threaten a primitive man with a small pistol, he would be less likely to respond compliantly than if threatened with a large stick. Ibid., 3. Having never seen nor otherwise known gunfire, he would be unable to link the image of the pistol with the prospect of pain or loss. By contrast, his everyday knowledge of big sticks and their menacing uses would almost ensure the latter threat's ability to inspire fear.
191. Ibid.
192. Ibid.
193. Although Freud repeatedly revised his account of instinctual life, he never deviated from his commitment to a model of human behavior as motivated by instinctual energy.
194. The following brief account of the link between instinctual frustration and traumatic experience in Freudian theory is drawn largely from S. Freud, "Inhibitions, Symptoms, and Anxiety," in *The Standard Edition of the Complete Psychological Works of Sigmund Freud*, 20th ed., ed. J. Strachey (New York: Norton, 1959): 87.

195. S. Freud, "New Introductory Lectures on Psycho-Analysis: Lecture XXXII: Anxiety and Instinctual Life," in *The Standard Edition of the Complete Psychological Works of Sigmund Freud*, 22nd ed., ed. J. Strachey (New York: Norton, 1964): 81.
196. This hypothetical scenario glosses over the complexity of the inquiry that psychoanalysts deem necessary to develop an adequate portrayal of the links between a person's behavior, conscious motivations, and unconscious fears. For example, a woman who quickly rejects her doctor's reproductive abstinence condition might, in the alternative, be seen as acting autonomously, free from infantile fear of abandonment, or as reacting defensively (and non-autonomously) to such fear by assuming a defiant stance. The recurrence of such "onion-peeling" problems in psychodynamic interpretation presents its practitioners with pervasive uncertainty.
197. Katz, *The Silent World*, 121–128.
198. M. Klein and J. Riviere, *Love, Hate and Reparation* (New York: Norton, 1953): 57–119.
199. Her choice would thus be accepted by some liberal (and bioethical) theorists as autonomous, albeit perhaps not authentic. See text accompanying notes 172–175.
200. Such influence can flow from perceived similarities between a clinician's personality and that of a prior authority figure or from conceptual parallels between the content of clinical advice and the beliefs of such an authority figure.
201. R. Schafer, *The Analytic Attitude* (New York: Basic Books, 1983): 97–112.
202. Ibid., 257. Schafer emphasizes that narrative imprisonment is the product of fantasy, not actual circumstance:

    [A]nything may serve as a prison. As we learn from that eloquent authority on imprisoning love, Juliet Capulet, even a silk thread will do. A job, a marriage, a tradition, a vow of vengeance, a stain of dishonor, a dream of glory, a promise made or a promise broken, a tense body or a beautiful face, a small town or the whole wide world; every one of them and many more are potential prisons."

203. Ibid.
204. Ibid., 263.
205. Ibid., 183–203.
206. Ibid. Schafer emphasizes that limitation is inevitable. Psychoanalysis, he holds, can enhance our autonomy by expanding our consciousness of narrative confinement, but "limitation is inherent in being anything at all." Ibid., 263. He adds,

    To be something is to be different, to remain different reliably enough to be identified as who and what you are, to have an identity in the most general sense of that term. . . . Limitation is . . . inherent in family and group belongingness, in having any kind of definable past and values, and in undergoing any kind of development one way rather than another.

207. There is an obvious parallel between this vision and the process of conscious identification with one's own preferences demanded by strong models of authenticity in liberal theory. See text accompanying notes 169–171.
208. An additional factor weighing against the appeal of psychoanalytical theory in this context may be the impact of feminist and other types of criticism of Freud. Although psychoanalysis has moved much beyond Freud, this criticism has probably undermined its cultural standing in recent years.
209. This preoccupation of psychoanalysts with the personal invites the frequent complaint that their clinical work ignores the moral significance of social and economic determinants and thereby reinforces injustice. Conversely, some critics warn that

the tolerant intimacy of psychoanalytical work invites, in Alan Stone's words, "a kind of reflection in which the outside world shrinks and the self expands," encouraging too facile a disregard for moral duties to others. A. Stone, *Law, Psychiatry and Morality* (Washington DC: American Psychiatric Press, 1984): 231.

210. Psychoanalytic theory, however, has often been employed as an analytic tool for radical critique, most notably by the philosophers of the Frankfurt School. See, generally, H. Marcuse, *Five Lectures: Psychoanalysis, Politics and Utopia*, J. Shapiro and S. Weber, trans. (Boston: Beacon Press, 1970); H. Marcuse, *Eros and Civilization* (Boston: Beacon Press, 1966). See also Lawrence, "The Id, the Ego, and Equal Protection," 317; C. F. Alford, *Melanie Klein and Critical Social Theory* (New Haven, CT: Yale University Press, 1989).

211. As Wertheimer notes, this claim is contrary to the "preanalytic sense" that coercion has to do with the degree of pressure on a decision-maker. See note 145.

212. See text accompanying notes 142 and 143.

213. Wertheimer, *Coercion*, 310.

214. Ibid. (citing R. Nozick, *Philosophical Explanations* [Cambridge, MA: Harvard University Press, 1981]: 628)

215. The quest for accounts of human rationality that distinguish us from other animals (and thus by implication single out persons for special regard) continues in our time with an empirical twist. Efforts by rational choice theorists to show that humans engage in distinctive strategic behaviors—e.g., waiting and indirection—represent one example. See, e.g., J. Elster, *Ulysses and the Sirens: Studies in Rationality and Irrationality* (New York: Cambridge University Press, 1984): 9–28 (arguing that humans engage in "global maximization," while other animals are capable only of "local maximization" or "gradient-climbing"). A trace of Kantian metaphysics remains in this work—e.g., in Elster's proposition that *"in creating man natural selection has transcended itself."* Ibid., 16 (emphasis in original). Yet such efforts fit nicely with Rawls' call for the recasting of Kantian regard for persons as ends in terms of a "reasonable empiricism." J. Rawls, "The Basic Structure as Subject," *American Philosophical Quarterly* 14 (1977): 159, 165.

216. Richard Rorty's reconstruction of liberalism as the avoidance of cruelty represents one prominent example. Rorty builds his case for non-instrumental deference and regard upon our "feelings of solidarity" with other persons. Our "ability to think of people . . . different from ourselves as included in the range of us," Rorty argues, is evoked by narrative accounts of "particular varieties of pain and humiliation." R. Rorty, *Contingency, Irony and Solidarity* (New York: Cambridge University Press, 1989): 192. This ability, potentiated by the evocative power of such accounts, rests upon myriad historical contingencies and shapes the limits of our noninstrumental regard for others. Ibid., 189–198.

217. A loose analogy might be drawn to the insight that risking human life to pursue an economic opportunity endangers the myth that life is priceless. Unwilling to discard this myth, which itself expresses the sense that persons merit noninstrumental regard, we look for ways to hide the tension between it and our worldly aspirations. We fear, moreover, that visible affronts to the myth that life is priceless will erode our collective respect for life. Such concerns animate the law's attempts to construct subterfuges—doctrines and decision-making procedures that allow us to hold to conflicting aspirations. Calabresi, *Ideas, Beliefs*, 87–91. More generally, such concerns may inspire us to develop conceptual systems able to contain those contradictions most threatening to our deeply felt values.

218. See M. Nussbaum, *Love's Knowledge: Essays on Philosophy and Literature* (New York: Oxford University Press, 1990): 41–42 (arguing that emotions are "intelligent parts of our ethical agency" because they reflect our deeply held views about what is important).
219. Not surprisingly, the law presents multiple examples since courts are principal mediators of such conflict. Unconstitutional conditions cases are perhaps the most prominent. The emergence of the welfare state against a constitutional backdrop of cherished negative rights created myriad, novel possibilities for state influence over personal choice with respect to the exercise of these rights. Other examples from the recent past include the development of plea bargaining (see, generally, A. W. Alschuler, "Plea Bargaining and Its History," *Columbia Law Review* 79 [1979]: 1) and the advent of large business organizations able to gain contractual advantage through the use of vastly superior bargaining positions. See J. P. Dawson, "Economic Duress—An Essay in Perspective," *Michigan Law Review* 45 (1947): 253, 282–288 (observing that the doctrine of duress has evolved to incorporate unequal exchanges achieved through superior bargaining power).
220. See B. Steinbock, *The Concept of Coercion and Long-Term Contraceptives* (1993) (unpublished manuscript on file with the author, focusing on efforts to promote the use of Norplant).
221. See text accompanying notes 209 and 210.
222. We might, however, aspire toward a better understanding of the fears and yearnings that might make such ugliness contagious in the hope that by addressing them we can prevent its spread to those not infected.
223. The conversational attitude I have in mind is nicely captured by Thomas Kuhn in a comment on intellectual engagement with claims that seem implausible:

> When reading the works of an important thinker, look first for the apparent absurdities in the text and ask yourself how a sensible person could have written them. When you find an answer, . . . when those passages make sense, then you may find that more central passages, ones you previously thought you understood, have changed their meaning.

T. S. Kuhn, *The Essential Tension: Selected Studies in Scientific Tradition and Change* (Chicago: University of Chicago Press, 1977): xii.
224. The idea of a distinctly dialogic rationality, unbound by the wills of isolated individuals, has been richly developed by Hans-Georg Gadamer. See, generally, H.-G. Gadamer, *Dialogue and Dialectic*, P. C. Smith, trans. (New Haven: Yale University Press, 1980). In Gadamer's words:

> When one enters into dialogue with another person and then is carried along further by the dialogue, it is no longer the will of the individual person, holding itself back or exposing itself, that is determinative. Rather, the law of the subject matter is at issue in the dialogue and elicits statement and counterstatement and in the end plays them into each other.

H.-G. Gadamer, *Philosophical Hermeneutics*, D. E. Linge, trans. (Berkeley: University of California Press, 1976): 66.
225. See text accompanying notes 81–83.
226. For purposes of delineating such deviation, I count as social costs not only monies spent for medical treatment or public assistance but also the suffering of children who endure the misery of terminal illness or the tragedy of maternal deterioration and death.

227. See M. G. Bloche, "Psychiatry, Capital Punishment, and the Purposes of Medicine," *International Journal of Law and Psychiatry*, 16 (1993): 301, 317–319.
228. Ibid., 327–328, 356–357.
229. See text accompanying note 88.
230. See, e.g., President's Commission for the Study of Ethical Problems in Medicine and Biomedical and Behavioral Research, *Securing Access to Health Care*, 20 (setting forth, as an ethical standard, an adequate level of health care for everyone); U.N. GAOR 3rd Comm., 21st Sess., Supp. No. 16, at 167 U.N. Doc A/6316 (1966) (International Covenant of Economic, Social, and Cultural Rights, assuring to all "medical service and medical attention in the event of sickness." The United States is not a party to the covenant). It is frequently pointed out that the United States is the only industrialized nation aside from South Africa that has failed to guarantee universal access to medical care.
231. As noted above, medical advice commonly serves public health ends, even at the expense of individual patients' interests. However, such counseling tends not to take a frankly "directive" form (at least as I defined this term earlier, see text accompanying note 25) unless linked to the actual or potential exercise of state compulsion—e.g., in cases of mandatory treatment for psychiatric or infectious disease.
232. See note 35.

12

The Moral Right to Have Children

MADISON POWERS

> Because you are HIV, that doesn't mean you don't have no right to have a baby. You have every right like everyone else.
>
> *woman from Los Angeles*

Much of the contemporary discussion of reproductive rights has occurred in the context of a pregnant woman's decision whether or not to have an abortion. For example, although the United States Supreme Court decision in *Roe* v. *Wade* refers more broadly to a woman's right to decide whether or not to have children, for many the language of reproductive rights is virtually synonymous with the right not to have children against one's will, and this right often is identified with the particular right to have an abortion. However, another, somewhat less frequently explored dimension of reproductive rights is a right to have children. The issues raised in this chapter relate to the right to have children.

Some of the reproductive rights arguments most widely discussed are strictly legal ones. They involve questions regarding the interpretation of the U.S. Constitution and debates about the institutional competence of judges to enumerate fundamental rights that, arguably, neither are found in the text of the Constitution nor derivable from the history of the Constitution and its amendments.

However, the focus of this chapter is on the underlying moral rights of individuals, as opposed to the merely legal or constitutional rights, relating to reproduction. This chapter presents a basic introduction to the more abstract philosophical aspects of these discussions and provides a background for understanding the broader ethical context of the medical, legal, and policy chapters of this volume.

It should be noted, however, that the distinctions between moral and legal rights, as well as the relevance of the distinctions, are themselves controversial and vexing questions. Accordingly, it is important to note some of the possibilities.

Some, for example, argue that there are fundamental moral rights to reproduce without interference by others and, accordingly, that the government is not morally justified in interfering with decisions to have or not have children, however strong the fetal or societal interests may be. A second view opposes abortion as morally wrong, saying that because there is no moral right to have an abortion there should be no legal right to abortion.

However, some who oppose abortion agree with those who conclude that the government is not morally justified in interfering with decisions not to have children. This last position agrees about the personal immorality of abortion but favors recognition of at least some legal rights to abortion, perhaps out of some higher-order moral commitment to a principle of respect for individual autonomy. Similar positions with respect to the right to have children are imaginable. One view categorically rejects any moral limits on the right to have children, and accordingly, legal limits would be seen as morally impermissible. Some may hold that individuals have no moral right to reproduce without restriction, perhaps because of the harm to future generations or to society, and thus they may claim that society's laws ought to reflect the immorality of such choices. Others may agree with views about the immorality of some instances of having children, but they may claim that the depth of unresolved (and perhaps unresolvable) conflict argues against any legal restriction on an individual's decision to have children.

Hence, those who advocate a split between legal and moral rights may favor the recognition of unrestricted reproductive rights in a legal system, while insisting that it would be individually morally wrong for women to have abortions for certain reasons (e.g., sex selection) or to have children in some cases.

These examples show that there is no straightforward and uncontroversial way of establishing the proper relation between law (or what the law ought to be) and the moral requirements governing individual conduct. Although the arguments of this chapter are not meant to resolve questions regarding the relation between law and morality in general, some underlying, foundational philosophical issues arising from any attempt to justify and defend a moral right to have children are explored. Hence, the primary focus is on two significant moral arguments, which, if persuasive, would count in favor of at least some forms of legal interference with a woman's decision to have children in some instances.

In the first section, I briefly explore some preliminary points about the centrality of the language of rights in contemporary debates over the control of reproduction. Although the task of developing a theory which can justify a moral right to have children is well beyond the scope of this book, there is a need to indicate why so many people have thought that there are such rights and why many may think it appropriate to cast arguments about reproductive morality in terms of moral rights.

In the second and third sections, I address the issue of when it is wrong to have children. In the second section, I consider the wrongness of having children when doing so will result in harm to the child. In the third section, I consider the wrongness of having children when doing so will have significant implications for the distribution of scarce resources within society at large.

Although many of the arguments of this chapter do not focus specifically on AIDS or HIV infection, they go to the heart of some of the fundamental questions in ethical and social theory that underlie much of the current public policy debates about the reproductive choices of HIV-infected women.

Justifications for Reproductive Rights

Protected choices and protected interests

A commonly held conception of reproductive rights recognizes a right to have children and a right not to have children, and it views both rights as arising from a unitary justificatory basis. Many, for example, assume that both flow from a more general right of decisional freedom over whether or not to have children and that the two are inextricably linked. The two rights can be seen as inextricably linked only if it is true that the core right to be protected is the ability to decide either way. On this view of rights, it is protection against interference with the woman's decision itself that is secured by the right, even though the actions undertaken, the interests at stake, and the consequences of noninterference may be very different, depending upon whether we are concerned with a decision to have children or a decision not to have children.

The commonly accepted view is a conception of reproductive rights which has received a degree of recognition in American law, often classified as a "protected choice" conception of rights.[1] At the heart of this conception of rights is the idea of the right-holder having the freedom to choose among a set of options without interference by others. Thus, the primary function of any reproductive right, on the protected choice conception, is the protection of a woman's reproductive choice. As some constitutional scholars have noted, without the continued legal recognition of a broader right to decide either way, there would be no recognized legal basis for protecting a woman's right to have children.[2] Thus, the state would be free to interfere in either respect.

Although the primary function of any reproductive right in the protected choice conception of rights is the protection of a woman's reproductive choice, this does not entail that the *rationale* for the right is based on a commitment to the overriding moral significance of unrestricted exercise of autonomous choice. The deeper rationale for protecting those choices may lie elsewhere in the set of human interests that arguably make such choices especially valuable to safeguard.

A second conception of rights shifts the primary focus from protected choices to protected interests. The reason for this shift is that it is thought to provide a deeper, more fundamental account of the normative significance of labeling some moral standard as a right. On this alternative view, we do not begin with an assumption that it is the central importance of individual choice that is the primary function of rights. Instead, the protected interests conception supposes that the main function of rights is to give special weight to some interests in preference to others. As Joseph Raz defines it: "X has a right if and only if X can have rights, and other things being equal, an aspect of X's well-being (his interest) is a sufficient reason for holding some person(s) to be under a duty."[3]

Raz's definition, however, does not rule out the importance of protecting autonomy. For example, the interests which support a right to have children may justify duties to respect the exercise of individual choice over such matters, and autonomy may be among the interests that justify rights to have children. Among the rights a protected interest conception may generate are rights of control or an ability to make reproductive choices without interference.

The mandatory rights thesis

A less familiar claim about the right to have children involves no companion right not to have children (or, derivatively, a right to have an abortion). Those who subscribe to what Joel Feinberg calls a mandatory rights thesis may defend a right to have children, compatible with a rejection of abortion rights, on the grounds that a woman has a right to have children because she has a duty to have children.[4] On this account it is assumed that because it is a mandatory duty to have children, say a duty imposed by God, and because it is a logically prior, nonwaivable duty, it creates a right against others who would interfere with carrying out that duty.

The mandatory rights position does not rely upon arguments based upon autonomy or freedom of choice, which typically provide at least a part of the theoretical foundation for more comprehensive reproductive rights claims on either the protected choices or protected interests conceptions. Nor is it compatible with the protected choices conception. Rather, it sees the woman's right to have children free from interference or restriction by others as a consequence of a duty imposed upon the right-holder which cannot be evaded by an act of choice. This view admits of no basis for support of a companion right not to have children. Because the right functions only to protect from interference in what is taken to be the morally required activity of having children, it does not function to protect an individual from interference with reproductive decision-making generally.

Rights and interests

An important feature of all of the major views of rights is that they depend on some further framework of justification. It is within some justificatory framework that the relevant interests can be identified as the rationale for a specific right. However, the question of the best justification for rights generally is a notoriously controversial one, and many have doubts about whether such a justificatory theory can be found. Skeptical critics may view all talk of moral rights as incoherent unless the needed justificatory theory can be defended.

The leading contenders for such a theory have included natural rights, contractualist, and consequentialist theories. The task of natural law theory would be to specify those interests which are in some sense natural components or essential elements of human flourishing. A contractualist might be concerned to identify those interests that would be the basis for agreement among rational hypothetical deliberators who set out to design the basic set of rights and duties for a society. The consequentialist would need an account of those interests which figure in the conception of value to be maximized, say by a set of rights and duties, the acceptance of which would produce the best overall consequences (as judged by that conception of value).

In short, however one conceives of the ultimate basis for justification of moral rights, if there are any moral rights, we will need to know something about the kinds of interest which figure centrally in the justificatory scheme to know the content and strength of whatever rights there are. Although the task of developing such a justification is beyond the scope of this chapter, we nonetheless need to know something about the kinds of interest a justificatory theory might take into account in defending the existence of a right to have children.

Why talk about rights?

If one considers the need for a deeper justificatory framework to support rights, then it is reasonable to ask what theoretical role rights have in our moral discourse. One cynical answer is that rights have tremendous strategic rhetorical advantage. Rights are much more difficult to take issue with than other more temperate moral claims. Indeed, one widely shared concern is that rights language has become so much the common currency of moral debate that it may simply escalate the rhetoric rather than illuminate moral controversies. However, it cannot be the strategic advantage itself that makes rights talk appropriate, for rights do play a special role in moral discourse.

To assert that someone has a right involves a number of important judgments about the underlying interests and their importance in relation to other moral concerns. Two most relevant to this discussion are as follows.

First, rights entail that there are no contrary considerations that by themselves are sufficient to defeat the claim that there is a basis for imposing a duty on others. Thus, we are necessarily involved in making judgments regarding the presumptive weight of an asserted interest in light of all other interests with which it competes. There simply is no basis for talk of a right that does not begin its inquiry with an assessment of underlying interests and their relative priority. The usual understanding of a right is that its violation is an injustice, not simply conduct which falls short of a moral ideal or standard of what would be desirable.

Second, on any account of the purpose or function of rights, rights do serve as a kind of constraint on the pursuit of other goals, such as the maximization of collective welfare. They establish the special importance of some considerations in a way that sets them apart from other calculations of social interest. This is not to say that the recognition of rights must treat some interests as absolutely immune to other trade-offs; but if rights are to have any distinctive theoretical role, as Ronald Dworkin argues, they at least must raise the threshold before competing reasons to override rights will be entertained.

Is autonomy reason enough?

One kind of objection to reproductive rights reflects a kind of weariness about blanket appeals to autonomy. This complaint may be based in the idea that autonomy interests alone are not enough to ground such rights. Even if autonomy interests add a considerable measure of support for certain rights, critics may claim that the fundamental basis for rights is never what may be called a bare appeal to autonomy or the moral significance of freedom of choice. How might this objection be answered?

Autonomy is surely one of the most important values in Western culture. Its moral significance has been defended on a variety of grounds. It is an ideal which emphasizes the importance of individual freedom for both personal and political development.[5] It has been treated as an irreducible element of human flourishing.[6] Others have viewed respect for autonomy as an essential aspect of human dignity in its recognition of the intrinsic value of each person's capacities and perspectives, including his or her right to hold certain views, to make certain choices, and to take certain actions based on personal values and beliefs.[7] Some have emphasized the centrality of autonomy to self-development as that which makes persons the "creators of their own lives . . . shapers of their own values . . . originators of projects and plans."[8] Others have argued that the real value of autonomy lies in the fact that "it makes each of us responsible for shaping his own life according to some coherent and distinctive sense of character, conviction, and interest."[9] In short, there is no lack of powerful justifications offered on behalf of taking autonomy interests seriously.

Nonetheless, some critics still may doubt the plausibility of grounding rights solely on autonomy-based considerations. The essential core of an alternative view of the moral significance of autonomy can be recapitulated as follows: (1) freedom of choice is of inherent moral importance; (2) but what makes freedom of choice valuable is not the mere fact of choice alone; (3) otherwise, more choice would always be better than less choice; (4) the alternative way of understanding the value of choice is to assume that choice matters morally when there are genuinely valuable options; and (5) what matters morally is that there is an adequate range of truly valuable options, rather than an unlimited set of options.

Thus, the proponent of the alternative conception views it as a mistake to assume that one can speak meaningfully about the inherent value of freedom of choice apart from a deeper justification which explains why choices of a particular sort are worth protecting. This view forges an essential link between the moral value of freedom of choice and the properties which make certain options choiceworthy. Hence, the claim is that ultimately a defender of reproductive rights (or rights of any sort) will have to give an account of the other interests to fully explain the moral importance of the kinds of choice it identifies as protected.

However we view the moral significance of choice, the best account of the function of rights in moral discourse, or the role of autonomy in human well-being, the plausibility of arguments for overriding reproductive rights will in part depend as much on spelling out the interests that figure in the justification of the rights as it does on specifying the kinds of interest in competition with the right. Accordingly, we turn next to a review of some of the interests that may be thought to support reproductive rights.

Some familiar arguments

Arguments narrowly addressed to the right not to have children are better developed in the literature of legal, philosophical, and public policy debates than arguments focusing on the right to have children. Typically, the arguments rely upon a recitation of the interests that may be compromised by not being able to avoid having children.

A striking aspect of many of the arguments frequently advanced on behalf of the right not to have children is the extent to which some are not as readily adaptable in support of a right to have children. My purpose in calling attention to these differences is not to judge which of the two rights is stronger or best supported by reasons. I am not certain that is possible. Nor is it to claim that the two rights can be pried apart. The more general point is to illustrate the need for separate and distinct arguments on behalf of a right to have children. A survey of standard reproductive rights arguments reveals some important differences.

Some of the arguments for a right not to have children focus upon the potential for harm to the interests of the woman from having children. Having children may involve the physical and psychological consequences of childbearing and delivery, including significant risks to health from pregnancy. Also identified are the emotional demands and sacrifices that may arise as a consequence of childbirth; the potential adverse effects of pregnancy on intimacy and emotional commitments to others; the financial and social responsibilities of being a parent; and the effect of dependents upon a woman's ability to pursue economic, professional, and other personal goals.

Other arguments for rights not to have children obtain an important measure of their weight from considerations of equality. As many have argued, the ability to control one's fertility and to avoid the burdens of unwanted pregnancy is one of the most significant elements of personal choice necessary to secure a degree of autonomy for women comparable to that enjoyed by men. For example, Sylvia Law argues that restrictive governmental policies on abortion "affect the ability of women to plan their lives, to sustain relationships with other people, and to contribute through wage work and public life."[10] Kenneth Karst argues that such policies undermine a woman's right to equal citizenship by restricting her "ability to make responsible choices in controlling one's own destiny."[11] Law also notes:

> [n]ature demands that women alone bear the physical burdens of pregnancy, but society, through the law, can either mitigate or exaggerate the costs of these burdens. When the state denies women access to abortion, both nature and the state impose upon women burdens of unwanted pregnancy that men do not bear.[12]

In addition, laws requiring women to have children against their will are said to impose stringent legal duties on women not imposed on men, which are not reflected elsewhere in the law. Donald Regan and others have argued that as a general principle of both conventional morality and American law no one is required to come to the aid of others when aid can be provided only at significant risk to the rescuer.[13]

Most of the arguments listed above do not provide the same degree of support for a right to have children. One cannot rely upon the potential for various physical and psychological harms of pregnancy and childbirth for a right to have children. A woman's interest in limiting reproduction as a general condition for ensuring equality between men and women does not add support to the right to have children in quite the same way. Such arguments concentrate upon the removal of impediments to equality that arise from policies that ensure that women do not have to bear children against their will. In short, rights not to have children seem to have specific theoretical justifications that do not lend themselves to the support of rights to have children.

All of this is not to say that other arguments bearing some resemblance to some of the ones made on behalf of rights not to have children cannot be made on behalf of rights to have children. For example, unacceptable interferences with a woman's bodily integrity can result from policies that prevent a woman from having children (e.g., forced sterilization) just as they can result from policies that prevent a woman from not having children (outlawing abortion).

Additionally, others have argued for a right to have children that also appeals to related considerations of equality. John Robertson, for example, has argued that full procreative freedom, including the freedom to "reproduce when, with whom, and by what means" is "necessary to permit some women to fit pregnancy and childbirth successfully into their lives."[14] This suggests that equality with men in the pursuit of those things which contribute to well-being in a life demands a similar protection from interference with plans to have children.

An important point, however, is that many of the relevant arguments will be somewhat different, and the competing interests they engage will vary as well, depending on whether we are concerned with defending the right to have children or the right not to have children. This does not mean that the right to have children is any less secure than the right not to have children. Indeed, a curious feature of many international rights declarations and of much of the philosophical literature on the right to have children is that the value associated with the right is simply taken as a given.[15]

In addition, the thrust of most of the philosophical literature is either to discuss the possible limitations on such rights or to address further issues of what duties children and parents owe one another in light of an understanding of the significance of that relationship.[16] Perhaps the relative lack of explicit discussions of the value of having children reflects the deeply intuitive and widely shared judgment of its importance for human flourishing. Nonetheless, some powerful insights into the special value of having children can be inferred from the general assumptions behind such discussions.

It is important to note at the outset that not all kinds of motivation for having children should be relied upon as the basis of interest one would offer in support of a right to have children. Some critics of what has been called a "pronatalist bias" have pointed to the fact that we may desire to have children for the wrong reasons.[17] One ought to be cautious in making assumptions about either the prevalence or the motivational significance of such reasons in the decision-making of men and women, but it may be useful to mention the kinds of "interests" that are not claimed as the basis of a right to have children.

For example, one would not appeal to desires to have children to save a troubled marriage, to please or defy one's parents, or to prove one's adulthood or sexual maturity. Nor must one include what could be described as pathological desires for children, such as the gratification of excessive needs for affection and attention or to overcome feelings of worthlessness or loneliness.[18] Similarly, one would not defend rights to have children by appealing to a desire for a source of status or self-identity derived from associating oneself with the achievements of others[19] or to the fantasies of adults who want to overcome their own unhappy childhoods by creating a "heaven on earth" for their children.[20]

Fortunately, several very compelling interests can be cited in support of a right to have children, and these interests are easily fitted into many of the underlying theories designed to provide the justification for moral rights.

First, the relation of parent to child can be seen as central to human emotional life. Both the biological and social dimensions of parenthood offer a kind of pleasure and satisfaction not easily replicated in other human relationships.

Second, having children can be valuable for its contribution to a qualitative difference in the relationship between parents. Bertrand Russell noted that rearing children can "produce so deep a tie between a man and a woman that they will feel something infinitely precious in their companionship."[21]

Third, the relation between a parent and a child is one of a class of strong personal attachments which have special consequences for psychological growth and development. Jeffrey Blustein argues that it is a relationship which contributes to and "integrates several parts of the human personality" and allows its participants to "interact in an uninhibited and unforced way."[22]

Fourth, parenthood can deepen the capacity for friendship through development of affection, intimacy, empathy, and trust in a context not involving the degree of competition, struggle for power, and concern for fairness in the distribution of burdens that often characterizes other relationships. Because of the dependence of the child, one experiences the opportunity to act truly for the sake of another.

Many other interests surely could be cited, but these four are enough to make a compelling case for the existence of rights to have children. Moreover, the argument does not depend upon the claim that it is freedom of choice alone that grounds the right to have children. If arguments of this sort are successful, one can defend the existence of a right to have children without thereby committing oneself to any particular view of rights with respect to abortion.

I turn to the second and most important phase of my task, which is to discuss two types of argument that critics may claim are sufficient to outweigh the kinds of interest that underlie rights to have children.

Harm to Future Generations

When is it wrong to have children? One possible answer is that it is wrong to have children when doing so results in harm to the child. For example, some have argued that it is wrong to have children who will suffer from a severe illness or disease such as HIV infection. The core of such an argument would be that the wrongness of having children consists in harm caused to the child who is born and that it is the child's existence itself which constitutes the harm. However, the relevant notion of harm is exceedingly complex in such cases, and our ordinary moral intuitions on these matters provide us with remarkably little guidance.

The best place to begin is with an analysis of the concept of harming more generally. Joel Feinberg's influential definition will be adequate for our discussion. He broadly defines harm as any setback to the interests of another.[23]

Three implications of this general definition should be noted.

First, because the focus is upon the person affected by the action of another, the mental state of the person causing harm to another is irrelevant to the analysis. In Feinberg's broadly inclusive definition, harm may be caused intentionally, negligently, accidentally, or even without any knowledge or awareness of the person responsible for the setback to another's interests.

Second, the definition of interests is left purposely open. It is meant to comprehend any adverse impact upon anything pertaining to the physical, emotional, financial, spiritual, or any other conceivable aspect of the well-being of another.

Thus again, the definition is meant to be as inclusive as possible; it is designed to avoid begging any essential questions, as for example, by simply stipulating that an adverse impact of some particular sort does not count as a harm.

Third, the definition itself is morally neutral. Although all moral theories agree that harm to others is what makes at least some acts wrong, none concludes from the mere fact of harm that the action which resulted in the harm was wrong. All moral theories recognize that sometimes we are morally justified in causing harm to others, and most moral theories view some harms as morally irrelevant (e.g., harm to business competitors in a capitalistic society). The task of moral theory is, as Annette Baier observes, to decide which harms to notice.[24]

The definition of harm as a setback to the interests of another raises thorny questions about the identities of those who are capable of having interests of a morally relevant kind. Moral theorists notoriously disagree on these matters, but at least some familiar views should be rejected as inadequate on the grounds that they are question-begging.

For example, some utilitarians (and others as well) adopt a version of what Jan Narveson calls a person-affecting view.[25] One version of this argument claims that only those with "lives in being" are capable of having interests which may be harmed. Thus, all moral duties, either to benefit or to prevent harm to others, are construed as duties to existing persons. One reason for advocating such a restricted account of moral duty is clear: by definition, only existing persons have interests which may be harmed or benefitted. Thus, the person-affecting view would provide a quick and decisive way to settle some controversial questions arising in population ethics. One implication of such a view is that future generations (i.e., those not yet conceived), and perhaps fetuses, cannot be harmed or benefitted—and hence cannot be the subjects of moral protection—because they cannot be said to have interests.

Let us start with the easiest example. It would be impossible that a failure to conceive could be counted as a harm to those not yet conceived. This conclusion follows from the core assumption that the not-yet-conceived do not have interests which could be set back. Hence, potential members of future generations who are never conceived simply have no ground for complaint about not being brought into the world. Not only do future generations not have a complaint for not being born but they have no complaint for being born, even, say, with a severe illness. In the person-affecting view, it is impossible to argue that being born harms the child for, by definition, harm is possible only where there are interests and only lives in being have interests. Because the not-yet-conceived are not lives in being, the fact that some child who is later born may suffer is treated as morally irrelevant.

Accordingly, conceiving a child with a serious illness could never be wrong on the grounds that to do so would cause harm to the only entity that matters—namely, a life in being at the time of the harm. The not-yet-conceived also lack interests which could be advanced. Just as the not-yet-conceived cannot be harmed by being born (or not being born), neither can the not-yet-conceived be benefitted by either choice. Such a view entails that we can never say that the creation of a life is a good for the person brought into being.

In short, the implication of the person-affecting view is that no action (e.g., having children) nor any refraining from action (e.g., failing to conceive) can be either morally prohibited or morally required for reasons having to do with the well-being of those not yet in existence.

The person-affecting view has more difficult philosophical problems to solve in the case of a fetus. It has to defend a view of whether the fetus is a person according to the life in being criterion and, hence, someone having interests that matter morally. Either fetuses are treated as persons with interests that can be harmed or benefitted or they are assigned the same moral status as the not-yet-conceived, who lack any such interests. However, if the person-affecting view itself is suspect, we need not take a position on which of two possible interpretations of the person-affecting view is best, and the thorny issue of whether a fetus is a life in being is avoided. I argue that the life in being standard embodied in the person-affecting view should be rejected in any case.

The main difficulties with the person-affecting view are its deeply counterintuitive implications. It is grossly inaccurate to suppose that harm cannot be done to the unborn simply on the ground that they presently lack interests which may be harmed or promoted. For example, it seems quite natural to describe as a harm a debilitating medical condition manifested later in adulthood but caused by a medication prescribed (to the mother) before conception (e.g., diethylstilbestrol). If harm to the interests of persons is a morally significant event, there is no obvious reason to exclude from consideration the harm that will be caused to persons who do not now, but will in the future, have interests which can be harmed.

The above view is strengthened by the recognition that it is possible to intentionally harm the interests of those who do not yet exist. For example, we can imagine a scientist creating a developmental toxin designed to adversely affect newborns who are exposed to the body of the mother who received the toxin prior to conception. What matters morally it seems is the prospect of interests being adversely affected in the future by actions of persons at a time clearly prior to the existence of actual interests of lives in being. No one has even been conceived on this example, and yet the notion of an intentional harm to a future person is a readily comprehensible possibility.

Absent a compelling argument for accepting the person-affecting view on other grounds, it seems implausible to exclude from moral consideration all potential harms to the interests of fetuses or even the unconceived. The conclusion then would be to admit that, in principle, it is possible to cause harm to the interests of a child who is not yet born but who will be in existence at a later date.

The person-affecting view is thus discarded as arbitrary and counterintuitive. The question then becomes the narrower one of whether by virtue of either being born or not being born someone can be harmed. We can divide this question into two parts.

First, is it possible to argue that anyone is harmed by not being born? The problem is that no identifiable interests have been adversely affected, say, by a decision not to conceive. It seems that it is impossible to suppose that the interests of any child are harmed by not being conceived, for it is difficult to make sense of the idea that there ever will be anyone whose interests can be said to have been affected for the worse. Only those who in fact come into existence at a later date can have interests which may be harmed or advanced.

The second question involves consideration of possible harm from being born to those who in fact come into existence at a later date. Unlike those never conceived, it is, in principle, possible to claim that being born may constitute a harm to the child because there will be a life with interests which may be harmed as a consequence of an action taken prior to the beginning of life. However, we now need a standard by which we can determine what kind of life, if brought into existence, constitutes a harm to that life.

One prominent view is that it is plausible to claim harm only under very limited conditions. We cannot say, for example, that being born with an extremely severe and debilitating illness harms a child in all instances. Even on the assumption that the child suffers greatly, we cannot say that the child is worse off than he or she otherwise would have been, for the alternative is that he or she "wouldn't otherwise have been."[26] Thus, the only way we can say that a child is harmed by being born is to say that "this child's life is worse than nothing—would be worth not living."[27]

The correlative of this proposition is that the creation of any life, as long it is at least barely worth living, is a benefit to the child created. As long as we can truly say that it is at least barely worth living, we are committed to the view that it is better than nothing and thus of net benefit to the child to be alive. For many, this account seems consistent with the views expressed by persons with severe disabilities, even when others who imagine themselves in a similar position express a preference for nonexistence. If it is plausible to suppose that life itself can be a benefit when there is a net balance of good over harm, then we must also suppose that, in principle, the creation of life itself can be a harm to the person who is born with a severe medical condition. However, can we also agree with the conclusion that the only way in which a life itself can be viewed as a harm is when it is worse than not living?

Perhaps a different kind of benchmark for measuring harm should be adopted. Instead of comparing the net balance of benefits and harms of life with a particular condition against the net balance of benefits and harms associated with nonexistence, we could consider some other point of reference.

One alternative would be to compare the quality of life of a child born with some medical condition against the quality of life of the child one would have had without the condition. This approach would allow us to suppose that if the condition results in a life of a lower quality than otherwise would have been, then we could judge that the child has been harmed.

There are numerous problems for this view, which can be called "the counterfactual quality of life standard." This approach relies upon the highly speculative use of a counterfactual assumption: we have to assume that there would have been an alternative life and that we can accurately know what the quality of life of that alternative child would have been but for a particular causal factor. Matthew Hanser, for example, claims that "if a child born now would be defective, and a child born later would be perfectly healthy, she [the mother] *would* have a good reason for waiting."[28] The estimated counterfactual quality of life of the alternative child is thus the baseline for measuring harm to an actual child. The implication is that the extent that the quality of life of an actual child falls below the quality of life of this hypothetical alternative child is the measure of the harm caused by being born.

One problem with this counterfactual test is that there are potentially unlimited causal factors that may influence the quality of life of a newborn. We would have to judge for each mental or physical condition of a newborn that, but for the causal factor identified, the child would have been better off. Thus, by definition, any and all causal factors that could be identified as ones that reduce a child's quality of life below what it otherwise would have been must be viewed as sources of harm. The implication is a remarkable one. There is no limit to the number of ways in which the child must be seen as harmed by what we do (or fail to do). We would be forced to conclude that any child is harmed by virtue of being born, at least any child born short of perfection (whatever that is), simply because there always would be some causal factors we could point to as reducing an actual child's quality of life below what is hypothetically possible.

Moreover, another problem for this counterfactual standard is that just because someone is harmed by our action does not mean that it is morally wrong. Even if bringing a child into existence can be said to harm that child, it remains an open question whether, all things considered, it is wrong to do so. We know that surgery, antibiotics, and other medical interventions cause harm to patients. In many of these cases, what we want to know for purposes of moral judgment is whether we have harmed them, all things considered.[29] Only the first counterfactual standard, which compares the quality of life of a child with a given condition to the alternative of nonexistence, can supply a meaningful answer to this question. Only if we can say that a life is not worth living—i.e., worse than nonexistence—can we confidently say that the child has experienced net harm from being born.[30]

Consider two further plausible lines of argument with respect to the HIV context.

The first issue is raised by John Arras. He considers the claim that "the greater the magnitude and probability of predicted harm, the less justifiable it is to have children."[31] Although Arras is inclined to suppose that this kind of argument is valid in theory, he nonetheless finds it difficult to apply in the context of reproductive decision-making by HIV-infected women. He argues, and I think persuasively, that for such an argument to succeed it must be shown that "all (or at least the vast majority) of infected children will have lives so brief and so filled with suffering that they qualify as 'wrongful.'"[32] Without medical intervention, about 25% of children born to HIV-infected mothers will be HIV-infected; with intervention, at least among certain women, the transmission rate may be under 10%. The acceptability of this risk is a matter about which reasonable people will disagree. Moreover, the use of a probability of harm-to-benefit ratio test is further complicated by the fact that the prognosis and general health status of prospective HIV-infected mothers, as well as the quality and extent of support available to the mothers from family and friends, also will vary considerably. Hence, the prospects for a life worth living, both for those who will be infected and those who will not, will vary greatly among children born to HIV-infected mothers, depending on how well their mothers fare.

Measuring the harm of being born against nonexistence has implications we cannot ignore. It is a very lenient standard, at least for those who agree that the idea that persons can be harmed by being born makes sense. There are many ways in which one's existence can be made worse than it might have been, even if we agree that the life one has is a great deal better than barely worth living.

A second way some of these problems might be met is by shifting to the alternative baseline standard suggested by Laura Purdy. She argues that we cause harm to a child in a morally significant way when the life brought into existence is one whose potential for quality falls below a range she calls the "normal opportunity for a good life."[33] Although this standard provides no precise benchmark, it does provide a basis for judging that at least some acts of having children can be morally wrong in virtue of the health-related harms caused to the child. In this view, we need not suppose that the only harm accrues when the resultant life is not worth living. At least in those cases where the severity of debilitation is so great, the suffering so profound, the prospects for longevity so low, and the likelihood of consequences of this sort ensuing so high it is wrong to have children.

If we applied Purdy's normal opportunity range standard to cases of men and women with HIV infection, no clear answer emerges. Even if, for the sake of argument, we assume that the course of all newborn HIV infections matches the first three requirements—severity of debilitation, profound suffering, and poor prospects for longevity—the fourth condition ensures that the test yields no obvious answer to questions about the wrongness of having children in the context of HIV. The likelihood of such consequences ensuing, estimated at about 25% in the context of HIV, is still far less than with some genetic conditions. Although the burden of moral justification for exposing others to risks of great harm is heavy and although it is especially objectionable to expose anyone to grave risks without prospects for compensating benefits, it is not clear that having children is wrong when the probability of such a child's falling outside of the normal opportunity range is not what all would judge as unacceptably high.

Indeed, if as preliminary data suggest, the administration of AZT to pregnant women proves successful in reducing the probability of vertical transmission of HIV to the fetus, the case for wrongfulness of reproduction on Purdy's standard is further eroded.[34] The probability of harmful consequences may fall well below current ranges, and the case for the moral unacceptability of HIV-infected mothers having children is diminished further.

More fundamentally, however, the normal opportunity standard has counterintuitive implications which are hard to defend. We would be in the curious position of arguing that bringing a child into existence can be morally wrong by virtue of its falling below the normal opportunity range for a good life, while acknowledging that it still is a life worth living because it represents a net balance of benefit over harm. It is difficult to suppose that his or her life can be regarded as worth living and simultaneously to insist that someone has done something morally wrong by bringing it into existence.

A further morally troubling feature of such a standard is that it is so stringent that it treats a large number of reproductive choices, ordinarily thought morally acceptable, as morally culpable simply because the children born fall below what is described as a normal opportunity for a good life. The specification of the level of well-being which defines the floor of a normal opportunity range itself is a matter of great controversy, and the scope of a normal opportunity range for a given society is a function not only of health status but of social and economic arrangements which make one's health status especially disadvantageous.

In summary, it seems that the best account of when being born is a harm to a child is one that reckons quality of life from a baseline of comparison with nonexistence. Only when we can say that a child is worse off than never having lived can we confidently say that he or she has been harmed in a way that casts strong doubt on the morality of having children. However, determining when life is worse than not living—or indeed, if this kind of judgment should ever be made—is an extraordinarily vexing problem, and Arras has shown that it is an especially difficult claim to sustain in the context of HIV infection.

Distributive Justice

Is there a right to have as many children as one wants? Does the right encompass a freedom to have any kind of children one wants? The asserted rights to have as many children as one wants and to have children of a particular kind raise ethical issues generally described as questions of distributive justice. Arguments of this sort claim that it may be wrong to have children when doing so has adverse consequences for the equitable distribution of scarce societal resources.

The creation of more children or children with especially expensive medical conditions may reduce the amount of resources that could be used for the benefit of others. The main concerns, it seems, are with the share of social resources that each additional child will require. The issue of maintaining a fair share of social resources for others is dramatically raised in the case of the number of children each may have. If social resources are sufficiently scarce, then arguably society has as much of a stake in limiting reproduction as it does in controlling whether individuals choose not to have children. Similarly, society may have substantial interests in limiting the kind of children that are born. Just as more children place increased demands on social resources, the birth of children with costly medical conditions may place similar burdens on resources.

Two broad distributive justice arguments must be distinguished at the outset. One objection, which I will call a level-one objection, is based upon concerns that the birth of some children with expensive medical conditions will require the redistribution of scarce resources from the economically better-off members of society to those who are economically worse off. In short, a familiar concern is that tax revenues will be used to care for the children of poor HIV-infected mothers and their HIV-infected children. A second, or level-two, objection raises more fundamental issues of distributive justice. If we assume that having children can be an action or activity that has significant implications for resource allocation among members of a society, then we want to ask under what conditions it is morally acceptable for individual members to engage in activities that have substantial resource implications for society, independent of the question of whether forced redistributive schemes are morally permissible.

The question "When is it morally acceptable to have children?" is thus treated as a species of a larger set of moral questions regarding activities that lessen the overall pool of resources available for others. Accordingly, level-two inquiries neither assume nor deny that the current distribution of resources is morally justified; instead, they ask under what conditions any kind of activity with significant resource implications for the rest of society is morally justified. In what follows I articulate several possible ways of answering this second-level question, first by comparing possible rationales for limiting rights to reproduction to rationales for limiting rights to ownership of private property. I will return to the first-level issue at the end.

Limiting property rights and reproductive rights

The societal interest in limiting reproduction for the purpose of conserving resources is partially analogous to the theoretical underpinnings some have offered as a justification for limiting the scope of individual property rights. The analogy may at first seem strained or peculiar in as much as children are not ordinarily seen as property. However, this is not the point I wish to make.

The relevant analogy consists in the fact that there are other activities besides private ownership of natural resources which may have adverse distributive consequences for the rest of society. The analogy lies in the fact that the privatization of the world's resources (i.e., conversion to individual property) has profound implications for society overall. The more that is removed from the common domain, the less there is available for others. Having children is an activity which can have similar implications. The creation of new persons equally may lessen the proportion of resources available for use by others, just as the direct appropriation of resources by individuals does. Without an expansion of the world's capacity to produce the necessities of life, the consequence of having more children is that there is less in the common pool of resources available for others.

Just as we might ask if there are some justifiable restrictions on the rights of individuals to acquire and use property for their exclusive use, we may ask if there are similar justifications for restricting the rights of individuals to produce new persons whose existence likewise reduces the aggregate of the world's resources, which are, in principle, available to others.

The most familiar justification for the right of private property and its limitations is that offered by John Locke.[35] A simplified reconstruction of the Lockean argument begins with two premises. First is the premise of individual self-ownership. Even if we do not yet have an exclusive claim on any of the world's resources, we are entitled to the exclusive domain over our own persons.[36] Second, we gain exclusive rights of dominion and disposition of the resources necessary to sustain ourselves by mixing our labor with the undeveloped resources previously available to humankind in common as unowned goods.[37] From these two premises, Locke concludes that individuals acquire complete and exclusive control over these resources without needing the consent of all whose well-being may be restricted by those rights. This is a simplified form of Locke's initial argument for private property in the abstract (leaving aside for our purposes whatever philosophical problems might adhere to the defense of these first two premises).

However, Locke recognized that there may be limits to such rights, and he sought to supply the justificatory basis for restricting the scope of the right to private property by interposing a qualification on such rights, which has come to be known more recently as the Lockean proviso. It holds that each may enjoy exclusive rights to private property as long as there is enough and as good left over for others after the act of acquisition. The proviso is an important qualifier in as much as it can limit the justifiable claims of individuals to engage in unrestrained appropriation for reasons having to do with distributive consequences for others.

As many have noted, application of the Lockean proviso would create an especially stringent limitation in the modern world, in which there is no longer the abundant supply of unowned resources that Locke supposed available in the New World during the seventeenth century. Once a certain amount of appropriation has occurred, there may not be as much and as good left over for others.[38]

A version of the Lockean proviso could be applied to the right of reproduction as well. One might claim that the justification of one's right to have children is similarly constrained by a requirement that the resulting distributional pattern of social resources must provide as good and as much left over for others. Similarly, the application of such a restriction to reproductive rights would be equally stringent in the modern world, in which there are already more than five billion persons living and where it is projected that in the near future there will be more persons currently living than have previously lived in the whole of human history.

I begin with the Lockean proviso not because I think it offers a promising criterion for limiting either property or reproductive rights. It does, however, reflect a general concern that arises in both contexts. Even if societal interests in distributive justice, as reflected in the Lockean proviso, are too stringent in the context of property rights, arguably some lesser restriction would still have considerable theoretical support. Even if it is too demanding to require that there be as much and as good left over, the force of the argument for some restriction on rights of private property remains an attractive one. Although I have no concrete suggestion for the precise principle that would limit the scope of private property to ensure that what we may call a fair share of social resources remains available for others, the threshold appeal of such a claim must be acknowledged.

Moreover, there seems to be no obvious difference between adopting a principle limiting rights to property to ensure that a fair share of social resources remains, in principle, available for others and adopting such a principle limiting the right of reproduction for the same end. One can see that the core of one kind of concern for limiting rights to reproduction lies in the idea that some limits may be justified in an appeal to one's responsibility to not engage in activity that uses up more than one's fair share, however that vague notion might be filled out.

Additionally, such a principle would seem to have application equally when the demand on resources is a consequence of the number of children that are born as when the demand is a consequence of medically costly children being born. Thus, it seems that if the rights to reproduce without state interference are implicated by arguments of this sort, they have possible relevance to two quite different kinds of case.

In the first instance, it is the rights of potential parents who are likely to bear children with special medical, developmental, and social service needs that are at stake, for these clearly disproportionately affect the available resources left over for others. As many probably assume, these may include a large number of persons who use illicit drugs and poor persons, who are more likely to give birth to children with low birth weight, HIV infection, and other conditions correlated with poverty.

In the second case, the rights of wealthy and middle class potential parents in wealthy nations, for whom it can be expected that a disproportionate share of social resources will be expended on behalf of their children, also are implicated. This is because children born of middle to upper class parents of first-world nations consume approximately 20–100 times the social resources either of children born to average-income parents in third-world nations or low-income parents in the United States. Hence, they too would be the subject of any restriction based upon Lockean considerations of distributive justice. Like the children born with special medical needs, the children of the better-off disproportionately reduce the proportion of a society's resources available for the benefit of others.

If any limits on the right to reproduce based upon distributive justice arguments are to be viewed as morally acceptable, they may not be ones which limit only the rights of the worst-off members of society. However, the claim that such restrictions are likely to have an especially adverse impact upon these two groups and that these two groups may stand in morally similar positions may seem somewhat surprising. It may seem that the restrictions constituting something like a modified or weakened Lockean proviso on reproductive rights would apply solely to those who by virtue of their own poverty impose these additional costs upon society at large. The problem of affluent reproducers will seem to many not to constitute a similar problem of distributive justice in so far as they do not place similar demands upon the public purse.

However, this kind of argument conflates the level-one and level-two arguments distinguished earlier. The point to be emphasized here is the restriction meant as a constraint on any type of activity may, in principle, reduce the aggregate amount of resources left over for others. Thus, the concern of such a principle is to establish the justifiable limits to private property rights on the grounds that there must be a fair share of social resources left over for others. A conclusion that the propertied and the unpropertied are in different moral postures with respect to reproductive behavior ignores this threshold role, which a proviso on acquisition of private property plays in a justificatory scheme.

It is of no use to appeal to the mere fact that the demand attributable to reproductive behavior is upon private rather than public resources. Unless the distribution of resources after privatization is itself justified by some distributive principle of the sort I have called a modified Lockean proviso, one cannot yet complain that the taking of private resources for the benefit of medically and economically disadvantaged children brought into the world is unjust. Only then would the affluent have the sort of moral claim on their own resources which would allow them to retain for their own use enough resources to support either more children or more expensive children of their own.

Provisionally, it seems that lacking such an argument for the moral entitlement the affluent have to the resources they privately possess, any plausible Lockean principle restricting reproduction would apply with equal force to reproductive decisions of the most affluent parents, whose children also consume a large share of available resources. Any threshold constraint on reproductive behavior, based on the idea that one must leave a fair share of social resources for others, would apply to anyone's reproductive behavior.

One possible way to avoid the result I have supposed would be to adopt something like Robert Nozick's blanket rejection of all patterned conceptions of distributive justice.[39] Patterned conceptions are ones which seek to promote a certain distributive outcome, such as the type supposed appropriate by the Lockean proviso or by a similar principle which aims to ensure that a fair share of social resources are in principle available for others. One might follow Nozick in elevating a principle of autonomy to the role of a side constraint. Such a principle would hold that any resulting patterns of distribution are not unjust as long as there is no injustice in the manner of acquisition and transfer of resources. As long as no other rights are violated in the acquisition of private resources, one is entitled to those resources, whatever the distributive consequences for others.

One could then make the same case for the reproductive conduct of the affluent. As long as no other rights are violated in the acquisition of private resources, they may consume as much as they wish on their children. The affluent who meet Nozick's conditions for just acquisition of property would be free to have as many children as they want (or spend as much on their children as they want), and their reproductive options would not be constrained by any further demands of distributive justice. Even the fact that their unrestrained reproduction might make others worse off than they otherwise would have been would not be morally relevant.

Moreover, those who cannot provide for their children have the same right to reproduce on the Nozickean view because the strong principle of autonomy equally permits them to engage in activities of their own choosing. However, as a consequence of the strong principle of autonomy that preserves their rights to noninterference, they have no rights against others for any share of social resources that might be needed to support their children. Since in Nozick's view it would be an injustice to deprive persons of their property justly acquired, it would be an injustice to tax them for the support of children born to parents who cannot meet their needs from private resources.

For Nozick, any demand upon the public purse is an especially grave moral problem when it requires the affluent to meet others' needs through involuntary taxation. The reason is that involuntary taxation violates his strong principle of autonomy. That strong principle of individual autonomy would require us to judge any unconsented interference with individual choice to be morally prohibited. Only by taking such a view could one resist all arguments for limiting reproduction on the grounds of its distributive consequences for others. It would, incidentally, preclude any interference with a woman's right to have children either for the social resource reasons or for the sake of the child (unless we can show that being born is a harm of the relevant sort).

The conclusion seems to be that either one must accept in principle some legitimate limits on the right to reproduce—and with it the implication that those most likely to be affected by such limitations will include many of the richest and the poorest members of society—or one must accept no limits on the right because of a strong principle of autonomy—and with it the implication that the very worst-off will enjoy no rights to a distributive share of social resources for the benefit of their children.

The second alternative seems difficult to accept. Although it preserves for all an across-the-board right to reproduce, its distributive consequences are severe and for many deeply counterintuitive. Arguing for a strong libertarian position—i.e., categorical commitment to the supreme moral importance of individual autonomy—is a very high price to pay for defending an unrestricted right to reproduce.

The first alternative, by contrast, admits of some striking exceptions to a right to reproduce. Although it leads us to accept only such limitations that can be justified on the basis of some more general principle of distributive justice, the impact could be to severely limit the rights to reproduce for those who are most likely to have more, or more costly, children.

If the arguments in this section have been successful, two conclusions might be drawn for public policy.

First, an absolute principle of autonomy must be defended if the restriction of reproduction on distributive justice grounds is to be rejected categorically. I doubt the prospects for success of that project for many of the same reasons cited by those skeptical about the bare appeal to autonomy as the justification for such rights.

Second, it is not clear that it would be morally acceptable to adopt public policies specifically designed to limit the reproductive rights of the worst-off members of society on the grounds of their added cost to the public purse. Unless it can be demonstrated that the resources that would be required to benefit the worst-off exceed a fair share of social resources to which they are entitled under some general principle of distributive justice, and unless a firm case can be made for the idea that the affluent fully deserve their resources, such a policy would lack a firm philosophical basis. This challenge is unlikely to be met in the current social and political context.

Conclusion

In this chapter, I have argued that there are many reasons to suppose that a right to have children can be defended, even if we are unable to put forward a comprehensive theory justifying rights generally. Although I have noted the inapplicability of some of the standard reproductive rights arguments to the justification of a specific right to have children, I have argued that a variety of interests can be seen as plausible grounds for such rights under a variety of justificatory schemes.

Moreover, many of the counterarguments designed to show that it may be morally wrong to have children provide no compelling basis for restricting the rights of HIV-infected women to have children. Neither the potential for harm to children nor the adverse distributional consequences for society overall offer the kind of arguments that provide a secure foundation for restrictive or punitive public policies aimed at limiting women's rights to have children.

Notes

1. H.L.A. Hart, *Essays on Bentham: Studies in Jurisprudence and Political Theory* (Oxford: Clarendon Press, 1982); L. W. Sumner, *The Moral Foundations of Rights* (Oxford: Oxford University Press, 1987).
2. J. Robertson, "Embryos, Families, and Procreative Liberty: The Legal Structure of the New Reproduction," *Southern California Law Review*, 59 (1986): 954–967.
3. J. Raz, *The Morality of Freedom* (Oxford: Oxford University Press, 1986): 166.
4. J. Feinberg, *Rights, Justice, and the Bounds of Liberty: Essays in Social Philosophy* (Princeton, NJ: Princeton University Press, 1980): 157–158.
5. T. L. Beauchamp and J. F. Childress, *Principles of Biomedical Ethics*, 3rd ed. (New York: Oxford University Press, 1989): 67.
6. J. S. Mill, *On Liberty* (Indianapolis: Bobbs-Merrill, 1958).
7. I. Kant, *Groundwork for the Metaphysics of Morals*, trans. H. J. Paton (New York: Harper and Row, 1964).
8. G. Dworkin, *The Theory and Practice of Autonomy* (Cambridge: Cambridge University Press, 1988): 110.
9. R. Dworkin, "Autonomy and the Demented Self," *Milbank Quarterly*, 64, suppl. 2 (1986): 8.
10. S. Law, "Rethinking Sex and the Constitution," *University of Pennsylvania Law Review*, 132 (1984): 1017.
11. K. Karst, "The Supreme Court 1976 Term, Forward: Equal Citizenship Under The Law," *Harvard Law Review*, 91 (1977): 58.
12. S. Law, "Rethinking Sex," 1016.
13. D. Regan, "Rewriting Roe v. Wade," *Michigan Law Review*, 77 (1979): 1569; J. Thomson, "The Right to Privacy," *Philosophy and Public Affairs*, 4 (1975): 295–314.
14. J. Robertson, "Procreative Liberty and the Control of Conception, Pregnancy, and Childbirth," *University of Virginia Law Review*, 69 (1983): 406.
15. See, e.g., Universal Declaration of Human Rights, 1948, Article 16; The European

Convention on Human Rights, Article 12; Covenant on Civil and Political Rights, Article 23, all reprinted in the Appendix, J. W. Nickel, *Making Sense of Human Rights* (Berkeley: University of California Press, 1987).

16. See, e.g., M. Bayles, "Limits to a Right to Procreate," in *Ethics and Population* (Cambridge, MA: Schenkman, 1976): 41–55; O. O'Neill, "Begetting, Bearing, and Rearing Children," in *Having Children*, eds. O. O'Neill and W. Ruddick (New York: Oxford University Press, 1979): 25–38.
17. A. Silverman and A. Silverman, *The Case Against Having Children* (New York: David McKay Company, 1971); E. Peck and J. Senderowitz, eds., *Pronatalism: The Myth of Mom and Apple Pie* (New York: Thomas Y. Crowell Company, 1974).
18. B. Lerner, R. Ruskin, and E. Davis, "On the Need to Be Pregnant," *International Journal of Psychoanalysis*, 48 (1967): 295.
19. F. Wyatt, "Clinical Notes on Motives of Reproduction," *Journal of Social Issues*, 23 (1967): 51.
20. M. Flapan, "A Paradigm for the Analysis of Childbearing Motivations of Married Women Prior to Birth of the First Child," *American Journal of Orthopsychiatry*, 39 (1969): 410.
21. B. Russell, *Marriage and Morals* (New York: Bantam, 1968): 96.
22. J. Blustein, *Parents and Children: The Ethics of the Family*, (New York: Oxford University Press, 1982): 191–192.
23. J. Feinberg, *Harm to Others. The Moral Limits of the Criminal Law*, vol. I (New York: Oxford University Press, 1984): 32–36.
24. A. Baier, "Poisoning the Wells," in *Values at Risk*, ed. D. MacLean (Totowa, NJ: Rowman and Allanheld, 1986): 49–74.
25. J. Narveson, "Utilitarianism and Future Generations," *Mind* 76 (1967): 62–72. Although this is one way some have read Narveson's claim, he later suggests that this was not his intended claim. "Moral Problems of Population," in *Ethics and Population*, 73. He argues that all moral reasons are grounded in the existence of persons who may be harmed or benefitted by our actions. We might interpret that claim restrictively to mean "presently existing" or to include those who will exist in the future as well. Narveson suggests that his person-affecting argument is of the latter sort; I use the term as a convenient shorthand expression for the former, more restrictive view.
26. D. Parfit, "On Doing the Best for Our Children," in *Ethics and Population*, 101.
27. Ibid.
28. M. Hanser, "Harming Future Generations," *Philosophy and Public Affairs*, 19 (1990): 69–70.
29. It should be noted that there are other cases in which most of us will claim that even when an action helps someone more than it harms him or her, it is still unjustified. For example, I abduct you against your will and the consequence is that you are safely removed from a building which collapses. Arguably, I have harmed you even though it is false that you experienced a net surplus of harm over loss.
30. For a discussion of this second counterfactual standard, which compares existence to nonexistence, see J. Feinberg, "Wrongful Life and the Counterfactual Element in Harming," *Social Philosophy and Policy*, 4 (1988): 145–178.
31. J. D. Arras, "AIDS and Reproductive Decisions: Having Children in Fear and Trembling," *The Milbank Quarterly*, 68 (1990): 364.
32. Ibid., 365.
33. L. Purdy, "Genetic Diseases: Can Having Children Be Immoral?" in *Genetics Now:*

Ethical Issues in Genetic Research, ed. J. Buckley, Jr. (Washington DC: University Press of America, 1978): 25–39.
34. E. Connor, R. Sperling, and the ACTG 076 Protocol Team, Memorandum entitled "Discontinuation of Enrollment in ACTG 076," Feb. 20, 1994.
35. J. Locke, *Two Treatises of Government*, ed. P. Laslett (New York: New American Library, 1965): treatise II, sect. 24–47.
36. Ibid, sect. 26.
37. Ibid.
38. Robert Nozick has acknowledged this prospect and has suggested that even if there are no longer any unappropriated resources available to others, private property may still be justified as long as their overall position is not worsened thereby. I do not discuss the details of his interesting amendment of Locke's rationale.
39. R. Nozick, *Anarchy, State, and Utopia* (New York: Basic Books, 1974).

13

Reproductive Choices of Adolescent Females with HIV/AIDS

PATRICIA A. KING

> That's why you see when I came out pregnant and I was fifteen and I was very young and I did not know what I was doing. I didn't even know about birth control. That's why I became pregnant at such a young age.
>
> woman from New York

The HIV/AIDS epidemic poses significant challenges to law and other public policies that regulate or support familial and other intimate relationships.[1] This is especially true of laws and policies that govern reproductive decision-making for adolescents. In my view, these laws and policies must be reformed to permit adolescents to make and to carry out the decisions that govern the sexual and reproductive aspects of their lives. Otherwise, efforts to prevent further horizontal and vertical spread of HIV/AIDS will be significantly impeded.

The prevailing liberal view in this society has been that individuals should have freedom of choice in reproductive matters. Whether and how to reproduce has been a private matter with which government and health-care providers should not interfere. A darker reality, however, has existed alongside this view. A persistent belief that in some circumstances individuals should not be permitted to reproduce or should be strongly discouraged from doing so also endures. A challenge posed by the HIV/AIDS epidemic is whether being HIV-infected is such a circumstance.[2]

By contrast, with adolescents there has been no predominant assumption about freedom of choice in reproductive matters. Instead, there is widespread confusion and controversy about whether, and to what extent, parents, government, or adolescents themselves should influence or control reproductive decision-making. As a consequence, arguments that support freedom of choice in reproductive matters for women who are infected with HIV/AIDS cannot be automatically applied to adolescent females. Thus, before I can reach the special case of HIV/AIDS, reproduction, and adolescents, it is necessary initially to stake out my position with respect to the reproductive options of adolescents generally. Accordingly, I argue first that laws and policies must be reformed to permit adolescents to control the sexual and reproductive aspects of their lives. I then argue that, in the context of the HIV-infected adolescent, clinical interventions should be designed to acknowledge and support the adolescent herself as the ultimate decision-maker. More important, however, than the legal allocation of decision-making authority is the process by which adolescent reproductive decisions are made.

This chapter is divided into three parts. The first part reviews what is currently known about the sexual and reproductive behaviors and experiences of adolescents, against which the urgency of the problem of HIV infection and vertical transmission among adolescents can be evaluated. The second part describes some of the difficulties inherent in the development of coherent and defensible public policies concerning adolescent sexuality, in which my position favoring legal reform is defended. The third part turns specifically to issues of reproductive choice for the HIV-infected adolescent, particularly in the clinical context. I contend that for pragmatic reasons adolescents should ultimately make the reproductive choices that affect their lives. At the clinical level, however, services must be offered in a way that takes account of the nature of reproductive decision-making and the nature and characteristics of adolescence, including, where possible, the need to involve parents or other supportive adults. Offering clinical services in this manner does not result in distinguishing adolescents from adults in the provision of services. Rather, it serves to underscore that adults in similar circumstances are also in need of supportive and caring services that take account of individual circumstances and preferably involve other family members or loved ones.

A Looming Epidemic Among Adolescents

The most important lesson to draw from the medical and social data about HIV/AIDS and the sexual and reproductive behaviors of adolescents is that adolescents and (if the adolescent is female) their offspring are at serious risk of becoming infected with HIV/AIDS.

In the early stages of the HIV/AIDS epidemic, the possibility that adolescents might be at risk of contracting the disease was seldom, if ever, raised. The demographics of the epidemic did not alert policy-makers to the possibility that HIV/AIDS among adolescents might become a significant issue. Instead, attention was focused on infants born to HIV-infected mothers or children who were infected as a result of being transfused. In addition, there was little appreciation of the fact that the sexual and drug practices of adolescents not only put them at risk of the disease but were also likely to increase the numbers of children born to HIV-infected mothers. Today, however, there are reasons to believe that there is a looming HIV/AIDS epidemic among adolescents. The National Commission on AIDS has warned that the "HIV/AIDS epidemic threatens a new generation of Americans. Adolescents are vulnerable to infection owing to a combination of behavioral, social, and in some cases economic forces."[3] Should HIV infection take hold in the adolescent population, incomparable havoc and harm will occur in the lives of our young and in the lives of their offspring. Clearly, everything possible should be done to prevent this epidemic from occurring.

Although the data for the United States are sparse, there is evidence that HIV infection is rising among adolescents and that minorities and females are especially vulnerable. The number of adolescents diagnosed as having AIDS is indeed small but the number is growing. The Center for Disease Control (CDC) defines a teen as being from 13 to 19 years of age.[4] In 1981, there was one reported case of an adolescent with AIDS. In 1992 there were 159 cases.[5] Cumulatively through June 1994, 1,768 cases of AIDS in adolescents were reported.[6] In addition, these figures doubtlessly understate the prevalence of HIV infection among teens. In many communities in the United States, HIV infection is the leading cause of death among young men and young women aged 25–44 years.[7] One in five of all reported AIDS cases is in the 20–29 year age group.[8] In view of the median incubation period of ten years between HIV infection and AIDS diagnosis, some proportion of these persons were infected during their teen years. Since it is not likely (depending on time of infection) that teens will have an AIDS-defining illness during the years they are chronologically adolescents, it will continue to be difficult to get a true picture of the prevalence of HIV/AIDS in this population.

Of significance is the fact that minority teens seem to be at greater risk than whites. Among teenagers applying to the military between 1985 and 1989, the overall infection rate was 1:3,000. However, it was 1:1,000 for African-American teenagers. In 1987–1990, the overall infection rate for Job Corps applicants was 1:300, but for African-American applicants it was 1:80. Native American applicants also had a higher rate of infection than whites.[9]

While most teens with HIV/AIDS are older and male, it is a matter of some consternation that females seem to be particularly vulnerable to infection.[10] This vulnerability is troubling not only for what it portends for the lives of young females but also because it may translate into increased levels of perinatal transmission of the virus.

The proportion of female adolescents diagnosed with HIV/AIDS has more than doubled, from 14% in 1987 to 32% in 1994.[11] The CDC reports that of the 565 adolescent female AIDS cases reported cumulatively, 292 are from heterosexual contact.[12] Although studies indicate varying infection rates among teens overall, they consistently indicate the prominence of HIV infection in young females. One study of applicants for U.S. military service indicates that females are experiencing rates of HIV infection comparable to adolescent men.[13] Another study of Job Corps trainees indicates that, while the seroprevalence rate was higher in males (3.7 per 1,000) than in females (3.2 per 1,000), among trainees aged 16 and 17 years, females had the higher rate (2.3 per 1,000 vs 1.5 per

1,000).[14] Yet another study reported that in heterosexual adolescents ages 15–19 years who attended sexually transmitted disease (STD) clinics, the median prevalence rate in females was significantly higher (8.3%) than in males of the same age (4.4%).[15] Finally, a greater percentage of adolescents than adults with AIDS are female (34% vs. 13%).[16]

There is evidence to suggest, by analogy to some venereal diseases, that there are anatomical and physiological reasons why adolescent women may be at greater risk for HIV infection. It is hypothesized that their maturing ovarian function and cervical environment are more penetrable by certain organisms.[17] Mucous production, cervical ectopy, and genital tract maturity are proposed as anatomical reasons why young women are particularly susceptible to HIV infection.[18] This is in addition to the fact that HIV seems to be more easily transmitted from men to women than the reverse.[19]

There are also social factors that contribute to the risk of female adolescents to HIV infection. First, adolescent females often have sex with older men who have had multiple sexual partners.[20] Second, there is evidence that some teens acquire the infection as a result of sexual abuse.[21] There are already data to indicate that adult women who have been abused are more likely to be infected with the virus.[22]

What we know about adolescent sexual practices indicates that, unless modified, these practices will facilitate transmission of HIV/AIDS in this population. Sexual abstinence is the only completely effective way of avoiding both STDs and pregnancy. Significantly, nearly 20% of adolescents do not have intercourse during their teenage years.[23] Many adolescents, however, are sexually active.

The CDC's Youth Risk Behavior Survey indicates that of all surveyed students in grades 9–12, 54.2% reported having had sexual intercourse and 39.4% reported having had sexual intercourse during the 3 months preceding the study. This represents 39.6% of ninth graders, 47.6% of tenth graders, 57.3% of eleventh graders, and 71.9% of twelfth graders.[24] A recent study reports that more than half of women and almost three-quarters of men have had intercourse before their eighteenth birthday.[25]

The only effective strategy to prevent heterosexual transmission of HIV/AIDS other than sexual abstinence is consistent and correct use of condoms during sexual intercourse.[26] Pregnancy is an indication that no contraceptives are being used or that contraceptives are being used inappropriately. Significantly, approximately one million adolescent females become pregnant each year. This number represents 12% of all females aged 15–19 years and 21% of those who have had sexual intercourse.[27] While contraceptives other than condoms are effective in preventing pregnancy, they do not prevent transmission of HIV/AIDS and other STDs. An encouraging note is that contraceptive use among adolescents, especially condom use, increased considerably between 1982 and 1988.[28] Among the adolescents in the CDC survey who were currently sexually active (3 months before the survey was conducted), 77.7% of female and 77.8% of male students had used contraception during their last sexual intercourse. The proportion of white female students who used contraception (81.1%) was significantly higher than that of black (71.4%) and Hispanic (62.6%) female students. According to the CDC survey, 49.4% of male students and 40.0% of female students reported that they or their partner had used a condom during their last act of sexual intercourse.[29]

A disturbing note is that for many teens sex is not a voluntary choice. This is especially true for the youngest teens: 74% of women who had sexual intercourse before the age of 14 and 60% of those before age 15 report having had sex involuntarily.[30] These data suggest that even if adolescent females want to use contraceptives, they may not always be able to do so.

The prevalence of STDs is another indication of unprotected sexual intercourse. As might be expected, the prevalence of STDs in adolescents has increased dramatically in recent years. Of all STDs (including HIV/AIDS) 86% occur among persons 15–29 years of age.[31] Three million teens—one out of eight—are infected with an STD.[32] In addition to indicating the practice of unprotected intercourse, the presence of an STD is itself believed to facilitate transmission of the HIV virus.[33]

In short, the data strongly suggest that as a result of their sexual and reproductive behaviors adolescents are at serious risk of becoming infected with HIV/AIDS. The only way to prevent HIV/AIDS from taking hold among adolescents is to encourage them to abstain as long as possible before engaging in sexual intercourse and once sexually active to use condoms. Adolescents must be helped to alter their risky sexual and reproductive behaviors. If successful, such efforts would not only preserve the lives of many of our young but might also reduce vertical transmission of HIV/AIDS to the next generation by reducing the number of unintended pregnancies.

Developing Public Policy for Adolescent Sexuality

Adolescence is conceptually and for public policy purposes a difficult developmental period.[34] Mistakes and mishaps that occur (and to some extent are expected to occur) in the move toward adulthood may have profound and lasting consequences for the adolescent, family, and society. Increasingly, the consequences are of concern to the state, whose role in ameliorating or preventing harsh consequences generates controversy. A looming HIV/AIDS epidemic is likely to emphasize further the state's need to focus on the consequences of adolescent sexuality. Such a focus, should it occur, will come at the expense of parental autonomy.

Allocating decision-making for adolescents

". . . adolescence is a relatively recent and culturally specific concept."[35] This period is broadly characterized, on the one hand, by the relative immaturity of adolescents in relation to adults and their prolonged economic dependence on others, typically their parents. On the other hand, adolescence is a period in which a teen is biologically mature and thus capable of engaging in sexual intercourse and bearing children. Sexual activity was traditionally associated with other markers of adulthood—employment, economic independence, and marriage. Today, puberty occurs at earlier ages, while the other indicia of adulthood occur much later than before. Thus, the time at which sexual activity is considered appropriate has increasingly become a matter of enormous controversy. Some view this issue as a moral one: sex should only occur within the confines of marriage. Others worry more about the negative consequences to the adolescent and potential offspring that often accompany sexual activity. Still others worry about the costs to society of providing services, especially welfare, to those adolescents who have children.

Another major problem from a public policy perspective is the great variation in the age and capacities of those we label adolescents. Obviously, sexuality, pregnancy, and childbearing have different meanings and impacts for a 13 year old and a 19 year old. Meaning and impact also vary considerably in accordance with social, economic, and cultural circumstances. Similarly, the capacity for mature judgment is not merely a function of chronological age but varies considerably from adolescent to adolescent.

Yet another problem is the competing expectations that society has for this developmental period. Although not an adult, the adolescent is expected to learn how to be an adult and to assume adult responsibilities. Such knowledge is acquired through a process of trial and error, of taking risks and experimenting. This process requires that to some extent adolescents be treated as though they were adults and be permitted to engage in adult activities. At the same time, however, we believe that adolescents need guidance and support in navigating through this difficult period.

The adolescent is expected to make mistakes. The hope is that the mistakes will aid learning and not be too costly in long-term consequences. The impact of the mistakes adolescents make depends critically on the social and economic context in which they occur. Parents and society try to protect adolescents from the most serious mistakes and consequences, especially those that flow from behaviors such as sexual intercourse, drug use, and drinking, which are generally considered inappropriate for adolescents. There is broad understanding, however, that adolescents can and do engage in these behaviors. The prolonged economic dependence of adolescents gives parents some clout with teens but does not necessarily give parents control over the behaviors and activities of youth. It certainly does not insure open communication between parents and children. Therefore, with respect to adolescent sexuality, whether a focus on consequences should be a priority and who should have primary responsibility for guiding adolescent behavior—parents, the state, or adolescents themselves—is hotly disputed.

Traditionally, parents have been charged with the care, support, and rearing of children, including the right to make decisions about health care.[36] There are many reasons to justify giving authority to consent to medical treatments to parents,

> but at the root of the common law rule was the narrower notion that parents are legally responsible for the care and support of their children. Among other things, the parental consent requirement protects parents from having to pay for unwanted or unnecessary medical care, and from the possible financial consequences of supporting the child if unwanted treatment is unsuccessful.[37]

The state acknowledges the primary role of parents. Yet, it retains a wide range of power to regulate the family in matters affecting the welfare of children, including matters related to sexuality and reproduction.

In general, government's role in the regulation of sexual and reproductive behaviors is controversial.[38] There is disagreement about what sexual practices are acceptable. There is even more debate about who should be permitted to engage in sexual behaviors and with whom and under what circumstances. Even historically, governmental attempts to modify sexual behaviors to reduce the incidence of STDs have been controversial.[39] The controversy reaches new heights when government attempts to regulate adolescent sexual and reproductive behaviors.

Increased sexuality, pregnancy, and childbearing among teenagers has fueled the debate. There are sharply divergent views on the role of government, the authority and responsibility of parents with respect to the sexual activities of youth, and the competence and capacity of adolescents to make their own decisions and to take responsibility for the consequences of their acts. Disagreements about sex education provide a useful illustration. Conservative traditionalists see abstinence as the only effective means of preventing the spread of HIV/AIDS. They urge that sex education is best left to parents and family. They oppose sex education and school provision of condoms.[40] A recent judicial decision prohibiting New York City from dispensing condoms as a part of an AIDS education effort to unemancipated minor students without the prior consent of their parents or guardians or without an opt-out provision reflects this position.[41] Public health practitioners often argue that, in view of the data indicating that many adolescents are sexually active, government should provide teens with information and condoms to better protect themselves from disease and pregnancy. They are reluctant to rely on parents because they fear that communication between adolescents and parents is often difficult, if undertaken at all.[42] Others affirm the choice of adolescent females to be sexually active and to have children. They advocate that the state's role should be to empower and support young women to make good choices for themselves.[43] As a consequence, in the United States there are no consistent, comprehensive, or coherent governmental policies about sex education or other matters concerning adolescent pregnancy and childbearing.[44]

The potential impact of HIV/AIDS

A looming HIV/AIDS epidemic should have an impact on these disagreements. The nature and characteristics of the disease and its mode of transmission should direct attention to the consequences of adolescent sexual and reproductive behaviors and specific strategies needed to prevent further spread of the disease. A potential epidemic should also accelerate existing trends in law and policy toward adolescent control over sexual and reproductive behaviors. There are, however, countervailing forces that might mitigate this expected impact.

Although the same behavior—unprotected sexual intercourse—is implicated in both the spread of HIV/AIDS and high levels of pregnancy and childbirth among adolescents, the consequences are radically different. Pregnancy and childbearing may adversely impact the economic and social status of adolescents and their young. By contrast, HIV/AIDS infection is followed by the death of the person who is infected and, if that person is a female who gets pregnant, the birth of a child who will be orphaned or possibly infected as well. It is one thing to produce a stalemate on what are appropriate interventions while adolescents continue to engage in sexual activity, get pregnant, or give birth. It is quite another to have first-hand experience with the prolonged dying and death of the youngest and potentially most productive members of society.

There is no effective treatment for HIV infection nor any method to block further transmission of the disease, except possibly the use of zidovudine during pregnancy, which may reduce or prevent transmission to offspring.[45] Thus, pragmatically, modification of risky sexual and reproductive behaviors is currently the only means of preventing further spread of the disease.

Modifying risky and potentially harmful sexual and reproductive behaviors is at best a difficult and lengthy process. Sexual and reproductive behaviors generally occur in private. They are not especially amenable to governmental or even parental control and oversight. It is practically impossible to insure that adolescents practice abstinence. Whether sexual intercourse has occurred is detectable (as in allegations of rape), but detection is not likely to be utilized on any broad scale. If sexually active, only persons having sexual intercourse can insure (if they are available) that condoms will be used. Some consequences of sexual activity, such as pregnancy or the presence of a venereal disease, can be detected. In addition, parents or governments could act to prevent pregnancy altogether by requiring sterilization or the use of long-term contraceptives. However, with the possible, but unlikely, exception of persons with mental disabilities, such measures seem at odds with constitutionally mandated norms governing bodily integrity and reproductive freedom. Thus, to modify behaviors it seems that individuals must be targeted. Individuals have to be motivated to act, based upon accurate and complete information and access to skills and needed services.[46] Altering risky behaviors, therefore, seems to require that individuals have control over the sexual and reproductive aspects of their lives.

In recent years, despite persistent controversy, two trends have emerged that have import for the traditional structuring of decision-making between parents and the state. These trends should be reinforced if HIV/AIDS concentrates attention on ameliorating the adverse consequences of sexual activity among teens. The first trend is government's increased recognition of the decision-making authority of minors. It remains the case, however, that claims of adolescents to self-determination against both their parents and the state in matters of particular concern to adolescents have met with mixed success. This is particularly true with respect to those adolescent behaviors that are implicated in the HIV/AIDS epidemic—regulation of sexuality and reproductive decision-making. The second trend has been the establishment of adolescent pregnancy and childbearing as priorities for national and state governments.[47] Implementation of government-funded programs addressed at these priorities, however, has met with increasing controversy. Moreover, as noted in a recent report, these programs and policies

> are fragmented and oriented toward specific problems rather than toward the constellation of problems that characterize adolescents . . . the current U.S. health care system does not yet have a strategy for dealing with adolescents or for dealing with the broad concept of health embodied in the World Health Organization (WHO) definitions.[48]

As a matter of constitutional law, adolescents have been given greater authority in decision-making related to contraception[49] and abortion.[50] Lower federal court decisions have beaten back efforts to require parental notification as a condition to receipt of contraceptives.[51]

At the state level, there also has been progress in extending to adolescents the general power to consent to medical treatment. For example, in some situations, such as those resulting in emancipation or in emergency circumstances, parental consent to medical treatment is not required. Some states have lowered the age of majority (generally 14–16 years old), recognized the power of mature minors, or specified birth of a child as the time at which a person may consent to medical treatment.[52] This trend toward greater liberty of minors in part represents real appreciation of the fact that the capacity for mature judgment is not a function of chronological age.

Still other states specify the particular conditions, such as pregnancy, venereal disease, drug abuse, or abortion, for which minors may give effective consent to related diagnosis, treatment, and services. These conditions or diseases involve behaviors such as sexual intercourse, drinking, or drug use that when engaged in might carry serious and long-term consequences. If parental consent were a requirement for treatment, many adolescents might go untreated and suffer harm. Allowing adolescents access to contraceptives or medical treatment is a means of mitigating the harm that might result from participation in such behaviors.

Recognition of a minor's right to consent to medical care generally or for specific purposes is not necessarily, however, social recognition that minors are to be treated in all respects as though they were adults. There are indications that enabling minors to give effective consent to medical decisions reflects a balancing of state interests in child welfare and the general public health with respect to parental autonomy. In short, minor consent is allowed for very practical reasons.

In *Carey v. Population Services International*, for example, the concurring opinions of Justices Stevens and White describe as "frivolous appellees argument that a minor has the constitutional right to put contraceptives to their intended use notwithstanding the combined objection of both parents and the state."[49] Both justices were able to concur in the result because it was unreasonable to assume that the state prescribe that adolescents were to be put at risk of unwanted pregnancy and venereal disease.

Although *Planned Parenthood v. Danforth* made it clear that parents did not have an absolute veto over a minor's choice to terminate pregnancy, this decision did not permit all minors to elect to have an abortion. The minor could be required to go to court as an alternative to requiring parental consent. One author put the matter this way:

> Bypass procedures may be viewed as a way to facilitate a minor's ability to obtain an abortion, without having to grant to her explicitly the same degree of autonomy possessed by adult women. This view recognizes both that most minors are immature, and that it is never in the best interests of a minor to be forced to carry a pregnancy to term. To extend to all minors the right to abortion, however, represents too great an assault on our notions of parental autonomy. Judicial bypass procedures allow the law to maintain the fiction that someone else will decide for the immature minor, while providing a procedure to ensure that if she persists, she will in fact be able to obtain an abortion.[53]

Perhaps the strongest evidence that legal empowerment of minors is not so much recognition of their claims to self-determination as concern about their welfare is that minors may not insure that the treatments they consent to will be kept confidential. The Supreme Court has allowed states to require parents to be involved in abortion decision-making of their adolescent children.[54] Indeed, it is still unclear as a matter of constitutional law whether a minor's access to contraceptives can be conditioned on parental notification.

Notification requirements are also found in state statutes that authorize minors to consent to medical treatment. Where notification is mandatory, however, the effect may be to undermine the welfare of minors.[55] Mandatory notification is as burdensome as parental consent provisions because such requirements discourage adolescents from obtaining needed care. Some states give health-care providers discretion with respect to whether parents should be involved in adolescent care. While such laws may also discourage adolescents from seeking needed care, they are an improvement over mandatory notification requirements that do not take sufficient account of the possibility in some circumstances that parental involvement may be at odds with the welfare of minors.

In short, increasing the liberty of minors has an instrumental value in helping to insure their welfare. What is referred to as "privacy" for adolescents in reality represents state, as opposed to parental, guidance of adolescents. This approach to decision-making for adolescents is urgently needed if a looming HIV/AIDS epidemic is to be averted. The data with respect to adolescent sexual and reproductive practices demonstrate the need to identify, counsel, and perhaps test youth at increased risk of infection. Given the nature of HIV/AIDS and its modes of transmission, these needs can be met most effectively if parental consent and disclosure of diagnosis are not mandated.[56]

Adolescents have made some strides in obtaining recognition of their decision-making authority, at least in the areas of medical and reproductive decision-making. Sadly, in the area of being able to implement the medical and procreative decisions they are legally permitted to make, adolescents have made little or no progress. Although adolescents have choices in theory, in reality they may have difficulty convincing others to provide them with services if they cannot pay for them. In general, parents cannot be required to pay for services that they do not authorize; otherwise, their parental autonomy would be breached. Even where a family insurance policy might cover services desired by an adolescent, it is most often the case that the parent who is insured will receive notification of some sort from the insurance carrier if a claim is filed. As a consequence, the adolescent desire for privacy is undermined if she or he seeks assistance from an insurance company. Moreover, often the specific services that adolescents need are not available.[57]

Problems associated with the economic dependence of adolescents could be alleviated if adolescent health care were publicly funded. While such support does serve to transfer power away from parents, it is clearly less of an intrusion on family autonomy than requiring the parents to pay for services they have not authorized. However, public funds have not been made available on a wide-scale basis.[58] A recent Institute of Medicine study states that two of the four characteristics of the structure of the U.S. health system that inhibits the provision of health-care services to adolescents are "the tangle of health insurance arrangements that define who can afford care and what services are eligible for reimbursement . . . [and] a large majority of adolescents have no financial access to care independent of their families."[59]

Authority to consent is not enough. To modify their behaviors and to take care of the health and medical needs associated with HIV infection, adolescents will need services that they can access in spite of their economic dependence. As English notes:

> [o]ne of the most critical issues is the necessity for establishing a linkage between testing and treatment in order to encourage adolescents who are at high risk of infection to learn their HIV status, while providing a benefit to justify the increased risks of loss of confidentiality and discrimination that may occur as a result of identification.[60]

In short, increases in adolescent decision-making authority and in access to some services can be justified as being in the best interests of youth and society. However, existing law and policy, especially the areas of confidentiality and notice provisions, reflect ambivalence about the extent to which parental autonomy should, or can, be ignored. Hopefully, at the policy level, the looming HIV/AIDS epidemic will focus greater attention on the impact of policies on the health and well-being of adolescents themselves, rather than their impact on family values or parental autonomy. From the perspective of public policy, the best way to minimize the potentially devastating effects of the HIV epidemic for our youth is for government to play a major role in providing adolescents with information and access to, and control over, the services that are required to reduce or prevent transmission of the disease.

Despite compelling reasons provided by a looming HIV/AIDS epidemic to expand adolescent control over their sexual behaviors, the specific nature and character of the behaviors involved in transmission of HIV/AIDS and the social settings in which they occur also pose serious obstacles to making the required changes in law and policy. Two of the obstacles deserve special mention. These barriers are, first, the reluctance of society to discuss openly and frankly sexual and reproductive matters and, second, the tendency to stigmatize victims of STDs. Both barriers have been encountered in trying to prevent the continued spread of the disease among adults.[61] They have special force with respect to the behaviors of adolescents.

In our society, the social implications of sexual behavior are typically ignored. Sexual behavior is regarded as essentially private behavior. There is reluctance to discuss openly sexual and reproductive behaviors. As a consequence, relatively little is known about this very sensitive and private area of human interaction. Fortunately, because of rising concern about teenage sexuality, pregnancy, and childbearing, more is known about adolescent than adult sexual behaviors. Even among teenagers, however, much more needs to be done. For example, most of the information about adolescents is about intercourse, not other sexual behaviors.[62]

Society's reluctance to come to grips with sexuality, especially adolescent sexuality, may be reinforced by the tendency to stigmatize victims of STDs. This tendency might override any commitment to protect youth from the adverse consequences of their sexuality. This is particularly worrisome in view of connections between adolescent sexuality and traditionally stigmatized groups and other controversial matters such as abortion.

Alongside a tradition of caring for the sick and those most vulnerable to disease has been a countervailing tradition of regarding epidemic disease as punishment for sin. While this latter view has softened over the centuries, it has retained special resonance with STDs.[63] In addition, HIV/AIDS has tended to concentrate among groups—gay men, drug users, racial and ethnic minorities, and the poor—that have been traditionally stigmatized in this society.

In the public mind, there already exists an association between sexually active teenagers and some traditionally stigmatized groups. The "problem" of unwed mothers is commonly perceived to be an issue for inner-city teens only. In addition, single parenting is viewed as resulting from pathologies within African-American family structures or deficiencies in African-American culture generally. Clearly, adolescent pregnancy, childbearing, and single parenting are serious problems for the African-American community.[64] It is equally apparent, however, that these matters are mistakenly perceived as being problematic for minority communities only.[65] Nonetheless, these perceptions linger despite data that indicate that rates of single motherhood have increased overall in the United States.

The effects of stigma are many,[66] but the possibility of greatest relevance here is that the dominant society may not perceive itself as being at risk and thus react to the prospect of an AIDS/HIV epidemic among adolescents in a punitive manner. Adolescent females at risk or already infected with HIV/AIDS closely resemble their adult counterparts. The punitive impulse evident in responses to reproductive matters in connection with women who are HIV-infected and who are of reproductive age is likely to be directed at adolescent females as well.

Societal interest in perinatal transmission has focused almost exclusively on the suffering or costs associated with the care of infants and children, not their mothers. Data indicate that only about one-third of children born to infected women will have the disease. Research suggests that the use of AZT during pregnancy may lower this rate even further.[67] However, the plight of children free of the disease is equally compelling. Not only will they lose their mothers but in many cases the father, too, is infected and will die.

The unwillingness to focus on the suffering and frequent abandonment of loved ones sustained by adult females is linked to public perceptions of infected women—prostitutes, drug users, and the sexually promiscuous—as being morally blameworthy. By contrast, children, like blood transfusion recipients, are perceived to be innocent victims. Moreover, women who are HIV-infected are likely to be members of racial or ethnic minorities and often poor. These facts have no doubt increased women's vulnerability to negative stereotypes.

Since adolescents are also children, one might expect that it would be easy to institute protective measures because their relative youth would prevent them from being tagged with negative stereotypes. Yet the opposite seems to be true. Sexually active or drug-using adolescents do not generate the sympathy that infants and younger children evoke.[68] Indeed, their youth and relative immaturity often serve as justification for proposals to control sexuality, pregnancy, and childbirth that would clearly be considered inappropriate for adult women.

In Zimring's words, "As a period of semi-autonomy, [adolescence] places special burdens on legal reasoning and public choice."[69] As already argued, there is reason to expect that the entrenched differences that characterize the contenders in the teenage sexuality debates will be minimized in the face of a looming HIV/AIDS epidemic among adolescents. Yet it also is likely that many will continue to object to laws and policies shaped to facilitate adolescent control over sexual matters even in the face of HIV. Their objections may flow from beliefs that their young are not at risk or because, even while recognizing the devastating consequences of HIV/AIDS infection, they value government restraint and family privacy more highly. As one commentator has noted, it is likely, "that no significant progress can occur as long as Americans view the issue [teenage pregnancy] in terms of individual rather than societal responsibilities and insist on policies that reflect traditional family values rather than contemporary adolescent needs."[70] Hopefully, the threat of HIV/AIDS will move public policy for adolescent sexuality in this direction. In time, perhaps, we will come to understand that the problem is not so much who has the authority to make decisions but rather the nature of the process in which the decisions are made.

When Adolescents Become Infected with HIV/AIDS: Guidance for Policy-Makers and Health-Care Providers

I have argued that law and other public policies should permit adolescents to control the sexual and reproductive aspects of their lives—in short, that in this context adolescents should be treated as though they were adults. This argument is not premised on the view that adolescents are capable of autonomous choices, though some adolescents may, in fact, have this capacity. On the contrary, it recognizes that many adolescents are immature and economically dependent on others. The argument does assert. however, that it is not reasonable for the state to allow adolescents to be put at risk of HIV/AIDS infection and premature death.

The question now arises of whether this same argument should be extended to cover adolescents who are infected with the virus. In particular, if we allow adult women who are infected to retain authority to control the reproductive aspects of their lives, should infected adolescent females be similarly treated? At the level of policy, I urge that the arguments made above apply with equal force to the circumstance where the adolescent is infected with HIV/AIDS. At the program or clinical level, I argue that adolescents should be presumed to have control over the sexual and reproductive aspects of their lives. At this level, however, society's concerns about the relative immaturity of minors can be accommodated by making provision for the involvement of adults in the decision-making process.

At the policy level, the issue of whether the state should proscribe childbearing for adolescents is posed. It is beyond the confines of this chapter to engage the question of under what circumstances, if any, the state should proscribe childbearing. Elsewhere in this book the Working Group argues that requiring females with HIV/AIDS not to reproduce would be morally wrong and likely legally impermissible. Since adolescents also have constitutional rights that must be recognized, I would urge that those arguments apply with equal force to adolescents. Issues of bodily integrity, privacy, and reproductive freedom are as essential ingredients of self-identity and self-respect for adolescents as they are for adults. Moreover, because of their relative immaturity and inability to participate fully in the political process, adolescents are particularly vulnerable to the initiation of policies that might not be as respectful of their physical and mental integrity as they would be of adults in comparable situations.

The question of whether the state should try to shape the reproductive choices of HIV/AIDS-infected adolescents is much more complex. Many advocate that the state undertake efforts to persuade or influence the reproductive choices of adolescents. For example, some would argue that as a condition of receiving public support for their children, unwed adolescents should be required to live with their parents. Others have urged that adolescents be given positive incentives, such as money, to refrain from childbearing.

Whatever the merit of such policies in the context of general efforts to reduce teenage pregnancy and adolescence, it would be inappropriate to single out female adolescents who are infected with HIV/AIDS in this regard. The premise behind these incentives seems to be that postponed childbearing is in the best interest of the adolescent and her offspring. The premise itself is contested by some who argue that any adverse effects to the adolescent or her offspring are likely attributable to the girl's social or economic status and not to her being an adolescent per se.[71] Even if the premise is accepted, however, postponed childbearing for an HIV/AIDS adolescent is not a realistic alternative. Since reasons for, and the importance of, having children vary across cultures and experience,[72] it cannot be stated with assurance that forgoing childbearing is in the best interest of all adolescents. Additionally, the social characteristics of infected adult females suggest that they are just as likely as adolescents to be economically dependent on others. Moreover, the plight of infants born to adolescents who are infected is not in any relevant way distinguishable from children born to adult females similarly infected. All offspring are at risk of being infected. All are at risk of being orphaned at an early age.

Thus far my comments have been restricted to public policy. Clinical services differ from public policy in at least one important respect. The clinical context permits individualized assessment of the adolescent's relative immaturity and economic independence. There is the opportunity to influence or shape adolescent choices and behaviors in the course of one-on-one interactions. Thus, the question of what the nature of the interaction between clinicians or health-care providers and adolescent girls who are HIV-infected should be arises.

It is extremely difficult to posit a model that would govern all interactions between counselors and patients, given the wide variation among adolescents and their life experiences. It is possible, however, to provide broad guidelines that should be followed in the clinical encounter.

The first general principle is that adolescents should be presumed to be able to make reproductive choices to the extent permissible under governing state law. First, as I have argued above, such an approach is likely to be in the adolescent's best interest. Second, there are reasons to believe that, despite their minor status, many adolescents in this situation are in fact capable of making autonomous choices with respect to their welfare. Obviously, competency varies according to the situation and over time. Cognitive–developmental theory and research strongly suggest, however, that minors aged 14 and older are comparable to adults relative to competency. Weithhorn summarizes, "[i]n general . . . we might conclude that minors age 14 and older should be considered by professionals to be as competent as adults to make decisions about their own welfare."[73] Moreover, the data are particularly compelling when one considers that our legal and ethical assumptions about adult decision-making may not conform to what actually occurs in practice.[74] Competency, however, is just one of the conditions necessary to make legally valid choices. There is reason to believe that minors are more susceptible than adults to persuasion and inducements with respect to the choices that they make.[75] There is support for the view that this susceptibility is influenced by the social environment,[76] though data on the developmental aspects of voluntariness are scant. While the problem of voluntariness is worrisome, it does not invalidate the position that adolescents should have ultimate responsibility for making reproductive choices. It does suggest, however, that differences among adolescents and the nature and characteristics of the choice at issue should be considered in the counseling context.

Although the implementation of specific reproductive choices may involve medical interventions and medical professionals, reproductive decisions at their core are not "medical" ones. These decisions are essentially personal and are influenced by subjective values and experiences. They also "occur within a complex interaction of socioeconomic, ideological, and family influences, which can vary considerably across class, racial, ethnic, and cultural boundaries."[77] Thus, childbearing means different things to different people and at different times in their lives. What is in a person's best interests is indeterminate and highly speculative. Moreover, although reproductive decisions are intensely personal, they are not necessarily arrived at in self-interested isolation from others, particularly if the desire is to have, rather than not have, a child. Partners and spouses are often involved, and the decision to bear a child leads to the establishment of a new relationship.

In the HIV/AIDS context, these primarily personal and private decisions take on additional dimensions. The various relationships that infected persons have with others also take on new significance. At some point, an infected person will need to be cared for and supported psychologically and economically. These functions are typically carried out by family members. Any offspring also will need to be provided for in view of the expected premature death of the mother. Such support is of critical importance if the child also is infected with HIV/AIDS. In most cases, these functions will be borne by family members or significant others. Importantly, family members may not necessarily perceive these responsibilities as burdensome. For example, in light of the likely premature death of a child, a parent might affirmatively desire the birth of a grandchild. In view of the nature and meaning of a reproductive decision, it can be argued that the adolescent's reproductive choices should be made jointly with those most profoundly affected by the adolescent's decision. In such circumstances, the possibility of influence or persuasion is of less concern.

Ultimately, however, the legal allocation of decision-making authority is less important than the process by which the decision is made. Within existing legal and policy frameworks, there is enormous flexibility in structuring the actual participation of others in the decision-making process. There are minimally two important goals that any process should attempt to achieve. First, the process should promote reasoned and reflective reproductive decisions by adolescents. Second, to the extent that there is likely to be ongoing collaboration, the process should facilitate the establishment and maintenance of a close, caring, and trusting relationship between the health-care provider or counselor and the adolescent.

The ideal process for reproductive decision-making by an adolescent would involve participation by parents or other significant adults in that adolescent's life. There are advantages to such participation. First, participation would be in accord with traditional views of parental roles as guiding and supporting the adolescent. Involvement would promote family harmony. It would also foster mutual respect between parent and adolescent, which will be important in any ongoing relationship with a person infected with HIV/AIDS.

The role of the clinician or counselor would be to facilitate this involvement. This can be done by providing pertinent information, such as medical data, and by assisting all parties to understand the full implications of childbearing. To the extent the adolescent's choice is influenced by others, such influence should come from parents or other significant adults, who are more likely to appreciate the values and circumstances of the adolescent's life.

Two possible exceptions might lead to decision-making without adult involvement. The adolescent could refuse to involve parents or others in the decision-making process. Where the adolescent is competent, the adolescent should be treated the same as an adult woman permitted to make reproductive choices. Where the adolescent is not competent, the health-care provider should take whatever steps are taken with incompetent adults. An option to include parents or significant others at the discretion of the clinician and over the adolescent's objection should be considered. This option has the advantage of providing assistance and support for the adolescent who may be in need of it but is too immature to appreciate that fact. It has the disadvantage of possibly generating the adolescent's hostility and jeopardizing ongoing collaboration. As a consequence, it should be used sparingly. When used, the adolescent should have the opportunity to suggest adults other than parents to involve. Another exception is where the involvement of parents or other adults proves to be unproductive. In such circumstances, if there is an ongoing and trusting collaboration between provider and patient, it is possible that the provider assumes the role of a significant adult. If this happens, it would be appropriate for the provider to try to influence the adolescent's choice through reasoned argument and honest and empathetic counseling.

It should be noted that the ideal model is equally appropriate for adults. The nature of the reproductive decision does not change. Others are always implicated. Moreover, adult females with HIV/AIDS are not significantly different from their adolescent counterparts. Although they are presumed to be capable of making reproductive decisions for themselves, the impact of illness, prior drug use, or other stress-related factors may impair their capacity. Many are also psychologically and financially dependent on others.

In short, the model for interaction between provider and patient should be essentially the same for adults and adolescents. The clinical encounter is an appropriate point in which to assist both adults and adolescents to make reasoned, reflective, and responsible reproductive decisions.

Notes

1. C. Levine, "AIDS and Changing Concepts of Family," *Milbank Quarterly* 68 (1990): 33–58.
2. J. Arras, "AIDS and Reproductive Decisions: Having Children in Fear and Trembling," *Milbank Quarterly* 68 (1990): 353–382.
3. National Commission on AIDS, "AIDS: An Expanding Tragedy," *The Final Report of the National Commission on AIDS* (Washington DC: National Commission on

AIDS, 1993); United Nations Development Programme, "Young Women: Silence, Susceptibility and the HIV Epidemic," (New York: United Nations Development Programme, 1993); S. W. Henggeler, G. B. Melton, and J. R. Rodrigue, *Pediatric and Adolescent AIDS* (Newbury Park: Sage Publications, 1992); K. Hein "Adolescents at Risk for HIV Infection," in *Adolescents and AIDS: A Generation in Jeopardy*, ed. R. J. DiClemente (Newbury Park, CA: Sage Publications, 1992), 3–16; K. Hein, "AIDS in Adolescents: A Rationale for Concern," *New York State Journal of Medicine* 87 (1987): 290–295; U.S. Congress, "A Generation in Jeopardy: Children and AIDS," *A Report of the U.S. House of Representatives, Select Committee on Children, Youth and Families*, (Washington, DC, 1987).

4. Centers for Disease Control, *Facts about Adolescents and HIV/AIDS* (Atlanta, GA: CDC, 1993).
5. Centers for Disease Control, "Update: Acquired Immunodeficiency Syndrome—United States," *Morbidity and Mortality Weekly Report* 42 (1993): 547–557.
6. Centers for Disease Control, *HIV/AIDS Surveillance Report*, 6 (1994): 12.
7. R. M. Selik, S. Y. Chi, and J. Buehler, "HIV Infection as Leading Cause of Death Among Young Adults in U.S. Cities and States," *Journal of the American Medical Association*, 269 (1993): 2991–3001.
8. Centers for Disease Control, *Facts About Adolescents*.
9. National Commission on AIDS, *Preventing HIV/AIDS in Adolescents* (Washington, DC: National Commission on AIDS, 1993).
10. United Nations Development Programme, "Young Women"; M. E. Guinan, "Commentary: HIV, Heterosexual Transmission, and Women," *Journal of the American Medical Association*, 268 (1992): 520–523.
11. Centers for Disease Control, *HIV/AIDS Surveillance Report*, 6 (1994): 1–33, 8.
12. Ibid.
13. D. S. Burke, J. F. Brundage, M. Goldenbaum, et al., "Human Immunodeficiency Virus Infections in Teenagers: Seroprevalence among Applicants for U.S. Military Service," *Journal of the American Medical Association* 263 (1990): 2074–2077.
14. M. E. St. Louis, G. A. Conway, C. R. Hayman, et al., "Human Immunodeficiency Virus Infection in Disadvantaged Adolescents: Findings from the U.S. Job Corps," *Journal of the American Medical Association* 266 (1991): 2387–2391.
15. D. A. Wendell, I. M. Onorato, E. McCray, et al., "Youth at Risk: Sex, Drugs, and Human Immunodeficiency Virus," *American Journal of Disease of Children* 146 (1992): 76–81.
16. Centers for Disease Control, *HIV/AIDS Surveillance Report*, (Atlanta, GA: CDC, 6 (1994): 1–33, 8.
17. K. Hein, "Adolescents at Risk," 3–16.
18. United Nations Development Programme, "Young Women."
19. T. V. Ellerbrock, T. J. Bush, M. E. Chamberland, et al., "Epidemiology of Women with AIDS in the United States, 1981 through 1990: A Comparison with Heterosexual Men with AIDS," *Journal of the American Medical Association* 265 (1991): 2971–2975.
20. Wendell et al., "Youth at Risk," 76 at 80; Burke et al., "Human Immunodeficiency Virus," 2074 at 2077.
21. G. A. Gellert, M. J. Durfee, C. D. Berkowitz, et al., "Situational and Sociodemographic Characteristics of Children Infected with Human Immunodeficiency Virus from Pediatric Sex Abuse," *Pediatrics* 91 (1993): 9–44.
22. S. Zierler, L. Feingold, D. Laufer, et al., "Adult Survivors of Childhood Sexual

Abuse and Subsequent Risk of HIV Infection," *American Journal of Public Health* 81 (1992): 572–575.
23. Alan Guttmacher Institute, *Sex and America's Teenagers*, (New York: Alan Guttmacher Institute, 1994).
24. National Commission on AIDS, "AIDS: An Expanding Tragedy."
25. Alan Guttmacher Institute, *Sex and America's Teenagers*.
26. I. De Vincenzi (for the European Study Group on Heterosexual Transmission of HIV), "A Longitudinal Study of Human Immunodeficiency Virus Transmission by Heterosexual Partners," *New England Journal of Medicine* 331 (1994): 341–346.
27. Alan Guttmacher Institute, *Sex and America's Teenagers*.
28. Ibid.
29. Centers for Disease Control, "Sexual Behavior among High School Students—United States, 1990," *Morbidity and Mortality Weekly Report* 40 (1992): 885.
30. Alan Guttmacher Institute, *Sex and America's Teenagers*.
31. Centers for Disease Control, "Sexual Behavior among High School Students," 885.
32. National Commission on AIDS, *Preventing HIV/AIDS in Adolescents*.
33. Ibid.
34. F. Zimring, *The Changing Legal World of Adolescence* (New York: Free Press, 1982).
35. D. L. Rhode and A. Lawson, eds., "Introduction," in *The Politics of Pregnancy: Adolescent Sexuality and Public Policy* (New Haven, CT: Yale University Press, 1993) 2.
36. *Prince v. Massachusetts*, 321 U.S. 158 (1944).
37. R. H. Mnookin and D. K. Weisberg, *Child, Family and States*, 2nd ed. (Boston: Little, Brown and Company, 1989): 458.
38. National Research Council, *The Social Impact of AIDS in the United States*, eds. A. R. Jonsen and J. Stryker (Washington, DC: National Academy Press, 1993): 202.
39. A. M. Brandt, *No Magic Bullet: A Social History of Venereal Disease in the United States Since 1880* (New York: Oxford University Press, 1987).
40. N. Astone, "Thinking about Teenage Childbearing," *Philosophy and Public Policy* 13 (1993): 8–13.
41. *Alfonso v. Fernandez*, 606 N.Y.S.2d 259 (1993).
42. H. G. Miller, C. F. Turner, and L. E. Moses, *AIDS: The Second Decade* (Washington, DC: National Academy Press, 1990): 14.
43. D. M. Pearce, "Children Having Children: Teenage Pregnancy and Public Policy from the Women's Perspective," in *The Politics of Pregnancy: Adolescent Sexuality and Public Policy*, eds. A. Lawson and D. L. Rhode (New Haven, CT: Yale University Press): 46–58.
44. National Research Council, *Risking the Future: Adolescent Sexuality, Pregnancy, and Childbearing*, ed. C. D. Hayes (Washington, DC: National Academy Press, 1987): 19.
45. E. Connor, R. S. Sperling, R. Gelber, et al., "Reduction of Maternal–Infant Transmission of Human Immunodeficiency Virus Type 1 with Zidovudine Treatment," *New England Journal of Medicine* 331 (1994): 1174–1180.
46. National Research Council, *AIDS: Sexual Behavior and Intravenous Drug Abuse*, eds. C. F. Turner, H. G. Miller, and L. E. Moses (Washington, DC: National Academy Press, 1989): 260.
47. Rhode and Lawson, *The Politics of Pregnancy*, 316–318.

48. National Research Council, *Losing Generations: Adolescents in High Risk Settings* (Washington, DC: National Academy Press, 1993).
49. *Carey v. Population Services International*, 431 U.S. 678 (1977).
50. *Planned Parenthood of Central Missouri v. Danforth*, 428 U.S. 52 (1976); *Carey v. Population Services International*; *Bellotti v. Baird*, 332 U.S. 622 (1979).
51. The two decisions are *State of N.Y. v. Heckler*, 719 F.2d 1191 (1983) and *Planned Parenthood Federation of America v. Heckler*, 712 F.2d 1196 (1983). The courts concluded that the requirements were inconsistent with Congress' intention to make family planning services available to adolescents. Neither decision reached the issue of whether a notification or consent requirement violated a minor's constitutional rights.
52. Mnookin and Weisberg, *Child, Family and States*, 456–467.
53. I. Ellman, P. Kurtz, and K. Bartlett, *Family Law*, 2nd ed. (Charlottesville, VA: The Michie Company, 1991): 1109.
54. *Planned Parenthood v. Ashcroft*, 462 U.S. 476 (1983); *Hodgson v. Minnesota*, 110 S. Ct. 2926 (1990).
55. Rhode and Lawson, *The Politics of Pregnancy*, 12, 318–321.
56. R. L. North, "Legal Authority for HIV Testing of Adolescents," *Journal of Adolescent Health Care* 11 (1990): 176–187.
57. P. Budetti and C. Feinson, "Ensuring Adequate Health Care Benefits for Children and Adolescents," *The Future of Children: Health Care Reform* 3 (1993): 37–59.
58. Mnookin and Weisberg, *Child, Family and State*, 467–468.
59. National Research Council, *Losing Generations*, 85.
60. A. English, "Expanding Access to HIV Services for Adolescents: Legal and Ethical Issues," in *Adolescents and AIDS: A Generation in Jeopardy*, ed. R. J. DiClemente (Newbury Park, CA: Sage, 1992): 279.
61. Miller et al., *AIDS: The Second Decade* 112–117.
62. Alan Guttmacher Institute, *Sex and America's Teenagers*, 19–29.
63. National Research Council, *The Social Impact*, 124–129.
64. M. C. Simms, "Adolescent Pregnancy among Blacks in the United States: Why Is It a Policy Issue?" in *The Politics of Pregnancy: Adolescent Sexuality and Public Policy*, eds. A. Lawson and D. L. Rhode (New Haven, CT: Yale University Press, 1993): 241–256.
65. A. Phoenix, "The Social Construction of Teenage Motherhood: A Black and White Issue?" in *The Politics of Pregnancy: Adolescent Sexuality and Public Policy*, eds. A. Lawson and D. L. Rhode (New Haven, CT: Yale University Press, 1993): 86–93.
66. National Research Council, *AIDS: Sexual Behavior and Intravenous Drug Abuse*, 390–399.
67. Connor et al., "Reduction of Maternal–Infant Transmission."
68. National Research Council, *The Social Impact*, 211.
69. F. Zimring, *The Changing Legal World*, 82.
70. Rhode and Lawson, *The Politics of Pregnancy*, 321.
71. Ibid., 1–19.
72. N. E. Adler and J. M. Tschann, "Conscious and Preconscious Motivation for Pregnancy among Female Adolescents," in *The Politics of Pregnancy: Adolescent Sexuality and Public Policy*, eds. A. Lawson and D. L. Rhode (New Haven, CT: Yale University Press, 1993): 144; C. Levine and N. N. Dubler, "Uncertain Risks

and Bitter Realities: The Reproductive Choices of HIV-Infected Women," *Milbank Quarterly* 68 (1990): 321–352.
73. L. A. Weithorn, "Involving Children in Decisions Affecting their own Welfare: Guidelines for Professionals," in *Children's Competence to Consent*, eds. G. Melton, G. Koocher, and M. Saks (New York: Plenum Press, 1983): 246.
74. C. H. Fellner and J. R. Marshall, "Kidney Donors—the Myth of Informed Consent," *American Journal of Psychiatry* (1970): 1245–1251.
75. D. Scherer and N. Reppucci, "Adolescents' Capacity to Provide Voluntary Informed Consent," *Law and Human Behavior*, 12 (1988); T. Grisso and L. Vierling, "Minors' Consent to Treatment: A Developmental Perspective," *Professional Psychiatry* 9 (1978): 412–427.
76. A. Meisel, L. H. Roth, and C. W. Lidz, "Toward a Model of the Legal Doctrine of Informed Consent," *American Journal of Psychiatry* (1977): 285–289.
77. Rhode and Lawson, *The Politics of Pregnancy*, 7.

14

Moral Multiculturalism, Childbearing, and AIDS

ANITA ALLEN

> People treat us like we're shit, like we're not human. You know? At least when we have our babies, we know that they love us, they need us. And no matter what, they will not turn away from us. You know, we need that. We need that. We need that love, you know.
>
> *woman from New York*

In 1995, the World Health Organization estimated that 16 million people around the world were infected with AIDS. Of these, 7–8 million were women of childbearing age and 1 million were infants who contracted AIDS from their mothers. In the United States, it is reported that most of the 6,000 HIV-infected infants born each year are born to urban African-American and Hispanic women. Many mothers of infected infants acknowledge that they or their sexual partners have injected illegal drugs.[1]

Public health education aimed at injection drug users (IDUs) and women of childbearing age has not reduced the incidence of pediatric AIDS attributable to perinatal transmission. Despite the volume of government and private research, no cure or vaccine for AIDS is on the immediate horizon. A study sponsored by the National Institute of Allergy and Infectious Diseases (ACTG-076) links the drug zidovudine (AZT) to a dramatic two-thirds reduction in the risk of perinatal HIV transmission among the women enrolled, when administered during pregnancy.[2] Unfortunately, at about $50 per week, AZT is a prohibitively expensive drug, the use of which by the poor is not publicly subsidized in some states. In addition, although the initial results are positive, researchers have not ruled out the possibility that children who had been exposed to AZT in utero could experience adverse side effects. Moreover, it has not been determined whether equally dramatic results would be achieved in all populations of HIV-infected women, given the strict entry criteria for ACTG-076. Nor have researchers determined pregnant women's willingness to test for HIV infection and to elect AZT, were it readily available and proven reasonably safe. For now, the ultimate impact of AZT-based therapies on pediatric AIDS is uncertain. Authorities expect the annual percentage of infants born with HIV infection to remain significantly high.

The pregnancies of women with HIV infection are usually unplanned.[3] However, some women who know that they are HIV-infected become pregnant deliberately:

> We wanted a baby. My husband . . . knows he's positive. I know I'm positive. . . . He wanted a baby, and I wanted a baby. We both wanted a baby. . . . I got pregnant when I knew I was positive.[4]

Whether a pregnancy is planned or unplanned, the result will be the same: a full 20%–30% of the babies born to HIV-infected mothers not receiving AZT during pregnancy will develop AIDS and die as infants or children.

Maternally transmitted pediatric AIDS has spawned the moral question of whether HIV-infected women ought to give birth to children. Ordinarily, the life a mother gives to her child is called a "gift." Under the extraordinary circumstances of AIDS, the life a mother gives to her child often is described as a "harm." Childbearing by HIV-infected women thus implicates widely accepted moral principles proscribing avoidable harm or risk of harm to others.[5] If childbearing is immoral because of the harm it allegedly causes, then the risk of having a child who may develop AIDS turns celibacy, contraception, sterilization, or abortion into moral imperatives.

Maternally transmitted pediatric AIDS has spawned another moral question: whether members of society ought to stand in judgment of HIV-infected women who become pregnant and give birth. A morally grounded refusal to stand in judgment has been among the societal responses to HIV-infected childbearers. In fact, some people adopt with respect to HIV-infected childbearers the same stance one HIV-infected woman adopts with respect to IDUs who bear children: "I can't pass judgment because you have to walk in somebody's shoes to understand."[6]

To "walk in someone else's shoes" is to see the world from her vantage point, from her perspective. Ideally, with a willingness to learn and to care, anyone would be able to see the world as others see it. Yet, seeing the world from others' perspectives may require more than a sympathetic outlook and knowledge of, for example, others' personal, economic, or cultural characteristics. It may require substantial similarity of social characteristics and/or experiences. Conceivably, only IDUs can really learn to see the world as other IDUs see it; conceivably, only poor women of color with HIV infection can really learn to see the world as other poor women of color with HIV infection see it. Walking in someone else's shoes is a powerful precondition of accurate moral judgment, which, if embraced, would threaten to disqualify most middle-class moralists from passing judgment on HIV-infected women. Moreover, taken seriously as a precondition of sound moral judgment, walking in someone else's shoes appears to contradict aspects of the influential modern Western philosophical tradition that I will call "moral universalism."

Moral universalism includes the epistemological thesis that virtually any rational adult is competent to know moral truth and make accurate moral judgments. It also includes the normative thesis that persons can and should be judged on the basis of universally applicable or objective standards of conduct. Moral universalism implies that sound moral judgments do not typically require similar social characteristics or life experiences. It also implies that people from different social groups are, by and large, subject to identical standards of conduct. The idea that you have to walk in someone else's shoes before you can know how to judge them is thus seemingly at odds with moral universalism's emphasis on the equal moral competence of typical adult members of the human community.

Indeed, moralists who embrace moral universalism rarely identify walking in someone else's shoes as a condition of moral judgment. Nevertheless, the need to walk in someone else's shoes to warrant judging them is a prominent theme in moral theories that take a skeptical attitude about both the ability of one person to judge another accurately and the existence of universally applicable or objective standards of conduct.

Moral multiculturalism refers to the currently popular perspective that culturally divergent groups may have divergent moral perspectives, divergent capacities of moral judgment, and divergent obligations.[7] Although culture is a complex and ambiguous concept, contemporary moral multiculturalists include race, ethnicity, gender, religion, and even sexual orientation among the salient markers of cultural difference. Like moral universalism, moral multiculturalism combines epistemological and normative claims. Moral multiculturalism's epistemological claim is that social characteristics and life experiences profoundly limit the capacity of members of one group to acquire moral knowledge and make right judgments concerning members of other groups. Moral multiculturalism doubts that outsiders to a social group have the epistemological access to the world of insiders necessary to make accurate moral judgments. On the basis of that doubt, moral multiculturalism discourages and disparages outsider judgment of insiders. The normative claim of multiculturalism is that if people are to be judged, they should be judged in accordance with group-relative standards of conduct that reflect their group's own values.

Some moral multiculturalists are relativists who do not categorically deny the existence of objective moral values. Rather, they say that what objectively is right for a person depends upon, or is relative to, the values of that person's group, which may be poorly understood by members of different cultural groups. However, other moral multiculturalists categorically reject objectivism. These antiobjectivists view allegedly objective moral values as contingent ideologies that often serve the needs and interests of dominant cultural groups at the expense of subordinate ones. Predictably, say the antiobjectivists, appeal to a dominant group's morality will lead to the classification of the nonconforming behavior of subordinate groups as problematic and immoral.

Moral theories seldom are explicit in public discussion. However, public responses to maternally transmitted pediatric AIDS clearly reflect commitments to the strikingly oppositional theoretical perspectives of moral universalism and moral multiculturalism: condemnation of women with HIV infection has tended to flow from moral universalists, while refusal to condemn has tended to flow from moral multiculturalists. As this chapter explains, some of the most frequently cited defenders of HIV-infected women choosing pregnancy and childbirth are moral multiculturalists. These defenders have strongly implied that middle-class white moralizers who condemn poor black and brown women are racially intolerant. The charge that racial prejudice pervades AIDS policy perspectives makes maternally transmitted pediatric AIDS a compelling practical context for assessing deeply opposed universalist and multicultural approaches to moral judgment.

The central goal of this chapter is to reexamine the moral claim that HIV-infected women ought to avoid reproduction in light of the prominent role that competing multicultural and universalist understandings of moral judgment play in the debates. I highlight respects in which, as applied to the morality of childbearing in the context of AIDS, both universalist and multicultural understandings of moral judgment have proven deficient.

To their credit, moral multiculturalists have properly emphasized economic class and membership in minority subcultures as "contextual" factors capable of shaping moral judgments. However, multiculturalists have overstated the inability of universalism to incorporate wide-ranging concerns about "context." In addition, moral multiculturalists sometimes presuppose far more distinctive perspectives on childbearing among women of color than the evidence supports.

Moral universalists have been appropriately cautious about assuming disparate perspectives on metaphysics, morals, or motherhood. However, universalists have not always considered the possibility that their ascriptions of moral blame are products of limited knowledge, limited sympathies for the poor, or unconscious political biases against particular minority groups and women. In addition, the universalists have not focused closely on the relevance to judgment of the broader social context of reproductive decision-making that poor black and brown women share with other women—namely, a society that encourages motherhood by strongly endorsing heterosexual intercourse, pregnancy, childbirth, and childrearing as defining experiences for women.

Indeed, in light of what our society teaches about needs and responsibilities, moral universalists and moral multiculturalists should concur in the judgment that the decisions of HIV-infected women to have children are not blameworthy. An individual is not blameworthy for acting or making decisions against a background of reasonably required and sincerely held beliefs, though morally blameless conduct nonetheless may impose social costs that make it undesirable. However, HIV-infected women should not be singled out for censure or restraint because of the social costs they impose unless society is prepared to respond in the same way to analogously costly reproductive decisions, such as decisions to give birth to children with permanent mental and physical disabilities.

In the first part of the chapter, I describe moral judgment as a complex social practice with "lay" and "professional" practitioners and with universalist and multicultural variants. I suggest that the bioethical literature on maternally transmitted HIV includes perspectives by universalists who do not take prejudice or differences of race, ethnicity, class, and gender into account to the extent that their critics urge and their own theories allow.

In the second part of the chapter, I present an overview and analysis of interviews with HIV-infected women conducted by Johns Hopkins University researchers. My analysis points to the difficulty moral multiculturalists face in supporting their empirical claims that poor women of color have distinctive moral perspectives. The interview data arguably suggest that poor women of color with HIV infection share key perspectives on childbearing with other groups. If moral multiculturalists cannot show distinctive moral perspectives among poor women of color, they lack one possible foundation for opposing cross-group moral judgment.

Finally, in the third part of the chapter, I call for reasoning with *and* judging American women with HIV infection on the basis of their participation in an ethnically and racially diverse common moral community. To see childbearing in the context of AIDS as morally justifiable, as I urge we should, it is not necessary to disavow traditional values proscribing avoidable harm or to avow impenetrable barriers of race, ethnicity, religion, class, and gender. We need only bring some of the salient features of the social world into sharper relief.

Universalism and Multiculturalism in Moral Judgment

AIDS emerged as a public health concern in the United States at a time when the virtually ubiquitous social practice of moral judgment had both "lay" and well-developed "professional" faces. Ordinary lay moral judgment is the dimension of moral practice through which we express our basic values in informal settings outside of our professional roles. We judge conduct, character, and institutions. We say that this or that person's conduct is right or wrong, good or bad. We ascribe virtues, like honesty, loyalty, and responsibility. We praise governments for justice and condemn them for injustice. It seems that even those of us who do not view ourselves as moralizers or moralistic make moral judgments framed around our secular or religious values all the time.

Moral finger-pointing was among the first reactions of the American public to the announcement of the AIDS epidemic.[8] In this instance, the routine lay expression of secular and religious values commonly took the form of condemnatory moral judgment. HIV-infected individuals, their families, and their friends regarded moralism as a poor substitute for medicine. "Blaming the victim" was perceived as cruelly slowing the delivery of health care and social services to persons debilitated by the virus. At the same time that some segments of the public, perhaps a majority, worried that pregnant women with HIV infection would harm their children, others worried that society's moralism about AIDS would harm pregnant women.

Some Americans have depicted AIDS as God's punishment for degraded conduct by immoral people. Although AIDS does occur in men and women who engage in commonplace but disapproved practices, such as homosexuality, bisexuality, injection drug use, and prostitution, AIDS also occurs among many who do not engage in these practices. Victims have been blamed for their disease on the mistaken belief that AIDS is contracted only by "bad" people who knowingly flout the moral ideals of society.

The finger-pointing observed in the earliest years of the AIDS epidemic may have contributed to the stigmatization of individuals who developed HIV infection or AIDS through heterosexual, marital, maternal, and professional relationships. If hemophiliacs and dental patients sometimes escape guilt by association, poor, urban, black and brown mothers with infected newborns seldom do. Of course, even apart from AIDS, there is reason for concern about our ordinary moral judgments relating to the conduct of women, women of color, and mothers.[9] Black and Hispanic women were once widely stereotyped as promiscuous, hyperfertile, irresponsible, and unhygienic.[10] A residue of negative stereotypes may foster the conclusion that maternal immorality is the chief cause of pediatric AIDS. Minority groups stereotype their own members as immoral by virtue of AIDS, and even the medical profession can make a woman with AIDS feel "dirty" like a "slut."[11]

Professional moral judgment

"Professional" moral judgment is careful, often theoretically grounded, moral assessment by experts. Academic philosophers, theologians, physicians, and institutional policy analysts join bioethicists in the practice of expert judgment. Bioethics is a joint product of the pervasiveness of ordinary lay moral judgment and the desire of a self-critical, liberal society for a cadre of experts skilled at moral analysis related to medicine, public health, and the life sciences. Although many bioethicists have distinct loyalties to organized religion, bioethics came to the forefront in the 1970s in response to liberal pluralists' demands for nonpartisan secular ethical expertise.

The field of bioethics has descriptive and normative aspects. In its descriptive aspect, bioethics seeks to identify, analyze, and illuminate the values that inform human understanding. In its normative aspect, bioethics advances judgments about moral right and wrong and about professional ethics. With respect to AIDS, bioethicists and other public health policy analysts have offered normative

The moral critique of childbearing by HIV-infected women

In the professional bioethics and public health policy fields, moral critics opposed to childbearing by HIV-infected women offer what has become a familiar set of arguments. Lay moralists have made these arguments too. First and foremost, the moral critics argue that once HIV-infected women know the risk of perinatal transmission, they ought never to give birth. Moral critics see malfeasance in the creation of a child whose life one knows may be tragically short because of AIDS. They also see harmful immorality in the creation of a well child when one's own AIDS-related death or disability may prevent one from parenting. Moral critics argue, second, that the moral duty of women to protect their own health countermands childbearing. Pregnancy is stressful, and some studies suggest that it may hasten the onset of full-blown AIDS. A third and final argument links the moral duties ascribed to HIV-infected women to a thesis about the ethical duties of the health-care providers who serve them: because it is morally obligatory for women who are HIV-infected to refrain from harming themselves and their offspring, it is ethical, perhaps even obligatory, for health professionals to counsel them against maternity.

Why do professional moralists judge? The reasons are not so different from the reasons that lay moralists judge. Professional and lay moral judgments are not always for the sake of judgment alone. One practical goal of moral judgment is deterrence. Ascribing praise and blame potentially deters individuals responsive to the force of moral reasoning or sanctions from engaging in presumably harmful and offensive conduct. Thus, if the moral argument against childbearing by HIV-infected women were to reach and persuade those women, it might encourage voluntary sexual abstinence, birth control, and abortion, resulting in a reduction of the incidence of perinatal transmission. Knowing that transmission may occur can be expected to have behavioral implications for at least some infected women:

> I just can't see bringing a baby (into the world). . . . (A)nd as much as I('d) love a baby, if I got pregnant I would have to have an abortion. . . . I think it's cruel to subject them to a little bit of life. . . . I just don't think it's right.[12]

A second goal of moral judgment is influencing public policy. Ascribing praise and blame may lead lawmakers and other policymakers to reshape positive law and institutional practices. Policymakers morally opposed to childbearing in the context of AIDS could create incentives for morally preferable behavior. In the extreme, moral arguments could serve as part of the public policymaker's case for laws mandating criminal punishment, tort liability, loss of public benefits, directive counseling, abortion, or sterilization.

Very often, professional and lay judgments seem to presuppose what I have called moral universalism: the claim that moral judgments are true or false by virtue of conformity to universally applicable or objective values which ordinary individuals or experts are generally in a position to discover. As noted in the introduction to this chapter, when professional and lay moralists have condemned childbearing by HIV-infected women, their judgments have often had a distinctly universalist tone. Although many moral philosophers reject the relativism and antiobjectivism of moral multiculturalism in favor of moral universalism, "a tide of skepticism concerning the possibility of universally valid claims in ethics" prevails.[13] Adopting the moral multiculturalist perspective, a number of social scientists and humanists have been critical of universalism among lay and professional moralists who condemn HIV-infected women for bearing children.

Multiculturalism and the suspicion of judgment

In the 1980s, contemporaneous to the identification of AIDS, a multicultural movement began to take hold, particularly in education and the humanities.[14] Multiculturalism affirms and celebrates pluralism and the many differences that shape Americans' identities. Differences linked to race, ethnicity, religion, group history, sexual orientation, and regional heritage are among the identity-creating differences that multiculturalism asserts. The multicultural movement highlights inclusion of the perspectives and experiences of women and traditionally subordinated minority groups.

Multiculturalism is not a precise creed. However, in typical manifestations it suggests a distinct understanding of morality, here dubbed relativist (or "soft") and antiobjectivist (or "hard") moral multiculturalism. Both soft and hard moral multiculturalism offer a certain complex of cultural differences—chiefly, race, class, religion, sexual orientation, and gender—as a basis for positing divergent moral values and moral judgments. Both soft and hard moral multiculturalism recognize that some moral values may be held in common by divergent, and even antagonistic, cultures. Still, difference rather than similarity is the theme of the multiculturalists. Soft moral multiculturalism is highly skeptical of claims that particular moral values—especially the values of socially and economically dominant groups—have universal, as opposed to culturally relative, application. Hard moral multiculturalism pushes skepticism to the limit, rejecting outright the idea of objective values, whether of universal or culturally indexed application.

Although moral multiculturalism is new in terms of its emphasis on including the perspectives and experiences of women and traditionally subordinated minority groups, it is old when viewed as a repackaging of relativist theories advanced in some ancient Greek philosophy. Moral multiculturalism incorporates aspects of what philosophers refer to as "subjectivism," "cultural relativism," and "ethical relativism." *Subjectivism* views knowledge, perception, and judgment as constrained and shaped by a person's own mind as much as, or more than, by an external world of metaphysical or moral reality. *Cultural relativism* maintains that a person's moral values are the contingent result of that person's cultural background and experiences. *Ethical relativism* maintains that the truth, validity, or legitimacy of a person's moral judgments can be assessed only in reference to that person's own moral values, which are unique.

Moral multiculturalism also is old when viewed as a postmodern resuscitation of the Enlightenment tradition of liberal toleration. The liberal principle of tolerance holds that each person is entitled to live freely, in accordance with his or her own values, subject only to an obligation to refrain from harming others. Moral multiculturalism urges tolerance as the just political response to the values of traditionally excluded, disadvantaged, or subordinated people.

Moral multiculturalism encourages a general suspicion of cross-cultural moral judgments and the people who make them. In particular, moral multiculturalism cautions that when members of traditionally dominant social groups judge members of traditionally subordinate ones, they may judge wrongly in reliance on inapplicable outsider perspectives and values, but moral multiculturalism is not unique in its suspicion of normative judgment. Even apart from moral multiculturalism, the practice of moral judgment has come to have negative moral connotations. A general suspicion of moral judgment is afoot, of which moral multiculturalism is but one variety. What the British philosopher Mary Midgley astutely explains about her society also applies to ours: for some in society the expression "moral judgment" connotes unfavorable, uncharitable criticism that "moralistic" and "judgmental" people inflict on others from the detached, unsympathetic perspective of a superior or outsider.[15]

Moral multiculturalists and other moral skeptics have come to the defense of people with HIV infection and AIDS. Leading defenses of men and, especially, women with AIDS and HIV infection repeat moral multiculturalism's call for restraint in judgment and toleration of moral differences. They suggest that HIV-infected African-American and Hispanic women have cultural values about childbearing that justify their seemingly cruel decisions to risk pregnancy and bear children. Defenders of the HIV-infected women who choose to give birth despite the risk of transmission to their offspring contest the epistemological competence and the moral right of white, middle-class, or other mainstream moral critics to judge the reproductive choices of culturally diverse blacks, Hispanics, drug users, prostitutes, and poor people.

The temporal coincidence of the AIDS epidemic, moral multiculturalism, and the general suspicion of judgment may have insulated people with AIDS and HIV infection from the full heat of moral condemnation; but just as moral multiculturalism was on the ascendancy in the first decade of the AIDS epidemic, so too was the power and influence of the religious and political right. In the 1980s, people with AIDS were widely condemned as immoral by strong-minded universalists who believed they had a right and a duty to condemn. Although somewhat abated, such condemnations continue to be made.

Judgment in context

Moral criticism of women with AIDS and HIV infection strikes a raw nerve with some, especially some moral multiculturalists. At the same time, refusal to criticize women with AIDS and HIV infection is problematic for others, especially some moral universalists. Blanket refusal to criticize seems to understate the role that individuals can play in preventing the spread of AIDS. It also seems to imply that women with AIDS and HIV infection are not accountable as responsible moral agents.

The starting points of my response to moral criticism of women with HIV infection are the following assumptions. As a range of moralists—universalists and multiculturalists included—could agree, in light of the prejudice and ignorance that influences public reaction, condemnatory moral judgments about women with AIDS merit special scrutiny. Moreover, as moralists of varied stripes could also surely agree, neither lay nor professional condemnation of HIV-infected women is sound if it fails to meet the precondition that judgment about threats to public health be unbiased, factual, and contextually well informed.

With these assumptions in mind, there is reason to reexamine the conclusion reached by many observers that HIV-infected women should eschew childbearing to avoid harm to children. A chief reason for reexamination is the need to take seriously a charge that I believe could be, and arguably should be, made by both universalists and moral multiculturalists: that in framing the duties of infected women, typical moral critics pay inadequate attention to both their own social and cultural settings and those of infected women.

An obvious category of contextually relevant fact has been underemphasized by moral critics: the predicament of HIV-infected, minority group childbearers, as women in a maternalist society, being suddenly "disqualified" from maternal roles by the results of a blood test. Maternalism, as intended here, refers to the disposition to value being, becoming, or having been a mother. The maternalist is not neutral about, or tolerant of, mothering. She views the opportunity to mother as something for which she would make important sacrifices. The maternalist even may view motherhood as a moral obligation for herself or other women.

Maternalism pervades our culture.[16] It is reflected in the choices of poor pregnant teenagers and equally in the choices of the affluent women over 40 who invest in expensive infertility treatments. Upon reflection, it should not be surprising that women with AIDS and HIV infection continue to become pregnant and have children. A full account of the social and cultural settings in which questions of the morality of reproduction arise would emphasize society's maternalism as a powerful definer of the identities and roles of women.

Inadequate contextualization

Critics of John D. Arras's universalist-style assessment of the morality of reproduction in the context of AIDS have alleged cultural bias and inadequate contextualization.[17] The allegations are striking since Arras expressly calls for a sensitive and contextual balancing of morally relevant factors. Moreover, he concludes that blanket moral conclusions cannot be drawn about the choices of HIV-infected women as a class and that public and private policymakers, therefore, should refrain from categorically advising or requiring abstinence, contraception, birth control, and sterilization.

Arras argues that "contextualized assessment of several morally relevant variables might nonetheless justify judgments of reproductive irresponsibility."[18] According to Arras, in the field of reproduction, elements of "any ethical assessment" concerning human reproduction include the following: (1) the ability and willingness of parents to assume their proper responsibility for the child, (2) the magnitude of the threatened harm, (3) the probability of harm actually occurring, and (4) the weight of the burden that parents must assume in order to avert the threatened harm.[19]

For Arras, analysis of elements (2) and (3), the harm/probability ratio, would indicate that some women are culpable of what, in the law, is called "wrongful life." In general,

> (i)f the intentional and avoidable actions or health status of pregnant women cause predictable damage that will manifest itself in illness and disability for the children who will be born, we can legitimately criticize them for failing to respect their children's separate dignity and entitlement to protection.[20]

The strongest argument against HIV-infected women having children, Arras maintains, is the wrongful life argument that the women's choice "places future offspring at unacceptable risk of catastrophic harm"—harm so great that "no one would want to live such a life."[21] Applying his analysis, Arras concludes that a crack-addicted, homeless woman without a husband and with children already in foster care "has no business having additional children, particularly children who would be at risk for HIV infection."[22] Such a person's childbearing decisions clearly would be irresponsible, he suggests. Moreover, if a "reliable (80 to 100% accurate) prenatal test for eventual pediatric seropositivity" were to be "developed in the absence of vastly improved therapeutics for AIDS," Arras believes there would be a moral reason to go beyond "moral education" and to counsel all women with high-risk fetuses against childbirth.[23]

Based on these conclusions, one group of researchers cited Arras's analysis as an instance of

> (p)ublic discourse, reflecting middle-class values and sensibilities, (that) has focused almost exclusively on an assumed opposition between potentially infected infants and their mothers, portraying the latter as selfish drug users who lack moral scruples.[24]

Carol Levine and Nancy Dubler believe that relevant to any analysis of the morality of perinatal AIDS transmission is "the framework of values, norms, and practices encompassing women's sexual and reproductive lives—a moral universe—and the economic, cultural, and social reality from which it is derived."[25] Concluding that government and society "have no moral right to intervene" in the decision-making of HIV-infected women, Levine and Dubler have sought to refute anyone, presumably including Arras, who believes that the birth of HIV-infected babies is sometimes "inexplicable, unjustifiable, or immoral."[26]

Even if one thought Arras had reached the right conclusion about the condemnability of HIV-infected mothers, one could join these critics and quarrel with his failure to explain the full relevance or irrelevance of certain sociocultural factors. In truth, Arras does not emphasize ethnic or other cultural diversity as a source of morally relevant variables. Nor does he consider diverse perspectives on the kinds of lives that are deemed worth living. Arras shapes his argument for moral condemnation without detailed discussion of the cultural premises that may influence minority women's reproductive conduct, such as nonmainstream attitudes about sex, contraception, and abortion; nonmainstream attitudes about the meaning of illness, families, and death; and nonmainstream expectations of extended family and community assistance. Indeed, and I will return to this point, some studies indicate that the moralities of black and Hispanic women are not in every respect identical to those of middle-class whites.[27]

Arras's discussion mentions gender subordination and minority economic disadvantage. Arguably, however, he underemphasizes the moral relevance to reproductive ethics both of gender roles and of race and gender subordination. Arras subscribes to bioethics in the liberal tradition. This tradition regards autonomy—rationality and voluntarism—as a prerequisite of moral agency. One who lacks the capacity for rational judgment cannot be praised for responsibility or blamed for irresponsibility, nor can a person be praised or blamed if his or her conduct is compelled or coerced rather than free. Key, then, to the moral assessment of women with AIDS and HIV infection is the question of their procreative autonomy. Moral condemnation of women who become pregnant and give birth while HIV-infected is arguably unwarranted if they lack autonomy.

Ever since *Griswold* v. *Connecticut* and *Roe* v. *Wade* established a right of reproductive privacy, a frequent assumption has been that pregnancy and childbirth are experiences over which adult women normally have a morally significant degree of control and, thus, for which they normally have a significant degree of moral responsibility.[28] It is commonplace to regard both becoming pregnant and carrying a pregnancy to term as a matter of a woman's free, autonomous choice. Presumably capable of refusing sex, utilizing contraception, and obtaining medical abortions legally, women are viewed as having reproductive autonomy. As formulated, this assumption about autonomous choice expressly applies to adult women in normal circumstances. It assumes that very young girls lack the self-control and understanding that give rise to moral responsibility. It also assumes that forcible pregnancy is not the norm and that no one who becomes pregnant as the result of rape is responsible for her pregnancy.

Feminists have challenged the thesis of reproductive autonomy with a thesis of reproductive inequality and gender subordination.[29] They also have challenged the model of women as self-interested and unitary decision-makers.[30] In the face of women's historically subordinate social status, they deny that "autonomy" is an adequate description of women's reproductive experiences.[31] The choices of HIV-infected women to become pregnant or bear children are not fully autonomous to the extent to which women cannot refuse heterosexual intercourse, afford or comfortably use reliable birth control, or obtain abortions. Women in a socially subordinate position do not enjoy some of the highly meaningful forms of autonomy privileged men and women enjoy. For this reason, blaming poor minority women for pediatric AIDS may miss the boat.

Arras is overly attentive to factors he believes undercut autonomy and justify paternalism. His hypothetical homeless, sick, crack-addicted woman, "Joan," is scarcely an autonomous moral decision-maker as her "choice" to have the child she conceived by trading sex for drugs is "really a nonchoice." Arras wants us to think that Joan is the sort of woman for whom childbirth clearly would be immoral. However, even assuming that her choice is a "nonchoice," the point of, and justification for, moral condemnation of someone like Joan is unclear.

My criticism of Arras goes beyond concerns about female autonomy to encompass concerns about female identity. Arras is underattentive to the maternalist social construction of female roles and identities. As explained below, maternalism undercuts culpability for pregnancy and childbirth in the context of AIDS.

Is moral universalism a blinder?

Moral discourse about AIDS goes wrong when it undercontextualizes—that is, when it fails to acknowledge relevant situational variables. Undercontextualization is a weakness of Arras's analysis, though not necessarily a fatal weakness. His underrecognition of maternalism, or other situational variables, is an information deficit that conceivably could be cured by adding available information to his analytical framework and rethinking his conclusions in light of it.

One detects in the literature, however, another conception of the condemnations of HIV-infected women's reproduction. The charge of cultural bias and the consequent call for the contextualization of one's own and others' moral judgments about women with AIDS and HIV infection most typically have come from observers who are moral multiculturalists or who implicitly embrace another skeptical version of cultural and ethical relativism. For the skeptics, the universalists' assumption of a single moral standard is the cause of the undercontextualization in moral discourse concerning women with HIV infection.

Levine and Dubler react harshly to what they term the objectivist, a-contextualist assumptions of normative analysis opposing HIV-infected women's pregnancies.[32] They maintain a seemingly relativist, multiculturalist theory of moral judgment that rejects moral criticism to the extent that it is inconsistent with "the validity of different, class-based moral judgments rather than a single standard."[33] They strongly "do not agree that there is an absolute standard by which the birth of an HIV-infected baby is morally unacceptable."[34] Levine and Dubler maintain, in effect, that relativism requires that normative moral judgment of HIV-infected women be limited to their own moral framework.

Researchers also attacked moral universalism in an anthropological analysis of HIV-infected women in New York City, cited earlier.[35] This study was designed to get beyond putatively objective "middle-class values and sensibilities" that portray mothers "as selfish drug users who lack moral scruples." The effective delivery of health care requires identification of "some of the social and cultural factors that affect the reproduction decisions of poor, drug-using, HIV-infected women."[36] Typically, anthropological social science refrains from making moral judgments about insider women with HIV infection.

Relativism, and especially the moral multiculturalist version of relativism, tends to discourage cultural outsiders' evaluations of insiders' behavior since outsiders applying the insiders' morality inevitably labor under epistemological disadvantages. Levine and Dubler seem to conclude that moral judgment by outsiders has no legitimate role to play in shaping societal responses to reproductive decision-making by HIV-infected minority group insiders. Yet this broad response—understandable in light of the previously cited moralism, misinformation, and prejudice—is not the only logical and humane one.

In the final analysis, I believe it is misleading to cast the debate over childbearing by HIV-infected women as one between universalists (who condemn childbearing on the basis of their putatively objective values) and multiculturalists (who tolerate childbearing as justifiable as an expression of the values of HIV-infected women). The reason is that universalists, like multiculturalists, can and frequently do acknowledge respects in which normative evaluation benefits from information about the social and cultural settings of the evaluator and the persons evaluated. Extreme economic hardship is relevant to the moral guilt of a thief. Fear of continued battery and sexual abuse is relevant to the moral guilt of children who kill their parents. In principle, both universalists and multiculturalists can view as relevant to moral judgment the beliefs held by minority group members about parental or family responsibility and risk-taking in the context of reproduction. Both universalists and multiculturalists can complain that Arras's condemnation of some HIV-infected childbearers is short on details about the normative beliefs of men and women in the communities most affected by AIDS. Both universalists and multiculturalists can entertain the possibility that people are not blameworthy for acting or making decisions against a background of reasonably acquired and sincerely held beliefs about their roles and responsibilities.

The call for adequate contextualization, then, applies to both universalism and multiculturalism. What is important here is not the debate between universalism and multiculturalism but, rather, assessing the claim some multiculturalist studies make—a claim that universalists, in principle, also could make—that appropriate consideration of race, economic class, religion, drug use, and other social and cultural variables invalidates the moral condemnation of HIV-infected mothers. Moral multiculturalists and other relativists who defend HIV-infected childbearers say these variables create separate moralities. Universalists who defend HIV-infected childbearers could say these variables create situations that exempt, excuse, justify, or permit controversial conduct.

Assessing the claim that moral condemnation stems from undercontextualization is vital since studies of the context of reproductive decision-making purport to place health professionals on notice that clinical effectiveness is compromised by the assumption that middle-class or white values should govern the behavior of low-income, nonwhite patients. Contextual studies carry a message for policymakers as well: prejudice may obscure the extent to which unpopular reproductive choices are consistent with defensible conceptions of morality.

A Common Moral Community

The call for greater consideration of the context of childbearing by HIV-infected women implies that there are contextual differences, that these contextual differences matter, and that we can specify the ways in which these contextual differences matter. Folk wisdom, anecdote, and social science report behavioral and perspectival differences between and among various cultural groups, yet it is not always easy to identify meaningful differences or to determine their significance.

Social scientists slowly have begun to investigate whether there are measurable behavioral differences in how African-Americans and Hispanic women approach sex, pregnancy, childbirth, and family life when compared to whites.[37] A number of studies posit behavioral differences between and among these three groups. Scholars are divided on the question of whether different groups exhibit perspectival differences. According to African-American philosopher William A. Banner, "the conduct of the science of medicine or the conduct of the science of ethics is incompatible with anything called 'ethnic perspective.'"[38] Another African-American philosopher, Jorge Garcia, rejects the idea that differences in behavior and experience imply differences in morals or moral perspectives.[39] Although I do not agree with Banner's sweeping rejection of "ethnic perspective," I think he and Garcia are correct to question whether behavioral differences between minority group members and nonminority group members signal differences in moral perspective.

Some observers believe that African-American and Hispanic women exhibit significant moral differences when compared to other groups.[40] Positions range from the belief that there are group differences in concrete moral perspectives on particular issues to the belief that there are group differences in abstract moral philosophy and patterns of moral reasoning. It is said, for example, that a higher percentage of Hispanic-American women disapprove of abortion than do African-American and Asian-American women.[41] More generally, studies by Carol Stack maintain that some blacks have an altogether different pattern of moral reasoning than whites.[42] In Stack's research, women belonging to certain African-American subgroups did not conform to the pattern of care-oriented moral reasoning Carol Gilligan believes she observed in her mainly white female study groups.[43] Gilligan's white female respondents voiced what she calls an "ethics of care," not the "ethics of justice" typical of men. By contrast, Stack's female respondents voiced both the "female" ethics of care and the "male" ethics of justice with about equal frequency, as did her male respondents. One could conclude that, when it comes to moral reasoning, black men and women are more like one another than like either white men or white women. An explanation for this is suggested by Annette Dula's assertion that whites do not and cannot share the moral perspectives of blacks because whites do not share the same "history and . . . experiences in unequal power relationships."[44]

A priori, one might suppose, with Dula, that every group's moral values are as different from every other group's as their social experiences are different. One might presume that because the social experiences of poor, urban, black and brown HIV-infected women are, in many respects, very different from the social experiences of their mainstream middle-class critics, their moral values are correspondingly different. However, it is not clear that the moral perspectives of HIV-infected women differ significantly from those of other women.

Open to the idea of ethnic perspectives, I am nonetheless impressed by the paucity of evidence that African-American and Hispanic women with HIV infection accept unique sets of moral values or moral frameworks about reproduction. Social diversity is real in the United States. Yet, when it comes to pregnancy and childbirth, American women of divergent social groups similarly value many aspects of the motherhood experience. For this reason, those perceived to be cultural outsiders may be cultural insiders, so far as the ethics of reproduction are concerned. To the extent that a set of identifiable procreative and family values is held in common, there may be fewer outsider–insider concerns.

What does it mean to hold in common a value, or a standard, or morality for that matter? Abstractly, A and B both may value motherhood. This common value may be discernable from what they say about how much they enjoy mothering or the trouble to which both go to give birth to several children. But if A believes she personally must care for her children to be an adequate parent and B believes she may send her children to full-time day care and boarding schools while pursuing a legal career, it is not clear that A and B both hold motherhood as a value.

The problem of specifying when persons hold values, standards, or moralities is central in the debates over moral universalism and multiculturalism. I cannot offer here a complete account of what it means to share moral norms. However, claims of shared norms seem to make the most sense in the presence of similar behavior, professed adherence to similar general norms, similar normative judgments about concrete cases, similar prioritization of concerns, and/or similar background conceptions of the physical or metaphysical world. Conversely, claims that two individuals or groups share a normative moral realm make little sense where the individuals or groups behave differently, profess dissimilar general norms, judge concrete situations dissimilarly, display divergent priorities, and/or hold conflicting understandings of physical or metaphysical reality.

Under the foregoing conception of what is entailed in holding common moral norms, a series of interviews conducted in 1992 with HIV-infected women offers no unequivocal support for the claim that, compared to middle-class whites, HIV-infected African-American and Hispanic women subscribe to substantially different insider reproductive moralities. These interviews could be interpreted to provide evidence that HIV-infected women view moral questions about reproduction much as others do, appealing to familiar concepts, values, and standards.

The interviews: an overview

Both the Preface and Chapter 16 of this volume describe in detail a qualitative interview study of HIV-infected women. In brief, over 150 HIV-infected women were interviewed in Baltimore, New York City, Miami, and Los Angeles. I draw here primarily on the first 80 of these interviews; as noted in Chapter 16, the range of experiences and values of these women generally reflects those of the entire sample. The study subjects mainly were African-American and Hispanic women, ranging in age from early twenties to late forties. The women were questioned in English or Spanish about when and how they learned of their HIV infection; how knowledge of infection had affected their lives; and how friends, family, and others reacted to their conditions. The women also were asked about the quality of care they had obtained since learning of their HIV infection, about bearing and caring for children in the context of AIDS, and about policy proposals to criminally sanction pregnant drug users.

All but a few of the women interviewed said that they were mothers or grandmothers of minor or adult children. Some were pregnant at the time of the interview. A number were accompanied by children with whom they lived, including HIV-infected infants. Several who said they had young children reported that they were not their children's custodial parent and that their children were being reared by relatives, foster parents, or adoptive parents. A number of women had given birth to children who later died of AIDS.

Most of the women were shouldering family responsibilities. Some were single heads of households, responsible for as many as six or seven children.

Several described themselves as married, although in one case "married" proved to mean that the woman lived with a long-term partner. One woman said she was engaged to a man with whom she had had an intimate relationship for nearly a decade. A number spoke of long-term relationships with supportive husbands or male companions.

The women in the study were not consistently questioned about their educational backgrounds, but a few offered this information. One woman reported only an eighth-grade education, while another said she had completed two years of college and another that she had a bachelor's degree. The women were not consistently asked about employment, and very few mentioned current or past employment outside of the home. Three women said they had lost good jobs after their employers learned of their HIV infection. Some of the women mentioned receiving public assistance.

Many of the women said they had been illegal drug users; a few specifically indicated injection drug use. Most of those who described past addiction described themselves as currently free of drugs. A number said they currently were or previously had been enrolled in drug and alcohol treatment programs. Some stated that they had engaged in prostitution to support their drug addiction.

The women generally attributed their HIV infection to drug use or heterosexual contact with a drug user. Several women thought they might have contracted the virus through sexual contact with their husbands or long-term partners. One said she had had a blood transfusion after a miscarriage that might explain her illness.

Some of the women had sought AIDS testing because they believed that they were members of a high-risk group. Some of the women learned of their HIV status through routine prenatal care. Others found out when their sick children tested positive for HIV. Still others found out in the context of medical care or drug abuse treatment unrelated to pregnancy and childbirth. One woman said she had gone in for testing with a friend because cash incentives were being offered to persons who submitted to voluntary testing and returned for the results. Another said she and six friends and relatives went for testing to get money to buy drugs; all six tested were infected.

Some of the women in the study had discovered that they were HIV-infected within the past few months or years of the interview and remained asymptomatic. A few had lived with HIV for 5–8 years. Several of the women reported a history of illness, some HIV-related, some not. Only a handful of the women felt that they had developed symptoms of AIDS. In fact, a number stressed how well they felt:

> My health now is . . . great. And I'm feeling fine . . . the virus itself has not really started to affect my body in any way. I haven't had any major changes. My T-cells are up very high, which I am very thankful for. So, in general, my health is great.[45]

According to interviewers, a few of the respondents looked ill, and a number reported rashes, herpes, feeling tired, bouts of pneumonia, cervical cancer, and lymphoma. One woman said she was being treated with Prozac for a compulsive cleaning disorder, and several said they were on medication for depression.

The women's impressions varied as to whether they had been adequately informed about AIDS or their own health. One African-American woman interviewed in Baltimore said she knew little about the virus or her condition:

> I need to learn more about the virus that I have. Because . . . I went to a meeting, and there was a (lot of) HIV-infected people. And they were talking about T-4 count, I didn't even know what they was talking about.[46]

However, another black woman interviewed at the same facility seemed to know a lot about her illness and emphasized the availability of good information:

> (I)t's not hard at all (to get information about HIV). It's just wanting to know. Wanting to know is the key. Some women—and I'm saying this through talking with other HIV-positive women and being with (them) . . . —some go into denial. And they don't want to know. They won't ask for information. Information is offered to them. And they refuse . . . but that's on them, and not the doctors.[47]

Differences of opinion about facts (like the availability of medical information) and values (like the norms of abortion and punishment of pregnant drug users) emerged from the interviews. Yet a striking convergence of beliefs and values also emerged when it came to some fundamental aspects of health, religion, reproduction, and family life.

What the interviews show

The interviews provide evidence of lives that, to varying degrees, are framed by a cluster of five distinguishable, but interrelated, traits and values that by no means are unique to minority women with HIV infection and AIDS:

1. *Maternalism*, a marked tendency to value being, becoming, or having been a mother.
2. *Private antiabortionism*, a strong disinclination to terminate one's own pregnancy combined with a moderate "pro-choice" policy perspective.
3. *Family-centrism*, a tendency to view oneself in the context of family networks that are expected to function as pivotal sources of mutual socioeconomic and emotional support throughout the life-cycle.
4. *Theism*, belief in a god and in reproductive outcomes as related to divine will.
5. *Optimism*, the disposition to believe that one will overcome or cope well with adversity.

Empirical evidence that HIV-infected poor women of color do not have moralities that are plainly and relevantly different from those of middle-class white women weakens some multicultural objections to middle-class moralists exercising judgment. Such evidence weakens the class of objections that assumes moral difference always follows other cultural or ethnic differences. Left untouched by the evidence is the argument of hard moral multiculturalists that middle-class white moralists should not judge poor minority women with HIV infection because—even though the two groups in some sense share a common morality—racism, sexism, and classism are likely to skew judgment to the detriment of the subordinate groups.

I believe most American men and women, of all ancestries and socioeconomic classes, share enough of a common morality to be justified in judging one another. I also believe that it is possible to overcome one's own tendencies toward systematic moral prejudice. However, warrant to judge is not warrant to condemn. That is, observing that a certain set of moral values is shared by diverse groups and admitting that those groups may, therefore, have a common basis for mutual moral criticism is not to validate condemnation of HIV-infected mothers. On the contrary, recognition of shared values can be the starting point for understanding why having children in the context of AIDS is morally permissible. I propose conceiving of poor women of color with HIV infection as moral agents engaged by the values of "our" community no less than "theirs." When viewed as the outcomes of complex occasions for moral judgment about life, death, and the meaning of human happiness, the unpopular reproductive decisions of HIV-infected women are much harder to condemn. Well-informed moral assessment will find little to condemn in the reproductive choices of HIV-infected childbearers.

Maternalism

The overwhelming majority of the women interviewed were mothers, grandmothers, and maternalists. They conveyed the sense that to be a mother was a natural yearning common to all women, including women with HIV infection and AIDS:

> You always think of yourself as a giver of life. . . . That is how we view ourselves as women. We know this from the very start, that that is one of the things we do and probably will do. And you just can't one day when you don't really feel any different, be told you can't do that. I mean it's like it just doesn't sink in. Twenty or twenty-five years or thirty years of being conditioned to that is what you do. That is what you are. That is part of your function on this planet. . . . Most of the women I know want to have children . . . they can't talk about it without crying. They really can't. . . . When I wanted to have a baby, I wanted to have a baby. . . . I just physically wanted to have a baby. This is it. The time is right now . . . and I . . . did it.[48]

A woman who worried about perinatal transmission described motherhood as incomparable: "you can't compare the feeling."[49] Another who said her daughter cherishes her despite the irresponsible life she had led, described being a mother as "beautiful."[50]

Although relieved by her children's successes, one woman's feelings about motherhood were distinctly more ambivalent than others' in the interview group:

> (I)f I knew back then what I know now, I would not have (had) my kids. . . . I love my kids very much. But this was not planned. If I knew then what I know now, because life is so hard. Life is rough. So many things happen out there . . . drugs, killings, a lot of things . . . I would have stayed by myself.[51]

Another woman, a clear maternalist, said pressure to fulfill her obligations to her kids had "saved her" from drugs. She admitted that becoming a mother had been unplanned and unwanted:

> I wasn't planning to get pregnant. It was just something that happened, being out on the streets, selling my body just to get high.[52]

As stated, maternalists often are willing to make important sacrifices to have children. One woman made the ultimate sacrifice: her own health and life. She risked HIV infection for the sake of becoming a mother. After her husband was diagnosed with HIV infection, against all of her counselors' advice, she engaged frequently in consensual unprotected sexual intercourse. She continued attempting to get pregnant until she became HIV-infected:

> I sort of expected (to find out I was positive) because . . . I was trying to get pregnant at the time and (health-care workers) had cautioned me. . . . I was using no form of protection whatsoever . . . when we were having sex, so it wasn't that much of a shock (to test positive for HIV).[53]

Once she became infected, this woman's efforts to become pregnant lessened, but she said she still thinks "it would be nice to have a child . . . if possible."[54]

A 28-year-old, college-educated respondent said that she had always wanted a child and continued to want one after learning she was HIV-infected. She and a noninfected man met and fell in love. She carefully planned her pregnancy by him after speaking to a midwife and a physician, neither of whom affirmatively discouraged her. She stopped taking oral contraceptives, waited until the precise date of ovulation, had unprotected sex once, and, remarkably, became pregnant with twins. She viewed her easy impregnation in religious terms: "my religion comes in and maybe it's some kind of sign, you know, maybe it was meant to be."[55] Often emphasizing their high T-cell counts and good health, a number of other women said they had not yet ruled out pregnancy: "I sort of think I will have kids, biologically my own kids," said one.[56]

An HIV-infected condom user who had not ruled out a second child said she believes drug users should not have babies and should be jailed for doing so.[57] Several of the women distinguished the morality of having what one called an "AIDS baby" from having a "drug baby":

> (The drug user is) killing the baby, right there. The brain, the cells, everything is just tearing the baby apart, and when the baby comes out, the baby is sick. . . . I really believe that is totally different from a woman who wants to have a baby HIV. Even though the child is going to be in the same predicament, it's not gonna last long.[58]

Her point seemed to be that infants born addicted to drugs necessarily received damaging drugs in utero and typically matured into adulthood with nonfatal cognitive deficiencies. Infants born to HIV-infected mothers, however, may not develop AIDS at all. If an infant does develop AIDS, its suffering will be short-lived because its life will be short.

Unlike those just described, some of the women interviewed seemed to regard HIV infection as a definitive reason—for themselves and others—not to bear children. Several women had undergone tubal ligation after learning they were HIV-infected. One said she used Norplant because she already had lost a baby to AIDS and did not wish to repeat that painful experience.[59] Some women said they were using condoms or were abstinent to avoid pregnancy. A couple of women had undergone abortions to avoid bearing a child with AIDS. One woman, who did not wish to become pregnant because of her HIV infection, expressed pessimism about birth control, including Norplant, which she learned about for the first time during her interview:

> Myself, I don't trust birth control. I've gotten pregnant on the pill . . . on the IUD . . . with the rubber, so, no, I don't trust none of them. I figure if God means for you to have a kid, that's when you're going to have them. . . . So I wouldn't trust (Norplant) either.[60]

One woman said being a mother was "very important" to her and that if someone could assure her that her second child would not be infected, she would have one "quick."[61] Another said her "conscience would not let (her) bring a baby (into the world) knowing that (she is) sick and having her have to suffer."[62] "We must think of their little lives and when they don't have anything," she said. In the same vein, describing childbirth in the context of HIV as a "sin," one woman reasoned:

> To make him suffer, you really have to think about it. . . . Are you going to be there for this baby? . . . What's going to happen to this child? It's bad enough a normal child can't find a good home. . . . Now can you imagine a baby that's sick? Not everybody really cares. . . . They might have a chance of being normal . . . but how can you really be sure? I wouldn't advise it to nobody.[63]

An infected woman who had participated in support groups of childless HIV-infected women commented with a marked sense of tragedy that:

> I've given my shoulder to girls who are HIV-infected and don't have kids and wanted kids. It's tearing them up. It's tearing them up. Not the thought of having the virus . . . the more concern of theirs is the baby . . . not being able to have just one. It's killing them more than the virus is.[64]

The willingness of a maternalist to reproduce in the face of AIDS may be affected by her knowledge of the risks. One of the women in the study group seemed especially confused about the odds of perinatal transmission:

> It can be 50–50. It could be 100 and 90 (sic). That I wouldn't know. But, only way I could find out about it, I have one, which, I'm not ready to have it right now. (My previous child, to which I gave birth while infected) turned out to be healthy. . . . We take good care of him.[65]

One woman seemed very well informed and said the rate of perinatal transmission was about 30%. She still seemed insecure in her knowledge and lamented the lack of solid information about the risks of transmission to offspring. Her impression was that physicians vary greatly in their estimates of risk and that the 30%–70% risk assessment could not be trusted.[66]

Most of the women seemed to oppose antichildbirth directive counseling by health-care professionals. They seemed to regard the decision to risk having a baby with HIV infection as the individual woman's to make. One woman opposed directive counseling on the grounds that "the majority of women do want more children" and that a counselor's opinions are "just her opinion."[67]

To satisfy their desires to mother, three women expressed an interest in alternatives to traditional biological parenting.[68] Adoption was a possibility some were considering. Stating that she was jealous of girlfriends with babies, this woman said the risk of HIV infection in biological parenting was too great. She wants to adopt an HIV-infected infant: "Why bring another baby into this world when there are so many of them already sitting in the hospital waiting?"[69]

Another woman seemed interested in surrogate motherhood as a way for HIV-infected women to care for genetic offspring without risking perinatal transmission:

> Wouldn't it be easier if the egg was . . . taken out of the mother and given to (a) surrogate? . . . I feel that would be the best way. . . . It would be easier if someone would volunteer to carry the baby for her . . . and that still be her child even though someone else is carrying it for her. . . . That would be the only way if I really desperately wanted a child and I didn't have a child. . . . But as far as carrying it in my womb, I couldn't.[70]

A recent study found a high correlation between childbirth by HIV-infected women and having healthy minor children in the custody of others.[71] The study suggests that the HIV-infected women who are most likely to carry a child to term are those who have lost custody of previous children due to maternal neglect or abuse. One way to reduce the incidence of pediatric AIDS, the study suggests, could be to reconnect HIV-infected women with their existing children living with relatives or in foster care. Although it is solely a matter of conjecture, some of the infected women in our interview group had lost children they might well have been seeking to replace. One woman with a heightened sense of the risks of lost custody commented that it is better to have an HIV baby than a drug baby because: "the drug baby, they gonna take away from you," but the HIV baby you can keep.[72]

Among the respondents who said they would not recommend pregnancy for HIV-infected women were several who had already lost children to AIDS or were currently taking care of children sick with AIDS. Although childbirth may be an attractive option for HIV-infected women who never have had children or who have lost custody of children, it did not appeal to several respondents who were caring for sick children or who already had lost a child to AIDS. One woman said she decided to use Norplant after losing a 4-month-old daughter to AIDS.[73]

Maternalism led some respondents, on one or more occasions, to risk perinatal transmission of HIV for the sake of having a child, but it would be a mistake to conclude from this that they were indifferent to HIV transmission generally. One woman said that out of concern for exposing her mother to the virus she wouldn't let her borrow her "cute lingerie" or "touch certain things."[74] Others, including a prostitute, said they tried especially hard to get their partners to use condoms, with mixed results.[75]

Finally, the mothers with HIV infection in our study seemed to worry a great deal about what would become of their children. One respondent said she worries about her kids' future and wants them to be together. She trusts no one but her mother to care for her kids, even though "(my mother's) moral judgments are . . . different from the way I raised my kids, so it's gonna be a hassle with her trying to raise teenage boys and girls."[76]

Private antiabortionism

The American public as a whole is divided on the morality of abortion. Polls suggest that most Americans prefer laws that permit at least some abortions. Abortion in cases of rape, incest, and extreme medical or economic hardship generally meets approval. The women interviewed in our study typically said they did not approve of abortion for themselves (though a number had obtained them) but thought it was up to the woman whether she opted for abortion. No one said she favored laws banning abortion. For this reason, I describe the personal opposition to abortion found in the group as "private" rather than "public policy" oriented antiabortionism.

Although several of the women had elected abortions, one stated that abortion had been her primary means of birth control: "My method of contraception when I was like from age 16 to 20 was abortions. I had like five abortions."[77] The women justified their decision to abort on a number of grounds, including lack of a responsible father to help care for the child: "I don't want to bring a child into the world that didn't have a father to support him."[78]

Drug use and HIV infection were additional reasons cited for abortion. One woman said she had had an abortion at age 19 while using drugs and experimenting with various forms of birth control.[79] HIV infection was a reason a number of women said they had aborted or would consider abortion.

A couple of women said they did not want to abort their fetuses, despite their HIV-infected status, because they had had what they deemed too many abortions in the past.[80] A 41-year-old woman who was 5 months pregnant and had several adult and minor children, including a healthy 3 year old, said she had been pregnant three times since finding out she was HIV-infected. She had aborted all three of these to avoid the risk to the child, but this time:

> I just feel that I have had too many abortions. . . . I just can't do it again. I really can't . . . lay there on that table again, and hear that humming of that machine. I just, I just can't go through it again. . . . I will get my tubes tied . . . but . . . this is my last chance for a girl. . . . I decided to go ahead with (the pregnancy) and take . . . what happens.[81]

A number of women stated categorical opposition to abortion for themselves and for others: "I don't believe in an abortion. They have to die on their own."[82] When asked whether she had considered terminating her pregnancy, one HIV-infected crack addict with three children answered, "There is one thing I don't believe in, killing, killing . . . killing no baby. I can't. I couldn't."[83]

One woman said she left her pregnancy in "God's hand" and that she "didn't think (she) had the right to decide whether (she) should abort the baby or not."[84] Having passed up an opportunity to abort in her third month, another woman said she "didn't believe in abortion."[85] She added that a woman who finds out she is pregnant in the fifth or sixth month may abort because "once the baby's born, it's going to die (anyway)." One respondent advised that women not obtain abortions because it is "good to have at least one child" to continue the "family line."[86] A couple of women, however, said they would recommend abortion to women with HIV.[87] When asked about childbirth in the context of AIDS, one woman said, "I know that the idea to have an abortion is not a good idea either, but I think it would be the best."[88] She qualified that if a woman finds out she's pregnant after the second month, "I would advise her not to have an abortion."

Women who had not aborted pregnancies conceived after they learned of their HIV status said they had been urged to abort by health-care professionals and family members.[89] One woman's mother had advised her to abort.[90] Another seemed to recall being advised by her health-care provider against carrying her child to term:

> But, when I got pregnant . . . at first I was thinking about abortion, but . . . I had made up my mind that I was going to have him and this was going to be my last baby

whether he's negative or positive. I wasn't going to have anymore. I was going to keep him.[91]

A young HIV-infected woman narrated the story of visiting an abortion clinic to get information and to confirm her pregnancy. She had been advised by various people to abort because of her youthful age, lack of economic resources, and lack of a spouse; but she met a "pro-life" blockade at the door:

> [T]here were people out in front of this clinic, that wouldn't let me in there. They said, "hey you're a child killer, you're a murderer." . . . I was scared to have an abortion. I thought, maybe I am a murderer. . . . I was scared . . . (especially) having those people showing me, you know, pictures of dead babies. You're a murderer. Oh my God, man, you know. They made me feel terrible about myself. . . . I didn't know I had this disease. But if I did know . . . what's worse? I ask you, what's worse? Having an abortion? Or bringing a child into this world with AIDS, that doesn't have that much of a chance to make it. Either way, will she die . . . ? That is such an important question.[92]

Family-centrism

As studies of the social resources of HIV-infected women have shown, it is a myth that African-American and Hispanic women necessarily have an extensive network of supportive family members.[93] Some of the women interviewed indicated that they were estranged from spouses, parents, or siblings. A number of the Hispanic women were immigrants whose families lived abroad in Puerto Rico, Venezuela, the Dominican Republic, or Haiti.

Some of the women whose families were close by had not yet told them about their disease. Yet, most of the women spoke of their families in ways that suggested a centrality of family relations in their lives. Maternalism, which many interviews reflected, is one kind of family-centrism; respondents also placed an affirmative value on other family relations, especially female relations, such as their mothers, grandmothers, sisters, and aunts.[94] Frequently, there was an implicit understanding that these were relationships that ought to provide mutual support throughout the life-cycle. When family ties were less enduring and central, there was disappointment.

Researchers elicited views about family from the respondents through questions about the reaction of those with whom they had discussed their HIV status. "I have a pretty strongly knit family, and I know that they will be there for (my children when I die)" was commonly implied.[95] One woman's family wanted to "pamper her like a little baby" when they found out about her HIV infection.[96] Another said her mother was very supportive and worked hard to eliminate stress from her life, but her husband couldn't face her disease.[97] Many women had chosen to inform only their families about their infection due to shame or fear of stigmatization and rejection. One woman said she had only shared the secret of her infection with the women in her family, including her five sisters.[98] She told her mother first because "you just know that your mom really cares and . . . you feel comfortable telling her. . . ." She felt her sisters still loved her:

> I ain't told my (four) brothers. . . . (I told my sisters, to whom I am closer and) they proved (sic) they protective of me. They still love me. They don't feel no different. . . . So they take care of (my son) . . . they feed him. They drink with him, you know?[99]

A younger woman said she immediately had told an older sister with whom she lives because her "mother and father are dead. And there's only five of us children. So we gotta support and look up to each other."[100] One woman had not yet told her family but planned to do so. She expected she would first tell her mother, who helps her care for her 10 year old, because "she was the closest friend I have."[101] Asked whether she would have a child if it would not be sick, this woman said she would because she knew the child would be taken care of by its father and grandmother "after I pass." A long-time drug user said she had gone "through hell" with her mother, who threatened to take her kids from her: "(T)hen she locked me out one time. . . . But I think because I was family . . . she couldn't really . . . lock me out completely."[102]

A Hispanic woman, whose husband had just been released from jail, said her mother had taken her kids away from her "because I wasn't taking care of them." She had a positive attitude about this family intervention:

> You have to have a family that love you. That's very important. . . . When you love your kids and when you have a family that cares for you, that helps you a lot. . . . My mother took my kids away from me, but she always tried to help me. She always tried to talk to me (about drug rehabilitation).[103]

Although she told her husband first, one woman said she felt best telling her sister about her HIV infection. Protective of her husband, she also said she wouldn't have a child as an HIV-infected person because "I wouldn't only be jeopardizing my baby but my husband."[104]

One woman said she had not told her family, only a lover.[105] Another said she had received no support from her family or friends since she discovered she was HIV-infected; her daughter would not let her near her grandchildren.[106] A mother of two said that her family's reaction "wasn't good, it wasn't bad, but they stand by me 100%."[107]

Although many of the women said their families were supportive and understanding, a number said they had been, at least temporarily, ostracized by them. One woman described her family's reaction:

> But my younger sister, she was like crying . . . she would keep her daughter away from me. If I was to call my niece to me and give her something . . . what I gave, I would find in the trash. . . . (S)he used to walk around with a bleach bottles (sic), everything she washing with bleach. Spoons, forks, she even ate separate. . . . But

now she's coming around. I guess she has accept it. And she let her daughter come to me now.[108]

Several women had not yet told their families, including their parents, siblings, and children. One said she would not tell her children until she became very ill because she feared they would become too clinging. Shame and fear of harm prevent some women from telling their families about their HIV infection:

> I feel ashamed of myself just thinking that I am HIV-positive. If you say you are not going to lead a normal life, everybody is gonna take care of you, my mother, my father. I can't even tell a word with them. Because if I say that to my mother, I might live longer than her because she might die because she loves me. . . . She cares about me. I have a 12 year old. I cannot tell her because I don't want to change her life. . . . I don't want to hurt her. . . . She's my baby. My heartbeat. My blood. You cannot live without blood. . . . She is in my blood.[109]

Theism

Polls show that as many as 80% of all Americans believe in God. More people in the United States than in western Europe attend church regularly. At least 10 of the 80 women whose interviews I reviewed expressly appealed to belief in an interactive God. Two identified a particular religious affiliation, one saying she was Catholic, the other that she was a born-again Christian.[110] A respondent who mentioned God several times expressly denied that she was religious.[111] Without mentioning God or a religion, one woman noted that "some people believe in miracles."[112] Another proved her right, saying, "I keep on praying for a miracle."[113]

One woman described giving birth, "(e)ven being infected with HIV," as "a blessing from the Lord."[114] A couple of women seemed to think that whether or not they got pregnant was up to God. Several others said they thought it was up to God whether they gave birth to an infant who would contract AIDS:

> Hopefully, thanks to The Man Upstairs, He might make him, smooth, you know, regular, as any other baby. . . . I can cope with an addict baby better than an AIDS baby.[115]

> It's your choice to have that baby . . . (but) God gives life and God takes it away.[116]

Six months pregnant, an infected woman said her child's future was:

> In the Lord's hand, even though we know what normalcy is about, man work and all that, but I look at it like it's in God's hand. It's up to Him whether He wants this child to survive.[117]

Some of the women asserted that whether they lived or died was also a matter of God's will. "If He wants me, He'll get me," said one.[118] Putting faith in God or accepting one's fate as God's will seemed to be a source of comfort to some respondents. One woman said she had not sought out support groups: "I just ask God to help."[119]

Optimism

The women interviewed very often were optimistic about their chances of fighting off full-blown AIDS. Given the usual course of the disease, their optimism may seem surprising. By optimism, I mean a tendency to believe that good outcomes are likely. The optimist believes it is possible to beat the odds, conquer obstacles, prevail where others might fail. In the biomedical context, optimism that one can fight a normally fatal illness is sometimes tagged "denial." Thus, the woman who said that she would survive if she stayed away from drugs, took AZT, and maintained good nutrition might be viewed as being in a state of denial rather than as being optimistic.

Religion was the source of some of the optimism. One woman said she had been "scared to death" when she found out she had AIDS because she thought she was going to die.[120] However, "I found out that I didn't have to die. Only once God was ready for me."[121] Another woman said:

> I'm a born-again Christian. . . . I found the Lord, and He kept me up. We believe in the Lord so much that, like, He is our healer. . . . So . . . I stand firm, (believing) that I am going to be healed, that I am being healed.[122]

A woman who cited staying healthy and believing in God as keys to longevity, also offered that:

> As long as I think positive, I'm alright. Just hopefully, I can last as long as I can last. I'm not going to give in to it, you know, cause your mind can make you give in and you're gone tomorrow. . . . So far, so good. . . . I haven't been sick at all.[123]

Many of the women appeared to have learned about the concept of denial in drug or AIDS counseling and used it liberally. One woman implied that she had been in a state of denial when her husband was diagnosed as HIV-infected. She did nothing to protect herself from disease: "I didn't protect myself in no way . . . which I now realize was stupid."[124] A number said that they had once been in denial about their own HIV status.[125] A mother of three said she had taken her children to be tested on three separate occasions before she believed they were really infected. Several women indicated that they were past the denial stage and quite hopeful of living "a good while and not dying tomorrow."[126]

Many of the women emphasized that, although they had passed the denial stage, their family members or friends had not. One woman said her three daughters were in denial about her HIV status, another that her boyfriend was in denial.[127] The husband of one woman resisted belief: "he was in big denial." He told his wife: "You ain't got it. (P)eople messed up the test."[128] On the whole, the women seemed to think that denial was something to be overcome but that one ought not give up hope.

Constituting a moral community

The multicultural movement under way in the United States emphasizes social differences tied to ethnicity, race, gender, and class. Many would agree with the multiculturalists, as I do, that it is important to consider the implications of social differences for moral judgment. The question before us now is whether ethnic and racial differences undercut some groups' judgments about HIV-infected women of color.

The HIV-infected women of color interviewed in this study spoke with different words and accents of difference grounded in profoundly varied histories. In particular, the languages and linguistic idioms employed by the women reflected their social backgrounds, yet these women expressed fears and frustrations seemingly common to persons of varied backgrounds facing serious illness and death. Furthermore, the women revealed perspectives on motherhood, abortion, families, God, and hope that they shared with people who do not have similar histories. When viewed in this light, the interviews strongly suggest that, with respect to the broadly defined values we have identified, African-American and Hispanic women are members of a larger "moral community," a community of lay and professional moralists of varied social backgrounds, who hold similar perspectives relating to procreation, parenting, and illness.

These conclusions do not, of course, justify rushing to judgment about the reproductive choices of HIV-infected women of color. The knowledge that men and women of color have been victims of egregious bioethical misjudgment in the past counsels caution in making condemnatory judgments without a wide and tested basis of fact that one is prepared to view without prejudice. Moral multiculturalism doubts that members of the dominant social groups within a moral community have the capacity to view social subordinates in that same moral community without prejudice or racism. So, while it may be true that minority groups and majority groups participate in the same moral practice and subscribe to a complex of shared beliefs and values, it does not follow that majority group members are likely to judge minority group members accurately. If misjudgment is not only possible but likely, a reason arguably exists for not undertaking judgment.

There are other good moral reasons to refrain from making moral judgments about persons in one's own moral community. First, not knowing the details of a situation is a reason to refrain from judgment, pending fuller understanding. The judgments we offer have little to recommend them if they do not reflect knowledge of the factual context affecting the behavior of HIV-infected women. Sound moral judgment concerning HIV-infected women is impossible without education about the medical and public health aspects of HIV infection and the socioeconomic conditions facing these women.

Second, making—or at least publicly expressing—moral judgment may be morally inappropriate in certain situations of crisis or tragedy. The parent who leaves a 2 year old at home alone may deserve moral criticism but not at the scene of the fire in which the child has been killed. Even if people with AIDS are deserving of moral criticism in some respects, it may be morally inappropriate to burden them with one's moral condemnation as they struggle to make sense of their fatal illness. It is an open question whether restraint of judgment is necessary when its would-be subjects are not critically sick with AIDS but simply HIV-infected.

Those who have condemned HIV-infected childbearers may have condemned without warrant for the reasons surveyed. Likewise, those who have refused to stand in judgment of HIV-infected childbearers may have done so without warrant, failing to understand that Americans belonging to different ethnic and racial groups may belong to a common moral community of persons who share a broad range of values and practices.

Justified Maternity

When childbearing by HIV-infected women is described as immoral, the basis of the description is risk of harm to offspring and to the women themselves. I want to offer a perspective from which childbearing by HIV-infected women does not appear to be immoral, despite concerns about harming offspring and women's health. Mainstream moralities appropriately regard many forms of harmful conduct that flow from a background of pervasive and reasonably acquired beliefs as justifiable or excusable. To morally condemn HIV-infected women for imposing the risk of harm on unborn children and other costs on society is to ignore ingrained patterns of belief acquisition and identity.

Maternalism as cultural fact

Whether due to nature, nurture, or both, American women typically want to become mothers. American men typically want their women to become mothers. We are a society of maternalists. The identities of women are shaped, inter alia, by motherhood and expectations of motherhood. Patricia H. Collins notes that some see motherhood "as providing a base for self-actualization, status in the Black community, and a catalyst for social activism."[129] That there are 1.5 million elective abortions each year is consistent with the claim that we are a society of maternalists. A large percentage of the women who obtain abortions are women who already have children or who plan to have children in the future. Abortion is an agonizing choice precisely because of maternalism.[130]

Maternalism, a varied mix of philosophical, psychological, and moral characteristics, runs deep. Angela Davis has written of the contemporary imperative toward motherhood as a "bizarre and contradictory" ideology.[131] It cannot be turned on and off at will. One could not reasonably expect that a maternalist suddenly would cease to be a maternalist a month or a year after notice of a risk of disease. The interviews with HIV-infected women corroborate the suspicion that maternalism does not, in fact, abate with the first diagnosis of a fatal communicable disease. On the contrary, serious illness seems to heighten the desire of some HIV-infected women to bear children.

Many women's sense of self evolves around a felt personal and social "mission" to bear and rear children. For such women, procreation may be precisely the thing to which they turn for fulfillment and meaning as they face terminal illness. Some of the women interviewed seemed especially anxious to become pregnant. Recall the woman who contracted HIV infection while attempting to become pregnant by a spouse who was expected to die of AIDS. Recall the HIV-infected woman who had male children but risked pediatric AIDS and her own health because she longed for a daughter.

The ethical template for women's lives, society's maternalism implies that women have moral permission, if not a moral duty, to mother. Maternalism helps not only to explain childbearing by HIV-infected women but also to justify it. The HIV-infected women who have babies are acting authentically out of their socially fostered identities. Not every identity a society fosters generates moral permission to act. The identity of a youth-gang member as ruthless and lawless does not clearly justify or excuse random street violence with high-powered assault weapons. Women who reproduce in the context of AIDS, however, are not acting out of self-identities that require flouting what they understand to be the law as a condition of self-validation. They view childbearing, and themselves as childbearers, as well-meaning, caring, and lawful.

Arras states that ethical assessment of human reproduction always requires an appraisal of the "ability and willingness" of parents to assume their "proper responsibility" for the child.[132] He implies that HIV-infected women who do not make such an assessment or who fail to consider the harm they may do through childbirth can be judged morally irresponsible. However, maternalism functions to deny, or at least to obscure, the relevance of questions of "ability and willingness" to mother. Maternalism also denies or obscures the relevance of considerations of "responsibility to the child," apart from the primary responsibility to the child to give it life. The "proper responsibility" of a woman to her child is childbirth and child care (only) to the best of her ability. Differently put, in the mind of the maternalist, which is to say in the minds of vast segments of our society, there is normally a very strong, virtually irrebuttable, moral presumption in favor of motherhood. To reverse that presumption by condemning HIV-infected women of color looks suspiciously like irrational prejudice. More to the point, to reverse the presumption is to deny the rationality and sensitivity of women whose only "failing" is construing the demands of maternalism in the context of HIV infection differently from those within the same moral community who condemn them.

Burdens of proof

I have presented maternalism, without endorsement, as a fact about our society that undercuts the case for condemnation of HIV-infected women based on the harm principle. It bears emphasis, however, that many people endorse maternalism. Those who endorse maternalism as a regulative norm may want to go further than I have gone, arguing that the harm principle as a regulatory norm competes with a "maternalism principle." Indeed, it could be argued that the harm principle has its valid and uncontroversial sphere of relevance in, for example, the criminal law of battery between strangers, not in the sui generis field of human reproduction. To apply the harm principle to reproduction, perhaps one first must reconcile it with maternalist principles. Viewed in this way, it is not the HIV-infected childbearer who has the burden of justification in the face of the harm principle but her moral critic in light of the maternalism principle.

Last wishes

It was a cliché of the 1960s that dying children who were granted a last wish asked to go to Disneyland. It may be that dying women who do not feel sick and have no children, or no daughters or no sons or no custody of previous children, will ask for a baby. The analogy is not perfect. The trip to Disneyland is, at worst, a suboptimal allocation of a modest amount of money. The decision to bear a child is, at worst, the creation of a human being whose life will include a painful illness, early death, and loss of one or both parents. What may make the desire to go to Disneyland and the desire to have a baby analogous, and therefore deserving of a similar moral response, is the philosophical understanding that giving birth inherently is not an injury or harm.

The maternalist moral community that HIV-infected women share with others is divided on the question of whether giving birth is an absolute good. Some of the African-American and Hispanic women interviewed plainly regard giving birth to a child who dies of AIDS as harming the child. However, other respondents seemed implicitly to agree with the philosophy that giving birth to a child is not an injury. It has been suggested by Taunya Lovell Banks that, because of high rates of infant mortality, violent death, and illness in their neighborhoods, poor women of color may be less inclined to view the risk of illness and premature death as reasons not to bear children than middle-class white women.[133] The interviews did not contradict Banks's conjecture, but I would stress that belief in the absolute good of giving life is not universal among, nor limited to, poor urban dwellers, blacks, or Hispanics. Judeo-Christian religions, to which a cross-section of the society subscribes, promote belief in the inherent good of giving life.Some of the HIV-infected women interviewed depicted children's fates as in God's hands. These women seemed to fully appreciate the tragedy of short, painful lives but did not blame themselves for whether a life was short or long. Their words implied that pediatric AIDS is a tragedy but not a personal immorality.

Drug use and moral judgment

People addicted to drugs often make poor decisions about their own health and about the health and welfare of others. Many HIV-infected women profess past or current drug use. In light of these facts, it may seem surprising that I have not focused on the presumed relevance of drug addiction to moral judgment and childbearing by HIV-infected women.

The reason for rejecting such a focus is this: the reproductive decisions of the HIV-infected women interviewed were not directly linked, in obvious ways, to their past or current drug use. Active drug addiction may have very little to do with explaining why HIV-infected women choose and risk childbearing, when compared to maternalism, family-centrism, and belief in an interactive God. It doubtless is true that some HIV-infected women lack minimal rational competence because of drug addiction or severe active illness, but these women also lack meaningful moral agency. Their decisions to bear children are nondecisions, and their behavior is neither morally justified nor unjustified. Like children and other incompetents, they are exempt or excused from moral assessment.

Drug users do not lack competence in every sphere of judgment. Many drug users with HIV infection can be held morally accountable for their reproductive behavior, along with other HIV-infected women. At that point, the question becomes whether the fact of drug use works as an independent variable against the case for viewing childbearing as either justified or unjustified. Some of the HIV-infected women interviewed stated that having a child while using drugs was morally different from having a child knowing that one risks perinatal transmission. It would seem to follow that these women regard drug-using HIV-infected childbearers as less moral than others.

Conclusion

Moral multiculturalism is a significant new direction in American moral thought. Moral multiculturalism defends the choices of HIV-infected women by insisting that they belong to separate moral communities that outsiders are either incompetent to judge or unable to judge without prejudice. Some moral multiculturalists take their defensive stances further, arguing that HIV-infected women are blameless because historical mistreatment of poor, minority groups ultimately accounts for their high levels of pediatric AIDS. Because important historical differences exist between and among the various racial and ethnic groups, there is merit to moral multiculturalism's demand for the suspicion and contextualization of judgment. Even so it would be premature to conclude with some moral multiculturalists that women of color have unique moralities.

There is to a significant degree, I believe, a common moral community in the United States. Certain broad clusters of moral commitments and perspectives are shared, and potentially they permit mutual moral judgment within a moral community constituted by diverse peoples. It must be hoped that the future will see few instances in which shared Judeo-Christian values are recited as perverted justifications for moral condemnation of minority group members. Citing the broad value commitments of the American moral community, we can begin to understand why HIV-infected women do not deserve condemnation for cruelty and immorality. Their unpopular choice to bear children is founded on reasonable renderings of the shared morality.

In many respects, our society encourages belief in an interactive God who decides matters of birth and death. Our society treats creating families as a moral privilege and duty. In the past, some professional and lay moralists have attempted to judge childbearing by HIV-infected women in a cultural vacuum that gave these facts a surprisingly minor role. Women faced with death believe in good faith in an interactive God who makes decisions about the timing of births and deaths. Women faced with death believe in good faith that they may and should carry on their family lines. I do not recommend that HIV-infected women bear children. However, I believe the maternalist culture, combined with religion and family-centricism, explains and morally justifies childbearing by the HIV-infected women who choose to do it. In short, maternalism, especially when combined with family-centrism and theism, justifies childbearing.

Having children, even in the context of AIDS, is a highly personal matter, but some of the implications are far from personal. When children die from AIDS, it touches the hearts and wallets of the public. Those who counsel and care for HIV-infected women enjoy no platform of moral privilege. They must inform women of the risks and benefits of various courses as best they can. Then, if they feel they may or must press pregnancy avoidance or abortion, they must be prepared to reason with infected women against a background of complex norms that pit ideals and definitions of harm avoidance against ideals and definitions of responsible motherhood.

Notes

1. United Press International, "HIV Infection Trend Moving Toward Women," Feb. 8, 1995; L. Altman, "At AIDS Talks, Science Confronts Daunting Maze," *New York Times*, June 6, 1993, p. A1; L. Altman, "HIV Immunity Discussed at Berlin Conference," *New York Times*, June 9, 1993, p. A7; D. Brown, "2.5 Billion a Year Urged to Curb AIDS Cases: Officials at World Conference Cite Explosive Growth of HIV Infection in Some Countries," *Washington Post*, June 8, 1993, p. A17; D. Brown, "AIDS Conference Offers New Data but no Full Understanding of Virus," *Washington Post*, June 13, 1993, p. A22; J. Jacobson, "Beyond AIDS: The Worldwide Plague of Sexual Diseases," *Sunday*, June 7, 1992, p. C3.

2. L. K. Altman, "In Major Finding, Drug Limits HIV Infection in Newborns," *New York Times*, Feb. 21, 1994, p. A1.
3. See A. Pivnick, A. Jacobson, K. Eric, et al., "Reproductive Decisions Among HIV-Infected, Drug-Using Women: The Importance of Mother–Child Coresidence," *Medical Anthropology Quarterly* 5 (June 1991): 153–168 2NS; M. Hutchinson and A. Kurth, "I Need to Know that I Have a Choice: A Study of Women, HIV, and Reproductive Decision-Making," *AIDS Patient Care* (February 1991): 17–24; C. Levine and N. N. Dubler, "HIV and Childbearing—Uncertain Risks and Bitter Realities: The Reproductive Choices of HIV-Infected Women," *The Milbank Quarterly* 68 (1990): 321–351; P. Selwyn, R. J. Carter, E. Schoenbaum, et al., "Knowledge of HIV Antibody Status and Decisions to Continue or Terminate Pregnancy Among Intravenous Drug Users," *Journal of the American Medical Association* 261 (June 1989): 3567–3571.
4. Interview C-15, May 15, 1992, Miami. Quotations are from the series of interviews conducted by the Working Group, as noted in the Preface to this volume and described in greater detail in Chapter 16.
5. See J. D. Arras, "AIDS and Reproductive Decisions: Having Children in Fear and Trembling," *The Milbank Quarterly* 68 (1990): 353–382. For a general discussion of the obligation to avoid harm and risk of harm, see J. Feinberg, *The Moral Limits of the Criminal Law: Harm to Others* (New York: Oxford University Press, 1984).
6. Interview N-25, Nov. 19, 1992, Los Angeles.
7. H. Flack and E. D. Pelligrino, eds., *African American Perspectives on Biomedical Ethics* (Washington, DC: Georgetown University Press, 1992). This book contains chapters by W. Banner, "Is There an African-American Perspective on Biomedical Ethics?"; A. Dula, "Yes, There Are African-American Perspectives on Bioethics"; J. Garcia, "African-American Perspectives, Cultural Relativism and Normative Issues: Some Conceptual Questions"; and L. Thomas, "The Morally Beautiful."
8. See G. Corea, *The Invisible Epidemic: The Story of Women and AIDS* (New York: Harper Collins, 1992); D. Nelkin, D. P. Willis and S. V. Parris, eds., *A Disease of Society: Cultural and Institutional Responses to AIDS* (New York: Cambridge University Press, 1991); R. Carper, *AIDS: The American Roads of Denial* (Springfield, OR: Cross Cultural Press, 1990).
9. See S. Sherwin, *No Longer Patient: Feminist Ethics and Health Care* (Philadelphia: Temple University Press, 1992); E. Martin, *The Woman in the Body: A Cultural Analysis of Reproduction* (Boston: Beacon Press, 1987). See also Levine and Dubler, "HIV and Childbearing"; 337–342 R. Bayer, C. Levine, and S. Wolf, "HIV Antibody Screening: An Ethical Framework for Evaluating Proposed Programs," *Journal of the American Medical Association* 256 (Oct. 1986): 1768–1774; H. Minkoff, "Care of Pregnant Women Infected With Human Immunodeficiency Virus," *Journal of the American Medical Association* 258 (Nov. 1987): 2714–2717.
10. See D. E. Roberts, "Reconstructing the Patient: Starting with Women of Color," in *Feminism and Bioethics: Beyond Reproduction*, ed. S. M. Wolf (New York: Oxford University Press, 1994); A. Dula "Yes There Are African-American Perspectives," in *African American Perspectives*. 193–203.
11. H. Dalton, "AIDS in Blackface," *Daedalus: Journal of the American Academy of Arts and Sciences* 118 (Summer 1989): 205–227; Interview S-24, Nov. 19, 1992, Los Angeles.
12. Interview C-03, Feb. 28, 1992, Baltimore.

13. This remark is made by Ciaran P. Cronin in the introduction of his translation of J. Habermas, *Justification and Application: Remarks on Discourse Ethics* (Cambridge, MA: MIT Press, 1992): xi.
14. See C. West, *Keeping Faith: Philosophy and Race in America* (New York: Routledge, Chapman & Hall, 1993), for a rich account of multiculturalism as a postmodern movement.
15. M. Midgley, *Can't We Make Moral Judgments* (New York: St. Martin's Press, 1991).
16. For critical discussions of society's maternalism, see D. E. Roberts, "Racism and Patriarchy in the Meaning of Motherhood," *Journal of Gender and the Law* 1 (1993): 1–38; C. Sanger, "M is for the Many Things," *Review of Law and Women's Studies* 1 (1992): 15–67; D. Axelsen, "Women as Victims of Medical Experimentation: J. Marion Sims' Surgery on Slave Women, 1845–1850," *Sage* 2 (Fall 1985): 10–13. Describing the work of the "father of gynecology," Axelsen observed that "Sims also saw women as defined in large part by their capacity for reproduction; this attitude is reflected in his later preoccupation with problems of infertility in women."
17. Arras, "AIDS and Reproductive Decisions," 353–382.
18. Ibid., 354.
19. Arras, "AIDS and Reproductive Decisions," 362. See also M. D. Bayles, *Reproductive Ethics* (Englewood Cliffs, NJ: Prentice-Hall, 1984).
20. Arras, "AIDS and Reproductive Decisions," 360.
21. Ibid., 364–365.
22. Ibid., 370.
23. Ibid., 377.
24. Pivnick et al., "Reproductive Decisions Among HIV-Infected, Drug-Using Women," 2NS.
25. Levine and Dubler, "HIV and Childbearing," 322.
26. Ibid., 322.
27. See Hutchinson and Kurth, "I Need to Know that I Have a Choice," 22; and Dula, "Yes, There are African-American Perspectives," 322.
28. *Griswold v. Connecticut*, 381 U.S 479 (1965) held that, with respect to married people, the Constitution prohibits laws that criminalize the use or prescription of contraception. *Roe v. Wade*, 410 U.S. 165 (1973), held that the Constitution prohibits categorical bans on early medical abortions.
29. C. A. MacKinnon, "Refections on Sex Equality Under Law," *Yale Law Journal* 100 (1992): 1281–1328. See also R. Siegel, "Reasoning from the Body: A Historical Perspective on Abortion Regulation and Questions of Equal Protection," *Stanford Law Review* 44 (1992): 261–381; F. Olsen, "Unraveling Compromise," *Harvard Law Review* 103 (1989): 105–135.
30. R. Colker, "Feminism, Theology, and Abortion: Toward Love Compassion, and Wisdom," *California Law Review* 77 (1989): 1011–1075.
31. Legal theorists Robin West and Joan Williams explore misplaced emphasis on choice and autonomy in their work. In connection with reproductive autonomy and black women, see D. E. Roberts, "Racism and Patriarchy in the Meaning of Motherhood," *Journal of Gender and the Law* 1 (1993): 1–38.
32. Levine and Dubler, "HIV and Childbearing," 345.
33. Ibid.

34. Ibid., 346.
35. Pivnick et al., "Reproductive Decisions Among HIV-Infected, Drug-Using Women.": 154–155.
36. Ibid., 154.
37. See D. Bluestein, "The Unanticipated Pregnancy: A Preliminary Study," *Family Practice Research Journal* 9 (Spring/Summer 1990): 105–113; A. Diaz and L. R. Jaffe, "Frequency of Use, Knowledge, and Attitudes Toward the Contraceptive Sponge Among Inner City Black and Hispanic Adolescent Females," *Journal of Adolescent Health Care* 11 (1990): 125–127; G. Wasserman, V. A. Rauh, S. Brunelli et al., "Psychological Attributes and Life Experiences of Disadvantaged Minority Mothers: Age and Ethnic Variations," *Child Development* 61 (1990): 566–580; I. W. Banks and P. I. Wilson, "Appropriate Sex Education for Black Teens," *Adolescence* 24 (Spring 1989): 233–245; E. Hervey Stephen, R. R. Rindfuss, and F. Bean, "Racial Differences in Contraceptive Choice: Complexity and Implications," *Demography*, 25 (February 1988): 53–70; G. E. Wyatt, S. Doyle Peters, and D. Guthrie, "Kinsey Revisited, Part II: Comparisons of the Sexual Socialization and Sexual Behavior of Black Women Over 33 Years," *Archives of Sexual Behavior* 17 (1988): 289–332; L. DeSantis and J. T. Thomas, "Parental Attitudes Toward Adolescent Sexuality: Transcultural Perspectives," *Nurse Practitioner* (August 1987): 43–48; M. McCormick, J. Brooks-Gunn, T. Shorter, et al., "The Planning of Pregnancy Among Low-Income Women in Central Harlem," *American Journal of Obstetrics and Gynecology* 156 (January 1987): 145–149; G. Powell and G. E. Wyatt, "Mental Health Professional's Views of Afro-American Family Life and Sexuality," *Journal of Sex and Marital Therapy* 9: 51–66; H. Minkoff, "Care of Pregnant Women Infected with Human Immunodeficiency Virus," *Journal of the American Medical Association* 258 (Nov. 1987): 2714–2717; K. E. Bauman, "The Difference in Unwanted Births Between Blacks and Whites," *Demography* 10 (August 1973): 315–328; S. Gustavus, "Family Size Preferences of Young People: A Replication and Longitudinal Follow-Up Study," *Studies of Family Planning* 4 (Dec. 1973): 335–342; V. M. Mays and S. D. Cochran, "Methodological Issues in the Assessment and Prediction of AIDS Risk Related Sexual Behaviors Among Black Americans," in *AIDS and Sex: An Integrated Biomedical and Biobehaviorial Approach*, eds. B. Voeller, J. M. Reinisch, and M. Gottleib (New York: Oxford University Press, 1990): 97–120.
38. Banner, "Is There an African-American Perspective?" 191.
39. Garcia, "African-American Perspectives," 43.
40. Dula, "Yes, There are African-American Perspectives": 201.
41. National Council of Negro Women and Communications Consortium Media Center, "Women of Color Health Poll," Aug. 30, 1991, p. 59. Thirty-three percent of the Hispanic women polled said they disagreed with the statement that "The Decision to Have or Not to Have an Abortion is One That Every Women (sic) Must Make for Herself." Only 14% of African-Americans and 8% of Asians disagreed. The figures for low-income Hispanic women revealed even greater ethnic disparities. For a historical discussion of African-American women's support of legal abortion rights, see L. J. Ross, "African-American Women and Abortion: 1800–1970," in *Theorizing Black Feminisms: the Visionary Pragmatism of Black Women*, eds. S. M. James and A.P.A. Busia (London: Routledge, 1993): 141–159.
42. C. Stack, "Different Voices, Different Visions: Gender, Culture, and Moral Rea-

soning," in *Women of Color in U.S. Society*, eds. M. Baca-Zinn and B. Thornton Dill (Philadelphia: Temple University Press, 1994): 291–302.
43. C. Gilligan, *In a Different Voice: Psychological Theory and Women's Development* (Cambridge, MA: Harvard University Press, 1982).
44. Dula, "Yes, There are African-American Perspectives," 201.
45. Interview C-01, Feb. 28, 1992, Baltimore.
46. Interview C-02, Feb. 28, 1992, Baltimore.
47. Interview C-01, Feb. 28, 1992, Baltimore.
48. Interview N-22, Nov. 17, 1992, Los Angeles.
49. Interview M-26, Aug. 26, 1992, New York.
50. Interview M-13, May 14, 1992, Miami.
51. Interview M-24, Aug. 26, 1992, New York.
52. Interview C-08, May 13, 1992, Miami.
53. Interview N-06, July 9, 1992, New York.
54. Interview N-06, July 9, 1992, New York.
55. Interview S-17, Sept. 30, 1992, New York.
56. Interview N-07, July 9, 1992, New York.
57. Interview M-14, May 15, 1992, Miami.
58. Interview M-20, Aug. 26, 1992, New York.
59. Interview N-09, Aug. 19, 1992, New York.
60. Interview N-23, Nov. 18, 1992, Los Angeles.
61. Interview M-14, May 15, 1992, Miami.
62. Interview C-03, Feb. 28, 1992, Baltimore.
63. Interview M-26, Aug. 26, 1992, New York.
64. Interview C-01, Feb. 28, 1992, Baltimore.
65. Interview M-11, May 14, 1992, Miami.
66. Interview N-06, July 9, 1992, New York.
67. Interview M-20, Aug. 26, 1992, New York.
68. Interview N-05, July 9, 1992, New York; Interview M-25, Aug. 26, 1992, New York; Interview M-22, Aug. 26, 1992, New York.
69. Interview N-05, July 9, 1992, New York.
70. Interview M-22, Aug. 26, 1992, New York.
71. Pivnick et al., "Reproductive Decisions Among HIV-Infected, Drug-Using Women.": 161–162, 166.
72. Interview M-20, Aug. 26, 1992, New York.
73. Interview N-09, Aug. 19, 1992, New York.
74. Interview S-22, Sep. 30, 1992, New York.
75. Interview S-21, Sep. 30, 1992, New York; Interview S-19, Sept. 30, 1992, New York.
76. Interview M-22, Aug. 26, 1992, New York.
77. Interview N-05, July 9, 1992, New York.
78. Interview M-20, Aug. 26, 1992, New York.
79. Interview M-03, March 2, 1992, Baltimore.
80. Interview S-16, Sept. 30, 1992, New York.
81. Interview M-21, Aug. 26, 1992, New York.
82. Interview N-04, March 12, 1992, Baltimore.
83. Interview S-21, Sept. 30, 1992, New York.
84. Interview S-15, Sept. 28, 1992, New York.

85. Interview S-22, Sept. 30, 1992, New York.
86. Interview C-16, May 15, 1992, Miami.
87. Interview N-03, March 11, 1992, Baltimore.
88. Interview M-24, Aug. 26, 1992, New York.
89. Interview N-16, Aug. 19, 1992, New York.
90. Interview M-11, May 14, 1992, Miami.
91. Interview S-20, Sept. 30, 1992, New York.
92. Interview N-32, Nov. 19, 1992, Los Angeles.
93. E. Mutran, "Intergenerational Family Support Among Blacks and Whites: Response to Culture or Socioeconomic Differences," *Journal of Gerontology* 40 (May 1985): 382–389; K. Reeb, A. V. Graham, G. Kitson, et al., "Defining Family in Family Medicine: Perceived Family vs. Household Structure in an Urban Black Population," *Journal of Family Practice* 23 (Oct. 1986): 351–355; J. Reis, L. Barbera-Stein, E. Herz, et al., "A Baseline Evaluation of Family Support Programs," *Journal of Community Health* 1 (Summer 1986): 122–136.
94. Women are central in African-American extended families, and women's relationships with other women hold special importance. See P. Hill Collins, *Black Feminist Thought* (New York: Routledge, 1991): 118–120.
95. Interview C-01, Feb. 28, 1992, Baltimore.
96. Interview C-11, May 14, 1992, Miami.
97. Interview S-15, Sept. 28, 1992, New York.
98. Interview M-14, May 15, 1992, Miami.
99. Interview M-14, May 15, 1992, Miami.
100. Interview N-02, March 11, 1992, Baltimore.
101. Interview M-20, Aug. 26, 1992, New York.
102. Interview M-21, Aug. 26, 1992, New York.
103. Interview M-24, Aug. 26, 1992, New York.
104. Interview M-23, Aug. 26, 1992, New York.
105. Interview M-26, Aug. 26, 1992, New York.
106. Interview C-02, Feb. 28, 1992, Baltimore.
107. Interview C-12, May 15, 1992, Miami.
108. Interview C-3, Feb. 28, 1992, Baltimore.
109. Interview N-11, Aug. 19, 1992, New York.
110. Interview S-04, Nov. 19, 1992, Los Angeles; Interview N-33, Nov. 19, 1992, Los Angeles.
111. Interview M-26, Aug. 26, 1992, New York.
112. Interview S-02, March 5, 1992, Baltimore.
113. Interview N-11, Aug. 19, 1992, New York.
114. Interview N-01, Feb. 27, 1992, Baltimore.
115. Interview N-04, March 12, 1992, Baltimore.
116. Interview C-05, May 13, 1992, Miami.
117. Interview C-09, May 14, 1992, Miami.
118. Interview M-26, Aug. 26, 1992, New York.
119. Interview N-13, Aug. 19, 1992, New York.
120. Interview C-04, Feb. 28, 1992, Baltimore.
121. Interview C-04, Feb. 28, 1992, Baltimore.
122. Interview N-33, Nov. 19, 1992, Los Angeles.
123. Interview S-15, Sept. 28, 1992, New York.
124. Interview M-26, Aug. 26, 1992, New York.

125. Interview C-01, Feb. 28, 1992, Baltimore.
126. Interview C-01, Feb. 28, 1992, Baltimore.
127. Interview N-03, March 11, 1992, Baltimore; Interview N-05, July 9, 1992, New York.
128. Interview C-4, Feb. 28, 1992, Baltimore.
129. Hill Collins, *Black Feminist Thought*, 118.
130. K. Maloy and M. Jones Patterson, *Birth or Abortion: Private Struggles in a Political World* (New York: Plenum, 1992).
131. A. Davis, "Surrogates and Outcast Mothers: Racism and Reproductive Ethics," in *"It Just Ain't Fair": The Ethics of Health Care for African Americans*, A. Dula and S. Goering, eds. (Westport, CT: Praeger, 1994).
132. Arras, "AIDS and Reproductive Decisions," 353.
133. T. Lovell Banks, "Women and AIDS—Racism, Sexism and Classism," *Review of Law and Social Change* 17 (1989–90): 351–385.

IV
VOICES FROM THE COMMUNITY

15

Practices and Opinions of Health-Care Providers Serving HIV-Infected Women

NANCY KASS AND RUTH FADEN

Since it became evident that HIV can be transmitted from mother to child through pregnancy and birth, there have been increasing calls for women to be tested for HIV and for women known to be HIV-infected either to delay or refrain from childbearing. Such calls by policy makers, clinicians, and members of the public have been in striking contrast to an otherwise established practice of according women autonomy in reproductive decision-making. Any plausible policy directed at influencing the reproductive behavior of HIV-infected women would have to be implemented in part or in whole through the health-care providers—doctors, nurses, social workers, counselors, and others—who interact with HIV-infected women. Despite the pivotal role of these health-care providers, little is known about their views concerning childbearing and HIV infection, nor is it known how the providers who regularly care for HIV-infected women currently approach the topics of reproduction and childbearing with their clients. To gain a better understanding of how health-care providers actually counsel women and what providers' own beliefs and attitudes are concerning HIV infection and childbearing, we interviewed providers who care regularly for HIV-infected women.

Conduct of the Interviews

Fifty-one health-care providers who work with HIV-infected women were interviewed in Baltimore, Los Angeles, Miami, and New York. These cities were selected because each has a high prevalence of HIV infection among women and children and the combination of cities represents a geographic and ethnic mix. Providers were drawn from any site within each city at which care was provided to HIV-infected women. These included designated HIV clinics, designated women's health-care clinics, drug-treatment centers, academic clinical and research centers, homeless shelters, and family planning clinics. Providers included obstetricians, pediatricians, internists, nurse practitioners, nurses, physician's assistants, social workers, and counselors.

The interviews were conducted by four women, two of whom were members of the Working Group for this project. Each interviewer conducted interviews in either three or four of the cities. The interviewers ranged in age from early 30s to late 50s. One was African-American, one was Hispanic, and two were Caucasian. All interviewers were either graduate students or professionals in the fields of public health or anthropology. Interviews were conducted between May 1992 and November 1993.

The interviewers used two different instruments in their research. The first instrument was an interview guide intended to ensure that certain topics were covered with all providers. These topics included what the provider's professional role was; how the provider usually talked to women who were HIV-infected concerning pregnancy; how relevant it was for the provider whether a woman already had children, whether she had other social support, how her own health had been, or whether she used drugs; and how the provider thought other providers counseled HIV-infected women concerning childbearing. Topics were not necessarily covered in a fixed order, however, and interviews were conversational. If a provider raised issues that were not in the guide, these were pursued as well. Interviews were audiotaped and typically lasted 20–30 minutes.

The second instrument was closed-ended, self-administered, and took less than 5 minutes to complete. It included statements to which providers could respond along a five-point scale concerning the frequency ("never" to "always") with which they would make certain recommendations to HIV-infected or drug-using women (e.g., "I would recommend to a woman who is HIV-positive that she not get pregnant"; "I would recommend Norplant to a woman who uses drugs") as well as statements to which providers could respond along a five-point scale ("strongly disagree" to "strongly agree") concerning certain attitudes (e.g., "There should be a law requiring pregnant women who use drugs to be in drug treatment while they are pregnant"; "Once women learn they are HIV-positive, they should not have any (more) children").

In all, we spoke with ten doctors, nine nurse practitioners, 11 nurses, two physician's assistants, seven social workers, and seven counselors.* Fifteen of these providers were African-American, 13 were Hispanic, 13 were white, seven were Haitian, and two were Asian. Thirty-eight of the providers we interviewed were women and 12 were men. Thirty-one providers had worked with HIV-infected women for at least 3 years, ten said they had worked with HIV-infected women for 1–2 years, and only nine told us that they had worked with HIV-infected women for less than 1 year.

As might be expected, these providers did not all speak with one voice. At the same time, there was remarkable agreement among providers on several themes central to our inquiry.

---

*Demographics were not available for all respondents.

How Providers Counsel Women

One of the most striking features of the interviews was the similarity with which most providers in our sample reported how they counseled women. The vast majority of providers we spoke with maintained that their interactions with HIV-infected women were based on a commitment to the view that childbearing decisions ought to be left to the women. Over and over again, we heard phrases like, "We don't try to push it either way," or "It's the mother's choice if she wants to get pregnant," or "All I can do is give them the facts and then they have to weigh all those facts and decide what it is that they want to do," or "I present the facts to them, I let them know what it means to be HIV-positive, give them the statistics basically, and let the patient make up her mind as to what she wants to do."

In some cases, there was explicit acknowledgment of the importance of reproductive rights. As one provider put it:

> The issue is, regardless of who the person is and what has happened in their life, they have the right to make the decision on their own. As health-care providers, we are supposed to be there to support them in whatever decision they make.[1]

Another provider said, "I try to give as much information as I can. Because I don't know what I would do in the same situation."[2]

Intertwined with their commitment to not forcing women into any particular decision, however, was a clear belief from many providers that childbearing was an extremely serious issue for HIV-infected women and that this should be conveyed. One provider said, "We are extremely honest. We don't candy coat it."[3] Another provider, describing that women need to be informed of a multitude of relevant considerations, said:

> We talk about, again, the transmission rate to the child. If she's had a lot of other kids. And I go a little bit more into, you know, children are infected, they do get sick a lot more than other kids. . . . And the children, they need a lot of special care. And if you want to, maybe someday you could come to one of the clinics and talk to one of the moms or somebody who can tell you what it's about. Before you make that kinda decision. I ask if there's a father involved, is he, does he know that she's positive? Does he know that there's a risk for the child to be positive? How does he deal with sick kids? How does she deal with sick kids? I mean, does she have any experience with anything like that? Cause it's not a, you know, mothers have this perception of having babies as a great thing, and then normal babies turn out be a little hectic, and if you have a sick child, forget that. So, you know, we try to assess how realistic she's thinking about having children.[4]

A tension was apparent for many providers, however, between wanting to respect women's autonomy in making these decisions and a personal feeling of discomfort with HIV-infected women bearing children. For some providers, the discomfort stemmed from their experiences in caring for HIV-infected women and seeing the consequences for these women's children.

> I mean, that's just something out of the order of things, to see a child die. And when you are faced with that and you look at these women who decide to have the baby in spite of the disease, you would like to cry out, no, no, no, no, no, but it's not for us. It's for her.[5]

We heard, similarly, "I really think it's the woman's decision. So, I have to fight my own stuff. . . Part of me wants to say, 'You're probably not going to live to see your daughter grow.' Of course, I can't do that."[6] This tension was highlighted through another provider's question: "I think sometimes we are probably too lenient. We, I don't know, I don't know if we give them too much support?"[7]

For a smaller number of providers, there was less ambivalence. These providers believed that it was their place to tell HIV-infected women that they should avoid childbearing:

> We just try to encourage them not to get pregnant. I tell them why they shouldn't get pregnant because the babies can all be HIV-positive. So they don't want to risk disease to their baby. So they will try to follow our recommendation not to get pregnant.[8]

Another reported, "I think the message is pretty standard. And that message is not to have any more children once you find out that you're HIV-positive."[9] Still another said, "I think if she already has children, I would definitely say, 'Why do you want to risk it?'"[10] And another said, simply, "By saying no, it might help them not to go for the next pregnancy."[11] The issue is not clear-cut for many providers, however, as illustrated by one respondent: "I try to encourage them not to have any other kids. But at the same time, can I blame them?"[12]

For some providers, what was more relevant than the woman's HIV status per se was what kind of a mother she was. One provider said:

> Last time she was pregnant, I said, "Do you wanna get a termination? You know, you still have plenty of time?" And I think that I was trying really to influence her not having any more. Because . . . she's not a good mom. . . . And she really doesn't care. She just happens to get pregnant, and she keeps having it. So, to me, that's more difficult to deal with than the mother who just wants to have kids and you could kinda figure out that she's concerned, really caring.[13]

Another provider said:

> So even if it wasn't HIV-positivity or -negativity, my automatic reaction is let's think about it. You can't even take care of yourself, much less another baby or two babies or three babies.[14]

How Providers Think Other Health-Care Professionals Counsel HIV-Infected Women

We asked providers whether they thought other health-care providers interacted with HIV-infected women differently. Although many providers said that their style was similar to that of others, particularly others at their own institution, some were ready to disclose "horror stories" from other institutions. That providers were eager to describe this conveyed to us further that they saw their own counseling style as quite different from that in some of the stories they had heard."We have women who are referred to us from the other services who have been told to abort. Straight out."[15] Another said:

> The doctor is saying, you are positive, you have to get an abortion. You're gonna have a sick kid. Things like that. And really, they're not provided with the right information. So people are told if you're positive, you're definitely going to have a positive child. You know, a lot of the women over and over keep saying, you know, I'm so glad I came here because otherwise I didn't have enough information. . . We keep hearing horror stories of clients of ours who have gone to other clinics, and the people said, "You're gonna have an AIDS baby. And it's gonna die. And you're gonna get real sick." And they come in here crying, hysterical.[16]

Still another reported,

> Doctors will call us up and say, "How dare you tell her it's up to her and what she should and should not do about either aborting, having a miscarriage, carrying the baby, even getting pregnant." I mean, they call us and say, "Who in the hell do you think you are?" So as far as the medical profession, I know that they have a knee-jerk reflex about what should and should not be done. Um, and they don't know the facts. They don't know the percentages of conversion. And they don't know anything. It's just a real reflection of society's knee-jerk reflex that these HIV women should not have babies.[17]

Providers' Own Opinions Concerning Whether HIV-Infected Women Should Have Children

We were interested not only in how providers talked to women but in what their own attitudes were concerning HIV-infected women and childbearing. We knew that providers might have personal feelings about this issue, whether or not they thought it was appropriate to voice these opinions to their patients. Indeed, we learned that many providers felt uncomfortable with HIV-infected women having children. Again, that is not to say that they would necessarily counsel women not to have children or even that they were clear on what they would do if they were in the women's situation themselves, but providers did not convey indifference about this issue. One provider captured what many others described:

My own personal conversation about this is that I don't think HIV women ought to have children. You're infected and they don't have a cure for it and the child is going to be motherless at some point in the future.[18]

Among the strongest feelings were expressed by this provider: "In general, these are poor women having babies and the taxpayers are paying for it. And if it's HIV positive, poor women having babies, that's even worse."[19] Another said:

If the person does get sick, they will die and leave those kids. And then you have to think, well, is it fair to the child? You know? You go ahead and have that child and you die? And who's really gonna take care of the child? Most of the time they have to go to foster care.[20]

This was echoed by another provider:

I have a harder time with a positive woman than a negative woman, naturally. Because I don't want that baby to be positive or to be without a mother.[21]

And still another said:

When we sit back and we see the babies that we deal with and we see them born, we see them become ill, and we see them die, it hurts us. I mean, we grieve and we grieve hard, just as if the child was our own because in fact they are like our own.[22]

The ambivalence between providers' inner feelings and what they believe is the appropriate way to counsel women was reflected with this provider's statement:

We all know that they have the right to have kids. And we let them know that, if they get pregnant, even though they can feel that we don't really want them to have other kids, we let them know that, if, by any chance you get pregnant, we'll be here for you. We'll give you all the care that you need.[23]

Several providers felt their opinion about whether it was appropriate for HIV-infected women to have children was affected by whether the woman already had children: "I guess that's my prejudice, but I feel if you've had a lot of kids, it might not be as important to have another child."[24] Another said:

I will accept that if she has never had a baby, you want to take the chance to have one. You might be lucky and the baby still revert, that's fine. But if you already have two, three, or four kids, I don't think it's worth it to go for it. Because you don't know. There is the chance, that possibility that you might have an infected child.[25]

A minority of providers felt differently altogether; this subset firmly believed that it was fine for HIV-infected women to decide to have children. One provider framed it this way:

It's like telling a woman whose baby is going to have a birth defect to abort. She has the right to make her decision. So we can't say one thing for one portion of the population and another for a different portion of the population.[26]

Nonetheless, it is fair to say that the majority of providers interviewed conveyed at least some degree of discomfort with the notion of HIV-infected women having children, and some said directly that they thought that this was a bad idea. Most providers, however, were clear to say that this was their personal opinion, and many voiced their hope that the HIV-infected women they care for still would feel free to make their own decisions.

Findings from the Self-Administered Questionnaire Related to HIV-Infected Women

After the open-ended interview was conducted, providers were asked to respond to closed-ended items on a much shorter instrument. According to this questionnaire, 42% of providers said they "often" or "always" would recommend to a woman who was HIV-positive that she not get pregnant (Table 15.1). Forty percent said they "often" or "always" would recommend Norplant to a woman who was HIV-positive, though significantly fewer (13%) said they "often" or "always" would recommend abortion to a woman who was HIV-positive and pregnant. Thirteen percent of providers agreed or strongly agreed with the statement "There should be mandatory insertion of Norplant for HIV-positive women" and 29% agreed or strongly agreed with the statement "Once women learn they are HIV-positive, they should not have any (more) children" (Table 15.2). There was no difference in how providers of different professional backgrounds responded to these statements, nor was the ethnic/racial background or sex of the

TABLE 15.1. The Degree to Which Providers Would Make Recommendations Concerning Childbearing to Women Who Are HIV-Positive or Who Use Drugs

	Never/Rarely	Sometimes	Often/Always
I would recommend to a woman who is HIV-positive that she not get pregnant	38%	20%	42%
I would recommend Norplant to a woman who is HIV-positive	25%	35%	40%
I would recommend abortion to a pregnant woman who is HIV-positive	67%	21%	13%
I would recommend to a woman who uses drugs that she not get pregnant	24%	20%	57%
I would recommend Norplant to a woman who uses drugs	25%	29%	46%
I would recommend abortion to a pregnant woman who uses drugs	63%	29%	8%

TABLE 15.2. Providers' Attitudes Concerning HIV-Positive Women and Childbearing

	Strongly Disagree or Disagree	No Opinion	Strongly Agree or Agree
There should be mandatory insertion of Norplant for HIV-positive women	81%	6%	13%
Once women learn they are HIV-positive, they should not have any (more) chidren	55%	16%	29%
Women who use drugs should not have children	56%	24%	20%
There should be a law requiring pregnant women who use drugs to be in drug treatment while they are pregnant.	28%	14%	59%

provider or the length of time the provider had worked with HIV-infected women significantly associated with how he or she responded.

At first blush, it may appear that data collected from the interviews and from the self-administered questionnaires were inconsistent. Providers' responses to the closed-ended questionnaire items seem to suggest a more heavy-handed or directive approach to counseling than described by most providers in the interviews. Our belief is that both sets of data are accurate, however. That is, it was clear to us from talking to providers that they have a tremendous amount of ambivalence around this issue. They have discomfort with HIV-infected women having children, which would explain their saying that they would recommend to an HIV-infected woman that she not have children. At the same time, for the most part, these providers are committed to the belief that the choice about childbearing should be left to the woman. Providers might make a recommendation or might counsel in a way in which their own opinion is revealed, but they still want to ensure that their clients understand what their options are and feel that the choice ultimately should be made by them. That a smaller proportion of providers agreed or strongly agreed with the statement "Once women learn they are HIV-positive, they should not have any (more) children" than the proportion who would "recommend" not having children to an HIV-infected woman, and that a smaller proportion agreed that "HIV-infected women should have mandatory insertion of Norplant" compared with the proportion who would "recommend" Norplant to HIV-infected women further substantiates our thesis. Providers are resistant to agree with statements that hint at heavy-handedness. Providers seem to make a distinction between advising women not to have children compared with requiring them not to. It is our belief that just the difference in wording between "should not" in the first statement and "recommend" in the second resulted in fewer providers identifying with the first, more directive one. Time and time again, providers told us in interviews that they were strongly against any policy requiring HIV-infected women to not have children or to be sterilized, even when they seemed to hope that HIV-infected women would make that decision on their own.

Provider Attitudes and Practices Concerning Women Who Use Drugs

Generally, providers were less comfortable with drug-using women having children than with women who are HIV-infected having children. One provider expressed her own feelings as:

> I get really aggravated when I see a mother who knows but just ignores the fact that you are doing damage to yourself as well as your baby by using drugs. Let alone, what's gonna happen once you deliver that child. Are you thinking about that while you're out there using drugs? No.[27]

Another said that she and other providers at her clinic "don't do drug users well."[28] When asked what she meant, she said that providers are likely to listen to women who do not use drugs and try to sort out what is best for them. Drug-using women, she said, are less likely to get that care. "All of us in general don't like to deal with users playing the games that drug users play."[29]

Generally, more providers felt comfortable trying to exert influence with women who use drugs than with women who are HIV-infected.

> Sometimes we'll even take them up to the nursery and say, "Look, this is what happens when you use crack. You may put this in the back of your mind when you're smoking that rock, and you may not think of it because you can't see that baby . . . [but] it's in you. And you know it's living off of you, but you don't have to really see it or be responsible for it yet." I say, "But look at this little guy here. His mother smoked crack into her ninth month of pregnancy, and in the seventh or eighth month, the placenta separated and look how tiny that little baby is. And he's gonna have a hard time surviving. And he's gonna have some learning problems, and we always want the best for our children, as mothers. And this is something you have to think about if you're a drug abuser."[30]

Another provider said:

> If they're pregnant and they use drugs, yes, we do tell them a lot more. Because, beside the virus, the baby can come out with alcohol syndrome and all those things, crack babies. And at least I try to put them in a rehab center or at least during the time try to do as much as I can. What they're willing to do is a different story.[31]

Some providers used the threat of protective services in their discussions with drug-using women. One provider in particular said that it was important to make drug-using women feel guilt as a means of trying to influence their decisions.

> We have to report you. If the baby's urine is dirty, or yours is dirty, they're gonna take the baby from you automatically. And you're gonna have to finish a drug program. You might finish that drug program, but that baby still might be damaged when it's born. So they really, they're impacted a little bit by guilt. You have to make them feel guilt. Because IV drug abusers, or just drug abusers, don't feel guilt. The drugs can make the guilt feelings go away real easily.[32]

Clearly, providers had much stronger feelings about the ability of drug-using women to parent compared with that of HIV-infected women. One provider was describing that, generally, the HIV-infected women she knew were good mothers, "unless they are IV drug abusers, where they abandon their children."[33]

In describing how colleagues counsel women who use drugs, the sense generally was that colleagues, too, have strong feelings about this issue and tend to be directive in their interactions. One provider said:

> I think there are some people who feel that if the woman is a drug user and she's HIV-positive, that she's committing a crime if she has a baby. . . My impression is that the doctors have a prejudice against it and they would opt that these women have an abortion. But to say whether or not they actually convey this to the women when they are examining the women or talking with the women, I couldn't honestly say which way they go. But my own personal feeling is that they kind of try to talk the women into having an abortion. They feel, you are a drug user, you are HIV-positive, you don't need to have a baby. Abort this baby, why are you going to bring this baby into this world with all these negatives against it. That's the impression that I get from them. As to what they are actually saying, that's another story. But I always ask myself if that's the way you feel . . . even if you are not saying that . . . how much of that is really going to be conveyed to the person that you are talking to.[34]

There still were many providers, however, who thought that reproductive decisions should be left to women, even if the women used drugs. The following comments are representative of numerous providers: "We have a lot of substance abusers . . . it's a very common combination. I think they have the right to make that choice."[35] Another said, "No difference. . . . I have to give her the facts and it's her decision to make."[36] We also heard:

> You know the perception that people may have that because this woman is a drug user . . . they don't care about their children. You may have some that have that kind of mentality, but we see mothers who have been drug users for many years and have children and then they find out that they are HIV-positive and their children are positive. I've seen these mothers stand over these babies in the hospitals in these beds saying why, why my child. Innocent babies, and actually hurt that this has happened. They love their children just like any other women that give birth.[37]

Findings from the Self-Administered Questionnaire Related to Women Who Use Drugs

In response to items on the self-administered questionnaire, 57% of providers said they "often" or "always" would recommend to a woman who uses drugs that she not get pregnant (this is in contrast to 42% when the question concerned HIV-positive women). Forty-six percent said they "often" or "always" would recommend Norplant to a woman who uses drugs, and 8% said they "often" or "always" would recommend abortion to a pregnant woman who uses drugs (see Table 15.1). Twenty percent agreed or strongly agreed with the statement "Women who use drugs should not have children" and 59% agreed or strongly agreed that "There should be a law requiring pregnant women who use drugs to be in drug treatment while they are pregnant."

Generalizability of Findings

We interviewed providers who, for the most part, had chosen to work either with HIV-affected populations generally or with women in particular. As stated earlier, 62% of the providers we interviewed had worked with HIV-infected women for at least 3 years. As such, the providers included in this study were not representative of all health-care providers in this country, and it is likely that their attitudes and practices do not reflect those of health-care providers generally.

Unlike most health-care providers, who may rarely or only superficially interact with persons who are infected with HIV, the providers with whom we spoke had intense and long-lasting relationships with their HIV-infected clients. Providers explained that clients had medical visits quite frequently, and providers came to know their clients very well. Through this, understanding of the women's lives and a remarkable advocacy for the women themselves often emerged. This was described by two different providers:

> We try to follow these moms pretty closely, at least the ones that I have. So we know how many children they have, more or less, we know pretty much what the issues are at home. If there's anything new, we usually pick it up. . .[38]

> We have a tremendous advocacy for our women. We are very supportive of them. From the time that they're diagnosed to the time that they die. We develop an attachment and a closeness to them that they know, when they're in trouble, no matter if it's related to HIV or not, it's related to drug abuse or it's related to physical abuse. They're abandoned, they're homeless, they're hungry. They've got a place to go. And we have a full resource system. And we see them enough on this floor all day long, but they're not here because they're sick. They're here because they're homeless, they're hungry, they need food vouchers, they need formula or diapers for the baby. They just need somebody to say, "You don't need to stay in the house if he's beating you. We'll put you in a safe place." Anything. We really try to work on empowering our women and advocating for their needs. To me, that would be the single most important thing that we really try to do.[39]

Providers described the trust that develops in their relationship with women as extremely important in determining whether or not their care will be successful. If clients trust them, they are more likely to follow their recommendations, feeling more confident that advice is being given with what is best for them in mind.

While we do not believe that our sample is representative of all health-care providers, we do believe that it is representative of many providers who are working with HIV-infected women. That is, many HIV-infected women are receiving care at HIV-designated clinics or at sites at which providers have chosen to work with them and have vast experience doing so. As such, our sample and the views expressed probably are representative of most providers currently caring for HIV-infected women. Nonetheless, it may be that women who live in areas with a low prevalence of HIV infection or women who do not have a regular source of medical care are more likely to interact with providers who have less experience working with HIV-infected women. As HIV becomes more prevalent, providers may be less likely to refer their HIV-infected patients to specialists and more "mainstream" providers may be caring for HIV-infected women, even in large cities. While data on the attitudes and practices of such providers are presently unavailable, our findings suggest that providers less experienced in the care of HIV-infected women may be more punitive and directive in their interactions with them.

A limitation of this research is that it was conducted before the findings from ACTG 076 were known. That trial revealed that an intervention now is available that may significantly reduce the rate of vertical transmission, at least among certain categories of HIV-infected women. It is very likely that these findings already have changed how providers talk to HIV-infected women about reproduction and childbearing. Although the findings apply most directly to pregnant women, of course they have implications for women considering pregnancy as well.

For the most part, providers we talked to said that they would not make recommendations to women under any circumstance. Even when we pressed them concerning whether their counseling style would be affected by the number of children the woman had, whether she had Medicaid coverage, or how sick she was, providers said they would provide women with information and leave childbearing decisions to them. This leads us to suspect that findings from ACTG 076 would only reinforce that stance.

It would have been interesting to ask those providers who thought it was a bad idea for HIV-infected women to have children whether ACTG 076 results changed their attitudes. To what degree were their opinions due to the fact that HIV can be transmitted vertically, and if that was an important factor, was the reduction in vertical transmission from 26% to 8% sufficient to warrant a change in attitudes? Given the timing of the interviews, we were unable to ascertain whether, knowing an intervention was available, an even smaller proportion of providers would recommend that HIV-infected women avoid pregnancy or have an abortion.

Through this research, our goal was to learn more about providers' attitudes. Therefore, interviews were conducted with many types of provider who interact with HIV-infected women. It is a limitation of this approach, however, that only providers' self-reports of how they counsel women can be documented rather than our being able to record actual exchanges between providers and women. There is no way for us to know if providers represented accurately the content or tone of those interactions.

Conclusions

Most providers interviewed believed that it was not their place to tell HIV-infected women what to do about childbearing, in terms of either becoming pregnant or whether to continue an existing pregnancy. This is not to say that all of these providers felt comfortable with HIV-infected women deciding to have children; indeed, many (though not all) providers expressed great discomfort with the notion. Nonetheless, most held fast to the view that ultimately the decision had to be the woman's own. Expressing the understanding developed through caring for HIV-infected women, one provider said to us, "Can you blame them?"

A smaller number of providers, however, reported that they did tell women that they should not become pregnant or bear children. These providers justified their position by appealing to concerns that offspring would be sick and that mothers eventually would die, leaving their children orphaned.

The impact of maternal drug use on providers' attitudes was stark. Providers were considerably more likely to voice recommendations if women also used drugs. Indeed, providers generally had stronger feelings about the behaviors of drug-using women than about women being HIV-infected per se. Providers were more likely to think that it was wrong for drug-using women to have children, and there were more providers who reported being directive in their interactions with women who used drugs.

Also stark was how providers differentiated between terminating and preventing pregnancy. Providers generally felt uncomfortable with the idea of encouraging or promoting abortion. Even among providers who felt it appropriate to make recommendations about childbearing in certain situations, very few said they would recommend abortion to women under any circumstance.

It is clear that many health-care providers who work with HIV-infected women have tremendous affection for the women they serve. The majority of the providers we interviewed communicated the concern and empathy they feel for their patients. The often voiced commitment to respect the right of HIV-infected women to decide for themselves about childbearing undoubtedly is related to the respect of these providers for the women in their care. Although only a minority of our respondents volunteered that they were directive with their clients, many reported that they had heard stories of other providers interacting with HIV-infected and drug-using women in a forceful manner.

Anecdotes suggesting that all providers tell HIV-infected women not to have children clearly are not true. Nonetheless, although most of the providers with whom we spoke attempted either to gently advise or indeed to not at all direct the reproductive behavior of their clients, many considered themselves to be the exception. Of course, it may be that how providers described their counseling style was not always accurate or that we were talking to an unrepresentative group. We can conclude, however, that at least some HIV-infected women in cities of high prevalence are hearing that decisions about childbearing ultimately are theirs to make.

Notes

1. Interview S101, Aug. 5, 1992, New York.
2. Interview N103, July 9, 1992, New York.
3. Interview C102, May 12, 1992, Miami.
4. Interview M101, May 12, 1992, Miami.
5. Interview S104, Sept. 30, 1992, New York.
6. Interview N103, July 9, 1992, New York.
7. Interview M104, May 12, 1992, Miami.
8. Interview C110, May 14, 1992, Miami.
9. Interview C104, May 12, 1992, Miami.
10. Interview S105, Nov. 16, 1992, Los Angeles.
11. Interview S104, Sept. 30, 1992, New York.
12. Interview M104, May 12, 1992, Miami.
13. Interview M101, May 12, 1992, Miami.
14. Interview N112, Nov. 17, 1992, Los Angeles.
15. Interview C101, May 12, 1992, Miami.
16. Interview M101, May 12, 1992, Miami.
17. Interview N103, July 9, 1992, New York.
18. Ibid.
19. Interview C107, May 12, 1992, Miami.
20. Interview M104, May 12, 1992, Miami.
21. Interview N103, July 9, 1992, New York.
22. Interview S101, Aug. 5, 1992, New York.
23. Interview M104, May 12, 1992, Miami.
24. Interview M101, May 12, 1992, Miami.
25. Interview S104, Sept. 30, 1992, New York.
26. Interview S101, Aug. 5, 1992, New York.
27. Interview M107, May 12, 1992, Miami.
28. Interview N112, Nov. 17, 1992, Los Angeles.
29. Ibid.
30. Interview C102, May 12, 1992, Miami.
31. Interview C101, May 12, 1992, Miami.
32. Interview C102, May 12, 1992, Miami.
33. Ibid.

34. Interview S102, Aug. 5, 1992, New York.
35. Interview M102, May 12, 1992, Miami.
36. Interview S102, Aug. 5, 1992, New York.
37. Ibid.
38. Interview C101, May 12, 1992, Miami.
39. Interview C102, May 12, 1992, Miami.

16

In Women's Words: The Values and Lived Experiences of HIV-Infected Women

NANCY KASS AND RUTH FADEN

We were guided in our work by the view that, to the extent possible, public policies should be informed by the values and experiences of those most directly affected by them. Therefore, over the course of 2 years, we interviewed HIV-infected women living in four cities in the United States. Women talked to us about their intentions concerning childbearing, whether they thought it was acceptable generally for HIV-infected women to have children, how health-care providers have discussed reproduction and childbearing with them, and what they think health-care providers should be saying to HIV-infected women. As might be expected, a rich set of data emerged. A summary of the findings as they relate most closely to the subject of our policy recommendations is presented in this chapter.

Between February 1992 and November 1993, 159 women from Baltimore, Miami, New York, and Los Angeles were interviewed. These four cities were chosen because each has a high prevalence of HIV infection among women and children and together these cities represent a geographic and ethnic mix among the women who are infected. Interviews were qualitative, open-ended, and conversational. They were audiotaped and typically lasted 30–45 minutes. Interviewers used a semistructured outline guide to ensure that certain topics always were covered, but topics were not necessarily covered in a regular order; moreover, if a woman raised issues that were not in the guide, these usually were explored with her as well.

Women were eligible to be included in our sample if they were receiving care from any organization within the city that served HIV-infected women (not necessarily a health-care organization) or if a provider or another client with whom we already had made contact identified a woman to us and sought the woman's permission to be contacted by us. Two of the women we interviewed were adolescents, 63 were 20–29 years old, and 83 were 30 years or older (we did not know the ages of 11 of the women). Twenty of the women (13%) currently were pregnant. The vast majority of the women (135 or 85%) already had at least one child. We learned the educational background of 111 of the women interviewed. Of these women, 20 (13%) had not attended any high school, 26 (16%) had attended some high school but never had graduated, 28 (18%) were high school graduates, 27 (17%) had attended some college but not graduated, and 10 (6%) were college graduates. Eighty-four of the women were African-American, 47 were Hispanic, 20 were white, five were Haitian, and we did not know the racial or ethnic background of three of the women.

Interviews were conducted by four women, two of whom were members of the Working Group. Each interviewer conducted interviews in either three or four of the cities. The interviewers ranged in age from early 30s to mid-50s. One was African-American, one was Hispanic, and two were Caucasian. All interviewers were either graduate students or professionals in the fields of public health or anthropology.

Having Babies: Personal Values and Intentions

Approximately one-quarter of the women we interviewed were not planning on having more or any children, and being HIV-infected had nothing to do with that decision. These women had decided long before that they did not want to have children or already had had as many children as they wanted or were unable to have children. Approximately half of the overall sample also did not want to have more or any children, and these women held those beliefs explicitly because they were HIV-infected. The remaining one-quarter of the sample either thought it was likely that they would have (more) children or at least would not rule out the possibility.

For many women, the tragedy of learning that they had been infected with HIV was their belief that they couldn't (or shouldn't) have children. "When I found out, I said, 'Damn. That means I can't really have no babies,' even though I wanted another one."[1] Another woman said, "It's hard because you want to have children."[2] Over and over we heard phrases like "I would not bring a kid into the world. I think it's unfair"[3] or "Is it fair to bring a child into this world who might have AIDS and die? Well, a person doesn't have that right."[4] One woman said:

> No, I can't have any more kids. Cause I have this disease and the longer, you know, the older I get, the worse my disease is getting, there's more chances of my baby even being worse, OK? She's healthy, she's fine. But what about my next baby?[5]

Women overwhelmingly cited the possibility of the children being infected as the reason they should not have children. Representative of many women's comments are the following: "That tiny infant to suffering, I wouldn't do that"[6] or "I hate to see a poor little child in that much, that kind of pain"[7] or simply

"That's cruel, that's cruel."[8] One woman said, quite specifically, "I think the biggest problem is worrying about whether your kid is going to be infected."[9]

Some women who already had had an infected child spoke of how they did not want to go through that experience again.

> I've had two that have died. I would really just help the other children that need it rather than keep destroying other lives. Every child that is brought to the world has the right to be born, but I don't think we have a right to bring them into the world if we know that they are going to be born with an illness. . . . I tried twice, and twice was enough.[10]

Another woman said,

> I would like to, but I can't do it. I don't want to take that chance. Maybe if [my daughter] wasn't positive, it would be much easier. But knowing that she's positive, it's harder . . . cause I know everything I have been through already with her, and it's not us that really suffer, it's them.[11]

Another woman told us,

> I had my first case of shingles last summer. That was the most humiliating thing I've ever gone through in my life. I cannot imagine their need for putting somebody through shingles. I've had PCP. I wouldn't wish that on a two or three year old.[12]

Still another woman said, "I have a friend who's out there now that's lost a daughter. And the pain . . . the only daughter she ever had . . . I couldn't handle that." Later, she said of her own situation,

> I feel like I've cheated them . . . especially my daughter. Because I couldn't give her the type of attention that I gave my son because I was [infected] . . . from the time she was born, and that really makes me sad. She was three years old when she first asked me "Mommy, are you going to die?"[13]

Among the women who did not intend to have children because they were HIV-infected, we were interested in pursuing the extent to which vertical transmission was their exclusive concern. Therefore, we asked the hypothetical question, "If there were a 'magic pill' that women could take that would prevent their babies from being infected but could not improve women's own health, would that alter how you felt about having children?" Indeed, many women did indicate that, were such an intervention available, they might change their intention and go on to have children. "If we knew the baby would come out negative, then we could have been parents again."[14] Another woman agreed:

> If it was that away, and they could help me and prevent it, cause I'd love to have another one. But, that, that chance haven't come yet. You know. And this is just a chance you taking. Yeah, if they come up with that, I would love to have another baby.[15]

Although with less frequency, some women also voiced the concern that children of HIV-infected women could be orphaned.

One woman said, "We think, what if we die? Who is the kid going to stay with? Is the baby going to suffer, too? You have to think so many ways of what to do. It's not easy to make a decision."[16] Other women said, "If the child is born healthy or not healthy, whatever, and then the mother go, who is going to take care of the child? So don't even have the child"[14] and "What if I got sick or something happened to me? Who is going to take care of my kids?"[18]

Other women spoke of the loss associated with their own mortality as a reason not to have children. "I wouldn't be there to see them grow up, go to school, finish school, get a job. I wouldn't be there for them. So, that would be a choice I wouldn't make."[19] We heard from another woman:

> You just wish you could be there all the time for him and just thinking that someday I'm going to go away and leave him alone, even though he'll have the family around, it seems that you're the special person for that child. You might think to bring up your kids one way and then if you leave, you're gone, or you die, that other person who stays with him might end up bring him up the wrong way or something.[20]

Even women who had not gone through the experience of mothering an infected child imagined that it would be very difficult for them to have a sick or dying infant. "How I'd be able to deal with the time when this baby is very, very ill, and this baby has to die. Death is final. And I don't know if I could have went through that, so I had an abortion."[21] Another woman said, "Having to have to give them medicine every day and suffering, I can't stand that. I wouldn't be able to stand that."[22]

We noted earlier that about a quarter of our sample could not rule out the possibility of becoming pregnant in the future. The majority, although not all, of these women framed this in somewhat religious terms. One woman said, "To give birth is a blessing from the Lord."[23] Two women offered almost identical thoughts, suggesting that the decision was not theirs to make: "I just have it all in God's hands"[24] and "I want my baby. I want a life. And, I leave it in God's hands."[25] Yet, a few women framed the discussion in terms of rights. "Because you are HIV, that doesn't mean you don't have no right to have a baby. You have every right like everyone else."[26]

Whether or not they had children, the women we interviewed usually agreed that whether a woman already had children was relevant not only to that woman's decision but also to whether it was acceptable generally for HIV-infected women to have children. Indeed, many women with children felt that it was only because they already had children that they could decide not to have more. A woman who learned she was infected after her daughter was born was asked if she would have wanted to become pregnant if she had found out beforehand that she was infected. "The first time I would have," she answered, "I would have had her anyway."[27] Other women said more generally:

I think for women who have never had a child and who have been diagnosed as HIV-positive, we [sic] ought to have at least one baby. I mean, they're due that. Before I got pregnant with my child, I was feeling like I wasn't a woman.[28]

Another woman said, "I think if they don't have any kids and they still want them bad enough, they could take the chance and have them."[29]

Importance of Motherhood

Feelings about motherhood are integral to discussions about HIV-infected women having children, and it is crucial to understand both the prevalence and the depth of those desires. Both women who had children and women who did not conveyed the importance of motherhood for them. "It's very, very important. I mean, you bring up this kid and it's so special to you."[30] "I think the HIV is harder on women cause we want to have kids. Sometimes I see babies and I think I would love having a baby, but I get scared."[31] In describing her relationship with her children, one woman said,

> I know they love me. It's like no pressure involved. It just feels good to have someone love you and to love someone back. It's like it's a part of you and you are part of that person and that person is a part of you.[32]

For some women, the importance of motherhood was heightened as a result of their illness.

> Now I see that it's the most important thing in my life because now I don't even know how long I would be able to be a mother. It was always important, but you really don't think about it like that until somebody hands you your pink slip.[33]

Along a similar vein, many women who had children said that, in the context of their infection, their children were their main reason for living. "I looked at him and I says, 'well he's here and I've got to take care of him. I have to be here for him.'"[34] Another woman said, "I refuse to get sick now that I have somebody to take care of."[35] We heard from another, "It's really hard to beat the battle between not wanting to fight it and having to fight it for my daughter,"[36] while another said, "No matter what I have, HIV, AIDS, whatever, they're going to love me."[37]

What Health-Care Providers Have Said About Childbearing

We were very interested in how health-care providers had discussed issues related to childbearing with women. Had they told women they shouldn't have kids? Had they told them their opinions at all? Along these lines, we heard quite a range from the women. Some women reported that their providers had given them information and made it clear that the decision was theirs to make. One woman said, "She was nice with me. She only advised me to be careful, because it was not certain that the baby was going to be born sick or not, that many things could happen."[38] Another woman said, "I never had a doctor or nurse say that I shouldn't have a child, no. They told me the risk factors."[39]

Several other providers, according to the women's reports, tried to exert influence. One woman responded, "When I was four months pregnant with Morris, they 'advised' me that I should think about having an abortion. Because the baby—no doubt about it—was going to be positive at birth."[40] Another woman reported,

> I got pregnant again, and my doctor said if you want to live to the end of the year—he put a guilt trip on me pretty much, telling me you've got to care about this one right now, you know, and care about yourself. He said if you want to be around to take care of this one, you can't have this baby.[41]

Another woman said, "Most of them tell you no. Because the doctor here, she's told me no. And so did another doctor."[42] One woman spoke of a provider she had seen previously: "The lady that I been seeing before I started to coming to this clinic, the regular doctor, doctor say 'How could you do that?' You know. I really hated the way she had talked to me."[43] One woman said that her doctors had told her she should have an abortion, but when she said she didn't want to, they were good about giving her prenatal care.[44] Another woman said,

> I was being told that, as a woman, how dare I bring a child into the world that was going to be born sick. Automatically they figured this child was going to be sick, you know. They labeled my baby, you know, as a sickly child, you know. They wouldn't see me, you know. He wouldn't see me. He wanted to refer me to someone who would perform an abortion.[45]

Another woman generalized doctors' counseling style beyond the context of HIV:

> I didn't want their opinion because . . . what I've noticed in most doctors is that if you tell them you want to have a baby and they know that you have a heart disease, you have a liver disease, you have high blood pressure, they say no. You a smoker they say no. Your gut ache, they say no. Well I have AIDS, so I know they were going to say no.[46]

Perhaps the most common way that women described how providers had talked to them about childbearing was with firm, but not forceful, advice that they should not have children. One woman said,

> I think they're giving me what they feel is good advice. Well, they tell me, like, you know, they don't say, "Don't get pregnant." You know, they talk to me and, you know, explain certain things to me and why it wouldn't be good. I mean, they can't make me not do it. So they just do what they can and explain to me in a nice way. And you take it however you want it.[47]

Another woman, when asked if she had been advised not to get pregnant, said, "Not in so many words, but they advise everyone to get it together. And they advise everyone not to have kids."[48]

What Women Think Health-Care Providers Ought To Say

Women then were asked what they thought health-care providers ought to say. Responses here were quite varied, though certain themes emerged. On the question of whether health-care providers should give advice, women were close to evenly split between providing comments like, "I don't think a doctor should tell a woman what to do, even if she's HIV-positive or not HIV-positive, I think it is up to her"[49] and "They should tell them not to have them at all."[50]

On other issues there was clear consensus, however. One theme that emerged from numerous interviews was that women want to be given the facts.

> Facts. What exactly could happen, how exactly it would happen. . . . I don't think the doctor has the right to say no. And they don't have the right to say yes. Because what they're thinking is their opinion. But it's your body, it's your system, it's your life. They should just tell them what the risks are. And by, by knowing the risk, that person is going to make the right decision.[51]

A similar comment was, "I think they should put everything in front of them, you know, the good points and the bad points, and let the woman make her own mind up."[52]

Another woman said she thought providers sometimes shied away from the truth.

> Doctors who sit there and beat around things and sugar coat them to gloss them over so they don't hurt as much when they tell them aren't doing any favors because it doesn't change the problem. All it does is change your way of thinking about it, and you may not take it as seriously as you should.[53]

Many women seemed desperate for information, and some expressed frustration that they couldn't be told more precisely whether *they* would have an infected child.

For many women, what was at least as important as what providers said was how they said it. One woman said, "So it's like the way you say it, you know. Yeah, you can give advice, not orders."[54] Another woman said, similarly, "I think when the person recommends, I think they should do it with care and kindness and say 'but, it's your choice.' . . . Recommending is fine, but you can't, like I said, you can't mandate it."[55] That seemed to be a message we heard from many women: it is fine for doctors and other providers to give advice, as long as it is done in a gentle and caring manner.

How Women Would Advise Other Women

We wanted to know not only what women thought health-care providers should say but also what they themselves would say to a friend who was HIV-infected and came to them for advice. This question was interesting because it revealed both women's own opinions about HIV-infected women having children and how appropriate they thought it was for people to give each other advice in this area. In response to this set of questions, we heard many of the same themes described above. Women often thought it was a bad idea for the friend to go ahead and become pregnant and often thought this because of concern for the well-being of the baby. For example, we heard,

> I just think if you're HIV-infected, don't have it. I don't like seeing little babies with tubes all here and there and everywhere. . . So I would ask any woman that's HIV-infected, please don't.[56]

Another woman said,

> I would tell her you shouldn't have no babies, not with HIV. I would tell her, don't have none. Don't have no kids. It's bad enough she's HIV, you know. And to have a baby? Uh-uh.[57]

We also heard, "There's a possibility the child won't have it, but then the child has a possibility of losing you."[58]

Nonetheless, even though many women thought that, if asked, they would tell a friend that it was a bad idea to have children, being HIV-infected, almost all of these women believed that ultimately it was the friend's decision to make. Expressing what was echoed by many others, one woman said,

> I guess I would tell them, well, if I was you, I wouldn't do it. I wouldn't want to risk the life of a baby, you know. Even though you have a chance that the baby can come out alright, with nothing, you know. Still, you never know. It's their choice. You can't tell somebody what you have to do or what you should do.[59]

Another woman said,

> I would tell her, "I don't think you should get pregnant. You know, because eventually the child is gonna die. Maybe even before the child get a year old. You know. It's gonna die. So why put pain on top of pain? You already have it. So why, you know, put the child through that?" You know, but I can't, I wouldn't tell her, "Go ahead get pregnant" or "No, don't get pregnant" cause that's not my place.[60]

Again, echoing how women said they themselves would act, one woman described what she would say to a friend if a hypothetical "magic pill" to prevent transmission suddenly were available.

> If they had a magic pill, and you're in fairly good health, I would say go for it, especially if you wanted to be a mom. That's the greatest gift in the world, bearing a child.[61]

A few other women thought it was acceptable for the friend to go ahead and have a baby, even absent a "magic pill." We heard,

> I say go for it. Take that chance because maybe that child might be brought into this world and not have nothing. And that child when it's raised would become something that would change the whole world. You don't have the right to say no. If you become pregnant, to me, you don't have the right to take that child away because God put the child in here. That child can be what saves your life instead of kills you. Because stress and being lonely, this is what killing AIDS patients. When your child gives a smile at you, it gives you so much more reason to live and you try harder.[62]

Another woman said,

> My advice to her would be if she really thought within herself that she could give that child the love and care and the need to fulfill its life, yes, by all means have that baby because it's not a guarantee that the baby will be infected. And if the baby is infected, still if you have that love, it will not matter.[63]

Not surprisingly, women sometimes had ambivalence. One woman responded, clearly thinking out loud,

> It's so confusing . . . cause it could make her happy if she didn't have any, it could fill that. And being happy now I've learned with being sick when I stress myself out or I'm worried . . . but then we have to think. How do we just use this child, you know?[64]

Views and Experiences of Pregnant Women

We were interested in the stories of the 20 pregnant women included in our study. Had they planned to get pregnant? Did they know they were infected at the time that they became pregnant? Were their views different from those of the women we interviewed who were not pregnant? Of the 20 HIV-infected pregnant women we talked to, seven learned they were HIV-infected while they were pregnant. Of these seven, one thought she already had had too many abortions to have another one; one learned from her provider that there was a chance that the baby would be alright and decided to take the chance. She said,

> In the beginning I [considered having an abortion] because I felt you wasn't able to have kids with a virus like that. I didn't think you was capable of having kids, but the doctor says you can. So once he told me that, I felt a little more secure . . . so I figured I would keep it. Plus I don't have any kids, too, and I won't be able to have any after this. So I would just take care of it like it was sick or anything else, like asthma or diabetes, something that you could run to the hospital. I just have to watch the baby more, anything little thing, even if it is a cold or something, they said to get them to the hospital because it could be something worse than just a cold.[65]

A third woman also said she wanted to take the chance. The fourth woman had no children and clearly wanted to have a child; she said that, even if she had known she was infected beforehand, she probably would have gone ahead and had one child. The fifth woman would not have become pregnant had she known she was infected but said simply that now she was leaving it up to God; the sixth woman said that she had sought an abortion but that it would cost too much. The last woman who learned of her infection while pregnant said that she became pregnant while using drugs: "Sometimes I be high, I just want the money, I don't think about it."[66] Her three previous children live with her mother because of her drug use. She has now decided she wants to get clean and go ahead and have this child.

Of the thirteen women who already had known they were infected before they became pregnant, ten had not planned the pregnancy, while three had. Among the ten who had not planned the pregnancy, we frequently heard phrases like, "It just happened" or the pregnancy happened "by accident." Several women told us that they had been using some kind of protection, though one woman said she didn't like to take her birth control pills. When the women learned they were pregnant, they had different reactions. Three of the women had tried to get an abortion and could not. A fourth wanted to have an abortion, but her husband did not want her to. Two women said they were antiabortion, though both said quite definitively that they would not have more children in the future. One woman said she had been pregnant three times since learning of her infection. She had had abortions the previous times but now couldn't face the possibility of another one. Besides, she said, "they really don't know, the kid may be fine."[67] Another woman hinted that she had been wanting another child anyway because her one child, a much older daughter, didn't treat her well. Moreover, she wanted a boy. One woman who had an unplanned pregnancy simply said that, now that she was pregnant, she was leaving it to God. The last woman was actually waiting to have an abortion when we interviewed her. She said that she didn't have the money or social support to have a baby. She lamented that choice:

> I mean, yeah, I could go and have this kid. I could be on welfare for the rest of my life, but is that the best thing for me? Is it the best thing for the child? No. It all comes down to doing what you think is best. And if you're wrong, you're wrong, but you do the best you can do against given situations.[68]

There were three women who had planned their pregnancies knowing they were infected with HIV. What is interesting is that their reasoning was similar to that of nonpregnant women when the latter described situations when it might be acceptable, or at least understandable, for an HIV-infected woman to become pregnant. One woman said that she had no children and really wanted to have at least one. Besides, she said, her T-cells were still very high. The second woman said that her first child had died of HIV, so she wanted several children because she knew she could be "stuck without any." The last woman had had children previously, but she had been using drugs when she had had those children and they were not living with her for that reason. Now she was clean, and she wanted to have one child, "doing it right." Although these last two women had borne children, they seemed to be saying the same thing, that they wanted at least one successful relationship as mother to child.[69]

Respecting Choices

Without a doubt, the most striking finding from the interviews was that, with few exceptions, no matter what women thought HIV-infected women ought to do, no matter what they thought providers ought to say to women or they themselves would say to women, and no matter what their own situation, they thought the decision should be left to the women. It was the very rare woman who thought it appropriate for women to be forced or even strongly influenced by others concerning childbearing. We heard comments like, "I don't think anyone should make that decision for you . . . I feel it is a personal decision"[70] and "I feel that's their choice. If they are prepared mentally and emotionally and physically to deal with whatever may be, then go ahead."[71] One woman said,

> I don't think there should be any laws cause, you know, when my boyfriend and I get in an argument, you know, he tells me to be quiet. I go, well, this is a country of freedom and speech and I'm going to say what I want. I always go, and he's like, what? You know, so it's like a country of freedom and speech, you know. You do have the right to have a kid or not, you know. And about having abortions, you know, well, it is kind of sad, you know, getting rid of a kid. If you think about it, you know. But I don't know, I think that women should have a right to have a kid if they want. You know, it's up to the woman, not to nobody else.[72]

What was interesting was that, at first blush, it seemed that some women were giving inconsistent responses. On the one hand, they seemed to convey that HIV-infected women should not have children or even that doctors should tell HIV-infected women not to have children; on the other hand, they seemed to think women should do what they wanted. For example, during the course of the same interview we heard from one woman:

> I would sit her down and tell her don't do it . . . being pregnant, it's gonna travel to her child's life . . . infection is gonna infect the baby . . . but then again it would be up to them cause some people might feel that they just want to go through it anyway, but it's best to let 'em know, you know, not to do it.[73]

Another woman said in her interview, "I would advise her not to. I would tell her not to have one" and then later, "I think that should be up to the individual."[74] What became clear was that the issue of childbearing among HIV-infected women is extremely complicated. During the course of the interviews, women often seemed to be sorting out what they were thinking. Sometimes a woman would start down one line of thought, elaborating, for example, on why HIV-infected women really shouldn't have kids. Later in the interview, however, she might shift to another theme, such as why an HIV-infected woman might really want to have a child and thus why providers should point out both the pros and the cons to her. Given that women often seemed to be thinking out loud and even formulating their opinions as they spoke, it was particularly striking that almost everyone articulated that the choice about childbearing ultimately must be left to the woman. Even women who quite forthrightly believed that HIV-infected women should not have children said that the choice must be left to the women.

This is not to say that these women believed that making the choice can be approached lightly, however. Indeed, many women stressed the need to make responsible choices and to think long and hard about the decision. For example, when we asked women how they would talk to an HIV-infected friend about childbearing, we heard comments like the following:

> What I would tell her is, think about it very well. Think about it so good that you know your pros and your cons. Speak to your physician. Make sure you know, it's like, get a second opinion. I would ask her to really think about it. And is she prepared, if the baby comes out sickly, you know, being positive. And within that 16 months that the baby got a chance to either go back to being negative. . . . Plus the baby being sick, meaning if he or she doesn't become HIV-negative, is she prepared? Because most likely she is going to be alone. The father ain't gonna be around. And any of her family members might not understand or be around, or his family member, whatever. It's just gonna be on her shoulders. Is she gonna be prepared? And the headache and stress and the B.S. that she is going to go through. And seeing your child sick, and you're helpless, you can't really do anything. Regardless of they give you medicine and all that, are you going to be able to handle all that? Knowing that you're positive also and you being . . . anxiety and stressed does not help your body, your immune system, and on and on and on. Are you ready for it? See, that's the thing. See, I was ready for it when I was positive. I was like, yeah, I better do it now and praying and hoping and wishing that if I did get pregnant that the baby would come out negative. But that is my advice to any female. Honestly, think about it.[75]

Another woman said simply, "I would just tell her if that's really what she wants, she got to look at the consequences."[76] Two women voiced almost identical opinions:

> If you think you can handle it, first, you have to always think if it's positive, and if you feel you can handle it, then have it.[77]

> All I can say for all the women who want to have kids is to think about it. Think about it. Nobody can guarantee that their kids won't be positive. And I mean you just have to deal with the heartache of taking care of them and dedicating a lot of that time to running back and forth.[78]

Finally, we heard, "If you make positive choices, healthy, responsible choices, you don't have to say I'm sorry afterwards. You don't have to feel guilty afterwards."[79]

Attitudes About Abortion

Not surprisingly, the issue of abortion arose in almost all of the interviews. Of interest was that women felt quite differently about terminating a pregnancy than they did about the avoidance of conception. Indeed, whereas the majority of women had said that they would not have more children because of HIV or that it was not a good idea for HIV-infected women generally to have kids, these feelings did not hold true concerning abortion. For many women, this, too, was framed in language relating to God.

> I think, "No, it would be better not to have children because of the virus." But if someone becomes pregnant, then I would say, "Stay with it, God wanted me to have it, because it is God who gives life, not us, we can't do it."[80]

Another woman said of her own experience, "I left it in God's hands. I didn't think I had the right to decide whether I should abort the baby or not."[81] Other women said, "If I was pregnant, well then, I'm already pregnant. I will pray to God, and there's a 70% chance"[82] or "If you become pregnant, to me, you don't have the right to take that child away because God put the child in there."[83] Another woman said, simply, "I don't believe in killing no baby."[84] Thus, many who thought it was not a good idea to get pregnant were clear that if they became pregnant, they would not have an abortion. At the same time, there were several other women who told us that, although they basically were "against" abortion, they would (or did) have one if they became pregnant, being HIV-infected.

Somewhat related was the clear difference in feelings, or even judgment, many women had between women who became pregnant knowing they were infected and women who became pregnant before they found out. Many women who had children were quick to tell us that they hadn't known they were infected at the time. One even said, "If I would have known that [my partner] was HIV-positive when I was pregnant with my daughter, I probably wouldn't have had her."[85]

Of the smaller number of women who thought abortion was acceptable, their reasoning usually was based on wanting to prevent harm to the child: "So you might as well just end it now instead of letting the baby come into the world and have to die"[86] and "I just don't really think that women should have them when they find out."[87]

Drugs and Babies: The Picture Changes

In contrast to the context of HIV infection, where opinions were mixed and varied in intensity, almost all women interviewed had strong feelings that women who use drugs should not have children. We heard comments like, "Well, I think if you're an addict, you shouldn't have any children, period, none. That's it. No."[88] and "I think that's the lowest."[89] Another said, "I say if you can't quit, go get your abortion."[90] Another woman said, "If you're using drugs—even if you didn't have HIV—if you're using drugs, I don't think you should have kids,"[91] and finally one woman said, "No, because the children will come addicted."[92]

For many, the intensity of their feelings resulted from personal experience of the harm that drugs can do. One woman said,

What do I think about women who use drugs getting pregnant? I hate 'em. I figure you got nine months. If you can't take nine months out of your life to bring a nice healthy little roly-poly infant, you know, you are destroying his whole life by drinking and drugging, those nine months. You're destroying, the brain damage, the function in school all that at slow pace. I've seen it, I live it. My brother's three [children] are all in special education and it's terrible. . . . I would rather for you to abort than to destroy that life like that.[93]

Another woman recalled, "Like my nephew was born out of two parents that were drug users. He's not a normal child . . . my godson also, both parents were drug users, and he's a lot like my nephew is."[94]

Still another woman told us,

I had a granddaughter that is a drug baby. She will never walk. She is retarded. She has cerebral palsy, and her body is twisted. One side is two inches shorter than the other. She's very thin. She has a very small head. She still can't talk or sit up. I had to have her taken out of the home. . . . But, after a while, they're going cut these funds because there's going to be no money. So I would say prevent it if at all possible.[95]

Another said, perhaps with the greatest heartache,

It don't work. It doesn't work. My daughter went through my addiction with me . . . when she was two, that's when it started, the roller coaster ride. . . . But when she was like in her teenage, like 11, 12 years old, that's most of the part she remembers. . . . And it's just hard. Then it got to the point, it got so bad with me that I had to send her to my mom's. Not only are we suffering, but they're suffering too, and that's not fair. . . . And I wish I could go back. I wish I could make up for all the suffering that I caused her, you know. I wish I could. All I can do is make amends to her. That's all I can do.[96]

One of the most poignant accounts came from this woman:

You are ashamed. . . . There is no way you cannot be ashamed, you know? I have been with like women in the street, and we have sat and cried together because we know we should not be out here like this, getting high, you know? We high, or we about to get high, whatever, but it just being with each other. We talk about our children. We know we shouldn't be out here and most of the women have children already . . . and it's a hurting feeling, it really is. Because you know that you doing wrong, that you know you doing wrong to yourself. You know you doing wrong to this little baby. You don't even know what you doing to this little baby. You know? But you don't stop! It's just, I can't even describe it.[97]

In general, the women we interviewed were much more likely to think that it was acceptable to be "heavy-handed" with women who use drugs than with women who are HIV-infected, and numerous women shared as justification: "Either you gonna use drugs or you gonna take care of your child. You can't do both."[98] One woman said that it was alright for HIV-infected women generally to have kids, unless the woman is "unhealthy and in denial, or doing drugs."[99]

Although there was a greater consensus that drug-using women should not have children, there was not complete agreement. Similar to when referring to HIV-infected women, the women we interviewed were hesitant to recommend abortion to a drug-using woman. One woman said, "I'd rather have the baby and give it up before I'd have an abortion,"[100] and another woman said, "I'd probably try to influence her to stop using drugs. 'Why don't you go to a program,' something like that. I still wouldn't tell her to get an abortion."[101]

Some women, particularly those who themselves had used drugs previously, advocated mandatory or recommended treatment for women who use drugs. One woman said that drug-using women should

> get in treatment. But I don't think that they should tell the mother no, you can't have a child just because you are on drugs. A drug addict doesn't mean that you're going to be a bad mother. Just the opposite sometimes. The drug addicts that have kids end up leaving drugs for the kids. And they make better mothers because they suffered before they became a mother and they were able to tell those children and explain to them about life and, you know, through their own learning.[102]

Somewhat similarly, a couple of women said that if a woman was using drugs, it was the responsibility of her health-care provider to discuss this further with her, particularly if she was considering having children. One woman argued, as others had in the context of HIV-infected women,

> I always have to go back to our basic rights and the right to make our own decisions. Although I'm not going to tell you I haven't been appalled by a woman who has had two or three coke babies . . . but it's a basic freedom, those things are. . . . I have to go back to saying wait a minute, if we start there, then where is it going to end. So I would have to say we don't have a right to impose that on any individual. And I have very mixed feelings about saying it, but I have to go back to that.[103]

Conclusions

Conducting these interviews made it clear, if we ever had had any doubt, that the issue of HIV-infected women having children is difficult and complicated. Women mourn the possibility of not being able to have children, they feel that the information they have received in many cases is incomplete, and they need to make decisions in the context of uncertainty about their own health and life expectancy. As is true among persons who are not HIV-infected women, we found that the opinions of our respondents were not uniform. Some women thought that HIV-infected women should not have children, while others thought that it was acceptable. Nonetheless, certain themes clearly emerged.

Women's greatest fear was vertical transmission. Most women care desperately for the well-being of their children. What pains them about either HIV-infected women or drug-using women having children is the possibility that the children will be sick, have a disability, or have a significantly shortened life expectancy. Consistent with this, many women said that if a "magic pill" were available that could prevent their child from being infected, even if it did not affect their own health, they would go ahead and try to have a child. These responses about vertical transmission and a "magic pill" were interesting, given that, at the time the interviews were conducted, the results from ACTG 076 (the research study suggesting that the risk of vertical transmission could be reduced through the administration of AZT) had not yet been released. That so many women said they would seriously consider having a child if there were a magic pill suggests that, in light of the findings from ACTG 076, more HIV-infected women may try to have children in the future.

We heard from women that they want to be given the facts. They want to be given honest information from their providers but for this information to be provided in a respectful manner. When asked, many of the women interviewed thought that it was acceptable for providers to give women advice but reiterated that it should be presented as advice, not orders. The majority of women interviewed shared what we heard also was the opinion of many providers (see Chapter 15), that HIV-infected women should not have children. Some women seemed to be willing to make an exception if the woman had not yet had any children, however, and in almost all cases women believed the decision should be left to the women themselves. Many other women framed the situation as "in God's hands" and therefore not their place to interfere. In general, we found no systematic differences in opinion, experience, or response based on the age, ethnicity, city, or pregnancy status of the women. The only exception was that Hispanic and African-American women were more likely than white women to invoke God, such as to say that she was "leaving it to the Lord" or "leaving it in God's hands."

That, of the thirteen women who became pregnant knowing they were infected, ten had not planned their pregnancies calls for better or more accessible interventions to prevent pregnancy among women who choose to do so. It also must be highlighted in reviewing our data, however, that only women who currently were pregnant were considered when we focused on pregnant women's circumstances and decisions. Naturally, this creates overwhelming bias that when HIV-infected women become pregnant, they choose to continue their pregnancies. Clearly, there were many other women in our sample who had become pregnant and terminated the pregnancy before the conduct of our interviews.

The heartache of this situation cannot be minimized. For the women who want to have children and believe they cannot, it is agony. For the women who have children and either do not live to see the children grow up or have to witness their children dying, it is agony. For women who do have children, however, they believe that there is nothing like the feeling of being a mother, and, for them, it is all worth that.

Notes

1. Interview N15, Aug. 19, 1992, New York.
2. Interview S22, Sept. 30, 1992, New York.
3. Interview M3, March 2, 1992, Baltimore.
4. Interview M36, Aug. 18, 1993, Miami.
5. Interview N32, Nov. 19, 1992, Los Angeles.

6. Interview N17, Aug. 19, 1992, New York.
7. Interview N31, Nov. 19, 1992, Los Angeles.
8. Interview S1, March 5, 1992, Baltimore.
9. Interview N49, Nov. 2, 1993, Los Angeles.
10. Interview N44, Nov. 1, 1993, Los Angeles.
11. Interview N14, Aug. 19, 1992, New York.
12. Interview M57, Aug. 21, 1993, Miami.
13. Interview M36, Aug. 18, 1993, Miami.
14. Interview N43, Nov. 1, 1993, Los Angeles.
15. Interview M9, May 13, 1992, Miami.
16. Interview N43, Nov. 1, 1993, Los Angeles.
17. Interview S5, Aug. 5, 1992, New York.
18. Interview S19, Sept. 30, 1992, New York.
19. Interview M40, Aug. 18, 1993, Miami.
20. Interview N43, Nov. 1, 1993, Los Angeles.
21. Interview N30, Nov. 19, 1992, Los Angeles.
22. Interview N39, Nov. 1, 1993, Los Angeles.
23. Interview N1, Feb. 27, 1992, Baltimore.
24. Interview N50, Nov. 2, 1993, Los Angeles.
25. Interview N16, Aug. 19, 1992, New York.
26. Interview N50, Nov. 2, 1993, Los Angeles.
27. Interview N38, Nov. 1, 1993, Los Angeles.
28. Interview M37, Aug. 18, 1993, Miami.
29. Interview S10, Aug. 5, 1992, New York.
30. Interview N43, Nov. 1, 1993, Los Angeles.
31. Interview S22, Sept. 30, 1992, New York.
32. Interview M22, Aug. 26,. 1992, New York.
33. Interview N49, Nov. 2, 1993, Los Angeles.
34. Interview S24, Nov. 17, 1992, Los Angeles.
35. Interview N35, Feb. 26, 1993, Los Angeles.
36. Interview S29, March 2, 1993, Los Angeles.
37. Interview M37, Aug. 18, 1993, Miami.
38. Interview S9, Aug. 5, 1992, New York.
39. Interview N44, Nov. 1, 1993, Los Angeles.
40. Interview M37, Aug. 18, 1993, Miami.
41. Interview S24, Nov. 17, 1992, Los Angeles.
42. Interview S26, March 1, 1993, Los Angeles.
43. Interview M12, May 14, 1992, Miami.
44. Interview N36, Nov. 1, 1993, Los Angeles.
45. Interview S35, Aug. 18, 1993, Miami.
46. Interview N44, Nov. 1, 1993, Los Angeles.
47. Interview M39, Aug. 18, 1993, Miami.
48. Interview M46, Aug. 19, 1993, Miami.
49. Interview M47, Aug. 19, 1993, Miami.
50. Interview N41, Nov. 1, 1993, Los Angeles.
51. Interview N44, Nov. 1, 1993, Los Angeles.
52. Interview N49, Nov. 2, 1993, Los Angeles.
53. Interview S29, March 2, 1993, Los Angeles.
54. Interview M45, Aug. 19, 1993, Miami.
55. Interview S24, Nov. 17, 1992, Los Angeles.

56. Interview N31, Nov. 19, 1992, Los Angeles.
57. Interview N12, Aug. 19, 1992, New York.
58. Interview S24, Nov. 17, 1992, Los Angeles.
59. Interview N39, Nov. 1, 1993, Los Angeles.
60. Interview N2, March 11, 1992, Baltimore.
61. Interview N30, Nov. 19, 1992, Los Angeles.
62. Interview N44, Nov. 1, 1993, Los Angeles.
63. Interview N1, Feb. 27, 1992, Baltimore.
64. Interview N20, Nov. 17, 1992, Los Angeles.
65. Interview S12, Sept. 29, 1992, New York.
66. Interview S21, Sept. 30, 1992, New York.
67. Interview M21, Aug. 26, 1992, New York.
68. Interview S29, March 2, 1993, Los Angeles.
69. For similar findings, see A. Pivnick, A. Jacobson, K. Eric, et al., "Reproductive Decisions among HIV-Infected, Drug-Using Women: The Importance of Mother–Child Coresidence." *Medical Anthropology Quarterly*, 5 (1991): 153–169.
70. Interview S17, Sept. 30, 1992, New York.
71. Interview S20, Sept. 30, 1992, New York.
72. Interview N40, Nov. 1, 1993, Los Angeles.
73. Interview N9, Aug. 19, 1992, New York.
74. Interview M9, May 13, 1992, Miami.
75. Interview N15, Aug. 19, 1992, New York.
76. Interview N20, Nov. 17, 1992, Los Angeles.
77. Interview N38, Nov. 1, 1993, Los Angeles.
78. Interview N14, Aug. 19, 1992, New York.
79. Interview M57, Aug. 21, 1993, Miami.
80. Interview S18, Sept. 30, 1992, New York.
81. Interview S15, Sept. 28, 1992, New York.
82. Interview M18, May 15, 1992, Miami.
83. Interview N44, Nov. 1, 1993, Los Angeles.
84. Interview S21, Sept. 30, 1993, New York.
85. Interview N39, Nov. 1, 1993, Los Angeles.
86. Interview S24, Nov. 17, 1992, Los Angeles.
87. Interview N33, Nov. 19, 1992, Los Angeles.
88. Interview N22, Nov. 17, 1992, Los Angeles.
89. Interview S15, Sept. 28, 1992, New York.
90. Interview N37, Nov. 1, 1993, Los Angeles.
91. Interview N39, Nov. 1, 1993, Los Angeles.
92. Interview M46, Aug. 19, 1993, Miami.
93. Interview N17, Aug. 19, 1992, New York.
94. Interview M36, Aug. 18, 1993, Miami.
95. Interview N28, Nov. 18, 1992, Los Angeles.
96. Interview N26, Nov. 18, 1992, Los Angeles.
97. Interview M21, Aug. 26, 1992, New York.
98. Interview M23, Aug. 26, 1992, New York.
99. Interview N22, Nov. 17, 1992, New York.
100. Interview M41, Aug. 18, 1993, Miami.
101. Interview M39, Aug. 18, 1993, Miami.
102. Interview N44, Nov. 1, 1993, Los Angeles.
103. Interview N25, Nov. 19, 1992, Los Angeles.

V

CONCLUSION

17

HIV Infection and Childbearing: a Proposal for Public Policy and Clinical Practice

RUTH R. FADEN, NANCY E. KASS, KATHERINE L. ACUFF, ANITA ALLEN, JEAN ANDERSON, TAUNYA LOVELL BANKS, M. GREGG BLOCHE, RICHARD CHAISSON, SYLVIA COHN, NANCY HUTTON, PATRICIA A. KING, MARSHA LILLIE-BLANTON, MARY E. MCCAUL, MADISON POWERS, KAREN H. ROTHENBERG, ALFRED SAAH, LIZA SOLOMON, AND LAWRENCE WISSOW

> What I would tell her is think about it very well. Think about it so good that you know your pros and your cons. And is she prepared, if the baby comes out sickly, you know, being positive. And within that 16 months that the baby got a chance to go back to being negative. . . . Plus the baby being sick, meaning if he or she doesn't become HIV-negative, is she prepared? Because most likely she is going to be alone. The father ain't gonna be around. And any of her family members might not understand or be around, or his family member, whatever. It's just gonna be on her shoulders. Is she gonna be prepared? And the headache and the stress and the B.S. that she is going to go through. And seeing your child sick, and you're helpless, you can't really do anything. Regardless of they give you medicine and all that, are you going to be able to handle all that? Knowing that you're positive also and you being—anxiety and stressed does not help your body, your immune system, and on and on. Are you ready for it?
>
> *woman from New York*

Should others interfere with or otherwise attempt to influence the reproductive choices of HIV-infected women and, if so, how? In this volume we have analyzed the numerous moral, legal, medical, and public policy issues that bear on this question. We have examined the relationship between HIV infection and the use of illegal drugs as well as precedents for interference with reproduction among women who use drugs. We also have presented the perspectives of women who are HIV-infected as well as the views of professionals who provide services to women who are infected. In this chapter we put forward a policy proposal for whether and how others should attempt to influence, counsel, or otherwise interfere with the reproductive choices of HIV-infected women based on the analyses, arguments, and findings presented in earlier chapters.

This chapter focuses first and most briefly on recommendations for public policy. Our proposal here is, we believe, straightforward.

The bulk of the chapter addresses our recommendations for clinical practice. Specifically, we present a particular model for how persons who provide services to HIV-infected women should approach questions of childbearing with their patients and clients. We then defend that model against alternative approaches to provider–client interaction.

Like the book itself, this chapter is framed around and for women. We focus primarily on women because that is where the public debate about HIV and reproduction has focused, not because that is where the debate *should* be focused. Childbearing requires both sexes. So, too, does the transmission of HIV to infants: the women who give birth to infected newborns in most cases have contracted their infection from men who are their partners in sex, drugs, or both. A central theme of this book is the importance of remembering that reproduction is an issue for men as well as women. As is explicated below, many of our recommendations apply equally to men and women. At the same time, however, women are more vulnerable than men to certain policy proposals. For example, compulsory sterilization of HIV-infected men will not have the same effect on the incidence of pediatric HIV as compulsory sterilization of HIV-infected women. Similarly, policies concerning Norplant and abortion have no analog for men.

Public Policy

What government should not do

We oppose any public policy in which HIV-infected women would be compelled by law to be sterilized, have abortions, or use any form of contraception. We also oppose any public policy in which entitlements to social or medical services for which HIV-infected women otherwise would be eligible—such as subsidized housing, welfare payments, drug rehabilitation services, or medical care—would be contingent on reproductive forbearance of any kind. We similarly oppose any public policy in which HIV-infected women would be advantaged with respect to access to such services based on an agreement to eschew childbearing—e.g., by jumping the queue on a waiting list for a slot in a drug-treatment center.

A policy of compulsory reproductive forbearance is morally wrong on its face and also likely would be judged legally impermissible. As argued in Chapters 8 and 12, although government has a legitimate interest in the welfare of children, the health of future generations, and controlling social costs and burdens, these interests are insufficient to warrant the extreme deprivation of liberty and invasion of privacy entailed by such a policy.

The option of connecting social entitlements to reproductive forbearance is more complex. Currently, there is considerable societal interest in the family and family values, including interest in the structuring of public policies intended to support these values. A principal target of this interest is welfare reform. Numerous proposals have been put forward, and in some cases implemented, intended to discourage childbearing among young, poor, unmarried women. Another arena of focus is drug policy, where, as noted in Chapter 10, there is considerable interest in discouraging drug use during pregnancy and also discouraging women who use drugs from having children. Still another arena is adolescent pregnancy, which, as noted in Chapter 13, has been the target of numerous preventive interventions. Although the arguments for interfering with reproduction in these different contexts vary, they are examples of an interest in involving government in the reproductive lives of citizens. Behind this interest is a vision of the family and what is best for children—i.e., that children are best raised by two adult, married parents who have the financial and emotional means to support them. Whether the desire to limit childbearing among poor women is an additional dimension of this vision of the family and the public policies it implicates is a subject of debate.

An analysis of this morally contentious question is beyond the scope of this inquiry. We do not here take a position on whether it ever is appropriate for a government to implement public policies intended to shape the reproductive choices of its citizens. We do, however, maintain that there is no justifiable reason for singling out women who are HIV-infected to be the target of such policies. There is nothing about HIV per se that warrants such intervention. If there is some characteristic that always or often is true about the HIV context that justifies intervention by government with reproductive matters, that characteristic also occurs in other contexts. Unless public policies are inclusive of all the contexts in which this presumably morally relevant characteristic is found and unless the execution of such policies does not disproportionately burden any particular group, these policies are unfair. For example, women who are HIV-infected are not the only women who have medical conditions that make it likely that their offspring will be orphaned while still children. If a parent's shortened life span is the animating consideration for state interference with reproduction, then public policies must be directed at all persons who have medical conditions for which this is a likely outcome or, depending on one's justificatory structure, all such persons whose children are likely to require public assistance once they are orphaned. Similarly, some have argued that the degree of suffering experienced by children who actually are infected is sufficient to warrant restrictive policies. Although the consequences of HIV infection for children can be devastating (see Chapters 4 and 5), women who are HIV-infected are not the only women who may give birth to children who will have a fatal or serious medical condition. If the possibility that offspring may be born with such a condition is adequate justification for state interference with reproductive choice, then again, restrictive public policies must be directed at persons who are carriers of numerous genetic conditions as well as persons who are infected with HIV.

As noted throughout this volume, many women who are HIV-infected are poor, on public assistance, and former or current users of illegal drugs. If we as a society conclude that it is appropriate to attempt through public policies to influence the reproductive choices of women who are poor or who use drugs, then many women who are HIV-infected may be included among those targeted for intervention but not because they are HIV-infected.

It could be argued that because all of these characteristics—shortened maternal life span, a risk of serious illness among offspring, drug use, and poverty—tend to cluster among HIV-infected women, government is justified in singling them out for special treatment. This argument fails, however, for several reasons. First, the life circumstances of many women who are HIV-infected do not include all of these characteristics. Second, the underlying assumption behind this "clustering" argument is that, even if no single characteristic warrants state intervention, the combined effects of these multiple characteristics are sufficiently awful and sufficiently burdensome on government to provide adequate justification. Once again, however, it is not only among some HIV-infected women that one finds such bleak prospects for children or such high dependency on government. Moreover, to target HIV-infected women for restrictive policies creates the social harm of inappropriately perpetuating the stereotype that all infected women have this range of unfortunate characteristics.

What government should do

It is the responsibility of government to enact policies whose purpose is to reduce the rate of infection among both men and women. Such policies will serve not only to prevent primary infection, thereby protecting and promoting the health of men and women, but also to be the most direct means of preventing pediatric HIV. Such policies also will contribute to other interests raised in debates about childbearing and HIV, including societal interests in reducing the costs associated with HIV infection in both adults and children and the costs that result when children who themselves are not infected are orphaned by the death of their HIV-infected parents.

Continued support by government of programs directed at the development of a vaccine that can effectively prevent individuals from becoming infected with HIV is one of several strategies critical to this effort. Should such a vaccine become approved for general use, government should enact policies promoting its use and guaranteeing universal access to it.

Equally important is the government's vigorous pursuit of policies whose purpose is to prevent men and women from becoming infected. Insofar as needle exchange programs have been demonstrated to reduce the rate of transmission among persons who use injection drugs, these programs should be supported. The promotion of condoms and other practices that can reduce the risk of transmission through sexual behavior also must continue. Safer sex and safer drug use campaigns should be directed at both men and women. If such efforts are to be both fair and effective, however, they must take account of the relative powerlessness of women in many sexual and social contexts. Unless and until women are positioned equally to men in the control of sexual dynamics, women cannot, and should not be expected to, bear the burden of preventing HIV transmission through the use of condoms or through changes in other sexual practices over which they have little or no control. Social policies, including educational campaigns, should be directed at bringing home the message of condom use to men and couples and toward providing women with the emotional and instrumental resources necessary to alter or leave oppressive sexual relationships where condom use is an anathema.

The government also should be aggressive in supporting the development of preventive methods that women can more easily control and effectively implement. Arguably, the U.S. Public Health Service came late to the development of research programs on interventions centered on women, including, for example, research on antivirucides. Promising research in this area should be vigorously pursued. Should a safe antivirucidal preparation be developed that is effective without concomitant condom use, the product should be widely promoted and widely available.

In the conduct of persuasive communication campaigns directed at promoting the practice of "safer sex," the Working Group has concluded that it is permissible to appeal to the natural desire to have healthy children by pointing out the risk of vertical transmission, though the response to such a motivational argument is not known. At the same time, however, the Working Group is mindful of the need to craft such appeals carefully[1] so as not to create an inflated impression of the rate of vertical transmission.

For men and women who already are HIV-infected, government should take responsibility for ensuring access to information and counseling about reproduction and childbearing, as well as access to contraceptive and sterilization services, abortion, and prenatal care. Later in this chapter we detail our position on the kind of counseling that should be offered in clinical settings. Our central concern here is with financial support for counseling and education. If these services are to be widely available to HIV-infected persons, they must be acknowledged components of HIV care, eligible for reimbursement through third-party and government health insurance programs. We appreciate that in this era of scarce resources and de facto rationing any proposal to add items to the list of "covered services" may be viewed as naive and doomed to failure. We are not prepared here to argue whether the offering of such services would save money, either for the health-care system or for society generally. Counseling and education may save money if, as a result, infected persons decide to avoid childbearing or if HIV-infected women decide to take AZT during pregnancy, thus possibly averting births of HIV-infected children; but whether counseling will have these effects is both unknown and in some respects irrelevant. The primary justifications for state support of education and counseling are the enhancement of personal control over reproduction and the prevention of suffering that can result when children are born into difficult circumstances without forethought, preparation, and planning.

Government also should ensure that all HIV-infected pregnant women be informed that AZT seems to reduce the rate of vertical transmission and be offered AZT without financial barriers to access. The position that all pregnant women should be offered HIV testing has broad support.[2] The Working Group has not debated whether the impact of AZT on transmission now warrants mandatory screening for HIV during pregnancy. In whatever manner prenatal testing is conducted, all pregnant women should be informed of the benefits of AZT.

Interactions Between Clients and Providers

The Working Group concentrated most of its efforts on the complex topic of how, in a clinical context, individual clinicians and counselors ought to interact with HIV-infected women concerning reproduction and childbearing. Whether providers should address these topics was never at issue; the Working Group believes that it would be irresponsible of providers to avoid questions of reproduction and childbearing, though we learned through our interviews that these discussions do not always happen. The issue considered by the Working Group was how these topics should be approached in the clinical setting and toward what objective.

Five models were debated and are summarized below.

Model 1: Reproductive forbearance as a condition of receipt of services

Care at a health-care facility would be contingent on the client agreeing not to have a child (by either not becoming pregnant or having an abortion). This requirement could be fulfilled through sterilization, Norplant, an agreement to not become pregnant through whatever means the client selected, or through abortion if an HIV-infected woman became pregnant.

Providers would explain to clients that, out of concern for the well-being of children who might be infected, concerns for uninfected children whose mothers (and often fathers) are infected and ultimately would not be available to raise them to maturity, and lingering concerns about the effect of pregnancy on the health of HIV-infected women, it is the policy of this facility to require HIV-infected women not to have children.

Model 2: Explicit counseling advocating reproductive forbearance

The receipt of care would not be contingent on remaining childless, and women who bear children would not lose access to medical services. The explicit goal of the policy, however, would remain the prevention of births among HIV-infected women. Counseling would be designed to persuade infected women to not have children. In this counseling, the disadvantages and moral dimensions of having a child when the woman or man is HIV-infected would be emphasized. The provider would focus on the potential suffering of the future child, would make sure the client is not underestimating the risk of transmission, and would understand the likelihood of her dying before the child reaches adulthood. The persuasive effect of the counseling may be bolstered by bringing HIV-infected adults to a hospital floor in which sick HIV-infected children receive care.

Model 3: Provider endorsement of both reproductive forbearance and personal choice

Providers who oppose childbearing would convey to clients their personal conviction that HIV-infected adults should not have children. Providers would explain that their view arises out of the combination of concerns about the risk of vertical transmission, the effect on the child of having a parent with a chronic condition and of having that parent die prematurely, and the potentially deleterious effect of pregnancy on the woman's health and ability to cope with her disease. Providers would emphasize that they are recommending that pregnancy not be undertaken but not that pregnancy or childbirth is physically problematic.

Providers also would acknowledge that having a child is a very personal decision and that each person's situation is different. Providers would assure clients that, whether the client accepts or rejects the provider's recommendation, the provider will stand by the client and continue to provide care to her.

Model 4: Contextualized counseling toward reasoned and reflective decisions about childbearing

The primary task of the provider would be to engage the client in a meaningful discussion of the implications of having a child and of not having a child for herself, for the client's family, and for the child who would be born. Providers would focus on the client's values and life circumstances and on what is most relevant to her and to her family. Providers would assist clients in examining what childbearing means to them and what it would mean to them not to have a child. Providers also would assist clients in gaining an understanding of the factual information relevant to decisions about childbearing in the context of HIV. However, the discussion would cover a range of topics that go far beyond what can be understood as the relevant medical facts, and the direction of the conversation would vary depending on each person's life circumstances and priorities.

Model 5: *Education about the medical dimensions of reproduction in the context of HIV*

The health-care provider's primary task would be to convey factual information relevant to decisions about childbearing in as objective or neutral a fashion as possible. Topics to be discussed would typically include the risk of vertical transmission, the role of AZT in reducing transmission, the prognosis for HIV-infected children, any medical implications of pregnancy for the course or treatment of HIV disease in women, and methods of birth control. For pregnant women and couples who express an interest in terminating the pregnancy, information about abortion, including how the procedure is performed as well as its availability to HIV-infected women, and information about alternatives to abortion, including adoption and foster care, would be provided.

Although models 1, 2, and 3 differ markedly in the methods of influence employed, they share the same objective—the prevention of births to HIV-infected women. The success or failure of these models would be evaluated by the same criterion: birth rates. By contrast, the objective of model 4 is to assist HIV-infected women to make and act on reasoned and reflective decisions regarding reproduction and childbearing. The success of model 4 would not be evaluated by the number of births averted but rather by the more elusive criteria of whether, as a consequence of counseling, women were more likely to make a conscious and reflective decision about reproduction and more likely to act on these decisions. Model 5 has yet a different objective—to provide women with a sufficient base of knowledge to make an informed decision about reproduction. In the interest of avoiding even the appearance of interference with reproductive choice, this model does not seek to engage women in discussions about reproductive choices, the reasons behind their choices, or the implications of their choices.

The Position of the Working Group

The Working Group endorses model 4 as the appropriate approach for addressing issues of reproduction and childbearing in clinical settings that serve HIV-infected women. We begin a defense of this position by describing why we reject the alternative models.

We reject model 1 for essentially the same reasons as we oppose any policy by government to make entitlements to social or medical services for which HIV-infected women would otherwise be eligible contingent on reproductive forbearance. Indeed, as a practical matter, model 1 likely would require state action to be legally permissible.

By contrast, models 2 and 3 could be implemented in clinical settings without assistance by government. These models have the same objective as model 1—lowering the birth rate among HIV-infected women—but the means they propose for achieving this objective are less controlling. Model 2, which draws heavily on a provocative position developed by John Arras,[3] assumes that it is morally wrong, or at least morally questionable, for HIV-infected women to have children. The model assumes further that it is morally appropriate, if not morally obligatory, for providers to attempt to persuade their clients to do the right thing by not having children. These assumptions are examined carefully in Chapter 14 in light of the values and priorities of the HIV-infected women we interviewed. What emerges from that analysis is the recognition that, rather than being clearly morally indefensible, the choices of HIV-infected women to bear children often are founded on reasonable interpretations of commitments that are widely shared in American society—commitments to motherhood, religion, and the family. The importance of these commitments in many if not most moral communities, coupled with the extraordinary variation in the circumstances of the HIV-infected women in which these commitments must be interpreted, makes a model claiming the universal wrongness of childbearing itself morally indefensible.

Model 3 differs from model 2 in two respects. First, it does not suggest that it is objectively or universally wrong for HIV-infected women to have children. Instead, it maintains only that it is the personal conviction of the provider doing the counseling that childbearing in this context is wrong or ill-advised. Second, there is potentially less interference with the value of respect for autonomy in model 3 than in model 2. For example, in model 3 the provider assures the client that he or she will continue to care for the client even if the client rejects the provider's recommendation not to have children. As noted in Chapter 11, there is profound disagreement about the potential for coercion or other autonomy-negating effects that may arise out of different counseling strategies in clinical settings. Often, these disagreements reflect differing normative visions and commitments. To some, the differences between models 2 and 3 may not seem morally significant. In either case, the persuasive and social powers of the provider are concentrated toward the same objective—influencing HIV-infected women to not have children.

It is the wrongness of this objective that is the primary basis of the Working Group's rejection of models 2 and 3, as well as model 1. As we argued earlier with respect to state policy, there is no justification for singling out those who are HIV-infected to be the target of campaigns to eschew reproduction. Women with HIV are not alone in imposing on potential offspring the risks of fatal illness or a disadvantaged upbringing, nor are they the only women who may burden government with some or all of the costs of caring for their children. Moreover, some HIV-infected women have children in circumstances that are not considered disadvantaged, and in many cases their children never draw disproportionately on government resources. At the same time, that HIV-infected women often are poor and from ethnic minorities compounds the potential for injustice. Moreover, it is likely that women would be much more likely than men to be the clients with whom these models would be implemented. This reality introduces yet another dimension of injustice to an already questionable practice. Any attempt to discourage childbearing among HIV-infected women thus raises questions of both racism and sexism—to what extent is HIV a politically acceptable justification for a generalized position that certain women should not have babies? Finally, as we already have noted, it cannot even be maintained that the decision to have a child when one is HIV-infected is necessarily morally wrong or indefensible. Chapter 16 poignantly presents in the words of women that having a child when one is HIV-infected is an understandable human desire. If the analysis in Chapter 14 is correct and it is not only understandable but also at least sometimes morally defensible to go forward with childbearing in this context, how can models 2 or 3 be justified?

Model 5, by contrast, raises none of these contentious questions of justice. It purports only to communicate the medical facts objectively, in a style consistent with at least some popularized understandings of the tradition of "nondirective" counseling in genetics.[4] While improving knowledge is important and laudable, it is by no means clear that information relevant to reproductive choice can be presented in a truly value-free manner. Moreover, our interviews with HIV-infected women (Chapter 16) bear out that information alone is not likely to meaningfully assist HIV-infected women with the complex issues raised by questions of childbearing. In addition, for reasons we describe below, we do not believe interventions that go beyond the provision of disembodied facts necessarily raise the specter of inappropriate interference with personal choice.

The objective of model 4, the model we endorse, is different in important respects from the objectives of both models 1, 2 and 3 and the objective of model 5. In model 4 counseling is intended to increase the likelihood that becoming a parent is the result of an active decision rather than something that merely happens and that the decision reflects a careful weighing of the implications of the choice in terms of the person's own values and life circumstances. At least with respect to complex, consequential choices that have profound implications for others as well as oneself, such as having a child when one is HIV-infected, we here assume that reasoned, reflective decisions are more likely both to be genuine expressions of self-governance and to produce good outcomes and less likely to produce regret and suffering than snap decisions or when reproduction is unplanned and unintentional. This assumption goes undefended in our analysis.

The Working Group not only endorses model 4 but endorses that such counseling be conducted with men as well as women. It is inappropriate to perpetuate the notion that childrearing is the responsibility only of women. The argument that vertical transmission is the rationale for focusing on women is weak. First, the transmission of HIV to infants generally requires both sexes: in most cases, HIV-infected women have contracted the infection from men who are their partners in sex, drugs, or both. Second, as suggested by recent findings with respect to AZT, it is likely that advances in medical interventions will significantly reduce, if not eliminate, the chance of vertical transmission. Increasingly, the central concern with reproduction among HIV-infected persons will not be the birth of infected children but the birth of children whose parents will not be alive to raise them to maturity. The problem of parents dying applies equally to potential fathers and mothers.

Table 17.1 presents an outline of the topics we envision would be the subjects of discussion in model 4. In addition to these topics, which we assume are relevant to almost all HIV-infected persons, a distinguishing feature of model 4 is that issues that are unique to the client's situation also would be raised in the counseling. For example, if the client also is using drugs, the provider would discuss whether the client is equipped to care for a child while using drugs, the special medical implications of having a child when addicted to drugs, and whether the woman or man should enter treatment before seeking to have a child.

TABLE 17.1 Elements of Counseling to be Included in all Interactions

1. The latest understanding of the rate of vertical transmission, including the effect of interventions and whether certain characteristics, such as the stage of the woman's illness or mode of delivery, may be associated with different rates.
2. The risk of transmitting HIV infection to a sexual partner when attempting to have a child, including methods for minimizing this risk, such as restricting unprotected intercourse only to those times when the woman is thought to be most fertile.
3. The possible scenarios related to prognosis of a child who is truly infected, including available treatments.
4. The effect of pregnancy on the course of the mother's own HIV infection and the effect of infection on pregnancy outcomes.
5. Whether and why the woman or man wants to become pregnant or have a baby.
6. What being pregnant and being a mother or a father mean to her or him.
7. Whether he or she has any children already, how those children are being cared for now and by whom, and how the client expects they (and any future child) will be cared for as she or he becomes (more) ill and after his or her death.
8. Whether she or he is in a relationship and the meaning of a pregnancy and childbearing to that relationship: do both persons want the pregnancy equally?
9. How having (another) baby would affect her or his family, including (where relevant) the effect on other children.
10. His or her current health status and current use of medical care and how having a baby might affect these considerations.
11. How well she or he is coping generally and the effect of having a baby on abilities to cope in the future.
12. Whether or how it would make a difference if the other parent or the baby was to become infected and, therefore and inevitably, to have a premature death, for the baby, the other parent, herself or himself, and the rest of the family.

Similarly, if the client has had children removed from her custody, the client would be asked to consider whether and why the prospects for parenting this child are different. One element of our position that distinguishes it from traditionally "nondirective" counseling is this affirmative requirement on providers to raise these difficult issues. What distinguishes model 4 from model 3, however, is that the value structure within which these difficult issues are to be addressed is that of the client and not that of the provider.

It is clear from the interviews that we have conducted, as well as from the experiences of the clinicians in our Working Group, that the extent to which these and other sensitive issues can be effectively discussed is crucially dependent upon both the relationship the client has with the provider and the manner by which both information and opinions are conveyed. This second issue is straightforward. We heard repeatedly in interviews with women that it was not necessarily what a provider said that was upsetting but how the provider said it. Sometimes women were offended by providers whose general style of interaction was perceived as disrespectful or condescending. In other cases, the offense was more specific and, for example, related to insensitive timing, as when a provider would start discussing abortion immediately after informing a pregnant woman that her HIV antibody test result was positive. For medical interactions generally, but especially when the discussion includes personal and difficult issues such as those raised by reproduction and HIV, all clients must be treated with respect and sensitivity. Second, an attempt must be made to "meet clients where they are": to determine how they are progressing in coping with their illness; what information they are able to process and with what sort of language; and how and when it is appropriate to convey which types of information, questions, and counseling.

The level of sensitivity required for this kind of counseling is easier to achieve if the provider knows his or her clients well. By the same token, clients who have been receiving regular care from a particular provider with whom they have developed a trusting relationship are more likely to want to discuss the personal dimensions of the decision. Moreover, both the provider and the client have an extended period of time over which to consider these issues. Through an ongoing relationship, the provider can have a much greater understanding of the client's life situation. The provider sees who accompanies the client to appointments, hears the client talk about what else is going on at home, sees or hears about who is caring for her or his children and how the children are faring, and indeed even may be a care provider for other members of the client's family (including any children). All of these contribute to the client and provider having the sort of relationship that would allow a conversation related to childbearing in which a provider could discuss with a woman unique aspects of the woman's situation; and, presumably, the woman would be more likely to trust that the provider has a sound basis for raising pointed questions.

Insofar as there is a relationship between the degree of intimacy of the client–provider relationship and the depth with which the topics included in model 4 can be discussed, two issues emerge. First, providers who have long-standing relationships of trust with their clients may form a deeply held conviction, based on a detailed understanding of a particular client's life circumstances, that the consequences are likely to be disastrous if that client has a child. That conviction likely would reflect the provider's knowledge about the experiences of other similarly situated clients and the provider's own values and commitments. In such a circumstance, the provider may feel a strong moral pull to persuade the client to not have a child, or at least to advise against it. At the same time, in a relationship of trust, the client may be more likely to value the provider's opinion as to whether she or he should have a child and to ask for that opinion. There is no bar in model 4 against a provider sharing his or her opinion if asked for it by the client. The only caution is that the provider make clear that this opinion reflects a broad base of considerations, including the provider's personal values. The question of whether a provider should volunteer her or his opinion about whether a particular client should have a child is more difficult. The Working Group did not reach consensus on this issue, except to conclude that the only circumstance where this might be permissible is where the provider has a high degree of confidence that the consequences are likely to be disastrous and to emphasize again that, if an opinion is offered, it must be clearly stated as rooted in the provider's personal values as well as the provider's professional experience. It is the Working Group's view that a prediction of disastrous consequences could not flow simply from the diagnosis of infection or the perception of client hardship. It would require a complex of unfortunate circumstances, such as debilitating and severe drug addiction, mental illness, and a history of child abuse or neglect of self, against which the client's being infected may play little or no part.

The second issue raised by the fact that model 4 is enhanced by a trusting provider–client relationship is the extent to which the model is practical in the absence of such a relationship. Indeed, one argument favoring model 5 is that the minimal level of interaction involved in this model is about all that can reasonably be expected in a busy clinical setting in which care is often delivered impersonally and rapidly. Moreover, many HIV-infected women do not have a regular source of medical care and therefore do not have ongoing relationships with health-care providers. At the same time, however, it is clear from our interviews with providers and clients alike that the staff in many settings in which care is provided to HIV-infected persons, although severely overworked, frequently are committed to their clients, see them repeatedly, and know them well. Also, there is nothing in model 4 that stipulates that the counseling must be done by a health-care professional. There is reason to believe that trained peer counselors may be effective at both establishing relationships of trust with clients and discussing with clients the sensitive issues around reproduction.[5] As noted previously, reimbursement for counseling services is essential to the successful implementation of model 4.

Two other challenges to model 4 also should be considered. First, why is there less potential for interference with autonomous choice in model 4 than in model 3? Second, why single out persons who are HIV-infected for this type of reproductive counseling? As noted in Chapter 11, by some accounts, the counseling dynamic affords the opportunity for manipulation, however it is constructed. The principal safeguard as we have constructed it is that, unlike model 3 in which the interaction is defined in terms of the values of the provider, in model 4 the touchstone for discussion is the values, commitments, and aspirations of the client.

If we are correct in our assumptions that reasoned, reflective decisions about childbearing are likely to be "better" than impulsive decisions or having children who are unplanned or unintentional and that model 4 can increase the likelihood of such decisions, then, ideally, all persons of reproductive age—not just those who are HIV infected—should have counseling like that presented in model 4. Where the stakes of reproduction are higher, however, such as in the context of HIV, other chronic or genetic illness, or among adolescents, there may be more justification for government support of such services.

The overall goal of our recommendation is to encourage HIV-infected women and men to make responsible decisions about childbearing. By "responsible decisions" we mean decisions that are reflective and deliberate and that, in terms of the client's own values, life circumstances, and commitments, take account of the implications of their choices for themselves, for their families, and for their potential children. This objective is grounded not only in the value of assisting persons to take control over their lives and empowering them to make choices that truly reflect their values and commitments but also in the desire to minimize the suffering that can result when actions such as having a child, particularly when one has a chronic and ultimately fatal illness, proceed without forethought.

Notes

1. N. Kass, R. Faden, A. Gielen, and P. O'Campo, "Pregnant Women's Knowledge of HIV: Implications for Education and Counseling," *Women's Health Issues*, 2 (Spring 1992): 17–25.
2. R. Faden, G. Geller, and M. Powers, eds., *AIDS, Women and the Next Generation: Towards A Morally Acceptable Public Policy on HIV Screening of Pregnant Women and Newborns* (New York: Oxford University Press, 1991); Institute of Medicine Committee on Prenatal and Newborn Screening for HIV Infection, L. M. Hardy, ed., *HIV Screening of Pregnant Women and Newborns* (Washington, DC: National Academy Press, 1991); Centers for Disease Control, "U.S. Public Health Service Recommendations for the Human Immunodeficiency Virus Counseling and Volun-

tary Testing for Pregnant Women," *Morbidity and Mortality Weekly Report* 44 (July 1995): 8.
3. J. D. Arras, "AIDS and Reproductive Decisions: Having Children in Fear and Trembling," *The Milbank Quarterly*, 68 (1990): 353–382.
4. F. C. Fraser, "Genetic Counseling," *American Journal of Human Genetics* 26 (1974): 636–659; National Academy of Sciences, Committee for the Study of Inborn Errors of Metabolism, *Genetic Screening: Programs, Principles and Research* (Washington, DC: National Academy Press, 1975); Institute of Society, Ethics and the Life Sciences, Research Group on Ethical, Social and Legal Issues in Genetic Counseling and Engineering, "Ethical and Social Issues in Screening for Genetic Disease." *New England Journal of Medicine* 286 (1972): 1129–1132.
5. R. J. Cabral, C. Galavotti, P. M. Gargiullo, et. al., "Paraprofessional Delivery of a Theory-Based HIV Prevention Counseling Intervention for Women," (in press 1995).

INDEX

Abdul-Quader, 135
Abe, T., 106
Abel, E. L., 132, 243
Abercrombie, P. D., 56
Abortion
  attitudes of HIV-infected pregnant women, 437–438
  coerced, 231
  in context of disability, 144–145
  decision-making, adolescent, 353
  directive counseling for, 162–163
  female drug abusers and, 117–118
  by HIV-infected women, 257
    health-care provider and, 192–193
    public policy and, 199–200
    vs. unaffected women, 42
  laws, 292
  maternalism and, 397
  negligently performed, 184
  outlawing, 327
  personal opposition to, 385, 390–392
  rights, moral vs. legal, 320–321
  for sex selection, 321
  Supreme Court cases, 146–149, 153, 320, 378. *See also specific cases*
Aboulker, J. P., 107
Abrams, J., 55
Abstinence
  as condition for medical care, 266–270
  counseling, 36, 260
    accommodation and, 294–295
    for adolescents, 351
    advisory vs. directive, 274–275
    conscious intent requirement, 277
    lack of reciprocity and, 294–295
    normative issues, 292–294
    quasi-coercion and, 277–278
    unconscious coercion in, 280

  promotion for HIV-infected women, 291–292
Abulafia, O., 55
Achola, J.O.N., 57
ACOG (American College of Obstetrics and Gynecology), 143, 186
ACTG. *See* AIDS Clinical Trials Group (ACTG)
Acuff, K. L., 241–243, 251–252
ADA. *See* Americans With Disabilities Act (ADA)
Adachi, A., 56
Adams, J., 107
Addiction as disability, 157–158
Ades, A. E., 59, 76
Adler, N. E., 365
Adolescents
  adulthood markers and, 350
  age of majority, 353
  AIDS incidence, 31
  childbearing by
    impact of, 350, 352
    responsibility for, 361
  contraceptives
    condom usage, 348–349
    long-term, 152–153
    usage of, 348–349, 353–354
  decision-making, reproductive, 345–346, 355–356
    allocating, 350–352
    clinician/counselor role in, 361–362
    competency and, 360
    government recognition of, 353
    ideal process of, 361
    legal allocation of, 360–361
    without adult involvement, 362
  economic dependence, 350, 355–356
  emancipation, 353–354

Adolescents *(continued)*
  expectations for, 350
  female
    anatomic susceptibility to HIV, 348
    HIV/AIDS incidence, 347
    pregnancy rates, 348
    seroprevalence rate, 347–348
  HIV-infected, 4, 151
    parents and, 358–362
    policy-makers and, 358–362
    prevalence of, 347
    public perception of, 358
  legal issues
    empowerment, 353–355
    for unintended pregnancy, 151–153
  male
    HIV/AIDS incidence, 347
    seroprevalence rate, 347–348
  medical treatment
    consent for, 353–355
    insurance and, 355
  parental control, 350–351
  potential impact of HIV/AIDS, 352–358
  pregnancy, 32, 151–153, 352
  risk, HIV/AIDS, 346–349
  sexual activity, 348
    detection of, 352
    involuntariness of, 349
    reluctance of society to discuss, 356–357
  sexually transmitted diseases, 348, 349
Adrien, M., 61
Africa, HIV seroprevalence, 11
African-Americans
  adolescent contraceptive usage, 349
  children, HIV incidence in, 63
  drug treatment program enrollment, 121
  families, child care in, 85
  female drug abusers, condom usage and, 117
  HIV-infected infants, 367, 399
  HIV-infected women, 4, 82, 178, 372
    cultural childbirth values and, 375
    drug abuse during pregnancy and, 112
    HIV/AIDS mortality, 8–9
    incidence of, 15, 143
    injection drug use and, 112
    maternalism and, 397
    moral values of, 381–382
  HIV seroprevalence, 10
  hopelessness and, 100–101
  incidence of HIV infection, 15
Agarossi, A., 56
Age
  AIDS-related death rates, 7–8, 31

  of diagnosis for AIDS in children, 67
  of HIV-infected women, 4, 31
  of majority, 353
  of onset of symptoms for children, 67
Agency for Health Care Policy and Research (AHCPR), 40
Agins, B. D., 77
Agresti, M. G., 107
AIDS. *See also specific aspects of*
  case definition
    in infants/children, 68
    revision of, 20
  epidemic
    finger-pointing in, 372
    religious rights and, 375–376
  first cases of, 97
  incidence in women, 31
  reported cases, 3–5
  surveillance data, 5
  surveillance definition of, 5–7
  in women
    complications, 6
    demographics of, 143
    first reports of, 3
    vs. heterosexual men with AIDS, 4–5
AIDS Clinical Trials Group (ACTG), 102
  128 protocol, 71–72
  152 protocol, 72
  076 study, 44–45, 47–48, 65, 367
    coerced treatment and, 234–235
    health-care provider interviews and, 422
    HIV-infected drug abusers and, 233–234
Ajuluchukwu, D. C., 136
Albert, J., 60
Alcabes, P., 29, 107
Alcoholism, 111
Alcohol use, maternal
  congenital anomalies and, 119–120
  fetal alcohol syndrome and, 119, 126, 130
  incidence, 111
  prenatal exposure, 218
Alexander, V., 206
Alford, C. F., 317
Allain, J. P., 76
Allan, J. D., 107
Allen, M. H., 205, 209–211
Allen, S., 13, 53
Almond, B., 210
Alschuler, A. W., 318
Alston, W. P., 303
Altman, L. K., 401–402
Amaro, H., 131, 136, 139
Amenorrhea
  depo Provera and, 33

INDEX

drug abuse and, 116–117
  in HIV-infected women, 40–41
American Academy of Pediatrics (AAP), 91, 237
American College of Obstetrics and Gynecology (ACOG), 143, 186
American Medical Association (AMA), 237
American Nurses Association (ANA), 237
American Prosecutors Research Institute (APRI), 229
American Public Health Association (APHA), 237
American Society of Addiction Medicine, Inc., 237–238
Americans With Disabilities Act (ADA), 163
  application to HIV-infected women
    access to fertility services, 158
    access to medical services, 156–158
    counseling against pregnancy, 158–159
    directive counseling, 159–160
    pregnant women, counseling of, 160–161
  involuntary sterilization and, 150
  Title II, 154
  Title III, 154–155
Amniocentesis, 48, 194
Amniotic fluid, HIV in, 44
Amos, C. I., 59, 74
Amsel, Z., 135
Anderson, J., 28, 52–55, 61–62, 107
Andrew, E., 30
Andrews, S., 94
Andrulis, D., 109, 241–242
Anemia, 69–70
Angarano, G., 52, 107
Angell, M., 176
Annas, G., 299, 300
Anstone, N., 364
Antiabortionism, private, 385, 390–392
Antidiscrimination legislation, patient-provider relationship and, 192
Anti-gp41, 45
Antiretroviral Pregnancy Registry, 45
Antiretroviral therapy, 22–23, 98
Anzen, B., 76
APGAR scores, 119, 124–125
Appetite stimulation, 41
APRI (American Prosecutors Research Institute), 229
Arditti, R., 165
Ariceta, J. M., 75
Armstrong, D., 62
Arno, P. S., 109
Arnold v. Board of Education of Escambia County, Alabama, 147

Arnow, P. M., 109
Arras, A., 207
Arras, John D., 201, 239, 297, 333–334, 343, 362, 377–380, 398, 402–403, 407, 461
Arrastia, C. D., 56
Arrhythmias, 69
Asaro, A., 165, 175
Asch, A., 166, 169
Ashley, R. L., 54
Asian/Pacific Islander children, HIV incidence in, 63
Astemborski, J., 108–109
Atrash, H. K., 61
Augenbraun, M., 55
Autonomy
  clinical, reinterpretation of, 288–295
  informed consent and, 258, 378–379
  moral significance, 325
  negating influence, 270, 288, 295–296
    alternative accounts, 276–288
    conflicting viewpoints, 290–292
    Faden and Beauchamp model of, 266
    normative aims of bioethical theory and, 275–276
  precluding influence, 295–296
  reproductive rights, 340–341, 378–379
    for HIV-infected women, 259–260
    justification for, 325–326
  respect for, 289
Autrey, M., 56
Avery v. County of Burke, 147
Axelsen, D., 403
Ayanian, J. Z., 106
Aylward, E., 77

Baca-Zinn, M., 405
Bach, 306
Bachicha, J., 137
Bacillary angiomatosis, 6
Bacterial infections
  in children, 68, 72
  gender differences, 22
  prophylaxis, 23, 72
Baende, E., 75
Bahr, G. R., 109
Baier, Annette, 329–330, 343
Baird, K. A., 139, 176
Baker, L. S., 93
Balfour, H. H., 107
Balfour, H. H. Jr., 106
Banks, I. W., 404
Banks, Taunya Lovell, 242, 399, 407
Banner, William A., 381, 402, 404
Barbacci, M. D., 25, 54, 58

Barbarini, G., 56
Barbera-Stern, L., 406
Barbour, S. D., 74
Barin, F., 59
Barnard, M., 135
Barnette, M., 243
Barrere, B., 14
Barrett, M. E., 132
Barrier contraceptive methods, 34–35
Barthes, R., 303
Bartlett, J. A., 106
Bartlett, K., 365
Bartlome, J., 62
Barton, S. E., 57
Bastian, L., 107
Bateman, D. A., 61
Battjes, R. J., 135
Bauman, K. E., 404
Baxter, G., 59
Bayer, R., 164, 166, 169, 175, 201, 239–240, 402
Bayles, M. D., 302, 305, 343, 403
Beal, R., 212
Bean, F., 404
Beauchamp, Tom, 264–267, 270–272, 274–277, 280, 298, 304–305, 307–308, 310–314, 342
Beckman, L. J., 138
Beers, V. S., 109
Behavior
  help-seeking, of female drug abusers, 120–122
  HIV-risk, 113
Beliefs, self-oppressing, 282
Benn, S., 313
Bennett, C. L., 107
Bentley, J. D., 109
Beral, V., 29
Berardi, V. P., 13
Bergman, A., 28, 55
Berkelman, R. L., 29, 164
Berkley, S., 57
Berkowitz, C. D., 363
Berman, S. M., 171
Berns, D., 13, 57
Bernstein, R. J., 309
Berrebi, A., 58
Besharov, D., 242
Bhat, G. J., 74
Bicarbonate, urinary, 69
Biddlecom, A. E., 54
Bigelow, G. E., 135
Biggar, R. J., 59, 74
Bigler, W., 52

Bignozzi, C., 59
Bingol, N., 137
Bioethical theory, normative aims, 275–276
Bioethics, 261, 372, 378
Biragli, P., 60
Birth. *See* Childbirth
Birth control. *See* Contraception
Birth weight, low, 46
Bisexual men, 21
Black, P. J., 166
Blackburn, R., 53
Blacks. *See* African-Americans
Blanche, S., 59, 74–77
Bleecker, T., 109
Bloche, M. Gregg, 242, 246, 315, 319
Bluestein, D., 404
Blustein, Jeffrey, 329, 343
Bodin, G. F., 52
Bohlin, A. B., 76
Bolan, G., 54
Boland, M. G., 94
Bolognesi, D., 74
Booth, D. K., 106
Bornstein, M. H., 138
Boschini, A., 56
Botkin, J. R., 206
Boulos, C., 61
Boulos, R., 61, 74
Bouno, D., 107
Bovicelli, L., 76
Boyce, J. G., 56
Boyer, J., 59–60
Boylan, L., 59
Bracken, L., 208
Brain involvement in HIV-infected children, 70–71
Brandon, W., 29
Breast-feeding, HIV transmission via, 44, 64
Brechot, C., 59
Brennan, T. A., 202, 210–211
Brettle, R. P., 25, 58, 135, 136, 138
Breyel, J., 139
Broder, S., 74
Brodman, M., 55, 57
Broliden, P. A., 59, 76
Brookmeyer, R., 26
Brooks, N. A., 166
Brooks-Gunn, J., 404
Brooner, R. K., 135, 139
Brossard, A., 59
Brotman, B., 165, 175
Broussard, A., 74
Brown, C., 60, 75, 206, 299
Brown, D., 401

Brown, L. S., 135–136
Brown, S., 57
Brown, S. B., 249
Browne, S. E., 166
Brownstein, R., 170
Brundage, J. F., 13, 363
Brunelli, S., 404
Brunham, R. C., 61
Brutus, J.-R., 61
Bruun, J. N., 107
Bryant, K. J., 131
Bryson, Y., 59
Buckley, J. Jr., 344
Buck v. Bell, 146, 149–150
Budetti, P., 365
Buehler, H. W., 28
Buehler, J. W., 29, 164, 363
Burgdorf, R. L. Jr., 173
Burger, H., 59
Burk, R. D., 55–56
Burke, A. C., 131
Burke, D. S., 13, 56, 363
Burna, K. A., 61
Burns, D. N., 60
Burns, K. A., 132, 136
Burns, S. M., 58, 75, 135–136
Burns, W. J., 132, 136
Burris, S., 203
Burrow, G. N., 137
Burwell, L. G., 52
Bush, T. J., 13, 57, 306, 363
Busia, A.P.A., 404
Butz, A. M., 62, 77, 136
Byers, R. H., 29
Byrne, M. A., 29

Cabral, H., 131, 136
Cabral, R. J., 461
Cahalane, D. Kenneally, 247
Cahalane, Denise, 227
Calabresi, G., 300, 307–308, 317
Caldwell, M. B., 93–94
Callahan, D., 166
Callahan, S., 166
Calvelli, T. A., 60
Cameron, D. W., 13, 52, 55
Cameron, W., 57
Campana J., 171
Campbell, S. W., 62
Cancer
  cervical, 6, 20, 40
  childhood, psychosocial adjustments of, 89
Candidiasis, 6, 21–22, 24, 40, 102
Canessa, A., 58

Caniglia, M., 59
Canner, J. K., 60
Cao, L., 74
Capron, A. M., 300
Carael, M., 52
Carey, J. T., 107
Carey vs. Population Services International, 354
Carovano, K., 62
Carpenter, 29
Carpenter, C. C., 27–28, 30, 57
Carpenter, C.C.J., 107, 108
Carpenter, C. J., 28
Carper, R., 402
Carratta, L., 56
Carrega, G., 58
Carroll, K. M., 131
Carter, R. J., 58, 402
Casolati, E., 56
Catania, J., 135
Cates, W., 52, 53
Caucasians, 4
Cavero, C., 62
Cavkin, David, 222
CD4 analogue, 46
CD4 lymphocytes
  cell count, 5, 16
    as AIDS-indicator, 20
    AZT therapy and, 23, 48
    HIV progression and, 16–17
    HIV prophylaxis during pregnancy and, 48–49
    in late HIV disease, 20
    low, management of, 72
    MAC prophylaxis, 23–24
    mucosal candidiasis and, 40
    normal, 16
    in opportunistic infections, 17
    PCP prophylaxis and, 23
    perinatal HIV transmission and, 65
    in pregnancy, 43–44, 48
    zidovudine treatment and, 97
  HIV destruction of, 67–68
  loss, frequency of injection drug use and, 112–113
CD8 lymphocytes, 16, 43
CD4 receptor, 67
Celentano, D. D., 108
Center for Disease Control (CDC), 63, 91
  AIDS definition, 20
  childbirth recommendations for HIV-infected women, 214–215
  diagnostic criteria for pediatric HIV infection, 64–65

Center for Disease Control (CDC) *(continued)*
  directive counseling and, 144, 186
  epidemiologic data, on adolescent HIV infections, 347
  Youth Risk Behavior Study, 348
  zidovudine guidelines, 97
Certified nurse-midwife (CNM), 50
Cervical cap, 34–35
Cervical carcinoma, 6, 20, 40
Cervical dysplasia, 6, 21, 39, 102
Cervical intraepithelial neoplasia (CIN), 39–40
Cervicitis, 41
Cesarean delivery, 65
Chaisson, R. E., 27, 28, 30, 62, 107
Chamberlain, W., 314
Chamberland, M. E., 13, 306, 363
Chancroid, 38
Chandwani, S., 76
Chapman, J. W., 302, 315
Chasnoff, I. J., 61, 132, 136–138, 242
Chatis, P., 55
Chavkin, D. F., 246
Chavkin, Wendy, 61, 240–241
Chemically dependent person, 226. *See also* Drug abusers, female; Drug abusers, male
Chen, J.-H., 53
Cherman, J.-C., 59
Cherukuri, I. J., 136
Cherukuri, R., 137
Chi, S. Y., 363
Chiasson, M. A., 57
Childbirth
  abandonment, personal values/intentions, 427–430
  in AIDS context, 401
  decision for, 197
  by drug abusers, 119–120
  HIV-infected, 41–42
  of HIV-infected child, 84–85
  by HIV-infected women
    harm from, 368
    health-care provider viewpoint, 430–432
    justified, 397–400
    moral critique of, 373–374
    public response to, 368
    transmission, mode of delivery and, 65
  as moral privilege/duty, 401
  postponement, personal values/intentions, 427–430
  process, HIV infection and, 64
  wrongful, 184
Child custody
  denial, to unwed father, 148

  drug treatment completion agreements for, 229–230
  loss of, by neonatal testing, 162
Childhood diseases, 68
Childhood experience, decision-making and, 285
Child-protective services (CPS)
  coerced birth control, 233
  interventions, 232–233, 235
  National Drug Control Strategy and, 215
  prenatal drug use reporting, 217
  stigma, 85
Children. *See also* Infants
  with AIDS, 3, 143
    maternal transmission, 368
    as tragedy, 399–400
  with chronic illness, psychosocial adjustments of, 88–91
  epidemiology of HIV in, 63
  with expensive medical conditions, right to give birth to, 335
  in HIV-affected families
    death of parent/sibling and, 87–88
    interventions for, 92–93
    uninfected siblings/children, impact on, 91–92
  HIV-infected, 73
    anti-HIV treatment for, 71–72
    comorbidity among, 82–83
    health care for, 71
    loss of, 390
    natural history, 66–71
    preventing infections in, 72
    problems, early identification/treatment of, 73
  of HIV-infected mothers, 78–79, 93
    custody/decision-making issues for, 85–86
    families and, 82
    outlook for, 87–91
    positive effect of, 86–87
    socioeconomic status and, 82
    stigma and, 81–82
    vignettes of, 79–81
  personal injury actions against parents, 197
  right not to have, 320, 326–327
  right to have, 320, 329
    distributive justice and, 335–341
    harm to future generations and, 329–335
Childress, James F., 264, 298, 304–305, 342
Child welfare system, 85
Chin, J., 297
Chiodo, F., 76
Chiphangwi, J. D., 14, 58, 60

Chlamydia infection, 37, 39
Chorioamnionitis, 44, 46
Chorionic villus sampling (CVS), 48, 194
Chraibi, J., 58
Chu, S. Y., 29, 164
Chutivongse, S., 53
Ciesieki, C. A., 29
CIN (cervical intraepithelial neoplasia), 39–40
Civil commitment, 224–227
Clark, A., 175
Clark, R., 29
Clarke, A., 165
Classism, involuntary sterilization and, 144–145
Clayton, E. Wright, 206, 211
Clin, J., 60
Clinical trials, 22–23. *See also* AIDS Clinical Trials Group (ACTG)
  exclusion of women from, 24
  participation of women in, 101–102
Clinton administration, 215
Clumeck, N., 107
CMV (cytomegalovirus), 21–22, 41
CNM (certified nurse-midwife), 50
Coalition on Alcohol and Drug Dependent Women and their Children, 238
Coates, J., 135
Coates, T. J., 109
Cobbs, C. G., 30
Coberly, J. S., 61
Cocaine abuse
  crack, 38, 115, 126–127
  criminal prosecution with coerced treatment, 227–228
  methadone treatment, 222
  obstetrical complications, 119
  in pregnant women, 111–112
Cochran, S. D., 171, 404
Coercion
  as conscious experience, 277–280
  counseling against pregnancy and, 159
  definition, by Faden and Beauchamp model, 263–266
  moral judgment and, 261–263, 288
  reductionism and, 289
  treatment
    civil commitment, 224–227
    coerced birth control or abortion, 230–231
    and criminal prosecution, 227–229
    de facto commitment, 230
    frequency, 223–224
    of pregnant drug abusers, 222–231
    for retaining/regaining child custody, 229–230
    types, 223
    unconscious, 280
Cohen, G. A., 314
Cohen, J. B., 27, 107, 135
Cohen, J.H.M., 26
Cohen, S., 165–166, 170
Cohn, D., 30
Coker, R. J., 26
Coles, C. D., 132
Colker, R., 402
Collier, A. C., 107
Collins. G., 132
Collins, Patricia H., 397
Colposcopy, 39–40
Comacho, T., 53
Community agencies, 93
Comorbidity, among HIV-infected children, 82–83
Compensatory damages, 181–182, 184, 195–196
Competency of adolescent decision-making, 360
Conant, M. A., 55
Conception, decision not to conceive, 191
Condoms
  female, 12, 34–35
  male, 4, 34–35
    adolescent usage, 348–349
    breakage rates, 35
    efficacy, public perception of, 36
    female drug abusers and, 117
    gender inequality in relationships and, 128
    for HIV prevention, 37
    HIV transmission and, 35
    injection drug users and, 114
    prostitutes and, 115
    provision by schools, 351–352
    with spermicide usage, 34, 191
    sterilized women and, 32
    usage factors, 35–36
    women's requests for partner usage of, 36
Condon, C. M., 249
Confidentiality
  breach, for protection of others, 189
  duty to maintain, 47, 181, 188–191
  of mother, neonatal testing and, 162
Congenital HIV infections, 63–67
Congenital malformations, maternal drug use and, 119–120
Congenital syphilis, 38
Conigliaro, J., 106

Connaughton J. F., 137
Connor, E., 74, 75, 177, 344, 364, 365
Connors, D., 166
Constitution, right to procreate, 146–149
Conti, M., 56
Contraception, 32–36. *See also specific forms of contraception*
  coerced use of, 223, 230–231
  court-ordered, 151
  decision-making, adolescent, 353, 354
  information, 191
  long-term, 152–153, 291
  practices, of female drug abusers, 116–117
  as probation condition, 233
  regulation, 147–148
Conway, G. A., 363
Coombs, R., 57, 76
Cooper, D. A., 74, 107
Coping mechanisms, 90, 183
Corbett, M. A., 62
Corcostegui, B., 75
Cordier, G., 26
Corea, G., 175, 402
Corey, L., 54, 57
Corgnaud, V., 74
Cornelius, L. J., 94
Costigliola, P., 76
Cote, R. J., 62
Cotton, D. J., 30, 108, 251
Coulter, S. L., 53
Counseling
  advisory, 293–295
    coercion in, 295
    vs. directive, 260–261, 274–275
  advocating reproductive forbearance, 453
  as coerced treatment, 235
  conceptual analysis/moral judgment, 261–263
  confidentiality, duty to maintain, 47, 181, 188–191
  decision not to conceive, 191
  directive, 214, 283, 293
    for abortion, 162–163
    ADA and, 159–160
    argument against, 161
    implications of, 186–188
    for sterilization, 230
    vs. advisory, 260–261, 274–275
  duty to provide
    breaches in, 184–188
    scope of, 182–184
  duty to warn, 188–191
  elements for all interactions, 457
  failure to provide, 183–186
  for HIV-infected women, 32, 291–295
    accommodation and, 294–295
    normative issues, 292–294
    during pregnancy, 47
  legal interventions and, 217
  methods
    of health-care providers, 413–414
    of other health-care professionals, 415
  negligent, 186–187. *See also Doe v. Jamaica Hospital*
  nondirective, 187–188, 214
  against pregnancy, ADA and, 158–159
  of pregnant women, ADA and, 160–161
  toward reasoned/reflective decision-making, 453–454
  Working Group position on, 454–460
Counselors. *See* Health-care providers
Counterfactual thinking, 267–268
  frames for, 268–269
  quality of life standard, 332–333
Courgnaud, V., 59
Covino, J. P., 57
Coyne, J. C., 94
Crack cocaine, 38, 115, 126–127. *See also* Cocaine abuse
Creagh, T., 27
Creagh-Kirk, T., 27, 30
Crenshaw, K. Williams, 314
Criminal prosecution
  and coerced treatment, 227–229
  for consensual sexual intercourse with underage women, 152
  of pregnant HIV-infected drug abusers, 219–222, 234, 237–238
    legal theories for, 219–221
    opposition, 220
Critchlow, C. W., 54
Cryptococcal meningitis prophylaxis, 24
Culbert, A. J., 300
Cultural relativism, moral multiculturalism and, 375
Cupitt, C., 135
Curran, J. W., 57
Custody, 85–86, 87
CVS (chorionic villus sampling), 48, 194
Cynamon, M., 30
Cytomegalovirus (CMV), 21–22, 41
Czarniecki, L., 94

Dahlgren, L., 138
Dallabetta, G. A., 14, 25, 58, 60
Dallascasa, P., 76
Dalton, H., 203, 402

Damages
  compensatory, 181–182, 184, 195–196
  punitive, 181–182
Dan-Cohen, M., 307
Danforth, S. B., 57
Danger
  to others, 224–225
  perception of, interpersonal differences in, 285–287
  to self, 224–225
Daniel, L., 26
Daniels, Norman, 277–279, 288, 308, 311, 313
Dapsone, for PCP prophylaxis, 49
d'Arminio, M. A., 75
Darragh, T. M., 55
Darrow, W. W., 52, 135
Datta, P., 75
Dattel, B. J., 29, 55
D'Aunno, T. A., 131
Davenny, K., 61, 107, 131, 136
Davidson, A. J., 53
Davis, Angela, 397, 407
Davis, E., 343
Davis, P. C., 313
Dawson, J. P., 318
D'Costa, L. J., 55
ddI (Didanosine), 23, 48, 72
Death
  AIDS-related, 31, 143
  HIV-infected children, 70–71
  of parent/sibling, children and, 88–89
  rates, 7–9
  symbolic equivalents, 284
Debanne, S., 132
Decision-making
  adolescent, 345–346
    government recognition of, 353
  allocating for adolescents, 349–352
  authenticity, 280–288
    liberal social theory and, 280–281
    psychoanalytic models and, 283–287
    radical social theory and, 281–283
  autonomous choices, 263–264
  autonomy-negating influence, 295–296
  childhood experience and, 285
  coercive vs. noncoercive, 259
  criminal law and, 234
  by drug-abusers, personal issues of, 128
  governmental intervention, 149–153
    contraception, court-ordered, 151
    involuntary sterilization cases, 149–150
    medical intervention, court-ordered, 151
  harm to children and, 334
  HIV-infected women advice for other women, 433–434
  legal interventions and, 217
  locus of, 183
  moral framework, 378
  nonautonomous, 265
  paradigms of influence without intent, 287–288
  reasoned/reflective, counseling toward, 453–454
  respect for reproductive choices, 436–437
  threat/offer distinction, 270–274
DeCock, K. M., 13–14
Deegan, M. J., 166
De facto commitment, 230
DeFerrari, E., 61, 62
DeHovitz, J. A., 209
DeLeeuw, H. W., 109
Deligdisch, L., 57
Delke, I., 61
Delusions, 84
de Martino, M., 76
Dementia, 20, 32, 84
Depo Provera (depot medroxyprogesterone acetate; DMPA), 33, 41
Deppe, D., 52
Depression
  death of parent/sibling and, 88
  of drug-abusing pregnant women, 120
  inability to seek medical care and, 83–84
  parental, 87
DeRemer, P. A., 56
Derish, P. A., 107
Dermatitis, seborrheic, 70
DeRossi, A., 76
DeSantis, L., 404
Deschamps, M. M., 58
DesJarlais, D., 26, 55
Desvarieux, M., 58
Deteis, R., 62
Detels, R., 106, 107
Devash, Y., 60
Deveikis, A., 59
De Vincenzi, I., 364
DeVore, S. L., 135
Diaby, L., 14
Diagnosis. See also HIV status
  communication of, 182
  disclosure. See Disclosure
  as family secret, 92
  neonatal testing, maternal implications, 161–162
Diaphragm, 34–35
Diarrhea, 6, 20

Diaz, A., 404
Diaz, V., 137
Dickinson, G. M., 58
DiClemente, R., 53–54, 363, 365
Dictor, M., 74
Didanosine (ddI), 23, 48, 72
Dideoxycytidine (ddC), 48
Dill, B. Thornton, 405
Dillon, M., 59
Dinamore, J., 220
Dinsmore, J., 250
Directive counseling. *See* Counseling, directive
Dirkes, K., 61
Disability. *See also* Americans With Disabilities Act (ADA)
  HIV infection as, 163
  of women, discrimination and, 145–146
Disadvantaged families, 82
Disclosure
  consequences, 189
  fear of, decision not to conceive and, 189
  of HIV status, by neonatal testing, 162
  by neonatal testing, 162
  risk-benefit analysis, 189–190
Discrimination
  of women with disabilities, 145–146
  history of
    for low-income women, 144–145
    for women of color, 144–145
Distributive justice, 335–341
Divine, G., 107
Dixon, S., 137
DMPA (depot medroxyprogesterone acetate; depo Provera), 33, 41
Dobbs, D., 173, 203, 205–208
Doctor-patient relationship, self-determination and, 264–265
Doe v. Jamaica Hospital, 156–158, 186–187, 192–193, 257–258
Doi, P., 30
Dolin, R., 107
Domestic violence, 32, 189–190
Dondero, T. J., 57
Donoghoe, M. C., 135
Dooling, E., 137
Dorrucci, M., 27
Dotino, P., 55
Douglas, J. M., 53
Dowling, P., 166
Downey, G., 94
Downing, R., 57
Drucker, E., 132, 136
Drug abusers, female. *See also* Injection drug users (IDUs)
  background of, 384

  child custody and, 87
  children of, 110
  of cocaine
    crack usage, 38, 115, 126–127
    criminal prosecution with coerced treatment, 227–228
    methadone treatment for, 222
    obstetrical complications, 119
    pregnancy and, 111–112
  contraceptive practices and, 116–117
  epidemic among pregnant women, 218
  health-care provider attitudes/practices toward, 419–420
  help-seeking behaviors of, 120–122
  incidence, 111
  maternal role and, 118
  perinatal transmission, 45, 222–223
  personal level effects, 110
  polydrug use and, 127
  pregnant, 32, 46–47, 119–120, 236–237
    adverse outcome and, 46–47
    coerced treatment for, 222–231, 234–235
    criminal prosecutions for, 237–238
    drug-treatment programs for, 127–128, 223
    neonatal outcomes and, 119–120
    public policy, 129–131
  representation in clinical trials, 102
  reproductive choices, 114–120
    new policy issues, HIV status and, 129–130
    policy/practices, present, 125–128
    pregnancy termination decisions, 117–118
    sexual activity and, 114–116
  societal level effects, 110
  syphilis incidence and, 38
  views/experiences of, 438–440
  vs. addiction, 157–158
Drug abusers, male
  adverse consequences for, 127
  as sex partners, 114
Drug toxicology screens, 126
Drug-treatment programs
  coercive, 217, 222–231
  completion, for retaining/regaining child custody, 229–230
  efficacy of, 115–116
  enrollment, African-American, 121
  integration with health-care services, 123–125
  lack of facilities for women, 222
  mixed-gender, 122–123
  for pregnant drug abusers, 127–128, 223
  referrals, 121, 124
  refusal to accept pregnant women, 179

targeted skills-building programs, 116
  for women, 216
    shortage of, 121
    specialized, need for, 122–123
Drug withdrawal, neonatal, 119
Drummond, J. E., 60, 75
Dubler, Nancy, 62, 171, 176, 201, 203, 209, 299, 365, 378–380, 402–403
Dula, A., 402, 404–405, 407
Duliege, A. M., 59, 74, 76
Dumestre, J., 29
Dunn, D. T., 59
Dunn, R. A., 54
Durbin, M., 53
Durfee, M. J., 363
Duty of care, breach of, 181–182
Dworkin, Gerald, 281, 301, 304, 314, 342
Dworkin, Ronald, 325, 342
Dwyer, B., 54

Easterbrook, P. J., 27, 30
Eaton, D., 204
Ectrodactyly, 145
Eczema, 70
Edelin, K. C., 132, 136–137
Edlin, B. R., 107
Education
  background, of HIV-infected women, 384
  for HIV-infected individuals, 32
  on medical dimensions of HIV-related reproduction, 454
  public health, for injection drug users, 367
  on risk factors/modes of transmission, 182–183
  sex, 351–352
  on sexual activity risks, 36–37
Efird, C. M., 62
Eglin, R. P., 52
Ehret, J. M., 52
Ehrlich, J. S., 172
Ehrlich, S., 137
Ehrnst, A., 74
Eldred, L. J., 27
Electrocardiogram, abnormal, 69
Ellerbrock, T. V., 13, 57, 61, 306, 363
Ellman, I., 365
El-Sadr, W., 77
Elster, J., 317
Elvy, G. A., 139
Embree, J., 75
Encephalopathy, in children, 68
Endocarditis, 22
Endometritis, 41, 46
English, A., 171, 365
Ensminger, M. E., 94

Epidemiology, HIV infection, 3–5, 63, 367
Epstein, A. M., 106
Epstein, R. A., 302, 309
Eric, K., 136, 402
Erickson, B., 54
Erlich, K., 55
Ernhart, C. B., 132
Escher, 306
Esophageal candidiasis, 40
Esophagitis, *Candida*, 21–22, 24
Ethical relativism, moral multiculturalism and, 375
Eversley, R., 108

Faden, Ruth, 52, 58, 108, 206, 252, 264–267, 270–272, 274–277, 280, 301, 305, 307, 308, 310–314, 460
Faden and Beauchamp model, 288–289
  advisory counseling, 274–275
  authenticity and, 281
  definition of coercion, 264–266
  directive counseling, 275
  manipulation and, 266
  resistibility and, 266–270
  threat/offer distinction, 270–274
Fahner, J. B., 74
Fahs, M., 56
Falek, A., 132
Family
  centrality of, 385, 392–394, 401
  children of HIV-infected mothers and, 82
  dissolution, after birth of HIV-infected child, 84–85
  encouragement, help-seeking behavior of drug-abusing women and, 121
  extended, unavailability of, 85
  HIV-affected, care issues for, 83–86
  responsibilities, 383–384
Fang, G., 59
Fann, S. A., 25
Fauci, A. S., 77
Feinberg, Joel, 30, 108, 206, 309, 323, 329, 342–343, 402
Feingold, A. R., 55, 61, 136
Feingold, L., 363
Feinson, C., 365
Felch, L. J., 135, 139
Feldman, J., 55, 61, 136–137
Fellner, C. H., 366
Felton, S., 59, 74
Female condom, 12
Feminism, 379
Feng, T. I., 57, 61, 136, 138
Fenyo, E. M., 60
Ferrence, R. G., 136

Ferris, T. F., 137
Fertility services, access to, 158
Fetal alcohol syndrome, 119, 126, 130
Fetal scalp monitoring, 45, 65
Fetus
  coerced treatment of pregnant women and, 235
  rights of, 147, 151
  safety, 194
Feuer, G., 56
Fever, persistent, 20
Feyerabend, Paul, 310
Fiddian, A. P., 107
Field, M., 176
Fife, D., 109
Financial aspects
  barriers to health care-services, 103–104
  burdens for HIV-infected women, 86
Fink, J. R., 251
Finkelstein, D. M., 30, 108
Finkelstein, N., 250
Finnegan, L. P., 131–132, 136–138, 241
Fiore, T. C., 57
First, M. B., 239
Firtion, G., 74
Fischl, M. A., 58, 106–107
Fisher, A., 57
Fisher, W. A., 53
Fishman, M., 94
Flack, H. E., 311, 402
Flapan, M., 343
Fleischman, A. R., 170
Fleisher, L., 206
Fleishman, J. A., 107–109
Fleming, I., 56
Fleming, J., 26
Fleming, P. L., 13, 29, 93
Fletcher, M. A., 58
Floridia, M., 107
Fojaco, R. M., 57
Fontelos, P. M., 75
Forrest, J. D., 52, 53
Forthal, D. N., 13
Foster, C. A., 135
Foster care, 86, 87
Fournie, A., 58
Fox, H. E., 59
Fox, R., 26–27, 54
France, A. J., 135
Francis, D. P., 297
Francoual, C., 74
Frank, D. A., 132
Frank, J., 60
Frank, R., 109

Franke, K. M., 58, 201
Frankfurt, H. G., 303
Fraser, F. C., 461
Frazier, R., 61
Freir, C., 137
Frenkel, L. D., 74, 77
Freud, S., 316
Freudian drive theory, 286
Fried, C., 302, 309
Fried, L. E., 131, 136
Friedland, G. H., 61, 107
Friedman, F., 55
Friedman, H. B., 27, 28
Friedman, S. R., 26
Friedmann, W., 56
Frigoletto, F., 298
Fruchter, R. G., 56
Fuchs, E. J., 27
Fuchs, M., 137
Fukunaga, K., 59
Fullerton, J., 62
Fundaro, C., 59
Funkhouser, A. W., 136
Furtado, M. R., 61
Future generations, harm toward, 330–331

Gabel, S., 94
Gabiano, C., 75–76
Gadamer, Hans-George, 310, 318
Gage, L. S., 109
Gail, M. H., 61
Gakinya, M. N., 13
Galavotti, C., 461
Gallagher, J., 165, 213, 242
Gallant, J. E., 28, 30
Galli, L., 76
Garcia, Anderson S., 225, 246, 247
Garcia, Jorge, 381, 402, 404
Gargiullo, P. M., 461
Garibaldi, K., 56
Gastrointestinal tract, involvement, in HIV-infected children, 69, 71
Gatell, J. M., 107
Gaur, S., 74, 77
Gay/bisexual men, 3
Gaylin, Willard, 284, 315
Gazaway, P. M., 135, 139
Geertz, Clifford, 310
Gelber, R. D., 177, 251, 364
Geller, G., 206, 252, 460
Gellert, G. A., 363
Gender differences
  in cytomegalovirus infection, 21–22
  in drug use, 111

INDEX

in HIV disease progression, 17
immunological markers, 16
in injection drug use, 111
pharmacokinetic, 24
in symptomatology, 19
Gender subordination, 377–379
Genetic counseling, 259
Genital herpes, 38
Genital ulcer disease, 11, 21, 41
Genotype, 45
Geographic distribution, 4–5
  HIV-infected childbirths, 41–42
  of HIV seroprevalence, in United States, 9–10
George, J. R., 13, 57, 76, 176
George, S. K., 243
Gerber, A. R., 59
Gerbert, B., 109
Giannelli, F., 107
Gianquinto, C., 60, 76
Gibbons, L. K., 165
Gibbs, J. P., 297
Gielen, A., 52, 58, 108, 460
Gill, P., 135
Gilligan, C., 405
Gilstrap, L. C., 132
Githens, P., 211
Giuliano, M., 107
Glasson, J., 203
Goden, 306
Goebel, F., 107
Goeder, J. J., 60, 74, 75, 76
Goedert, J. J., 59, 60–62
Goering, S., 407
Golar, K., 132
Gold, J., 74
Gold, J.W.M., 62
Goldberg, K. C., 106
Golden. N., 132
Goldenbaum, M., 363
Goldsmith, M. F., 170–172
Goller v. White, 198
Golombok, S., 53
Gonorrhea, 37, 38
Gonzalez-Lahoz, J., 107
Good, C. B., 106
Goodwin, S., 52
Gopalan, R., 138
Gostin, L., 108, 173, 174
Gottleib, M., 106, 107, 404
Goudeau, A., 59
Government. *See also specific federal legislation*
  drug policy, 215

  federal regulations, adolescents and, 345, 359
  public policy recommendations
    advised proposals, 450–452
    unadvised proposals, 448–450
  recognition of adolescent decision-making, 353
  sexual/reproductive behavior regulations, 351–352
  statutory protections, 153–161. *See also* State government
gp120 envelope protein, V3 region, 45
Grady, G. F., 13, 57
Graham, A. V., 406
Graham, N.M.H., 106, 107
Gramling, J., 57
Grandjean, H., 58
Granger, R. H., 138
Grant, J., 55
Graves, R. H., 249
Graves, S. R., 54
Gray, G. C., 25
Greco, D., 107
Green, J., 55, 109
Green, M., 94–95
Greenberg, 29
Greenberg-Friedman, D., 62
Greene, D. L., 244
Greenspan, J. R., 171
Grieco, M. H., 106–107
Griffith, D. R., 61, 137
Grimes, D. A., 298
Grimes, J. M., 25
Grimson, R., 59
Griscelli, C., 59
Grisso, T., 366
Griswold, 176
Griswold v. Connecticut, 378
Grodin v. Grodin, 199
Gromisch, D. S., 137
Groopman, J. E., 106–107
Grosboll, D., 165, 175
Grosch-Worner, I., 76
Grossman, 29
Grubman, S., 76, 176
Guardianship, 85–86
Guaschino, S., 56
Guest, F., 52, 53
Guillemot, D., 109
Guilt, moral, 380
Guinan, M. E., 132, 363
Gundrum, M. M., 297
Gupman, A., 138
Gurganious, L., 132

Gustavus, S., 404
Guthrie, D., 404
Gutierrez, C., 75
Guttmacher, Alan, 364, 365
Gwinn, M., 13, 57, 176
Gynecological disease, in HIV-infected women, 19–21. *See also specific gynecological diseases*

Habermas, Jurgen, 283, 310, 315, 403
Hackerman, F., 139
Hague, R. A., 75
Haiken, H. J., 94
Hair loss, in HIV-infected children, 70
Hairy leukoplakia, 6
Haitt, H. H., 202, 210
Hale, R., 313
Hall, J., 203
Hall, M., 138
Halpin, G. J., 61
Halsey, N. A., 60–61, 74, 76
Hamid, M. A., 132
Hammer, G. S., 54
Hammer, S. M., 30
Handley, M. A., 25, 58
Handte, J., 58
Hankin, C. A., 25
Hankins, C. A., 58
Hannan, E. L., 106
Hannon, W. H., 57
Hansen, J. O., 244
Hansen, N., 107
Hanser, M., 343
Hanson, R., 25
Hardy, A., 26, 54, 132
Hardy, L. M., 460
Hardy, W. D., 107
Harm
 of being born, *vs.* nonexistence, 334
 from childbirth by HIV-infected women, 368
 foreseeability to third parties, 190
 to future generations, 329–335
 maternalism principle and, 399
 by not being born, 332
 as setback to interests of another, 330
Harm-to-benefit ratio test, 334
Harris, A. M., 136
Harris, D., 95
Harris, L., 136, 138–139, 311
Harris, M. A., 61
Hart, H.L.A., 135, 342
Hartel, D., 29, 107, 131
Harth, J., 243
Hartley, T. M., 135

Hartmann, B., 164, 175
Hartz, A. J., 106
Hassig, S. E., 61, 75
Hatcher, R. A., 52–53
Hauer, L., 29, 55
Hayes, C. D., 364
Hayman, C. R., 363
Hayward, R. A., 109
Hazard, G. C. Jr., 204
He, W., 108
Health-care providers
 abandonment by, 192
 ADA and, 154–155
 advice, to HIV-infected women, 432
 anxiety, 194
 communication of diagnosis, 182
 doctor-patient relationship, self-determination and, 264–265
 duties, pregnancy-related, 192
 endorsement of reproductive forbearance, 453
 interactions with clients, 452
 liability, 180–194
  from acts or omissions, 185
  tort, assessing reality of, 195–196
 loyalty to patient, 293–294
 malpractice premiums, 179
 opinions, 421–424
  attitudes/practices toward drug abusers, 419–421
  on childbearing, 430–432
  conduct of interviews, 411–412
  counseling methods, 413–414
  on HIV-infected women and childbearing, 415–417, 418
  other professionals, 413–414
  self-administered questionnaire findings, 417–421
 refusal to treat HIV-infected person, 155–157
 reluctance to treat poor/minority women, 178–179
Health-care services
 accessibility, 24, 96, 102–106
  ADA and, 155–158
  for HIV-infected women, 24
  as moral entitlement, 294
 availability, 101–102
 financial barriers, 103–104
 and HIV-infected children, 71
 and HIV-infected women, 96, 101, 104–106
 integrated
  with drug-intervention programs, 123–125
  for women/children, 103
 need for, 99–101

INDEX

organization, 102–103
pregnant drug-using women and, 127–128
in rural areas, 104
system of barriers for pregnant drug abusers, 122
in urban areas, 104
utilization, evaluation framework for, 98–99
Health insurance, 103
Health-maintenance organizations (HMOs), 191–192
Hearst, N., 54
Heart involvement, in HIV-infected children, 69, 71
Hebert, L. E., 202
Hein, K., 363
Heins, Jr., H. C., 62
Held, V., 302, 303
Hellinger, F. J., 108
Heltzer, J. E., 131
Hematologic disorders, in HIV-infected children, 69–71
Henderson, C., 61
Henggeler, S. W., 363
Hepatitis B, 43, 48
Herbert, B., 54
Herbert, L. E., 210
Herbold, J. R., 13
Hermann, D. H., 203
Hernandez, S. R., 107
Herpes simplex virus (HSV)
  detection, 38
  gender differences, 21–22
  genital, 37
  prophylaxis, 24
Herpes zoster, 6
Herz, E., 406
Hessol, N. A., 26
Heterosexual transmission, 3–4, 12, 15, 36
Heyward, W. L., 55
Hickson, G., 211
Hidalgo, J., 27, 62, 107
Hilfiker, D., 202, 211
Hill, I., 139
Hill Collins, P., 406, 407
Hingson, R., 132
Hinter, A. G., 94
Hira, S. K., 53, 74
Hirozawa, A., 27, 107
Hirsch, M. S., 106
Hispanics
  adolescent contraceptive usage, 349
  children
    AIDS-infected, 399
    HIV incidence in, 63
  female drug abusers, condom usage, 117

HIV-infected infants, 367
HIV-infected women, 4, 82, 143, 178, 372
  AIDS incidence in, 15
  cultural childbirth values, 375
  HIV/AIDS mortality, 8–9
  HIV seroprevalence, 10
  injection drug use and, 112
  hopelessness and, 100–101
  moral values, 381–382
Hitimana, D. G., 75
HIV immune globulin, 46
HIV-infected women
  advice for other women, 433–434
  asymptomatic, 6
  demographics, 143
  maternal duty, 198–199, 236
  nongynecological manifestations, 21–22
  opinion, on what health-care advice should be given, 432
  parenthood/parenting by, 86–87
  positive effect of children on, 86–87
HIV infection
  clinical course, 15–24
  effect on pregnancy, 46–47
  incidence, 12
  incubation period, 66
  knowledge of recommended care, 99–100
  late complications, 20
  manifestations, early, 15
  natural history, 12, 16–18
  nongynecological manifestations, 21–22
  prognosis, 15–16
  progression
    CD4 cell count and, 16–17
    factors in, 16
    in injection drug users, 112–113
    pregnancy effect on, 373
    in women, 16–19
  seroconversion, 19–20
  seropositivity. See Seroprevalence
  staging system, 5–6
  symptoms, 19, 384–385
  transmission. See Transmission
  unique nature of, 81–83
  vaccine, 12, 46
HIV status
  concealment, 100
  disclosure. See Disclosure
  knowledge of
    pregnancy termination decisions and, 118
    as reason not to have children, 427
HIV variants/quasi-species, 45
Ho, G. Y., 56
Ho, J. L., 58
Ho, M., 106

Hodara, V., 60
Hoegerman, G., 242
Hoegsberg, B., 55
Hoff, R., 13, 57
Hofstadter, Douglas, 267–268, 306
Hogue, C.J.R., 61
Hollandsworth, J. G. Jr., 95
Holman, S., 61, 62
Holmes, K., 53, 54, 57
Holt, E., 61, 74
Homosexual men, clinical predictors of HIV disease progression, 20
Homosexual transmission, 3
Hook, E. W., 54
Hoover, D. R., 58, 60
Hopelessness, 100–101
Horger, E. O. II, 249
Horn, J., 28, 54
Horsburgh, R. C., 25
Hospitalization, of children, 89
Hotaling, G. T., 209
Howard, D., 55
Howard, R., 210
Hoyt, L. G., 74, 77
HPV (human papilloma virus), 21, 37, 39–40
Hsu, M. A., 136
HSV. See Herpes simplex virus (HSV)
Huchinson, M., 206
Human dignity, resistibility and, 270
Human leukocyte antigen (HLA), 45
Human papilloma virus (HPV), 21, 37, 39–40
Humiliation, 284
Hunter, N. D., 201
Hutcheon, N., 59
Hutchinson, C. M., 54, 403
Hutto, C., 61, 74, 76
Hutton, N., 61, 62, 77
Hyslop, N. E., 107

Icenogle, J. P., 55
Idiopathic thrombocytopenic purpura, 6
IDUs. See Injection drug users (IDUs)
Ikemoto, L. C., 170
Imam, N., 57
Imam, W., 28
Immorality of birth of HIV-infected infants, 377–378
Immunizations, childhood, 72
Immunosuppression, 20, 40, 68
Inborn errors of metabolism, 81
Infants
  with AIDS, 79–80
  of HIV-infected adolescent mothers, 359–360

newborn
  APGAR scores, 119, 124–125
  complications, from maternal drug abuse, 119–120
  of drug abusing mothers, outcome of, 119–120
  drug withdrawal symptoms, 119
  HIV infection, clinical signs of, 67
  HIV seroprevalence, in United States, 10
  testing, maternal implications, 161–162
Influenza immunization during pregnancy, 48
Informed consent, 258
Ingelfinger, F. J., 305
Inglis, J. M., 58
Injection drug users (IDUs)
  female, 3, 12, 15, 110, 216
  moral judgment of, 400
  pregnant, 179
  risk of sexual transmission and, 113–114
  former, disease progression and, 113
  gender differences in, 111
  HIV-infected
    disease progression, 112–113
    heterosexual contact with, 143–144
  male, as sexual partners, 114
  medical problems, 120
  needle-sharing partners, duty to warn and, 190
  pregnancy of, 42
  prostitutes, 115
  public health education, 367
  risk, HIV/AIDS, 112–113
  survival rates, 18
  syphilis incidence and, 38
Injection drug users (IDUs) bacterial infections and, 22
Insurance, adolescent medical treatment and, 355
Interpersonal relations, transformation of, 283
Interviews
  of health-care providers, 421–424
    attitudes/practices toward drug abusers, 419–421
    on childbearing, 430–432
    conduct of, 411–412
    counseling methods, 413–414
    on HIV-infected women and childbearing, 415–418
    opinions of other professionals, 413–414
    self-administered questionnaire findings, 417–421

INDEX

of HIV-infected women, 426
   childbirth, personal values/intentions, 427–430
   drug abuse views/experiences, 438–440
   findings, 385–386
   overview, 383–385
   sample characteristics for, 426–427
   setting for, 426
   structure of, 426
Intrapartum period, 45, 49
Intrauterine device (IUD), 34
Intrauterine growth retardation, 119
Intravenous immunoglobulin (IVIG), 72
Iron deficiency, 69
Isolatin, 284
IUD (intrauterine device), 34
IVIG (intravenous immunoglobulin), 72

Jacabsen, S. J., 106
Jackson, D. L., 313
Jacobson, A., 136, 402
Jacobson, J., 401
Jacobson, L. P., 27
Jacomet, C., 59
Jaffe, H. W., 28–29
Jaffe, L. R., 404
James, F. Jr., 204
James, M. E., 136, 138
James, S. M., 404
Janke, J. R., 132, 137
Jansson, L., 139
Jayle, D., 109
Jeffries, D. J., 297
Jensen, B. L., 28
Jessop, D. J., 95
Jewell, N. P., 54
Johnson, D., 170
Johnson, H. L., 132
Johnson, Jennifer, 219, 221–222
Johnson, M., 132
Johnson, P.D.R., 54
Johnson, R. O., 74
Johnson, T.B.R., 138
Johnson, W. D., 58
Johnstone, F. D., 58, 132, 136
Jondal, M., 60
Jones, E. F., 52, 53
Jones, J. H., 108
Jones Patterson, M., 407
Jonsen, A. R., 299, 364
Jovaisas, E., 74
Joyner, M., 55, 62, 77
Judeo-Christian tradition, 399, 401

Judson, F. N., 52–53
Junggren, K. L., 60

Kalant, O. J., 136
Kamanga, J., 53, 74
Kamenga, M., 60, 75, 299
Kant, I., 289, 310, 342
Kantor, G. K., 136
Kaplan, A., 279, 288, 305, 312–313
Kaplan, D., 166
Kaplan, J., 132
Kaposi's sarcoma, 19, 21
Karon, J. M., 28
Karst, Kenneth, 327, 342
Kaslow, R. A., 27–28
Kass, Nancy, 52, 58, 108, 206, 208, 299, 460
Katz, Jay, 106, 286, 298, 304, 311, 314, 316
Kaunitz, A. M., 52
Keeton, R., 173, 203, 205–208
Keeton, W., 173, 203, 205–208
Kegeles, S. M., 54
Keilitz, I., 225, 246–247
Keith, L., 137
Kellam, S. G., 94
Keller, J., 54–55, 61
Keller, M., 59
Kelley, K. F., 55
Kelman, M., 315
Kelves, D., 165, 175
Keruly, J. C., 27
Khabbaz, R. F., 135
Kidney, disease, in HIV-infected children, 69, 71
Kilburn, H. J., 106
King, M.-C., 60
King, R., 28, 54
King, V. L., 135
Kissinger, P., 61
Kitchen, V. S., 57
Kitson, G., 406
Kiviat, N. B., 54
Klein, L., 55, 57
Klein, M., 316
Klein, R., 55–56, 58, 61, 107, 165
Klein, V. R., 132
Kliks, S. C., 60
Klimas, N., 58
Klingel, D. M., 131
Klun, Melanie, 317
Kobuch, W. E., 58
Koch, M. A., 56, 74, 106
Kohler, B. A., 106
Kolata, G., 165, 175
Kolder, V., 165–166, 170, 175, 213, 242

Koocher, G., 366
Koonin, L. M., 61
Korber, B.T.M., 61, 75
Korn, A. P., 55–56
Korvick, J. A., 26
Kosten, 136
Koutsky, L. A., 54
Kowal, D., 52–53
Krakauer, H., 106
Krasnovsky, F., 53
Kreimer, S. F., 303, 309–310
Kreiss, J., 53–54, 57, 75
Kress, Y., 74
Krivine, A., 74
Kronman, A., 309
Kroon, S., 107
Kuhn, Thomas, 310, 318
Kunstman, K. J., 61
Kure, K., 74
Kurth, A., 206, 402
Kurtz, P., 365
Kyei-Aboagye, K., 132

Laden, B. I., 166
Laga, M., 55–56
Lagakos, S., 25, 106–107
Lai, S., 76
Laird, N. M., 202, 210
Lam, M., 171
Lamanna, M. A., 166
Lancaster, J. S., 132
Landau, J., 109
Landers, D. V., 55, 60
Landesman, S., 55, 58, 60–62
Landress, H. J., 132
Lapage, P., 75
Lape, M., 300
Larrieta, R., 75
Larson, E., 77
Laskin, O. L., 106–107
Laslett, P., 344
Laswell, Harold D., 265, 279, 288, 305, 312
Laufer, D., 363
Laure, F., 59, 74
Law, Sylvia, 326–327, 342
Lawrence, C. R. III, 313, 317
Lawson, A., 364–366
Lawthers, A., 202, 210
Lazarus, N., 53
Lazzarin, A., 52
Leape, L. L., 202
LeDeist, F., 59
Lee, A., 137
Lee, J., 139

Lee, R. V., 137
Leedom, J. M., 106–107
Leen, 138
Leen, C.L.S., 25
Legal issues
of adolescent women, 151–153
interventions, reproductive decision-making and, 217
representation, 195–196
in reproductive choices for drug-abusing women, 126–127
theories for criminal prosecution of pregnant drug abusers, 219–221
Leibman, B. D., 57
Lemp, G. F., 27, 107
Lenin, V. I., 315
LePage, P., 52
Lepri, A. C., 27
Lerner, B., 343
Leubsdorf, J., 204
Leukefeld, C. G., 131, 135, 246, 247
Leukopenia, 69
Levin, M. J., 52
Levine, Carol, 62, 94, 171, 175–176, 201–203, 209, 299, 362, 365, 378–380, 402–403
Levine, P. A., 56
Levine, R. S., 58
Levy, J. A., 60
Lewin, T., 169
Lewin-Epstein, N., 109
Lewis, 135, 138
Lewis, S. H., 59
Lex, B., 135
Liability
health-care provider issues, 180–194
issues for women, 196–200
reproductive, 180
Liberal social theory, 280–281
Lichtenberg, K. R., 239
Lidz, C. W., 366
Life, wrongful, 184
Lifson, A. R., 26, 28
Lillie-Blanton, M., 138
Lim, L., 107
Lindan, C., 13, 54
Linderking, W. R., 251
Lindgren, S., 74, 76
Lindman, K., 76
Lindsay, M. K., 55, 57
Linge, D. E., 318
Liomba, G., 14, 58
LIP (lymphoid interstitial pneumonitis), 69
Lipsitz, S. R., 202

Liskin, L., 53
Listeriosis, 6
Little, B. B., 132, 136
Little, R. E., 61
Localio, A. R., 202, 210–211
Locke, John, 337, 344
Lockean proviso, 337–340
Lofgren, R. P., 106
Logeli, P., 212
Lopez, C., 54
Louie, L., 60
Low-income patients, malpractice and, 179
Lucas, C. R., 54
Lukacik, G., 106
Lundgren, J. D., 251
Lungs. *See also specific pulmonary diseases*
 involvement, in HIV-infected children, 68–69, 71
Lwegaba, A., 57
Lyketsos, C. G., 94
Lyman, W. D., 74
Lymphadenopathy, peripheral generalized, 19
Lymphoid interstitial pneumonitis (LIP), 69

McAnaney, J., 109
McAuliffe, S. M., 94
McAuliffe, V. J., 107
McAvinue, S. M., 30
McBride, W. L., 315
Maccabruni, A., 56
McCalla, S., 61
MacCallum, L. R., 58, 75, 136
McCarthy, B. J., 62
McCarthy, T., 315
McCaughrin, W. C., 131
McCaul, M. E., 136, 138
McCormick, M., 404
McCormick, W., 57
McCray, E., 363
MacDonald, N. E., 53
MacGregor, S., 61, 137
McKeganey, N. P., 135
McKinney, K. C., 107
MacKinnon, C., 315, 402
MacLean, D., 343
MacLean, W. E. Jr., 94–95
McLoed, G. X., 30
McNulty, M., 202
McPhee, S. J., 109
McSherry, G., 74, 75
Madhavan, S., 58
Magana, J. R., 135
Maguire, B. T., 109
Mahoney-Trout, L., 13

Maier, J. A., 28, 55
Maiman, M., 29, 56
Makuch, R. W., 74
Malanda, N., 76
Malitz, F. E., 202
Malm, K., 95
Malnutrition, 45, 69
Malone, J. L., 25
Maloy, K., 407
Malpractice liability, 178–179
Mandatory rights thesis, 323
Mandelblatt, J. S., 56
Mangano, P., 208
Mangrola, U. G., 74
Manipulation, 266, 274
Mann, J. M., 13
Mano, H., 59
Manoka, A. T., 55
Manzila, T., 75
March, Sharon, 108
March of Dimes, 238
Marcuse, H., 317
Markers, immunological, 16
Markham, R., 60, 76
Marmor, M., 26
Marris, L., 136
Marsella, R., 55
Marsh, J. C., 131
Marshall, A. B., 246
Marshall, G. S., 74
Marshall, J. R., 366
Marte, C., 205, 209–211
Martier, S., 132
Martin, E., 402
Mascola, L., 94
Masur, H., 30
Maternalism, 376, 385–390
 abortion and, 397
 burdens of proof, 399
 as cultural fact, 397–398
 justification, by last wishes, 399–400
Matthews, J., 166
Matthews, T., 76
Mattingly, S., 212
Mayer, K. H., 27–28, 57, 107–108
Mayers, A., 93
Mayers, M. M., 61
Mayes, L. C., 138
Mayhan, K. G., 53
Mays, V. M., 171, 404
Mazzarello, G., 58
Medicaid, 103–104, 155
Medical problems, of female drug abusers, 116

Medical treatment
    consent, 248
    court-ordered, 151
Medical University of South Carolina (MUSC), 227–229
Megace, 41
Meheus, A., 54
Meisel, A., 366
Melchor, J. C., 75
Melica, F., 58
Mellado, M. J., 75
Melton, G., 363, 366
Melville, R. L., 107
Mendez, H., 60–62, 75
Meningitis prophylaxis, 24
Menstrual disturbances, in HIV-infected women, 40–41
Mental health problems, 83–84
Mental health services, 92
Mental illness, 88
Mentally impaired persons, involuntary sterilization for, 149–150
Mental retardation, 32, 126
Merigan, T., 74, 107
Messiah, A., 59
Metabolic acidosis, 69
Methadone patients, 114, 117, 120–121, 125, 222
Meyers, A., 94
Meyers, D. T., 313
Michael, M., 171
Michaels, D., 163–164, 174
Michelacci, L., 76
Midgley, M., 375, 403
Mielke, M., 56
Migrant farm workers, 4
Milazzo, F., 107
Mildvan, D., 106, 107
Mill, J. S., 342
Millard, J., 107
Miller, H. G., 364–365
Miller, L. H., 27
Miller, N. A., 131
Miller, S. I., 132
Mills, J., 55
Milunsky, A., 299
Minden, S., 165
Minkoff, H., 55, 58, 60–62, 136–137, 175–176, 209, 297–298, 402, 404
Minoque, J., 137
Minority groups. *See also* African-Americans; Hispanics
    adolescents, risk for, 347
    adverse outcomes and, 179
    children with AIDS and, 82
    economic disadvantage, 377–378
    health-care services for, 105
    hopelessness and, 100–101
    moral differences, 381–382
    stereotypes, 372
    women
        discrimination of, 144–145
        HIV/AIDS mortality, 8–9
Minors. *See* Adolescents; Children
Miotti, P. G., 14, 58, 60
Mirza, N. B., 61
Mitchel, L. S., 136
Mitchell, J. L., 135
Mitchell, M., 13, 137
Mitford, J., 300
Mnookin, R. H., 364–365
Mobidity, of women, sexually transmitted disease and, 37
Mohr, J., 307
Mok, J., 58, 75–76, 136
Mollica, R. F., 94
Mondanaro, J., 135, 138, 241
Montag, A. G., 57
Moore, J., 171
Moore, M. R., 27
Moore, R. D., 27, 30, 62, 107, 138
Mor, V., 107–108, 109
Moral community, common, 401
    constitution of, 396–397
    differences among minorities and, 381–382
    interviews of HIV-infected women and, 383–384
    family-centrism, 385, 392–394
    findings, 385–386
    maternalism, 385–390
    optimism, 385, 395
    private antiabortionism and, 385, 390–392
    theism, 385, 394–395
Moral guilt, 380
Moral judgment
    in context, 376
    for deterrence, 373
    drug use and, 400
    inadequate contextualization of, 377–379
    multiculturalism in, 369–372, 374, 376, 380, 383, 400
        contextualization, 381
        cultural relativism and, 375
        ethical relativism and, 375
        soft *vs.* hard, 374
        subjectivism and, 374–375
        suspicion of judgment and, 374–376
    professional, 372–373
    public policy and, 373

INDEX 483

rationale, 373–374, 378
universalism in, 371–372, 374, 383
  contextualization, 381
  relativism and, 380
  undercontextualization, 379–381
voluntarism, 378
Moral jugdment
  universalism in, 368–369
Morbidity
  AIDS-related pregnancy-associated, 46
  for drug-exposed neonates, 119
Morgenbesser, S., 302
Morlock, L., 202
Moroni, M., 107
Moroso, G., 58, 62
Morris, A., 27
Morrow-Tlucak, M., 132
Mortality, AIDS-related, 7–9, 15
Moscato, M. G., 74–75
Moschese, V., 59, 76
Moses, L. E., 364
Moss, A. R., 55
Moss, K. L., 220
Moss-Wells, S., 132
Mota, J. M., 137
Motherhood, importance of, 430
Mucosal candidiasis, 40
Muday, P. E., 29
Muenz, L. R., 60
Mugerwa, R., 57
Muggiasca, M. L., 56, 60, 75
Mukelabai, G., 53
Mulleady, G., 135
Multiculturalism, moral, 371–372, 374, 383, 400
Mulvihill, M., 136
Mundy, D. C., 59
Munk, G., 55
Munoz, A., 27, 62
Munoz, J. L., 61
Murray, J., 137
Murray, R. S., 300
MUSC (Medical University of South Carolina), 227–229
Musicco, M., 52
Mussman, M. G., 202
Mutran, E., 406
Mwale, C., 74
Mycobacterium avium complex infection, prophylaxis, 23–24
Myers, M. W., 106

Nachman, S., 59
Nagelkerke, N., 61
Nahmias, A. J., 59
Nancy, N. W., 62
Narveson, J., 330, 343
National Association of Public Child Welfare Administrators, 238
National Association of State Alcohol and Drug Abuse Directors, 222
National Council on Alcoholism and Drug Dependence, 238
National Drug Control Strategy of 1990, 215
National Education Association, 91
National Household Survey on Drug Abuse for 1991, 218
National Institute of Allergy and Infectious Diseases (NIAID), 23, 44
National Institute on Drug Abuse (NIDA), 218
National Pregnancy and Health Survey, 218
National Survey of Family Growth 1988, 34
Native American children, HIV incidence in, 63
Natural law theory, 323–324
Nauman, B., 60
Navaie, M., 59
Navarro, M., 94, 177
Ndinya-Achola, J. O., 61, 75
Ndovi, E., 14
Neal, D., 107
Neglect, child, 85
Negligence
  in counseling, 184–185
  legal elements, 180–181
  provider tort liability and, 195, 196
Negri, E., 56
Nehring, W., 95
Neil, K., 94
Nelkin, D., 402
Nelson, A., 55, 299
Nelson, J. A., 59
Neonatal abstinence syndrome, 119
Neonates. *See* Infants, newborn
Netter, T. W., 13
Neurodevelopmental monitoring, 73
Neurological deficits, in HIV-infected children, 70
Neurosyphilis, 38
Newell, M. L., 59
Newhouse, J. P., 202, 210
New York City Commission on Human Rights, 157
Ngugi, E., 53, 57
NIAID (National Institute of Allergy and Infectious Diseases), 23, 44
Nickel, J. W., 343
Nicolosi, A., 52
Nieman, R. B., 26
Nikora, B., 57

Niruthisard, S., 53
Nolan, K., 207, 210, 299
Noncoital sexual expression, 36–37
Nonoxynol-9, 34, 35
Normal opportunity for a good life, 334–335
Norplant
  for adolescents, 152–153
  advantages, 32–33
  as coerced treatment, 230–231
  genital tract infections and, 41
North, R., 108, 208–209, 365
Note, D. Koropp, 212
Notification requirements, for adolescent medical care consent, 354–355
Novello, A. C., 57
Novick, L. F., 13, 57
Nozick, Robert, 302, 305, 308–310, 314, 317, 340, 344
Nsa, W., 61, 75
Nsiah-Jefferson, L., 164–165, 175
Nugent, R. P., 60
Nurses. *See* Health-care providers
Nussbaumm, M., 318
Nutrition supplementation, for HIV-infected children, 69, 73
Nzila, N., 55
Nzilambi, N., 13

Oberman, M., 212
Object relations theory, 286
Obstetrical complications, of drug-using women, 119
Obstetrician/gynecologists (OB/GYNs) malpractice premiums, 179
O'Campo, P., 52, 58, 108, 460
Ochia, C., 55
O'Connor, M. C., 137
O'Donnell, J. F., 106
Oellerich, D., 132
Offers, welcome *vs.* unwelcome, 271–274
Ofstead, L., 61
Okware, S., 57
Oleske, J. M., 74, 76, 176
Oliver, R., 52
O'Neill, O., 343
Onorato, I. M., 363
Oppenheim, F., 301
Oppenheimer, E., 131, 137
Opportunistic infections. *See also specific opportunistic infections*
  CD4 cell count, 17
  coerced treatment, 235
  gender differences in, 21–22
  in HIV-infected children, 68
  in late HIV disease, 20
  mode of transmission and, 21
  prophylaxis, 23–24
  therapy, during pregnancy, 49
Optimism, 385
Oral candidiasis, 40
Oral contraceptives, 33–34
Orentlicher, D., 203
Oro, A., 137
Oropharyngeal candidiasis, 6, 20
O'Rourke, S., 59
Ortona, L., 107
Osterweis, M., 94
Owen, D., 203, 205–208
Oxtoby, M. J., 13, 93, 306

Paavonen, J., 54
Padian, N. S., 54
Palefsky, J. M., 55
Palmore, M. K., 132
Palomba, E., 75
Paltrow, L. M., 244, 246, 249
Paluzzi, P., 139
p24 antigen, 43–44, 64
Paone, D., 240–241
Pape, J. W., 58
Pappaioanou, M., 13, 57, 176
Pap smears, 39, 40, 48, 194
Para, M. F., 107
Paranoia, 84
Parazzini, F., 56
Parekh, B. S., 60, 76
Parens patriae doctrine, 224–225, 227
Parental immunity doctrine, 197–198
Parent-child relationship, 328
Parenting skills, of female drug abusers, 120
Parents
  of adolescents, 350–351
    decision-making and, 362
    with HIV infection, 358–362
  competency, 84
  inability/unwillingness to seek care, for child, 83–84
  participation in child's medical care, 92
  single, 85
  withholding of information, 91
Parfit, D., 343
Park, L. P., 106, 107
Parker, A. L., 61
Parks, W., 58, 61, 76
Parris, S. V., 402
Parsons, M., 165, 213, 242
Paskey, S., 208–209
Pass, K., 13, 57

Patient-provider relationship
    antidiscrimination legislation and, 192
    duty of care, 181
    existence, 191–192
    "special," duty to warn and, 189
    termination, 192
Paton, H. J., 310, 342
Pau, C. P., 60, 76
Payne, S. F., 107
PCR, 64
Pearce, D. M., 364
Pearson, J. L., 94
Peck, E., 343
Peckham, C. S., 59, 76
Pederson, C., 251
Pediatric AIDS. *See* Children, with AIDS
Pellegrino, E., 302, 304, 311, 402
Pelvic inflammatory disease (PID)
    with HIV infection, 6, 20–21, 37, 39
    IUD usage and, 34
Pennock, J. R., 302, 315
Pentamidine, aerosolized, 49
Perinatal drug exposure, 236
Perinatal transmission, 15, 43–46, 214
    court-ordered medical intervention, 151
    drug abuse and, 45, 222–223
    failure to inform of, 184
    predictors of, 64–65
    prevention, 143, 186
        zidovudine for, 194
    protection against, 45
    risk, 389
    societal interest, 357
Peripheral neuropathy, 6
Perkins, J., 202, 211
Perrin, J. M., 94–95
Person-affecting view, 330–332
Personality changes, 84
Personality disorders of drug-abusing pregnant women, 120
Persuad, D., 76
Peterman, T. A., 29
Peters, S. Doyle, 404
Peterson, H. B., 55–57
Peterson, L. M., 210
Peterson, L. R., 13, 57
Pettinelli, C., 106–107
Peutherer, J. F., 58, 136
Pezzotti, P., 27, 107
Phair, J., 27–28, 62, 106–107
Phibbs, C. S., 61
Philips, K., 135
Phillips, A. N., 27, 251
Phobias, 284

Physical barrier contraceptive methods, 34–35
Physicians. *See* Health-care providers
Pickens, R. W., 131
PID. *See* Pelvic inflammatory disease (PID)
Piechnik, S. L., 62
Piette, J., 107, 108
Pinching, A. J., 297
Pinto, R. P., 95
Piot, P., 61
Pivnick, A., 136, 402–405, 443
Placenta, HIV transmission across, 64
Placenta abruptio, 44
Planned Parenthood of Southern Pennsylvania v. Casey, 146–147
Planned Parenthood v. Danforth, 354
Plebani, A., 59
Plumley Rule, 198
Plummer, F., 52, 55, 57, 61, 75
Pneumococcal bacteremia, 72
Pneumococcal vaccine, 48
Pneumocystis carinii pneumonia (PCP)
    CD4 cell counts and, 49
    in children, 68–69
    gender differences, 21–22
    prophylaxis, 23–24, 98
        for children, 72
        pregnancy and, 193
        trimethoprim-sulfamethizole for, 23, 49
Pneumonia, 6, 20. *See also Pneumocystis carinii* pneumonia (PCP)
    bacterial, 22
Polio vaccine, 72
Polk, B. F., 26
Poor/minority women, HIV/AIDS, 179
Postconception injuries, 185
Postpartum management, HIV-associated pregnancy, 49–50
Pottenger, L. A., 109
Powderly, W. G., 107
Powers, M., 206, 252, 460
PPD skin test, 24
Preconception injuries, 185
Pregnancy, 191–192
    adolescent, 348
    continuation, 193–194
    desire for, 387
    drug use/abuse during, 46–47
        interaction with HIV infection, 120
    scope of epidemic, 218
    forcible, 379
    health-care provider duties, 192
    of HIV-infected women, 41–50, 218
        abortion attitudes, 437–438
        access to therapy during, 193

Pregnancy *(continued)*
  antepartum management, 47–49
  clinical course, 47–50
  effect of pregnancy on HIV infection, 43
  effects of, 46–47
  HIV progression and, 373
  intrapartum management, 49
  planned, 368
  postpartum management, 49–50
  psychosocial issues, 50–51
  refusal to treat, 179
  scope of epidemic, 218
  unplanned, 368
  views/experiences of, 434–436
  outcomes of drug treatment attenders vs.
    nonattenders, 124
  Pneumocystis carinii pneumonia
    prophylaxis, 193
  prevention, 32, 186
    vs. HIV infection prevention, 37
  termination, 42–43, 192–193. *See also*
    Abortion
    by minor, 354
  termination decision, female drug abusers
    and, 117–118
  tetracycline usage during, 199
  unintended, 47
    prevention of, 32
  wrongful conception, 184
  zidovudine usage during, 352
Pregnancy preference statutes, 223
Prematurity, 45–46
Prenatal care for HIV-infected women, 48
Prenatal diagnostic testing, 184
Prenatal drug use reports, 232–233
Prenatal screening, 15, 42
Prenatal transmission, risk, failure to inform,
  182
Preston, P., 243
Price. J., 243
Price, R. H., 131
Primm, B. J., 135
Private antiabortionism, 385, 390–392
Procreation rights, 146–149
Progestin-only implant, 32–33
Progestins, 41
Pronatalist bias, 328
Property rights, reproductive rights and,
  336–341
Prosser, 205–208
Prostitution, 115
Protected choice conception of rights, 322
Protected interests conception of rights,
  322–323
Proximal cause, 181

Pryzbeck, T. R., 131
Psychiatric illness, 32
Psychoanalytic models, decision-making and,
  283–287
Psychological manipulation, 275
Psychopathology of drug-abusing pregnant
  women, 120
Psychosocial adjustments of children with
  chronic illness, 88–91
Psychosocial development, 87
Psychosocial issues, in reproductive
  counseling, 183
Public health education, injection drug users,
  367
Public perception
  of HIV-infected adolescents, 358
  of infected women, 357–358
Public policy, 426
  adolescents and, 345
  for adolescent sexuality, development of,
    349–358
  for drug-using women, HIV status and,
    129–130
  makers of, guidance for HIV-infected
    adolescents, 358–362
  moral judgment influence, 373
  recommendations, what government should
    not do, 448–450
  reproductive choices of HIV-infected women
    and, 163
Puel, J., 58
Puissant, F., 74
Punitive damages, 181–182
Purdy, L., 334, 343

Quale, J., 55
Quality of life, counterfactual standard,
  332–333
Quasi-coercion, 277–278, 288
Quinn, S. C., 108
Quinn, T. C., 61
Quinti, I., 59

Race
  HIV/AIDS distribution, 4
  HIV seroprevalence and, 10
Racism, involuntary sterilization and, 144–145
Radical social theory, 281–283
Rafferty, J. A., 131
Ralph, N., 135
Randall, H. W., 59
Randall, T., 202
Rashbaum, W. K., 74
Rauch, K. J., 13
Rauh, V. A., 404

Ravizza, M., 75
Rawls, J., 317
Raz, J., 322–323, 342
Reagan, K. J., 60
Recine, U., 57
Rectovaginal fistula, 41
Redfield, R. R., 56
Redus, M. A., 57
Reeb, K., 406
Reed, B. G., 135, 139
Rees, M., 165–166, 175
Reeser, D., 137
Reeves, W. C., 55
Refaeli, Y., 60
Regan, Donald, 327, 342
Rehabilitation Act of 1977, 153–154, 160–161, 163
Reichart, C. A., 54
Reichman, R. C., 106
Reiman, J., 314
Reinisch, J. M., 404
Reis, J., 406
Reitmeijer, C. A., 52
Rejection, 284
Religious rights, 375–376, 429
Remy, J. C., 56
Repke, J. T., 25, 58
Reppucci, N., 366
Reproduction
  choices
    Faden and Beauchamp model and, 266
    of female drug abusers, 114–120, 125–130
    for HIV-infected women, 178, 291–295
    justification for directing, 143
    legal issues for drug abusers, 126–127
    personal, provider endorsement of, 453
    respect for, 436–437
    social issues for drug abusers, 126–127
  in context of disability, public sentiment against, 145–146
  counseling. See Counseling
  decision-making. See Decision-making
  decisions, of HIV-infected women
    moral multiculturalism and, 369–370
    moral universalism and, 369, 370
  disorders of female drug abusers, 116
  ethical assessments, 377, 398
  forbearance, 448
    counseling, 453
    provider endorsement, 453
    as receipt of services, 452
  freedom of choice, 345
  HIV-related, education on medical dimensions of, 454

inequality, 379
liability. See Liability, reproductive
responsible choices for, 178
rights for. See Rights, reproductive
Resistibility, 266–270
Reuland, M., 208
Reyelt, C., 59
Reynolds-Kohler, C., 59
Rezza, G., 27
Rhame, F. S., 107
Rhoads, J. L., 56
Rhode, D. L., 364–366
Ricci, E., 76
Rich, S., 173
Richman, D. D., 25, 106–107
Rifabutin, 23
Rigaud, M., 76
Rights, reproductive, 320, 342, 413
  autonomy and, 340–341
  justifications, 322–329
    autonomy, 325–326
    familiar arguments, 326–329
    mandatory rights thesis, 323
    protected choice, 322
    protected interests, 322–323
    rights and interests, 323–324
    theoretical role of rights and, 324–325
  moral vs. legal, 320–321
  property rights and, 336–341
Rimm, A. A., 106
Rinaldo, C. R., 107
Rindfuss, R. R., 404
Risby, J., 55
Risk, HIV/AIDS
  for adolescents, 346–349
  drug-related, 112–114
  fetal/maternal, 194
  gender specific factors, 114
  minority adolescents, 347
  responsibility not to bear children and, 178
  sex risk-reduction strategies, 115–116
  of state government interventions for HIV-infected women, 233
Ritter, J., 208
Riviere, J., 316
Roberts, D. E., 166, 402–403
Roberts, J.J.K., 135
Robertson, J., 135, 168, 327, 342
Robertson, V. J., 58, 61, 136
Rocco, L., 61
Roddy, R. E., 53
Rodgers, B. D., 137
Rodrigue, J. R., 363
Roe v. Wade, 146, 153, 320, 378
Rogers, M. F., 58, 61

Roldan, E. O., 57
Rolfs, R. T., 54
Rorty, Richard, 310, 317
Rosen, J., 60
Rosen, T. S., 132
Rosenberg, M. J., 53
Rosenberg, Z. F., 77
Rosenblum, L. L., 61
Rosenstein, B. J., 136
Rosenthal, E., 174
Rosett, H. L., 137
Ross, L. J., 404
Ross, M. G., 28, 55
Rossi, P., 59–60, 76
Roter, D., 203
Roth, L. H., 366
Rothenberg, K., 108, 203, 207–209
Rothman, D. J., 303
Rounsaville, B. J., 131
Rouzioux, C., 59, 74–75
Royall, R. M., 106
Rozsenich, C., 52
Rubenstein, W. B., 201
Rubin, C. P., 136
Rubinstein, A., 60–61, 74
Ruddick, W., 343
Ruff, A., 61
Ruhle, M., 212
Rush, C. S., 176
Ruskin, R., 343
Russel, M., 137
Russell, Bertrand, 328, 343
Rust, J., 53
Rutherford, G. W., 26, 28, 107
Rutigliano, P., 139
Ryan, L., 137
Ryder, R. W., 55, 61, 75

Saag, M. S., 26
Saah, A. J., 14, 59–60, 106
Sabbagha, R. E., 137
Sabine, J. A., 172
Sachs, B. P., 298
Sacks, H. S., 27
Sade, R. M., 309, 313
Safrin, S., 29, 55
St. Louis, M. E., 13, 60, 75–76, 299, 363
Saks, M., 366
Salmonella bacteremia, prophylaxis, 24
Salwen, M., 61
Sande, M. A., 30
Sanders-Woudstra, J.A.R., 95
Sanger, C., 403
Sangrillo, P., 251
Santelli, J. S., 52

Saracco, A., 52
Saunders, W. B., 137
Scarlatti, G., 60
Schafer, A., 56, 74
Schafer, Roy, 287, 316
Schedler, G., 231, 250
Scherer, D., 366
Schilling, 135
Schinazi, R. F., 59
Schizophrenia, 88
Schmidt, C. W., 135
Schnoll, S., 132, 242
Schoenbaum, E., 58, 61, 107, 108, 136, 402
Schoenstein, R., 204
School, for HIV-infected children, 90–91
School Board of Nassau County v. Arline, 153
Schooley, R. T., 106, 107
Schreibeis, D., 62
Schreiber, K., 55
Schultz, Maguire, 305
Schusters, C. R., 131
Schut, J., 137
Schwartlander, B., 56
Schwartz, R. M., 61
Schwarz, R. H., 297–298
Sciandra, M., 75
Scott, G. B., 58, 74, 76–77
Sedlis, A., 55, 56
Self-actualization, motherhood as, 397–398
Self-determination, 263–264
Self-oppressing beliefs, 282
Selik, R. M., 28, 363
Selwyn, P., 29, 58, 61, 107, 136–137, 402
Semba, R. D., 60
Sempala, S., 57
Senderowitz, J., 343
Senekjian, E. K., 57
Senie, R. T., 56
Septimus, A., 93, 95
Seroprevalence, 4, 5
    adolescent, 347–348
    female-to-male ratio, 15
    international, 11
    in pelvic inflammatory disease, 21
    in United States, 9–11
Serufilira, A., 13
Serur, E., 56
Sex education, 351–352
Sexual activity, 31–32
    adolescent, 348
        detection of, 352
        involuntariness of, 349
        reluctance of society to discuss, 356–357
        risks, education on, 36–37

INDEX

Sexually transmitted diseases (STDs). *See also specific sexually transmitted diseases*
  adolescents and, 348–349
  condom usage and, 35–36
  in HIV-infected *vs.* noninfected women, 37
  HIV risk and, 38
  HIV seroprevalence and, 11
  morbidity, in women, 37
  physical barrier contraceptive methods and, 35–36
  screening, for prenatal care, 48
  treatment without parental consent/notice, 152
Sexual partners
  bisexual men, Kaposi's sarcoma in women and, 21
  of female methadone patients, 114
  harm, duty to warn and, 190
  HIV status, injection drug user risk and, 113–114
  male injection drug users, 114
  number of
    for drug abusers, 114–115
    HIV seropositivity and, 4
    for injection drug users, 115
Sexual transmission, 3
  in female injection drug users, 113–114
Shaffer, N., 60, 76
Shah, P. N., 57
Shapiro, J., 317
Shapiro, M. F., 109
Shapiro, T. M., 306
Shaul, S., 166
Shaw, M., 213
Sheeley, G. A., 210
Shende, S., 244
Sherwin, S., 402
Shiboski, S. C., 54
Shield, E. P., 106
Shilts, R., 93
Shindledecker, R., 94
Shipley, B. A., 139
Shorter, T., 404
Shryer, T., 170
Shulman, J. F., 61
Shultz, M. Maguire, 298
Shusters, C. R., 131
Siblings, uninfected, 91–92
Siegal, F. P., 54
Siegel, D., 53
Siegler, M., 109, 299
Silverman, A., 343
Siminon, A., 75
Simms, M. C., 365
Simms, T. E., 25
Simonds, R. J., 176
Simonon, A., 75
Simonsen, J. N., 13
Simonsen, N. J., 52
Sinicco, A., 75
Sketchley, J., 53
Skidmore, C. A., 135
Skin disorders in HIV-infected children, 70–71
Skinner, J., 137, 176
Skinner v. Oklahoma, 146
Slade, B. A., 57
Sloan, F., 211
Slutsker, L., 137
Smith, G. P., 168
Smith, I. E., 132
Smith, J., 251
Smith, J. C., 61
Smith, J. E., 109
Smith, J. R., 57, 174
Smith, M. D., 108
Smith, P. C., 318
Smith, W., 94
Smoking, disease progression and, 113
Snell, L. M., 132
Social issues in reproductive choices for drug-abusing women, 126–127
Social workers. *See* Health-care providers
Society
  costs for care of HIV-infected children, 129–130
  costs of childbearing
    by drug-using women, 127
    by HIV-infected women, 292–293
  implications, of sexual behavior, 356–357
Soeiro, R., 74
Sokol, R. J., 132, 243
Solnit, A. J., 95
Solomon, F., 94
Solomon, L., 108–109
Sommer, A., 106
Sorenson, J. R., 300
Soumenkoff, G., 74
Spector, S. A., 107
Sperling, R., 55, 62, 177, 210, 344, 364
Spermicides, 34
Spiegel, L., 93
Spigner, C., 135
Spinillo, A., 56
Sponge, spermicide-impregnated, 34–35
Sprecher, S., 74
Stack, Carol, 382, 404
Stall, R., 135
Standard of care
  for genetic counselors, 259
  mother's health status and, 198–199

Standard of care *(continued)*
  profession-specific, 181
  for reproductive counseling, 181, 182–183
Stanley v. Illinois, 148
Stanton, D. L., 28, 30
State government
  civil commitment statutes, 224–225
  interventions
    by child-protective services, 232–233
    for HIV-infected women, risks for, 233
    for pregnant drug abusers, 219–222, 237
    for prenatal drug use, 215, 217–218
    reproductive decision-making for HIV-infected women, 233–237
  involuntary sterilization cases, 149–150
Stavudine (D4T), 48
STDs. *See* Sexually transmitted diseases (STDs)
Steer, P. J., 57
Stein, D. S., 26, 107
Stein, M., 27, 28, 57, 107–108
Stein, R.E.K., 95
Stein, Z., 59, 209–210
Steinbock, B., 318
Steiner, G., 306
Stephen, E. Hervey, 404
Sterilization, 32
  coerced, 130
  forced, 327
  involuntary, 144–145, 149–150
    Fourteenth Amendment and, 146
  mandatory, 353
  of minor women, 152
  negligently performed, 184
Stern, N., 166
Stevens, C. E., 54
Stevens, J. W., 107
Stevens, R., 13, 57, 61
Stewart, F., 52–53
Stewart, G., 52–53
Stewart, L., 54
Stiehm, E. R., 74
Stigmatization, 81–82, 100, 357, 372
Stingl, G., 107
Stocking, C. B., 109
Stokes, E. J., 138
Stoll, K., 202, 211
Stone, Alan, 317
Stone, K. M., 53
Stone, R. K., 137
Stratton, P., 61–62, 210
Straus, M. A., 136
Strauss, A., 94
Streissguth, A. O., 61

Streptococcus pneumoniae, 72
Stricof, R., 13, 57
Stryker, J., 364
Suarez, J., 56
Subjectivism, moral multiculturalism and, 374–375
Substance abuse. *See* Drug abusers, female; Drug abusers, male; Drug-treatment programs; Injection drug users (IDUs)
Sugarman, D. B., 209
Sugland, B., 27, 62
Sugland, S. W., 107
Suicide, 88
Sullivan, K. M., 302, 309–310
Sullivan, Louis W., 240
Sumner, L. W., 342
Sunderland, A., 58
Suppes, O., 302
Surrogate motherhood, 389
Survival
  AIDS-defining illness and, 18–19
  of AIDS-infected women, 97
  Kaposi's sarcoma and, 19
  rates, 5
  of women, 19
  zidovudine (Azidothymidine; AZT) and, 19
Suspicion of health-care system, 101
Svikis, D. S., 138, 139
Swart, A. M., 107
Sweet, R. L., 55
Syphilis, 4, 37, 38
Systems of thought, 183
Szabo, S., 27

Tan, W., 56
Tarantola, D.J.M., 13
Tardieu, M., 59, 76
Tarricone, N., 29, 56
Taub, N., 165, 166, 170
Taylor, Charles, 310
Taylor-Brown, S., 94
Taylor-Robinson, D., 29
Telzak, E. E., 62
Temelso, T., 107
Temmerman, M., 61
Tenti, P., 56
Teplitz, E., 55
Terminal illness, 81
Terragna, A., 58
Tetracycline usage during pregnancy, 199
Theism, 385, 394–395
Thomas. J. T., 404
Thomas, L., 402
Thomas, S. B., 108

Thompson, J., 342
Thompson, M., 27
Thompson, R., 136
Thomson, E., 207
Thorpe, K. E., 202
Threat/offer distinction in Faden and Beauchamp model, 270–274
Thrombocytopenia, 69–70
Thrush, 6, 20
Thurman, S. K., 166
Tibaldi, C., 75
Tielsch, J. M., 106
Tims, F. M., 246, 247
Tolerance, liberal, 375
Tomino, C., 107
Tort law
  defined, 180
  health-care provider liability, assessing reality of, 195–196
Tovo, P. A., 60, 76
Toxoplasma gondii prevention, 23
Transmission
  anatomic susceptibility of adolescent females, 348
  breast-feeding and, 44
  heterosexual, 3–4, 12, 15, 36
  homosexual, 3
  modes, education on, 182
  mother-to-child, 63–66
  oral contraceptives and, 33–34
  perinatal. *See* Perinatal transmission
  prevention strategies, 348–349
  vertical. *See* Perinatal transmission
Transportation problems, 86
Treisman, G. J., 94
Trichomonas, with HIV infection, 37–38
Trimethoprim-sulfamethizole, for PCP prophylaxis, 23, 49
Tropper, P., 59
Trowbridge, G. L., 74
Trussell, J., 52, 53
Tschann, J. M., 365
Tubal ligation, 32
Tuberculosis, 4, 20, 24
Tuomala, R., 298
Turner, C. F., 364
Twins, 44, 65

Ugen, K. E., 60
Ukl, C. N., 61
Ulanowsky, C., 210
Unger, R., 311
United States, HIV seroprevalence, 9–11
Universalism, moral, 371–372, 374, 383
Urine, bicarbonate, 69

Vaginal candidiasis, 19, 24, 40, 102
Vaginal pouch, polyurethane. *See* Condoms, female
Van de Pierre, P., 52, 75
Vanderveen, E., 131
Van Dongen-Melman, J.E.W.N., 95
Vannicelli, M., 138
Vasectomy, 32
Vaughn, T. E., 131
Vella, S., 107
Vermund, S., 26, 55, 106–107
Vertical transmission. *See* Perinatal transmission
Vida, D. H., 62
Vieira, J., 29, 56
Vierling, L., 366
Villota, J., 75
Vink, P., 74
VIN (vulvar intraepithelial neoplasia), 40
Violence, 117
  domestic, 32, 189–190
  interpersonal, 87
Virucidal agent, vaginal lavage, 46
Visces, K. H., 59
Visco, G., 107
Vlahov, D., 108–109
Voeller, B., 53, 404
Vogelhut, J., 62, 77
Volberding, P., 106–107
Vranizan, K., 55
"Vulnerable child" syndrome, 91–92
Vulvar intraepithelial neoplasia (VIN), 40
Vulvovaginal candidiasis, 6

Wachtel, T. J., 107–108
Wahren, B., 60, 76
Walker, C., 251
Walsh, J. H., 60–61
Wamola, I. A., 61
Wara, D. W., 60
Warn, duty to, 188–191
Warren, R., 54
Waskin, H., 107
Wasser, S. C., 13, 57
Wasserheit, J. N., 54
Wasserman, G., 404
Wasting syndrome, 20–21, 68
Watson, H., 135
Watters, 135, 138
Webber, M. P., 108
Weber, S., 317

Webster, L. A., 171
Weiblen, B. J., 13
Weight loss, 20
Weiler, P. C., 202, 210
Weiner, L., 137
Weinstock, H. S., 54
Weisberg, D. K., 364–365
Weiser, B., 59
Weisman, C. S., 202
Weithorn, L. A., 366
Welfare reform, 448–449
Wells, C., 57
Wells, G. A., 53
Wells, J. E., 139
Wendell, D.A., 363
Wenneker, M. B., 106
Wertheimer, Alan, 259, 272, 289, 300, 302, 308–310, 312, 317
West, C., 403
Western, P., 309
Wethers, J., 13, 57
Wetli, C. V., 57
Wharton, C., 53
White, D., 135
White, M., 302
White-Hamilton, J., 61
Whitehead, P. C., 136
Whittle, J., 106
WHO (World Health Organization), 31
Widy-Wirski, R., 57
Wigzell, H., 60, 76
Wike, C. M., 61, 75
Willander, A., 138
Williams, A. B., 55–56, 94, 136
Williams, H., 55, 57
Williams, W. V., 60
Williams-Russo, P., 58
Willis, D. P., 402
Willis, S., 57, 136
Willoughby, A., 57, 60, 61–62
Wilsnack, S. C., 138
Wilson, P. I., 404
Winch, Peter, 310
Winslade, W., 299
Wise, P. H., 94
Witte, J., 135
Wofsy, C. B., 135, 138
Wolf, S., 402
Wolff, R. P., 302
Wolinsky, S. M., 61, 75
Women. *See also* Pregnancy
  legal duties, 327
  liability issues, 196–200
  pregnant, drug abuse in, 111–112

Wong, B., 107
Wood, D. G., 60
Working Group
  client-provider interaction models, 452–454
  position of, 454–460
  public policy recommendations
    what government should do, 450–452
    what government should not do, 448–450
World Health Organization (WHO), 31, 367
Worth, D., 53
Wright, C., 56
Wright, T., 57
Wright-Spolarich, A., 241–242
Wrongful birth suits, 184–185
Wrongful conception/pregnancy suits, 184
Wrongful life, 184–186, 377
Wrongful pregnancy suits, 185
Wyatt, F., 343
Wyatt, G. E., 404

Yap, P. L., 75
Yogev, R., 74
Young, A., 61
Younger, S., 313

Zalcitabine, 23
Zanussi, C., 107
Zappatore, R., 56
Zarembka, A., 201
Zawistowich, L., 202
Zeger, S. L., 106–107
Zekeng, L., 52
Zembaty, J. S., 300
Zenilman, J. M., 54
Ziarati, N., 75
Zidovudine, 22–23
  FDA-approval, 23
  guidelines, 97
  for HIV-infected children, 71–72
  for reduction of perinatal transmission, 65–66
  resistance, 23
  survival and, 19
  use in pregnancy, 44–48, 194, 217, 335, 352. *See also* AIDS Clinical Trials Group (ACTG), 076 study
  as coerced treatment, 234–235
  perinatal transmission and, 367
Ziegler, J. B., 74
Zierler, S., 363
Zimmerman, D., 302
Zimring, F., 364–365
Zuckerman, B., 131–132, 136–138
Zylke, J. W., 201, 299

www.ingramcontent.com/pod-product-compliance
Ingram Content Group UK Ltd.
Pitfield, Milton Keynes, MK11 3LW, UK
UKHW041902230426
12049UKWH00001B/7